Sixth Edition

Research Methods in Education: An Introduction

William Wiersma
University of Toledo

Allyn and Bacon
Boston • London • Toronto • Sydney • Tokyo • Singapore

To
JOAN and SUSAN and LISA

Vice President, Education: Nancy Forsyth
Production Administrator: Marjorie Payne
Editorial Assistant: Christine Nelson
Marketing Manager: Ellen Mann
Cover Administrator: Linda Knowles
Composition/Prepress Buyer: Linda Cox
Manufacturing Buyer: Megan Cochran
Editorial-Production Service: Chestnut Hill Enterprises, Inc.
Cover Designer: Susan Paradise

Copyright © 1995, 1991, 1986, 1980, 1975, 1969 by Allyn and Bacon
A Simon and Schuster Company
Needham Heights, Massachusetts 02194

Library of Congress Cataloging-in-Publication Data

Wiersma, William.
    Research methods in education / William Wiersma. — 6th ed.
        p.   cm.
    Includes bibliographical references and indexes.
    ISBN 0-205-15654-1
    1. Education—Research.   I. Title.
LB1028.W517   1995
370′.7′8—dc20   94-11080
                                                          CIP

Printed in the United States of America

10 9 8 7 6 5 4 3   99 98 97 96 95

Contents

Preface

Purpose

Some work in research methods is required in almost all graduate programs in education, in the United States and in other countries. The professional literature of education is expanding every year, and much of that literature deals with research results. Professional educators should be familiar with the research in their special areas and, as the opportunity presents itself, participate in doing research.

To that end, the purpose of this book is the same as the purposes of previous editions and that is to present the language, principles, reasoning, and methodology of conducting educational research in such a way that the reader or student will be able to understand the logic of conducting educational research, read the research literature with understanding, distinguish between different types of research and how they apply, understand how research studies are designed and conducted, and design and conduct the research required in a graduate program.

Audience

Research Methods in Education: An Introduction is written primarily for graduate students in education, because the graduate level is usually the point in education at which the student first encounters formal training in research methods. However, because it is an introductory book, it is appropriate at any point at which research methods are introduced in a program. Students in undergraduate programs that emphasize research should find the book useful, even if there is no formal course in research methods. Education draws on several disciplines for its research methods, and for that reason students in related disciplines will find application for the book, especially students in the behavioral sciences. Of course, the book can be used independently as a professional reference.

Approach

The approach of this text is to provide the rationale for commonly used research procedures and to provide illustrations by means of numerous examples. Exercises, provided at the ends of all chapters, can be used by students to check their mastery of content. Solutions to selected exercises are provided in an appendix. Specific research methodologies are addressed and the discussion is comprehensive in that it attempts to bring the reader from the beginning of a research study to successful completion of the report. The procedures discussed have wide applicability, and the ideas presented are general enough to apply in many specific research situations.

Organization

The early chapters of the text follow approximately the sequence in which a research study is conducted. The introductory chapter describes the nature of educational research and introduces the steps in the research process. Because adequate identification of a research problem is so important, the entire second chapter is devoted to this topic. This chapter also introduces basic research terminology. Chapter 3 describes how to review the literature, including the identification of information sources.

Chapter 4 discusses research design for quantitative research; then Chapters 5, 6, and 7 are devoted to different types of research—experimental, quasi-experimental, and survey—that are considered quantitative in nature. Chapter 8 deals with research design for qualitative research. Chapter 9 discusses historical research and Chapter 10 ethnographic research, the two qualitative research methodologies considered most applicable to education. With this organization, the middle chapters focus on unique characteristics of specific types of research. Readers using the book independently can concentrate on the chapters that fit their particular types of research. These chapters represent the types of research most commonly used in education.

Because many studies involve samples, Chapter 11 is devoted to sampling designs. This is followed by a chapter on measurement and data collection; Chapter 12 provides an overview of several approaches to measuring variables and also discusses the preparation of data sets for computer analysis.

When quantitative research methods are used, sooner or later some type of statistical analysis is applied to the data. Chapters 13 and 14 describe statistical procedures commonly used; Chapter 13 discusses descriptive statistics and Chapter 14, inferential statistics. It should be emphasized, however, that this is not a statistics text. Therefore, the emphasis in the two statistics chapters is on the underlying reasoning of the various statistical procedures and the conditions under which they apply. There is no intention of developing computational mastery; in fact, little computation appears. Because most research data are analyzed by computer, the general procedures for using computer facilities also are described in connection with statistical procedures.

At various points in the research process, it is necessary to communicate about research. Much of this is done through written proposals and reports, and some of it is done through oral communications. Chapter 15 provides suggestions about how to prepare a research proposal and a research report. The discussion deals not only with the content of proposals and reports but also provides suggestions for how to put a report together in a correct and efficient manner. Guidelines are given in Chapter 15 for presenting research at conferences, and for graduate students when they are the center of attention for the defense of a dissertation (thesis) proposal or the dissertation (thesis) itself in a committee meeting.

Appendix 1 discusses "Ethical and Legal Considerations in Conducting Research." This appendix contains important information about how to obtain approval of a research proposal from an institutional review board and the principles of protecting human participants when they are involved in research. Appendix 2 contains answers to selected end-of-chapter exercises. Appendix 3 contains five statistical tables for handy reference. Finally, a glossary of research methods terms is provided for the reader's convenience.

The Sixth Edition

Any new edition of a text contains the usual updating of examples, references, and the like. It is not necessary to list the specific changes here. The basic organization of the text remains the same as for the fifth edition, except for the inclusion of separate chapters on research design for quantitative and qualitative research. This resulted in an expanded discussion of qualitative research, including the possibilities of using computers for the analysis of qualitative data. All in all, users of the fifth edition should feel comfortable with this edition.

The use of computers is discussed in connection with the three functions such use may serve. Statistical analysis and the analysis of qualitative data have been mentioned above. Microcomputers can be used as word processors for preparing research reports. Suggestions for using computers for this function are given in Chapter 15.

The text contains over one hundred figures and tables. Diagrams of research designs are used to illustrate their structures and underlying concepts. Examples, taken from a wide variety of educational research types and settings, are used throughout. Many examples are taken from the research literature. Important concepts are summarized and set off throughout the book, and key concepts are listed at the end of each chapter. So, the pedagogical features of this sixth edition should serve the user well.

Acknowledgments

I wish to acknowledge Dr. Edward Nussel and Dr. Philip Rusche for their permission to reproduce material from a research project we completed jointly. Special acknowledgment goes to Dr. Merrill Mehan of the Appalachia Educational Laboratory and Dr. Daniel Stufflebeam, Director of the Evaluation Center, Western Michigan University, for permission to reproduce a cover letter and example items from the FY 1992, External Evaluation Report. Also, the American Psychological Association granted permission to reproduce the principles from, "Ethical Principles of Psychologists and Code of Conduct."

For assistance with computer software I would like to acknowledge Dr. Michael Reed of CSR, Inc., Washington, DC, and Dr. Barbara McMillen of Bowling Green State University. For their helpful reviews of the fifth edition, acknowledgment goes to Douglas W. Yarbrough of Boise State University and Doris L. Prater of the University of Houston at Clear Lake.

Finally, I am grateful to the Literary Executor of the late Sir Ronald A. Fisher, F.R.S.; to Dr. Frank Yates, F.R.S.; and to Longman Group Ltd., London, for permission to reprint Tables III, IV, and VII (abridged) from their book *Statistical Tables for Biological, Agricultural and Medical Research* (6th edition, 1974).

William Wiersma

Educational Research: Its Nature and Characteristics

Introduction

Research has become such a prevailing phenomenon of our civilization that all of us are impacted by it. Scholars and practitioners of various levels of sophistication in the academic disciplines and professions engage in research. Students do not progress very far in our formal education system without encountering the necessity to do some type of research. Research is conducted in many, many settings: laboratories, classrooms, libraries, the city streets, and foreign cultures just to mention a few. Some research is of short duration, other research spans long periods of time. Industries, businesses, and funding agencies such as the Department of Education and the National Institutes of Health, spend vast sums of money on research activity. Yet, much research is done with little funding, "on a shoestring," so to speak. Advances in many fields of endeavor are attributed to research, and for much of this research activity there is the inherent assumption that research fosters improvement.

Graduate students may find it difficult, at least early in a graduate program, to identify with research situations and to key into a process of conducting research. Financial resources usually are limited, as are the opportunity, expertise, and experience for conducting research. Yet to pursue a degree, it is often required to produce some original research. Realizing that research is necessary—and having heard the term repeatedly—provides little direction for how to go about doing it.

When it comes to matters of research, the situation of the average elementary or high school teacher, counselor, or administrator is not much different from that of the graduate student. In fact, a considerable portion of the graduate student population is often made up of school personnel pursuing graduate programs on a part-time basis. So there may be an immediate need for participating in educational research required by the graduate program. But if we take a longer range view and accept the argument that the results of educational research will lead to the improvement of educational practice, professional educators should maintain a continuing interest in research. Educational research is prompted by external funding programs, such as those of federal and state agencies, and much of it is generated within the profession itself. Decision making in the schools is based on a combination of experience, expert opinion, and research results, and the professional educator should be knowledgeable about research methodology and results.

Much educational research is reported in such a way that a knowledge of the methodology is invaluable, and in almost all cases, such knowledge is essential for a meaningful implementation of research results. Although graduate students may have a short-term or immediate need to conduct research for a thesis or dissertation, a long-term result of the research experience should be that they become better professional educators and that they use research results increasingly in decision making.

Educational research is to some extent complex and demanding. However, the broad spectrum of research activities uses various research methods, ranging from relatively simple, single operations to complex combinations of procedures, both qualitative and quantitative. With organized and concentrated study, the aspiring educational researcher should be able to master necessary research methods. Basically, the only way to become competent in research is by doing it, but before research can be put into practice, some skills must be acquired. Knowing what to do in specific situations is important. How is the research problem identified? What procedures apply in pursuing the solution of the specific problem? How are the data to be collected and interpreted? How can a satisfactory, lucid report be produced? In the context of a specific research effort, all these questions call for certain skills.

The approach of this text is essentially one of emphasizing the application of procedures. To a large extent, what is done in educational research is based on common sense. We try to structure things so that we can tell what is going on, so that we can understand the information contained in the data. This text discusses general procedures and methods, but the practicing researcher must project them into the specific situation. To some extent, the idea of a "typical" research project is a misconception. There is no typical project; each has unique problems and conditions. Although there may be considerable similarity among various types of projects, doing a research project is not like baking a cake from a recipe.

The educational researcher should always aim for a respectable, competently done product. However, a researcher should not become discouraged if the results are less than perfect—it is not likely that there has ever been a perfect study. Therefore, any finished product will not be totally exempt from criticism. In doing research, there are potential pitfalls, and errors are likely to occur. Any researcher should be willing to accept the suggestions of peers. Criticism of research should be offered and accepted in a strictly constructive sense for the purpose of improving a particular project or improving future research in the area. A receptive attitude should be maintained toward the research and toward the suggestions of others.

The Nature of Educational Research

Research essentially is an activity, or process, and even though research procedures are many and varied, certain general characteristics help define its nature. Because educational research also has these characteristics, they are described and illustrated here among educational examples. The few general characteristics are as follows:

1. Research is empirical.
2. Research should be systematic.
3. Research should be valid.
4. Research should be reliable.
5. Research can take on a variety of forms.

These characteristics are related in that, as a composite, they describe the nature of research. They are somewhat separated in this discussion to focus on their individual meanings.

A strong empirical approach characterizes educational research. Technically, *empiricism* is the concept that all knowledge is derived from sense experience. But the result of this experience must take some kind of informational form so that knowledge can be generated. Information takes the form of data. There are many possible forms of data, including test scores, field notes, responses to questionnaire items, and computer printouts, to mention just four. The researcher works with these data. That work may involve organizing data, generating hypotheses from the data, testing hypotheses, and so on.

The Systematic Process of Research

Research is a process, and in order to enhance conducting research, it would seem reasonable to make it as systematic as possible. Indeed, many writers describe research as a systematic process. McMillan and Schumacher (1989) define research as "a systematic process of collecting and analyzing information (data) for some purpose" (p. 8), and Kerlinger (1986) defines scientific research as "systematic, controlled, empirical and critical investigation of natural phenomena guided by theory and hypotheses about the presumed relations among such phenomena" (p. 10).

Certainly, we would like to believe that educational research is systematic, but what can we do to make it so? We can use the approach of scientific inquiry, the search for knowledge through recognized methods of data collection, analysis, and interpretation. Associated with scientific inquiry is the scientific method, a research process considered, at least to some extent, to consist of a series of sequential steps. Opinions may vary as to the exact number of steps in the scientific method, but typically anywhere from four to six general steps are identified. These begin with identifying the problem through interpreting results and drawing conclusions. Five steps are compatible with the scientific method and provide the elements of a general, systematic approach to research: (1) identifying the problem, (2) reviewing information, (3) collecting data, (4) analyzing data, and (5) drawing conclusions. First, for a research study to be systematic, the nature of the problem to be studied must be defined, even if only in broad terms. Related knowledge is identified, and, in essence, a framework is established in which to conduct the research. Closely related to establishing the framework or foundation for the research is the identification of any necessary assumptions or conditions related to the research problem.

The second step is gathering information about how others have approached or dealt with similar problems. Certainly, one can and should profit from the work of others; it is not necessary to "reinvent the wheel" each time a research problem is attacked. The research literature is the source of such information.

Collecting data relevant to the problem is the third step in systematic research. However, data cannot be collected in any available, haphazard, or ad hoc manner. The process of data collection requires proper organization and control so that the data will enable valid decisions to be made about the research problem at hand. The fourth step is analyzing data in a manner appropriate to the problem. The fifth step is the process of drawing conclusions or making generalizations after the analysis has been made. The conclusions are based on the data and the analysis within the framework of the research study.

The five steps that characterize the systematic nature of the research process can be illustrated as follows:

The process just described is systematic and ordered, but it should not be inferred that research is a lock-step process. There may be overlapping and integration among the steps. In some studies, such as an experiment, hypotheses to be tested may be identified when the research problem is defined. In other research studies, those more qualitative in nature, generating hypotheses may not occur until data are collected and then hypotheses may be revised when data are analyzed. So the specific conditions of the research study impact upon the steps, but to some extent, all educational research studies are systematic.

> Educational research is systematic and within a broad framework follows the steps of the scientific method. However, across different types of studies there is extensive flexibility in how the steps are implemented.

The Validity of Educational Research

Regardless of the form research takes or the ends to which it is directed, we want research to be valid—that is, to possess validity. What is validity of research? In general, for something to be valid we want it to be based on fact or evidence, that is, "capable of being justified." Becoming more specific, validity involves two[1] concepts simultaneously, internal validity and external validity. Internal validity is the extent to which results can be interpreted accurately, and external validity is the extent to which results can be generalized to populations, situations, and conditions. Consider examples illustrating the concepts of validity.

Internal Validity.   Suppose a physical education teacher is interested in possible effects of two different exercise programs upon the physical performance test scores of eighth-grade boys. The teacher is scheduled for two morning physical education classes, and has the option of randomly assigning twenty-eight students to each class. The teacher implements one program in each class for a sixteen-week period and at the end of the period administers the same physical performance test to both classes. This research study has good internal validity. The overall scheme of the study is diagrammed in Figure 1.1.

Why does this study have good internal validity? Because, if the physical performance test scores of the two classes differ, say that the mean[2] for Class 2 is much higher than that for Class 1, we can interpret this result with confidence and conclude that Program 2 is the more effective program. Whatever the results, they can be interpreted with confidence, because *overall* the only difference between the two classes is the program. Both are morning classes taught by the same teacher in the same school, and both classes consist of eighth-grade boys. To be sure, any two boys might differ on their inherent physical ability, but fifty-six boys were assigned randomly, twenty-eight to each class. As classes, overall the two classes should be very similar on factors other than the programs that might affect physical performance. For example, possibly some boys get more sleep than others, but overall the averages should be about the same for the two classes. In essence, the random assignment "evens out" the two classes on these other factors, and we say that the groups are equivalent within random fluctuation.

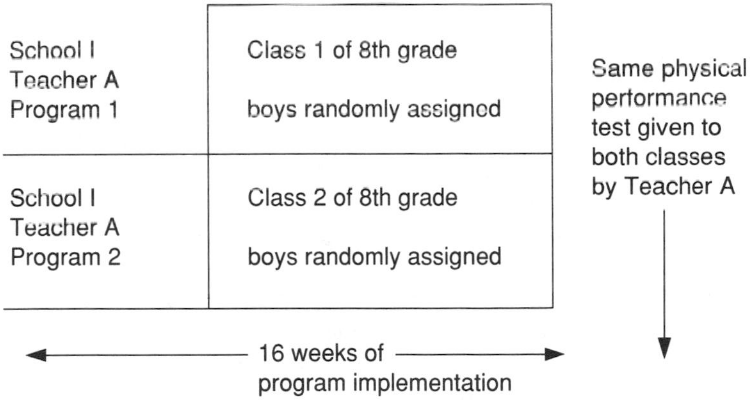

School I Teacher A Program 1	Class 1 of 8th grade boys randomly assigned	Same physical performance test given to both classes
School I Teacher A Program 2	Class 2 of 8th grade boys randomly assigned	by Teacher A

◄——————— 16 weeks of ———————►
program implementation

**FIGURE 1.1   Overall Scheme of a Hypothetical Research Study
That Has High Internal Validity**

Consider another example, which in contrast presents a situation lacking internal validity. Research is being conducted on the differing effects of three types of materials on performance in eighth-grade science. Three teachers are recruited for participation in the study. The teachers teach in different schools; two have four classes each of eighth-grade science, and the third has three classes. In one school, classes are assigned on the basis of ability grouping. It so happens that the participating teacher in this school has high-ability classes.

Each teacher uses one type of material for a period of nine weeks. The teachers use different materials, and no teacher uses more than one type of material. At the end of nine weeks, the students are tested on science achievement, each teacher using his or her own test. The overall scheme of the research study is presented in Figure 1.2.

Average science achievement scores are computed for the students taught using each of the three materials. What conclusions can be drawn about the relative effectiveness of the three types of materials? Essentially none. Suppose that the students in School III have the highest average score. Is it because they are high-ability students or because Teacher C is a superior teacher? Or is the test used by Teacher C easier than those used by the other teachers? Or are Materials 3 more effective than the other materials? There is no way these results can be validly interpreted, regardless of the pattern of results. Too many plausible and competing explanations of the results cannot be discounted to be able to conclude that Materials 3 are the most effective. Thus, this research study lacks internal validity because the results cannot be interpreted.

Internal validity is the extent to which the results of a research study can be interpreted accurately and with confidence.

External Validity.   As defined earlier, external validity is the extent to which research results can be generalized. To a large extent, internal validity is a prerequisite for external validity because if results cannot be interpreted it is not likely that they can be generalized. Consider an example.

In a school district which has five elementary schools a survey is conducted of parents' perceptions of the school—quality of the curriculum, effectiveness of the administration, discipline, etc. A telephone interview is developed with well-constructed items and an adequate number of items to cover the school characteristics of interest. Within each elementary school 25 parents of students enrolled are selected randomly and interviewed. For any parents not available or unwilling to be interviewed there is a defined procedure for random replacement. The interviews are conducted and 125 interviews are completed with only six of those being replacements for unavailable parents.

The population to which the results of this study are to be generalized is the population of parents who have children in the five elementary schools. With the manner in which the survey was conducted and the number of completed interviews, the results can be generalized with confidence to this population. The research study has high or good external validity. It is not likely that there would be much interest in generalizing the

Science Achievement Tested

School I Teacher A Materials 1	4 Classes Heterogeneous Ability	Test constructed by Teacher A
School II Teacher B Materials 2	3 Classes Heterogeneous Ability	Test constructed by Teacher B
School III Teacher C Materials 3	4 Classes High Ability	Test constructed by Teacher C

◄———————— 9 Weeks Instruction ————————►

**FIGURE 1.2   General Scheme of a Hypothetical Research Study
That Lacks Internal Validity**

results to other elementary schools, those in other school systems. If this were done, it would need to be done on a logical basis, providing an argument for the similarity between the parents of students in these schools and those in other school districts.

Suppose that in the study described above, the survey was conducted poorly, and for possibly other reasons, only 27 parents or about 22 percent of the intended 125, had been interviewed. Under this condition the study would be lacking in external validity. It cannot be argued that the 27 parents interviewed are a representative sample of the intended 125 parents, the population of parents of the students in the schools, or any other population for that matter. There may be unknown factors operating that caused the low interview response rate.

Because external validity can involve generalizations to populations and/or conditions, it is useful to consider another example, admittedly one rather extreme and one lacking external validity. A study is conducted on the effect of length of visual exposure on the recall of nonsense symbols. (A nonsense symbol might be five letters randomly sequenced.) The researcher obtains ten volunteers from a graduate student population in educational psychology. There are five different lengths of exposure, so two volunteers are used in each. A volunteer participates in the study by being exposed to twenty nonsense symbols individually; after each exposure, the volunteer is to reproduce the symbol. A total performance score is then generated from the number of symbols correctly reproduced. The overall scheme of this study is shown in Figure 1.3.

Suppose the results show that the performance scores generally increase with increased length of exposure. But to what populations and conditions can this result be

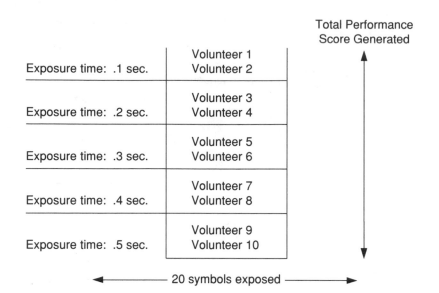

**FIGURE 1.3   General Scheme of a Hypothetical Research Study
That Lacks External Validity**

generalized? Can it be generalized to elementary or secondary students learning meaningful materials? Can it be generalized to young adults working on meaningful tasks in a highly structured situation? Not likely. The results (for recalling nonsense symbols) may not even be generalizable to the graduate student population, since the participants in the study were volunteers. In summary the results may be generalizable only to the ten volunteers who recalled the nonsense symbols. The study thus lacks external validity.

External validity is the extent to which research results are generalizable to populations and/or conditions.

It should not be inferred that to have external validity, results must generalize to many and varied populations and conditions. If a study involving only gifted students were conducted, the intent of the study could be to generalize to a gifted student population, not to all students. If a school system were doing a needs assessment, the results might generalize only to that system. Typically, when doing qualitative research, the researcher is not concerned with broad generalization of the results. So, external validity depends upon the conditions and purpose of the specific research study.

Validity of research is always a matter of degree. It is practically impossible to attain "perfect" internal and external validity in a study. As will be shown in later chapters, attempts in research design to enhance internal validity may decrease external validity, and vice versa. The researcher attempts to attain a balance so that results can be inter-preted with reasonable certainty and still have some useful generalizability.

> *Validity* of research deals with the accurate interpretability of the results (internal validity) and the generalizability of the results (external validity). Both types of validity are matters of degree.

The Reliability of Educational Research

When discussing validity, it is appropriate to consider a related concept—reliability of research. *Reliability* refers to the consistency of the research and the extent to which studies can be replicated. We sometimes distinguish between internal and external reli-ability. *Internal reliability* refers to the extent that data collection, analysis, and interpre-tations are consistent given the same conditions. For example, if multiple data collectors are used, a question of internal reliability is, "Do the data collectors agree?" Suppose a study of teacher performance is being conducted using a classroom observation inventory for data collection. The question of internal reliability would be, "Do the two or more observers agree when recording the same performance?" This is called the extent of *observer agreement*. If internal reliability is lacking, the data become a function of who collects them rather than what actually happened.

External reliability deals with the issue of whether or not independent researchers can replicate studies in the same or similar settings. Will researchers be able to replicate studies, and, if so, will the results be consistent? If research is reliable, a researcher using the same methods, conditions, and so forth should obtain the results as those found in a prior study. To be replicable, a research study must include adequate descriptions of the procedures and conditions of the research. The amount of definition necessary may vary across studies.

> *Reliability* of research concerns the replicability and consistency of the methods, conditions, and results.

Reliability is a necessary characteristic for validity; that is, a study cannot be valid and lack reliability. If a study is unreliable, we can hardly interpret the results with confidence or generalize them to other populations and conditions. Essentially, reliability and validity establish the credibility of research. Reliability focuses on replicability and validity focuses on the accuracy and generalizability of the findings.

Research Has a Variety of Forms

By just listening to others, it quickly becomes clear that research takes a variety of forms. Sometimes we hear an individual say, "I have researched this problem," which means that the person has considered various solutions to a problem. An elementary school student may say, "I am supposed to so some research on Brazil." This means the student has been assigned a report that will involve reading resource materials about Brazil. A graduate student in educational psychology may be conducting an experiment in a learning laboratory that involves engaging young adults in a complex learning task. Reading teachers in a school system may try different approaches to compensatory reading instruction for students who are poor readers. An educational sociologist may be studying the social interaction patterns in a large metropolitan high school.

Identifying and describing different forms or types of educational research is helpful for developing an understanding of the scope of educational research and the differences involved across research studies. Different forms or types of research involve classification systems and these are discussed in more detail next.

Classification of Educational Research

There are many ways to classify educational research studies and authors use classification systems of varying degrees of complexity. Essentially, classification systems are valuable to the extent they are useful for enhancing the effectiveness and efficiency by which research is conducted. Two systems are described here, one based on the goal or purpose of the research and the other on the way the research is conducted. The latter is a two-category classification scheme with general methodologies placed within this system.

Basic and Applied Research

Basic and applied research are differentiated by their goals or purposes. The purpose of *applied research* is to solve an immediate, practical problem. Such research is oriented to a specific problem. *Basic research* has a more general orientation: adding to the existing body of knowledge in the discipline. Basic research does not necessarily provide results of immediate, practical use, although such a possibility is not ruled out. If this result does occur, however, it is supplemental, not the primary purpose. On the other hand, in producing a solution to a specific problem, applied research may contribute to the general knowledge of the field. Both basic and applied research are important, they should not be differentiated by a hierarchy of value judgments.

An example of basic research would be to conduct an experiment concerning learning in a laboratory setting. The purpose of such an experiment would be to contribute to the knowledge about how learning takes place. The experiment might be focused on one or a very limited number of factors associated with learning, such as the differences that result when learning materials are presented in a figural or a verbal manner.

An example of applied research would be to conduct a survey of the elementary school teachers in a school system to determine their preferences and opinions about several available reading programs. The survey would be conducted by a curriculum committee or by the school system's administration, who are concerned with the problem of selecting the reading program or materials to be purchased. The results of the survey would provide information necessary for decisions about the purchase.

Unfortunately, misconceptions have developed with the use of terms *basic* and *applied research*. One such misconception is that basic research is complex and applied research is simple in its methodology. A related misconception is that applied research is carried out by unsophisticated practitioners, whereas basic research is performed by abstract, impractical thinkers. Another misconception is that applied research is often sloppy and haphazard but of great practical value, whereas basic research is precise and exacting but of little or no value in a real situation. As indicated earlier, however, basic and applied research arc differentiated not by their complexity or value, but by their goals or purposes.

> Basic and applied research are differentiated by their purposes. The primary purpose of *basic research* is the extension of knowledge; the purpose of *applied research* is the solution of an immediate, practical problem.

One type of applied research is *action research*—research conducted by a teacher, administrator, or other educational professional to aid in decision making in the local school. Action research focuses on the solution of day-to-day problems at the local level. There is little concern about generalizing the results of action research to other educational settings. Often, only a small, accessible population is used, such as the biology classes in a single high school.

Suppose the science teachers in a junior high school are considering whether to use additional group work in conducting experiments or an individual, programmed workbook that simulates experiments. They conduct action research with the students enrolled in the science classes at their school to determine the relative effectiveness and efficiency of the two methods. The teachers are concerned about their own situation; they are not concerned about generalizing to other schools.

Action research usually is less rigorous in terms of design and methodology than other educational research. Often, intact groups are used; in some cases, only a single group or an individual is involved in the study. Nevertheless, action research, combined with what is known from the research literature, provides a useful and viable approach to making educational decisions at the local level.

> *Action research* is usually conducted by teachers, administrators, or other educational professionals for solving a specific problem or for providing information for decision making at the local level.

Some authors, for example McMillan and Schumacher (1989), include a third category of evaluation or evaluative research. For the purposes of this introductory discussion, evaluation research can be considered close to applied research. Evaluation uses many of the same methods as research. Typically, the function of evaluation is to assess the merits of a practice or program in a specific situation. The application of the results is at a given site or sites and this is the primary focus for the evaluation. Evaluation results aid in decision making in a specific situation as with applied research.

> Basic and applied research provide a difference in general orientation based on the purposes of the research.

General Methodology: Qualitative and Quantitative Research

Up to this point, the terms qualitative and quantitative research have been used on occasion, without definition. Although the terms qualitative and quantitative are generally well known in our society, these as types of research, especially qualitative, are somewhat difficult to define, especially as specific practice that covers a variety of studies. We can take a definitive approach as provided by Krathwohl (1993):

> *Qualitative research: research that describes phenomena in words instead of numbers or measures. . . . Quantitative research: research that describes phenomena in numbers and measures instead of words. (p. 740)*

However, a description of these two approaches to research and an identification of their differences aids in understanding them.

The approach taken in this text is that although there are conceptual and methodological differences between qualitative and quantitative research, the distinction in terms of conducting research is not a dichotomy but a qualitative-quantitative continuum. Qualitative research has its origins in descriptive analysis, and is essentially an inductive process, reasoning from the specific situation to a general conclusion. Qualitative research, on the other hand, is more closely associated with deduction, reasoning from general principles to specific situations.

As Lancy (1993) points out, qualitative research is typically thought of as a method with a set of procedures for conducting research. From a practical standpoint of doing research this may be a useful approach, but there are underlying differences in the epistemologies of qualitative and quantitative research. They are based on different paradigms, a paradigm being a model consisting of assumptions, concepts, and propositions. Qualitative research in its purest sense follows the naturalist paradigm, that research should be conducted in the natural setting and that the meanings derived from research are specific to that setting and its conditions. The approach is that of a holistic interpretation of the natural setting.

Quantitative research has its roots in positivism and is more closely associated with the scientific method than is qualitative research. Reese (1980) defines positivism as:

a family of philosophies characterized by an extremely positive evaluation of science and scientific method. (p. 450)

The emphasis is on facts, relationships, and causes. Quantitative researchers place great value on outcomes and products; qualitative researchers have great concern for the impact of the process as well, typically more so than quantitative researchers.

It is not desirable to get sidetracked on a discussion of the role of theory in educational research at this point. That issue, along with a formal definition of theory, merits more elaboration as is done later in the chapter, but a few comments are in order here. Qualitative research does not emphasize a theoretical base for whatever is being studied at the beginning of the research. A theory may develop as the research is conducted, if it does it may be changed, dropped, or refined as the research progresses. If a theory develops based on the data, we have a "grounded theory," that is, a theory grounded in the data rather than based on some a priori constructed ideas, notions, or system. If no theory emerges, the research will be atheoretical, but will retain its descriptive value.

Quantitative research on the other hand, because of its deductive nature, tends to be more theory-based from the onset. In fact, when theory-testing research is being done it is likely to be quantitative research. Certainly, theories are not always identified explicitly in quantitative research but the theoretical underpinnings exist in one form or another.

Qualitative research is context-specific with the researcher's role being one of inclusion in the situation. As Smith (1987) indicates, qualitative research is based on the notion of context sensitivity, the belief that the particular physical and social environment has a great bearing on human behavior. Qualitative researchers emphasize a holistic interpretation. They perceive facts and values as inextricably mixed. On the other hand, quantitative researchers look for more context-free generalizations. They are much more willing to focus on individual variables and factors, rather than to concentrate on a holistic interpretation. Typically, quantitative researchers separate facts and values.

Overall, quantitative researchers are more attuned to standardized research procedures and predetermined designs than qualitative researchers. The latter are more flexible once they are into the research, and qualitative research involves multiple methods more frequently than quantitative research. Quantitative research has more of a catalog of designs than qualitative research. According to McMillan and Schumacher (1989), the most obvious distinction to a reader is the form of data presentation, and although Krathwohl's definitions given earlier may be somewhat extreme and oversimplified as to how phenomena are described, the presentations of data are different. Quantitative research relies heavily on statistical results represented with numbers; qualitative research relies heavily on narrative description.

Underlying the distinctions between qualitative and quantitative research is a difference in purpose. Qualitative research is done for the purpose of understanding social phenomena, *social* being used in a broad sense. Quantitative research is done to determine relationships, effects, and causes. When considering educational research, both of these purposes have relevance, indeed great relevance, for the improvement of education. So, both types of research are valuable and, in fact, can be supportive of each other in understanding the many factors that impact on education.

Figure 1.4 presents characteristics of the qualitative-quantitative research continuum. This is not necessarily an exhaustive set of distinctions, and many additional terms may appear in the literature. But this discussion should provide the reader with a basic conceptualization of the differences. Near the bottom of the figure, the methodology categories discussed below are placed on the continuum. Although qualitative and quantitative research have different underlying assumptions, and certainly different procedures, it is useful to place the methodology categories on the continuum because from the practical standpoint of conducting research, quantitative and qualitative procedures are often mixed. Nevertheless, the methodologies can be placed on the continuum as they tend toward the qualitative or quantitative end. The placement of the methodologies on the continuum of Figure 1.4 should be viewed as relative and not any type of exact spacing.

> Qualitative and quantitative research have their own characteristics, but as applied to educational research the distinction is more on a continuum than a dichotomy.

Experimental Research.   Educational research that is labeled "experimental" involves situations in which at least one variable,[3] the *experimental variable,* is deliberately manipulated or varied by the researcher to determine the effects of that variation. This implies that the researcher has the option of determining what the experimental variable will be and the extent to which it is varied. It is possible to have more than one experimental variable in a single experiment. In addition, in order to have what has become to be accepted as a "true experiment," the participants in the experiment must be assigned randomly to the experimental treatments.

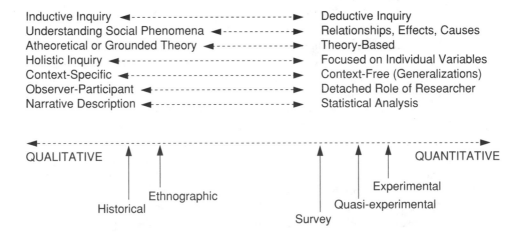

Inductive Inquiry ◄----------------------------► Deductive Inquiry
Understanding Social Phenomena ◄-------------► Relationships, Effects, Causes
Atheoretical or Grounded Theory ◄-------------► Theory-Based
Holistic Inquiry ◄-----------------------------► Focused on Individual Variables
Context-Specific ◄-----------------------------► Context-Free (Generalizations)
Observer-Participant ◄-------------------------► Detached Role of Researcher
Narrative Description ◄------------------------► Statistical Analysis

QUALITATIVE   QUANTITATIVE

Historical   Ethnographic   Survey   Quasi-experimental   Experimental

FIGURE 1.4   Characteristics of the Qualitative-Quantitative Research Continuum in Education

Suppose a researcher in health education is interested in the effects of three different exercise periods (periods of varying length) on resting heart rate. Sixty young adults are randomly assigned, 20 to each period. The 60 participants exercise as specified each day: 20 for one-half hour, 20 for 45 minutes, and 20 for 1 hour. The exercise for each period is specified. The exercise program is in effect for two months. The participants are measured on resting heart rate before and after the program so that a measure of change can be taken.

The experimental variable here is the period of exercise. This variable—that is, the three levels of exercise—was constructed by the researcher and then administered to the participants, 20 for each level. If different periods of exercise have an effect on heart rate, this effect should be manifested by differences in the (average) heart rates of the three groups.

Quasi-Experimental Research.   Quasi-experimental research is similar to experimental research in that one or more experimental variables are involved. However, instead of having participants randomly assigned to experimental treatments, "naturally" assembled groups, such as classes, are used in the research. Members have self-selected themselves into the groups. Single-subject designs that include the use of experimental treatments also are included in quasi-experimental research. Because of the difficulty often encountered when attempting to form groups by random assignment, quasi-experimental research is quite common in education.

Suppose a researcher is studying the effects of an instructional program in logical problem solving on sixth-grade performance on a mathematics concepts test. The experimental treatment is one-half hour of instruction in logical problem solving per day over a ten-week period. The researcher cannot randomly assign sixth-graders to classes, but eight intact classes receive the instructional program and eight classes serve as a comparison group. At the end of ten weeks, the students in the 16 classes are tested with a common mathematics concepts test.

Survey Research.   A variety of research studies can come under the heading of survey research. Generally, survey research deals with the incidence, distribution, and relationships of educational, psychological, and sociological variables. No experimental variables are manipulated. Variables are studied as they exist in the situation, usually a natural situation. Some surveys are limited to describing the status quo, while others attempt to determine the relationships and effects occurring between the variables. In the latter case, we have what is called *ex post facto research.*

A researcher conducting a study of the professional practices of college-level counselors in the private colleges of Ohio would be engaged in survey research. One way to do this study would be to construct an appropriate instrument, most likely a questionnaire, that could be completed either by a selected group of counselors or by the entire population of counselors. The responses of the counselors would provide a picture of the professional practices. From this information, the researcher could describe such characteristics as the relative importance (as perceived by the counselors) and the frequency of the practices. The study would emphasize the characteristics of the practices.

Consider an example of a survey involving ex post facto research. A study is conducted of the relationship between attitude toward school and achievement of upper elementary school students in various cognitive and skill areas (mathematics, verbal skills, etc.). The researcher would administer to the students included in the study an appropriate attitude inventory and achievement measures for the cognitive and skills areas. No variables are manipulated; that is, the researcher does not administer any treatments to students to change or influence attitude scores or performance scores. The data are collected, and the researcher attempts to identify any effects that may exist and tries to explain how the effects are operating. For example, one question that would undoubtedly be considered is, "Are certain attitude patterns consistently associated with specific achievement scores, and, if so, are the attitudes influencing the achievement scores?"

Historical Research. Historical research consists of studying a problem, an issue, a phenomenon, a movement, etc., in the past, and information collected from the past serves as the data to be interpreted. Historical researchers cannot relive the past so they must use documents and other artifacts to reconstruct the past through a process of critical inquiry. Historical research consists of describing what was, rather than what is or what effects certain variables may have on others. But historical research is much more than an attempt to reconstruct accurately the past. Historical research involves much interpretation and a projection of results and interpretation onto current issues, problems, procedures, and the like. In the context of education, historical research deals with educational "matters" of the past.

An example of historical research might be a study of federal assistance programs for secondary education during the period 1945–1960. The researcher would inquire about the programs through various sources, such as legislative documents and historical summaries. Then the researcher would describe the programs and consider their possible effects, both good and bad. Specific factors might be considered in tracing the history of these programs, such as their economic impact, and the implications of such impact for educational decision making and policy in the present and for the future. The context would be the events of some past period but the interpretation and implications of the results would not be limited to that period.

Ethnographic Research. Ethnographic research is commonly associated with anthropology, but it is finding increasing use in education. An *ethnography* is an in-depth, analytical description of a specific cultural situation, in the broad meaning of *culture*. Put into the context of education, we can define ethnographic research as the process of providing scientific descriptions of educational systems, processes, and phenomena within their specific contexts.

Ethnographic research relies heavily on observation, description, and qualitative judgments or interpretations of whatever phenomena are being studied. It takes place in the natural setting and focuses on processes in an attempt to obtain a holistic picture. Often, ethnographic research does not have a strong theoretical base, and few hypotheses are specified before the research is conducted. Theory and hypotheses are generated as the research proceeds.

Suppose a study of the nature of science instruction in a junior high school is being conducted. The research question is, "What is science instruction like in this school?" Observation is conducted in the science classrooms over the period of the school year. The observers take extensive field notes and interview students and teachers. On the basis of these results, they attempt to provide an accurate description and interpretation of science instruction in the school.

The classifications of educational research described above are attempts to provide some useful organization for an introduction to educational research. It is recognized that there are other classification systems of varying degrees of complexity. Some authors use categories such as descriptive research and causal-comparative research. Others may extend the methodologies to include types such as case studies. This text does not separate case study as a general research methodology because case study is recognized more as a way of reporting research and can cut across other types of research. Essentially, a case study involves a detailed examination of a single group, individual, situation, or site. Ethnographic research, when a single group is studied in depth, involves a case study. Case studies are commonly associated with, but not limited to, qualitative research. A single-subject study using quasi-experimental research is a case study.

The foregoing examples are brief and superficial descriptions of different types of research using the general methodology classification, but they illustrate the definitions involved. Of course, any specific study would require a more detailed statement of the research problem and hypotheses, as appropriate. More detailed examples are provided in the chapters that deal with these types of research. However, for the purposes here, the definitions do provide some contrasts between the various types. The classification of research by methodology is summarized in Table 1.1.

TABLE 1.1 Classification of Research by General Methodology

Type	Characteristics	Question Asked
Experimental	At least one variable is manipulated to determine the effect of the manipulation. Subjects are randomly assigned to experimental treatments.	What is the effect of the experimental variable?
Quasi-experimental	At least one variable is manipulated to determine the effect of the manipulation. Intact, naturally formed groups are used.	What is the effect of the experimental variable?
Survey	The incidence, relationships, and distributions of variables are studied. Variables are not manipulated but studied as they occur in a natural setting.	What are the characteristics of the variables? What are the relationships and possible effects among the variables?
Historical	A description of past events or facts is developed.	What was or what happened?
Ethnographic	A holistic description of present phenomena is developed.	What is the nature of the phenomena?

The Role of Theory

The term *theory* is used often in educational research; for example, we talk about *curriculum theory* or *learning theory.* Kerlinger (1986) defines a theory as "a set of interrelated constructs (concepts), definitions and propositions that present a systematic view of phenomena by specifying relations among variables with the purpose of explaining and predicting the phenomena" (p. 9).

Brodbeck (1963) includes many of the same ideas in her discussion of theory, adding that a theory is a set of laws and that all statements in a theory, both explained and explaining, are generalizations. The laws doing the explaining are the *axioms;* the generalizations explained are the *theorems.* Theories can range from a single, simple generalization to a complex formulation of laws.

> A *theory* is a generalization or series of generalizations by which we attempt to explain some phenomena in a systematic manner.

How are theories obtained or where do we get theories? Certainly one source is the research literature and the conceptual writings in a discipline. For example, theories of learning are often associated with educational psychology. If a theory did not exist or was not well developed, one could conceptualize a theory based on a logical analysis of prior research applied to the phenomenon under study. These approaches might be called "from the top down" as the theory emerges.

Earlier grounded theory was mentioned, and this might be characterized as, "from the bottom up," theory development. A grounded theory comes from the inductive analysis of the data as the research is conducted. The theory is grounded in the data and there are no preconceived ideas (at least nothing solidified) about what the theory will be. Suppose research is being done on teacher evaluation practices, and one question raised is, "What theory or theories of teacher evaluation underlie the teacher evaluation practices in the schools?" Using the grounded theory approach, evaluation practices in one or more school systems would be analyzed and the theory or theories would emerge from the data. The use of grounded theory is more closely associated with qualitative than with quantitative research.

The use of theory is more commonly associated with basic research than with applied research, and with quantitative research more than with qualitative research. Sometimes the term theory-testing research is used as a part of basic research. Consider an example. An educational psychologist is doing research on the relationship between frequency of encountering instructional materials (for example, word lists or mathematics problem solutions) and retention of the concepts included in the materials. A hypothesis is formulated that increased use enhances retention. Along with this hypothesis are hypotheses about several conditions relating to such factors as the complexity of the materials and the level at which continued use would no longer affect retention. Some relationships among factors may be hypothesized as well. Theory-testing research would enable us to test the theory with its primary and related hypotheses and, presumably, would either confirm or refute the theory, thus providing needed information for revising or extending the theory if necessary.

What is the role and purpose of theory in research? Basically, theory helps provide a framework by serving as the point of departure for the pursuit of a research problem. The theory identifies the crucial factors. It provides a guide for systematizing and interrelating the various facets of the research. However, besides providing the systematic view of the factors under study, the theory also may very well identify gaps, weak points, and inconsistencies that indicate the need for additional research. Also, the development of the theory may light the way for continued research on the phenomena under study.

In educational research, theory serves a synthesizing function, combining ideas and individual bits of empirical information into a set of constructs that provides for deeper understanding, broader meaning, and wider applicability. In a sense, a theory attaches meaning to facts and places them in proper perspective. Through this process, the theory aids in defining the research problem; that is, it helps identify the proper questions to be asked in the context of the specific project.

As indicated in Kerlinger's (1986) definition, a theory also serves the purposes of explaining and predicting. It suggests an explanation of observed phenomena, and it can also predict as yet unobserved or undiscovered factors by indicating their presence. Operating under the assumption that the theory is consistent, the researcher is then "tipped off" in terms of what to look for.

Another function of theory is to provide one or more generalizations that can be tested and then used in practical applications and further research. This development of generalizations is based on the assumption that generations do exist in education (or in any area under study) and that individual observations are special cases of such generalizations.

Conditions under which research is conducted and data are obtained within and across studies tend to be more valuable when incorporated into a meaningful whole; standing alone they may not mean much. As the facts of the research study, the data derive significance from the theory or theories into which they fit. Conversely, the theories become acceptable to the extent that they enhance the meaning of the data. Through this process, more adequate theories and unobstructed facts are secured; theory stimulates research, and conversely, research stimulates theory development and theory testing. The criterion by which we judge a theory is not its truth or falsity, but rather its usefulness. Theories sometimes decrease in usefulness in the light of new knowledge, and they are combined, replaced, and refined as more knowledge is made available.

A good theory is developed in such a way that the generalizations can be tested. The theory must be compatible with the observations made relative to it and with already existing knowledge. It must adequately explain the events or phenomena under study. The greater the generalizability of the theory, the more useful it will be because of its wider applicability.

Another characteristic of a good theory is reflected in the *law of parsimony,* which holds that a theory should be stated in the simplest form that adequately explains the phenomena. This does not mean that all theories should be simple statements; rather, they should be stated succinctly and precisely, avoiding ambiguities and unnecessary complexity. Important factors must not be overlooked, and the comprehensiveness of the theory must be adequate for its purpose.

The above discussion seems to make a strong case for "theory-based" research, and theories can be very useful, but therein lies the key—theories are valuable only to the extent that they are useful. Education draws on many disciplines and practices for its research base, both content and methods. So, the extent to which theory is valuable depends upon the specific purposes and type of research being conducted. Some research studies can benefit more than others from a strong theoretical base. Some studies develop theory from the data of the study itself. Other studies, at least on the surface, appear to be atheoretical, yet make valuable contributions to the research effort. All of this attests to the diversity that makes up educational research.

> A theory provides a framework for conducting research, and it can be used for synthesizing and explaining (through generalizations) research results.

The Activities of the Research Process

The systematic process of research leads to the general activities involved in conducting a research study. The activities, which correspond with the five steps of the scientific method described earlier, are elaborated on in this section. These activities are not limited to a specific type of research, such as ethnographic or experimental research, but apply generally. (Activities may receive varying emphasis, however, depending on the type of research.)

In summarizing the general activities involved in conducting a research study, we may appear to be emphasizing the sequential nature of the research process. To a certain extent this is fine, but as mentioned earlier, we do not want to leave the impression that the research process is rigid or completely structured. Activities overlap to some degree, and at times two or more activities can be in process simultaneously. For example, in ethnographic research, hypothesis formulation often takes place throughout the study, from data collection on. In many studies, preliminary analysis begins while data collection is still in process. Nevertheless, it is helpful to impose some order on the various activities.

Figure 1.5 presents a sequential pattern of activities in flowchart form to provide an overview of the various activities. The top row of boxes represents the general activities, and in order to accommodate flexibility in the research process and variations in different types of research, there is some overlap among the activities. For example, an experiment may be conducted for which all hypotheses are formulated and data identified before any data are collected. On the other hand, an ethnographic researcher might be reformulating hypotheses and identifying additional data well into the research process. This charac-teristic is indicated by the overlapping boxes in the figure.

The lower boxes (broken line) are not activities, but in essence are products of research. The arrows reflect the relationships between the activities and existing knowl-

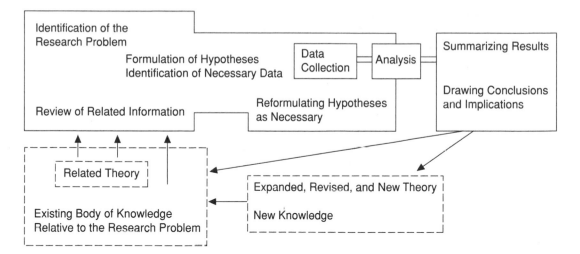

FIGURE 1.5   Sequential Pattern of General Activities in Conducting a Research Study and the Relationship of Such Activities to Existing Knowledge

edge, related theory, and expanded, revised, and new theory and knowledge. Related theory is considered to be a part, but not necessarily all, of the body of knowledge relative to the research problem. Expanded, revised, and new theory, if forthcoming from the research project, then becomes part of the existing body of knowledge, as does new knowledge not considered to be theory. All general activities draw on existing knowledge, but for the purpose of this figure, we associate the major impact of the body of knowledge with the research problem.

> The research process may be viewed as a sequence of activities, with the possibility of some overlap and fluctuation among the activities.

At this point, each of the activities will be described in more detail. However, this discussion is introductory and is designed only to provide an overview. In the following chapters, activities are described in detail and illustrated with examples.

Identification of the Research Problem

This is the beginning activity of the research process (at least, is should be), and it is often the most difficult The problem must be identified with adequate specificity. It is at this point in many studies that hypotheses—tentative "guesses" or conjectures about whatever is being studied—are generated. Variables must be identified and defined adequately for their use in the context of the study so that necessary data can be identified in preparation for data collection. This is done on the basis of existing knowledge. The literature is reviewed for information related to the research problem and to the possible methodology for conducting the research, basically to determine what others have done and have discovered that might be useful. The review of literature is a substantial task, and an entire chapter of this book (Chapter 3) is devoted to it.

Data Collection

Before data are collected, any necessary measuring instruments must be identified and perhaps developed; or if the data are going to be contained in a descriptive narrative, the researcher must prepare for taking field notes. If an ethnographic study is being done, the researcher collects the data through various procedures such as interviews and observation. If an experiment is being conducted, the experimental treatments are administered or manipulated just before or during the data collection process. In essence, the experiment is being conducted at this point; the measures are taken. In the case of a survey, measuring instruments, such as achievement tests or questionnaires, are administered. If instruments are developed, they must be tried before the major data collection for the study is undertaken. Then the data must be assembled, coded, and prepared for analysis.

Analysis

Results of the study are generated when analysis is done. Field notes are organized and synthesized at this point. Data are summarized, manipulated, and in essence reduced so they provide necessary information for description and hypotheses testing. If statistical analyses are done, they are completed at this point.

Summarizing Results and Drawing Conclusions

After the data have been analyzed and the results generated, the researcher must decide what information they provide. Results must be summarized and tied together, analyses must be interpreted, and conclusions must be drawn as they relate to the research problem. Conclusions are drawn about hypotheses if hypotheses were tested. The research report is prepared—a task that often requires rewriting. The importance of this task can hardly be overemphasized because it is the way in which the research results add to new knowledge and theory, and are incorporated into the existing body of knowledge.

The culminating activity of drawing conclusions and implications is in one sense the most important, because in essence this was the purpose for doing the research. Yet it is in this activity that many research studies are weak. Graduate students find writing the conclusions sections of theses or dissertations a difficult activity. (However, by no means is this difficulty unique to graduate students.) In the earlier steps, prescribed procedures seem to be followed and it is a matter of doing the tasks. But drawing conclusions requires interpretation, synthesis, and insights, activities that are difficult to specify as tasks. Evidence that drawing conclusions is difficult is the fact that many initial drafts of the final chapter of a dissertation, for example, read like a rewrite of the results chapter.

Although we cannot ensure that drawing conclusions will be insightful there are suggestions to follow to improve this activity and enhance the value of the research. These suggestions are:

1. Know the area in which the research has been conducted—in essence, know what is in the research literature, not simply have a passing acquaintance.

2. Address the issue of the external validity of the research. (Internal validity should have been established earlier.) Discuss the generalizability of the results and do not hesitate to extend external validity on a logical basis. Make whatever reasonable case possible for generalizing the results. This typically requires a broader perspective than the variables and procedures of the study.

3. Focus on the meaning of the results rather than the results per se.

4. If theory is involved, either existing or if new theory was generated, show explicitly the correspondence between the results and the theory.

5. Search for consistencies between the results and results of other studies and explain how these consistencies might extend the external validity of research in the area.

6. Search for inconsistencies between the results and results of similar studies, and identify factors that may be causing the inconsistencies.

7. Make the chain of reasoning evident by which the conclusions are reached—do not assume that the reader can read the writer's mind.

8. If possible, suggest future research that might address unresolved issues, and provide the next logical extension of knowledge.

Summarizing results and drawing conclusions should reflect scholarship throughout. Of course, we want to avoid unwarranted conclusions, but we want to maximize the information from the research results. It is always a good procedure to have one's conclusions reviewed by one or more colleagues familiar with the research in the area.

The naive researcher may attempt to begin the research study by breaking into the sequence at a point such as data collection (a data collector in search of a research problem). Sometimes researchers formulate hypotheses on the basis of some data and then attempt to extract a problem from the hypotheses. Breaking the sequence in this manner tends to result in confusion and inefficiency. Certainly there is flexibility in the research process and there may be overlap and repetition of activities depending on the requirements of the specific research. However, adherence to the process as organized in Figure 1.5 tends to enhance the efficiency of conducting research.

Summary

This chapter provided an overview of the nature of educational research and introduced numerous concepts. In subsequent chapters, concepts and procedures will be expanded and described in detail. The intent of this chapter was to introduce the reader to educational research, thus providing the "big picture."

Two classification systems for educational research were described to give some notions of the breadth and variety in educational research. The terms *basic* and *applied research* have been around a long time and apply to the purpose of the research. Qualitative and quantitative research is another way to classify research, but it is more useful to view this distinction as on a continuum rather than as a dichotomy. The various general methodologies of research all have their place in educational research. The purpose of the research dictates the type. Educational research can be put into the context of the scientific method; however, neither educational research nor the scientific method should be viewed as a rigid and invariable lock-step set of procedures.

The general activities of the research process were identified, described, and, in Figure 1.5, interrelated. Educational research involves many activities, some of which are simple, others complex. In fact, an entire continuum is encompassed, from simple to complex. Research is done in many different areas, such as curriculum, learning, and educational administration, to mention just a few. Research takes place at many different levels, from the individual action research conducted at the local school level, to large-scale projects conducted at universities or other agencies. Therefore, the description of educational research must be broad and must include many components. Even broad concepts, when projected into reality, are made up of specifics, however, and it is the specifics of research methods (activities, procedures, underlying reasoning, and so on) that are of major consideration in this text.

The Function of Educational Research

At the conclusion of the first chapter, it is well to consider the general role of educational research. A question might be raised by an already overloaded teacher: Why bother with educational research at all? What type of role or function does educational research have in the overall enterprise of education and in its specific facets.

In a general sense, all educational research is oriented toward one or both of two ends: the extension of knowledge and the solution of a problem. These two ends are not mutually exclusive, especially in education, and the orientation is one of emphasis. Is the research being done to solve an immediate, defined problem, or is it being conducted primarily for the purpose of extending the knowledge base, regardless of the immediate usefulness of the results?

Consider two contrasting examples from education. The mathematics supervisor of a large city school system is grappling with the problem of poor mathematics achievement by a segment of the student population in grades 5 through 8. The supervisor has the option of implementing any one of three teaching approaches (materials and methods) that may improve achievement. A decision must be made about which approach to use. If an experiment can be conducted using the approaches with samples of the population, useful information would undoubtedly be generated. If an experiment is not an option, the supervisor will have to rely on the data of others to make a decision. In any event, research is needed to solve an immediate problem.

Suppose that an educational psychologist is doing research in the area of learning—specifically, the mastery of abstract concepts—by conducting experiments in a learning laboratory that test young adults' ability to deal with unfamiliar concepts. Various contrasts in the type of materials, amount of information, and so forth, may be included in the experiment, the results of which may not be directed at any specific problem. Although this experiment may not be directly useful for developing curriculum materials at any particular school level, it adds to knowledge about learning and may be useful in extending or developing a theory of learning.

In a general sense, all research in education is directed to one or both of two ends: (1) the extension of knowledge and (2) the solution of a problem.

It might be said that the overall function of educational research is to improve the educational process through the refinement and extension of knowledge. The refinement of existing knowledge or the acquisition of new knowledge is essentially an intermediate step toward the improvement of the educational process. This step is extremely important and may occupy a considerable proportion of the time allotted to the research endeavor. The refinement of existing knowledge should not be taken lightly, since in many situations the initial ideas and procedures of a research study may be relatively crude and may remain adequate for only a short time.

Within the broad framework of educational improvement, the specific roles of educational research are viewed differently by the people associated with various aspects of education. Two examples illustrate this point. A researcher concerned with a learning experiment may be attempting to reinforce or refute a theory of how learning takes place. The function of research here is to aid in making a decision concerning the refinement or extension of knowledge in this particular area. The classroom teacher, on the other hand, grappling with the problem of coming up with a more effective technique for teaching slow learners how to read, looks to research for tangible evidence that will help solve the immediate problem. Both are appropriate roles for educational research. That is, research should aid the theorist in making a decision about the theory, and it should provide the teacher with information that will lead to the solution of the nontheoretical classroom problem. The long-range goal of both theorist and teacher is to improve the educational process —the teacher in a much more immediate situation and the theorist on the assumption that knowing more about learning will increase the effectiveness of the learning process.

The teacher, the administrator, the specialist of any kind in the schools, the college professor, specialists in research and development centers and in regional educational laboratories are all taking part; all concerned should be consumers of research findings. At some stage or another, almost everyone should be an active participant in research studies. The practitioner, such as the teacher, will use research primarily to shed light on some immediate problem. Research involvement may make that individual a better educator. For the educator, some involvement with research, if only as a consumer of research results, should be a part of professional activity and growth. To be sure, there will be different types of research and different amounts of involvement, but all educators should view educational research as a helpful mechanism that all can use, one way or another, for the improvement of the educational process.

KEY CONCEPTS

Qualitative research
Quantitative research
Systematic research
Scientific method
Internal validity
External validity
Reliability of research
Basic research
Applied research
Action research

Role of theory
Grounded theory
Law of parsimony
Experimental research
Quasi-experimental research
Ex post facto research
Survey research
Historical research
Ethnographic research

EXERCISES

1.1 Identify the primary difference between basic research and applied research.

1.2 Define internal and external validity of a research study.

1.3 Why is it true that if a research study is completely lacking in internal validity, it also lacks external validity?

1.4 For each of the following, identify which type of validity (internal or external) is most likely lacking:

    a. An experimenter finds there are four equally plausible interpretations of the results.
    b. The possible effects of different materials cannot be separated from the effects of the teachers who use them.
    c. A sixth-grade teacher finds the results of a learning experiment do not apply to sixth-graders.
    d. In an ethnographic research study for which multiple observers are used, the observers cannot agree on their conclusions.

1.5 Define reliability of research. Describe how reliability might be threatened in (a) an experiment involving four experimenters administering the experimental treatment at different times, and (b) a study of teacher performance using ten different observers.

1.6 What distinguishes an experiment from nonexperimental types of research?

1.7 What do we mean when we say that the general approach of qualitative research is that of inductive inquiry?

1.8 A critic of the schools in a large school system asserts that the procedures for evaluating principals and assistant principals of the system have no theoretical basis. Describe how a researcher would develop a grounded theory of principal evaluation in this system. What might be some of the components of the grounded theory?

1.9 Describe how the focus of historical research differs from that of ethnographic research.

1.10 Develop an argument against the position: "Theory is useless in educational research."

1.11 In the research literature, identify a report for (a) an ethnographic research study and (b) an experiment. Since experimental research tends to be on the quantitative end and ethnographic research on the qualitative end of the qualitative-quantitative research continuum, identify the contrasting characteristics of Figure 1.4 as found when comparing the two studies.

NOTES

1. Some writers conceptualize validity into more than two concepts, but the two concepts of internal and external validity are adequate for an introductory discussion, and provide a useful distinction when conducting research and interpreting research results.

2. Statistical analyses are discussed later in the text, but it is useful to use some simple statistical concepts for illustration. The mean is a very common measure, and in this case it represents the average score of the class. This is the arithmetic mean which is the sum of the test scores divided by the number of scores.

3. A *variable* is a characteristic that takes on different values (or conditions) for different individuals. Variables are described in greater detail in Chapter 2.

REFERENCES

Brodbeck, M. (1963). Logic and scientific method in research on teaching. In N. L. Gage (Ed.), *Handbook of research on teaching* (pp. 44–93). Chicago: Rand McNally.

Kerlinger, F. N. (1986). *Foundations of behavioral research* (3rd ed.). New York: Holt, Rinehart & Winston.

Krathwohl, D. R. (1993). *Methods of educational and social science research: An integrated approach.* New York: Longman.

Lancy, D. F. (1993). *Qualitative research in education: An introduction to the major traditions.* New York: Longman.

McMillan, J. H., and Schumacher, S. (1989). *Research in education: A conceptual introduction* (2nd ed.). Glenview, IL: Scott, Foresman.

Reese, W. L. (1980). *Dictionary of philosophy and religion.* Atlantic Highlands, NJ: Humanities.

Smith, M. L. (1987). Publishing qualitative research. *American Educational Research Journal 24*(2), 173–183.

C h a p t e r 2

Identification of a Research Problem

A good part of the research process deals with obtaining good answers—that is, solutions to research problems. However, the research process involves asking good questions or adequately identifying the problem or the phenomenon to be investigated. This may be a difficult step in the research process because at this point there has been little organization of the study. Adequate identification is necessary to get the research process underway. The extent of detail in problem identification may vary somewhat with the type of research. For example, experimental studies usually have very specific research problems with accompanying hypotheses, whereas ethnographic research has more general problem statements, and hypotheses may be generated throughout the study.

The identification of a research problem involves more than simply providing an ad hoc statement or question about the area of interest. The first step in the identification involves selecting a research topic. Then a specific statement of the problem is generated from the topic. If hypotheses are identified, these along with the statement of the problem involve the use of specific terminology about variables and conditions. Education, like any profession, has a professional language (parts of which at least, are sometimes called jargon), and it is essential that meanings of terms in that language be consistent within the context of the research problem. In this chapter, numerous basic terms are defined, and it is important for the reader to understand those terms because they are part of the foundational language of educational research.

Selection of a Research Problem

The selection of an appropriate research problem is a matter of asking good questions—that is, questions that are relevant and important in the educational context. This general comment may seem reasonable enough, but there are many important educational issues to be researched at any given time. So, how does one go about selecting a research problem?

There are different ways by which research problems are selected, not all of them due to the internal motivation of the researcher, desirable as that may seem. Graduate students seeking research problems in order to complete the requirements for a graduate degree typically zero in on a research problem in one of two ways. They associate themselves closely with the research efforts of one or more professors serving as their mentors, and identify a related problem or one that comprises a subset of that research effort. The assumption is that the reason the students are studying with specific professors is because of mutual interests.

The second way is through discussions with other graduate students, some of whom are farther along in the graduate program and can provide insight into the selection process. Areas of research interest develop over time and when someone initially begins thinking about doing research, the process of selecting a research problem becomes one of successive approximations to defining the problem. A teacher who is in a graduate program may want to do research related to some aspect of classroom instruction. Discussing a possible research problem with colleagues and professors and becoming familiar with the area or topic help in identifying more specifically a researchable problem. But research problems, typically, are not identified overnight. They require becoming informed about a possible topic, thinking about it, and discussing it with others. Problems become modified and refined. Sometimes problems are expanded, sometimes restricted. A related but different direction may be taken. All of this is done to "zero in" on the problem.

Although the selection of a research problem may seem to be somewhat of a "broad" process as described above, there are certain factors that facilitate the process. The research problem should be of interest to the researcher, and to at least some recognized segment of the education profession. Its place in the context of education should be assured. Originality should also be considered, especially if the research topic is being selected for a thesis, but a completely original research idea is rare. It is more likely that the research will be an extension of some already completed project. The extent of duplication or replication that is desirable in such studies depends on the specific area and the conditions of the research.

Another factor is the significance of the research problem for education from either a practical or a theoretical viewpoint. Trivial problems—for example, the proportions of elementary students who wear canvas or leather shoes and the relationship of this choice of footwear to achievement—can be researched procedurally. But such a problem has no theoretical framework and no significance, regardless of what the resulting proportions happen to be. A research problem should add to the existing knowledge or contribute to education in a meaningful way.

Not all problems in education are researchable. Some are philosophical in nature and can be discussed but not researched. An example is a question such as, "Should the history requirement in the senior high school be one or two courses?" Chances are that if the requirement is two courses, the students will learn more history, but the question remains whether it is important that they have two courses. Answers to such questions are for the most part based on value judgments. If additional conditions are not stipulated, the questions are not researchable.

Even if problems are researchable, doing the research may not be feasible. The necessary data for the study may be excessive or may be too difficult to obtain. Ethical considerations may be involved; for example, the testing required to obtain the necessary data may be an invasion of the individual's privacy. Necessary resources, such as laboratory facilities and funds, may not be available. Many of these kinds of conditions can make it impractical to research a specific problem.

Colleges of education in universities often have specific research "thrusts," so to speak. Some colleges may have special interests in curriculum research, research related to mathematics instruction, for example. Others may have interests in teacher performance, policy development in higher education, or the effects of physical training programs, to mention three additional examples. These thrusts can be effective sources for research problems. But there are other sources. The researcher's professional experience and situation can suggest problems, especially in applied research. Current educational issues may generate any number of research problems as can social and political issues related to education. The research literature contains implications for continued research on a topic, and theories from education or disciplines related to education can suggest research problems. For example, organizational theory as applied to education requires research for testing the theory. In summary, research problems are selected in a context and this includes information about a possible problem and the researcher's experience.

> The selection of a research problem involves reading, discussing, and conceptualizing. Typically, the process is one of successive approximations to the problem as factors related to the problem are considered.

Statement of the Research Problem

Selection of a research problem does not necessarily mean that it is adequately stated. Usually, a problem requires some reworking to get it into a suitable form for the study to proceed effectively. A problem may be stated broadly and then systematically restricted through a review of the literature in the initial stages of the research effort. It is better to work in this direction than to begin with a problem that is too narrow and then attach pieces to expand it.

Research problems may be stated in a declarative or descriptive manner or in question form. Many researchers, possibly the majority, prefer the question form, but either form is acceptable. The question form may aid in focusing the problem, and it is especially effective when subproblems are included within the larger research problem. The most important characteristic of the problem statement is that it must provide adequate focus and direction for the research.

At this point, it might be useful to illustrate some unsatisfactory and satisfactory problem statements. A statement such as "the elementary school curriculum" is far too broad to serve as a problem statement; in fact, it really contains no problem. A satisfactory statement might be: "A study of the effects of elementary school curriculum practices on the reading achievement of fourth-grade students in City A." Or, in question form, we might have: "What are the effects of elementary school curriculum practices on fourth-grade reading achievement in City A?" Following are several examples of original statements and their subsequent restatements into more manageable statements of the problem, including the question form:

Original Creativity of elementary school students.

Restatement A study of the relationship between divergent thinking scores and selected characteristics of fifth-, sixth-, and seventh-grade students.

Question form What are the relationships between scores of fifth-, sixth-, and seventh-grade students on a divergent thinking test and scores on (1) a general IQ measure, (2) a reading achievement test, and (3) a measure of physical dexterity?

Original Achievement and teaching techniques.

Restatement A study of the effects of three teaching techniques on science achievement of junior high school students.

Question form Do three different teaching techniques have differing effects on science achievement scores of junior high school students?

Original High-school dropouts.

Restatement An ethnographic study of the school environment of regular and learning disabled students to determine factors related to potential dropout.

Question form What factors of the school environment are related to the potential dropout of regular and learning disabled high school students?

Original A history of College A.

Restatement A study of the impact of federal aid to higher education on the expansion of the science and mathematics curriculums in College A during the period 1955–1972.

Question form What was the impact of federal aid on the expansion of the science and mathematics curriculums in College A during 1955–1972?

Original The role of the guidance counselor in the high school.

Restatement A survey of the practices of the guidance counselors in the high schools of City B.

Question form Four questions are given to illustrate the identification of subproblems:

What proportion of guidance counselors' working day is taken up with non-guidance activities?

What are the major strengths of guidance counselors' practices as perceived by the students?

What are the major weaknesses of guidance counselors' practices as perceived by the students?

What practices are perceived by guidance counselors as most effective in advising students about college selection?

A good statement of the problem should provide the researcher with direction in pursuing the research. The statement should indicate the general focus and the educational context of the problem. Key factors should be identified along with a general framework for reporting results. For example, in the first of the preceding restatements, the word *relationship* implies certain procedures and certain types of results. The three grade levels limit and define the population under study, and the term *divergent thinking scores* is certainly more specific than the word *creativity,* which was used in the original statement. Divergent thinking requires a definition such as the score on a specific divergent thinking test.

It should be noted that in the restatements of the problems, considerable definition of terms would be necessary. The selected characteristics in the first example would require identification and definition, and the three teaching techniques of the second example would require definition for the specific situation. Such definitions should accompany the statement of the problem, but they are usually not included in the statement because they would make it excessively long and cumbersome. Assuming that adequate definition accompanies the statement of the problem, there should be no ambiguity about what is to be investigated.

Whether or not research problems are stated in question form depends, to a large extent, on the preference of the researcher. If the question form appears to be helpful, it should be used. Actually, the form for stating the problem is relatively unimportant; what is important is that the statement be precise and definitive, so there is no confusion about what is under study.

It often helps in understanding the nature of the statement of the research problem to consider examples. Following is a list of problem statements developed by students in a research methods course:

1. A survey of reading program components and practices in selected school systems of Ohio.

2. What are the effects of cerebral, hemispheric overload on auditory and motor performance in young children?

3. An ethnographic study of science instruction in a girls' college-preparatory high school, grades nine through twelve.

4. What are the relationships between different types of praise and attitude toward school of students in an integrated elementary school?

5. A survey of the scholastic achievement of students from nine elementary schools entering Junior High School A.

6. What are the effects of age, type of material, and amount of available information on performance on a concept attainment task?

7. What are teacher and administrator perceptions of the professional growth credits program in the City A public schools?

8. What are the extent and nature of the educational backgrounds and professional qualifications of the chief personnel officers in private, four-year colleges in the United States?

9. A survey of teacher perception of and attitude toward the teacher competency testing program in State A.

10. A history of state-supported inservice programs for elementary and secondary teachers in Ohio during the period 1970–1980.

The statement of the research problem should be concise and should identify the key factors (variables) of the research study.

Constants, Variables, and Operational Definition

By itself, the statement of the problem usually provides only general direction for the research study; it does not include all the specific information. There is some basic terminology that is extremely important in how we communicate specific information about research problems and about research in general. A *constant* is a characteristic or condition that is the same for all individuals in a study. A *variable,* on the other hand, is a characteristic that takes on different values or conditions for different individuals. If a researcher is interested in the effects of two different teaching methods on the science achievement of fifth-grade students, the grade level is a constant, since all individuals involved are fifth-graders. This characteristic is the same for everyone; it is a constant condition of the study.

After the different teaching methods have been implemented, the fifth-graders involved would be measured with a science achievement test. It is very unlikely that all of the fifth-graders would receive the same score on this test, so the score on the science achievement test becomes a variable, because different individuals will have different scores; at least, not all individuals will have the same scores. We would say that science achievement is a variable, but we would mean, specifically, that the score on the science achievement test is a variable.

A *constant* is a characteristic or condition that is the same for all individuals in a study. A *variable* is a characteristic that takes on different values or conditions for different individuals.

There is another variable in the example above—the teaching method. In contrast to the science achievement test score, which undoubtedly would be measured on a scale with many possible values, teaching method is a categorical variable consisting of only two categories, the two methods. So, we have different kinds of variables and different names or classifications for them. There are many classification systems given in the literature; so many that there is considerable overlap and opportunity for confusion. The names we use are descriptive; they describe the roles that variables play in a research study. The variables described below by no means exhaust the different systems and names that exist, but they are the most useful for communicating about educational research.

Independent and Dependent Variables. Some of the most important and widely used descriptors for variables are independent and dependent variables. The terminology comes from mathematics. In a general sense, it is said that values of the dependent variable depend on the independent variables. Dependent variables are the variables that we measure, such as science achievement. Independent variables often simply are classifying variables, classifying the individuals of the research study. In the science achievement example, teaching method would be an independent variable. A fifth-grader in the study would be taught by one of the two methods, which would comprise the two classifications, or levels, of this variable. (Two is the minimum number of levels for a variable.) The score on the science achievement test—the dependent variable—presumably will somehow be affected by the teaching method. In fact, the purpose of the study would be to determine if the teaching methods have different effects on science achievement. The researcher attempts to explain performance on the dependent variable in light of the independent variable.

The following example further illustrates the use of variables and constants. In a study conducted to determine the effect of three different teaching methods on achievement in elementary algebra, each of three ninth-grade algebra sections in the same school, taught by the same teacher, is taught using one of the methods. Both boys and girls are included in the study. The constants in the study are grade level, school, and teacher. (This assumes that, except for method, the teacher can hold teaching effectiveness constant.) The independent variables in the study are teaching method and gender of the student. Teaching method has three levels that arbitrarily can be designated methods A, B, and C; gender of the student, of course, has two levels. Achievement in algebra, as measured at the end of the instructional period, is the dependent variable.

Consider other examples of independent and dependent variables:

Example 1: A study of teacher-student classroom interaction in different levels of schooling.

> Independent variable: Level of schooling, four categories—primary, intermediate, junior high school, senior high school.

> Dependent variable: Score on a classroom observation inventory which measures teacher-student interaction.

Example 2: A study of location of school effect upon attitudes toward school of seventh-grade students.

Independent variable: Location of school, three categories—urban, suburban, rural.

Dependent variable: Score on an attitude toward school inventory.

Example 3: A study of the effects of type of material upon solving concept attainment problems.

Independent variable: Type of material, two categories—figural, verbal.

Dependent variable: Time required to solve the concept attainment problems.

Example 4: A study of the professional attitudes of men and women teachers.

Independent variable: Gender of the teacher—male, female.

Dependent variable: Score on a professional attitude inventory.

Independent and dependent variables are descriptors of variables commonly used in educational research. The independent variables may be affecting the dependent variables, and in that sense, dependent variables depend on independent variables.

Other Possible Types of Variables. In any research study, a number of influencing factors may be present, appearing in the form of variables. For convenience, these variables are given descriptive names and are often called by these names in the literature.

An *organismic variable* is a preexisting characteristic of the individuals under study. It is not a variable that can be randomly assigned to individuals. The gender and intelligence of the individuals are examples of organismic variables.

An *intervening variable* is one whose existence is inferred, but it cannot be manipulated or measured. If it has an effect, it must be inferred from a prior knowledge of what the effect might be in the context of the independent and dependent variables of the study. In the algebra example, learning style of students is an intervening variable. Intervening variables may go by other names, such as nuisance variables, mediator variables, or confounded variables. They are variables whose presence may confuse the interpretation of other variable effects.

A *control variable* is a variable other than the independent variables of primary interest whose effects are determined by the researcher. In the algebra example, if the difference between boys and girls on the dependent variable is determined, gender of the individual would be a control variable as well as an organismic variable. Control variables are independent variables.

Other names used for variables overlap with the foregoing terms. An example is a *moderator variable*. Suppose a study is done on the effects of three reading programs on fourth-grade reading achievement. There may be considerable difference between students on prior reading achievement, and one program may be more effective than the other two for students who have high prior reading achievement. In this case, prior reading achievement is a moderator variable, since program effects may be different for different levels of this variable; that is, program effects are moderated by prior reading achievement. If a moderator variable is uncontrolled, it is essentially an intervening variable. If it is controlled—that is, its effects have been determined—it becomes a control variable.

It can be seen from the foregoing examples that the descriptions of variables are not mutually exclusive. For example, organismic variables may also be control variables. These kinds of variables often take on the form of independent variables in a study, although they usually are not the independent variables of primary interest. If the algebra example were extended to include two or more schools, and if the differences between schools were determined, school would become a control variable. (However, school could not be an organismic variable.)

Any given study is not limited to a single independent, organismic, control, intervening, or dependent variable. Suppose that the fifth-grade science achievement example were extended to include five schools; that the students were grouped, on the basis of previous performance, as high, average, and low; and that both boys and girls were included and their differences determined. Another independent variable—type of material, with two kinds of materials—is introduced. It is decided to do a more comprehensive achievement study to measure the same group on both reading achievement and spelling achievement. These achievement scores also would be dependent variables—not because there are two or more measures of achievement, but because scores vary for any one type of achievement and may be affected by the independent variables. Possible intervening variables now would become the students' learning styles and the teaching styles of the teachers. This is a relatively complex example; the variables are summarized in Figure 2.1. Note that the control variables are independent variables.

It should not be inferred that organismic variables are necessarily control variables. They are control variables only if their effects are determined—that is, controlled, as indicated in the example. The learning style of the students is an organismic variable, and it probably would appear as an intervening variable.

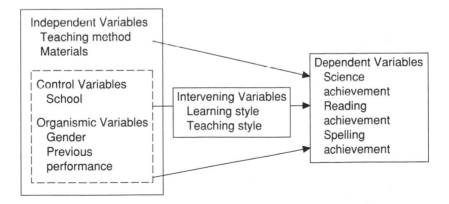

FIGURE 2.1   Different Types of Variables Operating in a Fifth-Grade Achievement Study

Variables as They Are Measured. When all the possible variables in education are considered, it soon becomes apparent that they are measured in different ways. In the science achievement example, the variable teaching method is simply a categorical variable; we know that the methods are different and can be given different names. On the other hand, if the dependent variable of the score on a science achievement test is considered, the measurement is not simply categorical; there is some kind of ordering and quantifying of the scores.

Essentially, there is a hierarchy of measurement scales—with four general categories, based on the amount of information contained in a score. The lowest type of scale is the *nominal scale,* which simply categorizes without order. Gender of the individual is a variable that is measured on a nominal scale.

Consider a variable such as attitude toward school. If one individual indicates a highly favorable attitude toward school and another individual indicates a neutral attitude, we not only know that they are different, but we also can order the individuals on the degree of favorableness in their attitudes toward school. Thus, besides having a difference, we also have order. A variable so measured is on an *ordinal scale.*

Suppose we measure a variable such as IQ or performance on an achievement test in reading or mathematics. If three individuals have scores of 105, 110, and 115, respectively, the difference of five points between the first two individuals is considered equivalent to the difference of five points between the second two individuals. This gives not only difference and order but also a unit of equal differences established in the measurement. This level of measurement is called *equal-unit* or *interval scale.*[1]

A variable such as age is an example of a fourth level of measurement. If an individual is exactly thirty years old, that individual is twice the age of someone exactly fifteen years old. We can say twice because the time of birth is the zero point in age. Thus, we have not only difference, order, and an equal unit, but also a comparison in terms of the ratio of one observation to another. Hence, this level of measurement is called *ratio scale.* To establish a ratio, the scale must have a true zero point.

Ratio scale variables, except for physical measurements, seldom occur in educational research. For most practical purposes, however, ratio scale measurement is equivalent to interval scale with regard to statistical procedures. Therefore, whether measurement is interval or ratio scale is usually not an important distinction in educational research.

The four levels of measurement, which are hierarchical in terms of the amount of information contained in a score, also can be viewed as the number of conditions needed to attain the scale. The ratio scale is the highest level in the hierarchy and contains the most information. The measurement scales are summarized in Table 2.1.

Variables whose measurement scales are ordinal level or higher may be divided into those that are numerically scaled and those that are not. For example, observations for variables such as weight in pounds are on numerical scales. However, if more general categories were used, such as light weight, medium weight, and heavy weight, the variable weight would still be ordered, but it would no longer be numerically scaled. A variable measured as poor, fair, good, or excellent is another example of one that is ordered but not numerically scaled.

TABLE 2.1   Measurement Scales and Their Conditions

Scale	Conditions	Example
Nominal	Measures without order; simply indicates that two or more classifications are different	Types of secondary schools: comprehensive, vocational, private, college prep, etc.
Ordinal	Measures with order; indicates that the measurement classifications are different and can be ranked	The letter grading system
Interval (or equal unit)	Measures with order and establishes numerically equal distances on the scale	Performance on a standardized achievement test in science
Ratio	Contains an absolute or true zero point in addition to an equal unit	Height

The discussion of measurement scales at this point was provided to elaborate on the meaning and nature of variables in education. Measurement of variables is a relevant issue in educational research and a later chapter is devoted to measurement.

Operational Definition.   In any research study, the variables and conditions of the study must be defined operationally. Educators often deal with variables that do not readily manifest themselves. If a school nurse were interested in the weights of first-grade pupils, they could be measured using a common weight scale. Similarly, if we want to measure and quantify ability to learn or reading comprehension, we must have some tool to do so. Perhaps we could set up a chain of definition for ability to learn and thus reach a consensus. But to achieve measurement, we must include the processes or operations that are going to be used to measure the phenomenon or variable under study. Such a definition is called an *operational definition*. In essence, an operational definition of a variable describes how or by what means we are going to measure the variable.

Operational definitions are not only desirable in educational research, they are essential. They are essential for defining how the variables are measured. We know that creativity is a variable among school-age children, and all people for that matter. But creativity cannot be measured until it has an operational definition. There may be more than one operational definition of a variable such as creativity and herein lies another value of operational definitions. They enable researchers to identify similarities and differences in research studies on the same topic or issue. Some variables are measured in different ways and thus may lead to apparent contradictions in research results. Anxiety is a phenomenon that can take on different operational definitions. If anxiety is defined as the score on a paper-and-pencil test, its relationship to other variables (for example, test performance) may be very different than if it is defined as a galvanic skin response. So, operational definitions provide for the replication of studies and they enhance the interpretations of results. Operational definitions aid in establishing the external validity (or lack of it) of research results, by helping define the limits for generalization.

The following are examples of operational definitions:

1. Ability to learn: score on the LM Form of the Stanford-Binet Intelligence Scale.
2. Science achievement: score on the science subtest on the Iowa Test of Basic Skills.
3. Divergent thinking: score on the Brick Uses Test.
4. Concept attainment performance: time required to solve correctly five concept attainment problems.

Conditions or characteristics of a research study may also require operational definition. For example, if high school seniors are to be surveyed, who is a high school senior? A possible operational definition of a senior is a student who is presently enrolled in a recognized high school, has not yet graduated, but has earned 12 or more high school course credits. In this case, a senior is defined in terms of certain observable or identifiable characteristics or properties.

An *operational definition* is stipulative in that it specifies the operation or characteristics necessary to identify the variable or condition being defined.

Hypotheses and the Statement of the Problem

Now that the concepts of variables, constants, and operational definitions have been described, we can continue with the elaboration of the specifics of the research study through the use of hypotheses. Attempting to include all specific information in the statement of the problem would make the statement cumbersome and unmanageable, so we develop hypotheses for more specificity and direction. Hypotheses may be derived directly from the statement of the problem, they may be based on the research literature, or in some cases, such as in ethnographic research, they may (at least in part) be generated from data collection and analysis. Ethnographic research also involves foreshadowed problems which, although they are not hypotheses, are statements of what to look for in doing the research. Foreshadowed problems are not replacements for hypotheses, but in ethnographic research they are supplemental to hypotheses and certainly provide direction for the research.

A hypothesis is a conjecture or a guess at the solution to a problem or the status of the situation. In a general sense, hypotheses take on some of the characteristics of a theory, which is usually considered a larger set of generalizations about a certain phenomenon. Thus, a theory might include several hypotheses. Logically, the approach is to proceed so a decision can be made about whether or not the hypotheses are tenable.

This is called *testing the hypothesis;* the results of such a test either support or refute the hypothesis.

Borg and Gall (1989) identify four criteria that hypotheses should satisfy:

1. The hypothesis should state an expected relationship between two or more variables.
2. The researcher should have definite reasons based on either theory or evidence for considering the hypothesis worthy of testing.
3. A hypothesis should be testable.
4. A hypothesis should be as brief as possible consistent with clarity (pp. 68–69).

A weakness of many hypotheses is that they are too broad to pinpoint the specific problem under study—as, for example, in the following hypothesis: "Bright students have good attitudes toward school." The terms *bright, good,* and *attitudes* represent types of broad, undefined generalities. Some type of vague relationship between brightness and good attitude is implied, but little direction for research is provided. To convert the statement into an acceptable hypothesis, it might be changed to read:

> *Students aged nine through eleven who score in the upper 25 percent of their class on the (standardized) IQ test have a higher mean score on the "X-Y-Z Attitude Toward School Inventory" than students who score in the lower 75 percent of the class on the IQ test.*

Note that this statement has specificity and that it states an expected relationship (the upper 25 percent on the IQ test have higher mean attitude scores than the lower 75 percent on the IQ test). Assuming that the measurement can be made, the hypothesis is testable.

Another version could be:

> *A positive relationship exists between the scores on the (specific) IQ test and the (specific) attitude inventory for students aged nine through eleven.*

This statement of the hypothesis is shorter than the initial statement. It includes an expected relationship and it is testable.

In both instances, the hypothesis contains the operational definitions of the variables involved: academic aptitude (brightness) and attitude toward school. These variables are defined by scores on a specific test and a specific inventory. If the operational definitions make the statement of the hypothesis too cumbersome, they can be presented in a separate statement or section. However, the variables should be clearly identified so that the expected relationship is defined—that is, that it will be positive or that the mean of a certain group will be higher than that of another group. The hypothesis is testable; that is, procedures exist for analyzing the data that will give results either supporting or refuting the hypothesis. (However, the two versions presented here would be tested in different ways.) The hypothesis declares the anticipated direction; supposedly, this is not just a wild guess. Overall, the hypothesis meets the criteria for a good statement, assuming that there are reasons that make the hypothesis worthy of testing.

A *hypothesis* is a conjecture or proposition about the solution to a problem, the relationship of two or more variables, or the nature of some phenomenon.

Types and Forms of Hypotheses

Kerlinger (1986, p. 189) indicates that, in a broad sense, researchers use two types of hypotheses—substantive and statistical. *Substantive hypotheses,* sometimes called *research hypotheses,* are tentative statements about the expected outcomes for the variables of the research study. An example of a substantive or research hypothesis is, "As punitive, disciplinary methods are increased in an elementary school, student achievement will decrease." In research in science education, a hypothesis might be: "Laboratory instruction enhances the student's understanding of scientific processes over an instructional approach limited to lecture, discussion, and theoretical problem solution."

A *statistical hypothesis* is given in statistical terms. Technically, in the context of inferential statistics, it is a statement about one or more parameters that are measures of the populations under study.[2] Statistical hypotheses often are given in quantitative terms, for example: "The mean reading achievement of the population of third-grade students taught by Method A equals the mean reading achievement of the population taught by Method B."

The preceding statistical hypothesis is an example of a hypothesis stated in *null form;* that is, no difference in the means is hypothesized. It is also called a nondirectional hypotheses because no direction is indicated for the results. The *null hypothesis* is sometimes described as the *hypothesis of no difference* or *no relationship.* Technically, when a statistical hypothesis is tested using inferential statistics, it is a null hypothesis that is being tested.

For any statistical hypothesis, there is an *alternative hypothesis* that expresses the remaining possible outcomes. The alternative hypothesis for the reading achievement example would be: "The reading achievement means of the populations of third-graders taught by Method A and Method B are not equal." Note that the null hypothesis and the alternative cover all the possibilities, in this case either the means are equal or they are not equal.

Suppose we had initially hypothesized, "The mean reading achievement of the population of third-graders taught by Method A is greater than the mean of the population taught by Method B." In order to cover all possible outcomes of the two means we have:

The mean of the population of third graders taught by Method A is less than the mean of the population taught by Method A, and
   The mean of the population of third graders taught by Method A equals the mean of the population taught by Method B.

These are two alternative hypotheses and the latter statement is the null hypothesis. We can combine the two statements for a single alternative hypothesis:

The mean of the population of third-graders taught by Method A is less than or equal to *the mean of the population taught by method B.*

The null hypothesis is contained in this single alternative, and again all possible outcomes are covered.

We can also distinguish between *directional* and *nondirectional hypotheses.* For the former, a direction of results is implied, whereas no direction is specified for the latter. The null hypothesis is a nondirectional hypothesis. Substantive or research hypotheses more often than not are directional because they indicate the anticipated direction of results.

Suppose a teacher experimenting with a new technique for teaching third-grade spelling hypothesizes that the spelling achievement of third-grade pupils being taught with the new technique exceeds that of pupils being taught with traditional methods. Specifically, the hypothesis would be:

The mean score on the ABC Spelling Test of third-grade pupils taught by the new method will exceed the mean score of pupils taught by traditional methods.

The alternative hypothesis is:

The mean score on the ABC Spelling Test of third-grade pupils taught by the new method will be less than or equal to the mean score of pupils taught by traditional methods.

The original hypothesis is a directional hypothesis in that a direction of results is implied—namely the greater achievement (higher mean score) of pupils taught by the new method. The alternative hypothesis contains the null hypothesis.

Consider additional examples of hypotheses and their alternatives:

1. The mathematics achievement of high-ability students equals that of average-ability students, or there is no difference between the mathematics achievement of average- and high-ability students.
1a. The mathematics achievement of high-ability students is not equal to that of average-ability students.
2. The reading level of first-grade girls is the same as that of boys.
2a. The reading level of first-grade girls is not equal to that of boys.
3. Science achievement of students taught by inductive inquiry exceeds that of those taught by deductive inquiry.
3a. The science achievement of students taught by inductive inquiry is less than or equal to those taught by deductive inquiry.
4. There is a positive relationship between academic aptitude scores and scores on a social adjustment inventory for junior high school age students.
4a. There is a negative relationship or no relationship between academic aptitude scores and scores on a social adjustment inventory for junior high school age students.

5.   Males, ages eighteen through twenty years, participating in Exercise Program A will have greater mean scores on the XY Physical Performance Test, than those participating in Exercise Program B.

5a.   Males, ages eighteen through twenty years, participating in Exercise Program A will have mean scores on the XY Physical Performance Test, less than or equal to the mean scores of those participating in Exercise Program B.

The first two hypotheses are null hypotheses, and these hypotheses and their alternatives are nondirectional. The latter three hypotheses are directional, and the null hypothesis for each is contained in the alternative hypothesis.

Should hypotheses be stated in directional or nondirectional form—or does it make any difference? The form used should be determined by the expected results. If the research literature in the area indicates that we can expect a difference or a direction of results, a directional hypothesis is called for; if the research literature does not present convincing evidence for a direction, or if an exploratory study is being done, a non-directional hypothesis should be used. Because of the emphasis on null hypotheses in inferential statistics, educational research—and behavioral sciences research in general—has probably overused the nondirectional hypothesis and underused the directional hypothesis.

Statistical hypotheses are used in the analysis of data; *substantive* or *research hypotheses* indicate the direction of results. Hypotheses may be stated in *directional* or *nondirectional* form. The null hypothesis is the hypothesis of no difference or no relationship.

These comments about hypotheses apply more to quantitative research than qualitative research. In quantitative research, hypotheses typically are identified at the beginning of the research study, prior to data collection, and if modified such modification is minimal. On the other hand, hypotheses in qualitative research are much more likely to emerge as the research is being conducted. There may or may not be some tentative, general hypotheses at the outset, but qualitative researchers are very willing to add, delete, modify, and refine hypotheses as data are collected and analyzed. Hypotheses in qualitative research are conjectures, but there is not much concern whether they are directional or null hypotheses. Their wording fits the context of the phenomenon under study.

Foreshadowed problems were mentioned earlier as statements, usually associated with ethnographic research, that supplement hypotheses, at least to get the research underway. Consider the research problem statement given earlier: "An ethnographic study of the school environment of regular and learning disabled students to determine factors related to potential dropout." Examples of foreshadowed problems associated with this statement are:

1. Interaction among regular and learning disabled students during instruction.
2. Role of the teacher in enhancing student learning.
3. Student social systems.
4. Opportunities for student success in the academic subjects.

Note that the foreshadowed problems do not specify anticipated results. Essentially, they identify factors for the researcher to observe as the research gets underway.

Examples of Hypotheses Related to Problem Statements.   A statement of a research problem may have one or more (usually more) hypotheses associated with it. Hypotheses are formulated from the research problem statement and should follow directly from it. Each of the following examples provides a problem statement, hypotheses, and operational definitions or comments on the operational definitions of the variables or conditions. The ethnographic research example (Example 2.3) contains foreshadowed problems, as examples of the phenomenon focused on by the researcher. Two example hypotheses are given, although if there were no basis for hypothesizing about the nature of the phenomenon under study, there would be no initial hypotheses. Example variables are given but they are not categorized as to type. Since ethnographic research takes a holistic and descriptive approach rather than a cause-and-effect approach, we would not be concerned about the distinction between independent and dependent variables. There are not likely to be any control variables in ethnographic research, but there would be many intervening variables, such as the elementary school science backgrounds of the students.

The hypotheses of Example 2.1 are stated in directional form. In Examples 2.2 and 2.4, both types of hypotheses are used. Both forms can be used, although a single form is sometimes preferred for consistency. Example 2.5 has null hypotheses, which of course, are nondirectional.

Example 2.2 would apply to action research, if it were conducted by the third-grade teachers in a single school to help them make a decision about which program to use in the school. Note that the dependent variable in this example is gain score in reading achievement, not simply reading achievement score. To determine gain scores, prior reading achievement scores must be known; therefore, prior reading achievement could be a control variable. Example 2.5 is an illustration of experimental research most likely conducted in a learning laboratory setting.

To illustrate the different types of variables discussed earlier in the chapter, the variables are listed and operationally defined as necessary. In each example, the hypotheses, operational definitions, and variables follow directly from the statement of the problem.

EXAMPLE 2.1 _____

Problem Statement

A survey of grading practices and patterns in academic areas of the senior high schools in Ohio.

Hypotheses

1. Average grades in the science areas of chemistry and physics are higher than those in biology and earth science.

2. Average grades in history and other social studies are higher than those in biological and physical sciences.

3. Average grades in advanced mathematics (second-year algebra and beyond) are higher than those in introductory algebra and consumer mathematics.

4. There is a positive relationship between grades received in English courses and those received in foreign language courses.

5. There is a positive relationship between grades received in Algebra II and those received in chemistry.

6. Grading patterns for courses in academic areas are higher as the size of the high school increases.

Operational Definitions

Academic areas: Sciences, mathematics, English, social studies, history, and foreign languages.

Senior high school: Grades 10, 11, and 12 of any accredited high school in Ohio.

Grades: The possible categories of the letter grading system A, B, C, and so forth, which may be converted to numerical scores.

Size of high school: Total enrollment in grades 10–12; categories are: less than 200 students, 200–499, 500–799, 800–1099, 1100, and greater.

Independent Variables	Dependent Variables
Academic areas	Grades
Specific courses in certain areas	Grading patterns/proportions of grades by category
Size of high school	

Possible Intervening Variables	Possible Control Variables
Type of school	Size of school
Gender of the student (organismic)	
Location of school	

EXAMPLE 2.2

Problem Statement

A study of the effects of two reading programs (A and B) on the reading achievement of third-grade students in School A.

Hypotheses

1. With students of heterogeneous reading achievement, there, will be no difference in the mean gains in reading achievement for students taught by Program A and those taught by Program B.

2. For students scoring in the lower 30 percent on prior reading achievement, those taught by Program A will have a greater mean gain than those taught by Program B.

3. For students scoring in the upper 30 percent on prior reading achievement, those taught by Program B will have a greater mean gain than those taught by Program A.

4. For students scoring in the middle 40 percent on prior reading achievement, there will no difference in mean gains for students taught by Program A and those taught by Program B.

Operational Definitions

Individuals included in the study: All third-graders of School A.

Program A: The set of reading materials purchased from Publisher Y and its suggested activities.

Program B: The set of reading materials purchased from Publisher Z and its suggested activities.

Independent Variable	Dependent Variable
Reading program—A and B	Gain score in reading achievement—for example, the difference between scores on two forms of a standardized reading test, one form given prior to the study, the second form given after the study
Possible Intervening Variables	Possible Control Variables
Teacher	Prior reading achievement (organisimic)
Teaching style (organismic)	Gender of the student (organismic)
Learning style (organismic)	
Student scholastic ability (organismic)	

EXAMPLE 2.3 _____

Problem Statement

An ethnographic study of the functions of laboratory work in science instruction for junior high school students in School A.

Foreshadowed Problems

1. The interaction among students as laboratory work takes place.
2. The interaction between students and teacher during laboratory work.
3. Student and teacher preparation for laboratory work.
4. The relationship between laboratory work and other aspects of science instruction.

Hypotheses

1. A function of laboratory work is to have students participate in a cooperative activity.
2. More academically able students will monopolize the control of the laboratory work.

Operational Definitions

Participating in the study: All students enrolled in science courses in School A.

Science instruction: All courses including as their emphasis instruction in physical, earth, or biological sciences; the general science and the earth science courses in School A.

Laboratory work: Any activity in which the student is directly involved (either singly or with other students) in conducting experiments, manipulating scientific apparatus, dissecting biological specimens, and so on.

Variables: The functions of laboratory work.

Types of interaction taking place during laboratory work.

Extent of laboratory work.

Type of laboratory work, for example, dissecting animals, physics experiment, and materials analysis.

The timing of laboratory work relative to other instruction in science.

EXAMPLE 2.4

Problem Statement

A survey of teacher opinion of the school board policies in the City C Metropolitan Area.

Hypotheses

1. The proportion of teachers in agreement with the policy on compensation for inservice work exceeds .75.
2. At least .50 of the teachers are in agreement with the policy on teacher transfer.
3. There is no difference between the proportions of elementary and secondary teachers in agreement with the policy on sick leave.
4. There are differences among the proportions of elementary teachers in agreement with the policy on transfer for suburban systems and the city system.

Operational Definitions

School board policies: Statements of procedures and/or conditions of employment and activity as found in school board minutes or directives.

City C Metropolitan Area: City C and its suburbs, as defined in State Publication No. 1234.

Independent Variables	Dependent Variables
Type of teacher—elementary, secondary (organismic)	Proportions (or percentages) of teachers responding favorably to policy items
Location of teaching or school system—the city and various suburban systems	

Possible Intervening Variables	Possible Control Variables
Age of the teacher (organismic)	Location of teaching
Gender of the teacher (organismic)	
Marital status of the teacher (organismic)	
Amount of graduate work completed by the teacher (organismic)	
Size of the specific school	

EXAMPLE 2.5

Problem Statement

A study of the effects of type of material, age, gender, and problem complexity upon performance on a concept attainment task.

Hypotheses

1. There is no difference in the mean performance of individuals using figural materials and those using verbal materials.

2. There is no difference in the mean performance of individuals in the age range twenty to twenty-five years and those in the range of twenty-six to thirty years.

3. There is no difference in the mean performance of males and females.

4. Concept attainment problems containing two and three relevant dimensions are of equal difficulty.

Operational Definitions

Since a concept attainment task is very specific, it would need to be described as part of the procedures for doing this research.

Type of material: figural: pictorial 3×3 cards in which the concepts are embedded; verbal: 3×3 cards with verbal statements corresponding to the pictorial cards.

Relevant dimension: A characteristic common to all cards that exemplify a concept (dimension might be a solid border).

Performance: Time in minutes (to two decimal places) required to attain the concept.

Problem complexity: The number of relevant dimensions in the concept; the greater the number, the more complex the problem.

(Age and gender are operationally defined in the hypotheses.)

Independent Variables	*Dependent Variable*
Type of material	Time in minutes required to attain the concept
Age (organismic)	
Gender (organismic)	
Problem complexity	

Possible Intervening Variables	*Possible Control Variables*
General intelligence of the individual (organismic)	Age
Spatial relations skill of the individual (organismic)	Gender
Efficiency and accuracy of the experimenter administering the task	

The preceding examples have not exhausted the numbers of possible hypotheses, which depend on the extent and conditions of the research study. In identifying the variables, possible intervening variables are listed. Note that gender is an independent variable of primary interest in Example 2.5, a possible control variable in Example 2.2 and a possible intervening variable in Example 2.1. That is because in Example 2.2 any differential performance between males and females would be determined, whereas in Example 2.1, if there is an effect of gender, it is not separated from the effects of other variables. In any event, gender is an organismic variable, as identified in parentheses.

Summary

This chapter has discussed the identification of a research problem from the initial selection of a problem through the process of generating a workable research problem statement, elaborated with related hypotheses and operational definitions of variables and conditions. It was implied that researchers select research problems in different ways. Certainly, there should be interest in an area of research and internal motivation to pursue the research, but external factors, too, influence the selection of a problem.

The various components for identifying a research problem are connected and their interrelationships can be summarized as in Figure 2.2. The statement of the problem is the springboard for developing the hypotheses, or in the case of ethnographic research, possibly foreshadowed problems in addition to or in lieu of hypotheses. Hypotheses then lead into doing the research. The process of generating hypotheses not only defines the problem more specifically, it also can effectively limit the research problem. Hypotheses are stated in the context of variables, operational definitions, and conditions. All of this is done on a base of relevant theory and existing knowledge. Research problems are not identified and pursued in an informational vacuum. They have a place in the educational world—either theoretically or practically, or both.

Hypotheses are not ends in themselves; rather, they are aids in the research process. Occasionally, a report of a research project may seem short on hypotheses. Possibly the researcher was working in an area with very little background information, or perhaps considerable theory development was necessary. In qualitative research, for example, initial hypotheses are often general and limited in number; as the research progresses, however, new hypotheses are generated and prior hypotheses may be revised, retained, or discarded. To the extent possible, hypotheses should be stated concisely and used as the framework for the research.

The concepts of variables, constants, and operational definition were described in this chapter, but these concepts are used not only when identifying the problem, but also

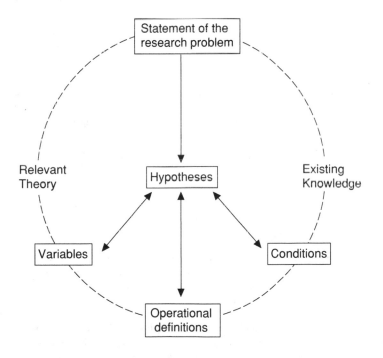

**FIGURE 2.2   Connections Between the Components for
Identifying a Research Problem**

throughout the research process. These are extremely important concepts, because they are part of the basic language of research.

The next chapter discusses the review of literature. The placement of the discussion of the review is somewhat arbitrary; it could have appeared before the discussion about identifying the problem, because some review often is done before the problem statement is refined and put into final form. However, the researcher must have some idea of what to look for, so the problem usually is identified before doing any extensive review of the literature.

KEY CONCEPTS

Constant	Interval scale
Variable	Ratio scale
Independent variable	Operational definition
Dependent variable	Statistical hypothesis
Organismic variable	Substantive hypothesis
Intervening variable	Research hypothesis
Control variable	Directional hypothesis
Moderator variable	Nondirectional hypothesis
Nominal scale	Foreshadowed problems
Ordinal scale	

EXERCISES

2.1 A study is conducted to determine the effects of three sets of instructional materials on fourth-grade reading achievement. Three random samples of fourth-grade boys are selected within the same school. These three groups are then taught by three different teachers, each teaching only one group and using one set of instructional materials. At the end of ten weeks of instruction, the students are tested on reading achievement. Identify the constant(s), independent variable(s), and dependent variable(s) of this study. Identify possible intervening variables that might be operating in this situation.

2.2 Suppose that in the study described in Exercise 2.1, the instructional materials are used with six classes each of fourth- and fifth-graders. Both boys and girls are included. The study is conducted at two different schools using three classes of each grade level in each school, each class being taught with a different set of materials. Identify the organismic variable(s) and the possible control variable(s) that are now included.

2.3 The problem statement of the study in Exercise 2.2 might be: "A study of the effects of different instructional materials on the reading achievement of fourth- and fifth-graders." Using the variables identified in the first two exercises, develop two or more related hypotheses. The hypotheses may be stated in directional or nondirectional form.

2.4 Suppose an ethnographic research study is to be done on the nature of social behavior of children in a racially integrated kindergarten. Develop four or more foreshadowed problems related to this research. If appropriate, develop one or more hypotheses that might be tested in this study.

2.5 What is the difference between hypotheses stated in a nondirectional or null form and those stated in a directional form?

2.6 A science educator is interested in doing research on whether or not a constructivist approach to science teaching improves science achievement of high school students over other approaches. Would it be more appropriate to use directional or nondirectional hypotheses in this situation? Why? Suppose the research is planned for the biology, chemistry, and physics classes in a single high school with at least two classes in each subject. Identify independent and dependent variables for this situation. For those variables identified, provide operational definitions. Identify one or more constants and one or more possible intervening variables.

2.7 Suppose a researcher is interested in doing a study on the effects of "open classroom" instruction on scholastic performance of elementary school students. What terms would require operational definitions? Provide examples of operational definitions for these terms.

2.8 For each of the following research problem statements, develop two or more related hypotheses, identify the different possible variables by type, and provide operational definitions for those identified. There is some flexibility in responding to those statements, but please identify any assumptions or special conditions.

  a. A survey of parent perceptions of the four elementary schools in a suburban school system.
  b. An ethnographic study of the role of the counselor in a large middle school serving inner-city students. You may identify foreshadowed problems in addition to, or in lieu of, hypotheses.
  c. A study of the effects of three physical training programs upon the upper body strength of senior boys in high school.

2.9 Classify each of the following variables in terms of type of measurement scale (nominal, ordinal, interval, or ratio):

  a. Performance on the essay section of an American history test.
  b. Ratings assigned by supervisors to the performance of student teachers.
  c. Strength of junior high boys on a physical task, as measured in pounds of force by an electronic device.
  d. Scores on a teacher-constructed, multiple-choice test of seventy-five items, for which all items are weighted equally.
  e. Ethnic background.
  f. Socioeconomic level.

2.10 From a professional journal, select an article that deals with a research study. Read the article and attempt to identify the statement of the problem and any hypothesis that may be tested in the study. Are the variables explicitly identified, and are operational definitions provided when needed?

NOTES

1. Some writers argue that many, possibly most, test scores are not quite interval scale level, but approach such measurement, and that, for research purposes, they can be considered interval scale. In a given situation, the meaning attributed to the measurement should be clearly identified.

2. The use of statistical hypotheses, including the null hypothesis, is discussed in greater detail in Chapter 14.

REFERENCES

Borg, W. R., and Gall, M. D. (1989). *Educational research: An introduction* (5th ed.). New York: Longman.

Kerlinger, F. N. (1986). *Foundations of behavioral research* (3rd ed.). New York: Holt, Rinehart & Winston.

Chapter 3

The Review of the Literature

One of the early activities in the research process is the review of the research literature — the body of research information related to the research problem. After the problem has been identified, at least tentatively, information is needed about the problem so it can be put in the proper context and the research can proceed effectively.

With the amount of information available from a variety of sources, the review of the literature is by no means a trivial task. It is a systematic process that requires careful and perceptive reading and attention to detail. In the review of the literature, the researcher attempts to determine what others have learned about similar research problems and to gather information relevant to the research problem at hand. This process centers on three questions:

1. Where is the information found?
2. What should be done with information after it has been found?
3. What is made of the information?

The first question deals with the specific sources of written reports or, possible reproductions such as microfiche. For most students, these sources can be found in or obtained through the library. Finding the information often involves using reference works such as indexes of periodical literature. Computer searches are very helpful in focusing the search and speeding up the process of sorting through the literature and identifying the potentially most useful sources. The sheer volume of available information on most topics makes a computer search almost imperative for any extensive review.

The second question deals with how information is assembled and summarized. Assuming that the content of a report is relevant to the research problem under study, the information must be retained in a usable manner.

Dealing with the third question is somewhat more abstract. To answer the first two questions, the researcher finds information and sets up a procedure for retaining it. Answering the third question requires making a judgment about the information in a research report. What parts of the reported results are relevant to the research problem?

How well was the research conducted? Thus, answering the third question requires a somewhat critical analysis of the reports reviewed. Then information from the related reports can be put together.

What is the value of a review of the literature? Besides providing a context for the research study, the review may be useful in any or all of the following ways:

1. More specifically limiting and identifying the research problem and possible hypotheses.

2. Informing the researcher of what has already been done in the area.

3. Providing possible research design and methodological procedures that may be used in the research study.

4. Providing suggestions for possible modifications in the research to avoid unanticipated difficulties.

5. Identifying possible gaps in the research.

6. Providing a backdrop for interpreting the results of the research study.

> The review of related literature serves multiple purposes and is essential to a well-designed research study. It generally comes early in the research process, and it can contribute valuable information to any part of the research study.

The Activities of the Review of the Literature

As Figure 1.5 indicated, the existing body of knowledge relative to the research problem provides information for identifying the problem. In that figure, the general activities of conducting a research study were ordered in their most likely sequence of occurrence. The review of the literature itself consists of several specific activities that, to a large extent, also take place in a sequence. These activities, shown in the flowchart in Figure 3.1, are initiated after the research problem has been identified, at least tentatively. The order of activities follows the flow of the arrows in the figure.

Like most activities or steps in a process, there are efficient and inefficient ways to review the literature. Rather than going to the library and haphazardly beginning to take notes, the researcher should follow a systematic process, as represented by the activities in the flowchart. Although even this process may involve some inefficiency in locating sources and reports, efficiency will be enhanced by following the process. Another important procedural point in conducting the activities is, for each activity, to do as complete and accurate an initial job as possible. For example, when a relevant report is located and an abstract is prepared, a complete bibliographic entry for the report should be included. This saves going back later just to complete the bibliography of the reference. If a report is relevant enough to include in the review, sufficient information should be obtained from it so that there is no confusion later about what was done (conditions,

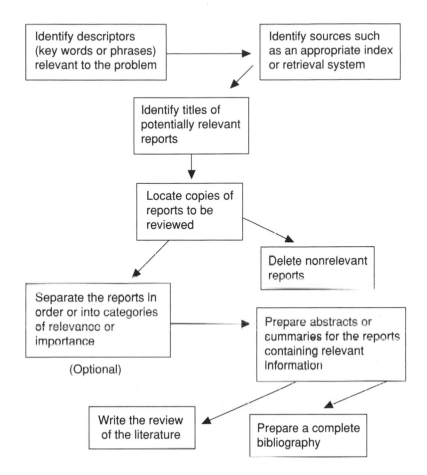

FIGURE 3.1   Flowchart of Activities in the Review of the Literature

procedures, individuals involved, etc.) or about the results. Doing the review of literature in the manner suggested not only reduces frustration but also saves time.

Sources of Information

The library is the most likely physical location for the research literature. There is no scarcity of reports of research studies related to education. Studies are published in books, periodicals, technical reports, and academic theses, available either in print or through a library's information retrieval system. This section deals with examples of sources commonly used in educational research.

Periodical Literature

Professional journals and periodicals regularly publish a large volume of research information, although some journals are more oriented to this type of material than others. The periodical indexes available in libraries provide concise and efficient guides to published contents. Of course, not all indexed content is research information, but the researcher may be interested in more than research results, such as discussion of theory. Following are some periodical indexes of particular interest to the educational researcher.

Education Index

The *Education Index* is one of the most widely used periodical indexes. It covers more than 360 educational periodicals. Published since 1929, the *Education Index* is a cumulative author-subject index to educational material in the English language. It is published monthly except July and August. Monthly issues are combined into quarterly issues, which in turn are combined in the annual volume for the year running from September through June. The entries include literature in periodicals, proceedings, yearbooks, bulletins, monographs, and governmental materials on education and education-related topics. The entries are arranged in alphabetical order in a combined author-key-word index. Under subject headings, such as "Learning, Psychology of" are alphabetically ordered subheadings such as "Attention" and "Conditional Response." Under these subject headings are references to the related literature, including title, author, and complete bibliographic information. Author entries list all titles of the author's published works that have appeared since the previous volume of the *Education Index*.

Examples of entries from the *Education Index* are shown in Figure 3.2. The information contained in the entry, including abbreviations, is identified in the legends at the side. The *Education Index* provides only bibliographical information; it does not provide an abstract or summary. In the example in Figure 3.2, "Learning, Psychology of" is the subject heading and then the subheadings provide further breakdown. From the title alone, it is sometimes difficult to judge the potential value of an entry's content to the research study at hand. However, even though all selected entries may not prove valuable when reviewed, the *Education Index* does provide a useful source for a manual search.

Educational Resources Information Center (ERIC)

ERIC is a national information center with central headquarters in Washington, DC., and currently twenty-one clearinghouses located throughout the country. The ERIC mandate is to screen, organize, and provide access to educational reports and documents by continual monitoring of the pertinent literature. Each clearinghouse is established for a single, broad topic; for example, the Clearinghouse for Elementary and Early Childhood Education is located at the University of Illinois in Urbana. ERIC clearinghouses have responsibility for acquiring the significant educational literature in their areas, selecting the highest quality and most relevant materials. Clearinghouses are responsible for processing the selected items for input into the ERIC database. The monthly listing of *Current*

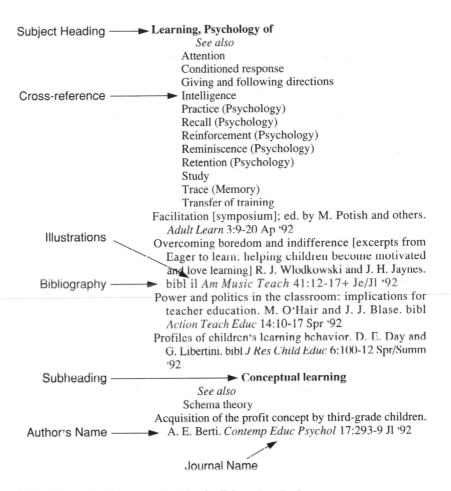

Subject Heading → **Learning, Psychology of**
See also
Attention
Conditioned response
Giving and following directions
Cross-reference → Intelligence
Practice (Psychology)
Recall (Psychology)
Reinforcement (Psychology)
Reminiscence (Psychology)
Retention (Psychology)
Study
Trace (Memory)
Transfer of training
Facilitation [symposium]; ed. by M. Potish and others.
Adult Learn 3:9-20 Ap '92
Illustrations → Overcoming boredom and indifference [excerpts from
Eager to learn: helping children become motivated
and love learning] R. J. Wlodkowski and J. H. Jaynes.
Bibliography → bibl il *Am Music Teach* 41:12-17+ Je/Jl '92
Power and politics in the classroom: implications for
teacher education. M. O'Hair and J. J. Blase. bibl
Action Teach Educ 14:10-17 Spr '92
Profiles of children's learning behavior. D. E. Day and
G. Libertini. bibl *J Res Child Educ* 6:100-12 Spr/Summ
'92
Subheading → **Conceptual learning**
See also
Schema theory
Acquisition of the profit concept by third-grade children.
Author's Name → A. E. Berti. *Contemp Educ Psychol* 17:293-9 Jl '92
Journal Name

FIGURE 3.2   Example Entries in *Education Index*

Source: Education Index. 64 (Sept. 1992) 174. (H. W. Wilson Co. New York). (Taken from the paperback monthly edition.)

Index to Journals in Education, an ERIC publication, contains the names and addresses of the clearinghouses.

ERIC publishes two sources of information. The source that covers the periodical literature is *Current Index to Journals in Education (CIJE),* just mentioned. *CIJE* is published monthly with accumulations every six months. It was established in 1969, so it covers the periodical literature since that date. *Resources in Education (RIE)* is the other source that covers educational documents such as papers presented at conferences and final reports of projects. *RIE* contains information about research not reported in the periodical literature. It, too, is published monthly and has semiannual accumulations for previous years.

The researcher gains access to *CIJE* and *RIE* through the *Thesaurus of ERIC Descriptors* (1990). This document contains an alphabetical list of terms and concepts used by the ERIC system for indexing. These terms are called *descriptors*. When documents are submitted to ERIC, experts categorize the report using key-word descriptors. The key-word descriptors are the basis for the ERIC indexing system. Other descriptors that are not key-word descriptors are also listed, and these might be considered by the researcher. Each *Thesaurus* updates the descriptors from the previous editions for new descriptors and deleted descriptors. The topics and concepts of the research problem must be translated into the descriptors of the *Thesaurus* in order to identify relevant information in *CIJE* and *RIE*.

An Example Using CIJE and RIE

In order to illustrate the use of the ERIC documents, consider the following research problem statement:

> *A study of facilities, content and procedures of learning laboratories in under-graduate college programs.*

First we go to the *Thesaurus* and find that "Learning Laboratories" is a key-word descriptor. The information concerning this key-word descriptor is given in Figure 3.3. The abbreviations in the left-hand column have the following meanings:

SN (Scope Note): A brief statement of the intended uses of the descriptor; for example, there may be restricted usage of a term.

UF (Used For): Terms following UF are *not* to be used in indexing. They represent terms that are synonymous or variant terms of the main descriptor or specific terms that, for purposes of storage and retrieval, are indexed under a more general term. The dates, 1967–1980, indicate that auto-instructional laboratories was a former descriptor used during this period.

BT (Broader Term), and NT (Narrower Term): Indicate the hierarchical relationships between classes and subclasses of descriptors.

The postings note at the top gives the numbers of times the descriptor was used in *CIJE* and *RIE*.

Next we go to *CIJE* or *RIE*. Consider *CIJE*. It contains a source journal index, a main entry section, a subject index, an author index, and a journal content index. We go to the subject index using the key-word descriptor, Learning Laboratories. Three entries are listed, and for the purpose of this example, we select one entry,[1] namely,

> Involvement in Learning: Its Impact on Student Outcomes. Community/Junior College Quarterly of Research and Practice. vl5 n4 p 391–94 Oct–Dec. 1991.
>
> EJ 434 828

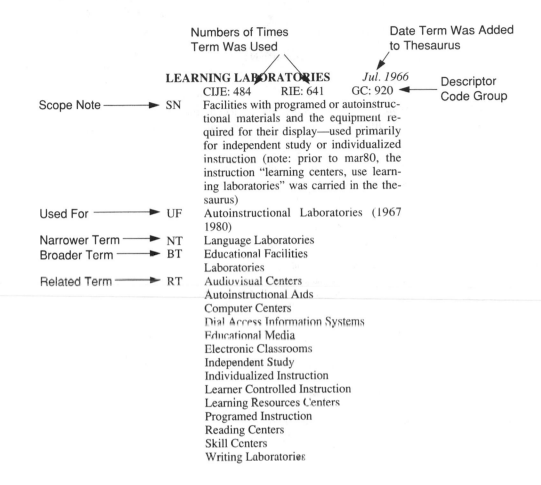

FIGURE 3.3 **Example Descriptor from the *Thesaurus of ERIC Descriptors***

Source: Thesaurus of ERIC Descriptors (12th ed.). Phoenix: Oryx Press, 1990, p. 145.

The EJ number at the end is the accession number, assigned by ERIC, for finding the entry in the Main Entry section. (EJ stands for educational journal.) The entry from that section is given in Figure 3.4. Most of the information is straightforward. The accession number is the number assigned by ERIC as documents are processed. Descriptors are the terms used by ERIC. Some entries, not this one, also have identifiers which are additional terms not found in the *Thesaurus of ERIC Descriptors*. The clearinghouse number identifies the clearinghouse through which the document entered ERIC, for this entry, the Junior College Clearinghouse. The annotation contains an abstract of the article; on the basis of the abstract, the researcher can decide whether or not to obtain a complete copy of the reference, either in hard copy or microfiche.

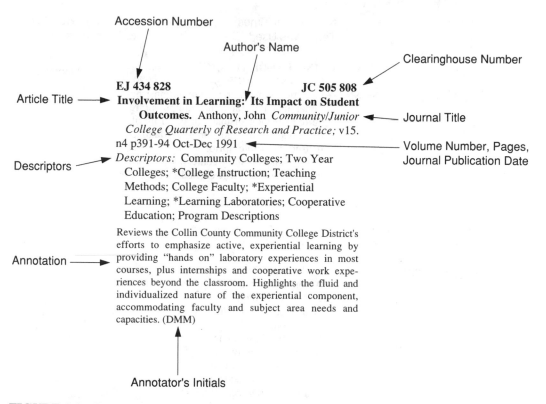

FIGURE 3.4   Example Entry from *CIJE*

Source: *CIJE*, Semiannual Cumulation, January–June 1992, p. 253. Phoenix: Oryx Press.

The author index would be used if the researcher is interested in any other publications by a particular author. Entries in the author index contain the author's name, article title, and accession number.

Consider *RIE*. We go to the subject index using the descriptor and locate two entries under Learning Laboratories in the November 1992 issue. The subject index contains the reference information and the accession numbers or ED numbers. (ED stands for education document.) We select the first entry and use the ED number to locate the entry in the Document Resumes section. The information from the Document Resumes section is given in Figure 3.5.

The *descriptive note* in this entry gives only the number of pages, but it might also contain other information, such as the date and location of a paper presented at a conference. The MF and PC after EDRS Price indicate that the document is available in microfiche and in paper copy. Prices are not given because they are subject to change; however, the latest price list can be obtained in the most recent issue of *RIE*. Of course, the abstract is of primary interest, since a decision about whether or not to pursue the

ERIC Accession Number

Clearinghouse Accession Number

ED 346 916

JC 920 345

Author → *Platt, Gail M.*

Title → **Assessing Program Effectiveness: It's a Tough Job, but Somebody's Got To Do It. The Annual Report of the South Plains College Learning Center, Levelland, Texas, 1991-92.**

Originating Organization → South Plains Coll., Levelland, Tex.

Publication Date → Pub Date—Jul 92

Note—59p. ← Descriptive Note

Publication Type → Pub Type—Reports - Evaluative (142)

EDRS Price - MF01/PC03 Plus Postage. ← ERIC Document Reproduction Service Availability

Descriptors → Descriptors—Basic Skills, Community Colleges, *Learning Laboratories, *Learning Resources Centers, Program Descriptions, Program Evaluation, *Reading Centers, Reading Improvement, Reading Instruction,*Reading Programs, *Remedial Programs, Self Evaluation (Groups), Tutorial Programs, Two Year Colleges

Identifiers → Identifiers—*Texas Academic Skills Program

Abstract → An assessment of the activities of the Learning Center (LC) at South Plains College is provided in this 1991-92 annual report. Introductory material describes the scope of the LC's operations, including reading and study skills remediation, developmental communications instruction, collegiate instruction in reading and human development, peer tutoring, computer-aided instruction, independent study opportunities, and workshops and seminars for all students at the college. Next, the report presents demographic information on the students served, including their Texas Academic Skills Program (TASP) status and scores. Following a section which reports the results of a survey soliciting faculty evaluations of the Center, tutoring activities and courses taught in the LC are reviewed. An assessment of program effectivenesss is provided in the next section, which looks at reading remediation in terms of course completion rates, passing rates on exit tests, retention rates, student evaluation of courses, and faculty evaluations. This section also discusses other effectiveness measures, other remedial courses ("Developmental Communications" and "College Success"), and noncourse-based remediation. The next two sections analyze data on the LC Lab and success seminars. Following discussions of program goals for 1992-93 and the effects of TASP implementation, the report concludes with activities and remedial instruction at community colleges. Appendixes include data on remedial reading courses, guidelines for non-center-based remediation, and a sample student contract for reading improvement. Additional attachments provide LC statistics, a statistical overview, and verbatim faculty comments. (JSP) ← Abstractor's Initials

FIGURE 3.5 Example Entry from *RIE*

Source: RIE, 27(11) NW. 1992, p. 115. Washington, DC: U.S. Government Printing Office.

reference would be based on the abstract's content. RIE also contains an author index, an institution index, and publication type index.

If a researcher desires the complete document, it can be ordered through the ERIC Document Reproduction Service; the address of the service and the price list are given in the latest issue of *RIE*. A document needed quickly can be ordered on microfiche (MC) or hard copy (HC). Microfiche is usually less costly and it is smaller, of course, but it requires a special microfiche reader, which is available at most universities. University libraries often have collections of ERIC microfiches, in which case documents may be available immediately.

These examples were given to illustrate the information in *CIJE* and *RIE* and a single descriptor was used. Other broad descriptors that apply to the research problem could be used. Going back over a considerable period, say several years, any one broad descriptor would undoubtedly produce a large number of references. In order to focus the search and limit the number of references, combinations of two or more descriptors could be used. References so located would simultaneously contain the two or more descriptors. Using multiple descriptors is illustrated in the computer search described later in the chapter.

ERIC has published *CIJE* since 1969 and *RIE* since 1966. For searching prior to these dates, the *Education Index* can be used. An advantage of *CIJE* and *RIE* over indexes such as the *Education Index* is that they include abstracts or short summaries of the articles and reports.

Other Indexes and Abstracts

Numerous other indexes and abstracts reference documents about educational research, in related disciplines or in particular areas of education. An example from a related discipline is *Psychological Abstracts (PA)*, a bimonthly publication that contains abstracts of reports or articles in more than 1000 journals, technical reports, monographs, and scientific documents. Many of the periodicals from which articles are abstracted for *PA* are educational journals. Biannual issues of *PA*, with author and subject indexes, are published for the six-month periods January to June and July to December.

An example from an educational area is *Exceptional Child Education Resources (ECER)*, published quarterly by the Council for Exceptional Children, which reviews more than 200 periodicals for information on exceptional children. The format for indexing in *ECER* is similar to that used in *CIJE*. Custom computer searches are also available; included in the computer search is an abstract of about 200 words.

Abstracts and indexes of other professions often contain educational information. For example, *Crime and Penology Abstracts* references current research into school violence, school vandalism, and school absence. The *Nursing Index* contains references to research into school health, diet, and nutrition, which have implications for education.

The citation indexes are somewhat different than those just described. If in a literature search one or more key references of several years ago appear, the citation index will give all the works that have since cited the reference. A citation index can be especially helpful in locating what other authors had to say about a controversial article. The search is initiated with the author's name and year of publication. The most widely used citation index for education is the *Social Science Citation Index (SSCI)*. The listings are for a given year, and then summarized in five-year accumulations.

Indexes and abstracts are available in almost all university libraries, and the procedures for using them are very much the same. The introduction to an index usually contains detailed information about availability and costs of documents and addresses for obtaining information. Detailed information is also provided about codes used in the entries and about how to locate references.

Review of Educational Research (RER)

Some of the most valuable and useful sources of information about a research problem are reviews on various topics and issues. There are reviews published on a regular basis, and others appear in periodicals as appropriate and as needed. One of the most useful is *RER*, issued quarterly by the American Educational Research Association, which publishes critical integrative reviews of research literature bearing on education. From its inception in 1931 through 1969, each issue of the *RER* contained solicited papers organized around a single educational topic or subdivision, such as "Educational and Psychological Testing." Topics were reviewed in three-year cycles; more active topics were reviewed every cycle and less active ones on alternate cycles.

Beginning with Volume 40 (June 1970), the *RER* has published unsolicited reviews of research on topics of the reviewer's own choosing. The papers in both the pre-1970 and post 1970 issues include excellent bibliographies that contain many references to the educational research literature. As an example of topics covered, the reviews that appeared in Volume 62 (Levin, 1992) were as follows:

"Shifting Conceptions of Validity in Educational Measurement: Implications for Performance Assessment"

"Framing a Theory for Social Studies Foundations"

"The Nature of Knowledge in Composition and Literacy Understanding: The Question of Specificity"

"Teachers' Beliefs and Educational Research: Cleaning Up a Messy Construct"

Other Reviews

As indicated above, there are reviews that appear in periodicals on an irregular basis. A good example is one by Koepsell, et al (1992), which was published in the *Annual Review of Public Health*. The topic of the review was, "Selected Methodological Issues in Evaluating Community-Based Health Promotion and Disease Prevention Programs." The review was twenty-seven pages in length and had ninety-five references. Although this review did not deal with an educational issue per se, it is related to education in the health sciences.

Reviews are very useful to researchers who want to locate a substantial quantity of research literature on a broad research topic without conducting an initial search. Reviews are helpful, but they do cover broad topics. As usual, the researcher must go through the content and retain information that is relevant to the research problem at hand. Other disciplines related to education also have their own reviews or review journals; an example is the *Annual Review of Psychology.*

Reports of Meta-Analysis

Meta-analysis is a statistical procedure for synthesizing research results across a number of studies which deal with the same research question and include similar variables. Because of the statistics involved, meta-analysis focuses on quantitative results, and in the analysis process includes a common measure of effect, called the effect size. The definitive description of meta-analysis was provided by Glass, McGaw and Smith (1981).

More will be said about the process of meta-analysis in a later chapter, but the point for the review of the literature is that a report of a meta-analysis relevant to the research problem at hand, can be very useful. Meta-analyses typically address consistencies and inconsistencies of results across studies. When there are inconsistencies there may be an attempt to identify possible factors causing the inconsistencies. In order for studies to be considered for the meta-analysis, minimum criteria usually are identified for the manner in which the research was conducted. Meta-analyses are not as comprehensive as reviews on a research topic, but they can be useful, not only for summarizing results, but also for comparing the conditions of studies reviewed. Of course, a meta-analysis includes a bibliography of all studies in the analysis. Meta-analyses appear in periodic literature, but not on any systematic schedule, as is the case with some reviews.

Abstracts and Reports in Periodicals

Numerous periodicals are devoted almost exclusively to abstracts or reviews. Some of them are in the academic disciplines, and others are in professional education. Any university library will have at least some of these periodicals on hand and, in most cases, can provide access to all of them. Examples of such periodicals are as follows:

Sociological Abstracts, published 1952–

Child Development Abstracts and Bibliography, published 1927–

Biological Abstracts, published 1926–

Educational Administration Abstracts, published 1922–

These periodicals include, but are not limited to, abstracts of articles dealing with research.

There also are many periodicals in education-related disciplines and in professional education that contain research articles, some of them more so than others. It would be impractical to present a comprehensive listing of such periodicals, but following is a representative sampling:

American Educational Research Journal (Washington, DC: American Educational Research Association)

Anthropology and Education Quarterly (Washington, DC: Council on Anthropology and Education)

British Journal of Educational Psychology (London: British Psychological Society)

British Journal of Educational Studies (London: Faber & Faber)

California Journal of Educational Research (Burlingame, CA: California Teachers Association)

Canadian Education and Research Digest (Toronto: Canadian Education Association)

Educational and Psychological Measurement (Durham, NC: copyright by Frederic Kuder)

Florida Journal of Educational Research (Tallahassee: Florida Educational Association)

International Journal of Qualitative Studies in Education (London, New York: Taylor and Francis)

Journal of Educational Measurement (Washington, DC: National Council on Measurement in Education)

Journal of Educational Psychology (Washington, DC: American Psychological Association)

Journal of Educational Research (Washington, DC: HELDREF Publications)

Journal of Educational Sociology (New York University, New York: Payne Educational Sociology Foundation)

Journal of Experimental Education (Washington, DC: HELDREF Publications)

Journal of Experimental Psychology (Washington, DC: American Psychological Association)

Journal of Research in Science Teaching (National Association for Research in Science Teaching and Association for the Education of Teachers in Science; New York: Wiley)

Louisiana Education Research Journal (Natchitoches: Louisiana Education Research Association)

Measurement and Evaluation in Guidance (Washington, DC: Association for Measurement and Evaluation in Guidance, a division of the American Personnel and Guidance Association)

NEA Research Bulletin (Washington, DC; National Education Association)

Psychological Bulletin (Washington, DC: American Psychological Association)

Psychological Review (Washington, DC: American Psychological Association)

School Science and Mathematics (Tempe, AZ: School Science and Mathematics Association)

The Research Quarterly (Reston, VA: American Association for Health, Physical Education, Recreation, and Dance)

Theses and Dissertations

Theses and dissertations prepared to meet the requirements for a graduate degree usually contain descriptions of completed research. The university library contains copies of theses completed at that university. To obtain information about dissertations completed at other universities, the most widely used comprehensive source is *Dissertation Abstracts* and its related services.

Dissertation Abstracts was renamed *Dissertation Abstracts International (DAI)* beginning with Volume 30, No. 1 (1969). *DAI* is a reference tool that provides a monthly compilation of abstracts of doctoral dissertations submitted to University Microfilms International (Ann Arbor, Michigan) by almost 500 universities in North America and worldwide. There are three sections under which dissertations are abstracted: Humanities and Social Studies (A), The Sciences and Engineering (B), and Worldwide (C). Section C formerly was called European Abstracts, but in 1989 it was expanded to include universities worldwide. It is published quarterly.

Beginning with Volume 30 and ending with Volume 33, each section was cumulated annually by key-word title index and author index. Starting with Volume 34, only author indexes are cumulated annually. From Volume 36 on, each of Sections A and B is divided into five main parts, as follows:

Humanities and Social Studies

  IA.   Communications and the Arts
 IIA.   Education
IIIA.   Language, Literature, and Linguistics
 IVA.   Philosophy, Religion and Theology
  VA.   Social Sciences

Sciences and Engineering

  IB.   Biological Sciences
 IIB.   Earth Sciences
IIIB.   Health and Environmental Sciences
 IVB.   Physical Sciences
  VB.   Psychology

Each main part is divided into numerous subject categories, the names of which are given at the beginning of each volume. Education has thirty-five subject categories, including, for example, "Early Childhood."

Entry to *DAI* is through the key-word title index. Key words are printed in alphabetical order, followed by the titles of dissertations in which they occur. Key words may be used in combination. Potentially useful entries can then be followed up in the document resumes section which provides an abstract of the dissertation. If the search goes back to Volume 29 or earlier, the researcher can use the *DAI Retrospective Index,* which contains bibliographic references in nine subject volumes for *DAI* Volumes 1–29. One of those subject volumes is titled *Education.*

University microfilms offers a computer search service for dissertations. It is called DATRIX II and is an efficient service for locating dissertations related to a research problem.

Selected Books

The host of books dealing with research—both education and education-related—can be located through various bibliographies, reviews, book indexes, and so on. It would be impossible, of course, to provide a comprehensive listing of books that partially or entirely deal with educational research; three publications are briefly described here because they are comprehensive and can be especially useful to the educational researcher.

Encyclopedia of Educational Research (EER).　The publication of the *EER* is a project of the American Educational Research Association (AERA) that represents a compendium of research covering five major issues in education. Six editions of the *EER* have been published, the most recent in 1992. The original edition appeared in 1941, with subsequent editions at approximately ten-year intervals.

The *EER* does not simply catalog the research that has been done on a topic; each entry provides critical evaluation, synthesis, and interpretation of much of the literature on the topic. The entries are prepared by noted educators who are familiar with the literature and research in their chosen topics. The most recent edition of the *EER* is the sixth, published in 1992 by Macmillan Publishing Company, with Marvin C. Alkin as editor-in-chief.

Handbooks of Research on Teaching.　There are three *Handbooks of Research on Teaching;* the first two were published by Rand McNally and Company (Skokie, Illinois), and the third was published by Macmillan Publishing Company (New York, New York). The preparation of the handbooks has been a project of the American Educational Research Association. The original was edited by N. L. Gage and published in 1963; the second, edited by R. M. W. Travers, was published in 1973; and the third, edited by M. C. Wittrock, was published in 1985. Both the second and third handbooks are original volumes, not subsequent revisions of the first.

The handbooks contain comprehensive presentations of research on teaching, including higher education and the teaching of subject matter. A variety of topics are given in-depth coverage in all three volumes, which are large and comprehensive—the first contains 23 chapters; the second, 42 chapters; and the third, 35 chapters. Not only is the content valuable to educational researchers, but each chapter has an extensive bibliography of references (in some cases, over 200 entries). The bibliographies themselves represent extensive searches of the research literature.

Review of Research in Education.　This is a publication of the American Educational Research Association; some of the early issues were published in cooperation with F. E. Peacock Publishers (Itasca, Illinois). The purpose of the *Review of Research in Education* is to survey disciplined inquiry in education through critical and synthesizing essays. Each of the essays, written by an author selected for expertise in that area, represents an attempt to appraise, evaluate, and criticize the more recent important empirical studies in the area. About ten areas are covered in each issue, categorized under broader topics such as curriculum.

The first volume of the *Review* was published in 1973, and it has been published yearly since then. To a large extent, the *Review* replaces the pre-1970 editions of the *Review of Educational Research,* which was described earlier in this chapter. Indeed, the *Review of Research in Education* was initiated by AERA to fill the void left by the *Review of Educational Research* when it adopted its new editorial policy of publishing unsolicited manuscripts on a variety of topics.

The *Review* is intended to be a source of information that highlights the strengths and weaknesses in educational research and provides direction for future research in the areas discussed. Although it is intended only secondarily to serve as a bibliographic reference source, it does contain a wealth of information and detailed reference lists with each article.

There are many other reviews, encyclopedias, and handbooks that directly or indirectly contain information about education. Most commonly, these are found in the reference section of university libraries. As just a few examples, these include:

Encyclopedia of Higher Education
Handbook of Child Psychology
Annual Review of Anthropology
Handbook of Teaching and Policy
Handbook of Research on Teacher Education
Educational Research, Methodology and Measurement: An International Handbook

This section presented several different sources of research information. Any difficulties encountered at this stage of a literature review are usually due not to lack of information, but to an inability to find the relevant references. Because there is such a large quantity of educational research information, it is important to conduct a systematic search, using the indexes, retrieval systems, reviews, and so forth, that are available. A manual search can be helpful in getting a review started, and it may be adequate for a limited review, but for any comprehensive review, a computer search is much more efficient.

Conducting a Computer Search

Computer-assisted searches of the literature are available through university libraries, many public libraries and state departments of education, and some school systems. Educational service organizations such as the Appalachia Educational Laboratory,[2] the regional educational laboratory serving Kentucky, Tennessee, Virginia, and West Virginia, provide computer-assisted searches of the literature on educational issues and research topics. A number of databases are available that contain educational research information. Probably the most frequently used database for education is the ERIC database. There are also databases in selected areas of education, such as the Bilingual and Bicultural Education Database, and related databases are available, such as *Psychological Abstracts* and *Social Science Citation Index*. Many university libraries have more than 200 bibliographic databases across all academic and professional areas that can be computer-searched. Thus, computer searches make available the maximum reservoir of information on a topic.

There are numerous advantages to a computer search; two obvious ones are comprehensiveness and speed. Descriptors used in "and" and "or" combinations can pinpoint or broaden the search as desired. Multiple databases can be searched, and bibliographic citations and complete citations with abstracts can be obtained. Finally, although a computer-assisted search may cost up to $50 (a more typical charge is in the $15 range, and some may be free of charge), it is highly cost-effective in terms of time and effort.

Typically, a computer search is conducted with the assistance of someone at the library who inputs the information through the computer terminal, monitors the search as necessary, and receives the printouts of the citations. However, many libraries now have a CD ROM[3] technology which can be used by an individual for inexpensive searches. In any event, a search requires planning so it can be properly focused. An example research problem is used here to illustrate the steps in the search.

Identifying the Research Problem and the Extent of Search

The research problem should be stated in specific terms so the problem is focused and so descriptors can be identified for the search. If a problem is too broad, an excessively large number of references may be identified, many of which will be irrelevant to the problem. If an exhaustive search is done, as would be the case for a dissertation, the problem would be narrowed. For the review of a journal article, the researcher might request only fifteen or twenty most recent references. The researcher has some flexibility in the extent of the search. If too many references appear, the search can be narrowed; if too few appear, it can be broadened through the use of descriptors. For the example, the research problem is stated as follows:

A study of measures of teacher effectiveness obtained through observation.

Selecting a Database

As indicated earlier, many databases are available. More than one database may be used, but descriptors must be applicable for the specific database. Of course, there is overlap among the database descriptors, and it is also possible to use certain descriptors for one database and other descriptors for another database. Related literature for most educational research problems is found in the ERIC database, *CIJE,* and *RIE.* The ERIC database is used for the example.

Selecting and Combining Descriptors

Descriptors are the search words used to tell the computer what to look for. Since the ERIC database is being used, descriptors are selected from the *Thesaurus of ERIC Descriptors*. Descriptors are used in combinations to broaden or narrow the search. The connecting words "and" and "or" can be used singly or in combination in the search.

Using the connector "and" between descriptors narrows the search, because all references must contain all terms so connected. The connector "or" broadens the search because references containing *any* of the descriptors will appear. For the example, we use "teacher effectiveness" and "observation" as descriptors. If we connect them with "or," we would obtain all references that contain either one or both descriptors. This would give us a very large number of references, many of which would be irrelevant. If we connect the descriptors with "and," a reference must contain both descriptors. This would greatly reduce the number of references. The relative volume of references using the two connectors is indicated by the shaded area in the two parts of Figure 3.6.

Before conducting the search using the "and" connector, as indicated in the lower part of Figure 3.6, we must consider that terms such as *teacher competence* and *teacher*

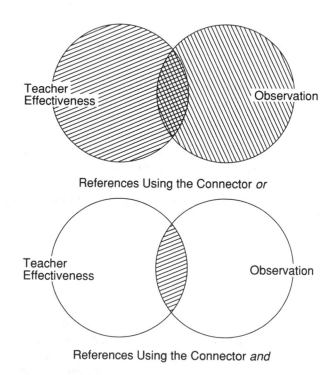

FIGURE 3.6   **Relative Volumes of References (shaded area) Using Connectors for Combining Descriptors**

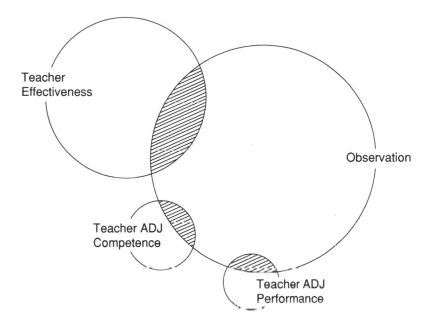

FIGURE 3.7   The Combination of Descriptors for the Example

performance arc sometimes used instead of *teacher effectiveness*. *Teacher competence* and *teacher performance* are not descriptors in the ERIC system, but "competence" and "performance" are. Using these terms singly is not feasible, however, because the number of references would be overwhelming. We can instruct the computer to scarch for "teacher" with "competence" *adjacent (ADJ)* to it and do the same for "teacher" and "performance." For the search, these descriptors are combined with "observation," using the connector "and." These combinations narrow the search considerably, as shown in Figure 3. 7.

Descriptors can be used in combinations with the connectors "or" and "and" to broaden or limit the search

---

Searching the Database for Numbers of References

As the descriptors are input through the computer terminal, numbers of references appear on the screen and these are used in deciding how to broaden or narrow the search. Figure 3.8 contains the numerical information for the example problem. This search was done using the BRS Search Service of BRS Information Technologies.[4] The information at the eight steps (indicated by RESULT) is as follows:

1. "teacher effectiveness" yields 10,206 references.
2. "teacher adj performance" (adj means adjacent to) gives 2,659 references.
3. "teacher adj competence" gives 220 references.
4. The combination of Results 1, 2, and 3 gives 12,051 references. Note that the combination is "1 *or* 2 *or* 3." The 12,051 is less than the total of results 1, 2 and 3 because some references are included in two or in all three of the previous steps.
5. "Observation" alone as a word yields 11,965 references.
6. Combining Results 4 and 5 with the connector *and* yields 923 references. These references are based on descriptors combined as "teacher effectiveness *or* teacher adj performance *or* teacher adj competence and observation."

```
BRS  SEARCH  MODE  -  ENTER  QUERY

    1_:  teacher  effectiveness

     RESULT    10206

    2_:  teacher  adj  performance

     RESULT    2659  DOCUMENTS

    3_:  teacher  adj  competence

     RESULT    220  DOCUMENTS

    4_:  1  or  2  or  3

     RESULT  12051  DOCUMENTS

    5_:  observation

     RESULT    11965  DOCUMENTS

    6_:  4  and  5

     RESULT    923  DOCUMENTS

    7_:  observation.mj.

     RESULT    800  DOCUMENTS

    8_:  4  and  7

     RESULT    26  DOCUMENTS
```

**FIGURE 3.8   Computer Printout Indicating
Numbers of References for
Descriptors and Combinations
of Descriptors.**

7. The 923 references are too many, so to narrow the search further, it is decided to include "observation" as a major descriptor (designated by mj). This means that in the initial indexing of the article or document, it was classified under the term "observation," rather than simply having the word appear in the document. This reduces the number to 800 references.

8. Finally, combining Results 4 and 7, we have 26 references. The same descriptors are used as for step 6, except "observation" is included in its more restricted form.

At this point we could include additional restrictions. For example, if we wanted recent references we could limit the search to those published within the past 10 years (or any designated period). We could get a listing of the references or we could obtain abstracts of any or all of them.

Figure 3.9 shows an abstract from the computer. The informational code is identified on the left. Some of the information is in numerical code. For example, 080 indicates that this document is a journal article and the 120 that it is considered reference material. The abstract is quite brief and on the basis of the abstract the researcher decides whether or not to obtain the entire document. Documents can be obtained in the usual manner, as desired—for example, on microfiche.

Broadening the Search, if Necessary

The example search was narrow, producing only 26 references from 1966 to the time the search was done. (The ERIC system was computerized in 1966.) If we decided that 26 references were not enough, the search could be broadened by reverting to "observation" as a word (rather than a major descriptor), and this would give us the 923 references of Step 6. But we do not want this many. Suppose we designate 40 references. We could keep the original 26 obtained from the narrow search and instruct the computer to add the 14 most recent references for a total of 40.

Use of the CD ROM

The CD ROM provides the opportunity for an inexpensive computer search, and with a few computer skills an individual can conduct the search without assistance. CD ROMs are limited in that they contain only one database (for example ERIC), depending on the compact disk inserted.

The researcher is taken through the steps of the search by the various menus appearing on the screen. For example, the first option is to "Select Main Activity" and one of those options is "Begin a New Search." Then there are several search options including "ERIC Subject Headings," which would be like using descriptors. Other example options would be to search on an author's name or a journal name. Then the search can be modified by including additional criteria, such as limiting the subject headings. Or only references in journals could be requested, limited to those with EJ numbers. The bibliographic references can be obtained on the computer screen, then abstracts of desired references can be printed for a nominal fee.

Accession
Number ——→ AN   EJ425117.
Author ——→ AU   Weade, Ginger; Evertson, Carolyn M.
Title ——→ TI   On What Can Be Learned by Observing Teaching.
Source ——→ SO   Theory into Practice; v30 n1 p37-45 Win 1991. 91.
Language ——→ LG   EN..
CIJE Issue ——→ IS   CIJAUG91.
              NO   RN: ISSN-0040-5841. ← International Standard Serial Numbering
Publication   CH   SP520342. ← Clearinghouse Accession Number
Type ——→ PT   080; 120.
              AV   UMI. ← Available from University Microfilms
Year ——→ YR   91.
Major ——→ MJ   *Classroom-Observation-Techniques.*
Descriptors   Evaluation-Methods. *Observation.*
                   Teacher-Evaluation.
Minor ——→ MN   Educational-Assessment. Elementary-Secondary-
Descriptors   Education. Instruction. *Performance.*
                   Teacher-Behavior.
Abstract ——→ AB   Examines *observation* as a process of systematic,
                   intentional action, exploring strategies for
                   observing within the classroom.
                   Implications for the practice of educational
                   evaluation, particularly *teacher* *performance*
                   evaluation, are noted. *Observation* as a process
                   of systematic, intentional action becomes
                   embedded within a larger agenda aimed at improved
                   schooling. (SM)

Annotator's Initials

FIGURE 3.9   Example Abstract from a Computer Search of the ERIC Database

CD ROM can be useful and efficient if the desired database is available. Some university libraries have the compact disk for government publications, which can be especially useful for areas such as policy research. Usually, the CD ROM terminal is in a prominent place and the researcher can sign up for a designated time period, say one-half hour.

A computer search is generally an efficient approach to identifying relevant references. It is not necessary to know how to operate the terminal; assistance will be provided by someone at the library. Various combinations of descriptors can be used to get some idea of the numbers of references available and whether or not they will be relevant. The available databases undoubtedly have something relevant to any educational research problem. There are limitations, however, to when indexes were computerized, and earlier references will have to be searched manually. Some indexes have been computerized for twenty-five years or more. When the printouts of abstracts become available, the researcher must still decide about the relevance of the reference and about whether or not to obtain a copy.

Selecting Studies for the Review of the Literature

The research literature on almost any educational topic is so extensive that it is not likely that all the studies related to a research problem can be included in the review. Also, there are time restrictions on how many studies can be reviewed, and reviews must be brought to closure. How then is a researcher to determine what studies to include in the review and at what point does further reviewing become unproductive?

There are no easy answers to these questions, but it is possible to make some suggestions. When a search is completed, it can be useful to check the eight or ten most recent references first. For one thing, these are the most current and should reflect the present state of thinking on the topic under study. Another advantage is that recent references will have the most current bibliographies. The reviewer can then determine which prior studies attracted the attention of others working on the same or similar topic. If an earlier reference repeatedly shows up in the bibliographies, it likely merits a review.

The review does not need to be done by "brute force," so to speak. Capitalize on the work that others have done. Consider the research problem, "A study of measures of teacher effectiveness obtained through observation," that was used as an example for the computer search discussed in this chapter. Anyone doing a review on this research problem would be wise to go to the *Handbook of Research on Teaching,* 3rd edition, and read Chapter 6. This chapter, written by Carolyn Evertson and Judith Green, is titled "Observation as Inquiry and Method." This chapter of 52 pages not only contains an excellent synthesis, but it has over 200 references in the bibliography. From the chapter and its references it can be determined who are the more recognized authors in the field, indicating whose publications may be most informative.

One disadvantage with a reference such as Chapter 6 mentioned above is that it was prepared in the mid-1980s, so it is not the most current. However, at least early in the review, a computer search could be done from the time the chapter was written until the present. A slightly different approach would be to identify the six or so most often referenced authors in the chapter, and do an author search to see what they have written since the review was completed. Once this activity gets under way, things will begin coming together; certain authors become associated with the research problem, various methods become apparent, and hopefully, there will be some consistency across results.

Just as use of a chapter from the *Handbook of Research on Teaching,* 3rd edition, was suggested above, reviews and reports of meta-analyses can provide much useful information. Of course, the more recent the reference, the more current the information. Whatever the publication date of the reference, the reviewer must bring the review up to date.

Reviews and meta-analyses essentially are secondary sources of the studies discussed. With primary sources, the reviewer is looking for well-designed studies and in some cases, studies that are highly original. Later in this chapter there is a discussion of critical review. To some extent, critical review is a subjective process, but usually the reviewer can tell if studies are well done and the results credible. We often pay close attention to recent studies, but there may be earlier studies which are highly relevant to the problem at hand. Some of these studies may be classics in the field and should be included in the review.

It is not unusual to discover mixed results in a review, even contradictory results in some instances. Such results require careful review to determine possible explanations; there may have been differences in the research conditions, the methods of at least one of the studies may have been deficient. Meta-analyses reports, when available, can be helpful for explaining mixed results. Such reports specify criteria for including studies, and usually provide comments about possible reasons for inconsistent results.

When has the review reached the point of "enough?" There is no single answer to this question in terms of number of references reviewed. The number is somewhat determined by the purpose of the review. A review for a journal article typically is considerably shorter than the review for a doctoral dissertation, for example.

There comes a point at which reviewing more references is going to provide little or no more useful information about the research problem. Intuitively, a reviewer pretty much knows when this point is reached. For example, when the patterns of research results of previous studies become consistent and additional studies simply reinforce these patterns, the results information has peaked. The methods used in the research studies may be quite similar and quite adequate for generating the necessary methods for the present study. Adequate here does not mean replicating exactly what has been done, but using the reviewed methods for extending the methods of the present study, possibly even coming up with a new and creative approach to addressing the problem. In general, when the information in the references reviewed seems to stabilize and seems quite complete in the context of the research problem, the review has reached closure. If the research study requires a considerable period, say several months, it will be necessary to update the review periodically to keep it current.

Assembling and Summarizing Information

After locating and reviewing the references from the literature search, the researcher must consider the question, "What should I do with the information?" The initial decision is to determine whether or not the content of the report (article, etc.) is relevant to the research problem under study. If it is not relevant, it can be deleted; if it is relevant, the information it contains must be summarized or somehow put into a usable form so that it is retrievable when the researcher needs it. In Figure 3.1, the separation of reports in order of importance was indicated as an optional activity. Sometimes it may be difficult to do this, because the distinctions between levels of importance may not be clear. Therefore, this activity may be omitted or it may be done after the abstracts or summaries have been prepared.

There are many formats or information recording procedures that can be used to assemble information from reported studies. Most researchers develop systems that seem to work well for them. For example, a straightforward note-taking procedure can be used. Regardless of the specific procedure used, it is best to use a systematic approach so that information is recorded consistently and important components are not omitted. Some formats and procedures are suggested here.

Bibliographic Entry

A complete and accurate bibliographic entry should be made for each relevant report reviewed. This entry is usually part of an abstract or summary; for quick reference, however, it may be best to place the bibliographic entry on a 3 × 5 card. If for no other purpose, such cards are useful for compiling a complete bibliography when the review of the literature is completed. The cards can be put in alphabetical order by the last names of the authors.

Bibliographic entries can be prepared as shown in Figure 3.10. Unless an individual has a lap-top computer, most entries are handwritten. A bibliographic entry contains the following information: the name(s) of the author(s), the title of the report (article, book, etc.), facts about publication, and, if an article is in a periodical, the inclusive page numbers. Facts about publication include the place, publisher, and date for a book, or the volume number and date of the periodical for an article. Titles of books, reports, and periodicals are underlined.

Whenever information from a report is to be used, a complete and accurate bibliographic entry should be made when the report is first used. This saves time and possible confusion. It is frustrating to have to look up a report again just because the bibliographic entry is not complete.

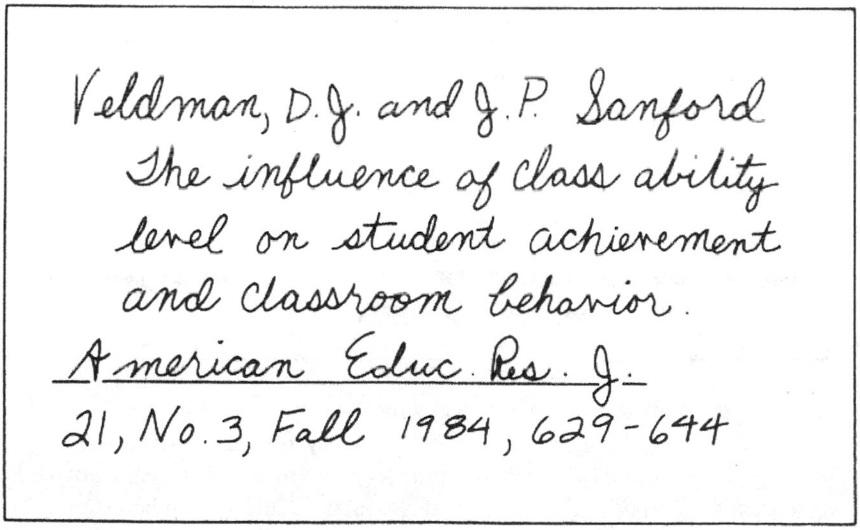
Veldman, D.J. and J.P. Sanford
The influence of class ability level on student achievement and classroom behavior.
American Educ. Res. J.
21, No. 3, Fall 1984, 629-644

FIGURE 3.10 Sample Bibliography Card

Abstract or Summary

A researcher reviewing the literature is faced with extracting the information from relevant reports and summarizing this information in a usable form. To use research results effectively—that is, to fit them into the context of the research problem—considerable information must be obtained from the report. For example, it is usually necessary to know something about the conditions under which the results were obtained. The problem of the reported research should be known, so that it can be related to the research problem under study. Thus, as the report is being reviewed, judgments must be made about which information will be retained—that is, written down.

Rather than just taking notes on research reports, the researcher usually uses some form of abstracting. An *abstract* is a summary of a research report that contains certain kinds of information. The form of the information should be consistent across the reports reviewed. There are slight variations among the components of an abstract suggested by different authors, but generally some form of the following are included:

Bibliographic Entry: An accurate and complete bibliographic entry heads the abstract.

Problem: This is a statement of the research problem of the report being reviewed; it may include statements of hypotheses.

Subjects: The individuals involved in research studies are often called "subjects" of the research; for example, "50 college sophomores enrolled in elementary education, 25 males and 25 females."

Procedures: This section describes how the research was conducted. It includes such items as the measurements used and the analyses performed. This section also may be called "Methodology."

Results and Conclusions: This section identifies the relevant results and conclusions of the study. A distinction may be made between results and conclusions—results being whatever occurred, such as certain statistics; conclusions being what the researcher has made of the results. In long reports with many results and conclusions, it is best to number them.

An *abstract* is a summary that contains the relevant information from a research report according to specified categories.

The length of an abstract must always be considered, because it is not efficient to retain the entire report. Many journals publish a very brief abstract at the beginning of each report. However, this abstract is limited in length and is usually not sufficient for the researcher's purpose. The abstract developed by the researcher should be somewhere between these two extremes.

When abstracting a report, the researcher attempts to condense the relevant information as briefly as possible while including all the necessary details. Although the abstract should be brief, the importance of having all necessary information must be emphasized. It is frustrating and inefficient to find that the information of an abstract is incomplete and that it is necessary to search out the report again. A number of factors affect the length of the abstract, including the length of the report, the complexity of the research, and the extensiveness of the findings. Some authors suggest limiting abstracts to a single page or to material that can be placed on a 5 × 8 card. There is some merit to these suggestions, since they facilitate manipulation of the reference information, but it may be difficult to stay within such strict space limitations. The content of the abstract should be as brief as possible, but including all necessary information will usually result in abstracts of varying length when several reports are abstracted.

The two sample abstracts in Figures 3.11 and 3.12 illustrate different abstract lengths. The first is an abstract of a nine-page article and the second is from a sixteen-page article. Although the length of the report does influence the length of the abstract, it is not the only determining factor. The number of conclusions drawn, the complexity of the research, and the extent of relevance to the research study at hand also affect the abstract's length.

Each of the sample abstracts has a complete bibliographic entry. The second abstracted article (Figure 3.12) had the research problem stated in the form of three

---

Yager, R. E. and R. J. Bonnstetter. "Student Perceptions of Science Teachers, Classes and Course Content." *School Science and Mathematics,* 84, No. 5, May–June, 1984. pp. 406–414.

Problem: To determine the perceptions of students of various ages and young adults, toward factors of their science instruction.

Subjects: Approximately 700 (total) Iowa students and young adults at ages 9, 13, 17, and (24–35) years old. Data from a comparison, natural sample of 2,500 from the National Assessment of Educational Progress (NAEP) study were also used.

Procedure: Subjects were surveyed in 1982 using an effective inventory including 13 items that were common to the inventory used in the 1977 NAEP study. Science consultants in Area Educational Agencies of Iowa were used for data collection. Responses to individual items were summarized using percentages, and compared to patterns of responses found in the 1977, NAEP study.

Results and Conclusions: Results of the 1982 survey in Iowa and those of the NAEP study were highly consistent. Almost one-half of elementary level teachers admit to now knowing answers to student questions, yet as students get older, decreasing percentages of students indicate that teachers make science exciting (68, 56, 45, 34 percent of the four age groups in order). It appears that as teachers become more knowledgeable in science, they are less successful in making it exciting to their students. As students advance through the grades there are substantial drops in the percentages that find science to be fun, interesting, or to make them feel successful. The lowest percentages (around 30%) were found among the young adults. Perceptions of the usefulness of course content, now and in the future, drop somewhat as students get older, but the big decline is between 17-year-olds and young adults.

FIGURE 3.11   Sample Abstract (Shorter Form)

Veldman, D. J. and J. P. Sanford, "The Influence of Class Ability Level on Student Achievement and Classroom Behavior" *American Educational Research Journal, 21,* No. 9. Fall 1984, 629–644.

Problem: The research problem was posed in three questions:
   (1) Are the classroom behaviors and achievement levels of students systematically different among classes of higher and lower ability?
   (2) Within classes, are the behaviors of higher and lower ability students systematically different?
   (3) Does student ability level interact with the ability level of the class to affect systematically students' classroom behavior and achievement?

Subjects: Junior high school students (grades 7 and 8) from 58 mathematics and 78 English classes (located in Texas), approximately 500 in math and 650 in English.

Procedures: An ex post facto study; achievement measures in math and English were analyzed along with 25 high-inference ratings of students by observers, and 25 low-inference measures of teacher and student behaviors; regression models (equations) were developed (math and English separately) to determine the contributions of grade, class mean ability, student ability and class ability by student ability interaction, criterion variables were class mean or student, achievement or behavior measure.

Results: A. For student achievement
   (1) High ability students performed better than low ability students in both math and English (certainly expected).
   (2) Interaction effects (for class ability by student ability) for both math and English; in math membership in a high ability class has more impact on low ability than high ability students; in English, the same pattern only stronger.

   B. For classroom behaviors, observer ratings
   (1) For 25 observer ratings of students, 14 showed significant relationships with class and pupil-within-class ability levels in both math and English; these ratings reflected behaviors associated with work habits, motivation, persistence, self-confidence, dependability, academic leadership and class participation, for which higher ability classes and students had lower ratings on student behavior problems, aggression, profane language and academic dependence, no significant class or student effect for ratings on extroversion, interaction with the teacher, physical maturity, unhappiness, cooperation and frequent talking to neighbors.
   (2) For interactions, math had 8 variables, English 4 with only 3 common to both, generally class ability level has more impact on the behavior of low ability students than on high ability students, placing low ability students with high ability students tends to have a positive impact on behavior of low ability students.

   C. For classroom process variables
   (1) Higher ability classes have fewer procedural contacts, less misbehavior and fewer call outs.
   (2) Higher ability students were given more response opportunities, gave more correct and few answers, had fewer adverse teacher contacts and less misbehavior.
   (3) Four of the five interactions that were significant showed the same patterns in math and English, generally lower ability students in lower ability classes tended to display more undesirable process behaviors than their counterparts in high ability classes; in English but not in math, lower ability students showed less misbehavior in higher ability classes.

FIGURE 3.12   Sample Abstract (Longer Form)

questions, which added to the length of the problem statement. Because the research problem was extensive, a considerable number of results were generated, and the results are separated more explicitly than the results of the first article. For the second article, the results are extensively synthesized. If the results were separated for the three questions, the abstract would be too long.

The abstracts shown in the figures are typed, but it is not necessary to type abstracts. Abstracts are a means to an end, not an end in themselves. They may be written on cards or on regular-sized paper, but the important thing is that they are useful and contain the necessary information. Although formats tend to be similar, there is enough flexibility for researchers to meet their individual needs.

Organizing Information

Research problems tend to have inherent and identifiable categories on which to group the studies reviewed. Such grouping of the studies facilitates the writing task, so that continuity can be achieved rather than a "back and forth" approach.

Consider the example research problem used for the computer search earlier in the chapter. Observation inventories or systems used to measure teacher behavior (and from behavior infer effectiveness) generally can be grouped into two categories: high-inference and low-inference systems. These terms refer to the amount of inference required on the part of the observer when recording the behavior. So, studies could be grouped as to whether either one or both of these systems were used, giving a three-category grouping.

Another possible grouping of studies dealing with teacher effectiveness is the grade level of teaching involved; for example, primary, middle school, high school or some combination of these levels. Even if the same observation system could be used for all levels, the patterns of results might be quite different depending on the level taught. Most of the studies likely would involve inservice teachers with varying years of experience. But there may be some studies involving teacher education students doing their student teaching. This may be another dichotomy on which the studies could be grouped, inservice teachers or teacher education students being observed. So, there are different ways to group the studies reviewed according to category systems somewhat unique to the research problem.

> Studies reviewed can be grouped according to categories that are somewhat unique to the research problem at hand, but that are identifiable. These categories will provide a logical organization of the information.

Interpreting and Using Information

The interpretation of results and other information found in research reports begins when the report is being reviewed. To begin, it is a good idea to skim a report to get an overview, without being too concerned with the specifics. From this overview, a decision can usually be made about the relevance of the report to the research problem being studied. Assuming that a report is relevant, the reviewer can then focus on the specifics and begin the abstracting process.

Critical Review

It is well known that there is considerable variability in the quality and comprehensiveness of reports in the educational research literature. Thus, as a researcher reads a report, it is necessary to take a somewhat critical perspective. But how does one read critically? Reviewing research reports requires an intellectual effort on the part of the reader, and the reader is responsible for having at least some familiarity with the area (not necessarily the research in the area) and some knowledge of research procedures. Indeed, one of the purposes of studying research methods is to better understand the research literature.

Nevertheless, there are characteristics of a report that a reader can look for, and if these characteristics are weak or lacking, the report is suspect. Smith and Glass (1987, p. 2) refer to these as *criteria* or *tools,* and they focus on different types of validity, beginning with logical validity. This validity deals with how the entire research study and report fit together. Do the various parts fit together logically and does the entire report make sense? Do conclusions follow logically from the results or are there inconsistencies? Were the procedures consistent with the research problem?

We have already introduced the concepts of internal and external validity of research. Internal validity deals with adequate and appropriate procedures so that results can be interpreted with confidence. Were the research procedures conducted appropriately? Were there possibilities for introducing bias? Are the procedures described adequately so the reader can understand what was done? Was the analysis appropriate?

External validity deals with the generalizability of results. Is the issue of external validity addressed? If so, do the results have adequate generalizability and do the generalizations seem reasonable? Was random selection or random assignment used, and if not, is representativeness argued on a logical basis?

Smith and Glass (1987, p. 4) also include the concept of *construct validity,* a concept from psychological measurement. A *construct* is a trait or an abstract quality of an individual, such as honesty. We do not see honesty directly but we can see evidence of it. When these constructs are used in research they should be defined in a way that is consistent with the prevailing thinking and research in the area. Measurement must be described and operationally defined.

This discussion included several questions, the kinds of questions a researcher has in mind when reading a research report. Many more specific questions could be raised, and those appropriate tend to come to mind as a report is read. This is part of the intellectual exercise of critical review. If a report has gaps in the discussion or the logical validity does not hold up, it will not be usable to the researcher. The internal validity must be adequate for interpreting results. External validity deals with generalizability and, specifically, the relevance of the report to the research problem at hand.

Critical review is an intellectual exercise in which the reader must judge the adequacy of the validity of the report.

Writing the Review

When the researcher has reviewed the reports to be used, or at least a substantial number of them, the information must be synthesized and put in the review of the literature. Now the researcher must decide what to make of the information. The abstracts of the studies reviewed can be grouped as was discussed earlier. If there are obvious gaps, it may be necessary to return to the literature and enlarge the search. It is at this point that the researcher uses the abstracts and pieces together the review puzzle.

The length of the review will vary according to the type of research report being prepared. The number of studies reviewed typically is greater than the number referenced in the review. In an article for a professional journal, the review is often limited, possibly to one page; essentially, it sets the context for the research problem and little more. In such situations, the review may contain only six or eight references, sometimes less. (In some articles, only two or three references are used because of space limitations imposed by the publication.) This does not mean that the researcher has reviewed only two or three reports. Many more may have been reviewed, but only the most relevant ones have been referenced. When a review is being done for an extensive research study, such as a doctoral dissertation, many reports, possibly 50 or more, may be included. In this case, the review of the literature becomes a major task. The written review itself usually contains subheadings, and information from the abstracts is organized according to the subheadings. Such reviews may cover 40 or more typewritten pages.

Regardless of the length of the review, the researcher should, if at all possible, include recent information. This does not mean that older information is not relevant, but the review should be up to date. For example, any review of the research on teacher effectiveness that had no entries more recent than ten years ago would certainly be suspect. Such a review would have a serious gap or deficiency.

Referencing

When information is reported from a source, it must be adequately referenced. A number of acceptable formats may be used, one of which is a footnote at the bottom of the page. In referencing information from the article abstracted in Figure 3.11, for example, a footnote might be used in the review narrative as follows:

> *Yager and Bonnstetter[1] found consistent results for the students in the 1982 Iowa survey and those surveyed in 1977 by NAEP.*

At the bottom of the page, the following footnote would appear:

> [1]*Yager, R. E. and R. J. Bonnstetter, "Student Perceptions of Science Teachers, Classes and Course Content."* School Science and Mathematics, 84, *No. 5 (1984), p. 409.*

For the narrative, if there are three or more authors of an article, the last name of the first author may be listed, followed by *et al.* (which means "and others"), rather than writing the names of all authors. A modification of this procedure is to list all of the names the first time the reference is used, then use et al. if it is referenced again. This is done simply for brevity. The footnote would contain the names of all authors.

A shorter format for references that does not require the footnote at the bottom of the page can be used. It involves a reference list or bibliography at the end of the chapter or report. One format is the author-date format. Using the sample reference, the author-date format would be:

Yager and Bonnstetter (1984) found consistent . . .

or, if the names of the authors are not to be emphasized in the narrative:

Other researchers (Yager and Bonnstetter, 1984) found consistent . . .

This format requires an alphabetical listing of references, which should be included in any case. If Yager and Bonnstetter were referenced more than once in the bibliography and if this reference was the second 1984 entry for them, the reference would be Yager and Bonnstetter (1984b). If the writer wishes to include the page number in the reference, it can follow the year, preceded by a comma.

The short method of referencing can also be used in an author-number format. In this case, the entries in the bibliography are numbered, and the reference number is used instead of the year of publication. The page numbers then follow the reference number if they are included. For example, if the Yager and Bonnstetter entry were number 30 in the bibliography, the reference would be:

Yager and Bonnstetter (30:409) found consistent . . .

or

Other researchers (Yager and Bonnstetter, 30:409) found consistent . . .

The author-date format is generally preferred to the author-number format because in the latter format, if a reference is added or deleted, all numbers of references following the addition or deletion have to be changed. If a reference is added after a good bit of the review is written, the necessary changes will be a bother and a potential source of error.

Referencing can be done in a number of ways—the traditional footnote or shorter methods, using the author-date or author-number formats.

Preparing the Bibliography

Usually, the final step of the review is putting together the bibliography. Some journals distinguish between a reference list and a bibliography; a reference list is limited to references cited in the report, whereas a bibliography may also include references for background information or further reading. The American Psychological Association (1983), for example, makes this distinction. Although a bibliography may include entries not cited directly in the review, it is not wise to include a large number of uncited entries.

The entries in a bibliography are ordered alphabetically according to the last name of the primary author (the one listed first). If the entries have been put on bibliography cards, as shown in Figure 3.10, the cards can be arranged in alphabetical order and the entries taken from them. This simplifies the task of typing the bibliography, especially if not all of the original sources are used. Abstracts can also be used, although they may be a little cumbersome.

An entry in a bibliography begins with the last name of the primary author, then includes any other authors before giving the title of the publication. Titles of articles or chapters are put within quotation marks (but note the difference in APA, 1983), and titles of books, names of periodicals, and so forth, are underlined. Publication date and volume numbers are given for periodicals. The city of the publisher, the publisher, and the publication date are given for books. Finally, page numbers are given, if necessary, as for articles in periodicals.

Several special situations can arise with respect to format and notation. For example, how are works with no author or an anonymous author referenced? How is a reference made to a statute in a state code? There are procedures for handling such situations, and they are discussed in manuals such as the *APA Manual* referenced at the end of this chapter.

Summary

This chapter described the process of reviewing the literature. A review serves a number of purposes—it puts the research problem in context; it provides information on what has been done; and it often provides information about how to conduct the research, including suggestions for instrumentation and research design.

The extent of a review of the literature depends on a number of factors, but it generally requires some time and attention to detail. Sometimes a researcher might comment, "There isn't anything in the literature on my research problem." What this means is that the researcher has not found a study exactly like the one being contemplated. A review of literature may include studies even indirectly related to the research problem, and it is the reviewer's responsibility to identify their relevance and synthesize the information from the several studies reviewed.

Figure 3.1 generally outlined the activities in a review of the research literature. Although a researcher may return to the literature at times for additional information and may rewrite parts of the review, the activities are generally done in order from top to bottom as in the flowchart in Figure 3.1. A review often occurs early in a research effort; if the study is conducted over an extended time period, additional entries may be necessary to bring the review up to date.

This chapter also provided several suggestions regarding where to find information, how to synthesize it, and what to do about it. Examples involving a manual search and a computer search were provided. Following consistent procedures enhances the review process by speeding the synthesis of information and reducing the likelihood of errors and repetition. In the final analysis, however, the researcher must write the review, organizing it and pulling things together in a way that will make sense to the reader. A well-organized review brings together the information on a single point or on similar ideas, provides some continuity among the results and conclusions of different research reports, and moves logically and smoothly from one point to another. Transition sentences, such as "Considering other factors that may affect teacher effectiveness, we move now to questioning behaviors," can be very helpful in leading the reader from topic to topic. After the review is written, it should be left alone for a week or two and then reread carefully. It will undoubtedly need some rewriting if it is an initial draft, but if it makes sense and there are no gaps or confusing sections, the researcher is well on the way to putting together a good review.

KEY CONCEPTS

Flowchart of activities

Periodical literature

Periodical indexes

Abstract

Computer-assisted search

Descriptors

Combination of descriptors

ERIC

CIJE

RIE

CD ROM

Bibliographic entry

Referencing

Bibliography

EXERCISES

3.1 Select a topic of interest and compile a list of possible references for this topic using the *Education Index* as a source. If you are doing this in connection with a real project, follow up on the references.

3.2 Suppose a teacher is interested in finding information about the content of mathematics programs for students aged eight to ten in Western European countries and the United States. If the teacher were using the ERIC system, what possible descriptors might be used?

3.3 A review of the literature is being done using a computer search for the following research problem:

A study of the relationship between teacher classroom behavior and student achievement in science, grades 6–12.

Using the ERIC database, identify descriptors that could be used in the search. What descriptors would broaden the search? What descriptors would narrow the search? Specify combinations of descriptors and the connectors.

3.4 Using the research problem in Exercise 3.3, or a research problem of your own choosing, conduct the initial part of a computer search, identifying the numbers of references for the descriptors as they are used either singly or in combination. Use any relevant database if you are using your own problem.

3.5 Consider the following research problem:

A study of the relationship between social adjustment and achievement in junior high school level academic areas.

If you have access to a CD ROM with an ERIC database, do a search for *research* reports on this problem. Limit your search using a criterion such as only EJ (educational journal) or the past ten years. Check about fifteen of the references to determine whether or not they actually deal with research or simply discuss the issue in the research problem. Now, do the same for the following research problem:

A study of the role of the principal in site-based management.

In comparing the results from the two searches, what do you find with regard to number of references, the nature of the references, and whether or not they describe research studies? (To some extent, the nature of a reference's content can be inferred from the title.)

3.6 Suppose a computer search of the literature is done related to the research problem:

A study of the effects of different questioning techniques upon achievement in senior high school history courses.

Identify descriptors from the *Thesaurus of ERIC Descriptors* that would be used in searching the ERIC database. Describe the order in which descriptors would be used and also the combinations using the *or* and *and* connectors. How might the search be narrowed? Broadened?

3.7 Select a journal article that does not exceed five pages and prepare an abstract of the shorter form.

3.8 Arrange a discussion among several graduate students, some of which are already working on dissertations or theses. In the discussion, address the following issues:

   a. The process by which the research problem was identified.
   b. The factors that motivated interest in the research topic.
   c. The assistance that can be expected from the graduate program advisor in identifying a research problem.
   d. The process by which the research problem was refined, either by narrowing it or broadening it, or revising it in some manner.
   e. The process by which the review of the literature was conducted.
   f. The manner in which studies reviewed were grouped for one or more specific research problems.

NOTES

1. Source: CIJE, Semiannual Cumulation. January–June 1992. Phoenix, AZ. Oryx Press.

2. The Appalachia Educational Laboratory is located in Charleston, West Virginia.

3. The acronym CD ROM stands for "Compact-Disk: Read Only Memory," which means that the system has no memory except what is read on the computer terminal screen.

4. The BRS address is 8000 Westpark Drive, Suite 500, McLean, VA 22102.

REFERENCES

American Psychological Association. (1983). *Publication manual of the American Psychological Association* (3rd ed.). Washington, DC: American Psychological Association.

Glass, G. V., McGaw, F., and Smith, M. L. (1981). *Meta-analysis in social research.* Beverly Hills, CA: Sage.

Koepsell, T. D., Wagner, E. H., Cheadle, A. C., Patrick, D. L., Martin, D. C., Diehr, P. H., and Perrin, E. B. (1992). Selected methodological issues in evaluating community-based health promotion and disease prevention programs. *Annual Review of Public Health,* 13, 31–57.

Levin, H. M. (Ed.) (1992). *Review of Educational Research* (Vol. 62, No. 3). Washington, DC: American Educational Research Association.

Smith, M. L., and Glass, G. V. (1987). *Research and evaluation in education and the social sciences.* Englewood Cliffs, NJ: Prentice-Hall.

Thesaurus of ERIC descriptors (17th ed.). (1990). Phoenix: Oryx Press.

C h a p t e r 4

Research Design in Quantitative Research

After a researcher has identified a research problem and has completed at least some review of the literature, it is time to develop a *research design*—a plan or strategy for conducting the research. As a plan, research design deals with matters such as selecting participants for the research and preparing for data collection—activities that comprise the research process. Research designs tend to be quite specific to the type of research, and the conditions that determine the specific research design to use are discussed in subsequent chapters. This chapter focuses on general concepts of design in quantitative research, and a later chapter, Chapter 8, does the same for qualitative research. There are process differences between qualitative and quantitative research. Quantitative research has its roots in positivism which Reese (1980) has defined as:

> *a family of philosophies characterized by an extremely positive evaluation of science and scientific method (p. 450).*

Thus, research design in quantitative research tends to be structured and prescriptive, much more so than in qualitative research. Also, as the name implies, the outcomes of quantitative research typically are to a large extent expressed as numbers, and research design is directed to enabling the researcher to make valid interpretations through comparisons and partitioning of those numbers.

The Purposes of Research Design

To a large extent, the need for research design is implicit. How could we proceed otherwise? There must be a plan by which the specific activities of the research can be conducted and brought to successful closure. Kerlinger (1986, p. 280) identified two basic purposes of research design: (1) to provide answers to research questions and (2) to control variance. This latter purpose is, to a large extent, unique to quantitative research.

The first purpose is general and straightforward—to provide answers to the specific research questions. But going through the motions of conducting research or engaging in research activities alone will not necessarily yield answers. This relates to a point made in Chapter 1 regarding our concern about making educational research systematic. Research should be valid, which includes being able to interpret results and, through those results, answer the research questions or problems being posed. Good research design assists in understanding and interpreting the results of the study and ensures that a researcher obtains usable results.

It has been said that all research is conducted for the purpose of explaining variance—the fact that not all individuals are the same or have the same score or measurement. In a broad sense, this may be true, although qualitative researchers may take issue with this assertion. Variance can be evident in a number of ways. For example, variance in elementary school students' achievement, motivation, attitude, age, and family background can be considered. Also, when the variance of any one variable is considered, it may be influenced by any number of factors. Variance in achievement, for example, may be due to aptitude and motivation, to mention two possible factors. In quantitative research design procedures are taken for controlling variance. Controlling variance means being able to explain or account for variance caused by variables being studied. Variance takes on quantitative meaning, and at least to some extent, is partitioned as attributable to variables included in the research study.

Explaining or controlling variance is an important part of quantitative research, and research design should address this issue.

The Concept of Controlling Variance

In quantitative research we attempt to quantify variance, and to the extent possible, partition it according to various sources or causes. But, how does variance manifest itself? Consider an example. A high school chemistry teacher is studying the effects of different methods of teaching on achievement in chemistry. The research problem could be stated as follows:

> A study of the effects of teaching method on the performance of high school students enrolled in chemistry.

The problem implies that an experiment will be conducted, since teaching method, the independent variable of primary interest, will be manipulated by the chemistry teacher. Teaching method has three different categories (also called levels), say M_1, M_2, and M_3. The dependent variable is performance on a chemistry achievement test administered after one semester of instruction. Ninety students, all juniors enrolled in the same school and taught by the same teacher, participate in the study. Thirty students are taught by each method. When the students are tested on chemistry achievement, there will be 90 scores, but these 90 scores will not all be the same. There will be a distribution of scores, the scores on the dependent variable, and because these scores are not all identical, this distribution will have variance.

Why are the 90 scores not all identical? This may be due to a variety of causes. The teaching methods may have different effects, and since method is the independent variable, the researcher certainly wants to be able to determine whether or not the three methods have different effects. Some students are undoubtedly more able than others, regardless of the instructional method. Possibly the time of day that instruction takes place has some effect. These are examples of variables that may be control variables or intervening variables, as discussed in Chapter 2. There undoubtedly is inherent variation in the way students respond to a chemistry test. Any number of factors might be operating to cause variance in the dependent variable scores.

Consider the variance of the 90 chemistry test scores. As will be seen in the chapters on statistical analysis, variance can be quantified; it is a real, positive number, a number such as 132 or 10,920. A variance of zero would indicate no variance, that is all scores in a distribution would be identical. The greater the number, the greater the variance; however, when analyzing variance we are more interested in "comparing" relative amounts of variance than in the actual values of the numbers. Suppose the variance of the 90 chemistry test scores is 360. Although variance does not come in circles, it can be quantifiably represented by the area in a circle as in Figure 4.2. The entire area of the circle represents all the variance (360) in the 90 chemistry test scores.

> Variance can be expressed quantitatively as a real, positive number. A variance of zero indicates that all scores in a distribution are identical.

Procedures for Controlling Variance

This section continues the chemistry example and illustrates procedures by which control of variance can be enhanced. The method of instruction is the independent variable of primary interest, and student ability will be considered as another variable to be controlled. There are basically four ways by which variance is controlled:

1. Randomization.
2. Building conditions or factors into the design as independent variables.
3. Holding conditions or factors constant.
4. Statistical adjustments.

The first three procedures are directly involved in structuring the research design. The fourth includes computational manipulations in an attempt to obtain control, so it is done at the analysis stage of the research, although preparation for it must be done when the research is designed.

Randomization.   Suppose in the chemistry example that the same teacher will teach the 90 students, having three classes of 30 students each, each class taught by a different method. The 90 students are a heterogeneous group with respect to ability level, which may well have some effect on performance on the chemistry test. Thirty students are randomly assigned to each of the three methods, as diagrammed in Figure 4.1. Thus, ability level is randomly distributed among the three methods, and one would expect its effect to be the same in each group of 30 students. In essence, the ability level effect has been spread evenly among the three groups, and the effect should be the same for all three groups. Although this procedure distributes the effect of ability level evenly, it does not allow the researcher to determine the differences caused by ability level.

Remember that the chemistry test score is the dependent variable and the variance of all 90 test scores is 360. Suppose that the means[1] of the thirty test scores for the three methods are 89, 75, and 96, respectively, for the methods, M_1, M_2, and M_3, and that the variance accounted for by these differences in means is 50 of the 360. Then the quantitative representation of the variance can be indicated as in Figure 4.2. The entire variance of 360 is partitioned with two parts, that due to method and all the rest, which is random or inherent variance. Quantitatively, the value of the former part is 50 and that of the latter, 310. Random variance contains the variance due to student ability, but because of randomization this variance is evenly spread among the three groups of students.

It can be noted that, in this example, randomization would also control other variables—primarily, organismic variables associated with the students. Motivational level, for example, would be randomly distributed among the three methods or groups. Mathematical knowledge or skill that might well be related to performance in chemistry would also be randomly distributed.

Randomization spreads an effect of a variable evenly across the groups of the study. Often, organismic variables are so controlled.

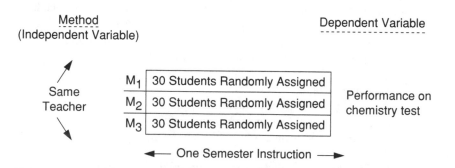

FIGURE 4.1   Research Design Using Randomization to Control for Ability Level

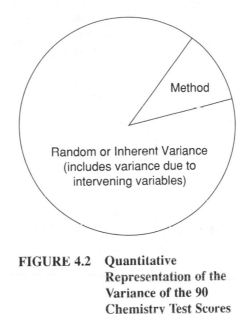

FIGURE 4.2   Quantitative Representation of the Variance of the 90 Chemistry Test Scores

A word at this point about terminology. Random or inherent variance also is called error variance, especially when statistical analyses are done. Error variance does not mean having made a mistake or anything like that. It simply means the inherent or natural variance that is due to random assignment or random selection.

Building in Factors as Independent Variables.   In the design in Figure 4.1, the students are separated into three groups according to method. If an ability level measure were available—possibly a score on a recent IQ test—the students could also be grouped according to ability level. If the top 45 students on the ability-level measure were designated as "higher" and the remaining 45 students as "lower" ability level, ability level would be an independent variable with two levels. Fifteen students of each of the two ability groupings would be randomly assigned to each method. This design is presented in Figure 4.3. Now it can be determined not only whether or not there is a difference among methods but also whether or not there is a difference between the higher and lower ability groups. The variance that might be caused by the ability-level effect can be accounted for. Suppose that ability level accounts for 75 of the variance. (This would be determined from the difference in the two ability level means of the chemistry scores.) Method[2] still accounts for 50 of the total variance, so the variance due to random variance is now 235 (360–50–75 = 235). This partitioning of the variance is presented in Figure 4.4.

The division of the students into only two ability-level groups is arbitrary in this example. (Three groups could have been used, designated high, medium, and low.) It should be noted that the researcher arbitrarily formed the groups so that equal numbers were maintained. To do this, the IQ test publisher's definition of higher and lower ability

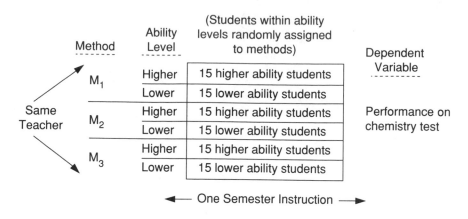

FIGURE 4.3   **Research Design with Ability Level Built In As an Independent Variable**

level would not be used (if a definition were available), because a published definition would undoubtedly make for considerable inequality in the numbers of students in each ability level. Indeed, for chemistry, one would expect few, if any, students of low ability level.

Building in a variable does allow the researcher to determine the effect of that variable, that is, to determine any differences attributable to that variable, or the variance accounted for by the variable. In the example, more of the variance has now been

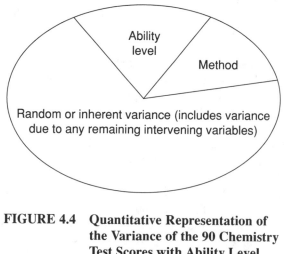

FIGURE 4.4   **Quantitative Representation of the Variance of the 90 Chemistry Test Scores with Ability Level Built In As an Independent Variable**

explained than when method was the only independent variable. The random variance has been reduced to 235. Then why is this procedure not always used? For one thing, measures on which the individuals can be separated, in this case the chemistry students, are not always available. For example, motivational level may have an effect, but motivation scores would be difficult if not impossible to come by. Therefore, motivational level remains an intervening variable, but it is randomly distributed if random assignment is used. Also, including increasing numbers of independent variables may make the design unnecessarily complicated. Therefore, factors so included are usually those that are expected to cause some variance in the dependent variable scores.

> Building factors into the design as independent variables enables the researcher to determine the effects of those factors. Too many independent variables, however, can unnecessarily complicate the research design.

Holding Factors Constant.   Holding a factor constant essentially consists of reducing a variable to a constant. In the chemistry example, the teacher could reduce ability level to a constant if only students with one defined ability level—say, those scoring between 100 and 108 on an IQ test—were included in the study. If ability level does tend to affect performance on the dependent variable, its effect would now be considerably diminished from what it would have been with the entire range of ability level included. Most of the variance in the chemistry test scores due to ability level would have been eliminated. The design would be essentially the same as that in Figure 4.1, except that only students within the designated IQ range would be randomly assigned to the methods. This number would likely be less than 30 per group if the teacher had started with the original 90 students. The variance of the chemistry scores of the remaining students would now change; it would tend to be reduced over what it was for all 90 students because the students now are more homogeneous in ability.

Holding factors constant can have some disadvantages. One has already been indicated: the possible elimination of individuals from the study, causing logistical problems or reducing the amount of data available on the dependent variable. Also, such results generalize only to the restricted group. Thus, external validity is reduced. The chemistry example already has several constants built into the design, such as teacher and length of instruction.

> When a factor is held constant, a potential variable is reduced to a constant. This eliminates, or at least substantially reduces, any effect the factor may have on the dependent variable.

Statistical Control.   Statistical control, when used, is attained through computational procedures applied when the data are analyzed, but the variable to be so controlled must still be planned for in conducting the research. For the purposes of this discussion it is not necessary to focus on the statistical procedures; they are taken care of through the analysis, usually done by computer. The important issue here is the concept of how variance can be controlled by this method. Turning again to the chemistry example, assume that an ability measure consisting of performance on a recently administered IQ test is available for all 90 students. It is likely that a relationship exists between performance on the IQ test and performance on the chemistry test such that high scores on one tend to go with high scores on the other and, similarly, low scores on one go with low scores on the other.

If we could somehow adjust the chemistry test scores for this difference in ability level, we would be controlling the effect of student ability on the chemistry test scores. This can be done with a relatively sophisticated statistical procedure. Depending on the strength of the relationship between the chemistry test and IQ test scores, high chemistry test scores would be lowered (by statistical computation) if the students had high ability-level scores, and students with low ability-level scores would have their chemistry scores raised. These adjusted chemistry test scores, now independent of ability level, would then be analyzed. *Independent of ability level* means that the effect of ability level has been removed.

The process of statistical control can be conceptually diagrammed as in Figure 4.5. Again, conceptually we can consider the total variance in the 90 chemistry scores. The statistical control would most likely account for more variance than building in student ability as a two-category, independent variable. Measuring students on an IQ test which is considered to have interval scale measurement is more sensitive to differences than categorizing students as higher and lower, which is ordinal measurement. Suppose the statistical control for ability level accounts for 130 of the original 360 variance in the chemistry test scores. Method still accounts for 50, so the random or inherent variance is now reduced to 180 (360–50–130 = 180). This is illustrated in Figure 4.6.

> Statistical control, in essence, consists of adjusting the dependent variable scores to remove the effect of the control variable.

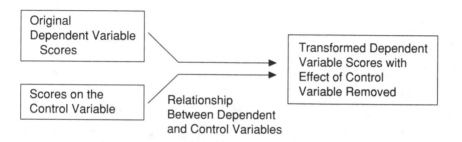

FIGURE 4.5   Conceptual Diagram of Statistical Control

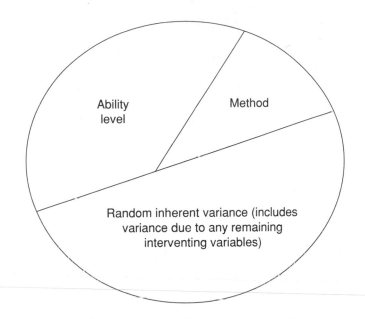

**FIGURE 4.6   Quantitative Representation of the
Variance of the 90 Chemistry Test
Scores with Ability Level Controlled
by Statistical Control**

If statistical control is simply a matter of putting an analysis through the computer, why is it not used more frequently? One reason is that it is often difficult to obtain adequate scores on a control variable. Scores must be available for all participants in the research. Preferably, the scores on the control variable should be obtained prior to conducting the research so that there is no possibility of the scores being affected by the independent variable—in the chemistry example, the teaching method. Then, too, control variables are effective only to the extent that they are related to the dependent variable and account for variance in the scores of that variable. Furthermore, certain statistical assumptions must be met; if they are not tenable, the statistical procedure should not be used.

Using Procedures for Control in Combination.   The four procedures for enhancing control can be used singly or in combination. One procedure might be used for controlling one variable and another procedure for a second variable. Extending the chemistry example somewhat will illustrate this point.

Instead of using only 90 students, a large high school in which there are at least 180 chemistry students will be used. Teaching method, with the same three levels, is still the independent variable of primary interest. Two teachers (T_1 and T_2) will be used, since there will be six chemistry classes. It is known that the students come from various science and mathematics backgrounds in the elementary schools they attended and in courses they have taken thus far in high school. (For example, some students may have taken Algebra

II, others not.) Scores on an IQ test given to all students when they were in eighth grade are available. There are two other high schools in this district, but there is considerable difference in the composition of the student bodies (for example, socioeconomic background) among the high schools. The four variables (in addition to the independent variable) and their methods of control are as follows:

Variable	*Method of Control*
1. Science background of the student	**1.** Randomization; the 180 students participating in the research are randomly assigned, 60 to each teaching method.
2. Teacher	**2.** Built in as an independent variable; each teacher uses the three teaching methods.
3. School	**3.** Reduced to a constant; students of only one school are included.
4. Ability level	**4.** Statistical control; the IQ test scores are used.

The research design is diagrammed in Figure 4.7. With the relatively high degree of control, if large enough differences occurred among the chemistry test scores of students taught by the three methods, the result would be an indication that the differences are in fact due to the methods. The research design has a high degree of internal validity; the results can be interpreted quite conclusively. However, it should be noted that the generalizability of results may be somewhat limited. Only one school and only two teachers in that school were used. The results generalize only to the extent that the student body and the teachers in this school are representative of some larger population. It may be that the intent is to generalize only to students of this school, but if wider generalization is intended, the external validity of the study must be argued on a logical basis.

When making decisions about the effects of independent variables, the variance they account for is compared with the random or error variance. If the random variance tends to be large because it contains variance caused by extraneous variables, the results may be difficult to interpret or be misinterpreted, thus jeopardizing internal validity. Although randomization does spread the effects of a variable evenly, it does not remove the variance caused by that variable from the random or inherent variance. Some variables, such as learning style of students, cannot he controlled practically by any other manner in most situations in which it might be involved. So, we want to guard against situations in which too much of the variance is unexplained, and therefore methods of controlling variance are used in combinations.

> Research design in quantitative research is directed to control or explain variance. This is done by including certain research conditions, an example being including additional variables as independent variables, and these become control variables.

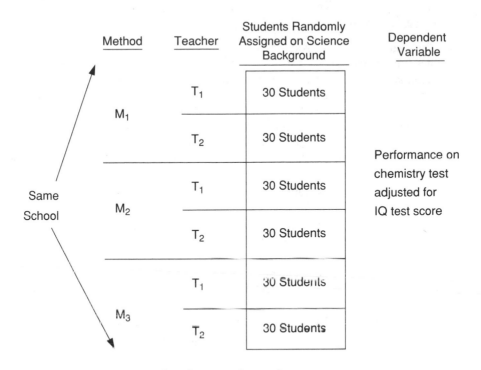

FIGURE 4.7   **Diagram of a Research Design in Which School, Science Background, Teacher, and Ability Level Are Controlled by Different Control Procedures**

The purpose of controlling variance is to enhance the interpretation of results so the researcher can tell what effects, if any, the variables are having. The time to think about control is when the research design is being developed. Carefully designing the research does much to enhance the validity of the research; failing to do so may well lead to uninterpretable or nongeneralizable results.

Characteristics of Good Research Design

What constitutes a good research design? There are some general answers, such as that the design should be appropriate for the hypotheses or that it should be feasible within available resources. However, to be more specific, four characteristics are discussed that enhance research design. These characteristics are not mutually exclusive, they have some overlap. We want research not only to be "do-able," but also to yield results that can be interpreted with confidence.

Freedom from Bias

One characteristic of a good research design is that it will provide data that are free from bias. This means that the data and the statistics computed from them do not vary in any systematic way, but only as would be expected on the basis of random fluctuations. Any differences that appear, therefore, can be attributed to the independent variables under study. If some type of bias exists in the data and differences appear that cannot be attributed to random fluctuation, it is not possible to determine whether this difference is due to the bias or to the effect of the independent variable.

Bias can enter into the data in a number of ways, including biased assignment of the individuals to the experimental treatments. For instance, in the chemistry example, if the higher ability students were all assigned to one teaching method, a bias would have been introduced.

Bias in the data may be eliminated by random assignment of individuals or random sampling, but the bias can be introduced independently of the random procedure. In the chemistry example, random assignment to the methods would have eliminated the bias of putting the higher ability students in one method. (The possibility of a "wild assignment" does exist, but its probability would be very small.) It would still be possible to introduce bias if, for example, three teachers were used, each using only one method, and there were considerable differences in their effectiveness. In that case, possible bias would have been introduced after the random assignment of students to methods. This leads to the concept of confounding.

Freedom from Confounding

One way bias can enter the data is through confounding of variables. Two (or more) independent and/or other variables are confounded if their effects cannot be separated. A good research design eliminates confounding of variables or keeps it to minimum so that effects can be separated and results can be interpreted without confusion. In the example with three teachers, each using only one method, teacher and method have been confounded. If the students of one method scored higher on the chemistry exam than those of the other two methods, we would not know whether the higher performance was due to the method or to the teacher. The effects of teacher and method cannot be separated, because each teacher uses only a single method.

Two or more variables are *confounded* if their effects cannot be separated.

Control of Extraneous Variables

Although extraneous variables are not the variables of primary interest in a research study, they may have an effect on the dependent variable. To control such variables is to be able to identify, balance, minimize, or eliminate their effects. The effects are manifested as they influence the variance in the dependent variable, so the control of extraneous variables is accomplished through the control of variance, as described earlier. In the chemistry example, the ability level of the students was considered an extraneous variable, and various approaches to its control were discussed. A good research design controls such variables, rather than confounding their effects with those of other variables or ignoring their effects altogether.

Statistical Precision for Testing Hypotheses

Analyses in quantitative research typically involve some types of statistical procedures, because quantitative research involves numbers and hypotheses that require statistical tests. It is important to have appropriate data with enough precision so hypotheses can be tested with confidence. In a statistical sense, precision is increased as the random or error variance is decreased. As we discussed in the chemistry example, when additional variables were controlled, the random variance tended to be reduced.

When statistical procedures are used to test hypotheses, for at least some hypotheses, it is necessary to obtain an estimate of random variance from the data. The more precise this estimate, the more sensitive the analysis will be to the effects of the independent variables. That is, the analysis will be more likely to indicate an effect if, in fact, one exists. Extraneous variables inflate the estimate of random variance and tend to make the statistical tests insensitive to existing, real differences.

The research design should provide data for testing all of the hypotheses of the study. Sometimes numerous and complex hypotheses are involved, so the researcher should check the design carefully and identify which part of the design will provide for testing such hypotheses.

Summary

The concepts discussed in this chapter apply to research design in quantitative research. Quantitative research typically has quite a structured design from the outset and there is little, if any, deviation from the design during the study.

In addition to providing answers to research questions, one of the purposes of research design is controlling variance. Controlling variance means being able to explain what is causing it, at least to the point that results can be interpreted with confidence. Variance is controlled in quantitative research by the structure of the design. Four general methods of controlling variance were described and illustrated, and these may be used in combination.

Four characteristics of a good research design in quantitative research, which are by no means independent of each other, were identified. For example, as we construct the design to avoid confounding, we may also be controlling extraneous variables. Although problems inevitably arise while conducting research, they usually can be circumvented or corrected with a well-planned design.

Of necessity, research designs are specific to the types of research. In subsequent chapters different types of research are considered, and each type has its underlying, general design with many possible variations.

Sometimes we talk about "selecting" a research design. Certainly designs are selected, but the variables, conditions, and so forth of a specific study flesh out the design. Thus, it is not correct to infer that selecting a design completes the task of obtaining an adequate research design. The selected design must be translated into the specifics of the study.

KEY CONCEPTS

Positivism

Variance

Random or error variance

Controlling variance

Bias

Confounded variables

Extraneous variables

Control of extraneous variables

Statistical precision

EXERCISES

4.1 Suppose the boys in a senior high school, grades 10–12, are measured on a physical performance test. Identify variables or factors which may contribute to the variance in the performance test scores.

4.2 A study is being conducted in which the dependent variable is student attitude toward school, defined operationally as the score on a specific attitude toward school inventory. There are sixteen elementary schools, four junior high schools, and two senior high schools in the district for which the study is conducted. Random samples of students are selected from all schools and administered the inventory. The independent variable of primary interest is the school, of which there are twenty-two. Considering the four methods of controlling variance described in this chapter, how would variance caused by the following factors be controlled? Suggest one method for each factor.

    a. level of school, elementary, junior high, senior high

    b. school district

    c. gender of the student

    d. academic motivation of the student

    e. intelligence or ability of the student

    f. time of year

4.3 In the research study of Exercise 4.2, are there any variables confounded with the independent variable of primary interest, school? If so, identify examples of such variables.

4.4 The research study of Exercise 4.2 is a survey. Why is this not an experiment?

4.5 Two high school history teachers who each teach two classes of American history have available two different packets of instructional materials. They are interested in whether or not the materials have differing effects on achievement in history, as measured by the final exam for the course (a common exam for all classes). A specific class will use only one packet of materials, but the teachers have the option of randomly assigning students to classes. In addition to the independent variable of primary interest (materials), it is desirable to control the variance due to (a) learning style of the student, (b) gender or sex of the student, (c) teacher, and (d) ability level of the student. The students are high school juniors, and no recent IQ test scores are available; but the grade point average (GPA) for the first two years of high school is available. Develop a research design to control the variance due to the four variables. Use at least two of the four basic methods of controlling variance in quantitative research. Diagram the design.

4.6 An educational psychologist is designing an experiment in which three different types of motivational techniques will make up the levels of the independent variable. The dependent variable is performance on a cognitive task that has been shown to be related to an ability-level measure. The participants (subjects) will be sixty randomly selected college freshmen enrolled in an introductory psychology course. Discuss possible variables that might be controlled in this experiment and suggest procedures for enhancing such control.

4.7 Define what is meant by *confounding of variables* and describe a research study in which confounding could occur.

4.8 From a professional journal, select an article about quantitative research in your area of interest. Read the article carefully and attempt to identify the design used for the research. Is there enough description about the design so that you can understand how the research was done? Does the article deal with variance in the dependent variable and describe how this variance was analyzed? Are issues of internal and external validity addressed?

NOTES

1. In the analysis, each method would be represented by the mean of the thirty test scores of students taught by that method. The mean would be determined by adding the thirty scores and dividing that sum by thirty.

2. In practice the numbers would not quite add this way because as we go from one procedure to the next, the design changes. However, the concept, not the numbers, are important here, so for simplicity we will keep the variance accounted for by method at fifty.

REFERENCES

Kerlinger, F. N. (1986). *Foundations of behavioral research* (3rd ed.). New York: Holt, Rinehart and Winston.

Reese, W. L. (1980). *Dictionary of philosophy and religion*. Atlantic Highlands, NJ: Humanities.

Chapter 5

Experimental Research

has a vaguely familiar, broad meaning in contemporary usage—so e tries a new approach or procedure to see what its effects will be, as an experiment or to the process as experimenting. In his attempts ulb, Thomas Edison tried different filament materials to determine He was experimenting.

esearch, rather specific descriptions are provided of how experiments ver, a basic concept from the broad usage of experiment is retained; tried—one or more independent variables are manipulated to deter- independent variable that is manipulated is called an *experimental*

s a research situation in which at least one independent variable, *imental variable,* is deliberately manipulated or varied by the

ental Design

se, an experimental design is a preconceived plan for conducting an specifically, an experimental design is the structure by which variables nged, or built into the experiment. The design includes the independent must include the experimental variable(s) and possibly other variables, variables. Since the measures (the data to be analyzed) are taken on iable(s), the points in the experiment where these measures are to be indicated. Experimental designs are often diagramed with symbols to indicate the arrangement of the variables and conditions. Such diagrams and their arrangements and symbols have certain meanings, which are explored in this chapter.

Consider an example. An educational psychologist uses three types of instructions—verbal, written, and combination verbal-written—to determine the effects of instruction on performance in solving abstract number problems. The participants in the experiment are college freshmen, twenty of whom are randomly assigned to each type of instruction. A participant comes to a learning laboratory, receives the instructions, and attempts to solve a series of number problems. The dependent variable is the score on the number of problems solved correctly in the series. Each participant goes through the experiment alone, rather than in a group, and the entire activity takes about one hour. The experimental variable is type of instruction, and there are three levels (the different types) of this variable.[1]

The experiment is diagrammed in Figure 5.1. In the upper part of the figure, the entire design is written out. The experimental procedure consists of administering the appropriate instruction and solving the problems. The measures on the dependent variable are collected during the experiment and usually recorded when it is completed. Depending on the experiment, the data may be collected while the experiment is in process or shortly after it is concluded. In this example, the data are collected after the instructions have been given and the participants are solving the problems.

Below the dotted line in Figure 5.1, the experiment is diagrammed in symbol form.[2] The R indicates random assignment to the three groups, designated by the Gs with subscripts. X is used as the symbol for the introduction or use of an experimental variable,

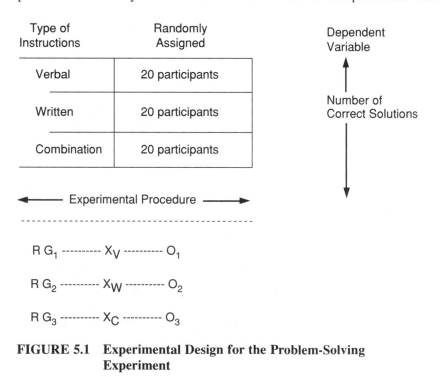

FIGURE 5.1   Experimental Design for the Problem-Solving Experiment

and the subscript on the X simply indicates the level of that variable. In the diagram, the V, W, and C subscripts on the X indicate the type of instructions—verbal, written, and combination. The Os indicate data collection (in a general sense, observation taken), and, in this example, the subscripts on the Os correspond with the numbers of the groups. In this diagram, O_1 indicates the data from Group 1 (G_1) the group that had verbal instructions (X_v). The Os are scores on the dependent variable—in this case, number of correct solutions.

The experiment diagrammed in Figure 5.1 is relatively simple. It contains only one independent variable, the experimental variable. Data are collected only at the close of the experiment. The experimental procedures with the instructions and problem solving might be somewhat complicated, but the design does provide the researcher with considerable control. If, in analyzing the scores, the researcher found those of G_3 to be consistently and considerably higher (more correct solutions) than those of G_1 and G_2 it would be quite conclusive that the combination type of instruction is more effective than the other two types in enhancing this type of problem solution.

Why bother with experimental design? It enables the researcher to interpret and understand the data of an experiment. The purpose of experimental design is no different from the purpose of research design generally—to be able to make sense of the results—and experimental design enhances control. In the example, the researcher can draw conclusions about the effect of type of instructions on problem solving because the design structures the instructions so that their effects are separated and can manifest themselves. Patterns of results can be directly associated with certain effects of the independent variable.

> An *experimental design* is the structure by which variables are positioned or arranged in the experiment.

Experimental Variables

In Chapter 2, various types of variables were discussed. One type introduced was the independent variable, which may have an effect on the dependent variable. Independent variables can take different forms, such as an organismic variable or variables that indicate different treatments or procedures to be administered to the participants in the research. An experimental variable is an independent variable; but not all independent variables are experimental variables. In the foregoing example, had the participants been identified according to their sex, so that ten boys and ten girls were administered each type of instruction, the sex of the participant could have been designated an independent variable. However, it is an organismic variable, not an experimental variable. The type of instruction was the experimental variable.

Any number of independent variables can serve as experimental variables. Conceptually, an experimental variable can have any finite number of levels, but in educational research, experimental variables usually have relatively small numbers of levels—perhaps two to five, and rarely more than seven or eight. The levels of the experimental variable are sometimes called *experimental treatments*. The following are some examples of possible experimental variables in educational research:

Experimental Variable	*Possible Levels*
1. Type of instructional organization	1. a. team teaching b. self-contained classroom
2. Type of materials for concept attainment	2. a. verbal b. figural

3. Drug dosage for experimental animals	3. a. 5 grams
	   b. 10 grams
	   c. 15 grams

4. Length of time on task with no break	4. a. 5 minutes
	   b. 10 minutes
	   c. 20 minutes
	   d. 30 minutes

5. Instructional strategy used in teaching history	5. a. lecture
	   b. group discussion
	   c. individualized instruction

6. Time of day for instruction	6. a. morning b. afternoon

7. Length of word lists used for spelling instruction	7. a. 10 words
	   b. 25 words
	   c. 40 words
	   d. 60 words
	   e. 100 words

8. Length of exercise period (per day)	8. a. 15 minutes
	   b. 30 minutes
	   c. 45 minutes
	   d. 60 minutes

9. Type of therapy	9. a. medication alone
	   b. exercise alone
	   c. medication and exercise in combination

For each of the examples of experimental variables, the researcher can manipulate or control the levels or experimental treatments. In number 7, for example, the word lists can be prepared and used with five groups of students randomly assigned to the lists. The purpose of the experiment undoubtedly would be to determine the effects of word-list length on student performance on a spelling exercise.

Use of the Term Subject

In research generally, but especially in experiments, the term *subject* is used to mean someone who participates in an experiment. Subjects are the participants in the experiment, those who receive the experimental treatments. Thus, the subjects of the instructions example were college freshmen. If fifth-grade students were used in an experiment, they would be the subjects. The symbol *S* is used to designate a subject. The term *subject* and the symbol *S* are commonly used in the literature.

Criteria for a Well-Designed Experiment

Before specific experimental designs are introduced, some general criteria for a well-designed experiment will be considered. Essentially, the characteristics that make for a good research design also apply to the design of an experiment. The criteria are listed here with brief comments for each criterion to explain what it means:

1. *Adequate experimental control*—This means that there are enough restraints on the conditions of the experiment so that the researcher can interpret the results. The experimental design is so structured that if the experimental variable has an effect, it can be detected. This may also mean controlling other variables through randomization or by building them into the design as independent variables.

2. *Lack of artificiality*—This criterion is especially important in educational research if the results of the experiment are to be generalized to a nonexperimental setting—for example, a classroom. It means that the experiment is conducted in such a way that the results will apply to the real educational world. We do not want the artificial or atypical characteristic of an experiment to cause the experimental effects.

3. *Basis for comparison*—There must be some way to make a comparison to determine whether or not there is an experimental effect. In some experiments, a control group is used—a group that does not receive an experimental treatment. The control group in an instructional experiment usually consists of a group of students taught by a traditional method. In a drug experiment with animals, a control group would consist of the animals that receive no drug. Certainly, not all experiments require control groups. Comparisons can be made between two or more experimental treatments and, on occasion, with some external criterion.

4. *Adequate information from the data*—The data must be adequate for testing the hypotheses of the experiment. The data must be such that the necessary statistics can be generated with enough precision to make decisions about the hypotheses.

5. *Uncontaminated data*—The data should adequately reflect the experimental effects. They should not be affected by poor measurement or errors in the experimental procedure. The individuals from the various groups should not interact in such a way as to cancel experimental effects or to cause misrepresentation of the experimental effects.

6. *No confounding of relevant variables*—This criterion is closely related to adequate experimental control. There may be other variables operating that have an effect on the dependent variable. If so, these effects must not be misinterpreted as experimental effects. Their effects must be separated or controlled, usually through the experimental design.

7. *Representativeness*—The researcher usually wants to generalize the experimental results to some individuals, conditions, methods, and so forth. To obtain representativeness, the researcher commonly includes some aspect of randomness, either through the selection of the subjects for the experiment or through the assignment of the subjects to the experimental treatments (and control groups, if used).

8. *Parsimony*—The criterion of parsimony means that, with all other characteristics equal, a simpler design is preferred to a more complex one. Of course, a design must be complex enough for the purposes of the experiment, but complexity is not encouraged for its own sake. The simpler design is usually easier to implement and possibly easier to interpret.

Experiments, like any type of educational research, are susceptible to technical and procedural errors. The development of an appropriate experimental design and its adequate implementation require considerable and careful planning, but they provide the best safeguard against errors. Experimental design requires simultaneous attention to a variety of details. This planning is done prior to conducting the experiment.

Experimental Validity

The criteria of a well-designed experiment can be summarized as the characteristics that enhance experimental validity. In Chapter 1, the validity of educational research was discussed, and the concept of experimental validity is essentially the same. Experimental validity is used here as defined by Campbell and Stanley (1963) and is considered to be of two types, internal and external.

Internal validity is the basic minimum of control, measurement, analysis, and procedures necessary to make the results of the experiment interpretable. Internal validity deals with being able to understand the data and draw conclusions from them. It questions whether the experimental treatment really makes a difference in the dependent variable. To answer this question, the researcher must be confident that factors such as extraneous variables have been controlled and are not producing an effect that is being mistaken as an experimental treatment effect.

External validity of an experiment deals with the generalizability of the results of the experiment. To what populations, variables, situations, and so forth do the results generalize? Generally, the more extensively the results can be generalized the more useful the research, given that there is adequate internal validity.

Experimental validity is of two types, internal and external. *Internal validity* is the minimum control necessary to interpret the results. *External validity* deals with the extent of generalizability of the results.

Although the purpose of experimental design is to have experiments high in both types of validity, in some cases securing one type tends to jeopardize the other. As more rigorous controls are applied in the experiment, less carry-over can be anticipated between what occurred in the experiment and what would occur in a natural educational setting. For example, in research on instructional techniques, the control of the experiment may be so extensive that an essentially artificial situation is created and only the experimental variables are operating. This would greatly enhance internal validity, but the generalization might be so limited that the results could not be applied to a real classroom situation. This does not imply that it is never desirable to achieve maximum control; the objectives of the experiment dictate the extent of the validity requirements. Clearly, an experiment whose results are uninterpretable is useless even if wide generalizability would be possible. On the other hand, it is unsatisfactory to do an experiment and then discover that the results cannot be generalized as anticipated in the objectives of the experiment.

Internal validity involves securing adequate control over extraneous variables, selection procedures, measurement procedures, and the like. The experimental design should be developed so the researcher can adequately check on the factors that might threaten the internal validity. To be sure, all possible factors are not operating in all experiments, but the researcher should have some knowledge about the variables and the possible difficulties that may arise in connection with internal validity. Then the experiment can be designed so the results can be interpreted adequately.

External validity certainly concerns the populations to which the researcher expects to generalize the results, but it also may include generalizing the findings to other related independent variables or modifications of the experimental variable. There may be factors such as size of class, type of school, and the like, across which the researcher hopes to generalize. For example, would the results of an experiment being conducted in a suburban school with fourth-grade pupils apply to an inner-city school? To eighth graders? Most likely not, but again this would depend on the variables and the details of the experiment. The researcher may also desire to generalize to different measurement variations. For example, would the results of an experiment including pretesting be applicable to a classroom situation without pretesting? External validity is concerned with these types of questions.

Threats to Experimental Validity

Experimental design should enhance experimental validity, but experimental validity does not depend on experimental design alone. The specifics of the experiment have an influence, and a number of things can happen to threaten experimental validity, both internal and external.

Campbell and Stanley (1963) have summarized the threats to experimental validity, identifying twelve threats, eight to internal validity and four to external validity. Table 5.1 lists and describes these twelve threats and provides an example of how each could occur. Because these are experiments, all examples assume that some experimental treatment has been administered.

The designs discussed in this chapter are general designs and they are fleshed out by the specifics of whatever experiment is being conducted. For this reason it should not be implied that certain designs will guard against all threats to experimental validity. For example, it does not make any difference what design is being used, if measurement breaks down and is inconsistent, instrumentation is a threat.

Experiments which include only one data collection such as those using posttest-only designs are not threatened by testing. The designs discussed in this chapter meet the

TABLE 5.1 Threats to Experimental Validity

Threat	Example

Internal Validity

1. History—unanticipated events occurring while the experiment is in progress that affect the dependent variable.

1. During a relatively short instructional experiment, one group of subjects misses some instruction because of a power failure at the school.

2. Maturation—processes operating within the subject as a function of time.

2. In a learning experiment, subject performance begins decreasing after about 50 minutes because of fatigue.

3. Testing—the effect of taking one test upon the scores of a subsequent test.

3. In an experiment in which performance on a logical reasoning test is the dependent variable, a pretest cues the subjects about the posttest.

4. Instrumentation—an effect due to inconsistent use of the measuring instruments.

4. Two examiners for an instructional experiment administered the posttest with different instructions and procedures.

5. Statistical regression—an effect caused by a tendency for subjects selected on the basis of extreme scores to regress toward an average performance on subsequent tests.

5. In an experiment involving reading instruction, subjects grouped because of poor pretest reading scores show considerably greater gains than the average and high readers.

6. Differential selection of subjects—an effect due to the groups of subjects not being randomly assigned or selected, but a selection factor is operating such that the groups are not equivalent.

6. The experimental group in an instructional experiment consists of a high-ability class, while the control group is an average-ability class.

7. Experimental mortality or differential loss of subjects—an effect due to subjects dropping out of the experiment on a nonrandom basis.

7. In a health experiment designed to determine the effects of various exercises, those subjects finding exercise most difficult stop participating.

8. Selection—maturation interaction—an effect of maturation not being consistent across the groups because of some selection factor.

8. In a problem-solving experiment, intact groups of junior high school students and senior high students are involved. The junior high students tire of the task sooner than the older students.

External Validity

1. Interaction effect of testing—pretesting interacts with the experimental treatment and causes some effect such that the results will not generalize to an unpretested population.

1. In a physical performance experiment, the pretest clues the subjects to respond in a certain way to the experimental treatment that would not be the case if there were no pretest.

2. Interaction effects of selection biases and the experimental treatment—an effect of some selection factor of intact groups interacting with the experimental treatment that would not be the case if the groups had been randomly formed.

2. The results of an experiment in which teaching method is the experimental treatment, used with classes of low achievers, do not generalize to heterogeneous ability classes.

3. Reactive effects of experimental arrangements—an effect that is due simply to the fact that subjects know that they are participating in an experiment and experiencing the novelty of it, also known as the Hawthorne effect.

3. An experiment in remedial reading instruction has an effect that does not occur when the remedial reading program (the experimental treatment) is implemented in the regular program.

4. Multiple-treatment interference—when the same subjects receive two or more treatments (as in a repeated measures design) . . . there may be a carry-over effect between treatments such that the results cannot be generalized to single treatments.

4. In a drug experiment the same animals are administered four different drug doses in some sequence. The effects of the second through fourth doses cannot be separated from possible (delayed) effects of preceding doses.

criterion of "true" experimental designs as defined by Campbell and Stanley (1963). That is, subjects have been selected randomly or assigned at random to experimental treatments. Thus, differential selection of subjects is not a threat for these designs, but it very well may be for quasi-experimental designs as described in Chapter 6. Random assignment enhances the equivalency of groups prior to administering experimental treatments. Statistical regression is not a threat if the subjects involved are not selected because of extreme scores. But if an experiment is conducted with such subjects, the possibility of this threat should be recognized and addressed. For example, if a statistical regression effect is confounded with the experimental effect, it may be possible to estimate the magnitude of the statistical regression effect from information in the research literature.

The shorter the duration of an experiment, the less likely history is to be a threat to validity. Careful specification and control over the measurement can do much to eliminate problems with instrumentation. If no subjects drop out of the experiment, experimental mortality is no problem. If only posttesting is used after the experimental treatment is completed, there is no opportunity for an undesirable interaction between testing and the experimental treatment. Thus, it is through the planning and the careful conducting of the experiment that the threats to validity are countered. Many times extraneous variables can be controlled as independent variables built into the design. It may not be possible to eliminate all threats, but it is important to recognize and interpret the results accordingly, entertaining alternate explanations of the data if such explanations are plausible.

Experimental designs in educational research are rarely, if ever, perfect. Through experimental design, the researcher attempts to attain adequate validity, both internal and external. Since enhancing one type of validity may tend to jeopardize the other, the researcher often must attempt an adequate balance, essentially by attaining sufficient control to make the results interpretable, while maintaining enough realism so that the results will generalize adequately to the intended situations.

Experimental validity must be considered in the context of each specific experiment. Attaining validity is not an all-or-nothing outcome. Possible limits to validity should be recognized and countered through the design and the way the experiment is conducted.

The following sections describe a number of designs commonly used in educational research. The designs are diagrammed in general and described, and an example is provided for each design discussed.

Posttest-Only Control Group Design[3]

In discussing experimental designs, two terms, *pretest* and *posttest,* are often used in connection with the data collection. *Pretest* refers to a measure or test given to the subjects prior to the experimental treatment. A *posttest* is a measure taken after the experimental treatment has been applied. Not all designs involve pretesting, but posttesting is necessary to determine the effects of the experimental treatment.

Experimental designs commonly involve two or more groups, one for each of the experimental treatments and possibly a control group. The posttest-only control group design in its simplest form involves just two groups, the group that receives the experimental treatment and the control group. The subjects are randomly assigned to the two groups prior to the experiment, and the experimental group receives the experimental treatment. Upon the conclusion of the experimental period, the two groups are measured on the dependent variable under study. Preferably, this measurement is taken immediately after the conclusion of the experiment, especially if the dependent variable is likely to change with the passing of time.

The posttest-only control group design is an efficient design to administer. It does not require pretesting, which for many situations is not desirable or applicable. Pretesting and posttesting require that each individual subject be identified so that pre- and posttest scores can be paired. The posttest-only design requires the subjects to be identified only in terms of their group and, possibly, other independent variables if such variables are included in the design.

The two-group design can be diagrammed as follows:

$$R \quad G_1 \quad X \quad O_1$$
$$R \quad G_2 \quad — \quad O_2$$

In this diagram, G indicates group and R indicates that the members of the group are randomly selected or assigned to each group. An X indicates an experimental treatment, a dash, no experimental treatment. The Os indicate a measurement (test, task, or observation) on the dependent variable, and the vertical positioning of the Os indicates when they take place. Since they are vertically aligned, they take place at the same point in the experiment. In this case, they are posttests, since they occur after the experimental treatment.

The posttest-only control group design may be extended to include more than two groups; that is, two or more experimental treatments may be used, increasing the number of groups to three or more. The subjects would be randomly assigned to the groups from the population, and the effects of the various experimental treatments could be investigated by comparing the performances of the groups. In the more general sense, the posttest-only control group design can be diagrammed as follows:

$$R \quad G_1, \quad X_1 \quad O1$$
$$R \quad G_2 \quad X_2 \quad O_2$$
$$\bullet \qquad \bullet \qquad \bullet$$
$$\bullet \qquad \bullet \qquad \bullet$$
$$\bullet \qquad \bullet \qquad \bullet$$
$$R \quad G_k \quad X_k \quad O_k$$
$$R \quad G_{k+1} \quad — \quad O_{k+1}$$

The subscripts on the Xs indicate the different experimental treatments. The number of these treatments in the specific experiment is k. Note that there is one group, the control group, which does not receive an experimental treatment. If no control group were needed, the design would be called a posttest-only randomized groups design.

EXAMPLE 5.1 _____

A fourth-grade teacher does an experiment on the effects of supplementary instructional materials on reading performance. Two kinds of supplementary instructional materials are to be used; along with the traditional materials, they make up the three levels of the independent (experimental) variable.

The research problem can be stated as follows:

> *A study of the effects of kinds of supplementary materials on the reading performance of fourth-grade students.*

Fifteen students in fourth grade are randomly assigned to each level of the independent variable; thus, forty five students participate in the experiment. During daily reading instruction, the fifteen students using each of the supplementary materials work with those materials for twenty minutes. The control group continues working with the traditional materials. After eight weeks of instruction, the students are tested with a reading test. Performance on this test is the dependent variable. The experiment is diagrammed in Figure 5.2. The symbols for the experimental treatments are X_1 and X_2 with a dash for the control group. Referring to the general design, in this case the number of experimental treatments, k, would equal two.

> The *posttest-only control group design* contains as many groups as there are experimental treatments, plus a control or comparison group. Subjects are measured only after the experimental treatments have been applied.

Pretest-Posttest Control Group Design

The addition of a pretest given prior to administering the experimental treatments essentially extends the posttest-only control group design to the pretest-posttest control group design. The subjects are randomly assigned to the two or more groups and tested just prior to the experiment on a supposedly relevant antecedent variable, possibly a second form of the test that measures the dependent variable.

What is gained by pretesting? It may be that the pretest score can be used as a statistical control in the analysis. In some experiments, especially in instructional areas, it is desirable to analyze gain scores—the differences between posttest and pretest scores. However, some authors caution against the use of gain scores, especially in a simplistic manner. For example, Cronbach and Furby (1970) suggest quite complex mathematical

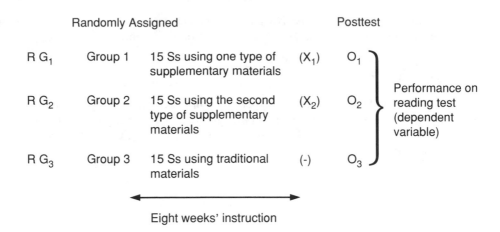

FIGURE 5.2 Diagram of Example 5.1 Posttest-Only Control Group Design, including Two Experimental Groups and a Control Group

models if gain scores are used at all. On the other hand, Zimmerman and Williams (1982) conclude that gain scores are quite useful. Whenever gain scores are contemplated, their meaning and reliability in the specific situation should be considered carefully.

In its simplest form, the pretest-posttest control group design contains two groups—one receiving an experimental treatment, the other not. It is diagrammed as follows:

$$R \quad G_1 \quad O_1 \quad X \quad O_2$$
$$R \quad G_2 \quad O_3 \quad — \quad O_4$$

Now there are twice as many Os as in the posttest-only design, so the Os with odd-numbered subscripts indicate pretests and those with even-numbered subscripts indicate posttests.

The pretest-posttest control group design can be extended to include more than two groups. It can be diagrammed in general form as follows:

$$R \quad G_1 \quad\quad O_1 \quad\quad X_1 \quad\quad O_2$$
$$R \quad G_2 \quad\quad O_3 \quad\quad X_2 \quad\quad O_4$$
$$\vdots \quad\quad \vdots \quad\quad \vdots \quad\quad \vdots$$
$$R \quad G_k \quad\quad O_{2k-1} \quad\quad X_k \quad\quad O_{2k}$$
$$R \quad G_{k+1} \quad O_{2k+1} \quad — \quad O_{2(k+1)}$$

The notation indicates k experimental treatments and a comparison group as a control group. If two or more experimental treatments are used and the experiment does not require a control group, the design would be called a pretest-posttest randomized groups design.

EXAMPLE 5.2 _____

A researcher is interested in the effects of length of intense instruction in geometric concepts on performance on a spatial relations test. The research problem can be stated as follows:

> A study of the effects of different length of instruction in geometric concepts on spatial relations performance of high school juniors.

The problem statement clearly implies an experiment, since length of instruction is a variable manipulated by the researcher.

Two parallel forms of the spatial relations test are used—one as the pretest, the other as the posttest. The experiment is set up as follows. Forty high school juniors are randomly selected, with the condition that all have taken a geometry course. The forty students are assigned to four groups of ten each, and the experimental treatments are administered as follows:

G_1 will receive one fifteen-minute period of instruction in three-dimensional geometric concepts.

G_2 will receive two fifteen-minute periods of instruction in three-dimensional geometric concepts.

G_3 will receive three fifteen-minute periods of instruction in three-dimensional geometric concepts.

G_4 (control group) will receive no instruction in three-dimensional geometric concepts.

The members of G_1, G_2, and G_3 will receive the instruction individually in a tutorial situation. (Care must be taken that the instruction is consistent for the members of a group; across groups, the only thing that should vary is the length of instruction.) The entire instruction will be completed over the period of one week. Before anyone receives instruction, the students are pretested; shortly after instruction is completed, the students are posttested. The experiment is diagrammed in Figure 5. 3.

The dependent variable in this experiment could be the gain scores between pre- and posttesting. Or the posttest scores could be the dependent variable, adjusted for pretest score. The adjusted scores would be generated through a statistical procedure. Using this design, the researcher can determine whether there are effects on spatial relations test performance from the different amounts of instruction in three-dimensional geometric concepts or, in comparison with the control group, whether instruction has any effects at all.

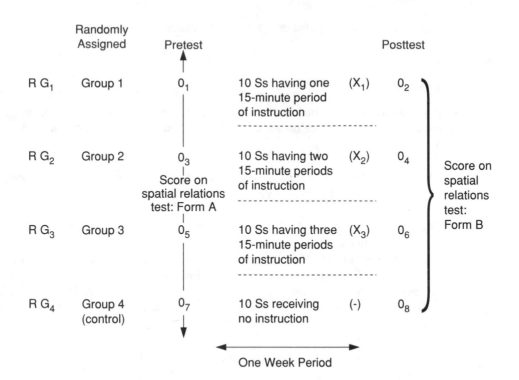

FIGURE 5.3 **Diagram of Example 5.2 Pretest-Posttest Control Group Design, including Three Experimental Groups and a Control Goup**

The *pretest-posttest control group design* contains as many groups as there are experimental treatments, plus a control group. Subjects are measured before and after receiving the experimental treatments.

Solomon Four-Group Design

Combining the pretest-postest control group design and the posttest-only control group design in their simplest forms produces a design described by Solomon (1949). This design, in its four-group form, includes two control and two experimental groups, but the experimental groups receive the same experimental treatment. Only one of each of the two types of groups is pretested, and all four groups are posttested at the conclusion of the experimental period. The assignment of subjects to all groups is random.

The diagram for the Solomon four-group design is as follows:

$$
\begin{array}{cccc}
R\,G_1 & O_1 & X & O_2 \\
R\,G_2 & O_3 & — & O_4 \\
R\,G_3 & — & X & O_5 \\
R\,G_4 & — & — & O_6
\end{array}
$$

Since it is a four-group design, only four groups are included and only one experimental treatment is used, the effects of which are determined by comparison of the posttest scores of the experimental and control groups. Since there is only one experimental treatment, no subscript appears on the X. Groups 1 and 3 are experimental groups, Groups 2 and 4, control groups (indicated by the absence of X).

The advantage of the Solomon four-group design is that it enables the researcher to check on possible effects of pretesting, since some groups are pretested and others not. It is possible that pretesting affects the posttest score or that pretesting interacts with the experimental treatment. That is, the effect of the experimental treatment is not the same in pretested and nonpretested groups. Since pretesting is not the rule in actual classroom practice, this is often an important consideration for validity.

EXAMPLE 5.3

An educational psychologist is experimenting with the effects of viewing a problem solutions film on performance on a logical reasoning test. The research problem can be stated as follows:

A study of the effects of viewing a problem solutions film on logical reasoning performance of young adults.

The experimental treatment is viewing the thirty-minute film. The subjects for the experiment are college seniors enrolled in an educational psychology class. The psychologist wants to pre- and posttest so that at least some gain scores can be analyzed. However, there is concern that the pretesting may trigger a certain kind of reaction to the film, such that the subjects being pretested may be cued about what to learn from the film. This is the reason for using the Solomon four-group design rather than a posttest-only design or a pretest-posttest design.

Thirty-two students are used for the experiment, and eight are randomly assigned to each of the four groups of the design. The design is diagrammed in Figure 5.4. The sixteen students in G_1 and G_2 are pretested at a single time. The next day, the sixteen students of the experimental groups view the film. Shortly thereafter, all thirty-two students are posttested. The pretest and posttest are parallel but different logical reasoning tests.

The psychologist can now check on possible effects of pretesting and the interaction of pretesting with the experimental treatment. Herein lies the advantage of the Solomon four-group design over the posttest-only and pretest-posttest control group designs. However, the Solomon four-group design has a disadvantage in that it requires more groups and consequently more subjects. The design can be extended to include more experimen-

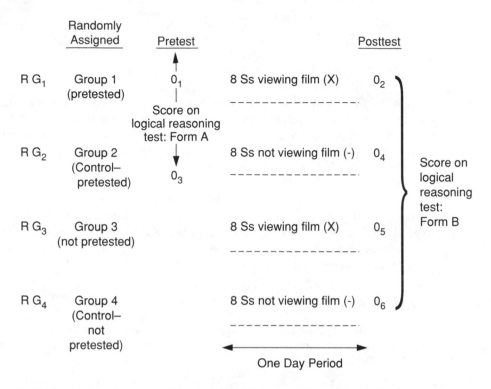

FIGURE 5.4   Diagram of Example 5.3 Solomon Four-Group Design

tal treatments, but for each additional treatment, two additional groups are required—one pretested and the other not. For example, if the experimental variable contained two treatments, six groups would be required; if it had three treatments, eight groups would be required.

The *Solomon four-group design* is a combination of the posttest-only control group design and the pretest-posttest control group design.

Factorial Designs

The Solomon-four group design actually belongs to a family of designs called factorial designs. These designs are used extensively in educational research, because essentially they are the designs when two or more independent variables are included in the design. The basic construction of a factorial design is that all levels of each independent variable are taken in combination with the levels of the other independent variables (technically referred to as *complete factorial*). The design requires a minimum of two independent variables, with at least two levels of each variable. This minimum design is called a two by two (2 × 2) factorial. The Solomon four-group design fits the 2 × 2 factorial because it has two independent variables (the experimental variable and the pretesting variable) and each variable has two levels.

Theoretically, there could be any number of independent variables with any number of levels of each. Using the numerical designation for a design, such as 2 × 4, the number of integers indicates the number of independent variables, and the numerical values of the integers indicate the number of levels for the specific independent variables. These numbers need not be the same for the independent variables. A 2 × 3 × 5 factorial has three independent variables, with two, three, and five levels, respectively. An example that fits this factorial is two teaching methods, three ability levels, and five grades.

The number of different groups involved in a factorial design increases very rapidly with the increase of the number of independent variables and number of levels. The 2 × 2 factorial has four groups. Adding just one independent variable with two levels would increase this to a 2 × 2 × 2 (denoted by 2^3) factorial with eight groups. If one level is added to each of the independent variables of a 2 × 2 factorial, resulting in a 3 × 3 factorial, the number of groups is increased to nine. Because the levels of the independent variable are taken in all combinations, the number of groups is the product of the integers that specify the factorial design. The 2 × 3 × 5 example above would require 30 groups.

The advantages of factorial designs over simpler designs are generally twofold: Factorial design provides the economy of a single design rather than separate designs for each of the independent variables, and it allows the researcher to investigate the interactions between the variables. For many research studies, a knowledge of interaction is of major importance, and investigating the existence of interaction is a primary objective of the study.

Interaction is an effect on the dependent variable such that the effect of one independent variable fails to remain constant over the levels of another. An interaction is present if the joint effect of two independent variables is not equal to their separate (additive) effects. This means that the effect of an independent variable by itself is not the same as when it is taken in combination with the levels of another independent variable. An example of interaction would be if students of different ability levels profited differently from different instructional content. Ability level and instructional content would be the independent variables.

The simplest type of interaction is that of two variables interacting. (This is sometimes called a *first-order interaction.*) More than two independent variables can be involved in an interaction. However, as more independent variables are involved in an interaction, it becomes increasingly complex, and interpretation becomes increasingly difficult.

Interaction in an experiment is an effect on the dependent variable such that the effect of one independent variable changes over the levels of another independent variable.

The factorial design allows for the manipulation or control of more than one independent variable. For this reason, it is often used as a design for enhancing control by including relevant factors as independent variables. Theoretically, the factorial design may be extended to include any finite number of variables and levels. However, complex designs should be considered with caution, one reason being that such a design may not be economically feasible in terms of the available subjects. Also, the interpretation of complex interactions involving more than two independent variables may, for all practical purposes, be impossible. For example, an interaction involving four independent variables—ability level, sex of the subject, instructional method, and type of material—would be very difficult to interpret.

Factorial designs involve two or more independent variables, called *factors,* in a single design. The cells of the design are determined by the levels of the independent variables taken in combination.

As indicated above, factorial designs can become complex and extensive with the inclusion of additional independent variables. Nevertheless, the concept of factorial designs is straightforward and they do appear extensively in the research literature. The example below includes only two independent variables, and because it is a 2×3 factorial, requires six groups.

EXAMPLE 5.4

A teacher is interested in the effectiveness of two different types of materials in learning American history—one highly graphic and pictorial, the other more abstract and more verbally detailed. The students available for the experiment are heterogeneous in ability, and academic aptitude test scores are provided for the students. Not only can academic aptitude serve as a control variable, but it is also possible that types of materials are not consistently effective across ability levels. That is, type of material and ability may interact. The research problem can be stated as follows:

A study of the effects of graphic and verbal materials on American history achievement when used with high-, average-, and low-ability high school students.

The 120 students are categorized into three groups on ability, arbitrarily designated high, average, and low. The 40 students with the highest academic aptitude test scores are designated high, the next 40 average, and the remaining 40, low. Then 20 students from each of the ability levels are randomly assigned to each of the two materials, and the instruction takes place over the period of one semester. The dependent variable is performance on a common history exam covering the content of the materials. The design is diagrammed in Figure 5.5.

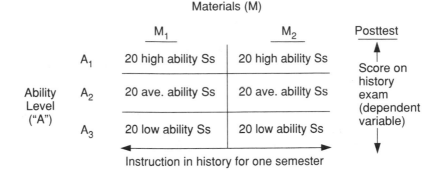

FIGURE 5.5   Diagram of Example 5.4 2 · 3 Factorial Design

The scheme used to diagram the factorial designs is slightly different from the designs diagrammed earlier. The groups are designated in the various cells of the design, rather than only on the rows, and the designation of independent variables is arbitrary. In the example, the types of materials are the experimental treatments, but M (for materials) is used instead of X. It is understood that all six groups of the example are tested at the close of the semester's instruction. Os are not included in the diagram.

In the example, random assignment is used only for assigning students to methods. Obviously, students cannot be assigned ability level at random, because it is an organismic variable. Also, ability level is arbitrarily defined so that 40 students would be in each category. It is not a requirement that the cells of a factorial have equal numbers, but they usually do, since analysis of the data and, to some extent interpretation of the results, are made less complicated if the cells have equal numbers.

Repeated Measures Designs

In some experiments, it is desirable to measure the same subjects more than once. In learning experiments, for example, a subject often performs a series of tasks, such as solving several problems in sequence, to demonstrate whether or not learning has taken place. Repeated measures designs can have the characteristics of designs discussed earlier. For example, pretesting could be done before any experimental treatments are administered. More commonly, the repeated measures are considered posttests only. As in a factorial design, other independent variables can be built into the design. In fact, most repeated measures designs are factorials, with the added characteristic of repeated measures.

The simplest form of a repeated measure design would consist of administering all the experimental treatments to all subjects. If there were k experimental treatments and n subjects, the design would be diagrammed as follows:

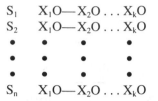

The S stands for the specific subject, and all subjects receive the same sequence of experimental treatments. The Os are placed in the diagram to indicate that measurement on the dependent variable takes place after each experimental treatment.

EXAMPLE 5.5

The example presented here is slightly more complex than the simplest design possible in that it contains two independent variables in addition to the experimental variable on the repeated measures. A learning experiment using college freshmen is being conducted in solving a series of four concept attainment problems. Subjects solve the problems individually in the learning laboratory setting. The problems can be solved using two types of materials, figural and verbal. This is one independent variable. The organismic variable, sex of the subject, is included as the other independent variable. The dependent variable is an efficiency of solution score, as defined by the experimenter. The research problem and related hypotheses can be stated as follows:

A study of the effects of type of material and sex on performance in solving concept attainment problems.
   H1: The mean performance of Ss using figural materials is greater than that of those using verbal materials.
   H2: There is no difference in the mean performance of males and females.
   H3: The mean performance of Ss improves across the four problem solutions.

The final hypothesis is that learning will take place in the experiment.
   A total of 40 subjects, 20 females and 20 males, is included in the experiment. The 20 males and 20 females are randomly assigned to the type of materials, with 10 of each to figural and 10 of each to verbal. The independent variables—sex of the subject and type of materials—are similar to a 2×2 factorial. Then there are four levels of the experimental variable problem, so that this could be called a $2 \times 2 \times 4$ factorial with repeated measures on the experimental variable with four levels. The design is diagrammed in Figure 5.6.
   Suppose the dependent variable in this example is the time required to solve the problem; the shorter the time, the more efficient the performance. In analyzing the data, we could compare the time means for figural and verbal materials. There would be 160 scores on the dependent variable, because there is a total of 40 subjects, each solving four problems. Eighty scores will be based on figural materials and 80 scores based on verbal

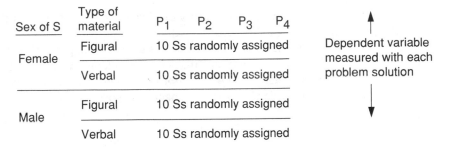

FIGURE 5.6   Diagram of Example 5.5 Repeated Measures Design

materials. Therefore, the two means for type of material will each be based on 80 scores. Likewise, we can check on an effect due to gender of the subject by comparing the means of males and females. Again, each of these means would be based on 80 scores, because there are 20 subjects of each sex and each subject solves four problems.

There will be four problem means, each based on 40 scores, one from each subject. If the mean times to solve the problems decrease from the first to the fourth problem, there is evidence that learning has taken place. So, the three hypotheses above can be tested using the data from a repeated measures design.

One characteristic of repeated measures designs is that they generate considerable data for the number of subjects involved. In the example above, 160 scores were obtained from 40 subjects. Repeated measures designs also have the characteristic that all observations are not independent; any two observations from different subjects are independent, but the observations from the same subject are not independent because they are from the same subject. This fact must be taken into consideration when the data are analyzed.

> *Repeated measure designs* are designs in which the same subject is measured more than once on the dependent variable.

There are variations and extensions to repeated measures designs that can accommodate certain characteristics. In the example above the four problems were solved by all subjects in the same sequence. If performance in solving the problems improved, it might be due to the problems becoming less difficult. The problems could be rotated so that each problem appears the same number of times in the four positions of the sequence. Such a design is called a counterbalanced design. More complex designs are discussed in advanced design texts such as Keppel (1991).

Designs Extended in Time

Sometimes, when working with educational variables and other variables in the behavioral sciences, it may be difficult to anticipate the time required for an effect to manifest itself. For some variables, the duration of an effect is unknown. Experimental designs can be extended to check on possible delayed effects or to check on the duration of an effect. This can be done by taking additional observations, extended in time. If we extended the posttest-only control group design in such a manner, a possible diagram of the design would be as follows:

$$R \quad G_1 \quad X_1 \quad O_1\text{---}O_2\text{---}O_3$$
$$R \quad G_2 \quad \text{---} \quad O_4\text{---}O_5\text{---}O_6$$

In this design, observations are taken on both groups after the experimental treatment has been administered to G_1. Then, at specified, regular intervals, subsequent observations are taken on both groups; although, no additional experimental treatments are administered. The length of intervals between observations would depend on the variables under study.

Designs so extended are susceptible to an effect of multiple observation, since groups are measured more than once. Earlier observations may have an effect on subsequent ones. Whether or not there is a multiple observation effect depends on the variables involved. Also, as designs are extended in time, they become especially susceptible to history and maturation effects as threats to internal validity.

Designs can be extended by taking additional observations on the groups. Such observations provide information about possible delayed effects of the experimental variable and about the duration of an effect.

EXAMPLE 5.6

A researcher is studying the effects of three different exercise programs (X_1, X_2, and X_3) on the resting heart rate, measured one minute after a brief, strenuous exercise. The research problem can be stated as follows:

A study of the effects, and duration of those effects, of three exercise programs on the resting heart rates of young male adults.

A random sample of sixty males, ages eighteen to twenty-two, is selected, and twenty are assigned to each of the three exercise programs. The subjects participate daily for two weeks in their respective programs; later, on the final day of the two weeks, they are measured on heart rate. When the heart rate data are being collected, a subject exercises strenuously for five minutes and rests for one minute; then the heart rate is measured. After the two-week period, the subjects no longer participate in exercise programs and are

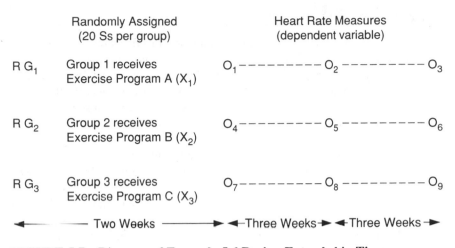

Randomly Assigned   Heart Rate Measures
(20 Ss per group)   (dependent variable)

R G$_1$ Group 1 receives   O$_1$ — — — — — — — O$_2$ — — — — — — — O$_3$
           Exercise Program A (X$_1$)

R G$_2$ Group 2 receives   O$_4$ — — — — — — — O$_5$ — — — — — — — O$_6$
           Exercise Program B (X$_2$)

R G$_3$ Group 3 receives   O$_7$ — — — — — — — O$_8$ — — — — — — — O$_9$
           Exercise Program C (X$_3$)

◄──────── Two Weeks ────────► ◄─Three Weeks─► ◄─Three Weeks─►

FIGURE 5.7   Diagram of Example 5.6 Design Extended in Time

instructed not to initiate exercise on their own. They are again measured on heart rate at three-week intervals after the final day of the exercise program. The design is diagrammed in Figure 5.7.

There is little likelihood of a multiple observation effect in this example. Simply having had heart rate measured three weeks earlier should have no effect on subsequent measures of heart rate. There may be a threat to internal validity if subjects continue to exercise on their own after the program has been completed. It would be desirable, almost necessary, to obtain the subjects' commitment prior to conducting the experiment that they will cooperate as instructed throughout the eight-week period of the experiment, including all observation.

Time Series Designs

Campbell and Stanley (1963) classify time series designs as quasi-experimental designs because they discuss the designs as being used with intact groups. However time series designs can be "true" experimental designs, so to speak, if the groups are formed randomly and there is provision for a valid comparison, such as a control group. Time series designs involve repeated measurement, usually some measures taken prior to the experimental treatment, and the insertion of the experimental treatment somewhere between two of the measurements.

> Time series designs involve repeated measurement with an experimental treatment inserted between two of the measurements.

EXAMPLE 5.7

A university professor teaches an "Introduction to Education" class which has seventy-eight students. The students have two discussion sections which meet once per week for two hours over the course of the semester. These sections meet for all students at the same time, and beginning with the third week, and at two-week intervals, the students are given exams covering the content of the previous two weeks. Seven such exams are given over the course of the semester. Graduate students conduct the discussion sessions and they rotate among the two groups.

The seventy-eight students are assigned randomly to the two discussion sections, thirty-nine to each section. One section receives the traditional treatment which is discussion of content covered and educational issues that may be raised. This is the control group. The experimental group receives traditional treatment except, between the second and third exams, the discussion section time is spent viewing and discussing videotapes of school situations. The use of the videotapes is the experimental treatment. The design may be diagrammed as:

$$R \ G_1 \quad O_1 - O_2 - X - O_3 - O_4 - O_5 - O_6 - O_7$$
$$R \ G_2 \quad O_8 - O_9 \text{———} O_{10} - O_{11} - O_{12} - O_{13} - O_{14}$$

The Os are given at the same time; for example, O_1 and O_8 are the same test. The different subscripts are used only to indicate that the Os come from different groups. The horizontal intervals between the Os all represent two weeks.

The primary interest in this example would likely be on the difference between O_3 and O_{10}. However, there might be some delayed effects of the experimental treatment which also could be checked. The differences between O_1 and O_8, and O_2 and O_9, those observations taken prior to the experimental treatment, should be no more than that due to random assignment.

Time series designs can be extended to additional groups and they may also involve multiple insertions of the experimental treatment. Of course, they can be extended in time. However, as designs are extended, they become increasingly susceptible to history and maturation as threats to validity. Time series designs also are discussed in the next chapter because they do find applications with intact groups, and single subject designs can be viewed as time series designs applied to an individual.

Interpreting Results of Experiments

If an experiment is designed properly, the researcher should be able to draw some conclusions about the existence and nature of an experimental effect. There are any number of specific analyses that are used to analyze experimental data. (Analysis procedures are discussed in later chapters. The role of statistics, both descriptive and inferential, is one of providing analyses; therefore, statistics are very important to the entire research effort.) However, in interpreting results, we want to consider some patterns of the data (the Os in the designs) and what these patterns indicate about the experimental treatment.

The interpretation of results can be approached in two ways: (1) given a certain result (or pattern of Os), what does it mean? and (2) what comparison would be made to determine whether or not a certain kind of effect exists? Sample designs and interpretations are considered below. The notation in the designs is the same as defined previously. Interpretation of results involves making comparisons between Os. Although Os consist of observations, such as pretest or posttest scores, in the design, they also represent group data summarized by computing a mean or some group measure. The symbol = means that these group measures are close to being equal; $\neq$ means that they are substantially different. (A substantial difference would likely be identified through the use of inferential statistics.[4]) In the examples, the a, b, . . . sets of results are considered independently.

INTERPRETATION EXAMPLE 5.1

A four-group pretest-posttest control group design is used with three different experimental treatments, X_1, X_2, and X_3, and a control treatment. All groups are pretested and posttested. The design is diagrammed as follows:

$$R \; G_1 \qquad O_1—X_1—O_2$$
$$R \; G_2 \qquad O_3—X_2—O_4$$
$$R \; G_3 \qquad O_5—X_3—O_6$$
$$R \; G_4 \qquad O_7———O_8$$

a. *Result:* $O_1 \neq O_2$, $O_3 \neq O_4$, $O_5 \neq O_6$, $O_2 = O_4$, but O_2, $O_4 \neq O_6$ and $O_1 = O_3 = O_5 = O_7 = O_8$.
   Interpretation: There are effects for all experimental treatments. The effects of X_1 and X_2 are the same, but they are different from that of X_3.

b. *Result:* $O_1 = O_3 = O_4 = O_5 = O_6 = O_7 = O_8$, but $O_1 \neq O_2$.
   Interpretation: There are no effects of X_2 and X_3, only an experimental effect for X_1.

c. *Result:* $O_1 = O_3 = O_5 = O_7$ and $O_2 = O_4 = O_6 = O_8$, but O_1, O_3, O_5, $O_7 \neq O_2$, O_4, O_6, O_8.
   Interpretation: There are no experimental treatment effects, but something, probably a maturation effect, is causing a change between pretest and posttest.

d. What comparison would be made to determine whether or not there is a change in subjects independent of the experimental treatment?
   Comparison: O_7 and O_8. If $O_7 = O_8$, there is no change; if $O_7 \neq O_8$, there is a change. (Comparisons could also be made between O_1, O_3, O_5, and O_8, since O_1, O_3, O_5, and O_7 are considered equivalent due to random assignment of subjects.)

It should be noted that there is no way to check on the effect of pretesting in this design, since all groups are pretested. There is no nonpretested comparison group. Also, when there are two or more experimental treatments (in this case, three), it is important to distinguish between them, because they may have differing effects. The sets of results for the example do not exhaust the possible patterns, but they illustrate possible outcomes.

INTERPRETATION EXAMPLE 5.2

A researcher uses a three-group design. There are two different experimental treatments, X_1 and X_2, and a control treatment. Groups are not pretested, but they are posttested twice, once shortly after the experimental treatments are completed and again later to determine whether there is a delayed effect of the treatments. The design is as follows:

$$R\ G_1 \quad X_1 \text{—} O_1 \text{———} O_2$$
$$R\ G_2 \quad X_2 \text{—} O_3 \text{———} O_4$$
$$R\ G_3 \quad \quad \text{—} O_5 \text{———} O_6$$

a. *Result:* $O_1 = O_3$, but O_3 and $O_1 \neq O_5$, and $O_2 = O_4 = O_6$.
   Interpretation: There are immediate experimental effects, and they are the same for X_1 and X_2. There are no long-term experimental effects.
b. *Result:* $O_1 \neq O_3$, and O_1 and $O_3 \neq O_5$, and $O_2 \neq O_4$, and O_2 and $O_4 \neq O_6$, but $O_1 = O_2$, and $O_3 = O_4$, and $O_5 = O_6$.
   Interpretation: There are experimental effects in both the short and the long term, and they are different effects for X_1 and X_2. However, the effects are consistent over time; that is, the short-term and long-term effects are the same.
c. *Result:* $O_1 = O_3 = O_5 = O_6$, but O_2 and $O_4 \neq O_6$, and $O_2 \neq O_4$.
   Interpretation: There are no short-term experimental effects. There are different long-term experimental effects for X_1 and X_2.
d. *Result:* $O_1 = O_3$, but O_1, $O_3 \neq O_5$ and O_1, $O_3 \neq O_4$, but $O_2 = O_4$, and O_1 and $O_4 \neq O_6$.
   Interpretation: There are short-term experimental effects, and they are the same for X_1 and X_2. There are long-term experimental effects, and they are the same for X_1 and X_2, but they are not the same as the short-term effects.
e. What comparison would be made to determine whether there are any long-term effects and whether they are the same for X_1 and X_2?
   Comparison: O_2 and O_4 with O_6. If O_2 and $O_4 \neq O_6$, then long-term experimental effects are indicated; then if $O_2 \neq O_4$, the effects of X_1 and X_2 are *not* the same.
f. What comparison would be made to check whether the passing of time effects the subjects on the dependent variable?
   Comparison: O_5 and O_6. These Os come from the control group, which receives no experimental treatment. If $O_5 \neq O_6$, there is some effect due to the passing of time; if $O_5 = O_6$, time has no effect.
g. Is there any way to check on the initial (preexperiment) equivalence of the three groups? Is this of concern? Why or why not?
   Answer: Since there were no pretests, there are no preexperimental Os to check equivalence, but this is of no concern, because the groups are considered equivalent due to the random assignment (R).

INTERPRETATION EXAMPLE 5.3 _____

This example is somewhat more complex since it involves six groups, three of which are pretested and three of which are posttested immediately after the experiment is completed. (It is a modification of the Solomon four-group design, extended in time.) All six groups are posttested some time after the experiment is completed. Only one experimental treatment (X) and a control treatment are used. The design is as follows:

$$
\begin{array}{ll}
R\ G_1 & O_1 \text{—} X \text{—} O_2 \text{——} O_3 \\
R\ G_2 & O_4 \text{—} X \text{————} O_5 \\
R\ G_3 & \text{——} X \text{—} O_6 \text{——} O_7 \\
R\ G_4 & \text{——} X \text{————} O_8 \\
R\ G_5 & O_9\ \text{—}\ O_{10} \text{——} O_{11} \\
R\ G_6 & \text{——————} O_{12}
\end{array}
$$

a. *Result:* $O_3 \neq O_5$, and O_3 and $O_5 \neq O_{11}$.
   Interpretation: There is an experimental effect in pretested groups in the long term. (This result gives no information about nonpretested groups or about short-term effects.) However, the effect is not the same for a group previously posttested and a group not previously posttested.

b. *Result:* $O_2 = O_6$, and O_2, $O_6 \neq O_{10}$, but $O_3 = O_5 = O_7 = O_8 = O_{11} = O_{12}$.
   Interpretation: There is an experimental effect in the short term, and it is the same for pretested and nonpretested groups. There is no long-term experimental effect.

c. *Result:* $O_2 \neq O_6$, but $O_6 = O_{10}$, and $O_2 = O_3 = O_5$, and $O_6 = O_7 = O_8$, and $O_{11} = O_{12}$.
   Interpretation: There is an interaction effect of experimental treatment and pretesting, and this effect persists in the long term. Note that this is *not* simply a pretesting effect, because $O_2 \neq O_{10}$.

d. What comparison would be made to check whether there is a change in a *nonpretested* control group over the long term?
   Comparison: O_9 and O_{12}. Since the groups are randomly assigned, had G_6 been pretested, it can be assumed that its pretest scores would have been similar to those of other groups. Pretesting occurs prior to the experimental treatment; therefore, O_4 and O_{12} or O_1 and O_{12} could also have been compared. If $O_9 \neq O_{12}$, there has been a change with the passing of time; if $O_9 = O_{12}$, there has been no change.

e. What comparison would be made to determine whether there is a long-term experimental effect in groups that are posttested only once?
   Comparison: O_5, O_8, and O_{12}. If $O_5 = O_8$, but O_5, $O_8 \neq O_{12}$, then there is an experimental effect that is not influenced by pretesting. If O_5, O_8, and O_{12} are all unequal, there appears to be an experimental effect, but there is also an interaction of the experimental effect and pretesting. If $O_5 = O_8 = O_{12}$, there is no long-term experimental effect.

f. What three effects, other than interaction effects, can be checked by this six-way design?

Answer: (1) the experimental treatment effect, in both short term and long term; (2) effects of pretesting; and (3) effects of prior posttesting.

Other comparisons could be made in the foregoing designs, and, of course, there could be other patterns of results. An important characteristic of design and interpretation of results is that there must be a comparison group for a contrast to check on a possible effect. Therefore, in the first example, since all groups were pretested, an effect of pretesting cannot be checked. In the third example, a pretest effect can be checked, but only by comparing groups that have and have not been pretested. We cannot check on a pretest effect by considering only G_1, G_2, and G_5.

The interpretation of experimental results is a common-sense process. The design aids the researcher in structuring the desired comparisons or contrasts so that effects can be checked. In any specific experiment, a knowledge of the variables and possibly of the results of related studies is also helpful in interpreting and understanding the data.

Randomness and Representativeness

In the designs described in this chapter, some aspect of random selection or random assignment of the subjects was included. This characteristic makes for what Campbell and Stanley (1963) call "true" experimental designs. By randomly selecting a sample, the sample represents the population from which it was selected. If a number of subjects are randomly assigned to the experimental treatments (including the control treatment, if there is one), then prior to the experiment, the groups of subjects differ only on the basis of random sampling fluctuation. The experimental groups are equivalent because of the random assignment.

However, if there is a pool of available subjects and they are randomly assigned to experimental treatments, what population do these subjects represent? Suppose that a researcher uses the 120 students enrolled in a beginning education course as the subjects for an experiment. The students are randomly assigned to experimental treatments, but they have not been randomly selected from some larger population. It could not be argued that they randomly selected themselves into the education course, so what population do they represent? This is a question of external validity that can be answered only by the researcher through a knowledge of the subjects and the variables under study. Do the 120 students represent college students who have been enrolled in beginning education courses during the past several years? Do they represent college students in education generally? Or do they represent young adults generally? Probably not the latter, but cases could possibly be made for the others.

The point being made is that the matter of representativeness, and hence generalizability, must often be argued on a logical basis. It would be nice if there was always the option of random selection from the population under study, but this is not the case. In the example here, if the 120 students participated in a learning experiment, the results would likely have considerable generalizability. They might even generalize to other age groups, depending on the conditions of the experiment.

In some experiments in educational research, intact groups are used. The groups have not been randomly selected, nor have the members been randomly assigned to the groups. For example, this situation occurs when intact classes of students are used in an experiment. When such groups are used, we have what Campbell and Stanley (1963) call a "quasi-experimental" design. (Such designs are discussed in the next chapter.) When groups are initially not equivalent in a random sense, this condition not only influences the generalizability, but it may also affect the internal validity of the experiment, since there may have been some initial differences between the groups relative to the variables under study.

In summary, it is preferable to have some condition of randomness in designing an experiment, but this is not always possible. Even if random assignment is used, the subjects may not have been randomly selected from some larger population, and generalizability must be argued on a logical basis. (The difference between random selection and random assignment is discussed in the sampling chapter, Chapter 11.) Of course, the case for external validity of any experimental results must be made in the context of the specific variables and conditions of the experiment.

Summary

This chapter provided some of the more general designs used in experimental research. The distinguishing characteristic of experimental research is the manipulation of variables. The experimental design provides the structure for the experiment in which the variables are deliberately manipulated and controlled by the researcher. It might be mistakenly inferred that complexity of design is a desirable characteristic of a more sophisticated experimenter, but a truly sophisticated experimenter need only come up with an experimental design that will do the job—meet the objectives of the research and be adequate for testing the hypotheses. An experiment must have definitely stated hypotheses, and the design should test these hypotheses, providing for the meaningful interpretation of results, whatever the pattern of the data.

At this point, the reader should have an understanding of the underlying reasoning of experimental design and the logic of the various design structures. Characteristics of a good experimental design were discussed early in the chapter. A well-conceived design will not guarantee valid results, but an inappropriate and inadequate design is certain to lead to uninterpretable results and tenuous conclusions, if any can be drawn. The design must be conceived prior to the experimentation, and it should be carefully planned and applied. No postexperiment manipulations, statistical or otherwise, can take the place of a well-conceived experimental design.

KEY CONCEPTS

Experiment
Experimental design
Experimental variable

Experimental treatment
Subjects
Experimental control

Contamination

Parsimony

Internal validity

External validity

Pretest-posttest control group design

Solomon four-group design

Factorial design

Repeated measures design

Threats to validity

Designs extended in time

Multiple observations

Randomness and representativeness

Posttest-only control group design

EXERCISES

5.1 Define the concepts of internal and external validity of an experiment. Why do we say that for some experiments, an attempt at increasing one type of validity tends to jeopardize the other type?

5.2 Several teachers plan to do an experiment in the school setting concerning the effects of class size on achievement in chemistry. Class size is an independent variable and has four levels of size—10–14, 18–23, 26–31, and 34–38 students. Four high schools are involved in the study, each with eight chemistry classes, two of each class size. Students can be assigned at random to a class within a school, but students cannot be assigned randomly to a school. Two chemistry teachers are used in each school, each teaching four classes. The dependent variable is chemistry achievement, measured after an instructional period of one semester. Develop and describe one or more experimental designs that would apply to this research study. Consider possible uncontrolled variables and variables that might be controlled. Is there a possibility of confounding of variables? State one or more hypotheses that might be tested by this experiment.

5.3 Discuss in detail an example of an experiment for which the posttest-only control group is appropriate. Consider such points as why you would not need pretests and the number of groups you would include. (You may want to extend the design to more than two groups.) Describe how you would enhance control in your proposed experiment. Also, identify the independent variable(s), dependent variable(s), and constants.

5.4 Discuss the possible gains in internal validity when going from a pretest-posttest control group design to a Solomon four-group design.

5.5 A teacher designs an experiment to determine the effects of programmed learning materials as supplementary aids in an advanced algebra course. The dependent variable is the amount of algebra learned during one semester of instruction. There are eighty-three students enrolled in four advanced algebra classes who are taught by this teacher, and these students were assigned randomly to the classes. The students make up the subjects for the experiment. One group of students has access to the programmed materials; the other group does not. Suggest an experimental design that would apply to this situation. Is it necessary for the teacher to use a pretest? How might the internal validity of the experiment be enhanced? Does this experiment have external validity, and if so, to what extent?

5.6 A five-group, posttest-only control group design is used. There are four experimental treatments and a control treatment. Using the notation introduced in the chapter, the design can be diagrammed as follows:

$$
\begin{array}{lll}
R \; G_1 & X_1 & O_1 \\
R \; G_2 & X_2 & O_2 \\
R \; G_3 & X_3 & O_3 \\
R \; G_4 & X_4 & O_4 \\
R \; G_5, & - & O_5
\end{array}
$$

a. Is there any need to be concerned about the preexperiment equivalency of the groups? Why or why not?

b. Is there any way to check on whether or not groups change on the dependent variable from before the experiment to after the experiment, independent of any experimental treatment? Why or why not?

c. What would you conclude from the following results and comparisons? The equals sign means that the observations are about the same; the not-equals sign means that they are substantially different. (*Note:* Consider only the results given. Do not read into the comparison results not specified.) Consider each set of results independently.

(1) No pair of Os are equal.

(2) $O_1 = O_3$ and $O_2 = O_4$, but $O_1, O_3 \neq O_2, O_4$, and $O_1, O_2, O_3, O_4 \neq O_5$.

(3) $O_1 = O_2$ and $O_3 = O_4 = O_5$, but $O_1, O_2 \neq O_3, O_4, O_5$.

(4) $O_1 = O_2 = O_3, = O_5$, but $O_1, O_2, O_3, O_5 \neq O_4$.

5.7 A researcher uses the following experimental design. It involves six groups and is, in essence, a takeoff on the Solomon four-group design. Only one experimental treatment, X, is involved.

$$
\begin{array}{llllll}
R\ G_1 & O_1 & X & O_2 & & \\
R\ G_2 & O_3 & — & O_4 & & \\
R\ G_3 & O_5 & X & — & O_6 & \\
R\ G_4 & O_7 & — & — & O_8 & \\
R\ G_5 & — & X & O_9 & & \\
R\ G_6 & — & — & O_{10} & &
\end{array}
$$

a. What is gained (apparently) by including the middle two groups?

b. What comparisons could be made to determine whether or not there is an effect of pretesting?

c. What would you conclude from the following results and comparisons?

(1) $O_2 = O_9$ and $O_6 = O_8$, but $O_2, O_9 \neq O_6, O_8$.

(2) $O_2 = O_6 = O_9$, $O_4 = O_8 = O_{10}$, but $O_2, O_6, O_9 \neq O_4, O_8, O_{10}$.

(3) $O_1 = O_2 = O_3$, and $O_3 = O_4$.

(4) $O_2 = O_4 = O_9$, $O_6 \neq O_2$, and $O_6 \neq O_8$.

5.8 The following design is used, including three groups, all of which are pretested once and posttested twice. Two experimental treatments, X_1 and X_2, are used.

$$
\begin{array}{lllll}
R\ G_1 & O_1 & X_1 & O_2\!\!-\!\!-\!\!-O_3 \\
R\ G_2 & O_4 & X_2 & O_5\!\!-\!\!-\!\!-O_6 \\
R\ G_3 & O_7 & — & O_8\!\!-\!\!-\!\!-O_9
\end{array}
$$

a. What is gained by including a pretest rather than only posttesting the subjects?

b. Is it possible to check on an effect of pretesting with this design? Why or why not?

c. What comparisons would be made to determine if there is an experimental effect in the long term?

d. Is it necessary to have the pretest to check on the preexperimental equivalence of the groups? Why or why not?

e. Suppose that $O_7 \neq O_8 \neq O_9$, the observations on the control group. What would you conclude from these results?

f. What would you conclude from the following results and comparisons?

(1) $O_2 = O_5$, but O_2 and $O_5 \neq O_8$, and $O_3 = O_6 = O_9$.

(2) $O_1 \neq O_2$, and $O_4 \neq O_5$, and $O_2 \neq O_5$, but $O_7 = O_8$.

(3) $O_2 = O_5 = O_8$, but $O_3 \neq O_2$ and $O_5 \neq O_6$, and O_3 and $O_6 \neq O_9$.

(4) $O_2 \neq O_5$, and O_2 and $O_5 \neq O_8$, $O_2 \neq O_3$, and $O_5 \neq O_6$, and $O_3 \neq O_6$, and O_3 and $O_6 \neq O_9$, but $O_7 = O_8 = O_9$.

5.9 Summarize the general characteristics of a well-designed experiment. Select one or more research articles that involve experimentation from such publications as the *American Educational Research Journal* or the *Journal of Educational Psychology*. Read the article carefully to determine the design used and the experimental procedure. Does the experiment seem to have high internal validity? Is there any indication of its external validity?

NOTES

1. The term *levels* is a holdover from the days when experimental variables were often such variables as drug dosages and fertilizer concentrations; that is, there were quantitative levels of the experimental variables. Now the term applies to qualitative and categorical variables, as well as quantitative variables.

2. The symbolism used here and throughout this chapter is similar to that introduced by D. T. Campbell and J. C. Stanley, "Experimental and Quasi-Experimental Designs for Research on Teaching," in N. L.

Gage (Ed.), *Handbook of Research on Teaching* (Chicago: Rand McNally, 1963), pp. 171–246.

3. The terminology and the diagramming format used here is very similar to that used by Campbell and Stanley in "Experimental and Quasi-Experimental Designs for Research on Teaching."

4. If inferential statistics are used in analyzing data from such designs, as they usually are, a substantial difference would be one that is statistically significant. Statistical concepts are discussed in Chapters 13 and 14.

REFERENCES

Campbell, D. T., and Stanley, J. C. (1963). Experimental and quasi-experimental designs for research on teaching. In N. L. Gage (Ed.), *Handbook of research on teaching* (pp. 171–246). Chicago: Rand McNally.

Cronbach, L. J., and Furby, L. (1970). How we should measure change—or should we? *Psychological Bulletin, 74,* 66–80.

Keppel, G. (1991). *Design and analysis: A researcher's handbook* (3rd ed.). Englewood Cliffs, NJ: Prentice-Hall.

Solomon, R. L. (1949). An extension of control-group design. *Psychological Bulletin, 46,* 137–150.

Zimmerman, D. W., and Williams, R. H. (1982). Gain scores in research can be highly reliable. *Journal of Educational Measurement, 19*(2), 149–154.

Chapter 6

Quasi-Experimental Research

The designs described in Chapter 5 are what Campbell and Stanley (1963) call "true" experimental designs. This is because they have the characteristic of random assignment of subjects to the experimental treatments (groups). Thus, equivalence of the groups is achieved and is within the limits of random fluctuation due to the random assignment. When conducting educational research, it is not always possible to select or assign subjects at random. There are many naturally formed intact groups of subjects in the educational world, such as the students in a classroom. When intact groups of subjects are used in an experiment, we have what is called *quasi-experimental research*. Such research can make valuable contributions, but it is important that the researcher be especially cautious about interpreting and generalizing results.

> *Quasi-experimental research* involves the use of intact groups of subjects in an experiment, rather than assigning subjects at random to experimental treatments.

The Problems of Validity

Lack of random assignment potentially introduces problems with the validity of the experiment—both internal and external validity. In Chapter 5, it was noted that one of the threats to internal validity is differential selection of subjects. Suppose that two intact classes of fifth-grade students were used in an experiment for which the dependent variable was performance in science, operationally defined as the score on a science test. The classes had initially been formed on the basis of ability grouping, one class with high ability and the other with average ability. The classes receive different experimental treatments. If there were an effect favoring the high-ability class, it would be difficult to argue that the effect was due to the experimental treatment. Ability level and experimental treatment are confounded, and there is no way to interpret an effect with confidence.

Any number of factors might be operating in the formation of intact groups, and it cannot be argued that such groups are random samples of some larger populations. Random selection or assignment is a process (described in Chapter 11), and it either has or has not been done. With quasi-experimental research, it has not been done, so there is the possibility that selection bias will jeopardize the generalizability of the results.

What is a researcher who uses intact groups to do? For the purposes of generalizability, representativeness must be argued on a logical basis. For internal validity, the researcher must attempt to establish the degree of equivalence between groups. This requires considering characteristics or variables that may be related to the variables under study. For example, if intact classes were involved in an instructional experiment in mathematics, the grade level probably would be included either as a constant or as another independent (control) variable. The researcher would also want evidence that the classes are of comparable ability level. If empirical data such as IQ test scores are available, they can be helpful in checking equivalence of groups. In fact, such data sometimes can be used for statistical control. Even with empirical data, checking and establishing equivalence always involves some subjective judgment on the basis of information about variables and conditions of the experiment. The lack of randomness must be given specific attention when interpreting the results, and the extent to which it can be countered determines the confidence in the internal validity of the experiment.

> When considering problems of validity of quasi-experimental research, limitations should be clearly identified, the equivalence of the groups should be discussed, and possible representativeness and generalizability should be argued on a logical basis.

Posttest-Only, Nonequivalent Control Group Design

Some of the quasi-experimental designs look very much like the experimental designs discussed in the preceding chapter, except that there is no random assignment of subjects to the groups. When the term *nonequivalent* is used, it means nonequivalent in a random sense. It does not mean that it will be impossible to make a case for the similarity of the groups on relevant variables or characteristics. Indeed, with quasi-experimental designs, the confidence that can be placed in the validity of results depends in large part on the case that can be made for the similarity of the groups.

Using the notation introduced in the preceding chapter, the posttest-only, nonequivalent control group design in its simplest form can be diagrammed as follows:

$$G_1 \quad X—O_1$$
$$G_2 \quad\ \ —O_2$$

The design indicates that one group receives the experimental treatment and another group, serving as a control group, does not receive the experimental treatment. Both groups are posttested at the same time, shortly after the experimental treatment is completed for G_1. The design can be extended to include any number of experimental treatments. For k treatments,

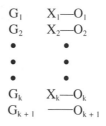

$$G_1 \quad X_1\!\!-\!\!O_1$$
$$G_2 \quad X_2\!\!-\!\!O_2$$
$$\bullet \qquad \bullet$$
$$\bullet \qquad \bullet$$
$$\bullet \qquad \bullet$$
$$G_k \quad X_k\!\!-\!\!O_k$$
$$G_{k+1} \quad \!\!-\!\!O_{k+1}$$

the design requires k + 1 groups. If two or more experimental treatments are used but no control group, the design would be called a posttest-only, nonequivalent multiple-group design.

The *posttest-only, nonequivalent control group design* contains as many groups as there are experimental treatments, plus a control group. Intact groups are used, and subjects are measured only once, after the experimental treatments have been applied.

The validity of any experiment depends on the specific conditions of the experiment, but experiments using the posttest-only, nonequivalent control group design generally are weak in validity. The difficulty arises from the possibility of selection bias and the lack of pretests prior to the experimental treatments. The design should not be used unless some antecedent data are available that provide information about the extent of similarity between the groups. Such data will not eliminate selection bias if it exists, but they provide information that may avoid a misinterpretation of the results.

EXAMPLE 6.1

A junior high school teacher who has four classes of eighth-grade science conducts a study using three different new approaches plus the traditional approach (control) to teaching the laboratory portion of the course. The teacher uses a different approach for reaching each of the four classes. The dependent variable is performance on an examination given at the end of the semester covering the laboratory content. The research problem can be stated as follows:

> A *study of the effects of instructional approach on the performance of eighth-graders on a science laboratory examination.*

The design is diagrammed in Figure 6.1.

No pretests were given, but to check on the similarity of the classes, other information was reviewed and the following data were discovered:

1. The proportions of boys and girls are about the same across the classes.

2. The previous seventh-grade science grades of the students were about the same for Classes 1, 2, and 4, but Class 3 students had somewhat higher grades. The same pattern was true for other areas of previous seventh-grade achievement, such as mathematics.

3. Although, for the most part, the school does not group students by ability, there is an honors program in English; because of scheduling restrictions, many of the students in Class 3 are also in the English honors program.

The time of instruction and the teacher are constants in this study. Two classes, 1 and 4, meet in the morning; the other classes meet in the afternoon.

It appears that Classes 1, 2, and 4 are quite similar on variables that may affect performance on the examination. However, Class 3 seems to be a more able class, which will have to be considered when interpreting the results. There is a partial confounding between experimental treatment and ability level, since any one class receives only one treatment.

Example 6.1 Results and Interpretation.   Suppose that the following pattern of results appears on the posttest: $O_1 = O_2$, but O_1 and O_2 are greater than O_4, and O_3 is greater than O_1 and O_2.

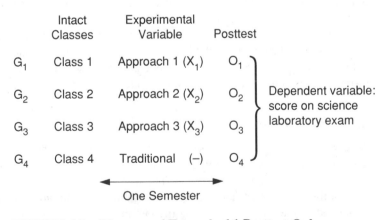

FIGURE 6.1   Diagram of Example 6.1 Posttest-Only, Nonequivalent Control Group Design, with Three Experimental Groups and a Control Group

Interpretation: Approaches 1 and 2 are more effective than the traditional approach, and they appear to be equally effective. These approaches do not seem to be affected by the time of day, since one class meets in the morning and the other in the afternoon. No definite conclusion can be drawn about Approach 3; in fact, it may not be as effective as the traditional approach, and the higher posttest scores of G_3 may be due to the students' abilities.

This example illustrates the fact that there may be alternative explanations with quasi-experimental designs, depending on the pattern of results. It may be that Approach 3 is the most effective approach, explaining the high O_3, or it may be that the high O_3 is due to the higher ability of G_3. Suppose that O_3 had been less than O_1, O_2, and O_4. Then it would be quite conclusive that Approach 3 is not as effective as the others, at least not with higher ability students. The similarity of Classes 1, 2, and 4 allows us to be relatively confident about the conclusions for Approaches 1 and 2 and the traditional approach.

Pretest-Posttest, Nonequivalent Control Group Design

The pretest-posttest, nonequivalent control group design is similar to the posttest-only, nonequivalent control group design, except that the subjects are also pretested. In its general form, if there are k experimental treatments, it can be diagrammed as follows:

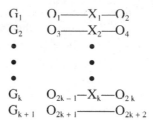

$$
\begin{array}{ll}
G_1 & O_1\text{———}X_1\text{—}O_2 \\
G_2 & O_3\text{———}X_2\text{—}O_4 \\
\bullet & \bullet \\
\bullet & \bullet \\
\bullet & \bullet \\
G_k & O_{2k-1}\text{—}X_k\text{—}O_{2k} \\
G_{k+1} & O_{2k+1}\text{———}O_{2k+2}
\end{array}
$$

Only two groups are required, an experimental group and a control group, for the design in its simplest form. If no control group is included, the design is called a pretest-posttest, nonequivalent multiple group design.

The inclusion of the pretest greatly aids in checking the similarity of the groups, because the pretest scores are on variables that have a strong relationship with the dependent variable. The pretest is administered to all subjects, under consistent conditions, prior to conducting the experiment. Pretest scores also can be used for statistical control, and in some cases gain scores can be generated.

> The *pretest-posttest, nonequivalent control group design* aids in checking the extent of group similarity, and the pretest scores may be used for statistical control or for generating gain scores.

EXAMPLE 6.2

An instructional experiment involves the use of two new reading programs and their possible effects on reading achievement in the fourth grade. The new programs are the experimental treatments, and the traditional program is the control treatment. Thirty fourth-grade classrooms in the elementary schools of a single district are to participate, and there is no random assignment. Ten teachers have agreed to use each of the reading programs, the two new programs and the traditional program. Of course, each teacher uses only one program. The students are pretested on Form A of a reading achievement test; the programs are used for an eighteen-week period; and then the students are posttested on Form B of the test. The design is diagrammed in Figure 6.2

The pretest score is helpful in checking on the similarity of the groups, but it is not the only variable that could be checked. Thirty teachers are involved, and no teacher uses more than one program. Are the groups of ten teachers similar on factors that may affect reading achievement? Although individual teachers may differ, groups of ten teachers may be quite similar when considering all the teachers. One factor to check might be the length of teaching experience of the teachers. If the most experienced teachers were all in one group, a systematic difference between the groups might exist.

If the schools in which the thirty classes are located differ on such factors as socio-economic regions, this would have to be considered. It would not be satisfactory to have one program limited to schools at a certain socioeconomic level, because there would be confounding between the effect of school and the effect of the reading program. A desirable arrangement would be for each of three schools at a socio-economic level to use one of the programs. It might be that some schools would have more than one program, although such an arrangement could lead to some contamination of the data due to interaction of students from different classes.

	Intact Classes	Pretest	Experimental Variable	Posttest (dependent variable)
G_1	Class 1 ⋮ Class 10	O_1	New Program 1 (X_1)	O_2
G_2	Class 11 ⋮ Class 20	O_3	New Program 2 (X_2)	O_4
G_3	Class 21 ⋮ Class 30	O_5	Traditional Program ($-$)	O_6

←———— Eighteen weeks' instruction ————→

FIGURE 6.2 Diagram of Example 6.2 Pretest-Posttest, Nonequivalent Control Group Design, with Two Experimental Groups and a Control Group

In Figure 6.2, although there are thirty classes, there are only three pretest Os and three posttest Os. When analyzing results, we initially check the group results, but in an extensive study such as this example, it is usually helpful—and even necessary—to break down or sort out results by making more detailed comparisons, such as the following:

1. Suppose that the pretest scores of classes in a program (group) are similar. Compare the ten posttest scores of the classes within a program. Are these scores close together or are they highly variable? If they are close together, the program appears to be having a consistent effect; if they are highly variable, the inherent variation is overriding any program effect, or the program effect is not consistent across classes within the program.

2. If classes vary on pretest scores, group the classes within a program into two or three categories (high, middle, low) on pretest score. Then check the posttest scores of these categories to determine whether the gains are consistent or different across categories within a program and across programs within a category. For example, suppose that for the classes scoring high on the pretest, the gains for New Program 1 are greater than those for New Program 2 and the traditional program. This is a comparison across programs within a category and it appears that New Program 1 is the most effective for those students who were initially the most able readers.

3. If the pretest scores of classes are similar, compare the posttest scores of the classes within a program. If they are about the same, external factors such as the teacher or school are having consistent effects; if they are different these external factors are having differing effects.

Example 6.2 Results and Interpretation. Suppose that the following pattern of results appears: $O_1 = O_3 = O_5$, but $O_2 \neq O_4$, and $O_2, O_4 \neq O_6$, but O_4 is greater than O_2 and O_2 is greater than O_6.

Interpretation: Based on pretest results, the groups appear to be quite similar initially. There are program effects: Both new programs are more effective than the traditional program, and New Program 2 is the most effective.

In many experiments involving nonequivalent groups, the design is extended to include control variables as independent variables. (If socioeconomic level could be included in this way, it would be an example of a control variable.) In essence, this extends the design to a factorial design. If some aspect of randomness could be included, the validity of the design would be enhanced. In the example, it would be helpful if the thirty classes could be randomly assigned to the programs. This still would not make for random assignment to the classes, but it would make the ten groups of teachers equivalent on a random basis. Such assignment would tend to equalize the differences among teachers over the experimental and control treatments. When using a quasi-experimental design, we attempt to build as much control as possible into the design. Then available information is used to check the equivalence of the groups. The results must be interpreted and generalized in the context of this information and the conditions of the experiment.

Time Series Designs

Time series designs were introduced in Chapter 5 as experimental designs if the groups can be formed through random assignment and there is a basis for comparison, such as a control group. However, quite commonly, time series designs are used with one or more intact groups, and with this condition they become quasi-experimental designs. The designs involve repeated measurement and an experimental treatment is inserted between two of the measurements for at least one of the groups. Time series designs are useful for situations in which there is periodic, naturally occurring measurement of the dependent variable over time, such as repeated testing in a class. Measurement should be consistent across the observations; with some dependent variables, it may be difficult to attain consistency.

Time series designs as quasi-experimental designs involve repeated measurement of one or more intact groups, with an experimental treatment inserted between two of the measurements of at least one group.

Single-Group Time Series Design

A single-group time series design can be diagrammed simply as follows:

$$G \qquad O_1—O_2—O_3—X—O_4—O_5$$

As indicated, there is no random assignment of subjects to the group. There can be any feasible number of observations or measurements, and the insertion of X should be done randomly. Observations may coincide with some routine measurement that takes place, such as a test every four weeks in a class.

One characteristic of time series designs is that there are numerous possible patterns of results. This introduces a problem with internal validity, especially with only one group in that there may be alternative explanations for the results other than the effect of the experimental treatment. Figure 6.3 shows three possible patterns of results. The Os on the horizontal axis represent the measurement occasions, and the vertical axis is the scale of the dependent variable.

For any particular experiment and dependent variable, there would be only one pattern. The interpretation of pattern A would be that the experimental treatment appears to have had an effect. There was a slight increase in the scores prior to the experimental treatment, but after the experimental treatment, the rate of increase was greater, especially between O_3 and O_4 and O_5. The smaller rate of increase between O_5 and O_6 may have been due to a diminishing experimental treatment effect with the passing of time.

On the surface, pattern B appears to include no experimental treatment effect. However, the marked increase between the final two measurements might be the result of a

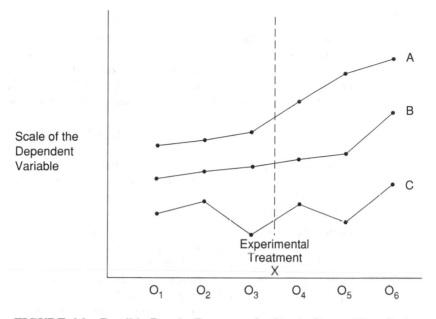

**FIGURE 6.3   Possible Results Patterns of a Single-Group Time Series
Design**

delayed effect. If no apparent external event could have produced this effect, an experimental effect is certainly plausible. For this reason, it is important to anticipate the time interval between the introduction of the experimental treatment and the appearance of its effect. For certain variables, the effect in pattern B is about as definite as it is in pattern A. It should be noted that as the time interval increases, the likelihood of an intervening extraneous event also increases.

The erratic pattern C almost excludes the possibility of drawing a conclusion about an experimental treatment effect. Since there is no control group, it is most difficult to infer the pattern without the experimental treatment. The fluctuation between observations may indicate that other factors are operating that override any experimental treatment effect. It is possible that the experiment would require an increase in control before there could be sensitivity to an experimental treatment effect. The conclusion of no experimental treatment effect cannot be drawn from pattern C, however.

The numerous observations of the time designs are useful, not only for locating a possible effect but also for avoiding inference of an effect when there likely is none. Consider pattern C. If O_3 and O_4 were the only measures taken, the researcher would conclude that there is an experimental effect, when the difference in the measurements may well be due to something else. In pattern B, the possible delayed effect would have been missed if only measures O_3 and O_4 (and even O_5) had been taken, so it is important to consider the entire pattern.

EXAMPLE 6.3

A physical therapist is working with a group of twelve patients in an eight-week rehabilitation program. Members of the group receive therapy every day, and the group is tested at the end of each week on a physical performance test. A traditional type of therapy is used, except for the seventh week (determined on a random basis), during which an experimental therapy is administered. The design can be diagrammed as follows:

$$G \quad O_1—O_2—O_3—O_4—O_5—O_6—X—O_7—O_8$$

Suppose that the results of this experiment produce the pattern shown in Figure 6.4. How would these results be interpreted? There is strong evidence that the experimental therapy is more effective than the traditional therapy. The pattern of improvement is quite consistent for the first six weeks, but it shows a large increase during the seventh week. Improvement returns to the earlier level during the eighth week. Thus, unless there is some other reason why there would be increased performance during the seventh week, there is a good case for an experimental effect.

In this example, maintaining consistency of measurement poses no problem, because the same physical performance test is used throughout. Consider another situation. An elementary school teacher uses a time series design to check the effects of individual versus group practice on performance in spelling. The class is used as the group. Each week the class is designated a certain amount of time for spelling practice (in addition to

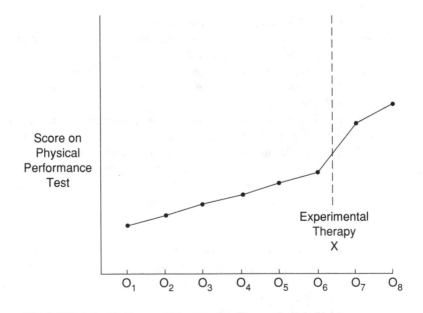

**FIGURE 6.4   Pattern of Results for Example 6.3, Using a
Single-Group Time Series Design**

the instruction), and a test is given every Friday. The usual format for practice is on an individual basis, but during one week over a six-week period, group practice is used as an experimental treatment.

One problem with this example is keeping the difficulty level of the spelling tests consistent. If the test after the group practice is easier than others and the class tends to perform better, the easier test is an alternative explanation for the results. Of course, the amount of practice time should be constant regardless of the practice format.

Multiple-Group Time Series Design

The single-group time series design can be extended to include two or more groups. A common practice is to include a control group in the design, in which case an example design could be diagrammed as follows:

$$G_1 \quad O_1—O_2—X—O_3—O_4—O_5—O_6—O_7$$
$$G_2 \quad O_8—O_9————O_{10}—O_{11}—O_{12}—O_{13}—O_{14}$$

Again, any number of observations can be taken, and the experimental treatment is inserted randomly for one group. The groups are measured at the same times.

> The *multiple-group time series design* includes two or more intact groups, one of which may be a control group, and an experimental treatment is inserted for at least one of the groups.

The inclusion of two or more groups strengthens the design because it provides for comparison, thus enhancing internal validity. For example, it provides a check for the possibility of an external event coinciding with the experimental treatment. Suppose that both groups in a control group design demonstrated an unusually large increase for the observations immediately following the administration of the experimental treatment to the experimental group. Since the increase occurred in both groups, it cannot be an experimental effect (since the control group had no experimental treatment), so it is likely due to some external factor that is affecting both groups.

The observations that occur prior to the experimental treatment can be used to check on the similarity of the groups. As with any multiple-group quasi-experimental design, the greater the similarity between the groups, the more confidence can be placed in the conclusions drawn from the results.

EXAMPLE 6.4

A teacher who has three classes of first-year algebra decides to do a study for which the research problem can be stated as follows:

A study of the effects of different types of feedback on performance in algebra.

During the semester, the teacher gives five equally spaced one-hour exams. The exams are of about the same difficulty overall, because the teacher carefully constructs the exams using items of about equal difficulty levels, even though the tests cover different content as the instruction progresses. Between the second and third tests, the teacher provides positive feedback (X_1) to one class, negative feedback (X_2) to another class, and no feedback (control treatment) to the third class. The experiment is diagrammed in Figure 6.5.

This design enables the teacher to make comparisons, not only between experimental groups but also with a control group. Note that the experimental treatments are applied only between two observations. At this point, we can consider possible patterns of results and interpretations that might be made. Because of the numerous Os, interpreting results requires sorting through them. The following patterns are to be considered independently.

Example 6.4 Results Pattern 1. $O_1 = O_2 = O_5$, and $O_3 = O_4$, but O_3, O_4 are greater than O_1, O_2, O_5, and $O_6 = O_7 = O_9 = O_{10}$, but O_8 is less than O_7, and $O_{11} = O_{12} = O_{13} = O_{14} = O_{15}$, and $O_1 = O_6 = O_{11}$.

Interpretation: Positive feedback (X_1) increases performance, and its effect persists through O_4; negative feedback (X_2) decreases performance, but it has only an immediate effect. Since performance in G_3 is highly consistent, it is unlikely that any external factors are causing changes in performance. Because the initial test scores of the classes were equal, the groups appear to be similar (on algebra test performance) prior to administration of the experimental treatments, even though there was no random assignment to the groups.

Example 6.4 Results Pattern 2. $O_1 = O_2$, and $O_3 = O_4 = O_5$, but O_3, O_4, O_5 are greater than O_1, O_2; $O_6 = O_7 = O_8$, and $O_9 = O_{10}$ are greater than O_6, O_7, O_8; $O_{11} = O_{12} = O_{13}$, and $O_{14} = O_{15}$, but O_{14}, O_{15} are greater than O_{11}, O_{12}, O_{13}; $O_1 = O_6 = O_{11}$, and $O_4 = O_9 = O_{14}$.

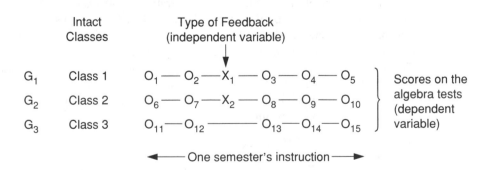

FIGURE 6.5   Diagram of Example 6.4 Multiple-Group Time Series Design, with Two Experimental Groups and a Control Group

Interpretation: Negative feedback (X_2) has no effect, in that the patterns for G_2 and G_3 are the same. Positive feedback (X_1) increases performance; at least it appears to have an immediate effect. It is difficult to infer anything about long-range effects of X_1, in that all classes increased performance at the fourth testing. That consistent increase across classes is most likely due to an external factor. Whatever caused the increase had a persistent effect through the fifth testing. Since initial test scores of the classes were equal, the classes appear to be similar at the beginning of the experiment.

Of course, with numerous observations, such as in the example, a large number of different results patterns are possible. If patterns are erratic, it becomes difficult to draw conclusions; for example, if the Os in classes keep fluctuating. Also, if test scores for classes prior to inserting the experimental treatments are different, there very likely is a selection bias.

Variations in Time Series Designs

The foregoing discussion focused on single-group and multiple group time series designs—the basic configurations for time series designs. There are variations, however, that can be incorporated into these designs. The number of observations in the series depends on the variables under study, but there should be sufficient observations so that the pattern can become established. One variation is to increase the number of observations in the series, possibly even as high as fifteen or twenty, for long-term experiments or for experiments in which observations can be sequenced closely. Extending the number of observations does increase the likelihood of external factors having an effect if time is extended.

Another variation is to insert the experimental treatment more than once in the series. This variation is more feasible if the series is lengthened. Multiple insertions provide a check on the consistency of an experimental effect if there is one. There are two ways to accomplish multiple insertion of the experimental treatment: (1) include it two or more times on a random basis, or (2) once it is inserted, persist with it for the remainder of the experiment. These two ways can be diagrammed as follows:

1. Multiple, random insertion of X:

$$G \qquad O_1—O_2—X—\ O_3—O_4—O_5—X—\ O_6—O_7—O_8$$

2. Persistent insertion of X:

$$G \qquad O_1—O_2—O_3—X—O_4—X—O_5—\ X—O_6—X—O_7—X—O_8$$

Either one of these approaches could have been used for the experimental treatments in the algebra classes example. The reinforcements, X_1 and X_2, could have been randomly inserted more than once in the series; or after their initial insertion, they could have been continued for the remainder of the semester.

Variations of multiple insertions can be included in time series designs.

Single-Subject Designs

Most experimentation in educational research involves groups of subjects; that is, we intend to generate results that apply to groups rather than to individuals. However, there are experimental situations in which it is desirable or necessary to use individual subjects—essentially, a sample size of one. In these single-subject situations, the basic experimental approach is to study the individual under both nonexperimental and experimental conditions.

Single-subject research can be useful for teachers who conduct research (probably action research) with individual students. Counselors who work with students on an individual basis may also have applications for single-subject designs. Researchers in such areas as rehabilitation and physical therapy encounter situations in which individual research is desirable. Generally, a subject is included in a study because of some condition or problem, and there is no random selection or assignment. Therefore, single-subject designs are usually considered quasi-experimental designs.

Single-subject designs commonly involve repeated measurement, sometimes several measurements of the dependent variable. Measurement is highly standardized and controlled, so that variations in measurement are not interpreted as an experimental effect. The conditions under which the study is conducted are described in detail, not only to enhance the interpretation of results but also to allow decisions about their generalizability.

Single-subject designs are characterized by what is sometimes called the *single-variable rule*. This means that only one variable, the treatment, is changed during the period in which the experimental treatment is applied. During the traditional or baseline treatment and the experimental treatment, all other conditions—such as length of time and number of measurements—are kept the same. This is necessary for interpreting the results so that some other effect is not misinterpreted as an experimental treatment effect.

The period during which the traditional treatment or normal condition is in effect is called the *baseline*. This period should be long enough that the dependent variable attains stability. If a dependent variable is fluctuating and the experimental treatment is applied, it is impossible to determine whether variation in the dependent variable is due to the experimental treatment.

Single-subject designs commonly involve repeated measurements, and they use the *single-variable rule*—changing only one variable at a time.

As with any quasi-experimental design, validity is a major concern in single-subject designs. Internal validity must be established to interpret the results. Alternative explanations of the results (other than an experimental effect) must be considered and, it is hoped, discounted. To deal with alternative explanations, it is necessary to maintain as much control as possible and to understand the nature of other variables that may be operating in the study. External validity depends on the similarities between the research study and other situations, and it must be argued on a logical basis.

A-B Design

Single-subjects designs are designated with a somewhat unique notation. The letters A and B are used to represent conditions; A indicates the baseline condition and B indicates the experimental treatment condition. Since individual subjects are used, there is no group notation.

The A-B design is the simplest of the single-subject designs. In general, it can be diagrammed as follows:

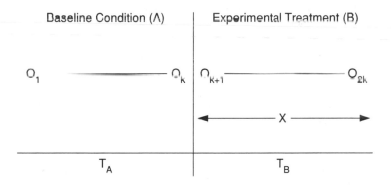

In this design, a single subject is observed under the baseline condition until the dependent variable stabilizes. Then the experimental treatment is introduced and the subject is again observed the same number of times. The T_A and T_B at the bottom of the design represent periods of time, and $T_A = T_B$.

The interpretation of results for the A-B design is based on the assumption that the observations would not have changed from those of the baseline condition if the experimental treatment had not been introduced. The design is susceptible to other variables, possibly those associated with history and maturation, causing an effect that may be a threat to internal validity. In a sense, the A-B design is the weakest of the single-subject designs with respect to internal validity, since the change between conditions is made only once.

EXAMPLE 6.5

A beginning teacher is having difficulty with classroom management, and an experienced teacher is helping the beginning teacher deal with this problem. The experienced teacher observes the beginning teacher twice per week over a period of four weeks, using a teacher performance observation inventory such as the Classroom Observations Keyed for Effectiveness Research (COKER). This period is the base-line period *(A)*, and the data from the eight observations comprise the baseline data. The classroom performance of the teacher is well stabilized during this four-week period.

The experimental treatment *(B)* consists of half-hour consultations between the two teachers, in which the experienced teacher discusses the classroom performance of the beginning teacher and attempts to shift it to behaviors that will improve classroom management. There are nine of these consultations, one before the first observation in condition *B* and then one immediately following each observation. Like condition *A,* condition *B* is in effect for four weeks, and the eight observations of condition *B* are taken under corresponding conditions (same classes, same length of time, same time of day, etc.) as those of condition *A,* the only difference being the experimental treatment. The design for this study is diagrammed in Figure 6.6. The data consist of the observation data using the COKER inventory.

Example 6.5 Results Pattern 1.   Observations O_1 through O_8 are stable and show few teacher behaviors that are believed to enhance classroom management. Then, beginning with O_9 through O_{14}, the observations show increasing behavior that would improve classroom management, and O_{14} through O_{16} are stable. The results are plotted in Figure 6.6.

Interpretation: With such a results pattern, there is quite conclusive evidence that the experimental treatment is having the desired effect. There has been an improvement in

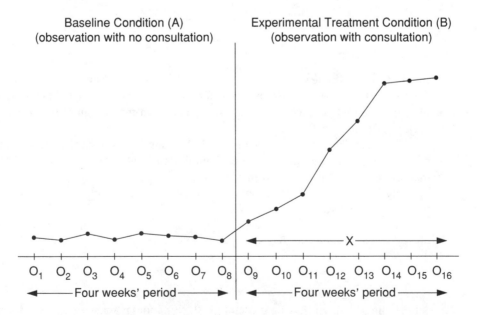

FIGURE 6.6   Diagram of Example 6.5 *A–B,* Single-Subject Design, with Results Pattern 1

classroom management to a stability point. However, it is possible that the results are due to a natural maturation of the beginning teacher, although this is quite unlikely as an alternative explanation due to the relatively short time periods.

Example 6.5 Results Pattern 2.   There is considerable fluctuation among O_1 through O_5, but O_5 through O_8 are quite stable. O_9 through O_{16} had the same pattern of fluctuation as O_1 through O_5, except that the observations were slightly higher in behaviors that enhance classroom management.

Interpretation: It is practically impossible to make a conclusive interpretation of these results. The beginning teacher's performance is quite unstable, and although the experimental treatment does seem to improve performance slightly, it does not enhance stability of performance during the four-week period. Apparently, there are other variables, such as conditions in the classroom or the feelings of the teacher, that have overriding effects.

What about generalizability of results from this study? If Results Pattern 1 had appeared—the results for which we concluded an experimental effect—they would be generalizable to other beginning teachers who have characteristics similar to those of the teacher in this study and who teach under similar conditions. Generalizability would have to be established through detailed description, which makes the case for such similarities. Since the teachers were attempting to solve an immediate local problem, there may not be much concern with generalizability.

A-B-A Design

The *A-B-A* design extends the *A-B* design so that another period of the baseline condition is included following the period of experimental treatment. The design also may be called a *reversal* or *withdrawal* design,[1] since the experimental treatment is withdrawn. Except for the change from baseline to experimental treatment and back to baseline condition, other characteristics—such as duration and number of observations—are kept the same. The added period of baseline condition tends to enhance internal validity over the *A-B* design, since the pattern of results is extended. The general design can be diagrammed as follows:

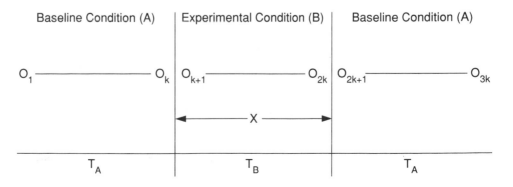

Note that in this design, there are the same number of observations for each duration of condition or treatment. Time would be constant, such that $T_A = T_B$.

EXAMPLE 6.6

A teacher has one student whose classroom behavior is highly negative—characterized by persistent, disruptive interruptions. The teacher keeps a weekly record of disruptive situations caused by this student. The behavior stabilizes over a three-week period, designated the baseline condition. Then for three weeks the teacher requires two individual counseling sessions per week with the student. These sessions, which are considered the experimental treatment, are conducted for one-half hour each on Monday and Thursday. After three weeks, the counseling sessions are discontinued and the teacher continues to collect data on the dependent variable (number of disruptive situations during the week) for another three weeks. Discontinuing the counseling sessions is reverting back to the baseline conditions. No other apparent changes occur between the three-week periods; the class, subjects taught, and so on, remain the same. The study is diagrammed in Figure 6.7.

Example 6.6 Results Pattern 1. (Consistent with the symbolism introduced in Chapter 5, = means about the same.) $O_1 = O_2 = O_3 = O_7 = O_8 = O_9$, and $O_4 = O_5 = O_6$, but $O_1, O_2, O_3, O_7, O_8, O_9$ are greater than O_4, O_5, O_6. (Note that the dependent variable is the number of disruptive situations caused by the student in class, so a low score is preferred.)

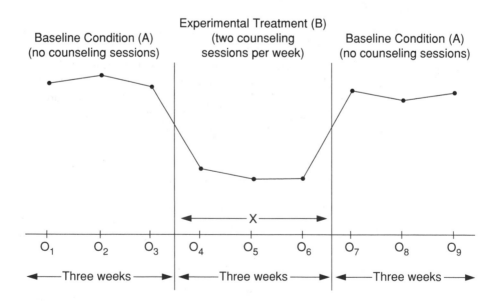

FIGURE 6.7   Diagram of Example 6.6 *A–B–A*, Single-Subject Design, with Results Pattern 1

Interpretation: The counseling sessions have the desired effect, but it is only an immediate effect. When the sessions are discontinued, the student reverts to the old behavior. It is not likely that an extraneous variable would have an effect that coincided exactly with the experimental treatment.

Example 6.6 Results Pattern 2. $O_1 = O_2 = O_3$, and $O_4 = O_5 = O_6$, and $O_7 = O_8 = O_9$, but O_7, O_8, O_9 are less than O_4, O_5, O_6, which are less than O_1, O_2, O_3.

Interpretation: This pattern of results gives rise to alternative explanations; therefore, we cannot be conclusive about an experimental effect. There may be an experimental treatment effect; if there is, it is immediate, but it also has an accelerating long-range effect, which may be difficult to understand. There is a possibility that some other variable associated with maturation is operating. This explanation would be more likely if there was a constant decrease in O_4 through O_9, rather than the single decrease between O_6 and O_7.

There are any number of possible patterns of results. If O_4 through O_9 fluctuated considerably, it would be impossible to conclude anything about an experimental effect. The experimental treatment may be interacting with an extraneous variable, or the behavior may have become unstable and this may or may not have been caused by the experimental treatment.

A-B-A-B Design

If we extend the *A-B-A* design to include one more experimental treatment period, it becomes the *A-B-A-B* design. Because of the extended observation, and because the baseline condition and the experimental treatment go through two cycles, so to speak, internal validity tends to be increased over the *A-B* and *A-B-A* designs. If the patterns of results are consistent for the two cycles, conclusions about an experimental effect can be made with considerable confidence.

The general *A-B-A-B* design can be diagrammed as follows:

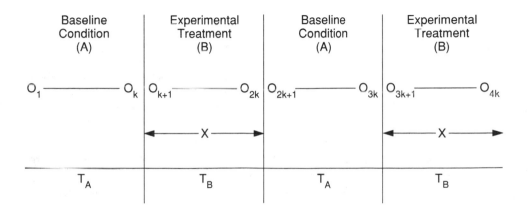

As with the preceding designs, characteristics are similar for the baseline condition and the experimental treatment, except for the introduction of the experimental treatment. The numbers of observations are the same, and $T_A = T_B$ in time, so that the single-variable rule is observed.

EXAMPLE 6.7

We will extend the example of the *A-B-A* design to the *A-B-A-B* design. The teacher decides to conduct counseling sessions with the disruptive student for a second three-week period after the second baseline condition period is completed. The research design is diagrammed in Figure 6.8. Note that the design is simply an extension of the design in Figure 6.7. The major difference is that the research study is extended from nine to twelve weeks, and an additional set of three observations is obtained for the experimental treatment.

Example 6.7 Results Pattern 1. $O_1 = O_2 = O_3$, and $O_4 = O_5 = O_6$, and $O_7 = O_8 = O_9$, and $O_{10} = O_{11} = O_{12}$; O_1, O_2, O_3 are greater than any other Os; O_{10}, O_{11}, O_{12} are less than any other Os; O_4, O_5, O_6 are less than O_7, O_8, O_9 but greater than O_{10}, O_{11}, O_{12}.

Interpretation: Since there are now twelve Os, it may be helpful to plot the dependent variable scores, as shown in Figure 6.9. In the figure, the scale of the dependent variable is the vertical axis, and the time periods are on the horizontal axis. The plot provides a pictorial representation of the data. We can conclude that the experimental treatment is having a positive effect. When the experimental treatment is discontinued, the student reverts partially to the old behavior, but when the experimental treatment is initiated again, the positive effect is present. Behavior is stable within the conditions for the three-week periods. It is unlikely that an effect of an extraneous variable would consistently coincide with the experimental treatment.

Example 6.7 Results Pattern 2. $O_1 = O_2 = O_3 = O_7 = O_8 = O_9$, and $O_4, O_5,$ and O_6 are unequal to each other and not equal to O_1, and $O_{10}, O_{11},$ and O_{12} are unequal to each other and not equal to O_1 or $O_4, O_5,$ and O_6.

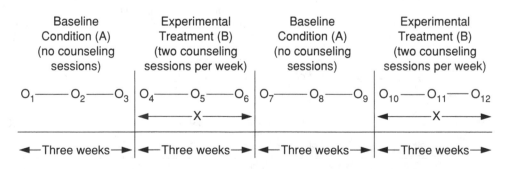

FIGURE 6.8   Diagram for Example 6.7 *A–B–A–B,* Single-Subject Design

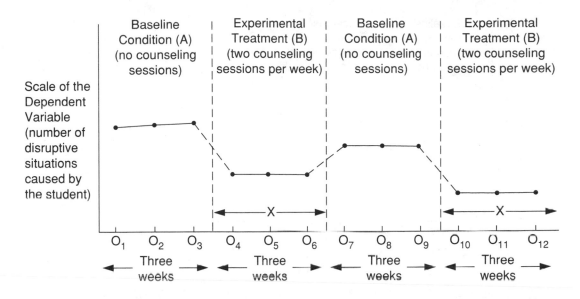

FGIRUE 6.9   Plot of Example 6.7 Results Pattern 1 for the *A–B–A–B*, Single-Subject Design

Interpretation: Again we will plot the dependent variable scores for this pattern of results (Figure 6.10). The erratic pattern of the dependent variable during the experimental treatment periods almost precludes drawing any conclusions about either a positive or a negative effect of the counseling sessions. The patterns for the two experimental treatment periods differ, so if there is an effect of the counseling sessions, it is not consistent. About the only conclusion we can make is that the counseling sessions cause the student behavior to vary or become unstable. This could be due to an interaction of the experimental treatment with some extraneous variable. We can also note that the counseling sessions have no long-range effects, since the results for the two baseline periods are the same with stable behavior.

How generalizable are these results? The teacher could generalize to other students of similar age and disposition who demonstrate the same type of disruptive behavior. Generalizations to other teachers, students, and behavioral problems would have to be argued on a logical basis. To do so would require a knowledge of counseling in such situations and the possible effects that might be expected. Since this is an example of action research, the teacher is probably not very concerned about generalization. If Results Pattern 1 had appeared, the teacher would have solved the problem. Other teachers might be interested in the results, and could make inferences to their own situations on a logical basis.

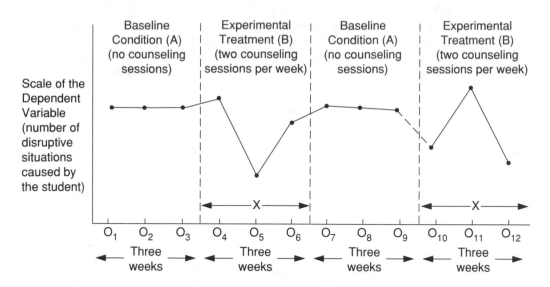

FGIRUE 6.10　Plot of Example 6.7 Results Pattern 2 for the *A–B–A–B,* Single-Subject Design

Multiple-Baseline Designs

There is a family of designs called *multiple-baseline designs*, which can be considered modifications of the single-subject designs. These designs use the *A-B* logic, but rather than being limited to one subject, one behavior, and one situation, they involve two or more behaviors, situations, or subjects, or some combinations of these. The multiple baselines are included because they come from the different behaviors, situations, or subjects. Generally, once an experimental treatment is introduced for a subject, it is continued, so these designs apply to studies in which it is undesirable to remove a treatment after it is started.

Multiple-Baseline Design Across Behaviors.　In this design, a single subject is observed on two or more behaviors in the same situation. After the baselines for the behaviors are stable, the experimental treatment is applied to one of the behaviors for a specified time; then it is applied to the second behavior for the same amount of time, and so on. If there is a consistent change in the behaviors after the experimental treatment is applied, a strong case can be made for an experimental effect.

An important consideration in this design is the independence of the behaviors. If the two or more behaviors are related in their occurrence, when the treatment is applied to the first behavior, it may cause change in the remaining behaviors. Thus, this design is best used for situations in which the behaviors are quite discrete and independent.

Multiple-Baseline Design Across Subjects.　This design uses two or more subjects, although they participate in the experiment as individuals. The multiple baselines come from the subjects. After the baseline behavior is stable, the experimental treatment is administered to one subject; then, after a specified period, the second subject begins receiving the experimental treatment, and so on. It is important that the subjects involved are independent in terms of the experimental treatment. That is, applying the treatment to one subject should not affect the others. If a teacher uses this design, it would probably be difficult to maintain independence between subjects unless they were students from different classes.

Multiple-Baseline Design Across Situations.   The baselines for this design come from different situations involving the same behavior and the same subject. The baseline behavior is established and then the experimental treatment is applied in one situation. After a specified period, the treatment is applied in the second situation, and so forth. This design is essentially the same as the multiple-baseline across behaviors, except that situations replace behaviors in being varied. As in the single-subject designs discussed earlier, the multiple-baseline designs have constant periods of time and numbers of observations during the administration of an experimental treatment, at least for any initial administrations of the treatment.

EXAMPLE 6.8 _____

The example presented here is of a multiple-baseline across situations design. A teacher is planning to use individualized instruction (the experimental treatment) in reading, mathematics, and social studies with a student who is having difficulties in these areas. The individualized instruction will be applied first in reading for a two-week period, then in mathematics, then in social studies. Once individualized instruction is begun in an area, it is continued for the duration of the study. There are three dependent variables in this study: the student's performances in reading, mathematics, and social studies. Four observations on each variable are taken during each two-week period. Operationally, the dependent variables are the percentages of instructional objectives attained of those specified by the teacher.

The design is diagrammed in Figure 6.11. Note that there is an initial baseline period of two weeks for all three areas. Then the baseline periods for mathematics and social studies continue for another two and four weeks, respectively, while the individualized instruction is phased in. The entire study requires eight weeks.

Example 6.8 Results Pattern.   Since there are three dependent variables and each is measured sixteen times, forty-eight scores are obtained on the subject. There are many possible patterns of results, with a pattern for each dependent variable, since each dependent variable has its own set of sixteen scores. Rather than listing forty-eight scores, a possible pattern of results is given in Figure 6.12.

Interpretation: The experimental treatment (individualized instruction) appears to be having an effect, but the effect is not consistent across situations (subject areas). In reading, there is a positive effect, which shows a gradual increase. In mathematics, the pattern becomes erratic after the experimental treatment is introduced. The increases at

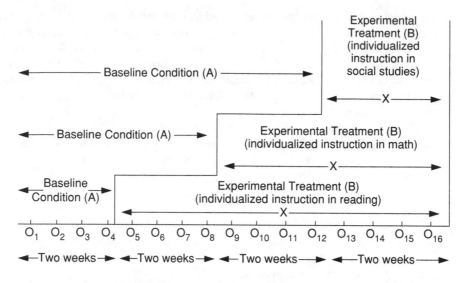

FIGURE 6.11   Diagram of Example 6.8 Multiple-Baseline Across Situations Design

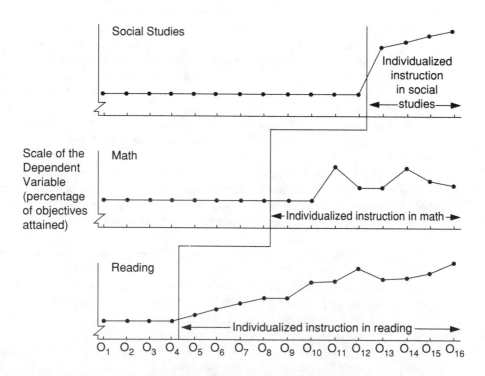

FIGURE 6.12   Plot of Results Pattern for Example 6.8 Multiple-Baseline Across Situations Design

O_{11} and O_{14} may have been due to an external variable; perhaps the objectives at these points were simply easier for the subject to attain. It is impossible to conclude that those increases are due to the experimental treatment. In social studies, the experimental treatment appears to have an immediate and sustained positive effect. In summary, we can conclude that individualized instruction does have an effect on performance in reading and social studies; the effect is positive for both areas, but more gradual for reading. If there is an effect in mathematics, individualized instruction causes performance to fluctuate and possibly increase slightly.

Multiple-baseline designs can become complicated very quickly, and interpretation may require considerable sorting of results. Depending on the variables studied, the designs can be modified to include reversal of conditions (withdrawal of the experimental treatment), but this complicates the designs even more. For such designs, *A-B-A* or *A-B-A-B* formats would be used. However, because of the complexity, such designs are generally used only if a simpler design cannot be developed for a specific study. Assuming that adequate internal validity can be attained, multiple-baseline designs do tend to have broader external validity than single-baseline designs. This is because of the multiple behaviors, subjects, or situations included in the designs.

Action Research and Quasi-Experimental Research

Action research was defined in Chapter 1, not as a separate methodology, but as research conducted by an education professional at the local level. Action research can utilize any methodology, qualitative or quantitative, but when experimentation is involved in action research, it most likely will be quasi-experimental in nature. Teachers, counselors, and administrators seldom have the option of random selection of subjects or assigning subjects randomly to treatments. Very often students are the subjects of action research, and they have been placed in classes or they are candidates for research studies because of certain characteristics that they did not acquire at random. For example, a student who receives an experimental counseling service does so because of a counseling need. If a teacher implements a new instructional procedure with a history class in order to determine the procedure's effects, the members of the class receive the procedure because they are in the class. They "self-selected" themselves into the class for whatever reasons, not because of random assignment.

Because action research often involves intact groups and individuals, and if experimental treatments are involved, such research is quasi-experimental, a good bit of action research is quasi-experimental research. Especially with regard to single-subject research, several extensions and modifications of designs are possible and were described in this chapter. Single-subject research can be especially useful for elementary and secondary school counselors as they work with individuals. Teachers can implement single-subject designs as they work with individual students on remedial instruction or enrichment instruction, for example. When one or more teachers implement experimental procedures with one or more classes, the most likely design will be some type of posttest-only or pretest-posttest, quasi-experimental design.

When experimentation is involved in action research, the design used will most likely be some type of quasi-experimental design.

Summary

This chapter discussed quasi-experimental research, which uses designs in which subjects are not randomly assigned or selected. The lack of randomization poses potential problems for establishing the validity of the research. When intact or naturally formed groups are used, there is a possibility of selection bias being introduced, and the similarity (or lack thereof) of the groups must be considered. In single-subject designs, the subject is usually selected because of some problem or condition associated with that subject. Rarely are the subjects used in single-subject designs selected at random.

Although the use of intact groups or specified subjects may pose threats to validity, they can be used effectively if adequate attention is given to the design of the research. In educational research, it is often impossible to apply random assignment when forming groups. Yet intact groups can provide valuable results, provided such results are interpretable.

When two or more intact groups are used, the credibility of the research depends on the extent to which the groups are similar on relevant variables. Relative to randomness, the groups are nonequivalent, but an argument may be made for their similarity. Therefore, it is important to have antecedent information about the groups, preferably through some kind of pretesting. Generalizability is argued on a logical basis.

Single-subject designs apply when the research centers on individuals rather than on groups—for example, when teachers or counselors are working with individual students. These designs involve multiple observations or measurements, taken across the baseline condition and the experimental treatment condition. Single-subject designs are characterized by extensive control over the administration of the experimental treatment and the collection of data on the subject, but since they are usually conducted in a natural setting, extraneous variables may have effects. Such research commonly involves extensive data collection, and the analysis of results may require considerable sorting through the data. It is often helpful to plot the data to identify the dominant pattern.

Concepts discussed in the chapter are especially applicable to action research as it is conducted in the schools and involves some type of experimentation. Action research commonly is conducted with intact groups or with individuals. Students as subjects involved in research, very often are not randomly selected from some larger group, or randomly assigned to experimental treatments.

Here and in Chapter 5, the more commonly used designs for experimental and quasi-experimental research have been discussed. However, many variations can be made to accommodate specific research situations. For example, as was discussed in Chapter 5, if a time series design were used with random assignment to the groups, we would then have a "true" experimental design, with some type of repeated observation. The important thing is to have a design that fits the objectives of the experiment, one that provides adequate control so that the results can be interpreted with confidence and generalized as intended.

KEY CONCEPTS

Quasi-experimental research	Baseline
Nonequivalent groups	A–B design
Posttest-only, nonequivalent control group design	A–B–A design
Pretest-posttest, nonequivalent control group design	A–B–A–B design
Time series designs	Multiple-baseline designs
Single-group time series design	Multiple-baseline across behaviors
Multiple-group time series design	Multiple-baseline across subjects
Single subject designs	Multiple-baseline across situations
Single-variable rule	

EXERCISES

6.1 The most desirable procedure for obtaining groups for an experiment is random selection or assignment of subjects, yet at times it is necessary to use intact groups and a quasi-experimental design. Discuss some of the difficulties that may be introduced when intact groups are used.

6.2 A biology teacher has three sets of laboratory materials available and decides to use one set with each of three classes over the period of one semester. The research question of interest is whether or not the different materials have differing effects on attainment of laboratory concepts, as measured by a section of the final examination given at the end of the semester. The score on this section of the test is the dependent variable. The classes are heterogeneous in ability, although students have not been randomly assigned to classes. The teacher decides to use a posttest-only, nonequivalent control group design. Diagram the design. How could the teacher apply a pretest-posttest, non-equivalent control group design, and what advantages would this design have over the posttest-only design? What are possible threats to the internal validity of this study? How generalizable are the results?

6.3 A study is conducted in three elementary schools on the effects of individual versus massed practice on fifth-grade spelling achievement. The fifth-grade teachers are allowed to use the method they prefer, but any one teacher uses only one method. After an eight-week period, the students are given a common spelling test. Discuss possible problems in interpreting the results of this experiment. Comment on both internal and external validity.

6.4 A teacher conducts a study on third-grade reading achievement with a class. Two methods of instruction are used, but not simultaneously. The students are tested every two weeks, and a particular method is used for each two-week period. The methods are randomly assigned to the two-week periods, and the study continues for an eighteen-week semester. Diagram this study as a time series design. Discuss its strong points and potential weaknesses. What might be a special measurement problem?

6.5 A study is conducted using intact groups to determine the effects of three different training programs. The groups are pretested, and the training programs are implemented for six weeks. The groups are posttested immediately following completion of the programs and again six weeks later. The design can be diagrammed as follows:

$$G_1 \quad O_1{-}X_1{-}O_2{-\!\!-\!\!-}O_3$$
$$G_2 \quad O_4{-}X_2{-}O_5{-\!\!-\!\!-}O_6$$
$$G_3 \quad O_7{-}X_3{-}O_8{-\!\!-\!\!-}O_9$$

Interpret the following sets of results. Consider each independently.

a. $O_1 = O_4 = O_7 = O_3 = O_6 = O_9$, and O_2 is greater than O_1, and O_5 is greater than O_4, and O_8 is greater than O_7, but O_2 is greater than O_5, which is greater than O_8.

b. $O_1 = O_4 = O_7$, and $O_2 = O_5 = O_8 = O_3 = O_6$, $= O_9$, but O_1, O_4, O_7, $\neq O_2$, O_5, O_8, O_3, O_6, O_9.

c. O_1, O_4, and O_7 are not equal to each other, in that O_1 is greater than O_4, which is greater than O_7; O_2 is greater than O_5, which is greater than O_8, but $O_3 = O_6 = O_9$.

d. Assuming that there is an experimental treatment effect immediately after the program is completed, what comparisons would be made to determine whether there are long-term experimental treatment effects?

e. Is there any way to check on whether or not there is an effect of pretesting in this design? If so, how would it be checked; if not, why not?

6.6   A two-group time series design is used in a health education study in which two senior high school classes participate. The dependent variable is attitude toward health maintenance habits; it is measured at the beginning of the semester and every three weeks during the eighteen-week semester. Thus, each class is measured seven times. An experimental treatment (X), which consists of showing a series of films about the medical effects of poor health habits, is randomly inserted in one three-week period for one of the classes. The design can be diagrammed as follows:

$$G_1 \quad O_1{-}O_2{-}O_3 {-}X{-}O_4 {-}O_5 {-}O_6 {-}O_7$$
$$G_2 \quad O_8{-}O_9{-}O_{10}{-\!\!-\!\!-}O_{11}{-}O_{12}{-}O_{13}{-}O_{14}$$

Interpret the following possible patterns of results:

a. $O_1 = O_2 = O_3 = O_8 = O_9 = O_{10} = O_{11} = O_{12} = O_{13} = O_{14}$, and O_4 is greater than O_3, but O_4 is less than O_5, which is less than O_6, which is less than O_7. The greater the score on the dependent variable, the more positive the attitude.

b. $O_1 = O_8$, and $O_2 = O_9$, and $O_3 = O_{10}$; none of O_8 through O_{14} are equal, and the pattern is such that the scores increase consistently from O_8 through O_{14}; O_4 is greater than O_3 and O_{11}; O_5 is greater than O_{12}, but $O_6 = O_{13}$, and $O_7 = O_{14}$.

c. What comparisons would be made to check whether or not the normal class instruction is having an effect independent of X?

6.7   A guidance counselor is working with a high school student who, though an able student according to Scholastic Aptitude Test results, is having difficulty in all subjects. The counselor has been meeting with the student once a week for four weeks. The counselor decides to have the student keep a detailed log of how his time is spent when not in school. These logs are then used in the counseling sessions in an attempt to get the student to concentrate more on subject matter. Each week, the counselor receives reports from the student's teachers and synthesizes this information. The logs are used for a four-week period, so this is an A-B design. Diagram the design. What pattern of results would be indicative of an experimental treatment (the use of the logs) effect? If there was an experimental treatment effect, how would the patterns of results differ if it was a one-time effect versus a consistent, accumulative effect? Present a pattern of results from which no conclusion could be drawn.

6.8 Describe a situation in an area of your own interest for which a single-subject design would apply. What are the advantages if an A-B-A or A-B-A-B design can be used instead of an A-B design? What are the advantages of going to a multiple-baseline design? Diagram your design.

6.9 Describe the differences between the following designs: (1) multiple-baseline across behaviors, (2) multiple-baseline across subjects, and (3) multiple-baseline across situations.

6.10 Several of the preceding exercises describe research situations that might be considered action research. Identify those exercises and describe why they are examples of action research. When action research is conducted, is it considered to be primarily applied or basic research?

NOTE

1. The *A-B-A-B* design discussed in the next section is also referred to as a reversal or withdrawal design, since there is a reversal of conditions in that design, too.

REFERENCE

Campbell, D. T., and Stanley, J. C. (1963). Experimental and quasi-experimental designs for research on teaching. In N. L. Gage (Ed.), *Handbook of research on teaching* (pp. 171–246). Chicago: Rand McNally.

C h a p t e r 7

Survey Research

The preceding two chapters dealt with experimental research. It was noted that, for a research project to be an experiment, at least one independent variable must be manipulated by the researcher according to some preconceived plan. However, many variables in educational settings do not lend themselves to deliberate manipulation. For example, intelligence, aptitude, and socioeconomic background cannot be randomly assigned to individuals or manipulated in an experiment.

Generally, there tends to be less control in nonexperimental research than in experimental research; therefore, interpretation of nonexperimental results may be less straightforward and more susceptible to ambiguity. But this is more a function of the general conditions under which nonexperimental research is conducted than a consequence of one or more independent variables being manipulated in an experiment. Nonexperimental research generally is conducted in a natural setting, with numerous variables operating simultaneously. Nevertheless, nonexperimental research can be carefully designed to enhance not only completion of the research but also interpretation of the results. It is the research problem and the conditions of the research that determine the appropriate methodology.

Survey Research: Its Scope and Description

Survey research is probably the single most widely used research type in educational research. It encompasses a wide variety of research studies: all the way from ex post facto studies that focus on the relationships of sociological variables as they occur in natural settings, to status surveys designed to determine the status quo of some phenomenon. Surveys are used to measure attitudes, opinions, or achievements—any number of variables in natural settings. Survey research has been around a long time and we owe much of its development to the field of sociology. Because survey research is broad in scope, it is useful to present some examples that illustrate its characteristics.

Survey research is broad in scope including status quo studies to those in which the relationships of sociological and psychological variables are determined and interpreted.

Ex post facto Research

Ex post facto means "from a thing done afterwards," and when ex post facto research is done variables are studied in retrospect in search of possible relationships and effects. There are no variables deliberately manipulated by the researcher. Ex post facto research goes by different names. Krathwohl (1993, p.514) includes ex post facto research as part of "After-the-fact, natural experiments." These are not experiments in the sense that the researcher manipulates variables, but under natural conditions in which are operating independent and dependent variables. Causal-comparative method or studies are other terms sometimes used for ex post facto research, but as Borg and Gall (1989, p.536) point out, in a sense, causal comparative is not a method but a particular way of analyzing relational data. Regardless of what it is called, ex post facto research can be considered a part of survey research because of its nonexperimental nature and the way data are collected; in essence, subjects are "surveyed."

Examples of ex post facto Research

The educational research literature abounds with examples of ex post facto research, but reports of studies are too long to reproduce in their entirety here. However, comments are made below on two studies in order to illustrate the nature of ex post facto research.

In research reported by Taylor, Frye, and Maruyama (1990), titled, "Time Spent Reading and Reading Growth," 195 fifth- and sixth-grade students were studied. The purpose of the study was to investigate the effects of time spent reading at school and at home on reading achievement. Students were tested on reading comprehension prior to beginning the study, and then daily reading logs were kept over a four-month period, mid-January through mid-May.

The information in the reading logs was coded, and four means calculated, all in mean number of minutes per day: (1) assigned reading at school (during the reading period), (2) pleasure reading at school, (3) assigned reading at home, and (4) pleasure reading at home. In essence, these amounts of time spent in four types of reading were the independent variables of the study. However, in the analysis, the independent variable was the mean number of minutes reading at home. The dependent variable was the score on a standardized reading comprehension test at the end of the study. The reading comprehension score taken prior to the study was used as a control variable in the analysis, essentially for statistical adjustment.

The report of this study was very well done. It is complete and the description of the procedures is straightforward and clear. One of the conclusions was, "The results support the conventional wisdom that it is valuable for students to actually read during reading class" (p.359). Any interested reader may consult the report for additional information about the study.

In a study of 1388 fourth graders, Finn and Cox (1992) investigated "Participation and Withdrawal Among Fourth-Grade Pupils." The research questions addressed were:

1. What specific behaviors distinguish those pupils judged by their teachers to be highly involved in classroom activities from their peers who are more withdrawn?
2. How is participation distributed among children from different races, gender, and socioeconomic groups?
3. Do differences in prior performance distinguish youngsters who are more involved in classroom activities in grade four from their less involved classmates?

The 1388 subjects of the study were enrolled in 72 schools across the state of Tennessee.

Teachers rated the individual students on the Student Participation Questionnaire, a 25-item inventory that reflects student classroom participation. Using the scores of this questionnaire, students were classified into three groups; nonparticipant, passive-participant, and active-participant. This three-category grouping was one of the "independent" variables, along with race and gender as additional independent variables.

Scores on achievement tests in reading and mathematics had been obtained for the pupils when they were in grades one through three. The Stanford Achievement Tests and the Basic Skills First Tests (curriculum-referenced tests developed by the state of Tennessee) were administered in the spring of each year. The scores on these tests were dependent variables of the study. Self-Concept and Motivational Inventory (SCAMIN) scores also had been administered at the end of grades one, two, and three. These scores served as additional dependent variables.

The analyses of the data were quite complex and the study generated numerous results and conclusions. One result was that there were highly significant differences in achievement at all three grade levels among the participation groups (p. 159). The more active participation, the greater the achievement. For additional information about this research the interested reader may consult the report. The important point here is the nature of the ex post facto research. The variables were not manipulated; they were measured as they occurred in the natural, school setting. The research focused on determining the relationships and effects among the variables.

> In ex post facto research the relationships and effects among variables are studied as they have occurred in a natural setting.

Other Survey Research

Practically all adults have been involved in surveys at some time or another. We are familiar with the political polls taken on almost a continuous basis during election years. People are surveyed about attitudes, opinions, perceptions, and often they are asked to evaluate something. General public populations are surveyed as well as more specific populations such as a professional population.

Education has its share of survey research. Certainly one of the most extensive surveys in education is the annual Gallup/Phi Delta Kappa Poll of the Public's Attitudes Toward the Public Schools (Elam, Rose, and Gallup, 1992), which is a national survey. Local school systems often do surveys that are called community surveys or school surveys. These surveys focus on numerous factors of school operation and the community's perception of the schools and how well they are being operated. A school census is also a survey, one designed to estimate future enrollments and needs of the school system. Colleges and universities conduct surveys of their graduates to obtain perceptions of the college experience and the value of the completed program. Education professionals may be surveyed about their opinions about educational issues. Evaluation research studies often include surveys of participants or clients. So, there are many educational research situations for which survey research is the appropriate methodology.

Survey Designs

Survey designs basically are of two types, longitudinal and cross-sectional. These designs are commonly used with samples,[1] although they can be used with an entire population. (When an entire population is included in the survey it is called a *census*.) The two characteristics that distinguish the designs are (1) the points at which data collection takes place and (2) the nature of the sample.

Longitudinal Designs

Longitudinal designs involve the collection of data over time and at specified points in time. Some longitudinal studies are of short duration, and others span a long period, possibly several years. In any event, data for such studies are collected at two or more points in time.

One type of longitudinal design is the *trend study*. In a trend study, a general population is studied over time. Random samples are taken at various points, and these are different samples, but the samples represent the general population. Trend studies often are used for studying attitudes or opinions over an extended period. For example, in a study of a community's changing attitude toward the schools, the general population would be the members of the community. Each time (possibly yearly) attitude is measured, a random sample is selected from the general population. An individual might be selected for more than one sample. The polls conducted over the course of a political campaign are examples of trend studies

---

A *trend study* is a longitudinal study in which a general population is studied over time. Usually, the population is sampled, and random samples are measured.

A variation on the trend study is the *cohort study,* which is also a longitudinal design. In a cohort study, a specific rather than a general population is studied, usually by drawing random samples at different points in time rather than including the entire population. The difference between trend and cohort studies can be illustrated by an example. A researcher is interested in studying the attitudes of the teachers in Region A toward professional unions. The survey is conducted every three years for fifteen years. At any given time, the random sample of teachers surveyed is selected from the teacher population at that time. The membership of the population would have changed, at least partly, from the previous time, but at any particular time it is the teacher population (in this case, called a *general population*). A survey conducted in this manner would be an example of a trend study.

If the researcher were interested in studying the attitudes toward professional unions of the 1995, beginning teacher population in Region A, this would involve studying a specific population. Three years later, the next random sample would be drawn from what remains of this population, which in 1998 would be teachers with three years' experience. Although some of the original beginning teachers would have left teaching along the way, the study would include only the attitudes of the population of teachers who were beginning teachers in 1995. A survey conducted in this manner would be an example of a cohort study.

A *cohort study* is a longitudinal study in which a specific population is studied over time.

In some populations that turn over rapidly, the actual members of the population may change almost entirely over time. For example, if a survey of undergraduate attitudes at a college were conducted every four years, there would be a large percentage of change in the actual members of the undergraduate population. However, the undergraduates at each point in time would still be the general population under study.

Trend and cohort studies enable the researcher to study change and process over time. However, because different random samples are selected each time data are collected, the trends are studied for the group, not for individuals. If changes are taking place, the researcher cannot specifically determine which individuals are causing the changes.

One variation on longitudinal designs, the *panel study,* involves collecting data on a sample of individuals at different times. The sample of individuals used is called the *panel,* which should be randomly selected at the outset of the study.

A *panel study* is a longitudinal study in which the same sample is measured two or more times. The sample can represent either a specific or a general population.

One advantage of panel studies is that they enable the researcher not only to measure net change but also to identify the source of change in terms of the specific individuals who are changing. Panel studies also can provide information on the temporal ordering of variables. Such information is important if the researcher is attempting to establish cause and effect, because an effect cannot precede its cause. Suppose we were interested in attitudes toward the central college administration and promotion patterns among college professors. If a full professor has as excellent attitude, is it because of promotion, or was the attitude there before promotion, and did it have some effect on whether or not promotion took place? Without some kind of ordering of what occurred first, there is no way to establish a possible cause and effect. (The ordering does not necessarily establish cause and effect; it merely indicates whether or not a cause-and-effect relationship is possible.)

Panel studies have some definite disadvantages, an obvious one being attrition in the panel across the data-collection points. Therefore, panel studies tend to be of relatively short duration compared to other longitudinal studies. Another disadvantage is that the panel study is demanding for both the panel members and the researcher, who must follow up and locate panel members. If the population from which the panel was selected is highly mobile and changing, the original panel may no longer be representative of that population at later data-collection points. Panel studies are most applicable with static populations over short time periods. For example, surveying school board members quarterly over one calendar year might involve a panel study. Another possible disadvantage is that the panel members might become conditioned to certain variables so that they are better at recall or exceptionally skilled in responding. Conditioning can also work the other way, causing panel members to become fatigued, bored, or careless.

Longitudinal designs are used for studying change or status over a period of time. The length of time and the number of data-collection points involved in a specific longitudinal design depend on the objectives of the study. For sampling, the trend study involves different random samples from a general population, the cohort study involves different random samples from a specific population, and the panel study involves a single random sample measured at several times.

Cross-Sectional Designs

In contrast to longitudinal designs, *cross-sectional designs* involve the collection of data at one point in time from a random sample representing some given population at that time. A cross-sectional design cannot be used for measuring change in an individual, because an individual is measured only once. However, differences between defined groups in the cross-sectional study may represent changes that take place in a larger defined population. Consider the following example.

Suppose a researcher is conducting a survey of mathematics achievement of senior high school students (grades ten through twelve) in a city school system or in a geographical region. Mathematics achievement is operationally defined as performance on a comprehensive, standardized mathematics test. A random sample is selected that includes tenth-, eleventh-, and twelfth-graders, and each individual is identified in terms of grade level. Another way of viewing the sampling is that random samples are selected from all grade levels. The sample is tested, and the researcher now has data on the three grades.

Even though the data are collected at the same point in time, because the three grade levels are represented, the data represent the pattern of mathematics achievement in senior high school. The differences between the grade levels represent gains in mathematics achievement across the three years. However, instead of using a single, grade-level population of students and measuring them three times longitudinally as they progress through the grades, three different grade levels are studied simultaneously.

> A *cross-sectional design* involves data collection at one point in time from a sample or from more than one sample representing two or more populations.

Selecting samples from two or more populations simultaneously and conducting a study related to the same research problem is called a *parallel-samples design*. Parallel-samples designs usually appear as cross-sectional designs, although they can be longitudinal. In the latter case, there would be two or more data-collection points, separated by a time interval.

As an example, a parallel-samples design used in a study of attitudes toward professional unions might include samples of teachers, school administrators, and school board members. Each of these three samples could respond to similar, if not identical, attitude inventories or questionnaires. The results of the different samples could then be compared.

Characteristics of different survey designs are summarized in Table 7.1. The cross-sectional designs have some logistical advantages over the longitudinal designs. Data collection is not spread over an extended time period, and potentially difficult follow-up of individuals is not necessary, as it is in a panel study. For these reasons, cross-sectional designs are more practical than longitudinal designs for master's thesis and doctoral dissertation research. If the time interval between data-collection points is very short—for instance, less than three months—a longitudinal design may be feasible for dissertation research. Most longitudinal studies are relatively large scale, however, and many take on the characteristics of continuing research that is conducted over a period of years. The

TABLE 7.1   Characteristics of Survey Designs

Design	Population Studied	How Sampled
Longitudinal	[Two or more data collection times]	
Trend	General	Random samples at each data-collection time
Cohort	Specific	Random samples at each data-collection time
Panel	General or specific	The initial random sample is used throughout the data-collection times
Cross-sectional	General or specific, and could include subpopulations[a]	Random samples from all populations at one point in time

[a]If two or more populations are studied simultaneously, this becomes a parallel-samples design.

characteristics of longitudinal and cross-sectional designs can be combined into a complex design that includes sampling two or more populations at two or more times. Comparisons could then be made at a given point in time and also across data-collection times.

The Methodology of Survey Research

The methodology of conducting a survey involves a series of detailed steps, each of which should be carefully planned. The initial step is to define the research problem and to begin developing the survey design. The definition of the research problem should include a good background in the variables to be studied, which of course includes a review of the literature. Variables included in the survey must be operationally defined, and the investigator should have information about the relationships of any sociological and psychological variables that may be involved. This information is valuable for constructing items or selecting measurement instruments, such as tests, for the survey.

The next step is the development of the sampling plan, if it has been decided to sample rather than measure the entire population. Various factors must be considered. The population to be sampled must be defined and the units identified for the sample selection. The sample must be selected so that valid inferences can be made to the population and to any subpopulations. Sampling procedures can be quite complex, and acquiring the sample may require considerable effort and resources.

Although some activities can be conducted simultaneously, the next major step is the preparation for data collection. For surveys involving interviews or questionnaires, this is a major step, because the instruments must be constructed. When data are to be collected using tests or inventories, such as an observation inventory, more than likely instruments will be available. It may also be necessary to train observers or testers.

Certainly, it is necessary to identify the specific types of data that will be generated by the questionnaire early in the construction of the items, and it is also necessary to consider how data will be tabulated, summarized, and analyzed. The procedures by which data are to be analyzed should be identified. Quantitative data analysis may be used, and many surveys involve qualitative data, so both quantitative and qualitative analyses may be necessary. The survey must produce data that can be used to test the research hypotheses or answer the questions raised by the research problem.

Especially for surveys using questionnaires and interviews, background or demographic information about the respondent is important in that it identifies the individual in terms of classifying variables for the analysis. For example, if the responses of men and women are to be analyzed separately or comparatively, it is essential to know the sex of the individual. Surveys vary as to the amount of required background information.

Initial drafts of a questionnaire or interview should be "tried out," so to speak, with a pilot run or trial run. Such a try-out should be done with individuals similar to the intended respondents. The purpose of the pilot run is to check for ambiguity, confusion, and poorly prepared items. Pilot run feedback can be very useful for finalizing the instrument. A pilot run is done with a limited number of individuals, usually five to ten, but seldom more than twenty.

When the measurement instrument is judged to be satisfactory, the data collection begins. The researcher should adhere to the sampling plan when collecting the data. If interviews are used, and depending upon the complexity of the interview, there may need to be provision for systematically checking the interviewers. This may be accomplished by having two interviewers interview the same individual. Such a measure of consistency is called *interrater reliability*. For certain types of interviews, it is also well to get a measure of the consistency of a specific interviewer, which is called *intrarater reliability*. This can be accomplished by taping responses and having the interviewer record the responses on two independent occasions.

Data, that is, the responses to the survey, will need to be tabulated and synthesized. For open-ended items, responses will need to be categorized, and category systems must be constructed for this purpose. Such systems may be based on a content analysis or on an a priori system of responses. The translation of data is known as *coding*. This task is greatly facilitated if the information from the questionnaire or interview form can be put directly into the computer.

Data analyses will depend on the nature of the data; to the extent that responses can be quantified, statistical analyses are appropriate. But qualitative description may also be done. Ultimately, the analyses must take forms that allow for testing the hypotheses and answering the research questions of the survey. If inferences are to be drawn to populations, the analyses should provide for them. A number of separate analyses commonly are conducted on the data of a single survey, and separate analyses as well as different types of analyses may be in order. For example, data composed of frequencies on factual information items would be analyzed differently than data from an attitude scale. The former might involve proportions, whereas the latter most likely would involve frequencies or means. Data from teacher interviews requesting their perceptions of social interaction among students might be synthesized through description. The final step of conducting the survey is preparing the report of results and conclusions.

Figure 7.1 summarizes the steps in conducting a survey. The left side of the figure includes the major steps, and the right side shows the activities that come under each step. In some cases, activities overlap into two steps. Not all activities would necessarily be applicable for a specific survey; for example, training of interviewers is necessary only for studies involving interviews.

The successful completion of a survey is not a simple task. Several possible pitfalls and problems can sabotage the survey. One common problem is the failure to allow enough time and resources for the various steps. The sampling procedure can break down, or there may not be enough resources to test and revise the items adequately. The items of the interview or questionnaire may be poorly constructed, resulting in unusable data. Failure to provide the follow-ups is a very obvious but common difficulty, and inadequate procedures for assembling and tabulating the data as the questionnaires are returned are often sources of inefficiency and confusion. Nonresponse may bias the results, and failure to consider the source of nonresponse may lead to unwarranted generalizations. Finally, if the researcher reports results as separate, isolated analyses without some synthesis, it is likely that the maximum information is not being obtained from the survey. Careful planning will go a long way toward avoiding serious difficulties when conducting the survey.

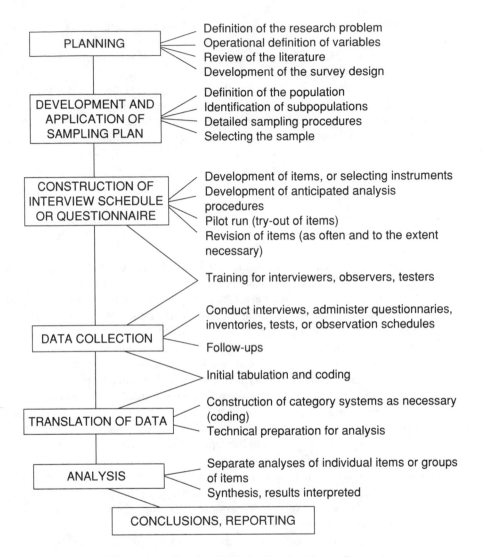

FIGURE 7.1   Flowchart for the Steps in Conducting a Survey

Questionnaire Surveys

One of the distinguishing characteristics among surveys is the method of data collection, and certainly the mailed questionnaire commonly is used for data collection. Questionnaires are used for surveys ranging in magnitude from national surveys to local surveys such as a community survey for a school system or even a single school. Questionnaires vary in length and complexity. But whatever the situation, surveys involving questionnaires require a series of sequential activities. The overall scope of these activities is presented in Figure 7.2. As indicated on the left side of the figure, early in the process some activities can be conducted concurrently, or at least overlap to some extent.

A good bit of the efforts of a questionnaire study are directed toward constructing good items and getting respondents to complete the questionnaire. But all activities are important and require attention to detail. The questions or hypotheses associated with the research study should be identified explicitly. This will facilitate the construction of questionnaire items and avoid both the inclusion of useless items and the omission of necessary items.

Item Construction

Item construction for questionnaires is a straightforward process, but without careful attention to detail, the items may be put together poorly and not provide the necessary data for the study. Before discussing item format, we consider general guidelines for item construction. These are:

1. Except for possibly a few items that request background or demographic information, have the items directly relate to the research problem, questions, or hypotheses.

2. Items are to be clear and unambiguous. Use terminology that the respondents will understand. Avoid vague words, technical terms, and jargon.

3. Include only one concept in a single item. An example of violating this guideline would be, "Are you in favor of minimum competency testing for students and career ladders for teachers?"

4. Avoid the use of leading questions. These are questions with implied assumptions or anticipated outcomes. Often such items suggest a preferred response. An example of a leading question would be, "Are you in favor of relaxed discipline in the schools, even though such discipline undermines the moral development of youth?"

5. Avoid questions loaded with social or professional desirability. In essence, do not ask questions so that certain responses make respondents disapprove of themselves. An example of violating this guideline would be asking a teacher, "Do you have difficulty maintaining a good learning climate in your classroom?"

6. Avoid questions that demand personal or delicate information. These items include requests for specific income information, possibly age of the respondent, or questions about the extent of involvement in illicit activities.

7. Request only information that the respondent is able to provide. All items should fit the informational background of the respondents.

8. Make the reading level of the items appropriate for the respondents. To the extent possible, use "soft" words rather than "hard" words. For example, when surveying teachers use "correction" or "corrective action" rather than "punishment."

9. Shorter items are preferred to longer items, and simpler items are preferred to complex items. Rather than using a single detailed and complex item, use two or more shorter items.

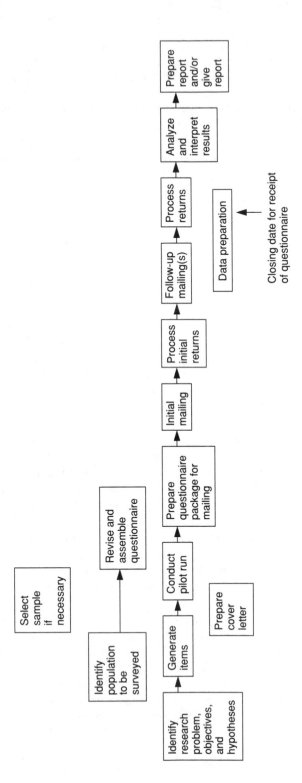

FIGURE 7.2 Sequential Activities of a Questionnaire Survey

10. When requesting quantitative information, ask for a specific number (such as an actual frequency) rather than an average. For example, ask, "How often during the past two weeks did you help your child with homework?" *Do not* ask, "On the average, how many times a month do you help your child with homework?"

11. The options for response to an item should be exhaustive; the options should be mutually exclusive. For some items, it is necessary to provide a middle-of-the-road or neutral response, such as "no definite feeling" or "undecided," to avoid forcing the respondent to make an undesirable response.

12. To the extent possible, avoid negative items and do not use double negatives. An example of a question using a negative item would be, "Which of the following instructional strategies do you not use?"

These guidelines may seem somewhat extensive, but in fact they are straightforward. Try to make the task of completing the questionnaire as easy as possible for the respondent so that it can be done efficiently and without confusion.

> Formulating items is essentially a matter of common sense. The law of parsimony applies: Keep things as simple as possible to obtain the necessary data.

Item Format

There are two general types of items used for questionnaires: (1) selected-response or forced-choice items for which the respondent selects from two or more options, and (2) open-ended items for which the respondent constructs a response. Selected-response items enhance consistency of response across respondents; data tabulation generally is straightforward and less time-consuming than for open-ended items. Selected-response items have the disadvantage of possibly "boxing-in" the respondent on the breadth of the response, but if the selected-response items produce the required data, this is not a problem. Adequately constructing selected-response items generally requires more time and effort, primarily because more of them are needed to cover a research topic. But this time is usually well spent and is more than made up when the responses are tabulated and interpreted.

Open-ended items allow the individual more freedom of response because certain feelings or information may be revealed that would not be forthcoming with selected-response items. A disadvantage of open-ended items is that responses tend to be inconsistent in length, and sometimes in content, across respondents. Both questions and responses are susceptible to misinterpretation. Irrelevant information may be included in the response. In any event, responses to open-ended items are usually more difficult to tabulate and synthesize than responses to selected-response items. Selected-response items should be used to the extent that they can obtain relevant information. They also require less effort from the respondents, because they do not need to construct the responses, and responding can be done in less time.

> The two general types of item format are selected-response items with two or more options and open-ended items for which the respondent constructs the response.

Of course, the open-ended item is more flexible and less structured than a selected-response item. But items can allow varying degrees of flexibility on a continuum from unstructured to completely structured. Consider the following items on a single topic, beginning with an unstructured item.

What do you think of the honors program in mathematics?

A corresponding partially structured item is:

What do you think about the effectiveness of the mathematics honors program relative to advanced placement in college?

A structured item is:

Do you feel that the present honors program in mathematics should be

a. continued without modifications?
b. continued but modified?
c. discontinued?

In this example, the term *honors program in mathematics* would refer to a specific program with which the respondent is familiar.

A selected-response format commonly used in questionnaire surveys is the Likert scale. A *Likert scale* is a scale with a number of points that provide ordinal scale measurement. A set of related responses, one for each point, is provided. Response is made by checking a point or circling a letter (or number) representing a point on the scale. When summarizing the results, these points are assigned numerical values, I to 5 or 0 to 4, which can be totaled over a number of items that concern the same issue or topic.

There are any number of possible sets of Likert responses. The important characteristic of a set is that the responses be appropriate for the items. Following are two example sets:

Strongly agree	Very satisfactory
Agree	Satisfactory
Neutral	Undecided
Disagree	Unsatisfactory
Strongly disagree	Very unsatisfactory

Examples of Likert scale items are given later in the chapter in the discussion of community surveys.

Pilot Run of the Items. Before preparing the final form of the questionnaire, the items should be tried out with a small group in a pilot run. This is a pretesting of the questionnaire, and deficiencies may be uncovered that were not apparent by simply reviewing the items. The group used for the pilot run need not be a random sample of prospective respondents, but the members of the group should be familiar with the variables under study and should be in a position to make valid judgments about the items. A class of students, possibly graduate students, can often serve effectively as a pilot run group. The results of the pilot run should identify misunderstandings, ambiguities, and useless or inadequate items. Additional items may be suggested, and mechanical difficulties in such matters as data tabulation may be identified. Difficulties with the directions for completing the questionnaire may also be uncovered. On the basis of the pilot run results, necessary revisions should be made for the final form of the questionnaire.

Besides eliminating ambiguities and clarifying directions, a pilot run can avoid results that provide little or no information. The following item, used in a pilot run with twenty-five respondents, is an example. The frequencies of responses are underlined following the category.

> *Please indicate your years of teaching experience (to the closest whole year) by checking the appropriate category*
>
> *0–10* <u>*21*</u>   *11–20* <u>*3*</u>   *21–30* <u>*1*</u>   *more than 30* <u>*0*</u>

These results provide little information, because the response categories do not separate the respondents. The possible responses might be changed, with the following results:

> *0–2* <u>*7*</u>   *3–5* <u>*5*</u>   *6–8* <u>*4*</u>   *9–11* <u>*5*</u>   *more than 11* <u>*4*</u>

Now the response categories provide more definitive information about the years of experience of the respondents.

A *pilot run* of the items provides the opportunity to identify confusing and ambiguous language, and to obtain information about possible patterns of results.

The Cover Letter

The cover letter is an essential part of any survey involving a questionnaire. It is the mechanism for introducing individuals to the questionnaire and motivating them to respond. The letter should be straightforward, explaining the purpose and potential value of the survey and transmitting the message that an individual's response is important. There should be nothing in the cover letter to arouse suspicions about the purpose or nature of the survey. The individual should be assured that the researcher is interested in the overall responses of the group and that the individual responses will not be singled out. A procedure may be set up by which replies remain anonymous, but in any event the individual should be assured that all responses are confidential.

The matter of who signs the cover letter can be of some importance. The cover letter should be on the letterhead of a professional organization or an institution with which the respondents would be likely to identify, or at least be knowledgeable about. If possible, the letter should be signed by someone in a professional position, who is (or appears to be) associated in some way with the respondents. For example, the cover letter of a questionnaire being sent to guidance counselors about guidance institutes might carry the signature of the institute director on the staff of a university that conducts such institutes. A graduate student who sends out a questionnaire and states that its purpose is data collection for a thesis can expect a limited and disappointing response.

Figure 7.3 contains the cover letter of a survey conducted as part of the external evaluation of the Appalachia Educational Laboratory[2] (AEL). This cover letter was quite effective in that the overall response rate for the client survey approached 80 percent. The following points can be made about the letter:

1. The purpose of the survey is stated succinctly early in the first paragraph, along with the reason for this particular recipient being selected.

2. The recipient is informed as to what will be done with the information provided through the questionnaires.

3. Confidentiality is assured.

4. Each questionnaire had a four-digit code number in the upper, right-hand corner. The purpose of this number is explained, and in the explanation it is clear that there will be follow-up of nonrespondents.

5. The importance of response is mentioned in the final paragraph.

6. A time estimate is given for completing the questionnaire. When such an estimate is given it must be an accurate estimate. Underestimates of time annoy respondents when they realize completion of the questionnaire is taking a lot longer than the estimate.

7. A "deadline" is given for the return of the questionnaire, which is three weeks from the mailing date. This deadline is arbitrary but there should be enough time for recipients to complete the questionnaire, but not so much that they put it aside and forget about it. A return deadline should be specified in all cover letters.

8. The recipient is reminded about the enclosed, postage-paid envelope, and enclosing such an envelope is a requirement.

9. Appreciation for completing the questionnaire is expressed.

10. The cover letter is signed by the person in charge of the external evaluation.

11. This cover letter is simply addressed "Dear Client." Of course it would have been possible to address each letter individually to the specific recipient. However, that would have required a lot of additional effort in preparing the survey packets. A decision must be made as to whether or not individual addresses on the letter are worth the effort. For limited surveys and with special populations such as certain professionals individual addresses are warranted. For example, a survey of the chief state school officers would warrant individual addresses.

12. The letter fits easily on a single page, which essentially is the maximum length for a cover letter.

WESTERN MICHIGAN UNIVERSITY

October 5, 1992

Dear Client:

The Western Michigan University Evaluation Center has been engaged by the Appalachia Educational Laboratory (AEL) to be its external evaluator. As part of our evaluation, we are surveying people who are receiving AEL materials and services. There are two sections to the questionnaire; the first is a section that deals with R & D Notes, whose masthead is reproduced at the top of Section 1. You have been identified as a recipient of R & D Notes and familiar with it. The second section of the questionnaire deals with your perceptions of AEL materials and services in general.

The information provided through the questionnaires will be presented to the AEL Board, the federal government, and AEL staff to help them improve AEL materials and services. Your responses to this survey will be confidential; no individual will be identified with his or her responses. The number on the questionnaire is a code so that we can identify those who have responded. This is to reduce the cost of follow-up and to eliminate the disruption of follow-up for those who have returned the questionnaire.

Your response is very important to the success of this evaluation. The information you provide is important to AEL, not only for program planning, but also in dealing with the funding agency. Completing the questionnaire should require no more than 20 minutes. We very much appreciate your completing and returning the questionnaire by October 26, 1992, in the enclosed, postage-paid envelope.

Sincerely yours,

William Wiersma

William Wiersma, Ph.D
External Evaluator for AEL

dm

enc

FIGURE 7.3   Cover Letter Used with Questionnaire Survey

Source: FY92 Report: External Evaluation of the Appalachia Educational Laboratory (February 1993) Kalamazoo, MI. The Evaluation Center, Western Michigan University. Reproduced by permission of the Appalachia Educational Laboratory and The Evaluation Center.

The cover letter merits careful attention and may require review and revision. It must inform the recipients about the survey and motivate recipients to complete the questionnaire in an accurate and timely manner.

Questionnaire Format

The questionnaire as a whole should be attractive and easily read. Multicolored printing can be used, although there is little evidence that such printing has much effect on the respondent's motivation. The questionnaire should not be so long that it makes responding a tedious or burdensome task or makes unreasonable demands on the respondent's time. The items should be in a logical sequence to hold the interest of the respondent.

Instructions for completing the questionnaire should be concise and clear, with examples for any complex or difficult items. If more than one item format it used, items with the same format are often grouped together. However, the logical sequence of the items should take priority over item format. That is, when completing the questionnaire, the respondent's chain of thought should be logical and organized, not "jumping around" from concept to concept.

The cover letter should set the stage for responding, and the early part of the questionnaire should begin immediately with the content related to the research problem. Most questionnaires include a section on respondent background or demographic information (for example, information about position, degrees held, etc.). This section should appear near the end of the questionnaire so that the transition from the cover letter is not broken. The items of this section should be selected-response format, and the options for any item should be mutually exclusive and exhaustive.

To the extent that it does not break the logical flow of the questionnaire, any open-ended items should appear toward the end of the questionnaire. Sometimes in questionnaires dealing with several concepts, open-ended items are dispersed throughout the questionnaire. In any event, the questionnaire should not begin with an open-ended item that requires extensive writing. If there are items that may be difficult for the respondent, place them near the end.

The questionnaire layout should not appear crowded, and the items should be easy to respond to. Items and pages should be numbered. An item and its response options must be on the same page, and the options must fit the item. If any special instructions are necessary, such as responding so that the questionnaire can be machine-scored, be sure that these instructions are clear and emphasized. Finally, at the end of the questionnaire, the name and address of the person to whom the questionnaire is to be returned should be given, reminding the respondent to place the questionnaire in the enclose stamped, self-addressed envelope.

> Questionnaire format should be attractive and straightforward, with the items ordered in a logical sequence. Responding to the items should be convenient and without confusion.

Procedures for Increasing Response Rate

One of the persistent problems with questionnaire studies is the possibility of a high rate of nonresponse. The validity of survey research involving questionnaires depends on the response rate and the quality of response. *Response rate* is the percentage of respondents returning the questionnaire, and *quality of response* depends on the completeness of data. The problem with nonresponse is that it introduces the possibility of bias, since the respondents might not be representative of the group intended to be surveyed.

> The possibility of nonresponse is a problem with questionnaire studies because nonresponse may introduce bias into the data.

Of course, the greater the response rate, the better the survey. Most surveys can tolerate some nonresponse, but what are acceptable rates of response? Writers differ on suggested minimum response rates, and the rates also may vary somewhat depending on the population being surveyed. Generally, however, when surveying a professional population, 70 percent is considered a minimum response rate. When surveying the general public, more nonresponse can probably be tolerated because the primary reasons for nonresponse may be apathy and lack of interest. For surveys conducted in the Austin (Texas) Independent School District, Jackson and Schuyler (1984) reported typical response percentage rates for staff surveys from the high 70s to low 90s. Response percentage rates of parents were in the 60s, and those of graduates were in the 60s and 70s, with a few lower.

Essentially, individuals will respond to questionnaires if the perceived cost of responding (in terms of time and effort) is low relative to the perceived reward. Dillman (1978) identifies the rewards a researcher can offer as follows:

1. Being regarded positively by another person.
2. Expressing appreciation to the respondent.
3. Being consulted on an issue of importance to the respondent. (p. 13)

Of course, monetary rewards also have been used on occasion, but these often are not feasible because of the cost. Hopkins and Gullickson (1992), in a meta-analysis of the effects of monetary gratuities on response rates, concluded that a gratuity can enhance the response rate, by as much as around 20 percent. The greater the gratuity the greater the impact, but even a $1.00 gratuity resulted in approximately a 20 percent increase. Enclosed gratuities were much more effective than promised gratuities. The findings held for both general and professional populations, and were consistent regardless of the saliency of the questionnaire content. Gratuities can have a positive impact even in a follow-up mailing (pp. 6–7).

It would stand to reason that an attractive, professional-looking questionnaire enhances response. Indeed, in a survey by Clark and Boser (1989) of experts in survey research, over 80 percent indicated high importance of appearance factors. Yet in a later study by Boser and Clark (1992), focusing on questionnaires mailed to teacher education program graduates, they found factors such as adequate margins and splitting a checklist over two pages were not particularly important to the respondents. However, when expending the effort of putting a questionnaire together, an attractive, professional looking questionnaire certainly does not reduce the response rate.

Contacting the respondent prior to mailing the questionnaire is another suggestion for enhancing response. A letter, postcard, or telephone call may be used for the contact. Colton and Kane (1989) conducted a national survey of newly licensed registered nurses. Three groups were used: (1) a control group receiving no prior letter, (2) an experimental group receiving a personalized pre-letter, and (3) an experimental group receiving a nonpersonalized pre-letter. The latter had no inside address and had "Dear Colleague" as the salutation. Otherwise the bodies of the pre-letters were identical. The response for the control group was 51.4 percent, and those for the experimental groups were 63.3 percent and 64.2 percent (p. 4). The group receiving the nonpersonalized letter had the highest response rate. Certainly the pre-letters produced higher response rates than the normal mailing alone. Precontacting respondents is an additional task, but it is worth considering if difficulty with response rate is anticipated, and the size of the sample is manageable for precontacting. Certainly, characteristics of the population surveyed will have an impact on response rate. If a professional population is being surveyed and the content of the questionnaire is professionally relevant, the response rate is usually greater than when the general public is surveyed.

Tollefson, Tracy, and Kaiser (1984) used three time-cue conditions: (1) thirty minutes, (2) fifteen minutes, and (3) no information, for completing a questionnaire that required about twenty-eight minutes for completion in field testing. They found the highest return rate with the thirty-minute cue, which led them to conclude: "While time cues increase the response rates, the time cues need to be matched to the average time required to complete the questionnaire" (p. 9). It can be inferred that individuals will not be tricked by an unrealistic time cue. Although reduced time for completing the questionnaire may increase the return rates, any time cues should be realistic.

Follow-up Procedures.   Follow-ups are a must for almost all questionnaire surveys, and the follow-up mailing should be timed to arrive at the respondents' addresses a few days after the deadline for return specified in the cover letter. They should be planned for in advance; in some cases, two or more follow-ups may be desirable. The follow-up letter should be pleasant but firm. Jackson and Schuyler (1984) found that fewer responses were received from graduates who received "cute" reminders than from those whose reminders were more businesslike. Again, the follow-up letter should encourage the individual to respond immediately.

> Follow-ups are considered necessary for questionnaire surveys, and they should be planned for in advance.

If financially feasible, a copy of the questionnaire along with a stamped, self-addressed envelope should be included with the follow-up mailing. Sometimes, a postcard reminder can be used effectively, but if so, it is sent within a week to ten days of the original mailing. Of course, it is not possible to include another questionnaire with the postcard, and this is a disadvantage. The individual is more likely to respond if a questionnaire is at hand, rather than having to find the one from the original mailing.

There are two approaches to a follow-up: (1) send a letter (or postcard) only to individuals who have not responded, or (2) send a blanket follow-up to everyone. The former approach is much preferred, because it is less expensive and eliminates the possibility of receiving two completed questionnaires from the same person. The latter approach should be used only if the nonrespondents cannot be identified. If the latter approach is used, the individuals must be told not to respond a second time if they have already responded.

Telephone calls, telegrams, or special-delivery letters may also be used for follow-up. However, they are expensive in terms of time and costs and, therefore, are not used extensively. Repeated follow-up mailings can be used, but the percentage gained by repeated follow-ups decreases with each follow-up. Unless response is low or an unusually high response rate is required, repeated follow-ups are not common.

In summary, for enhancing the response rate of mailed questionnaires, the researcher is well advised to construct an attractive, concise questionnaire with an informative cover letter and to provide for timely follow-up. If time cues are given, they should be realistic. A monetary incentive is helpful if this is an option. Of the procedures used to increase the response rate, follow-ups and monetary incentives seem to be the most effective based on the results of empirical studies.

Identifying Sources of Nonresponse

The difficulty with a high rate of nonresponse is that the data may be biased. Under no circumstances can it simply be assumed that the respondents are a random sample of the original questionnaire recipients. Also, increasing the size of the sample does not counter bias, it only increases the quantity of data.

When the data are biased, they do not represent the group under study. A survey on the need for mathematics teachers, conducted on a statewide basis with the following response, illustrates this point. The central administrations of almost all large school systems responded, but for some reason, those in small school systems did not return the questionnaire. Therefore, the data on the returned questionnaires indicated an average need for mathematics teachers in excess of the total number of mathematics teachers in most schools throughout the state. Thus, nonresponse can result in a data gap that markedly distorts the real situation. It is very tenuous to assume that nonresponse is randomly distributed throughout the group originally sent questionnaires.

Demographic information can be very useful for identifying possible bias due to nonresponse, and indeed, frequently demographic items are included specifically for determining sources of nonresponse. The researcher should be able to identify the sources of nonresponse in terms of respondent characteristics that may be related to the variables under study. Do certain subgroups of individuals—for example, men, junior high school teachers, suburban teachers, superintendents of small school systems—have a high non-response rate? It generally is not satisfactory to use a questionnaire without having a way of knowing who has returned it. Sources of nonresponse are identified by determining the response rates for categories of demographic variables—for example, secondary teachers versus elementary teachers.

Identifying subgroups with high nonresponse rates does not reveal the feelings of the nonrespondents, but it does identify the nonresponding groups. If nonresponse is associated with a certain type of feeling toward the questionnaire items—that is, nonrespondents have unfavorable attitudes toward them—the sample of responses definitely will be biased, since response and nonresponse are associated with the variables under study. It may be possible to interview a sample of the nonrespondents to acquire information about their characteristics and their reasons for not returning the questionnaire. Checking a sample of nonrespondents involves additional effort, although a sample of twenty-five or so is usually an adequate number. Borg and Gall (1989) suggest a check of nonrespondents if the nonresponse rate exceeds 20 percent (p. 443).

In some studies, it may be possible to argue that the nonrespondents are neutral in their feelings or disinterested in the issue. If this assumption is tenable, it can be used when interpreting the data, and a higher nonresponse rate would be tolerable before checking with nonrespondents. Such an assumption would more likely be valid when surveying a general public population rather than a professional population.

Nonresponse cannot be ignored, and the researcher must know the sources of the nonresponse. To the extent possible, it is important to determine the reasons for nonresponse.

Incomplete and Possible Dishonest Response

Although questionnaire recipients may be directed to respond to all items, there often are some respondents who omit one or more items. An omitted item may not be understood or a respondent may be unsure about the item. If there are just a few omitted items throughout and there does not seem to be any pattern to the omissions, the omissions should cause little difficulty. But if there are frequent omissions, they merit some checking.

Johnson, Gips, and Rich (1992) have observed that when respondents are asked to evaluate someone or something, there may be a tendency to omit items more frequently when the evaluation would be less positive than when it would be more positive (p. 1). So, with evaluative items that are frequently omitted, this may be a possibility to be recognized. If open-ended items are frequently omitted, this may be due to respondents simply not wanting to put forth the effort of responding. Or the omissions may be due to some other factor. One way to do an internal check on the responses to other items is to separate the questionnaire into two groups, one with the item answered, the other with it omitted. Then analyze the responses to the other items separately for these two groups. If the results differ then omitting the item is related to how the respondents responded to the other items.

There is no consistently prescribed method for dealing with omissions. It may be that an item is not easily understood. The researcher should check the extent of omissions and, if it seems noteworthy, look for patterns in the omissions or possible relationships to other variables. For example, if all the omissions of an item were on questionnaires completed by males (gender as one of the demographic information items), this result would be noteworthy.

> Omitted items are a nuisance and if there seems to be a noteworthy amount of omissions it is necessary to look for patterns that might explain the cause of omissions. Omissions essentially are nonresponse and may bias the results.

When surveys are conducted about sensitive topics, respondents may be motivated to be less than honest. Drug use is an example of a sensitive topic. Requesting information about any illegal or socially undesirable behavior is always tenuous, but much of this type of information can be obtained only through self-report. Wrona, Sanborn, and Constantine (1992) discussed four methods for identifying dishonest and careless respondents that were surveyed in a student drug-use survey. These four methods were:

1. Impossible response—respondents indicated using a nonexistent drug.
2. Implausible frequency and extent of use.
3. Unlikely response combinations—use of numerous items for inter-item consistency checks.
4. Honesty item—ask the respondent to indicate the extent of honesty in answering the items (pp. 3–4).

A somewhat subjective criterion can be set for excluding a respondent's data. For example, if any one of the four methods identifies a dishonest respondent the data are excluded. Or if, on an honesty item, a respondent indicates being dishonest, that is quite indicative of dishonest response. Of course, it is undesirable to discard data, but a reduced data set is an improvement over one that contains false information.

For probably most surveys done as educational research there is no reason to believe that the respondents would be dishonest when completing the survey. It is only likely to occur with sensitive issues, or topics such that certain responses reflect badly on the respondents. For example, topics involving behaviors that are against regulations, such as cheating or illegal behaviors. When these topics are addressed, there should be some type of check for dishonest and careless responses.

There are methods for including an "honesty check" of responses, and one or more of these should be used when addressing sensitive issues in the survey.

Examples

At this point we will consider some examples of questionnaire items. The first example is of a hypothetical survey of personnel in college counseling centers in Ohio private colleges. The research problem statement, hypotheses, and related items are given in Table 7.2. In an actual study, more items would be included for the hypotheses, and the hypotheses given are only examples of what would be a larger number included in an actual study.

Community Surveys.   School districts sometimes find community surveys—surveys of people in the district about their perceptions of the schools—useful and informative. Such surveys not only can provide information but they also can serve a public relations function.[3] When people are asked their opinions, this request often generates an interest in and a positive feeling toward the schools. School surveys can be conducted for the entire district or by school across the district or even for individual schools.[4] The entire community may be surveyed, or the survey may be limited to parents of children in the schools. In any event, questionnaires typically are limited in length, not to exceed the two sides of an $8\frac{1}{2} \times 11$-inch sheet.

Table 7.3 contains fifteen items from a community survey. (The name of the district has been changed.) The questionnaire for this survey had thirty-five items, thirty-two of them selected-response using the five-point Likert scale. The remaining three items were:

> *How do you receive information about the school?*
> (Three options, check all that apply.)
> *Do you have children attending the ABC Public Schools?*

and finally, an open-ended item:

> *If you wish, please provide any additional comments about the school system.*
> (About a two-inch space was available, but a respondent could use an additional sheet if necessary.)

The directions for this questionnaire specified that a neutral response indicated either that the respondent was uninformed about the item or had a neutral opinion. If it is important to differentiate between these two feelings, another opinion, "uninformed," could be provided. The registered voter list was used for selecting the sample.

Community surveys of the public's perceptions of the schools can provide useful information for boards of education in their decision-making process.

TABLE 7.2 Example of Research Problem, Hypotheses, and Questionnaire Items*

Research Problem
A study of professional preparation and activities of the personnel in college counseling centers in Ohio private colleges.

Hypotheses (examples)
1. The primary function of counselors is that of one-to-one counseling of students with academically related problems.
2. (a) The majority of counselors (50% or more) have an earned masters degree in a social services or professional area.
   (b) The majority of counselors have less than three years of counseling experience at the college level.
3. The work load in the centers is such that the average number of hours per week spent in center activities exceeds 50 (pro-rated on a full-time basis).
   These hypotheses imply questions about the functions of the centers, questions about the preparation of the professionals in the center, and questions on the work load.

With surveys involving questionnaires it is sometimes convenient to develop related research questions rather than specific hypotheses. Examples of questions corresponding to the three hypotheses above might be:
1. What are the professional functions of counselors in the counseling centers?
2. What is the distribution of highest earned degrees among the counselors in the centers; what is the distribution of counseling experience at the college level?
3. What is the distribution of work loads for counselors in the centers, and how is the work load partitioned among the professional functions?

Related Items (for each hypothesis [question], two example items are presented)
Hypothesis 1: I–1 Please check the one function you perceive as your primary professional function in your counseling center.
_____ a. Group counseling of students on non-academically related problems.
_____ b. Individual counseling of students on non-academically related problems.
_____ c. Group counseling of students on academically related problems.
_____ d. Individual counseling of students on academically related problems.
_____ e. None of the above.
I–2 Please rank the following functions in order of importance using rank 1 as the most important and rank 5 as least important.
_____ a. Group counseling
_____ b. Individual counseling
_____ c. Preparation for counseling sessions
_____ d. Follow-up after counseling sessions
_____ e. Routine paperwork associated with counseling sessions

Related Items
Hypothesis 2. II–1 Check the highest degree earned.
_____ Bachelors
_____ Masters in an academic discipline
_____ Masters in a professional area, including social services
_____ Doctorate
II–2 Indicate the number of years of counseling experience at the college level that you had as of July 1, 1995.
_____ none
_____ one or less
_____ more than one but less than three
_____ three or more

Continued

TABLE 7.2 *Continued*

Hypothesis 3. III–1 Indicate the total hours per week spent counseling clients—direct contact with clients.

_____ less than 10
_____ 10–20
_____ 21–30
_____ 31–40
_____ 41–50

III–2 During a typical week, indicate in the space provided the number of hours you spent in all center (professional) activities.

*Of course, in the actual questionnaire there would be more items, many more if this were a comprehensive study. The above items also illustrate different forms of response, select one of several options, ranking, and a short answer, although all are short responses and, with the exception of III–2, for Hypothesis 3, forced-choice. III–2, Hypothesis 3, could have included a number of item responses such as less than 10 hours, 11–15 hours, etc. However, it would be difficult to compute an average using such categories.

The items would not likely be consecutive in the questionnaire. The items for Hypothesis 2 could be placed with the background information of the respondent; if it were an extensive questionnaire the items could be placed under headings such as "Functions of Professional Center Personnel," and "Work Load of Center Professionals."

Client Surveys. Earlier in this chapter, the cover letter for the 1992, Appalachia Educational Laboratory (AEL) client survey was presented as an example cover letter. Table 7.4 contains seven items from the second section of the client survey, the section dealing with AEL products and services in general. The questionnaire (Evaluation Center, 1993, p. 56) contained items covering seven impact categories.[5] These categories were:

1. Overall satisfaction
2. Knowledge and/or skills
3. Information sharing
4. Use in planning
5. Use in implementation
6. Indirect benefits
7. Secondary clients' use in implementation.

The items of Table 7.4 all deal with use in planning. Items for an impact category were grouped together to facilitate the respondent's thinking when completing the questionnaire. The directions for this section are given in Table 7.4. The first twenty-two items, which dealt with the first three impact categories listed above, are omitted.

Interview Surveys

Questionnaire surveys are relatively inexpensive for reaching a substantial number of people, but they have some disadvantages associated with nonresponse, and occasionally

TABLE 7.3 Example Items from a Community Survey

Directions: Below are statements about characteristics, activities, and policies of the ABC School District. For each item, indicate the extent of your agreement, from Strongly Agree to Strongly Disagree, by checking the appropriate category. Neutral indicates that you are uninformed about the item or have a neutral opinion. Please respond to *all* items.

Statement		Strongly Agree	Agree	Neutral	Disagree	Strongly Disagree
1. The college preparatory curriculum is academically challenging.	(1)					
2. Students in the elementary schools are learning their basic skills.	(2)					
3. Efforts in recent years to improve the curriculum have been successful.	(3)					
4. The extracurricular activities in grades 7–12 are appropriate to the needs of the students.	(4)					
5. Home economics is an important component of the curriculum.	(5)					
6. Music is an important component of the curriculum.	(6)					
7. Physical education is an important component of the curriculum.	(7)					
8. Vocational education is an important component of the curriculum.	(8)					
9. I am in favor of remodeling portions of the High School Annex for vocational education.	(9)					
10. I am supportive of the Board's plans to implement a 4-year high school (9–12), middle school (6–8), and K 5 organizational plan in Fall 1991.	(10)					
11. I am generally satisfied with the work of the ABC Board of Education.	(11)					
12. I am generally satisfied with the central administration of the ABC Public Schools.	(12)					
13. School building administrators are generally successful in managing their responsibilities.	(13)					
14. The guidance department at the high school is functioning well in meeting student needs.	(14)					
15. The guidance departments at the junior highs are functioning well in meeting student needs.	(15)					

TABLE 7.4   Example Items from the FY 92, AEL Client Survey

AEL Products and Services Questionnaire

Please respond to the items in terms of AEL products and services in **general,** rather than only in the context of a specific program or project. Products and materials refer to any printed information (brochures, newsletters, workshop packets) and videotapes. Services involve contact with AEL personnel; for example, workshops, telephone conversations, technical assistance, referrals. Please read the statements **very carefully** and rate the items on the five-point scale. Please answer all the items in this section.

```
[———1———|———2———|———3———|———4———|———5———]
 Not at all          Somewhat          Much (Very) (Many)
```

						Circle One	
23. I have used materials from AEL when **planning** projects/activities.	1	2	3	4	5
24. AEL provides me access to other persons who are useful for **planning** my work.	1	2	3	4	5
25. I have considered AEL as one of my primary sources of information/assistance in **planning** projects/activities.	1	2	3	4	5
26. I have used AEL services when **planning** projects/activities.	1	2	3	4	5
27. I have accumulated materials from AEL to use when doing educational project **planning.**	1	2	3	4	5
28. I have used skills gained from AEL activities in **planning** my own projects/ activities.	1	2	3	4	5
29. AEL provides me access to others' materials that are useful in **planning** my work.	1	2	3	4	5

Source: FY 92 Report: External Evaluation of the Appalachia Educational Laboratory (February 1993), pp. 86–87. Kalamazoo, MI. The Evaluation Center, Western Michigan University. Reproduced by permission of the Appalachia Educational Laboratory and The Evaluation Center.

---

with careless response. The interview is an effective method of conducting a survey, and the use of an interview has the following advantages over use of a questionnaire:

1. If the interview is granted, there is no problem with nonresponse.

2. The interview provides opportunity for in-depth probing, and elaboration and clarification of terms, if necessary.

3. Completion of the survey can be standardized.

4. There tends to be more success with obtaining responses to open-ended items.

5. It is easier to avoid the omission of items.

6. Interviews can be used with individuals from whom data cannot otherwise be obtained.

With regard to (6) above, collecting information from educationally disadvantaged adults might require an interview, since such persons might lack the motivation to respond to a questionnaire, even if the items were written in an understandable manner.

However, interviews are costly in terms of time and effort. Within recent years, telephone interviewing has received increased usage as a replacement for face-to-face interviews. Telephone interviews typically reduce the cost of the survey, and they have other advantages over face-to-face interviews, as identified later. Interviews must be scheduled if they are face-to-face, because they involve an interchange between two people. Even with telephone interviews, unless the interviews are very brief, it is a good idea to schedule them in advance.

> The use of interviews has some advantages over the use of questionnaires, but interviews are costly in terms of time and effort.

Interview Items

Interview items, like questionnaire items, can be selected-response or open-ended format, and they can vary in the extent of structure. However, unstructured items would more likely be used in an interview than a questionnaire. The reason for this is that unstructured items leave much more interpretation to the respondent. In an interview, this interpretation can be somewhat controlled and directed, but with a questionnaire such direction is not possible. Generally, all respondents in an interview survey are asked the same set of questions. Wording could vary slightly to accommodate different respondents—for example if students, teachers, and principals were being interviewed in the same survey. A variety of item formats can be used in the same interview, and the interviewer has control over switching formats so there should be no confusion.

Whether items require an open-ended response or a selected response, they should be clearly stated in complete question form, with unambiguous terms that are meaningful to the respondent. Also, terms should have consistent meaning across respondents. The item should give the respondent adequate direction. Sometimes, optional wording or optional probes are given with items, but these should be used with caution. Consider the following open-ended item:

What do you like best about the schools in this district?

If the respondent hesitates, an optional probe might be given, such as:

We are interested in things such as the facilities, the quality of instruction, the schedule, the administration, whatever.

If this optional probe is used, those respondents who hesitate are answering a somewhat different question than those who do not receive the optional wording. At least, those who hesitate would be given more structure through the cues. A better approach would be to provide the same amount of structure for all respondents, such as:

Of the following, which do you feel are strong points of the schools in this district?

a. quality of instruction
b. facilities
c. schedule
d. central office administration
e. school (building) administration

Respondents could be invited to list others after the structured list is exhausted.

Items from the Gallup/Phi Delta Kappa Poll

One of the most comprehensive surveys in education is the annual Gallup/Phi Delta Kappa Poll of the Public's Attitudes Toward the Public Schools. The results of the twenty-fourth annual poll are reported by Elam, Rose, and Gallup (1992). The poll was an in-home interview survey, conducted in all areas of the United States and in all types of communities, during the period April 23 to May 14, 1992. The national sample consisted of 1,306 adults.

Examples of items from the twenty-fourth annual poll follow:

> *Do you think that preschool programs for children from low-income and poverty-level households would help them perform better in school in their teenage years? A great deal, quite a lot, not much, or not at all? (p. 48)*

The percentages of respondents selecting each option were given, and these were given separately for the national sample, respondents with no children in school, public school parents, and nonpublic school parents. This question was followed by a question about the willingness to pay more taxes for such programs. The same breakdowns of respondents were used as for the previous question.

An item about promoting racial/ethnic tolerance was:

> *In your opinion, are the public schools in this community taking the necessary steps to promote understanding and tolerance among students of different racial and ethnic backgrounds or not? (p. 50)*

The options were yes, no, and don't know. Again, percentages were reported using the same respondent breakdowns as for the question above. However, in a follow-up question about increasing the amount of coursework, etc., to promote understanding and tolerance, the respondents were divided by race and age.

Periodically, the poll has included questions about the length of the school year. A question in the twenty-fourth annual poll was:

> *In some nations, students attend school as many 240 days a year as compared to about 180 days in the U. S. How do you feel about extending the public school year in this community by 30 days making the school year about 210 days or 10 months long? Do you favor or oppose this idea? (p. 49)*

The percentages of responses were given for the national sample and also given were the percentages of responses to the same item for selected years going back to 1982.

The Gallup/Phi Delta Kappa Poll covers additional issues and provides a great deal of information. Since 1974, every Gallup/Phi Delta Kappa Poll has asked Americans to rate the public schools on a scale from A to F. So, in addition to current information, for some questions, patterns of results are presented across the years. Phi Delta Kappa's Center for Dissemination of Innovative Programs will provide materials on conducting community surveys (Polling Attitudes of Community on Education materials).

Conducting the Interview

As with any data-collection process, there must be preparation for conducting the interview. Interviewers must be trained in the procedures for conducting the specific interview, and these procedures must be "standardized" so that the respondents receive as consistent and identical interviews as possible. Because interviewing is demanding of time, unless a survey is very limited, multiple interviewers are used. They need to be trained, and they may need special knowledge for the survey. As with a questionnaire, the interview should be pretested and items revised until they are satisfactory. Interviewers require practice until the interviews are consistent across and within interviewers.

> Training the interviewer is a necessity. When two or more interviewers are used, the consistency in conducting the interview must be checked. In any event, an interviewee's responses should not be the function of the specific interviewer.

To schedule the interview, a mutually convenient time for the potential respondent and the interviewer must be identified. Interviewers should have flexible schedules so they are available at times convenient for the respondents. For example, if those surveyed are not available during the day, it is necessary to concentrate on evenings and weekends for the interviews.

After the interview is scheduled or initiated, it is necessary to obtain the respondent's cooperation. An advance letter informing the respondent about the study can be effective in obtaining cooperation. Such a letter is not only informative but it can reassure respondents, especially those who are concerned about their personal safety when admitting a stranger. The respondents should be informed about the purposes of the study and the importance of their contributions. Respondents should not be threatened by the interview or the subsequent use of the data. Making the respondent informed and comfortable about the interview does much to enhance cooperation.

Since the interview is a social encounter, it is important that the interviewer establish a good rapport with the respondent. The approach should be businesslike and efficient, friendly but not "chummy." Confidentiality of information should be assured, and the respondent should not be threatened by the questions. The interviewer must know the extent of probing desirable and the extent of elaboration allowed if the respondent has questions. Digressions should be avoided unless they relate directly to the items and are a part of probing for information.

The data-recording procedures used in the interview should be efficiently structured so that they do not interfere with the process of conducting the interview. A tape recorder can retain the entire oral communication, but the interviewer should get the respondent's consent before using one. If taping an interview is not practical or feasible, shorthand records of the interview must be developed. Structured questions may require only a check mark indicating one of several alternative responses, whereas responses to unstructured questions must be recorded briefly but completely, covering all main points. The recording of data should be as inconspicuous as possible and should not arouse suspicions in the respondent; for example, if a short response is given, the interviewer should not engage in extensive writing.

> The interview should be structured to obtain the necessary information efficiently in a friendly but businesslike atmosphere. If possible, there should be some accuracy checks on the responses.

Potential Sources of Error

Although the interview is well suited to probing the feelings and perceptions of the individual, the items of the interview itself do not ensure accurate measurement of those feelings. The individual must be able and willing to respond accurately with adequate oral expression; difficulties arise if the individual does not have the information necessary to answer the question or if there is an uneasy feeling about divulging the information. A tendency of the respondent to give inaccurate or incorrect information is called *response effect*. If a response effect exists, it is the difference between the actual response and the true response. The interviewer must be able to recognize misunderstanding and uneasiness and make on-the-spot decisions about any additional probing that may be desirable.

Weiss (1975) identifies potential sources of error when collecting interview data. One of these is the predisposition of the respondent to respond in a certain way, in essence producing a response effect. The respondent may lack motivation to respond, be threatened by the interview, or respond in a way perceived to put himself or herself in the best light. A respondent may give what is perceived to be a socially or professionally preferred response, regardless of his or her true feeling. There is no methodological technique that can ensure the accuracy of the data, but it may be possible to enhance truthful responses and to construct somewhat crude checks. The interviewer must be careful not to imply that there are preferable responses, and controversial questions should be avoided until the proper background and rapport have been established. In the context of the interview, the interviewer may form an opinion about whether the respondent is telling the truth, and it may be possible to construct questions that check on the consistency of responses. In so doing, the interview contains questions that ask essentially the same information, but in somewhat different form or wording, and appear at different points in the interview.

Another possible source of error is the predisposition of the interviewer toward the interviewee. Negative examples are if interviewers are ill at ease in the situation, talk down to the respondent, fail to establish rapport, or have stereotyped the interviewees. Interviewers should be selected carefully to avoid predispositions. To the extent possible, interviewers and interviewees should be matched on variables that may affect responses. For example, if the questions are such that responding to an interviewer of the opposite sex will inhibit response, then make sure that interviewer and interviewee are of the same sex.

Another possible source of error is associated with the procedures used in conducting the interview. There may be inconsistency across interviews. If the interview is too long the respondent may become bored or fatigued. The maximum length for an interview depends on the characteristics of the respondent and the intensity of interest in the interview items. A professional respondent can be interviewed for a longer period than someone from the general public. Generally, other people should not be present while the interview is being conducted. The location of the interview should be convenient and comfortable for both interviewer and respondent

> There are a number of possible sources of error in interview data: response effect of the interviewee, predispositions of the interviewer, and inconsistent or unfavorable procedures when conducting the interview.

Telephone Interviews[6]

As mentioned earlier, the telephone has received increased use in survey research within recent years, and when appropriate, it can be used effectively. The big advantage of telephone interviews over face-to-face interviews is cost—they are only about one-half to one-third as expensive. Generally, the lack of a telephone by potential respondents is no longer a problem (households in some rural areas might be an exception), and it certainly is not a problem with populations of professional respondents. However, in surveying some populations, unlisted numbers may be a problem. Sudman (1981) found that cooperation rates are about the same for telephone and face-to-face interviews, with possibly a slightly higher refusal rate for telephone than for face-to-face interviews. However, the telephone is more effective in locating hard-to-reach respondents. Quite often, professional respondents such as school personnel (teachers, principals, superintendents) are more accessible by telephone than by personal visits.

Telephone interviewing has other advantages over face-to face interviews:

1. Respondents can be sampled from a greater accessible population since travel time to individual respondents is eliminated.

2. Data collection can be centralized, and automatic data entry may be possible.

3. With the central data collection facility, monitoring for quality control is easier. Indeed, Lavrakas (1987) identifies the provision of quality control over the entire data collection process as the most important advantage of telephone surveying (p.10).

4. Data collection and data processing can be done with greater speed.

5. If in-home interviews are conducted, some potential respondents may be threatened by a visit from a stranger, while a telephone call would not be threatening.

6. If there is no answer to the call, much less time is lost than if a potential respondent does not keep an interview appointment.

Face-to-face interviews provide greater flexibility in conducting the interview and they can accommodate more complexity and length than telephone interviews. Most interviewees will tire of a telephone interview after twenty-five minutes or so, whereas face-to-face interviews can go longer without fatigue, even up to forty-five minutes to an hour. Visual cues, such as graphs and pictures can be used in face-to-face interviews. However, if the study requires respondents to react to some written material, this can be accommodated in a telephone interview by first sending the material to the respondent and then obtaining responses by telephone. Surveys that require such materials are seldom used with the general public; they are more applicable to populations of specialized professionals. Even then the researcher runs the risk that the interviewee has not received the necessary materials, or has not reviewed them.

Consider an example. Suppose a survey is being conducted of the school superintendents in a state. This is a specialized, professional population. A random sample is selected for the interview. Rather than traveling around the state conducting interviews, the superintendents selected for the sample could be sent necessary materials in advance and interviewed by telephone at mutually convenient times. The telephone interview would be less costly than a face-to-face interview.

In summarizing the comparison between telephone interviews and face-to-face interviews, Sudman (1981) concluded:

> *Response differences between phone and face-to-face procedures are small and can be ignored for most research applications. Using the appropriate methods and experienced interviewers, initial cooperation is the same on telephone and face-to-face interviews. There may be slightly higher refusal or don't know responses and shorter answers to open-ended questions on the phone because respondent suspicions may be higher while motivations to talk are not as great. (p.8)*

Thus, telephone interviews are certainly worth considering as an alternative to face-to-face interviews. They may not be quite as effective with sensitive or controversial questions, but this may be countered by the savings in effort, time, and costs.

Telephone interviews are less costly than face-to-face interviews. They can be used effectively under conditions that do not require a face-to-face encounter. There is no evidence that cooperation is greatly reduced by the telephone approach.

A Comment About Branching Items

Both questionnaire surveys and interview surveys may contain what are called "branching items." These are items which may cause the respondent to skip certain items depending upon the response. For example, in a local survey the question may be asked:

> *Do you favor extending the school year?*

The response options are yes, no, and don't know. If the response is "yes," there may be additional questions such as:

Do you favor extending it by twenty to thirty days?

If the response is "no" or "don't know," these questions would not be appropriate. If an interview is being conducted, branching items seldom cause any difficulties because the interviewer can skip to the next appropriate items. However, with a questionnaire survey the respondent must be directed explicitly about skipping items. For example:

If no, or don't know, skip to Item 16.

Even then, there is no certainty that all questionnaire respondents will skip items when they should do so. This is an example in which the quality control of data collection is better for the interview survey.

Other Surveys

Many surveys are conducted in education in which the data collection is conducted through means other than questionnaires or interviews. In these surveys, the data collection is highly "standardized" and controlled in that published tests and inventories are often used. Frequently, data are collected from what might be called "captive audiences," using intact groups such as classes. The standardized testing that occurs in many school systems in the spring of the year is an example of such a survey. Essentially, the students are surveyed to determine their achievement levels.

The measurement in surveys can take any number of forms. Standardized achievement testing was mentioned previously. Interest inventories and attitude inventories may be used. Inventories and tests may be constructed for local or regional surveys. The Ohio Statewide Testing Program for high school proficiency testing essentially is a survey of achievement in designated school subjects.

Federal and other agencies sponsor large-scale surveys including any number of variables such as achievement and attitude measures, and these surveys provide extensive data banks. The National Assessment of Educational Progress (NAEP) is a survey of American students' educational achievement. NAEP was started in 1969, and presently is being conducted biennially. For a description of the design of NAEP the reader is referred to Johnson (1992). Data banks from such surveys provide a rich source of educational research information.

> Many surveys involve the use of an available instrument such as a published test or attitude inventory. Data collection is highly structured and controlled.

Analyzing and Reporting Survey Results

Survey data can be analyzed using any appropriate procedures (data analysis is discussed in later chapters), and in many surveys at least part of the results are reported in a descriptive manner. Percentages or proportions of respondents selecting the options for an item are often provided. The results of the Gallup/Phi Delta Kappa Poll discussed earlier were reported using percentages. The percentages were broken down by numerous variables categorizing the respondents, such as by age, race, and whether or not respondents had children in school.

Because surveys often contain numerous items, the quantities of data are substantial and there needs to be some methods of data synthesis. Consider the AEL client survey, a part of which appeared in Table 7.4. The seven example items in that table (Items 23–29) comprise the subscale for the Use in Planning impact category. Although the individual items are measured on ordinal scales, it is possible to sum the scores for a subscale score. These scores could range from a minimum of 7 to a maximum of 35, the greater the score the greater the impact of AELs products and services on clients' planning. In the demographic variables part of the questionnaire, the respondent indicated state in which employed, type of employer, and professional role for which employed. These demographic variables identify different groups that were surveyed. In essence, the demographic variables can serve as independent variables for analyzing the subscale score, which is a dependent variable. Comparisons can then be made between groups, just as experimental groups, and possibly a control group, are compared in experimental and quasi-experimental research. Consider some hypothetical patterns of possible results and their interpretation.

Hypothetical Example 1

Three of the categories for professional role are teacher, central office staff (in a local education agency), and higher education professor. Suppose that the means for these three groups on the Use in Planning subscale are 28.6, 29.2, and 17.3 respectively. An analysis shows that the third mean is significantly lower than the other two, which are not significantly different. We can conclude that AELs products and services have more impact for planning in the local schools than in the teaching ranks of colleges and universities. Teachers and central office staff find about the same level of impact. There may be any number of reasons for these results. Possibly professors do not feel the need for assistance in planning. Or maybe AELs products and services for planning are better geared for local schools than for colleges and universities. There may be alternate explanations or a combination of explanations for the results.

Hypothetical Example 2

Suppose that the mean scores on the Use in Planning subscale are computed for respondents by the state in which they work: Kentucky, Tennessee, Virginia, and West Virginia, the four states served by AEL. State in which employed is now the independent variable with four categories, and score on the Use in Planning subscale remains the dependent variable. Suppose the four means are very close together, all around 25. The interpretation of this result would be that the impact on planning is consistent throughout the four-state region. Impact on planning does not seem to be affected by geographical proximity; West Virginia, where AEL is located, is no different than the more distant states.

Hypothetical Example 3

Results from individual items also can be informative. Suppose the means and standard deviations of the responses to items are computed. These are "rough" estimates of location and variability on the scale of measurement, because individual items are measured on an ordinal scale. The following results are obtained:

Item 23, mean = 4.2, standard deviation = 0.4
Item 24, mean = 2.6, standard deviation = 1.3

These results would indicate that AEL materials are used substantially more in planning, and consistently so by the small standard deviation, than does AEL provide access to other persons useful for planning. However, the large standard deviation for Item 24 responses indicates considerable variability. Apparently, some respondents did find AEL providing access to other persons useful for planning, but others found this not to be the case.

With the demographic variables, the numerous items, and the various impact category subscale scores, there are many analyses possible from a survey such as the AEL client survey. The researcher must sort through the variables and decide what analyses are most informative and useful, and meet the purposes of the survey. The reader is reminded that the examples above are hypothetical and should not be viewed as results of the actual survey.

Occasionally, it may be possible to use items or sets of items from other surveys. Items from large-scale surveys usually are well-constructed and reliable. A local school survey, for example, might use items from the Gallup/Phi Delta Kappa Poll. When this is done the analysis can include comparisons across the data sets, or the local results could be compared with the national results.

When achievement tests or attitude inventories are used in surveys, means, standard scores, and measures of variability typically are used to describe the distributions of scores. If numerous items measure a single concept or trait, scores on these items can be summarized to generate a total score. Relationships among variables can be explored, which is often the case in ex post facto research.

Survey results typically are summarized in tables including common descriptive information. The important characteristic is that the analysis and subsequent reporting of results fit the research problem. Planning for analysis and reporting should be done early in the survey, when the development of questionnaires or interviews takes place, or instruments are selected for collecting the survey data.

> Survey results typically are reported in a descriptive manner, but any appropriate analyses and subsequent reporting can be done to meet the purposes of the survey.

Summary

Survey research is undoubtedly the most widely used nonexperimental type of educational research. It is used in a variety of situations to investigate a large number of different research problems. Ex post facto research was included in this chapter because it is nonexperimental in nature, and the methodology used corresponds with that of survey research.

We often associate questionnaires and interviews with survey research, and rightly so because of their extensive use. Mailed questionnaires probably are used more than interviews because of the time and effort required for conducting interviews. However, telephone interviews are finding increased use.

Questionnaire surveys have gotten some bad press, partly because questionnaires at times are poorly constructed, and because they are susceptible to excessive nonresponse. A well-designed questionnaire survey requires several steps, from the identification of the research problem to the analysis and interpretation of the data. Careful attention to detail and using procedures to enhance response, especially conducting follow-ups, will do much to overcome the problems of a questionnaire survey.

The interview has an advantage over the questionnaire in that if the interview is granted and if the interviewer is adequately skilled, there should not be any missing or unusable data. Interviews also provide for probing and elaboration, if necessary. But interviews are costly and require the training of interviewers. Interviews must be consistent between interviewers, sometimes called interrater reliability, and within themselves. The latter is called intrarater reliability, and it is the extent to which an interviewer is consistent as he or she conducts two or more interviews. Pilot studies should be done before finalizing the items of either a questionnaire or an interview.

Survey designs were discussed; there are basically two types, longitudinal and cross-sectional. In longitudinal surveys, data are collected at two or more points over a period of time from the populations being studied. Trend, cohort, and panel designs are variations on the longitudinal survey, depending on the population studied. Cross-sectional surveys involve data collection at only one point in time, usually from two or more populations or subpopulations.

The successful completion of a survey is not a simple task. Several possible pitfalls and problems can sabotage the survey. One common problem is the failure to allow enough time and resources for the various steps. The sampling procedure can break down, or there may not be enough resources to test and revise the items adequately. The items of the interview or questionnaire may be poorly constructed, resulting in unusable data. Failure to provide for follow-ups is a very obvious but common difficulty, and inadequate procedures for assembling and tabulating the data as the questionnaires are returned are often sources of inefficiency and confusion. Failure to consider nonrespondents may bias the results and lead to unwarranted generalizations. Finally, if the researcher reports results as separate, isolated analyses without some synthesis, it is likely that the maximum information is not being obtained from the survey. Careful planning is essential for a successful survey; although such planning will not guarantee success, it will go a long way toward attaining this goal.

KEY CONCEPTS

Survey research
Survey designs
Cross-sectional designs
Longitudinal designs
Trend study
Cohort study
Panel study
Ex post facto research
Community surveys
Status surveys
Leading questions
Census

Selected-response items
Open-ended items
Pilot run
Likert scale
Cover letter
Follow-ups
Response rate
Telephone interviews
Interrater reliability
Intrarater reliability
Branching item

EXERCISES

7 1   A study of the effects of class size was conducted as a longitudinal study in Tennessee and the findings are reviewed by Pate-Bain, Achilles, Boyd-Zaharias, and McKenna (1992). The study was ex post facto in nature and included seventy-two schools throughout Tennessee. Of course, the independent variable of primary interest was class size. Without reading the report, identify possible additional independent variables and dependent variables. What is the value of conducting a study on class size as a longitudinal study? (Actually, the Tennessee study was a four-year study.) How often would data be collected on the dependent variables you identified? After completing this exercise it may be useful to compare your conceptualizations of a study with what was done in the Tennessee study.

7.2   In a liberal arts college of approximately 6000 undergraduate students, a study of student attitudes toward the general education requirement is to be conducted. The researcher is also interested in the change of attitude throughout students' college careers. One approach would be to design a longitudinal study, beginning with the present freshman class and surveying a sample of this population at four annual points. Another approach would be to use a cross-sectional design, selecting random samples from the four undergraduate class populations and surveying them at one point in time. Discuss the merits and disadvantages of the two types of designs.

7.3   Suppose that for the study of Exercise 7.2 it is decided to do a longitudinal study beginning with the freshman class. Describe how the survey would be done as a cohort study and as a panel study. Compare the advantages and disadvantages of doing the survey as a cohort study versus a panel study.

7.4   An educational products publishing firm is conducting a five-year longitudinal survey of teacher opinion and use of its products. The survey is conducted in a large city system, and a random sample of teachers is selected to serve as a panel for a panel study. Data will be collected from the panel every six months. What is to be gained by using a panel study as the longitudinal design? Discuss some disadvantages and potential difficulties of this panel study.

7.5   The director of institutional research at a college is concerned about the reasons undergraduates drop out before graduation. Each student who drops out is sent a questionnaire as soon as it is known that he or she is not returning. Construct items that might be used in this questionnaire. Would you use selected-response or open-ended items? Is nonresponse likely to be a problem? Why or why not? Suggest possible ways of following up on nonrespondents.

7.6 The department of guidance and counseling in a state department of education is planning to survey the state's secondary guidance counselors in an attempt to determine their specific professional duties and the time spent weekly on each duty. A random sample of guidance counselors will receive the three-page questionnaire by mail. Prepare a cover letter for this questionnaire. Whose signature (the position, not the individual) would you suggest for the cover letter?

7.7 Suppose that for the survey in Exercise 7.6, a random sample of one hundred guidance counselors was selected. Under what conditions would it be possible to conduct the survey by telephone? What would be the advantages of doing the survey by telephone? What would be the disadvantages?

7.8 A proficiency testing program is legislated and implemented in the schools of a state. The program provides standards of achievement for the advancement through the high school grades, and finally for graduation from high school. Proficiency must be demonstrated in selected academic subjects. A survey is to be conducted of educator perceptions and opinions about the program. There are different types of educators (teachers, principals, etc.) in the schools. A questionnaire is to be sent to a random sample of educators. Construct six or so items for the questionnaire to determine the extent of knowledge about, and acceptance of, the program. Identify possible dependent variables and independent variables, in addition to the type of educator. What comparisons among groups identified by independent variables might prove useful for policy decisions about the program?

7.9 For the survey suggested in Exercise 7.8, discuss provisions that might be made before sending the questionnaire for identifying sources of nonresponse. In this situation, what factor(s) might encourage educators to respond to the questionnaire? (Do not suggest a gratuity.)

7.10 A local school board wants to conduct a community survey of perceptions of the schools, especially as related to the curriculum, grades five through twelve, and the policies of the board relative to student issues such as the dress code. Develop ten or so items appropriate for a questionnaire survey. Would you suggest selected response or open-ended items? Who (position, not the individual) would you have sign the cover letter for the survey?

7.11 The parents of the students in a single school are to be surveyed about their opinions of a new grading system and report card. Under what conditions would you suggest a longitudinal design over a cross-sectional design, and vice versa? Assume that the school has about 350 students. Would you suggest selecting a random sample of parents or surveying the entire parent population? Why?

7.12 A health educator is designing a survey to determine the eating habits of the high school student population, in a city school system that has six high schools. Eating habits deal with factors such as what students eat and drink, and when they do so. Why would this be a difficult study to conduct as a questionnaire survey? Suppose it is decided to use an interview and a random sample of students will be interviewed. Develop three or four example questions for the interview. How would you check on the possibility of careless or dishonest response? Is such response likely to be a problem? If so, why? If not, why not?

7.13 Discuss the advantages and disadvantages of a questionnaire survey. Do the same for an interview survey, and then compare the circumstances under which each would be the preferable approach.

7.14 Review an article in the research literature that deals with a survey. Identify the research problem and review the procedures of the survey. How are the results summarized and reported? Do the conclusions seem reasonable based on the procedures and results?

NOTES

1. Many variations on random sampling and sampling designs are discussed in Chapter 11.

2. The Appalachia Educational Laboratory is a federally funded, regional educational laboratory. AEL is located in Charleston, West Virginia, and serves the four-state region of Kentucky, Tennessee, Virginia, and West Virginia.

3. For a discussion of the benefits of community surveys, the reader is referred to W. Wiersma and E. J. Nussel, "Tuning in to Your Community," *Journal of the Ohio School Boards Association,* 32(9), Nov. 1988, 22–27.

4. Surveying the constituents of an individual school usually is not recommended, especially if the questionnaire is sent from the board of education, because such a survey may imply that the school is being singled out because of problems.

5. Readers interested in more information about the client survey, the impact categories, and the content of the questionnaires may contact the Appalachia Educational Laboratory, P. O. Box 1348, Charlestown, WV 25325.

6. Many survey or polling agencies now use computer-assisted telephone interviewing (CATI) with sophisticated equipment. However, unless someone specifically is in the survey research business, CATI is not likely to be a feasible option.

REFERENCES

Borg, W. R., and Gall, M. D. (1989). *Educational research: An introduction* (5th ed.). New York: Longman.

Boser, J. A., and Clark, S. B. (1992). *Desirable mail questionnaire characteristics in teacher education research.* Paper presented at the annual meeting of the American Educational Research Association, San Francisco.

Clark, S. B., and Boser, J. A. (1989). *Seeking consensus on empirical characteristics of effective mail questionnaires: A first step.* Paper presented at the annual meeting of the American Educational Research Association, San Francisco.

Colton, D. A., and Kane, M. T. (1989). *The effect of pre-letters on survey study response rates.* Paper presented at the annual meeting of the American Educational Research Association, San Francisco.

Dillman, D. A. (1978). *Mail and telephone surveys: The total design method.* Toronto: Wiley.

Elam, S. M., Rose, L. C., and Gallup, A. M. (1992). The 24th annual Gallup/Phi Delta Kappa Poll of the public's attitudes toward the public schools. *Phi Delta Kappan,* 74(1), 41–53.

Evaluation Center (1993). *FY92 report: External evaluation of the Appalachia Educational Laboratory.* Kalamazoo, MI: Western Michigan University.

Finn, J. D., and Cox, D. (1992). Participation and withdrawal among fourth-grade pupils. *American Educational Research Journal,* 29(1), 141–162.

Hopkins, K. D., and Gullickson, A. R. (1992). *Response rates in survey research: A meta-analysis of the effects of monetary gratuities.* Paper presented at the annual meeting of the American Educational Research Association, San Francisco.

Jackson, E. E., and Schuyler, N. B. (1984). *Practice makes perfect? Skills gained in seven years of questionnaires.* Paper presented at the annual meeting of the American Educational Research Association, New Orleans.

Johnson, E. G. (1992). The design of the National Assessment of Educational Progress. *Journal of Educational Measurement,* 29(2), 95–110.

Johnson, G. A., Gips, C. J., and Rich, C. E.(1992). *"If you can't say something nice," Alternatives for dealing with survey item nonresponse.* Paper presented at the annual meeting of the American Educational Research Association, San Francisco.

Krathwohl, D. R. (1993). *Methods of educational and social science research: An integrated approach.* New York: Longman.

Lavrakas, P. J. (1987). *Telephone survey methods: Sampling, selection, and supervision.* Newbury Park, CA: Sage.

Pate-Bain, H., Achilles, C. M., Boyd-Zaharias, J., and McKenna, B. (1992). Class size does make a difference. *Phi Delta Kappan,* 74(3), 253–256.

Sudman, S. (1981). *Telephone methods in survey research: The state of the art.* Paper presented at the annual meeting of the American Educational Research Association, Los Angeles.

Taylor, B. M., Frye, B. J., and Maruyama, G. M. (1990). Time spent reading and reading growth. *American Educational Research Journal,* 27(2), 351–362.

Tollefson, N., Tracy, D. B., and Kaiser, J. (1984). *Improving response rates and response quality in educational survey research.* Paper presented at the annual meeting of the American Educational Research Association, New Orleans.

Weiss, C. H. (1975). Interviewing in evaluation research. In E. L. Struening and M. Guttentag (Eds.), *Handbook of evaluation research* (Vol. 1). Beverly Hills, CA: Sage.

Wrona, M., Sanborn, J., and Constantine, N. (1992). *Identifying dishonest and careless survey respondents.* Paper presented at the annual meeting of the American Educational Research Association, San Francisco.

Chapter **8**

_____

Research Design in
Qualitative Research

Just as with quantitative research, there are different methodologies of qualitative research, but there are common research design characteristics across different types of qualitative research. However, it should be noted that research design in qualitative research, when applied in a specific study, is less structured and generally considered to be more flexible than research design in quantitative research. This has nothing to do with whether designs are good or bad, or whether some are better than others. Research designs differ because of the context, purpose, and nature of the research.

The Epistemology of Qualitative Research

Before discussing the components of qualitative research design, it is useful to consider the epistemology of qualitative research. The dictionary[1] defines epistemology as a branch of philosophy that investigates the origin, methods, and limits of human knowledge. Essentially, when we are talking about the epistemology of qualitative research we mean underlying assumptions and basic ideas of how research is conducted. When being introduced to research methods there is a strong tendency to focus on techniques and procedures for getting the research done. This is fine, but it is important to realize that qualitative research is more than techniques, it is an approach to research which has somewhat different underpinnings than quantitative research.

Extensive descriptions can be written, and in fact are written, about the underlying epistemology of qualitative research (see for example, Lancy, 1993). For the purposes of this discussion, the major points can be summarized as follows:

1. Phenomena should be viewed holistically, and complex phenomena cannot be reduced to a few factors or partitioned into independent parts.

2. The researcher operates in a natural setting and to the extent possible should maintain an openness about what will be observed, collected, etc., in order to avoid missing something important.

3. It is the perceptions of those being studied that are important, and to the extent possible these perceptions are to be captured in order to obtain an accurate "measure" of reality.

4. A priori assumptions, and certainly a priori conclusions, are to be avoided in favor of post hoc conclusions.

5. That the "world," actually phenomena in the world, is perceived as described by Popper (1972) as cloudlike. This implies a somewhat loosely constructed model, one in which there is flexibility in prediction, for example, and one which is not run in a mechanistic manner according to a set of laws.

Of course, the points above could be elaborated, and their listing is somewhat repetitive with the discussion of qualitative research in Chapter 1. But the important point is that regardless of the specific techniques used, qualitative research has its set of underlying assumptions, its perspectives, its epistemology, if you will.

The epistemology of qualitative research provides the underpinnings for how qualitative research is conducted—how data are collected and analyzed and how conclusions are reached.

Educational research draws its content and methods from a variety of disciplines and traditions. We typically associate qualitative research with historical research and field-based research such as anthropology, and ethnography which is associated with anthropology. We often think of qualitative research as some type of unified, single approach to conducting research, but as Jacob (1987) in his review of qualitative research traditions points out, there are diverse traditions, which may be considered subdisciplines, within qualitative research. Although there is commonality across these traditions there are some differences, influenced by the purposes of the research. For the purposes of this discussion it is not necessary to categorize and describe the different subdisciplines; different writers will use differing category systems anyway. However, it is useful to define two of Jacob's (1987) identified traditions to illustrate the point about diversity. Ecological psychology and holistic ethnography are considered below.

Ecological psychology, as described by Barker (1968), is sort of the natural history component of psychology. It focuses on naturally occurring human behavior and relationships between human behavior and the environment (Schoggen, 1978, p. 33). The individual and the environment are viewed by ecological psychologists as having both subjective and objective components. Thus, in producing detailed descriptions of naturally occurring behavior, ecological psychologists are very willing to conduct quantitative analyses along with the more subjective, qualitative analyses.

Jacob (1987) describes what holistic ethnographers do as:

Holistic ethnographers seek to describe and analyze all or part of a culture or community by describing the beliefs and practices of the group studied and showing how the various parts contribute to the culture as a unified, consistent whole. (p. 10)

Culture is defined in different ways, but in a broad sense refers to what humans have learned that impacts upon behavior. The various parts of a culture are assumed to be interdependent. The culture of bounded groups are studied by holistic ethnographers. In educational research, bounded groups might be groups of specified students or teachers, for example. An educational research example of holistic ethnography was the study of an elementary school principal by Wolcott (1984).

Although qualitative research is viewed as a general approach based on its epistemology, we can identify traditions or subdisciplines which have some inherent differences related primarily to the purposes of the research.

Components of Research Design

Although there are different subdisciplines contained within qualitative research, for the purposes of this chapter, general components of qualitative research can be described. It should be kept in mind, however, that the extent to which these components apply will vary across specific research situations.

Qualitative researchers, for the most part, do research in natural settings; they do not manipulate or intervene (except possibly by their presence) in the situation. Therefore, research design requires flexibility and a tolerance for adjustment as the research progresses. Smith and Glass (1987, p. 259) refer to this as a *working design,* similar to what McMillan and Schumacher (1989, p. 179) call an *emergent design.* From the identification of the research problem, decisions must be made about beginning the study. Although the working design runs through the entire study, the components can be separated for discussion purposes, even though there is considerable overlap and integration of the research activities.

Working Design

The working design is the preliminary plan by which the research gets underway. Decisions are made about the subjects or sites to be studied, the length of time for data collection, and possible variables to be considered. For example, earlier in Chapter 2, an example research problem dealing with dropouts was stated as:

An ethnographic study of the school environment of regular and learning disabled students to determine factors related to potential dropout.

In order to pursue the research, the specific schools involved must be identified. These schools will not be selected randomly but because of their characteristics and availability. The schools are selected because they are considered typical of schools with high and average dropout rates. This is an example of *purposeful* (also called *purposive*) *sampling,* which means that the units, in this case the two schools, are selected because of their characteristics relative to the phenomenon under study, rather than being selected randomly. Decisions also would be made about whom to interview or observe, for example, students, teachers, and guidance counselors. Is the study going to require a couple of months, six months, or a school year? At least a preliminary decision needs to be made about the length of the study. Some adjustment may need to be made later, but based on the review of the literature and background information on the problem, a good estimate should be made.

The *working design* is a preliminary plan for getting the research under way.

Working Hypotheses

Qualitative research uses inductive inquiry, which for data collection means that it commences without any preconceived theories or hypotheses. However, all researchers are influenced by their own backgrounds, and some information is likely to be available about the research problems. Earlier the concept of foreshadowed problems was introduced. Although technically these are not hypotheses statements, foreshadowed problems come in at this point. Questions about the research problem may be introduced. There may be numerous questions, hypotheses, and foreshadowed problems, which may be reviewed, deleted, or extended as the data collection and analysis proceed.

Example working hypotheses from the dropout example might be:

> *As counseling sessions begin earlier and are more direct, the dropout rate decreases. What is the role of the faculty in attempting to reduce the dropout?* (question form) *Interaction of school administration and students.* (foreshadowed problem)

Data Collection

When preparing for data collection and during actual data collection the qualitative researcher deals with a host of issues, especially if data collection is done in a present situation such as with ethnographic research. The researcher must gain access to the situation, which may require special arrangements. If a researcher is conducting a study in her or his own institution, access may be automatic and data collection can be quite unobtrusive. However, for most situations the researcher needs to gain access more formally and decide on a particular role: Will the researcher be a participant-observer or simply an observer?

Data collection may be interactive or noninteractive, and these terms are what their names imply; interactive techniques involve the researcher interacting with subjects who are being studied, noninteractive techniques lack such interaction. Among the numerous methods of data collection, those most commonly used include observation, interview, collection and review of related documents, taking specimen records, and taking oral histories. Conducting an interview is an example of an interactive data collection technique. Reviewing historical documents is a noninteractive technique.

In the dropout example, the researchers might engage in the following data collection activities, although data collection certainly would not be limited to these.

1. Interview students and faculty, including guidance counselors.
2. Observe the interaction taking place between students and between students and faculty.
3. Review school records relative to factors such as grading patterns.
4. If in any way available, interview recent dropouts.

The data record of a qualitative research study can become quite massive with all the interview and observation protocols, document information, and so on. As recommended by some authors (Bogdan and Biklen, 1992), researchers should keep written accounts of their own thoughts about the data being collected. These accounts might include any possible personal bias, changes in the working design, and new hypotheses that are suggested by the data. As Smith and Glass (1987, p. 270) point out, a data record of 1000 pages or more is not unusual. Multiple copies may be useful as the researcher uses one for a chronological record and another for analysis, for example.

Methods of data collection are interactive or noninteractive depending on whether or not the researcher interacts with the subjects being studied. Observation, interview, and document collection and review are commonly used methods, and taking specimen records and oral histories are possible methods of data collection in qualitative research.

A comment about specimen records and oral histories is in order because these are not as familiar as observation, interview, and document collection. Schoggen (1978) defines a specimen record as:

A narrative description of one person, usually a child, in a natural, noncontrived situation as seen by skilled observers over a substantial time period (p. 43).

The first task is to record the stream of behavior, then the stream is divided into units and the units analyzed. Wright (1967) describes this as a three-stage process. To some extent, taking a specimen record is a special case of observation because the behavior is recorded though observation. Specimen records are most commonly used in ecological psychology, although they also apply to other qualitative research such as ethnographic studies.

Oral histories typically are interviews taken through the use of a tape recorder. This method eliminates the need for interviewer note taking, and it records the entire conversation. To the extent that any inflections in the comments and subject characteristics come through on a tape recording, these also are captured. Oral histories emphasize open-ended questions allowing the subject wide latitude in providing information. The most effective method of analyzing the interview, and certainly the most efficient, is to listen to the tape rather than to transcribe it.

Data Analysis and Interpretation

Data analysis in qualitative research begins soon after data collection begins, because the researcher checks on working hypotheses, unanticipated results, and the like. In fact, data collection and data analysis usually run together; less data are collected and more analysis is produced as the research progresses. There is considerable overlap of these steps in practice.

Qualitative data analysis requires organization of information and data reduction. The data may suggest categories for characterizing information. Comparisons can be made with initial theories or working hypotheses. Early data collection might suggest a hypothesis or theory, and then more data might be collected to support, disconfirm, or extend the hypothesis or theory. Initial descriptions of causes and consequences may be developed. Possible internal and external checks are made. All in all, analysis in qualitative research is a process of successive approximations toward an accurate description and interpretation of the phenomenon. The report of the research is descriptive in nature and contains little technical language. The emphasis is on describing the phenomenon in its context and, on that basis, interpreting the data.

Qualitative research often produces large quantities of descriptive information from field notes or interviews, for example. The information needs to be organized, and through this organization there should be data reduction. This process is called coding. The organizational part of coding can be likened to the preparation for a large rummage sale. Suppose a charity is having a large, community rummage sale of used clothing. Donations come in to a large room, for example a gym. Now the clothes need to be sorted and organized, in part to determine what is there; clothes are organized according to categories, but several categories could be used and may be used in conjunction with each other. A clothing category might include children's clothes, adolescents' clothes, and adults' clothes. These are then subdivided into boys' and girls' clothes and men's and women's clothes. Other subcategories might be dresses, slacks, blouses, etc., for women's clothes. Clothes also could be further categorized on quality or condition. So, there are any number of categories that could be used for organizing the clothes for the rummage sale. In like manner, there usually are multiple ways qualitative research data can be organized, that is, categorized. This process, deciding on one or more category systems and then organizing the data accordingly, is called coding.

> *Coding* is a process of organizing data and obtaining data reduction. In essence, it is the process by which qualitative researchers "see what they have in the data."

It may be possible in some studies to construct coding categories prior to data review, but more commonly the specific categories emerge from the data. The researcher searches for patterns of thinking or behavior, words or phrases, and events that appear with regularity or for some reason appear noteworthy. The words describing such phenomena become the coding categories. The data analysis of the dropout example would undoubtedly include categorizing the information from several faculty interviews, for example. Faculty likely would have varying perceptions of characteristics of potential dropouts, and faculty may have noted certain behavior patterns, social or academic. If, for example, three or four behavior patterns were evident these could become the categories for coding on behavior of potential dropouts.

Possible Codes.   Any number of possible codes may be used, and the coding categories become specific to the research study. The research problem and the purpose of the research influence the particular coding systems. For example, in the dropout study, teachers' perceptions of potential dropout characteristics suggest a basis for coding. Another basis would be potential dropouts' perceptions of school. A third basis would be patterns of potential dropouts' academic performance (behavior) patterns. The coding systems need not be mutually exclusive; in fact, they most likely would not be so. When perception of the subjects about how they perceive the situation is an important factor, as it is in a good bit of qualitative research, coding systems should capture these perceptions. In fact, the perceptions of the subjects about the phenomenon under study is a general code.

Setting or context codes are other general, often useful, codes. As the name implies these codes reflect the context or setting in which the phenomenon under study is observed. In the dropout example, the school environment would fit a setting code and categories might include a vocational school setting, a comprehensive high school setting, etc. Categories might also include information about factors such as the size of the school.

Another general code, which might be part of subjects' perception codes, is the subjects' perceptions of people or things. In the dropout example, potential dropouts may have different views of their teachers, and these views may differ from those of other students.

Process codes, which focus on the sequence of events and how changes occur, also can be useful. Again in the dropout example, there probably are different ways in which students go about dropping out of school. It would seem reasonable that different sequences of events would precede a learning disabled student dropping out than other students. If these processes exist, they should be captured by the data and their presence can be coded.

The above discussion by no means exhausts the possible general coding systems. The important characteristics of a coding system are: (1) the system accurately captures the information in the data relative to what is being coded, and (2) this information is useful in describing and understanding the phenomenon being studied.

> Data analysis in qualitative research is a process of categorization, description, and synthesis. Data reduction is necessary for the description and interpretation of the phenomenon under study.

The components of research design in qualitative research, which coincide closely with conducting the research, can be summarized as in Figure 8.1. It should be emphasized that the steps are highly integrated and interdependent. Qualitative research is very "researcher-dependent." For example, it has been said that for data collection the researcher is the instrument. This means that as data collection is ongoing, and during the entire research process for that matter, the researcher makes decisions about what data to

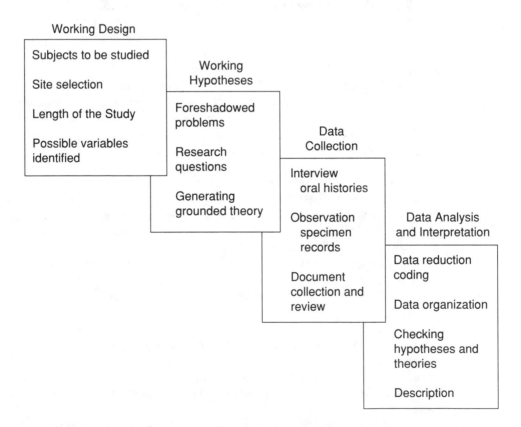

FIGURE 8.1 Components of Research Design in Qualitative Research

collect, whom to interview, and so on. Interviews and observation inventories are less structured and standardized than with quantitative research, so the researcher's perspectives are highly influential in qualitative research.

Perspectives for Qualitative Research

We have identified the components of research design primarily in terms of activities or tasks conducted during the research. Because research is a process, this is a useful way of thinking about research design. Yet, there are many different types of qualitative research studies, and with special considerations depending on the purposes and conditions of the research. Of course it is not feasible to describe each possible type in an overview chapter. However, qualitative research may be approached from two perspectives and the differences in these perspectives may be useful when considering research design. One perspective we will call the "funnel" approach, and the other, using the terminology of writers such as Bogdan and Biklen (1992), is described as "modified analytic induction." This latter approach is not quite a funnel in reverse, although when applied it does arrive at a universal explanation of some sort.

The funnel approach begins with general research questions that initiate the study. The researcher explores possible sites, subjects, sources of data, and procedures for data collection. On the basis of results from initial data collection, the groups/sites/conditions are identified more specifically, thus providing increased focus on the phenomenon under study. This process leads to more narrow data collection, concentrating on those data that reflect the specific phenomenon that has emerged. This process may be repeated, becoming more focused until the conclusions are concentrated on a specific component or a limited number of components of the study. The data collection, analysis, and interpretation has become more focused, directed or narrow, from a more general beginning.

In contrast, the modified analytic induction approach begins with more specific research problems or questions and then attempts to cover all cases of the phenomenon under study to arrive at a comprehensive, descriptive model. Data are collected on "cases," some of which fit the model, others that do not fit this initial model. There is a reformulation of the model to accommodate all cases, and more data are collected including a search for cases that do not fit this reformulated model. This process of data collection and reformulating the model is continued until a satisfactory, universal explanation is obtained of the phenomenon under study.

The funnel approach and the modified analytic induction approach are contrasted in Figure 8. 2. Note that the descriptors of the approaches deal with the focus of the research. They do not address issues such as specific data collection procedures. Observation, interviewing, etc., may be used for either approach.

> The funnel approach and the modified analytic induction approach are two contrasting ways in which we can consider the focus of qualitative research design.

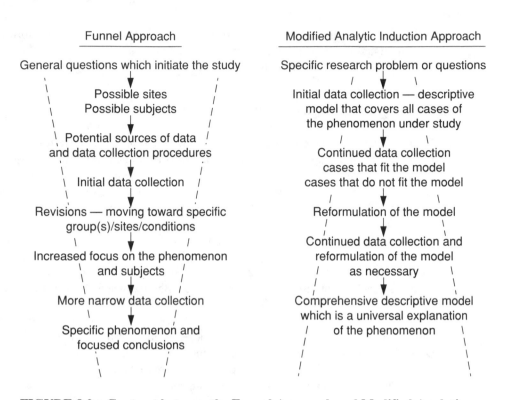

FIGURE 8.2   **Contrast between the Funnel Approach and Modified Analytic
Induction Approach**

The two approaches just described can be illustrated through examples of hypothetical but possible studies. During the 1970s and 1980s an alternative (to the self-contained classroom) instructional organization was implemented in thousands of U.S. schools, called Individually Guided Education[2] (IGE). IGE is a comprehensive instructional system involving team-teaching, multi-age grouping, and site-based management. The examples that follow are both presented in the context of IGE.

Example: Funnel Approach

Suppose it is decided to conduct research on the nature of schooling in IGE schools and three general questions to initiate the research might be:

1. What are the achievement patterns of students?
2. How do the staff, principal, teachers, aides organize for IGE instruction?
3. What are the patterns of interaction between students and teachers?

The research is being conducted in a school system that has four elementary IGE schools. These are the possible sites, and the possible subjects are the principals, teachers, aides, and students of these schools.

Data can be collected through interviews, observation, and review of student records, and other documents such as minutes of team meetings. Initial data are collected through visits to all four schools and on the basis of these visits the following revisions are made:

1. One school is selected as the site for the study because it most closely resembles the conceptual model of the IGE school.

2. The subjects to be studied are the principal, teachers, and aides—essentially these make up the group.

3. The phenomenon to be investigated is the "working" interaction between these subjects when implementing instruction.

4. The conditions under which this interaction will be studied are the instruction in reading and mathematics, the team meetings of instructional teams, and the meetings of the school-level management committee, of which the principal is the chairperson.

Now the data collection becomes more focused. Instruction, team meetings, and committee meetings are observed. The principal, teachers, and aides are interviewed. The data collected are directed to the interactions of these staff members under the conditions identified. The specific phenomenon is the interaction among the staff and the conclusions become focused on this phenomenon.

It should be noted that the revision or narrowing of the study may go through more than one step. In the interest of brevity, the example went from initial data collection, to the more narrow data collection, to the concluding focus of the study. However, this process might involve a series of successive approximations in arriving at the specific focus of the study.

Example: Modified Analytic Induction Approach

Again, consider an example in the context of an IGE school. The research question is phrased as, "What factors make for effective IGE school operation?" The researcher has available the staff and students of four elementary IGE schools. The following process is followed:

1. A teacher and the principal of one school are interviewed, in an open-ended manner, and a descriptive model developed of effective IGE school operation. The interviews concentrate heavily on the interactions of the staff, little on student activity.

2. The model from Step 1 sets the stage for interviewing the principal, two teachers, and a student from another IGE school. Some information from these interviews fits the previous model, other information does not, and the model is reformulated.

3. The researcher interviews an additional principal, six more teachers, two aides, and four additional students, some from the same two schools as in Steps 1 and 2, and some from the other two IGE schools. With each interview the model is reformulated as necessary.

4. The researcher conducts observation in all four IGE schools, the observation interspersed with conducting the interviews.

5. School records such as student achievement scores are reviewed.

6. Based on the interview and observation data, and information from the school records, the researcher obtains a descriptive model that explains in a universal manner the factors that make for effective IGE school operation. Essentially, the description is the model, and it is a comprehensive description, including for example, attention to student learning and student attitudes about school, staff attitude and morale, and procedures that enable the staff to work as a unit with a minimum of conflict.

For both examples, the question might be raised, "When has enough data been collected to bring the study to a close?" Sometimes it seems like data collection in qualitative research can go on and on. In fact, studies may require considerable time and effort, but most researchers can tell when they are reaching, or have passed, the point of data saturation. This is the point of diminishing returns for data collection, and additional data collection is not worth the time and effort. Field notes and other data may run several hundred pages, and as mentioned earlier, even over 1000 pages. When this happens, the data saturation point likely has been passed. There is no point in collecting data that will not be analyzed due to a lack of time or other resources.

Reliability and Validity of Qualitative Research

The traditional concepts of reliability and validity of research may cause some difficulties for qualitative researchers. Because qualitative research occurs in the natural setting it is extremely difficult to replicate studies. Nevertheless, a well-organized, complete persuasive presentation of procedures and results enhances external reliability. The reader should acquire an adequate understanding of the research so that a judgment can be made about its replicability within the limits of the natural context.

Internal reliability, that is, consistency in the research process, can be addressed in a number of ways. Much of qualitative research involves observation by multiple observers as at least part of data collection. Through proper training, consistency across observers can be enhanced, but there typically is some disagreement among observers. One way to obtain a measure of agreement is to complete the ratio of agreements to agreements plus disagreements. Lancy (1993) calls this concordance. Another procedure is to have a third observer analyze independently the material that is the source of disagreement. Videotapes can be especially useful for a reanalysis of data recorded thereon. If two or more researchers independently analyze the same data and arrive at similar conclusions, this is strong evidence for internal consistency.

Internal validity relies on the logical analysis of the results, as the researcher develops the description of the phenomenon under study. Because research is conducted in natural settings, often with complex phenomena, there is not the option of controlling variables, as might be the case in an experiment, for example. Verifying results and conclusions from two or more sources or perspectives enhances internal validity. As with any research, attention to detail is important for doing the research well.

Bogdan and Biklen (1992) raise the question:

Are qualitative findings generalizable? (p. 44)

Then in the ensuing discussion the answer essentially is "yes," but with qualifications, which is the position of most writers. When doing qualitative research, the researcher typically is not concerned with broad generalization of results. Rather, external validity is more concerned with the comparability of and the translatability of the research. *Comparability* refers to the extent to which the characteristics of the research are described so that other researchers may use the results to extend knowledge. *Translatability* refers to the extent to which adequate theoretical constructs and research procedures are used so that other researchers can understand the results. The case for external reliability must be argued on a logical basis. Some qualitative researchers may leave the issue of external validity to those that read the report of the study. If such is the case it should be so indicated, and of course, in order for the reader to make generalizations, the research must be well documented.

Validity of qualitative research for the most part is established on a logical basis, and providing an argument for validity requires well-documented research and a comprehensive description.

Use of Computers in Qualitative Research

The discussion of this chapter thus far has focused on how qualitative research is conceptualized and the components that describe research design in qualitative research. But qualitative research typically involves extensive descriptive data that require an intensive analysis. The analysis requires content analysis and interpretation. Characteristics, issues, and variables require categorization and coding, and as the analysis and corresponding writing proceed, they need to be retrieved and collated for summation and interpretation. Although all of this needs to be conceptualized and defined by the researcher, there are numerous mechanical tasks or phases which are part of the larger analytic process. Mechanical tasks may be likened to the "cutting and pasting" tasks of the writing process.

It is with these somewhat burdensome, mechanical tasks that computers with appropriate "software" can be helpful in analyzing large quantities of descriptive data such as field notes in ethnographic research. Software consists of the programs that instruct the computer on what is to be done. Although some of the first software that assisted in analyzing descriptive text (Stone, et al., 1966) was developed some twenty-five to thirty years ago, within recent years a number of quite sophisticated computer programs have been developed that can be helpful in conducting qualitative research.

Capabilities of Computer Software in Qualitative Research

For the qualitative researcher, it is important to recognize what it is that the computer and software packages can and cannot do. As mentioned above, computers can deal with mechanical tasks but they cannot perform the conceptual tasks requiring the traditional analytic skills of qualitative research. Computer programs are not capable of doing key tasks of interpretation, synthesis, and hypothesis testing. For example, a computer will not determine relevant codes for analyzing data. In essence, any task that requires conceptualization and systematic judgment is beyond the capability of the computer.

Of course the computer can be used for word processing in qualitative research, as it can be used when writing about any type of research. The computer can be used for organizing information, and in this way it functions as a database management system. Basically it can keep track of information that is filed and maintained. Beyond that, in general, computers are capable of searching, retrieving, manipulating, arranging, and rearranging descriptive data, that previously have been coded or in some way identified by the researcher. Computers can do these tasks quickly and efficiently. For example, computers can expedite time-consuming content analyses when directed by the researcher through the software. Content analysis might include quantifying the number of times an issue was mentioned by people being interviewed.

Computers used in qualitative research can be useful for conducting mechanical tasks such as searching and arranging descriptive data, but they cannot perform the conceptual tasks.

There are any number of available software packages or programs that can be used in qualitative research. In order to use any program it is necessary to obtain the manual or user's guide for the program, and this document also will contain a description of the requirements for use and the capabilities of the software. Comments are made below about two software programs that have been available for several years and have been used quite extensively. They are provided here as examples.

THE ETHNOGRAPH.   Originally developed by Seidel, Kjolseth, and Clark (1985), THE ETHNOGRAPH is actually a set of programs designed for a microcomputer that will assist in the analysis of descriptive, textual data. Its capabilities have been described by Seidel, Kjolseth, and Seymour (1988), and these can be summarized as:

1. Receiving and storing textual data such as field notes and interview transcripts; it will pick up textual data through a word processing program.

2. Numbering lines of text sequentially.

3. Coding any segments of data (e.g., a line) according to codes specified by the researcher.

4. Modifying or resorting based on modifications applied to codewords.

5. Searching for and retrieving coded segments of data.

6. Sorting segments of data by single or multiple combinations of codewords.

7. Counting frequencies of any number of variables and codewords as they appear in the data.

These seven tasks comprise a good bit of the work of qualitative research whether or not they are done with computer assistance. THE ETHNOGRAPH has the capability to complete tasks with speed and accuracy, especially any counting tasks, which is a definite benefit. It should be remembered that any coding system to be used, whether for THE ETHNOGRAPH or any other software, must be structured by the researcher, and programming the system for the computer may require considerable effort. For a discussion of the benefits and possible problems with the use of THE ETHNOGRAPH, the reader is referred to Tallerico (1991).

AskSam.   The acronym "askSam" stands for "Access Stored Knowledge via Symbolic Access Method." This software is available through Seaside Software, Inc., P.O. Box 1429, Perry, FL 32347, which also provides technical support and information about new product releases and upgrades. The program is considered a free-form, text-oriented, database system. "Free-form" means that few restrictions are placed on the format of the data. AskSam can perform searches on text, numbers, etc., in almost any format. The researchers can impose as little or as much formal organization on the data as they choose. Brown (1987) in his review of askSam, Version 2.3, sees this as a definite advantage. AskSam views characters, either alphabetic or numeric, as words or text. However, the program will distinguish between three types of words: (1) usual text—descriptive data, (2) numeric, and (3) calendar dates in several forms. AskSam is well documented in the manual that accompanies the program.

Using computer-assisted data analysis often is associated with ethnographic research, undoubtedly because of the preponderance of field notes and interview data collected in ethnographic research. But computer-assisted data management and analysis can be used for any area of qualitative research. Essentially, it applies whenever data consist of "textual" descriptions. As with any technology, the use of computers will be effective only to the extent that the users are knowledgeable about the software, and apply it within its capabilities.

Sources of Information about Computers in Qualitative Research

Any number of computer programs are available for use in qualitative research. New programs are being developed and existing programs are revised and updated periodically. In order to use a specific program, it is necessary to obtain the manual written for the program. Manuals typically are quite extensive and contain a lot of information, including descriptions of the requirements for, and the capabilities of, the program.

However, the manual usually is acquired when it has been decided to use a specific program. The prior step is to locate information about available programs. Computer magazines often contain information about programs and some of these are mentioned in Chapter 13 where computers are discussed in connection with statistical analysis. Software reviews appear in periodicals, some on a regular basis, others on an ad hoc basis. An example of such a review is the one cited earlier by Brown (1987).

An informative periodical that contains useful information on a continuing basis about using computers in qualitative research is *Qualitative Sociology,* published by Human Sciences Press, Inc., of New York. In fact, the Fall and Winter issues (Volume 14, Nos. 3 and 4, 1991), were devoted to computers and qualitative data as special issues. Renata Tesch was the guest editor and her introductory article (Tesch, 1991) provides a good background for the issue of using computers for analyzing qualitative data.

Books that address the issues and procedures associated with using computers in qualitative research also are available. Three such books are:

Fielding, N. G., and Lee, R. M. (Eds). (1991). *Using computers in qualitative research.* Newbury Park, CA: Sage.

Kennedy, J. J. (1992). *Analyzing qualitative research: Log-linear analysis for behavioral research.* New York: Praeger.

Tesch, R. (1990). *Qualitative research: Analysis types and software tools.* Bristol, PA: Falmer Press.

Summary

This chapter has provided an overview of research design in qualitative research.[3] Qualitative research design is not as prescriptive and structured as quantitative research design. Considerable flexibility is needed in decision making while the research is being conducted, and decisions on specifically how to proceed may be deferred to later stages of the research.

Nevertheless, general components of research design, which reflect the research activities, can be identified and described. In qualitative research there is considerable integration and overlap of these components. The discussion in this chapter described four components from an initial working design through data analysis and interpretation. Then too, two general approaches were described which showed contrasting directions that may be taken by qualitative researchers.

The chapter concludes with an overview of the use of computers when conducting qualitative research. Computer programs (software) have the capability of assisting with some of the technical tasks, especially those of analysis of descriptive data. However, software will not perform the "thinking" tasks; tasks of conceptualization and interpretation. These later tasks must be done by the researcher and these are the tasks, especially conceptualization, most directly associated with research design.

The following two chapters discuss two types of qualitative research, historical and ethnographic, in detail. Although the issue could be debated, these two types of research probably have the greatest application to education of the various types of qualitative research.

KEY CONCEPTS

Epistemology	Funnel approach
Ecological psychology	Modified analytic induction
Holistic ethnography	Data saturation
Working design	Reliability
Emergent design	Validity
Foreshadowed problems	Concordance
Specimen record	Comparability
Oral history	Translatability
Coding	Computer program—software

EXERCISES

8.1 An ethnographic research study is being designed for which the statement of the research problem is, "A study of the principal's role in school-based management at the elementary school level." Develop the working design for this problem by considering the specific decisions that can be made at this initial step of the research design.

8.2 For the research problem of Exercise 8.1, develop three or more working hypotheses. These may include foreshadowed problems and research questions.

8.3 When conducting the research of Exercise 8.1, teachers and the principal undoubtedly would be interviewed and other information would be obtained. Identify possible documents (within the school) that might be collected. What specific situations would merit observation, at least as a starting point?

8.4 A qualitative research study is to be conducted on the nature, efficiency, and effectiveness of site-based management in the schools of a large city district, one that has over seventy schools. Identify or describe each of the following:

    a. general questions to initiate the study
    b. possible sites, subjects, and potential sources of data
    c. how the funnel approach can be used to narrow the focus of this research
    d. a specific "phenomenon" that might emerge from this funnel approach

8.5 Compensatory reading programs for deficient readers in the primary grades often emphasize scores on standardized reading tests, and improvement in such scores as measures of program success. Thus, the focus tends to be on quantitative outcomes. However, the argument can be made that qualitative outcomes, for example, attitudes, motivation and the social-psychological factors of participating in the program, are of significant importance. Suppose a compensatory program is implemented in which small groups (maximum size of six) of deficient readers receive special instruction for one hour during the school day. A student participates in this instruction two times per week. In the elementary schools of a specific school system there are several of these groups. Suppose a qualitative research study is undertaken to determine the nature of the program and the way it is perceived by the students participating in it. Develop the research design, providing specifics for the four components of Figure 8.1. For example, comment on the site selection, considering that there are several groups, possible research questions, kinds of data to be collected, and how obtained, etc.

8.6 A research study is to be conducted about teachers' perceptions of an effective, fair, and appropriate model for teacher evaluation. The study will be done in a school system that has 218 teachers, grades K through 12. The teachers are the subjects of this study. Describe how the modified analytic induction approach would be used to arrive at a comprehensive descriptive model for teacher evaluation as perceived by the teachers. It would not be possible or desirable to interview all 218 teachers. Comment on issues such as how many, and specifically which teachers will be interviewed. Does the concept of grounded theory have any relevance in this situation? If so, how?

8.7 For the research study of Exercise 8.6, develop five specific research questions to get the study underway.

8.8 Select an article about a qualitative research study from a professional journal such as the *Anthropology and Education Quarterly* or the *History of Education Quarterly.* In reviewing the article, identify the specifics of the research design used for the research. How is the issue of external validity or generalizability addressed?

NOTES

1. *Random House Dictionary* (New York: Ballantine Books, 1980).

2. IGE originally was conceptualized at the R and D Center at the University of Wisconsin at Madison. There are any number of books and publications about IGE. One of the more comprehensive descriptions is found in H. J. Klausmeier, R. A. Rossmiller, and M. Saily, Eds., *Individually Guided Elementary Education: Concepts and Practices.* (New York: Academic Press, 1977).

3. For a comprehensive treatment, the reader is referred to *The Handbook of Qualitative Research in Education,* edited by M. D. LeCompte, W. L. Millroy, and J. Preissle (New York: Academic Press, 1992). This handbook contains 18 chapters and almost 900 pages. Thirty authors contributed to the handbook and these include leaders in qualitative research in education.

REFERENCES

Barker, R. G. (1968). *Ecological psychology: Concepts and methods for studying the environment of human behavior.* Stanford, CA: Stanford University Press.

Bogdan, R. C., and Biklen, S. K. (1992). *Qualitative research for education* (2nd ed.). Boston: Allyn and Bacon.

Brown, M. (1987) Software reviews. *Computers and the Humanities* (21), No. 3, 200–203.

Jacob, E. (1987). Qualitative research traditions: A review. *Review of Educational Research* (57) No. 1, 1–50.

Lancy, D. F. (1993). *Qualitative research in education: An introduction to the major traditions.* New York: Longman.

McMillan, J. H., and Schumacher, S. (1989). *Research in education: A conceptual introduction.* Glenview, IL: Scott, Foresman.

Popper, K. R. (1972). Of clouds and clocks: An approach to the problem of rationality and the freedom of man. In K. R. Popper, *Objective knowledge: An evolutionary approach.* Oxford: Clarendon Press.

Schoggen, P. (1978). Ecological psychology and mental retardation. In G. Sackett (Ed.). *Observing behavior. Vol. I. Theory and applications in mental retardation* (pp. 33–62). Baltimore, MD: University Park Press.

Seidel, J. V., Kjolseth, R., and Clark, J. A. (1985). *The Ethnograph: A users guide (Version 2.0) computer program.* Littleton, CO: Qualls Research Associates.

Seidel, J. V., Kjolseth, R., and Seymour, E. (1988). *The Ethnograph: A users Guide (Version 3.0) computer program.* Littleton, CO: Qualls Research Associates.

Smith, M. L., and Glass, G. V. (1987). *Research and evaluation in education and the social sciences.* Englewood Cliffs, NJ: Prentice-Hall.

Stone, P. J., Dunphy, D. C., Smith, M. S., and Ogilvie, D. M. (1966). *The general inquirer: A computer approach to content analysis.* Cambridge, MA: MIT Press.

Tallerico, M. (1991). Applications of qualitative analysis software: A view from the field. *Qualitative Sociology* (14) No. 3., 275–285.

Tesch, R. (1991). Introduction. *Qualitative Sociology* (14), No. 3., 225–243.

Wolcott, H. (1984). *The man in the principal's office: An ethnography.* Project Heights, IL: Waveland.

Wright, H. F. (1967). *Recording and analyzing child behavior.* New York: Harper and Row.

C h a p t e r 9

Historical Research

Historical research has been around a long time, possibly longer than most other types of research. When we think of historical research, a process of searching for, summarizing, and interpreting information from the past comes to mind. The past may be any time: as recent as within the immediately preceding year or it may go back several centuries. Specifically, historical research is a systematic process of describing, analyzing, and interpreting the past based on information from selected sources as they relate to the topic under study. Historical research is analytical in that logical induction is used by the researchers. For the most part, historical research is considered a type of qualitative research, although quantitative methods may be applied, and indeed are being used increasingly for historical research in education.

> Historical research is a systematic process of searching for the facts and then using the information to describe, analyze, and interpret the past.

Historical research may have a variety of foci. We may focus on issues, movements, and concepts in education. The history of the development of the teachers college in the United States would focus on a movement or a concept. However, we could do historical research about a specific teachers college, which would then focus on a specific institution. Biographies of educators would involve historical research. So, historical research can cover a wide spectrum as we consider past aspects of education.

Historical research deals with events of the past, for the most part those occurring in natural rather than contrived settings. The context of the event must be emphasized in its interpretation. Interpretation takes on special importance in historical research, because the events have occurred, and they occurred before the decision was made to study them. As documents were produced, such as a reporter preparing a newspaper story, interpretation was involved in preparing the document. As the researcher uses the document, interpretation again takes place.

> Interpretation is central to the research process when conducting historical research.

The historical researcher discovers data as the search is conducted through documents and other sources. This is in contrast to experimental research, for example, in which the researcher produces data. This requires the historical researcher to be especially sensitive to the existence of relevant data. It has been said that historical research is both science and art. The science part comes in the systematic process, the procedures of the research, that is used. But as Kaestle (1988a, p. 61) points out, making generalizations is more than inductive reasoning and requires creative interpretation, which invariably reflects the researcher's values and interests. So, producing historical research remains, to a large degree, subjective, and the process of historical research is primarily qualitative in nature.

The Value of Historical Research

Historical research deals with something that is over and done with, so why do it at all? The reason is that historical research in education is useful in a number of ways. Stricker (1992) discusses twelve reasons why the study of history is important and useful. Although the discussion is directed to the study of history at the high school and college levels, some of the reasons are directly relevant to the value of historical research. These reasons summarized and paraphrased are:

1. History is a storehouse of great ideas. (p. 296)
2. The past is a bulwark against contemporary confusion and overload. (p. 298)
3. Knowledge of the past is essential to understanding and judging current events and participating in current debates. (p. 302)
4. History shows what is and is not possible; thus a knowledge of history empowers, especially those with decision-making tasks. (p. 305)

Essentially, these reasons make the case that a knowledge of history, gained through historical research, can provide a perspective for decision making about educational problems, and it assists in understanding why things are as they are. Educational reform and even social reform are functions often served by historical research. Issues are often better understood—and probably better dealt with—if the historical perspective is known. Historical research can also be useful for predicting future trends. There is an old adage that those who are unfamiliar with the mistakes of history are doomed to repeat them. Thus, historical research can provide information necessary to avoid previous mistakes.

Historical research is valuable in identifying trends of the past and using such information to predict future patterns and implications for related trends. Thomas and

Moran (1992) provide an excellent example of historical research for this purpose. In their study they were testing the idea of superintendents being extremely vulnerable to myriad pressures and criticisms of various special interest groups (p. 22). They followed the career path of a single school executive from 1914 through 1922 as he served in three cities. In the conclusions section of the report the authors summarize their findings and then apply them to the educational scene today, especially with regard to the concern for school reform. In their conclusions they state:

> *Far from being weak and vulnerable, Hartwell (the superintendent whose career was followed) found strong support among like-minded, influential career super-intendents and conservative business and professional groups. . . . In the context of a period of reforms, punctuated by managerial efforts to dominate the work force, school superintendents constituted a powerful network of executives. Strengthened by their powerful school boards, they could ignore with impunity diverse interest groups, including teachers and working-class citizens demanding greater participation in the educational decision-making process. (pp. 48–49)*

Then in applying the results of their research to today's educational context;

> *The events that occurred in early 20th century St. Paul and Buffalo have important implications for contemporary superintendents. The issues and the actors remain much the same as they were in the period of progressive reforms, when superintendents gained and exercised greater control over school affairs. (pp. 49–50).*

In the remainder of their discussion they elaborate on this conclusion, recognizing changes between the 1914–1922 period and the present, and the implications of those changes for the school superintendent.

Graham (1980) argues for the contribution the study of history makes to the process of policy making. Policy making is principally concerned with two questions: "What is right?" and "What will work?" (p. 21). Answering these questions—that is, the formulation of policy—is often done through a judgment call, with the hope that a wise decision has been made. Graham concludes: "I believe that history, perhaps more than any other academic discipline, does make a valuable, though partial contribution. . . . I believe that history's contribution is two-fold: perspective and prevention" (p. 22). In this sense, the contribution of historical research to policy making is consistent with its value to informed decision making about educational issues and problems.

The value of historical research covers a wide spectrum, from providing an understanding of the past through accurate description to providing perspectives for decision making and policy formation.

Sources of Information in Historical Research

Because historical research concerns the critical evaluation and interpretation of a defined segment of the past, it is necessary to acquire some records of the period under study. The most common source is some type of written record of the past, such as books, newspapers, periodicals, diaries, letters, minutes of organizational meetings, and so on. However, written documents are not the only sources. Physical remains and objects (relics) of the past are other possible sources. Information may be orally transmitted through such media as folk songs and legends, and pictures, records, and various other audiovisual media can also serve as sources of information about the past.

When doing research of recent history, it may be possible to interview participants that actually were present for certain events. A study of school desegregation efforts and issues during the period 1950 through 1980 would be an example of historical research in which participants in relevant events could be found and interviewed about their experiences.

The sources of historical information are commonly classified as primary and secondary. A *primary source* is an original or first-hand account of the event or experience. A *secondary source* is an account that is at least once removed from the event. A court transcript of a desegregation hearing would be an example of a primary source for a study involving a desegregation problem; a newspaper editorial concerning the problem would be a secondary source. In a study including, among other things, the relationships between teachers and community members in nineteenth-century America, Clifford (1978) used teachers' written accounts of living with community families. These accounts were primary sources. A report on the same topic by another author would be a secondary source. The writings of John Dewey are primary sources of his views, whereas an interpretation by his students would be considered a secondary source.

Primary sources are first-hand accounts of the event or experience under study; *secondary sources* are accounts at least one step removed from the event or experience.

The Methodology of Historical Research

Edson (1986) came to the conclusion that "there is no single, definable method of historical inquiry" (p. 29). Kaestle (1992) supports this conclusion that historical research does not have highly developed methodology around which there is consensus, and historians are continually scavenging other disciplines for methods or theories (p. 362). Certainly, individual researchers vary in their approaches. Some search for historical information until all sources appear to be exhausted, and then begin organizing and interpreting extensive notes. Others work on a "search and write" cycle approaching the issue under study from two or more perspectives. There are any number of variations on specific procedures. Historical research tends to be a rather holistic process in which there is considerable overlap of activities. For example, interpretation runs throughout the process not only when making value judgments about the authenticity of sources but also when deciding the relevance of the sources.

Nevertheless, for the purpose of enhancing understanding of the historical research process, it is useful to describe the methodology in four steps. It is important to keep in mind that the steps may have considerable overlap, and although they can be defined, the steps tend to run together when conducting historical research.

The first step is the identification of the research problem, a typical beginning for any research study. The second and third steps are collection and evaluation of source materials and synthesis of information, respectively. These steps are closely tied together and may involve continued formulation and possible revision of hypotheses. The final step is analysis and interpretation with the formulation of conclusions. This final step includes drawing any generalizations. The four steps are diagrammed in Figure 9.1. The historical method of research is called *historiography.*

Identification of the Research Problem

The statement of the research problem may be such that hypotheses or questions are formulated along with the problem. If hypotheses are stated, they can be viewed as answers to implicit (or explicit) questions, or the problem may be stated as the purpose of the research without any explicitly stated hypotheses or questions. An example of the

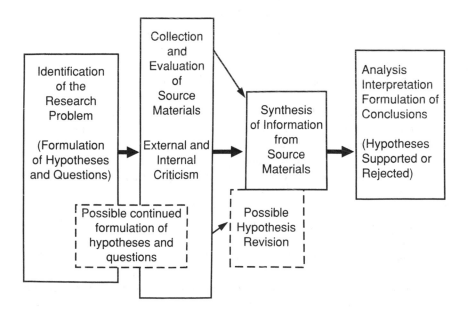

FIGURE 9.1   The Four Steps in the Methodology of Historical Research

latter is found in a study by Lewin and Hui (1989) entitled, "Rethinking Revolution: Reflections on China's 1985 Educational Reforms." This was a study of recent historical events in an attempt to enhance the understanding of the present educational scene. The purpose of the study is identified clearly in the first paragraph of the report:

> *The purpose of this paper is to give some insights into educational reforms that have developed as a result of the change in climate. It does so through a discussion of the context in which reforms have been introduced; an appraisal of factors that led to the announcement of educational reforms; a summary of key features of these reforms; and a critical analysis of their impact on the school system, on higher education and on teachers. (p. 7)*

There were no questions or hypotheses listed, but the statement of purpose implies several questions, among them:

1. *What were the reasons for the 1985 education reforms?*
2. *What were the education reforms?*
3. *What was the educational context at the time of the reforms?*
4. *What was the impact of the reforms on the school system?*

Cutler (1989), in a study of the schoolhouse in American education, listed five questions early in the report, which set the stage for the study. These questions were:

1. *When did the schoolhouse become important in American education?*
2. *Why did it become so significant?*
3. *Has it become symbolic of our national ideals?*
4. *Does it remind us of the importance we attach to either the environment or education?*
5. *Has it lived up to its promise? (p. 1, listed in order but not numbered)*

These questions were then answered and defended on the basis of historical perspective. The report includes over eighty references to sources. The use of questions is effective for organizing the content of the report and enhancing the continuity of ideas.

Nelson-Rowe (1991), in reporting on corporation schooling in the early twentieth century and the issues associated with factory-based trade education, states the purpose of the research as:

> *This essay examines these issues by focusing on the relationship between corporation schooling and the labor market in the early twentieth century United States. More specifically, it explores the labor market concerns that led employers to create such schools, the effects the schools had on the occupational outcomes and wage earnings of graduates, and the extent to which the schools met the needs of the sponsoring companies. (p. 30)*

The content of the report focuses on these issues, presenting the evidence and then drawing conclusions from the evidence. Forty-three footnotes provide the references for the research.

When hypotheses are stated, they usually are not stated in a statistical sense, although statistical information from the past could be used to support or refute hypotheses. Rather, in historical research, hypotheses are conjectures about the characteristics, causes, or effects of the situation, issue, or phenomenon under study.

Suppose a study is being conducted on the decline of the humanistic curriculum during the seventeenth and eighteenth centuries. Undoubtedly this decline was due to a combination of factors. One hypothesis might be that the elevation of the common person and his or her vernacular through the industrial revolution reduced the importance of the humanities as an avenue to culture. A second hypothesis might be that the advances of science made unwelcome inroads into the curriculum, and this was detrimental to the humanities.

It should be noted that these hypotheses rest on an assumption of fact—that is, that the humanistic curriculum did decline during this period. If this assumption were not correct, the hypotheses would have no basis. Having established any necessary assumptions (or facts) and stated the hypotheses, the researcher would then set out to assemble the necessary information to confirm or refute the hypotheses. In the foregoing example, when dealing with the initial hypotheses, the researcher would look for increased use of the common vernacular in the curriculum materials of the period. Different avenues to culture that developed during the period of the relationships between these and the humanities could be investigated. On the basis of the evidence, the hypothesis could be retained or discarded.

Another example would be a study of the historical development of professional education in the United States, specifically as it relates to secondary teachers. Undoubtedly, there would be several hypotheses; one might be that the teachers' college developed as an outgrowth of the normal school, due primarily to the inadequate supply of teachers produced by the colleges and universities. The researcher would then collect evidence about the various possible factors that influenced the development of the teachers college. Information would be needed about the supply and demand of secondary teachers and how this was related to the numbers of teachers produced by colleges and universities. The hypothesis is based on the assumption that the teachers' college was an outgrowth of the normal school and considers the inadequate supply not only as a factor, but as the primary factor.

The matter of basing hypotheses on accurate assumptions may seem obvious, but failure to do so can occur, and a false assumption is almost certain to lead to an erroneous conclusion. For example, in the late nineteenth century, many liberal arts colleges took the position that it was unwarranted to grant a baccalaureate to graduates of professional schools. This position was based on the assumption that it was not in the tradition of higher education to award bachelor's degrees for the profession of education. Careful historical research would have revealed that the arts degree of the medieval university originated almost exclusively for teaching purposes.

Kaestle (1988b) identifies four pervasive methodological concerns and one of these, the problem of defining key terms, applies to the identification of the research problem. Some terms generally have vague meanings and this can be a pitfall in discussions and conclusions if terms are not defined more specifically. The term educational reform has been around a long time, and it is almost always in vogue, but in any given context, its meaning must be specified.

A second potential difficulty with key terms is what Kaestle (1988b) calls presentism, described as:

> *the danger of investing key terms from the past with their present connotations, or conversely, applying to past developments present-day terms that did not exist or meant something else at the time. (p. 41)*

It could be argued that competency-based education, and correspondingly competency testing have been around for some time. But these terms may not have been used until relatively recently, and over the years the operational meanings likely would have changed had the terms been used.

When identifying the research problem, and throughout reporting the research, it is important to avoid vague and inconsistent use of key terms.

Collection and Evaluation of Source Materials

The collection of source material does not consist of simply assembling all available documents that appear to have some relevance to the research problem. A basic rule of historical research is to use primary sources whenever it is possible to locate them. The researcher must decide which are primary and which are secondary sources. This requires an analysis of the sources.

External Criticism.   Source materials must be subjected to *external criticism,* the tool for establishing the validity of the document. The question to be answered is: Is the document genuine, authentic, and what it seems to be?

External criticism in historical research evaluates the validity of the document—that is, where, when, and by whom it was produced.

Establishing the validity of materials involves several possible factors, any of which could make the document invalid. With written material, the status of the author in the context of the event is important. Was the author an on-the-spot observer, if the document appears to be a primary source? Are factors such as time and place consistent with what is known about the event?

Because the practice of using ghost writers is common, a document that appears to be the product of a direct observer may in fact be a secondary source. The ghost writer's unique contributions may inadvertently or deliberately threaten the validity of the document, and there also are possibilities of inadvertent mechanical errors. A word may be mistranslated or an error made in typing or transcribing documents. For source materials produced before the advent of printing, copy errors in reproduced documents are not unusual. Printing has not eliminated the possibility of such errors, but it has reduced their likelihood.

Internal Criticism. The second part of critical evaluation is *internal criticism,* which establishes the meaning of the material along with its trustworthiness. There may be some overlap between external and internal criticism, but the shift in emphasis is from the actual material as a source to the content of the material. To some extent, external criticism precedes internal criticism in the sequence, since there is little point in dealing with the content of the material if its authenticity is doubtful. However, consider the external criticism directed toward the author of what appears to be a historical document. In establishing the author's status, it may very well be necessary to evaluate some of the content. This essentially becomes internal criticism.

Internal criticism in historical research evaluates the meaning, accuracy, and trustworthiness of the content of the document.

The author is an important factor in evaluating the content of a document as well as in establishing the authenticity of the document. A pertinent question of internal criticism is whether the author was predisposed, because of position or otherwise, to present a biased rather than an objective account. Biographies and autobiographies may tend to shift the emphasis from the event to the person. Fictitious details may be included by the author because of some personal factor. An author who was opposed to an existing educational policy might have emphasized different factors than one who was favorable toward the same policy at the same time. For these kinds of situations, the position or status of the author is very important in ascribing meaning to the content.

An analysis of the author's style and use of rhetoric is important for internal criticism. Does the author have a tendency to color the writings by eloquent but misleading phrases? Is part of the writing figurative rather than a record of the real event? If the question of figurative and real meaning arises, the researcher must be able to distinguish between the two. Does the author borrow heavily from documents already in existence at the time of his or her writing? If so, is the document an objective restatement of the facts, or do the author's own interpretations come into the writings? The latter is more likely the case. The researcher should check the reporting of the author for consistency with the earlier sources. This process should also give indications of the separation of fact and interpretation.

The concern for accuracy is basic to all internal criticism (as well as external criticism). There are two parts to the question of the accuracy of a specific author: Was the author competent to give an accurate report and, if competent, was he or she predisposed to do so? A competent reporter may, for some reason, give a distorted account of an event. In checking several authors, there may be inconsistencies even about such facts as the date of a specific event. In such a case, the researcher must weigh the evidence and decide which account is more accurate.

A single document, even a primary source, can seldom stand on its own. Internal criticism involves considerable cross-referencing of several documents. If certain facts are omitted from an account, this should not be interpreted to mean that the author was unaware of them or that they did not occur. Each document should be evaluated in its chronological position—that is, in the light of the documents that preceded it, not in the light of documents that appeared later. If several sources contain the same errors, they are likely to have originated from a common erroneous source. If two sources are contradictory, it is certain that at least one is in error, but it is also possible that both are in error. The discounting of one account does not establish the trustworthiness of another. A specific document may prove valuable for certain parts of the overall research problem and essentially useless for other parts.

Both external and internal criticism are necessary for establishing the credibility and usefulness of the source. If the source is not authentic, it cannot be used. Even if it is authentic, if its content is not relevant to the research problem, it would be useless. The functions of external and internal criticism are summarized in Figure 9. 2.

Synthesis of Information

Internal criticism carries over into the third step of the methodology—synthesis of the information. The materials have now been reviewed and their authenticity established, at

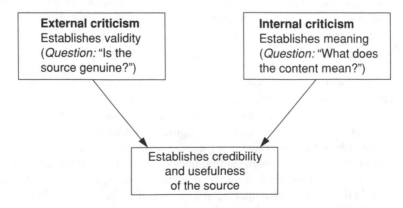

FIGURE 9.2 External and Internal Criticism in the Evaluation of Source Materials for Historical Research

least to the satisfaction of the researcher. The relative value of the various sources must be considered. For example, a primary source may be considered more important than a secondary one. If contradictory accounts appear, the inconsistencies must be resolved, which may require developing a case for discounting one version of the event.

Central ideas or concepts must be pulled together and continuity between them developed. If a substantial period of time—say, several years—is covered by the research study, the ideas often can be organized chronologically. In fact, chronological ordering commonly is required to avoid confusion between possible cause and effect among events. Several accounts of the same event may be included in the source materials. If the accounts are consistent, they provide historical support, and the researcher can summarize the information from these accounts with respect to the point being made.

As the researcher reviews the source materials and synthesizes the information from them, it may be necessary to formulate additional hypotheses or revise initial ones. Evidence may appear that refutes initial hypotheses; unanticipated information may support new hypotheses; and the materials also may generate new questions relevant to the research problem. If hypotheses and questions are not included but the research proceeds from a statement of purpose, it may be advantageous to introduce hypotheses when synthesizing the information. In any event, hypotheses should be introduced when they prove useful, especially as they provide direction for the research and assist in synthesizing information.

Analysis, Interpretation, and Formulating Conclusions

The final step of historical research methodology is characterized by decision making about the research problem. Historical research relies heavily on a logical analysis of the information from the documents. At the final step, the conclusions are formulated, and any hypotheses introduced earlier are either supported or rejected. Of course, it is necessary to make interpretations of the information, and the researcher should recognize the possibility of alternative explanations of the results if such explanations are reasonable. A case should be made for the most likely interpretation, but if other possible interpretations exist, they should at least be recognized. For all interpretations, the author should remain as objective as possible.

Earlier it was mentioned that Kaestle (1988b) identified four methodological problems and one of those primarily was associated with the identification of the research problem. The other three are most directly associated with interpretations and conclusions. They are:

1. Confusion of correlations (or associations) and causes.
2. A lack of distinction between ideas about how people should behave, and how ordinary people in fact behaved.
3. Failure to distinguish between intent and consequences. (pp. 40–41, paraphrased and numbered)

The first problem often is associated with quantitative research, that of interpreting an association or correlation between two variables, as a cause-and-effect relationship. There may be such a relationship, but the simple fact of association does not establish such a relationship.

Evidence about how people actually behaved may be lacking in historical documents. If during a certain period substantial legislation was passed, it cannot be inferred that people were pleased with the laws or even that they obeyed them.

We tend to think that knowing how things turned out gives hindsight a definite advantage over foresight. This may be so, but there may be danger in ascribing consequences to deliberate intentions. For school reforms of the past that have failed, it would be tenuous to conclude that failure was due to the deliberate intentions of educators. Many times other factors, over which educators have little or no control, contribute to failure and change. Also, in many situations, people may not have been aware of potential consequences of their actions.

Historical researchers cannot eliminate all potential difficulties in analysis and interpretation. However, researchers should be aware of potential problems and take these into consideration when interpreting results and drawing conclusions.

It is not practical to include here an entire conclusions section of a historical research report. These sections tend to be lengthy narratives, sometimes having the conclusions interspersed throughout the report. Occasionally, authors will not use headings within the report, although conclusions can be identified in the narrative.

As an example of conclusions from a historical research study, excerpts are taken from the report by Thomas and Moran (1992). This study was cited earlier in the chapter for applying results of the study to today's educational context. Additional conclusions from the study were:

> *Developments in St. Paul and Buffalo symbolize how conflicts may emerge during periods of reform as one group, seeking to enlarge its powers, enfeebles another group in its simultaneous bid for control. (p. 48)*

> *Hartwell and fellow superintendents claimed the need to depoliticize school governance. He called for a united front between his office and the teachers. Yet, he and many of his administrative cohorts throughout the country seized control of the schools and those who worked in them. (p. 49)*

> *Superintendents did not sympathize with the teachers' sense of deprivation when they removed the teachers from the center of power. Following a business model that made few allowances for democracy in decision-making procedures, superintendents called for stricter disciplinary measures against those who challenged their authority. (p. 49)*

Then after describing similarities and differences in school control between the early twentieth century and today, the authors conclude:

> *Participant and team management is the new coinage of the day in school administration. The new superintendent, whether place- or career-bound, will need to be schooled in effective leadership and community relations that forge consensus rather than divisions. (p. 50)*

The conclusions section consisted of five paragraphs which covered over two pages. This report is an excellent example of historical research reporting. Concepts are well-developed and the report has extensive documentation. There are 115 references in footnotes, many referencing newspaper articles published during the 1914–1922 period.

Quantitative Methods in Historical Research

As was mentioned earlier, historical research is usually considered a type of qualitative research, but quantitative methods may apply also. Indeed, within recent years there has been an increased use of quantitative methods, motivated in part by the availability of computers for summarizing and quantifying data. Historical research in education enables us to get in touch with the realities of schooling in the past and Kaestle (1988a) identifies this as the "great virtue of quantitative educational history." (p. 65) The description aids in learning about factors such as teacher supply and demand, the role of schooling across communities, and the impact of schooling on the individual. Quantitative methods help provide a description of the realities of schooling in the past.

Teese (1989), in a study of Australian public high schools, collected enrollment data from every post-primary school in the state of Victoria for the period 1946 through 1985. Then, in reporting the data, graphs were used in plotting completion rates across the years in percentages. Descriptive statistics such as percentages, proportions, and means are sometimes computed, but more sophisticated quantitative techniques can be used. Perlmann and Margo (1989) suggest using regression analysis in estimating the economic returns for teachers from their educational attainment.

Sometimes the volume of data from the past is such that sampling is necessary. In a study reported by Ringer (1978), a random sample of entries was selected from major biographical encyclopedias for Germany, France, England, and the United States. The entries were those for males born between 1810 and 1899 who might have reached advanced educational institutions between 1830 and 1930. Perlmann and Margo (1989), in their study "Who Were America's Teachers?" used two-stage, random sampling. At the first stage, they selected a 50 percent sample of census microfilm reels in 1860 and 1880. Then, at the second stage, they selected sets of pages from each reel. So, random sampling can be used effectively in order to keep the quantity of data manageable.

> Historical research is viewed primarily as qualitative in nature, but quantitative methods may be used effectively for some studies, especially those involving data sets (such as census data) that can be made machine-readable for computers.

Comments on the Reporting of Historical Research

In contrast to the reports of experimental or survey studies, which typically include generally accepted headings, reports of historical research commonly take the form of an unbroken narrative. For reporting historical research, it is often easier to enhance the continuity of ideas by not dividing the report. The research problem is usually identified early in the report, with a supporting context. Hypotheses or questions may be included, or a proposition (which is basically a hypothesis) may be presented that will be supported or refuted. Then the evidence is provided, synthesizing information from several sources. Finally, conclusions are presented, based on the evidence.

Reports in Professional Journals

A number of professional journals devote at least part of their space to reports of historical research. The most obvious journal for reports of historical research in education is the *History of Education Quarterly,* published by the History of Education Society. Numerous other journals publish reports of historical research, although they are not limited to this area. These journals include:

> *Educational Studies,* published by the American Educational Studies Association
>
> *Comparative Education,* published by the World Council of Comparative Education Societies
>
> *Comparative Education Review,* published by the University of Chicago Press
>
> *Harvard Education Review,* published by Harvard University Press
>
> *American Educational Research Journal,* published by the American Educational Research Association.

There are journals that are not specifically oriented to education, but do report historical research and include some educational studies. These journals include:

> *Historical Research,* published by the Institute of Historical Research (an institute in the University of London's Centre for Postgraduate Studies in History)
>
> *The Historical Journal,* published by the Cambridge University Press
>
> *History,* published by the Historical Association
>
> *Historical Methods,* published by HELDREF Publications and edited by the Department of History of the University of Illinois at Chicago.

The latter entry is identified as a journal of quantitative and interdisciplinary history.

Although it may be useful to illustrate some points from a research literature example, it is not necessary to reproduce an entire report from one of the professional journals. In a study entitled, "The English-Only Effort, the Anti-Japanese Campaign, and Language Acquisition in the Education of Japanese Americans in Hawaii, 1915–40," Tamura (1993), states the purpose of the study as:

> *This essay will show that the English-only effort in Hawaii, despite what its supporters said publicly, had little to do with language. Rather it was essentially an anti-Japanese drive, targeting the Japanese language and the Nisei-children*

of Japanese immigrants—while disregarding other non-English languages and the children of other immigrants. (p. 38)

The author then provides the historical record of immigration into Hawaii, with its large Japanese influx, and documents the origin and progression of the Americanization campaign. Issues such as attempts to reduce and even eliminate non-English language publications are discussed.

In the early part of the twentieth century, Nisei attended regular schools during the day, and after school, Japanese language schools. Organized opposition to these schools began around 1920, and the court battles that ensued are documented, both those in Hawaii and in other states. There is an extended discussion of the educational history, its conflicts and effects, upon the language acquisition of the Nisei. The interpretation of the events during this period focuses on other issues dealing with race and culture, rather than language alone, which motivated the Americanization campaign.

Student (Nisei's) lack of motivation to be fluent in Japanese supported the efforts to eliminate its use. However, the case is made that educators' lack of knowledge about a complex issue, and the cultural and social factors that were operating at the time, made the schools rather ineffective in promoting the Americanization campaign. In conclusion, Tamura writes:

> *This lack of effectiveness in influencing language acquisition combined with an anti-Japanese drive to produce a language policy that lacked clear focus. As a result, the English-only effort in Hawaii existed nominally rather than substantially, and had minimal if any impact on language use. (p. 58)*

The report contains fifty-seven references in footnotes and these references include a variety of sources. The court cases associated with the issue are documented. Newspapers and periodicals are cited, some from the period under consideration and others from a later period that contained information and commentary relevant to the issue under study. Numerous other sources, including secondary sources are cited. These sources are from writers who have written on the issue under study, or on related issues.

Reports of historical research in professional journals often tend to be somewhat longer than those of experiments or surveys, because historical research requires information from numerous sources that must be included with considerable detail. The information cannot simply be referred to and stated in a sentence or two. Historical research studies usually cover periods of several years (or longer) or deal with issues that involve considerable information. Using all of this information effectively, with good continuity of ideas, tends to increase the length of the report. The number of references cited in a historical research report tends to be quite large, in some cases over one hundred in a report of thirty pages or so in a professional journal.

Summary

Historical research, like any type of research, has some unique characteristics. Because historical research deals with events that have already happened, the historical researcher searches for data rather than producing data. The variables of the past have occurred; they are not subject to manipulation.

Educational research problems investigated by historical research can cover a variety of areas: general educational history, the history of an issue, the history of educational legislation, institutional history, and many others. In some manner, the problems generally deal with either policy or practices, and the nature of history and historical inquiry places this limitation on historical research. In a certain sense, the problems investigated by historical research have an ongoing characteristic. Many important educational issues are initially dealt with by relying on the perspective supplied by the history of the issue. Curriculum change often is viewed in the light of past philosophy, ideas, developments, and curriculums, and historical research is necessary to define the situation of the past and its meaning in the light of the present problem. Interpretations based on historical research thus can aid in defining a course of action for dealing with a present educational problem.

Historical research follows a systematic process called historiography, from the identification of the research problem through the formulation of conclusions. The process is quite integrated, characterized by a synthesis of information from the source materials. Internal and external criticism are used to establish the validity of source materials. In summary, historical research is a systematic process of reconstructing what happened and interpreting the meaning of events.

As with any period, there presently are many educational issues before the profession and before the public. Historical research in education can provide a perspective for issues, including information that can be used to avoid mistakes. The study of educational trends of the past may be useful for predicting similar or related trends for the future. Policy makers at any level in education can benefit from the contributions of historical research in arriving at decisions.

KEY CONCEPTS

Critical inquiry	External criticism
Source materials	Internal criticism
Primary source	Policy making
Secondary source	Historiography

EXERCISES

9.1 Select an article from a professional journal that reports on a historical research study. Review the article carefully, focusing on the author's procedures for collecting information. Consider such things as whether or not primary sources were used. Is there an adequate continuity between ideas? Did the author use hypotheses, either explicitly stated or implicit in the statement of the research problem? If so, what are they? Did the evidence used in making decisions about the research problems (or hypotheses) seem adequate?

9.2 For each of the following examples, indicate what type of research is most likely called for: experimental, survey, or historical:

a. An indicator of the likelihood of passing a school district's bond proposal.

b. The effects of drill exercises on the development of computation skills in arithmetic.

c. The basis for the age-graded school.

d. The relationship between psychomotor skills and achievement in academic success.

e. Precedents for the establishment of a dress code.

f. The effect of attitude toward school on achievement in science.

g. The attitude toward school of students enrolled in science courses.

9.3 Suppose you are interested in the history of requirements for graduation from elementary school that involved passing a common test of some kind. The period to be covered is 1900 to 1940, and the history within a single state is being studied. To some extent, this is a study of proficiency testing of the past, although it probably did not go by that name. What sources would you use for information? What are possible primary and secondary sources? Would there be any merit in reviewing educational legislation passed at the state level during the period?

9.4 Identify three or four educational key terms that might be susceptible to a problem of definition when considering these meanings today and what they meant fifty or seventy-five years ago. Are the difficulties in definition due to vagueness or presentism?

9.5 Suppose historical research is being done on the history of teachers' unions during the early days of their formation. Identify possible situations in which there may be problems making a distinction between how we interpret people may have behaved and how they actually did behave. Would research in this area be susceptible to possible confusion between intent and consequences? If so, how?

9.6 Review an article from a professional journal, such as *Historical Methods,* that involves the use of quantitative methods. Identify the methods used and note how they are used to support the conclusions of the study.

REFERENCES

Clifford, G. J. (1978). Home and school in 19th century America: Some personal history reports from the United States. *History of Education Quarterly,* 18(1), 3–34.

Cutler, W. W., III (1989). Cathedral of culture: The schoolhouse in American educational thought and practice since 1820. *History of Education Quarterly,* 29(1), 1–40.

Edson, C. H. (1986). Our past and present: Historical inquiry in education. *Journal of Thought,* 21(3), 13–27.

Graham, P. A. (1980). Historians as policy makers. *Educational Researcher,* 9(11), 21–24.

Kaestle, C. F. (1988a). Recent methodological developments in the history of American education. In R. M. Jaeger (Ed.), *Complementary methods for research in education* (pp. 61–78). Washington, DC: American Educational Research Association.

Kaestle, C. F. (1988b). Research methodology: Historical methods. In J. P. Keeves, (Ed.), *Educational Research: Methodology and measurement: An international handbook.* (pp. 37–42). Oxford: Pergamon.

Kaestle, C. F. (1992). Standards of evidence in historical research. *History of Education Quarterly,* 32(3), 361–366.

Lewin, K., and Hui, X. (1989). Rethinking revolution: Reflections on China's 1985 educational reforms. *Comparative Education,* 25(1), 7–17.

Nelson-Rowe, S. (1991). Corporation schooling and the labor market at General Electric. *History of Education Quarterly,* 31(1), 27–46.

Perlmann, J., and Margo, R. (1989). Who were America's teachers? Toward a social history and a data archive. *Historical Methods,* 22(2), 68–73.

Ringer, F. K. (1978). The education of elites in modern Europe. *History of Education Quarterly,* 18(2), 159–172.

Stricker, F. (1992). Why history? Thinking about the uses of the past. *History Teacher,* 25(3), 293–312.

Tamura, E. H. (1993). The English-only effort, the anti-Japanese campaign, and language acquisition in the education of Japanese Americans in Hawaii, 1915–40. *History of Education Quarterly,* 33(1), 37–58.

Teese, R. (1989). Gender and class in the transformation of the public high school in Melbourne, 1946–85. *History of Education Quarterly,* 29(2), 237–259.

Thomas, W. B., and Moran, K. J. (1992). Reconsidering the power of the superintendent in the progressive period. *American Educational Research Journal,* 29(1), 22–50.

Chapter 10

Ethnographic Research

Ethnographic research, which traditionally is associated with anthropology, has been around for a long time. Within the past two or three decades, ethnographic research in the educational context has been receiving increased attention. Undoubtedly, this is in part due to the increased acceptance of, and the increased interest in, qualitative research. Another contributing factor to the interest in ethnographic research has been the realization that there may be problems in education that can best be attacked, and possibly only can be attacked, through an ethnographic research approach. Ethnographic research sometimes goes by other names, such as *field research* or *qualitative research*. Although these terms are to some extent descriptive of ethnographic research, they are not synonymous with it. In this chapter, the nature of ethnographic research is discussed, along with procedures used in ethnographic studies. Also discussed are examples of educational research using ethnographic methodology.

The Nature of Ethnography in Education

The term *ethnography* refers both to a research process and the product of that process. The product is a written account, that is, the ethnography of what was studied. The term *ethnography* comes to us from anthropology. The *Random House Dictionary of the English Language* defines *ethnography* as "a branch of anthropology dealing with the scientific description of individual cultures." Anthropology is considered a science—specifically, the science that deals with the origins, development, and characteristics of humankind, including such factors as social customs, beliefs, and cultural development.

If we project this definition of ethnography into educational research, we can describe the ethnographic research process as:

The process of providing holistic and scientific descriptions of educational systems, processes, and phenomena within their specific contexts.

This is a broad definition, which is necessary because ethnographic research is applied in a variety of situations. As Wolcott (1988, p. 191) points out, "no particular research technique is associated exclusively with ethnography." Numerous research procedures are used in ethnographic research, and these can be described, but by themselves these techniques will not produce the desired product: the ethnography of what is under study. Ethnographic research is an inquiry process guided by experience in the research setting.

Although ethnographic research may at times involve quantitative procedures, it is considered a part of qualitative research. As such, its epistemology, that is, its origins and methods, is based in the epistemology of qualitative research. This topic was discussed in Chapter 8, and the underlying assumptions and basic ideas about how research is conducted of the qualitative epistemology applies to ethnographic research.

The Phenomenological Nature

Phenomenology is the study of phenomena; it stresses the careful description of phenomena from the perspective of those experiencing the phenomena. Phenomenologists do not assume that they know what things mean to the people they are observing. If behavior is being observed, the phenomenologist does not simply note that a certain behavior has occurred, but attempts to understand what the behavior means to the persons being studied, and this emphasizes the subjective aspects of the behavior.

Because ethnographic research is phenomenological in nature, it takes on the characteristics of that approach to research. These characteristics include the holistic and naturalistic nature of ethnographic research discussed below, so these characteristics overlap and are separated here only for emphasis. Essentially, the phenomenological approach is based on the concept that reality consists of the meaning of experiences by those being studied. For example, a good case can be made for the position that research on instruction in the schools should, at least in part, be ethnographic research. Consider fourth-grade mathematics instruction. The important focus for the phenomenological approach is to understand what mathematics instruction means—how it is perceived—by the fourth-grade students experiencing such instruction. There is little importance placed on what the educator thinks is going on; the importance is on understanding what the students are experiencing from their perspectives.

> The phenomenological approach emphasizes that the meaning of reality is, in essence, in the "eyes and minds of the beholders," the way the individuals being studied perceive their experiences.

The phenomenological nature of ethnographic research has certain implications for how research is conducted, and these can be listed as:

1. As much as possible, a priori assumptions about the phenomenon under study are avoided.
2. Reality is viewed holistically and complex phenomena are not reduced to a few variables.
3. Data collection procedures and instruments, although having some structure, should have minimum influence on the phenomena under study.
4. There is an openness to alternative explanations of the phenomenon, which may lead to alternative and changing concepts of reality.
5. Theory, as applicable, should emerge from the data as grounded theory rather than preconceived theories.

With regard to this latter characteristic, Lancy (1993) provides an excellent example of the emergence of grounded theory. In a study of parental influence on children's storybook reading, thirty-two parent-child pairs were videotaped as they read to each other. The process of identifying or developing grounded theory is summarized by:

> *We had few if any preconceptions of what we would find, only that we hoped that distinct patterns would emerge and that these would be associated with the children's evident ease/difficulty in learning to read. I spent literally dozens of hours viewing these videotapes: developing, using and casting aside various categories until I found two clusters of characteristics, which I called "reductionist" and "expansionist," which accounted for a large portion of the variation among parents' reading/listening styles. (p. 10)*

Thus, grounded theory is generated from the data, and developing grounded theory requires insight and understanding, and may require repetitive review of the data. Typically, this is not an easy task. Grounded theory does not lie like nuggets on the surface; it may require difficult extraction.

The Naturalistic Nature

Ethnographic research is conducted in a natural setting: a classroom, a school, a college, or some naturally occurring assembly of individuals. The researcher observes what is happening as it naturally occurs; there is no manipulation of variables, simulation, or externally imposed structure on the situation. Thus, ethnographic research is characterized as field research, with the "field" being the natural situation in which the research is conducted. For example, in an ethnographic study of social interaction among students in an integrated school, it would be necessary to observe student behavior in the school. The information could not be limited to teachers' opinion, and any social psychology theory that might apply should be grounded in the data.

Related to ethnographic research is the characteristic of *contextualization,* which requires that all data be interpreted only in the context of the situation or environment in which they were collected. Although all of educational research has a contextual emphasis to some extent, ethnographic research is probably more sensitive to context than other approaches. This has implications for the generalizability of research results. Ethnographic researchers often are not concerned about generalizability; to them, accurate and adequate description of the situation being studied is paramount. Of course, generalizability of results depends on the correspondence between the context under study and other situations.

Ethnographic research involves *field research* and requires *contextualization*—the interpretation of results in the context of the data collection.

The Holistic and General Perspective

Experimentation and survey research traditionally involve a priori hypothesis formation, followed by specific procedures designed to test hypotheses. In contrast, ethnographic research proceeds from the position that hypotheses may emerge as the data collection occurs. The implication for data analysis is that it will be inductive, rather than deductive, which typically concentrates on testing preconceived hypotheses. The ethnographic researcher attempts to suspend any preconceived ideas or notions that might undesirably influence the interpretation of what is being observed. The researcher concentrates on the entire context and thus maintains a holistic view, rather than focusing on bits and pieces. If hypotheses emerge from the data collection, they are retained for the time being, but an ethnographic researcher is willing to abandon tentative hypotheses if subsequent data collection fails to support them. The results of prior research also are held in abeyance until the researcher is convinced of their relevance to the research situation at hand.

Ethnographic research takes a general and holistic perspective. Hypotheses are more likely to emerge from the data than to be formulated prior to the research.

Given these characteristics, we can see that ethnographic research consists of naturalistic inquiry with a holistic emphasis. It is a phenomenological approach, emphasizing the subjective nature of behavior. Ethnographic research is conducted in the field setting, based on the premise that the situation influences people's interpretations, thoughts, and actions. The researcher attempts to interpret the situation from the perspective of the individuals being studied. Geertz (1973) characterizes the task of ethnography as "thick description."

To some extent, the methodology of ethnographic research emerges as the research is in progress. As indicated before, no particular research technique is associated exclusively with ethnographic research. But a variety of techniques are used, and it is helpful to put them into a conceptual schema in order to provide a general context for ethnographic research.

A Conceptual Schema for Ethnographic Research[1]

What kinds of research problems, issues, or topics are studied through ethnographic research? Typical ethnographic studies in education might have the following research statements:

1. A study of life in an urban classroom.
2. A study of decision making in an inner-city high school.
3. A study of student life in law school.
4. A study of student relations in an integrated school.
5. A study of peer interactions in racially mixed classrooms of a suburban high school.
6. A study of racial attitudes of children in a desegregated elementary school.
7. A study of interaction patterns among faculty in a private prep school.
8. A study of instruction in writing in the elementary school.
9. A study of socialization within a rural high school.

Note that these statements are general. They do not contain phrases such as "the effects of," nor do they imply cause-and-effect relationships. As research statements, they lack specificity, which would be undesirable if an experiment or a survey were anticipated. But ethnographic research does not begin from specified, preconceived hypotheses; it relies heavily on description as the research proceeds. The foregoing sample statements clearly imply description.

Given the nature of ethnographic research, what elements are present in an ethnographic research study? One commonality among ethnographic research studies is the focus on an organization—usually a social organization—or some part of it. For example, a school is a social organization, as is a classroom. We think of an organization as defined groups of people who interact in regular and structured ways. There is collective social action, based on rules and relations that have been developed by consensus. The behavior of any one group is influenced by how that group interacts with another or several groups. Furthermore, individuals in an organization tend to behave as the members of the groups to which they belong.

> Ethnographic studies focus on *organizations,* which consist of defined groups of people who interact in regular and structured ways.

In our conceptual schema, we can now begin breaking down an organization into its parts. There are a number of ways this can be done, depending on the criteria used. We will consider two divisions, cultures and perspectives.

An organization can be viewed as consisting of *cultures.* For example, a school has a student culture (possibly more than one student culture), a faculty culture, an administrative culture (assuming that the school is large enough), and possibly a teacher aide culture and a maintenance personnel culture. A culture consists of the collective understandings among the members of the group that are related to their particular roles. Whatever makes up the parts of a culture, there is coherence and consistency among these parts. We will call the parts that make up a culture *perspectives.*

Perspectives direct the behavior of individuals and groups; usually in ethnographic research, group perspectives are studied. The coordinated set of ideas and actions utilized by an individual in dealing with a situation is his or her perspective. Thus, perspectives are situation-specific. A group perspective consists of ideas and actions developed by a group that faces a common problematic situation. Ideas include beliefs and attitudes as well as conceptual schemes about how to deal with the problem.

Organizations are considered to be composed of *cultures,* and cultures are made up of *perspectives.*

To understand an organization or some part of it, ethnographic research is conducted from the inside, outward. That is, the researcher begins with the perspectives of one or more defined groups and uses them to describe one or more cultures. The purpose of the research may be to describe only one culture or to describe some aspect of one or more cultures in the organization. Unless the organization is small and sociologically simple, describing the entire organization might be quite ambitious. In the research statements listed earlier, the first implies description of an entire organization, the urban classroom. The second focuses on decision making, an aspect that cuts across cultures in a high school. The third focuses on student culture.

The relationship of perspectives, cultures, and organization is illustrated in Figure 10.1. The perspectives form the cultures, and the cultures make up the organization. The arrow indicates the direction of ethnographic research, beginning with perspectives to describe the cultures, which in turn describe the organization or some part of it.

Figure 10.2 illustrates an application of the conceptual schema to an ethnographic study of student life in law school. As indicated, three cultures are considered. These cultures may be made up of different numbers of perspectives—hence the use of k and k' and k''. This study focuses on a particular culture—the student culture—which is indicated by bold lines. The other two cultures are included because they are likely to affect student culture; although, they are not the cultures of primary interest.

Thus far, we have discussed ethnographic research primarily in terms of generally conceptualizing the nature of such research. The process has been alluded to, but specific procedures have not been described. At this point, we turn to the process and procedures of conducting ethnographic research.

The Process of Ethnographic Research

One characteristic of the process of ethnographic research is that the activities or procedures are more integrated than the procedures of other research methodologies. In Chap-

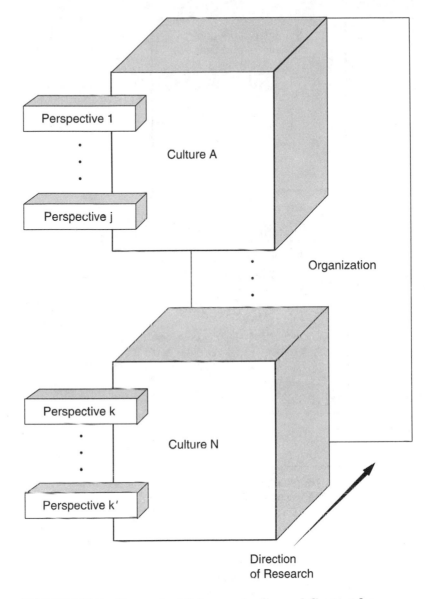

**FIGURE 10.1   Conceptual Schema of a General Context for
Conducting Ethnographic Research**

ter 1, a sequential pattern of general activities for conducting research was discussed. The activities were quite distinct, generally proceeding from identifying the research problem through drawing conclusions. Although we can identify specific procedures in ethnographic research, the procedures tend to run together or overlap throughout the process.

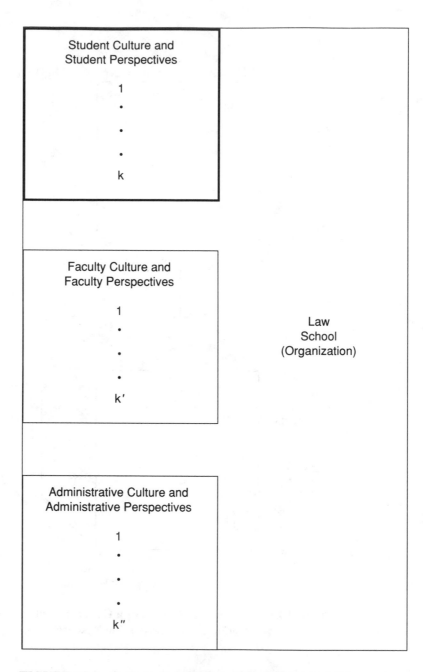

FIGURE 10.2   Sample Application of the Conceptual Schema to an Ethnographic Study of Student Life in Law School

For example, hypotheses may be generated throughout the entire data-collection process rather than being listed first and then collecting data to test them. Thus, the ethnographic researcher is little concerned with sequencing specific procedures.

> The process of ethnographic research is an integrated process in which procedures are conducted concurrently.

The activities of the ethnographic research process are diagrammed in Figure 10.3. The layering of the activities in the figure indicates that they overlap and that they may be conducted concurrently. Although ethnographic research does not have distinct sequencing of activities, there is a starting point and an ending point. The identification of

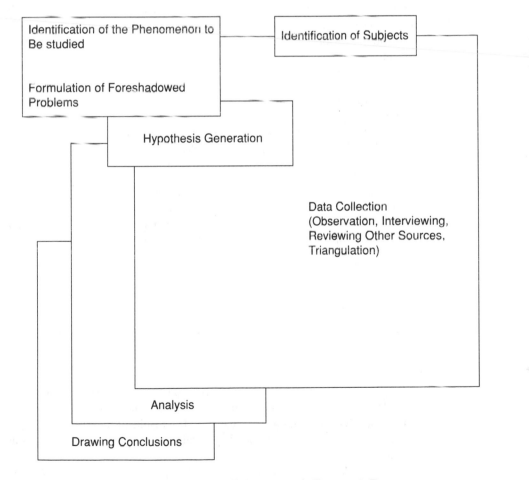

FIGURE 10.3   The Activities of the Ethnographic Research Process

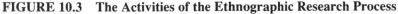

the phenomenon to be studied is the starting point, and the study terminates when the final conclusions are drawn. The activities are described and illustrated here in the context of a hypothetical study.

Identification of the Phenomenon to Be Studied

Suppose a study is conducted on:

The social interaction of students in a racially mixed urban high school.

This statement identifies the phenomenon to be studied as social interaction of high school students, specifically in a desegregated school. This is a general statement with few restrictions, but it does provide a starting point. Stated in question form it would be, "What happens socially to students in a racially mixed urban high school?"

Such a statement usually implies *foreshadowed problems*—somewhat specific factors and issues that apply to the phenomenon and provide a focus for the research. Essentially, there may be any number of foreshadowed problems, depending on the nature and extent of the study. The following are foreshadowed problems associated with the foregoing statement:

1. *Interaction among the students across races.*
2. *Interaction among the students across the sexes.*
3. *Faculty social systems.*
4. *Role of the faculty in the social interaction of students.*
5. *Established policies that encourage or discourage social interaction.*
6. *Acceptable codes of social behavior among students.*

Foreshadowed problems provide the researcher with something to look for. They provide direction, but they should not be considered restrictive. For example, as the study progresses, it might become apparent that grouping patterns for instructional purposes are also relevant, so these patterns would then be analyzed and discussed.

Foreshadowed problems follow from the more general statement of the phenomenon to be studied; they provide a focus for the research.

Identification of Subjects

Because the example deals with social interaction of students, students are the subjects of interest. However, the students are found in a high school and the school was selected because of its characteristics and availability. The results of this study might generalize to other designated urban high schools, but certainly not to all such schools. Generalization would be argued on a logical basis.

Getting back to observing students, it is not possible or necessary to observe everything. So, conditions and restrictions must be considered. Will students be observed:

1. As one class followed through four years, or as four classes simultaneously?
2. From the time they enter the school in the morning until they leave at night, or only for a specified segment of the day?
3. In class and out of class, participating in such activities as clubs and athletics, or only in specified "academic" activities?
4. Only in instructional situations and in situations such as eating lunch or walking in the halls, or in all the situations of the school day?

These questions illustrate the kinds of things that need to be considered when collecting the data. Decisions about conditions are somewhat arbitrary. The study must be feasible, but it would be undesirable to have restrictions that might distort or mask the phenomenon under study. For the example, the four classes would likely be observed simultaneously; following one class through four years would require a long study. Students would be observed in any situations that involve social interaction. They would be observed in large groups and small groups, some as small as one-on-one interchanges. To facilitate data collection, groups of students (possibly even individuals) would be selected and then observed for a specified period, such as a day or a week.

It would not be possible to observe all students. Although students or groups of students might be selected randomly, they would more likely be selected through purposeful sampling. Purposeful sampling, which is described more fully in Chapter 11, is a procedure of selecting individuals, or in this case small groups, because of certain characteristics relevant to the phenomenon under study. For example, a group might be selected because it contains both boys and girls of both races in a relatively informal setting.

Although the students are certainly the subjects of major concern in this example, other subjects, such as faculty members, also may be observed or interviewed. Faculty may affect the social interaction of the students, and they are a source of information. Again, faculty would most likely be selected through purposeful sampling. Certain faculty may be in a better position to observe social interaction than others. Essentially, the research is a study of the student culture, with a focus on social interaction, but other cultures in the school would undoubtedly contribute relevant information.

Subjects to be studied must be identified, and typically it is necessary to specify conditions and restrictions so that the study is feasible.

Hypothesis Generation

As the data collection proceeds in an ethnographic study, hypotheses may be formulated and modified. A study may begin with few if any specific hypotheses, but the data may imply hypotheses as the study continues. The ethnographic researcher is very amenable to introducing new hypotheses and discarding hypotheses that are not supported. There are no a priori limits on the number or nature of hypotheses.

A hypothesis that might be formulated in the social interaction example is, "Social interaction across racial lines increases as students become older." This hypothesis would be based on what is observed and initial data might support such a hypothesis, but it might be modified later to state, for example, that the increase occurs only within the sexes. The hypothesis modification procedure may become a process of successive approximations in an attempt to accurately describe the phenomenon under study.

> Hypothesis generation is a continuing activity throughout an ethnographic study. Unlike survey research or experimentation, for which hypotheses are initially specified and then tested, ethnographic research may begin with no hypotheses, and hypotheses may be formulated and modified along the way.

Data Collection

The mainstay of data collection in ethnographic research is observation conducted by the participant-observer, and a basic form of data is field notes. An observer may be identified openly as a researcher or may be in a disguised role. Wolcott (1988, p. 194) distinguishes among different participant-observer styles as active participant, privilege observer, and limited observer. As an active participant, the observer assumes the role of a participant. In the Becker, Geer, Hughes, and Strauss (1961) study, the observers actually assumed the role of medical student. For most ethnographic research in schools, the observer becomes a privileged observer. That is, the observer does assume the role of a participant but has access to the relevant activity for the study. The limited observer role would be used when opportunities for observation are restricted and other data-collection techniques, of necessity, take precedence. Limited observers should be used sparingly, if at all, in educational ethnographic research. Wolcott (1988) suggests that the active participant role has been underutilized in educational research and that researchers should attempt to become more active participants rather than passive, albeit privileged, observers.

Not all data collection in an ethnographic study is necessarily conducted through participant-observation. Interviews may be conducted with key individuals, and data may be collected through a survey that may support or refute information collected through observation. Written resources such as records may provide data. Like historical researchers, ethnographic researchers prefer primary sources over secondary sources. In fact, since ethnographic research deals with the present, there should be little need for secondary sources. Nonwritten sources such as videotapes, photographs, and artifacts also may provide data.

> Ethnographic research involves a variety of data-collection procedures, the primary procedure being observation.

Observation. Whatever their particular roles, observers try to be as unobtrusive as possible so that they do not interfere with normal activities. An important part of observation relates to the idea of contextualization; that is, to understand behavior, the observer must understand the context in which individuals are thinking and reacting. The observer must have the option of interpreting events. Thus, observation extends beyond objective recording of what happens. The participant-observer attempts to assume the role of the individuals under study and to experience their thoughts, feelings, and actions.

> The *participant-observer* attempts to generate the data from the perspective of the individuals being studied.

Observation in ethnographic research is comprehensive, that is, continuing and total. The observer attempts to record all relevant information in an unobtrusive way; consequently, observation is quite unstructured. It is not likely that an observer conducting ethnographic research would have a structured observation inventory. The emphasis is on capturing the perspective of the individuals being observed, which requires careful listening to pick up subtle cues and nuances. Observation is a continuing process; it is not limited to one or two sessions. In the social interaction example, observers might be in the school situation every day, all day, for an extended period—possibly an entire school year.

In the social interaction example, it would be difficult for the observer to assume the role of a student, so observation most likely would be conducted as a privileged observer. Possibly the observer could assume the role of a teacher which would make him or her a participant from a culture other than the one of primary interest. However, the task of teaching would divert energy from the research effort and also would limit the researcher's mobility about the school.

The recordings made by the observer while actually conducting the observations are called *field notes.* The content of field notes may be somewhat unorganized and rough. Immediately following observation, the observer should synthesize and summarize the field notes, include any interpretations that come to mind, and record any questions that may be implied. Any observation record should be carefully identified in terms of when, where, and under what conditions it was made.

> *Observation* in ethnographic research is continuing and total. It is quite unstructured. Field notes should be synthesized and summarized immediately after the observation.

The field notes are written as a narrative, which may contain abbreviations, some form of shorthand, and if the observer was rushed while recording, notes might consist of phrases. If positions or movements of subjects are important, the field notes may contain diagrams with arrows. Figure 10.4 contains a partial observation record that might apply to the social interaction example. A partial synthesis is provided in the lower part of the figure.

Videotaping.   Within recent years, videotaping has increased as a data collection procedure. Videotaping has definite advantages when it applies, the overriding advantage being that the situation may be reviewed repeatedly for the purpose of obtaining more information. In the Lancy example, described earlier, videotaping was very useful for generating grounded theory. It enabled the researchers to review and to compare repeatedly the parent-child reading situations. Grounded theory would have been much more difficult to develop based on one, in-person observation of each situation.

But videotaping has some definite disadvantages. It is hardly unobtrusive and the presence of the equipment and process may impact on the situation. Videotaping is more amenable to relatively compact situations, such as an interaction between two or three people. It is much more difficult to get a holistic picture of everything going on in a classroom or cafeteria, for example. The videotaping equipment must be available, and of course, there is some cost associated with videotaping.

Videotaping does take pressure off taking field notes. In essence, field notes may be taken at leisure as the tapes are reviewed. So given the conditions under which observation is being conducted, and videotaping is an option, a decision can be made whether or not it is feasible or even worthwhile.

Interviewing.   Interviewing might be quite open-ended and casual or it might be quite structured. However, in keeping with the phenomenological approach, at least some of the

---

Time: 11:45 a.m., January 15, 1994
Location: School Cafeteria, Ninth-Grade Students' Lunch Period

The groupings for lunch follow pretty much along gender lines: small groups of boys and small groups of girls. There were only two or three groupings of couples, in all cases both members of the same race (white). There was no mixing of the races for girls, but there was some for boys. In two instances there were white and black boys in groupings, and these boys were recognized as some of the aspiring athletes of the school. Students were orderly regardless of their groupings. . . .

After the observation—part of the summary and synthesis:
It appears that boys are more likely to interact socially across racial lines than girls. This difference may stem from the differences in traditional sex roles for students at this age of development. Girls tend to have a heightened interest in their appeal to the opposite sex and probably have little concern about making social contacts across races but of the same sex. Boys tend to be interested in factors such as physical competition; hence the groupings of athletes across racial lines. Question: In other situations, will groupings of boys occur along other factors? . . .

FIGURE 10.4   Example of a Partial Observation Record: Upper Part, Field Notes; Lower Part, Summary

interviewing should be quite open-ended and informal. Casual and informal interviewing can be done when an occasion presents itself during observation. Questions might be asked of those being observed in an attempt to clarify what is happening or in an attempt to capture the feelings of those observed.

Key-informant interviewing is a technique from anthropology in which the term *informant*[2] is defined by Wolcott (1988) as "an individual in whom one invests a disproportionate amount of time because that individual appears to be particularly well informed, articulate, approachable, or available" (p. 195). Wolcott also implies that ethnographic research in education may not be using the key informant to maximum benefit; partly because of the notion that truth resides in large numbers, and partly because of familiarity with education, researchers tend to see themselves as key informants.

Interviewing key informants would apply in the social interaction example. Certain students might be exceptionally well informed about the interaction or highly sensitive to it. Some faculty, such as one or more guidance counselors, also might serve as key informants. The principal or an assistant principal who deals with discipline is another candidate for key informant.

Formal, structured interviews may be conducted with a predefined set of questions. In the social interaction example, a number of students might be interviewed. Faculty and administrators also might be interviewed. Other people, such as cooks, lunchroom attendants, and janitors, might be interviewed to obtain their perceptions of the students' social interaction. Such interviews would be helpful in determining the tone of the social interaction, which might not be entirely apparent from observing behavior.

It is important that the interviewer be a good listener. At no time should interviewers indicate that they are being evaluative of the responses. An expression of genuine interest in what the informant is saying should be maintained. The informants should be at ease and inclined to talk freely. The interviewer should be flexible and ready to respond to whatever in the situation will produce useful information.

Reviewing Other Sources. There may be other sources of data that reflect on the research problem under study. These other sources often consist of records maintained on a routine basis by the organization in which the study is being conducted. Data from standardized achievement tests, attitude inventories, psychological tests, and vocational interest inventories might be useful. In fact, such measures could be administered in connection with the study; although, it is more common to use data from existing sources. Nonwritten sources such as photographs and films might provide information.

In the example, records of the incidence of discipline infractions involving interchanges between two or more students would be of interest. Such records might support (or fail to support) the observation data and the perceptions of the researchers. Students might be administered an attitude inventory to measure racial and socialization attitudes. (Such an inventory would likely need to be constructed for the study.) Videotapes of students interacting in a social situation would be an example of a nonwritten source.

Triangulation. Triangulation is part of data collection that cuts across two or more techniques or sources. Essentially, it is qualitative cross-validation. It can be conducted among different data sources or different data-collection methods. As Denzin (1978,

p. 308) points out: "Triangulation can take many forms, but its basic feature will be the combination of two or more different research strategies in the study of the same empirical units."

Figure 10.5 illustrates triangulation in two cases—one involving data sources and the other involving data-collection procedures. The figure applies to the social interaction example.

Basically, triangulation is comparison of information to determine whether or not there is corroboration. It is a search for convergence of the information on a common finding or concept. To a large extent, the triangulation process assesses the sufficiency of the data. If the data are inconsistent or do not converge, they are insufficient. The researcher is then faced with a dilemma regarding what to believe.

> *Triangulation* is qualitative cross-validation. It assesses the sufficiency of the data according to the convergence of multiple data sources or multiple data-collection procedures.

Consider an instance of triangulation from the social interaction example. The observation data in Figure 10.4, concerning ninth-grade students, led the researcher to a

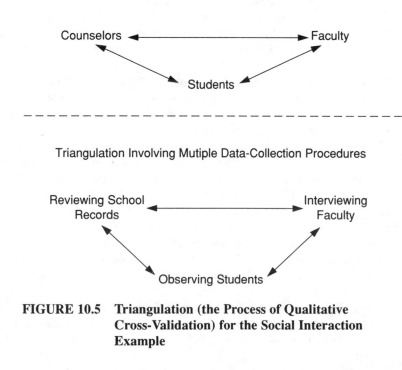

FIGURE 10.5   **Triangulation (the Process of Qualitative Cross-Validation) for the Social Interaction Example**

tentative hypothesis that there was more social interaction across the races for boys than for girls at this age. Some information collected from individual interviews with a ninth-grade boy and a ninth-grade girl was as follows:

> Ninth-grade boy: *Yes, I do things at school with both black and white boys. We practice basketball together and sometimes eat lunch together. When we talk in the halls it is mostly about sports. There are not many white kids in my neighborhood, but sometimes on Saturday we get together on one of the playgrounds at the big park and shoot baskets, and the white guys come over. One time a bunch of us went to a movie that the coach wanted us to see, but only guys went.*

> Ninth-grade girl: *The black girls in school pretty much stick together. We have nothing against the white girls, but they do different things. If we have a party or something outside of school, it's for the neighborhood which is mostly black. Sometimes in science class the teacher has us do projects together, and I might work with a white girl or guy, which is OK.*

This information from the interviews supports the hypothesis based on the observation data.

In reviewing school records, one type of information checked was the composition of the races in extracurricular activities, such as athletics and clubs. For activities in which ninth-grade students participated, the records showed that the proportional incidence of both black and white ninth-grade boys being involved in predominantly male-oriented activities was greater than the corresponding proportional incidence for black and white ninth-grade girls in predominantly female-oriented activities. Although this was relatively weak supportive evidence for the hypothesis, there were no data to refute the hypothesis. The results of the triangulation appear to be consistent.

Analysis

Analysis in ethnographic research consists of synthesizing the information from the observation, interviews, and other data sources. Typically, no hypotheses are tested using statistical procedures as is often the case with experimental and survey data. However, there may be some quantitative measures computed such as proportions and percentages, based on classifications of items from interviews or types of activities and events observed.

The quantity of data to be analyzed may seem overwhelming, at least initially. There are the field notes from observation and interviews, and data from records, etc. To begin with, it can be helpful to make some classifications of the data just to get a feel for what they contain. Becker et al. (1961) suggest a number of ways information can be classified, including the following:

1. Dichotomous categories indicating whether information obtained was directed by the observer's activities or was volunteered spontaneously by those being studied.
2. Number of responses to direct queries.

3. Dichotomous categories indicating whether information was obtained in the presence of the observer alone or when other individuals were present.

4. Proportions of information that consist of activities observed versus statements made.

Classifying data in such a manner is far from a complete analysis, but it does provide some direction. Presenting results in tabular form may be helpful, both frequencies and proportions. An example format for the social interaction example is given in Figure 10.6.

Bogdan and Biklen (1992) suggest two mechanical procedures for sorting through the data. The first suggestion is to number all the pages of material sequentially, most likely in chronological order. The numbering may be done separately for different types of data, such as observation data, interview data, etc. Page numbering helps to locate data. The second procedure is to take long undisturbed periods of time and read through the data at least twice. This procedure should give a sense of the scope and holistic nature of the data. By the second reading some preliminary ideas for developing a coding system should come to mind, and a tentative list of codes might be forthcoming. Because the quantity of data usually is large, it is useful to take notes about the data.

> Numbering the data pages and at least two readings of the data are two procedures to get the analysis under way.

Coding.   Coding the data is a necessary analysis task of practically any qualitative research study. Coding was discussed in Chapter 8, and it may be useful for the reader to

Statements	Volunteered	Directed	Total
To observer alone			
To other students with observer present			
To other students with observer and faculty present			

Activities	Same Race	Mixed Race
With one other student		
With more than one other student		
With one or more faculty		
With both other student(s) and faculty		

FIGURE 10.6   An Example Format for Classifications of the Data from the Social Interaction Example

review that section. Coding is a quite subjective activity and the codes basically come out of the data. Chapter 8 also suggests some general codes such as context codes or process codes.

Coding categories may be modified as the analysis proceeds. Major codes and subcodes may be used. The number of codes or categories in a system should be limited, but that does not mean that there will be only a few codes. Bogdan and Biklen (1992, p. 176) suggest limiting the number of codes from thirty to fifty. It is important that the codes cover all the data, yet provide a meaningful separation of the information.

A coding system that might apply to the social interaction example is "relationships codes." Relationships include friendships, cliques, leader/follower roles, etc., essentially the groupings and their interactions that make up the social structure of the school. Because the high school is racially mixed, the racial composition of relationships would be of interest as would the composition across the sexes.

Codes may be divided into major codes, subcodes, and supplemental codes. Major codes are broad categories and subcodes divide the major codes into more detailed categories. Supplemental codes are categories somewhat peripheral to the primary focus of interest, but, nonetheless, representing an influence on the phenomenon being studied.

In the social interaction example, a major category of the relationships codes would be friendships. Subcodes would be within the same race and within the same sex, and these could be further subdivided by African American and white. A supplemental code would be student/faculty friendships. This code is not directly a part of student interaction, but it may impact upon such interaction. Table 10.1 contains relationship codes for the social interaction research study. This is not an exhaustive list, but it does illustrate codes that focus the analysis on the research problem.

Codes are used for categorizing the information in the data. Major codes, subcodes, and supplemental codes may be used.

Coding is a means to an end, not an end in itself. Codes should be useful for organizing and synthesizing the data. They may be modified as necessary while the analysis is in process. Although some coding systems may be apparent due to the phenomenon under study, the data themselves, such as field notes, imply applicable systems and categories.

Use of Numbers.   In ethnographic research, terms such as *large, a long time,* or *quite rapid* often are used in describing phenomena. For certain types of phenomena, such as length of time, quantitative measures are available, and their use can increase the precision of the description. To say that the observation periods averaged about three hours is more precise than saying that they were "quite long" or that they lasted "most of the afternoon." In a study of high schools, if size of class is a characteristic used in the description, numbers such as averages are more informative than simple descriptive terms.

TABLE 10.1   Example Relationships Codes for the Social Interaction Research Study

Major Code: Friendships

  Subcodes: 1. Within same race, same sex
       1a. African-American girls
       1b. African-American boys
       1c. White girls
       1d. White boys
      2. Across races, same sex
       2a. Girls
       2b. Boys
      3. Within same race, different sex
       3a. African American
       3b. White
      4. Across races, different sex
       4a. African-American boy, white girl
       4b. African-American girl, white boy

Major Code: Cliques

 (repeat same type of subcodes, and continue this breakdown through the major relationship codes)

Supplemental Code: Student/faculty mentor

  Subcode: 1. Within same race, same sex
      1a. African-American woman faculty, African-American girl
      2b. African-American man faculty, African-American boy
      3b. White woman faculty, white girl
      4d. White man faculty, white boy

The subcodes may be continued as above. A second supplemental code category might be, Student/faculty, nonmentor friendship.

Ethnographic researchers engage in what is sometimes called *ballparking*—providing a very rough estimate of a phenomenon. An example of ballparking is, "Many students of both sexes engaged in conversations in the halls." For some activities and situations, it is impossible or undesirable to obtain numerical estimates, and ballparking is adequate. However, confusion can be introduced if numbers are specific when in fact they represent only ballpark estimates. Researchers should be clear about whether numbers are ballpark estimates or more specific estimates. If they are ballpark estimates, they may be indicating only order of magnitude.

Researchers should use caution in classifying individuals on variables whose frequency or existence involves a subjective perception. Schofield and Andersen (1984, p. 13) cite an example of ethnic identity: "Ethnic identity is, after all, a construct referring to one's subjective sense of self rather than to certain physical or cultural criteria that someone else might use to label one as belonging to a particular group."

A problem arises when certain counts or categorizations are based on operational definitions that are not in agreement with the perceptions of the individuals being studied.

For example, "official classification" may not be in agreement with the way the individuals studied perceive themselves, in which case, numbers based on official classification would be misleading.

> Numbers are useful in ethnographic research for providing more specific information than descriptive terms alone. Researchers must be clear about the level of precision contained in the numbers.

The analysis in ethnographic research relies heavily on description; even when statistics are used, they tend to be used in a descriptive rather than an inferential manner. Inferential statistics might be appropriate if random sampling of events or of some characteristic of the study had been done. But we would not expect the research context to be a random sample of some larger population of contexts. The ethnographic researcher is probably more willing than other types of researchers to accept the uniqueness of the research context and its conditions.

Drawing Conclusions

Experimental and survey research typically leave drawing conclusions as one of the final steps. In ethnographic research, drawing conclusions is integrated much more with other parts of the research process, especially the fieldwork. In fact, to the extent possible, it is a good strategy to incorporate the writing into the fieldwork even to the point of preparing a first draft while the fieldwork is in process.

Tentative hypotheses, theories, and explanations are generated during the fieldwork, but the ethnographic researcher guards against drawing final conclusions prematurely. Thus we have a successive approximation procedure of coming to conclusions when conducting ethnographic research. Wax (1971) suggests allowing as much time for analyzing and writing as was spent in the field. It is not the fieldwork that produces the ethnography, but the analysis and writing. What has been said and done does not have educational, psychological, sociological, or other meaning until such meaning is ascribed by the researcher. Producing the ethnographic account requires insight, reflection, and typically, some rethinking of initial conclusions.

> The conceptual schema for ethnographic research helps clarify the components involved in a specific study and aids in identifying the focus of the research.

Examples of Ethnographic Research in Education[3]

There are classic examples of ethnographic research, such as the Becker et al. (1961) study, *Boys in White: Student Culture in Medical School.* More recently in education, the comprehensive reports by Boyer (1983) and Goodlad (1984) are based on ethnographic research. However, not may educators are likely to conduct studies of such magnitude— not even for a doctoral dissertation. The extensive classic studies can provide useful information about methodology, but at this point, it should be helpful to consider examples of less extensive studies—those that are feasible for practicing educators and graduate program research. When considering examples, it is not feasible to reproduce entire reports, but the discussion below provides an overview of the nature of the research.

EXAMPLE 10. 1 CROSS CULTURAL COMMUNICATION IN SPECIAL EDUCATION

Harry (1992) reported on an ethnographic study of cross-cultural communication between educators and Puerto Rican-American families with children in the special education system. The sample, which was a purposeful sample, consisted of twelve Puerto Rican-American families, all of which had at least one child in special education. (Four families had more than one child in special education.) The description of the sample is complete, including details of the racial composition of the families, educational history of the mothers, and the location of residence, which was a medium-sized city in the Northeast. The children of the study were classified as learning disabled or mildly mentally retarded.

The report opens with several pages of background information on the phenomenon under study, and this information which is well-documented, includes views from other qualitative studies. The documentation is extensive; in fact, there is a total of forty-four footnotes throughout the report. The methodology of the study is summarized as:

> *Parents' views and experiences were sought through a recursive process of ethnographic interviewing, review of students' documents, and participant observation of parent professional conferences and community events. (p. 471)*

The interviews were unstructured, and being recursive, a minimum of three taped interviews were conducted with each parent. Interviews were from one to three hours in duration and all the interviews were conducted over a seven-month period. Interviews focused on the parents' perceptions of the special education process.

The examination of student records and participant observation provided additional data sources and these provided for triangulation of the data. As described in the report, there was corroboration of results across the data sources, thus enhancing the internal validity of the research. The method of interviewing is described in detail. In addition to the parent interviews, interviews were conducted with nine school district professionals and three Hispanic social workers from community agencies. The former were involved with developing policy for, or delivery of, services to limited-English proficient students and their families. One of these professionals became a key informant, so in addition to the interviews, this individual participated in six informal conversations.

The transcripts of interviews and field notes were analyzed by constantly comparing them to each other in order to uncover a general theoretical framework that would explain the data.[4] Essentially, this was a situation of developing grounded theory. The process led to a set of five higher-level concepts called themes, which provide the interpretation of the data on parent-professional interaction. These themes were:

> *Trust versus deference, written communications, communication and meaning, resignation/withdrawal, and pockets of excellence. (p. 478)*

Several pages are then devoted to discussing these themes individually; elaboration on the themes and their meanings is the context of the research study.

The final two major sections of the report are "Discussion" and "Conclusions." The discussion section contains an elaboration of the findings and their interpretations. The conclusions section contains exactly that, conclusions from the data. However, the section goes beyond simply stating conclusions. The conclusions are tied in with relevant concepts from other writers, including possible answers to questions raised by the study. Some of these suggested answers have policy implications for communication with the Hispanic community about special education systems, and even communication more generally. The report is brought to closure with conclusions about empowerment of parents and restructuring of communication practices.

EXAMPLE 10.2. ACADEMIC SUCCESS, THE SCHOOL, AND HOME ENVIRONMENT

In a field-based study, Schneider and Lee (1990) used ethnographic research in attempting to explain the academic success of East Asian students. The study was conducted with students in grades six and seven, and there was a comparison made with the academic performance of Anglo students in the same grades. Two elementary schools in Illinois were the sites for the study and these had at least twenty or more Chinese, Japanese, and Korean students in the two grades. All the East Asian students, a total of forty-six, were included in the study. A purposefully selected sample of forty-nine Anglo-American students also was included. No students with disabilities were included, and there were no other minority children in the study. All East Asian students had immigrated before September 1978. The study was conducted during the 1982–1983 school year, with ninety days of participant and nonparticipant observations of school activities. When in the school, an average of four hours per day was spent in observation, interviewing, and participating in special school activities.

The report begins with a discussion of related research and possible explanations of the academic success of East Asian students. In fact, a model is presented early in the report. In this study the researchers did not begin the research without any hypotheses. Hypotheses were part of the model for explaining success, and an example hypothesis given was:

> *We also hypothesized that East Asian parents were more likely to stress certain norms such as industriousness, diligence, and respect, which reinforce particular behaviors highly valued by teachers. (p. 364)*

The five methods of data collection used were:

1. Student census.
2. Review of school records.
3. Participant and non-participant observations.
4. Semistructured, in-depth interviews with students, parents, teachers, and administrators.
5. Collection of student essays (p. 365).

The census data were collected through the use of a questionnaire distributed to the homes through the student home rooms. School records included IQ test scores, achievement test scores, and report card grades. Short student essays were written on the subjects "my home," "my school," and "my future." In one of the schools, the superintendent would not allow teacher involvement with the essay preparation, and a limited number were obtained in that school.

This study is an excellent illustration of how a wide variety of data can be used in an ethnographic study. Some data were quantitative in nature, for example, annual family income from the student census. Over the period of the data collection—about nine months—the observation became more focused as certain factors and issues began to emerge. Although the researchers had some prior ideas for explaining academic success, they were open to any concepts and patterns indicated by the data.

The analysis presents information about family and parental factors, as obtained from the student census. The in-depth interviews provided insight into the attitudes, motivations, expectations, etc., of the students and families. Teacher interviews gave insights into student expectations, behavior, and performance. In the report, the results are provided in a descriptive manner including actual comments and examples.

The report closes with a "Discussion" section, and in this section the explanation of East Asian student success is pursued, based on the results of the research. There are over forty references cited in the report, an indication of how the research is tied in with other related research and relevant thinking about school success.

The Reliability and Validity of Ethnographic Research

As indicated in Chapter 1, the *reliability* of research involves the extent to which studies can be replicated. The concept applies to both procedures and results. If a study is reliable, another researcher who uses the same procedures, variables, measurements, and conditions should obtain the same results. The *validity* of research involves the interpretation of research results with confidence and the generalizability of the results. The former is called *internal validity* and the latter *external validity*. Reliability and validity influence the credibility of the research and the confidence that can be placed in the findings.

> *Reliability* is concerned with replicability of both procedures and findings. *Validity* refers to the interpretation and generalizability of results.

Chapter 8 has a discussion of reliability and validity of qualitative research in general, and those concepts also apply to ethnographic research. The following discussion of reliability and validity elaborates on these concepts as they apply to ethnographic research.

Reliability

Goetz and LeCompte (1984) distinguish between two types of reliability in ethnographic research—external and internal. External reliability involves the extent to which independent researchers working in the same or similar context would obtain consistent results. Internal reliability involves the extent to which researchers concerned with the same data and constructs would be consistent in matching them. Because it is conducted in naturalistic settings and often focuses on processes, ethnographic research is susceptible to problems of replication. However, these problems have been addressed and procedures have been suggested for averting them.

Ethnographic research usually is focused, not on the tabulation of frequencies of events or behaviors, but on obtaining an accurate description of the phenomena under study. In a specific study, internal reliability would depend on the extent to which two or more observers agree on what they saw and how they interpret what they saw. How can observers be made to agree? Basically, the way to enhance reliability (and validity, for that matter) in ethnographic research is no different from the way to do so in any other type of research—that is, through applying good methodology.

Ethnographic researchers may not be able to begin a study with as much design specificity as exists for other research, but the context of the research and the overall problem addressed should be specified as much as possible. Then access to data is an important factor, not only in terms of availability of the data, but also the status of the researcher. As one of the potential problems of fieldwork, Erickson (1986) identifies the limiting of the researcher's access to data due to inadequate negotiation for entry into the field setting. The researcher must develop a relationship with the participants that will provide access to data from the perspectives of the participants.

The use of multiple data-collection procedures, along with triangulation, tends to enhance internal reliability. There should be a variety of sources—observation, interviewing, site documents, and possibly other supporting sources—for data, and data must be in adequate quantity to have confirmed any assertions with confidence. Disconfirming evidence must also be sought and explained if such evidence exists. Videotaping, when it is applicable, can be useful. It allows the repeated viewing of situations or the phenomenon under study until underlying concepts can be identified consistently and with confidence. Also, if two or more observers are involved, repeated viewing can be a check on consistency of interpretation across observers, and it provides an opportunity for the resolution of differences.

The extensive description used in ethnographic research is a plus in terms of internal reliability; if there seems to be a lack of observer agreement, the sources of disagreement can be identified from the description. If observers are in disagreement, there should always be an opportunity for discussion to resolve the disagreement. Ethnographic research is often a cooperative effort among several individuals. There always should be opportunities for sharing insights, discussing interpretations, and reviewing the descriptions of others.

External reliability is a matter of degree, and some would argue that nothing can be replicated exactly. Many ethnographic researchers are not very concerned about whether or not others can replicate their studies. But, because ethnographic procedures are varied and are applied with varying degrees of sophistication, the ethnographic researcher must be particularly comprehensive in describing the methodology. It is not sufficient to use a shorthand description and then assert that data collection and analysis were carefully conducted. Goetz and LeCompte (1984, p. 217) summarize this point:

> *The researcher must clearly identify and fully discuss data analysis processes and provide retrospective accounts of how data were examined and synthesized. Because reliability depends on the potential for subsequent researchers to reconstruct original analysis strategies, only those ethnographic accounts that specify these in sufficient detail are replicable.*

Validity

Attaining reliability does not assure the validity of research—either internal or external. For example, observers could agree on their conclusions and yet the conclusions could be in error. If conclusions cannot be drawn with confidence, there are deficiencies in the research procedures, and the study lacks internal validity. If the results of a study do not generalize, the study lacks external validity, even if results were consistent internally and the study is replicable.

A research study may be both internally and externally reliable yet lack validity.

Consider internal validity first. In experimental design, we control extraneous variables to the extent possible—for example, through randomization or by including additional independent variables in the design. Because ethnographic research is conducted in the natural setting, it does not have this option of control. However, the naturalness of the data enhances validity. Smith and Glass (1987, p. 278) identify naturalness of the data as one of the qualities by which to critique a naturalistic study. The natural state of a study should be without reactivity and artificiality and should have a minimum of observer effects. There should be checking for possible observer effects.

Ethnographic research studies typically cover relatively long time periods, which increase the possibility of extraneous effects. However, longevity in the research context does enhance the search for causes and effects. The temporal ordering of events, the perspectives of various informants, and the possible effects of confounded variables are examples of factors that may affect internal validity, yet they are factors that tend to become better understood with exposure in the situation. Of necessity, in order to obtain adequate amounts of data, the data-collection period is quite long. There is no designated time period for ethnographic research; the length of time required for a specific study depends on the extent and complexity of the phenomenon being investigated. In summary, establishing internal validity is a process that involves both deduction and induction; the researcher systematically reasons through the possible causes for the data.

The concern of external validity is generalization; to what populations, conditions, contexts, and situations do the results generalize? LeCompte and Goetz (1982, p. 51) identify the problem as one of demonstrating "the typicality of a phenomenon, or the extent to which it compares and contrasts along relevant dimensions with other phenomena." There is no difficulty with this concept of generalization; the difficulty comes in attempting to use the concepts of random sampling or a formal mathematical model for argumentation, the later being used either knowingly or inadvertently. External validity in ethnographic research is, as the research itself, grounded in phenomenology and not in the positivism approach of quantitative research.

So, how then do we argue the generalizability of ethnographic research results? To take an extreme position that there is no generalization is not a functional position. Polkinghorne (1991) makes a very useful distinction between two types of generalizations:

Aggregate-type—generalizations limited to statements about the population considered as an entirety.

General-type—generalizations in which assertions are made that something is true for each and every member of a population. (p. 5, paraphrased)

Quantitative research uses the aggregate-type generalization; although, sometimes there is confusion and group results are interpreted as individual results. Ethnographic research uses general-type generalization.

This latter type of generalization is based on what is called assertoric argumentation (Polkinghorne, 1983). Such argumentation is based on the reasonableness of its claim given that its assumptions and evidence are acceptable. Assertoric argumentation accepts a full range of rationality. As examples, generalization may be based on the logic of similarity or dissimilarity in which something is understood as more or less like a prototype, and the logic of narrative relationships of events to a plot in which the meaning of an event is understood by its relationship to a designated outcome (Polkinghorne, 1991, p. 7).

External validity in ethnographic research is general-type generalization based on assertoric argumentation.

As an example of how external validity is addressed in a report of ethnographic research, a statement from the study by Harry (1992) is given below. That study was described earlier in Example 10.1. The statement appears relatively early in the report in a section on the interpretation of the data:

> *It cannot be claimed that the findings from a small sample of one cultural group can be generalized to other populations. However, the recurrent nature of the data-collection process and the considerable triangulation of data ensure that an accurate picture of participants' views has been obtained. It is therefore reasonable to assume that similar dynamics might be expected with similar populations under similar circumstances. Most important, since the study is concerned with the process of interaction between professionals and parents from poor and culturally different backgrounds, rather than with cultural understandings specific to any one group, it has much to offer to our understanding of how cross-cultural miscommunication can occur and, indeed, how it can be corrected. (p. 478)*

Although the author does not use the term assertoric argumentation, this essentially is being used. The opening sentence recognizes that a sampling argument cannot be used. But then the author makes a logical case for the generalizability of the results.

Another way of considering external validity in ethnographic research is that it is established through a posteriori judgment, which means an argument based on actual observation. In this type of generalization, the argument is that the results represent a reasonable possibility of being applicable in other situations. The generalization of the results is not conclusive until the results are actually tested in the situation to which the results are believed to apply. (This is sometimes called a generalization test.) This brings up another point about the responsibility of the reader of ethnographic research reports in establishing the external validity of the research. Lincoln and Guba (1985) comment on the transfer of findings from qualitative research:

> *The burden of proof (for the generalizability of results) lies less with the original investigator than with the person seeking to make application elsewhere . . . the responsibility of the original investigator ends in providing sufficient descriptive data to make such similarity judgments (with the "new" situation) possible. (p. 298)*

Thus, with ethnographic research—as with all qualitative research—the reader, or potential user, of the research results has a responsibility of interpreting the results and making judgments about its generalizability. This responsibility is greater than it would be for most quantitative research results. However, it is the responsibility of the researcher to specify conditions of the research setting and procedures, so that the basis for comparison (or lack thereof) can be established.

External validity of ethnographic research typically is argued on the basis of a posteriori judgment.

As a procedural matter, external validity can be strengthened by multisite studies. If a phenomenon seems to be consistent across a number of studies, its generalizability is increased. Even if there is inconsistency in the phenomenon, a study of the differences between the sites may reveal the limitations or specific conditions of generalization. Certainly, not all ethnographic studies in education can be multisite studies; in fact, few would meet that criterion. But the external validity can be enhanced by including variations of the research context in the same study. For example, if writing instruction in the elementary schools is being studied, including two or more elementary classrooms in the same study would enhance external validity.

Absolute reliability and validity are impossible to attain in any research study, regardless of type. Yet researchers establish reliability by using appropriate research procedures and through careful documentation of the research. This strategy applies to ethnographic research, and external validity is established, for the most part, on a logical argument.

The Role of Ethnographic Research

Ethnographic research involves a variety of procedures, giving it considerable flexibility and applicability in education. Ethnographic research emphasizes context, making it especially suitable for inquiry into educational issues that are heavily context-dependent. McMillan and Schumacher (1989) identify the impact of ethnographic research on educational inquiry as a dynamic one because "the methodology allows researchers to discover what are the important questions to ask of a topic and what are the important topics in education to pursue through empirical methods" (p. 423). So, ethnographic research can make an important contribution to a basic issue for all educational research, namely, "What are the important questions to ask?"

Because of the extensive and rich description coming from ethnographic research, such research provides a good potential for theoretical contributions, certainly theory development and, to some extent, theory testing. Extensive description provides a reservoir of evidence; if the fieldwork is well done, just from its sheer volume, it provides a preponderance of information about educational phenomena. Ethnographic research is appropriate for large-scale studies about the nature of education.

However, it should not be inferred that ethnographic research is applicable only for large-scale studies or for studies with extensive funding resources. The phenomenon under study requires observation to be understood; and teachers, part of whose role is that of classroom observer, are in an advantageous position for conducting research in the schools. Kantor, Kirby, and Goetz (1981, p. 305) address this point along with collaboration between teachers and researchers:

Experienced teachers have knowledge of children and classroom settings which makes them potentially strong researchers; ethnography allows them to use that knowledge and opens opportunities for dialogue between teachers and re-

searchers. Especially promising are collaborative efforts between teachers and researchers.

More recently, Cochran-Smith and Lytle (1990), although not limiting their argument to ethnographic research, make the case for not only the desirability but necessity of involving teachers in research on teaching.

Wagner (1990) makes the case that school administrators can serve effectively as ethnographers, especially in collaborative efforts with other educational researchers. In this article, the author examines several parallels between the work of educational administrators and school ethnography. Cited are examples of successful, collaborative research in which educational administrators have assumed the role of ethnographer. Accepting these arguments for the participation of teachers and administrators in ethnographic research, implies that this area of research is amenable to action research. Ethnographic research, by its very nature, requires a considerable time commitment, but teachers and school administrators are in an advantageous position to participate in such research.

However, just as any research approach has its limitations, ethnographic research should not be expected to be all things to all people. As Wolcott (1988, p. 203) points out, ethnographic research tends to focus on how things are and how they got that way. Of itself, ethnographic research does not prescribe courses of action; these are left for the researcher to develop, and the ethnographic account may or may not be helpful in this endeavor. Ethnographic research tends to reveal the complexity of educational phenomena, and, in the long run, this should be helpful in improving education. As more ethnographic research is done, the educational community should become better informed and become more sensitive to the importance of context in educational research.

> Ethnographic research makes contributions to education through empirical description of phenomena, the development of grounded theory, and theory testing. Ethnographic research focuses on how things are and how they got that way.

Summary

This chapter discussed ethnographic research in education, its rationale, and its methodology. Ethnographic research is conducted in a natural setting with emphasis on understanding the phenomenon under study from the perspective of those being studied. The product of ethnographic research is an ethnography, an account that might be described as a portrait of a culture or a *portraiture*. The ethnography is cultural description and interpretation.

Ethnographic research is concentrated heavily in fieldwork, and includes observation, interviewing, and other data-collecting procedures. The pre-fieldwork stage consists of focusing in on the research problem and selecting a research site. The ethnographic researcher does not necessarily formulate specific questions or hypotheses until the fieldwork is begun, but the available knowledge base relative to the problem is explored. The research site is not selected at random; it is selected because of characteristics that make it appropriate for the research.

Data are collected in the field, which necessitates on-site observation using field-based instruments. Observation may be more or less structured, and the results of observation are recorded in field notes. The processes of generating hypotheses, collecting data, and drawing conclusions are highly integrated. The research process is an attempt to enter into the conceptual world of those being studied in order to understand how and what meaning they construct about the phenomenon under study. The objective is to attain a holistic description of the phenomenon.

A conceptual schema for ethnographic research was discussed, involving the concepts of perspectives, cultures, and organizations. Such a conceptual schema aids in understanding the general characteristics of an approach to research. The methodological steps in ethnographic research include the usual activities of conducting research. These steps or activities tend to overlap and are more extensively integrated than they are in other types of research. For example, an experimenter typically begins with a specified set of hypotheses that will be tested by conducting the experiment. In contrast, the ethnographic researcher identifies the phenomenon to be studied and then develops the hypotheses through the data collection. Subsequently, the hypotheses may be retained, modified, or discarded. Theory may be generated from the data; this is known as grounded theory.

Ethnographic research's contribution to education is through "rich," empirical description. Through this description understanding is enhanced, and there is a potential for theoretical contributions. As a mode of inquiry, ethnographic research is inductive, which means that the analysis is based on the information that emerges from the data rather than being imposed on the data according to some prior theory or hypotheses. Ethnographic research emphasizes context, and since so many educational phenomena appear to be context-specific, ethnographic research has many applications in educational research.

Key Concepts

Ethnography	Triangulation
Field research	Ballparking
Contextualization	Field notes
Phenomenology	Reliability
Grounded theory	Validity
Organization	Portraiture
Culture	Inductive inquiry
Perspective	Key informant
Participant-observer	Aggregate-type generalization
Privileged observer	General-type generalization
Limited observer	Assertoric argumentation
Coding	A posteriori judgment
Foreshadowed problems	

EXERCISES

10.1   Contrast the nature of ethnographic research and the nature of experimental research. Identify differences in orientation and methodology. What are some conditions under which each type is appropriate?

10.2   If we identify the conceptual components of ethnographic research as perspectives, cultures, and organizations, describe how these components are related or connected. Select an example (either real or hypothetical) of ethnographic research in education, and identify these components for the example.

10.3   Define the process of triangulation. Suppose a researcher is conducting ethnographic research on instruction in elementary school mathematics. Describe how triangulation might be used.

10.4   A study is being conducted on student life in a private, residential prep school (assume grades nine through twelve). Identify the perspectives, cultures, and organization for this study. Develop two or more sample hypotheses that might be generated, based on the observation.

10.5   A fourth-grade teacher is interested in conducting research, essentially action research, on the nature of instruction in arithmetic compared to the nature of instruction in reading-language arts, from the students' viewpoints. The research is conducted with this teacher's class of twenty-seven students, beginning in October and concluding the next June. As an ethnographic study, identify the organization, cultures, and possible perspectives in this study. What phenomena would be observed within the instruction? Would interviewing be conducted, and if so, what types of questions would be asked and of whom? Comment on the external validity of the study. How important is generalizability of results, and on what basis could external validity be established?

10.6   For the study described in Exercise 10.5, suppose the teacher designates an hour each week for observation of instruction in each of the two subjects. At the completion of the hour, the teacher writes field notes about the instruction observed. Suggest possible coding systems that might be used for classifying the information in the field notes. What might be useful major codes and subcodes? Is it necessary to use the same coding system for instruction in both arithmetic and reading-language arts?

10.7   Describe the differences between a participant-observer, a privileged observer, and a limited observer. Provide an example of each that applies to ethnographic research in education.

10.8   An ethnographer is conducting a study of the "nature of foreign language instruction" in a senior high school, specifically instruction in French, Spanish, and German. Over the period of a school year, the researcher observes classes in each language on a continuing basis, observing at least two classes in each language each week. Describe what may be the content of the researcher's field notes. Develop three or four questions that might be included in a student interview. Do the same for a teacher interview.

10.9   Distinguish between the reliability and the validity of ethnographic research.

10.10   Describe what is meant when we say that external validity in ethnographic research is based on assertoric argumentation and is general-type generalization. Contrast this with aggregate-type generalization typically used for establishing external validity for most quantitative research.

10.11   Why is it sometimes difficult to establish external validity of ethnographic research? What can be done to enhance external validity in ethnographic research?

10.12   Select an article dealing with ethnographic research from a professional journal. Review the article carefully, identifying the research problem and the hypotheses generated. Is the methodology described in adequate detail so that the reader can understand how the study was conducted? How is the issue of generalizability addressed? Do the conclusions follow from the results?

NOTES

1. The schema discussed in this section is based on concepts discussed in Becker et al., *Boys in White: Student Culture in Medical School* (Chicago: University of Chicago Press, 1961). Although the Becker et al. book is based on an extensive study, one beyond the scope of most research conducted for a thesis or dissertation, the concepts underlying that study are useful for conceptualizing ethnographic research regardless of the scope of a specific study.

2. The term *informant* is not used as in police circles, when it means a person who informs on other people. Ethnographic researchers use informants for their knowledge, opinion, and interpretation.

3. The summer 1987 issue of the *American Educational Research Journal* (Vol. 24, No. 2) has a special section on qualitative methodology that includes discussions of reporting and publishing qualitative research. Anyone contemplating the publication of an ethnographic research study will find this section helpful.

4. This method of analysis is called the constant comparative method as described by B. Glaser and A. L. Strauss, *The Discovery of Grounded Theory; Strategies for Qualitative Research* (Chicago: Aldine, 1967).

REFERENCES

Becker, H. S., Geer, B., Hughes, E. C., and Strauss, A. L. (1961). *Boys in white: Student culture in medical school*. Chicago: University of Chicago Press.

Bogdan, R. C., and Biklen, S. K. (1992). *Qualitative research for education: An introduction to theory and methods*. Boston: Allyn and Bacon.

Boyer, E. L. (1983). *High school: A report on secondary education in America*. New York: Harper & Row.

Cochran-Smith, M., and Lytle, S. L. (1990). Research on teaching and teacher research: The issues that divide. *Educational Researcher,* 19(2), 2–11.

Denzin, N. K. (1978). *The research act: A theoretical introduction to sociological methods* (2nd ed.). Chicago: Aldine.

Erickson, R. (1986). Qualitative methods in research on teaching. In M. C. Wittrock (Ed.), *Handbook of research on teaching* (3rd ed.) (pp. 119–161). New York: Macmillan.

Geertz, C. (1973). *The interpretations of cultures*. New York: Basic Books.

Goetz, J. P., and LeCompte, M. D. (1984). *Ethnography and qualitative design in educational research*. New York: Academic Press.

Goodlad, J. I. (1984). *A place called school*. New York: McGraw-Hill.

Harry, B. (1992). An ethnographic study of cross-cultural communication with Puerto Rican-American families in the special education system.

American Educational Research Journal, 29(3), 471–494.

Kantor, K. J., Kirby, D. R., and Goetz, J. P. (1981). Research in context: Ethnographic studies in English education. *Research in the Teaching of English,* 15(4), 293–309.

Lancy, D. F. (1993). *Qualitative research in education: An introduction to the major traditions*. New York: Longman.

LeCompte, M. D., and Goetz, J. P. (1982). Problems of reliability and validity in ethnographic research. *Review of Educational Research,* 52(1), 31–60.

Lincoln, Y. S., and Guba, E. G. (1985). *Naturalistic inquiry*. Beverly Hills, CA: Sage.

McMillan, J. H., and Schumacher, S. (1989). *Research in education: A conceptual introduction.* (2nd ed.). Glenview, IL: Scott, Foresman.

Polkinghorne, D. E. (1983). *Methodology for the human sciences: Systems of inquiry.* Albany: State University of New York Press.

Polkinghorne, D. E. (1991). *Generalization and qualitative research: Issues of external validity.* Paper presented at the annual meeting of the American Educational Research Association, Chicago.

Schneider, B., and Lee, Y. (1990). A model for academic success: The school and home environment of East Asian students. *Anthropology and Education Quarterly,* 21(4), 358–377.

Schofield, J. W., and Anderson, K. (1984). *Integreting quantitative components into qualitative studies: Problems and possibilities for research on intergroup relations in education settings.* Paper presented at the annual meeting of the American Educational Research Association, New Orleans.

Smith, M. L., and Glass, G. V. (1987). *Research and evaluation in education and the social sciences.* Englewood Cliffs, NJ: Prentice-Hall.

Wagner, J. (1990). Administrators as ethnographers: School as a context for inquiry and action. *Anthropology and Education Quarterly,* 21(3), 195–221.

Wax, R. H. (1971). *Doing fieldwork: Warnings and advice.* Chicago: University of Chicago Press.

Wolcott, H. F. (1988). Ethnographic research in education. In R. M. Jaeger (Ed.), *Complementary methods for research in education* (pp. 187–210). Washington, DC: American Educational Research Association.

C h a p t e r **11**

Sampling Designs

The preceding chapters discussed research designs for various types of studies and mentioned samples and random assignment from time to time. On occasion, an entire population of individuals may be included in a research study, but in many educational research studies, it is simply not feasible to include all members of a population. The time and effort required would be prohibitive. This is certainly true in survey research when large populations are concerned. Thus, a sample is used much more commonly. This chapter describes procedures for selecting samples.

A sample is a subset of the population to which the researcher intends to generalize the results. To do this, the researcher wants the sample, or the individuals actually involved in the research, to be representative of the larger population. Selecting a random sample ensures representativeness from a mathematical perspective. However, it is not possible to select random samples for all possible educational research studies so, at times, purposeful samples are used. A sample either is or is not random, and a random sample must incorporate some aspect of random selection. Obtaining a random sample may be a relatively complex procedure, especially if large (and possibly diverse) populations are to be sampled. The first part of this chapter is devoted to a discussion of random sampling procedures, followed in the second part by a discussion of purposeful sampling.

The Concept of a Random Sample

A random sample involves what is called *probability sampling,* which means that every member of the population has a nonzero probability of being selected for the sample. In other words, all members of the population have some chance of being included in the sample. In complex sampling designs, the probabilities of selection may *not* be the same for all members, but the probabilities are all nonzero. A simple random sample is such that when it is selected, all members of the population have the same probability of being selected.[1]

A *random sample* is an unbiased sample, which means that those individuals selected vary only as they would due to random fluctuation. There is no systematic variation in the sample that would make this sample different from other samples. Of course, a random sample is representative of the population from which it was selected.

> A *random sample* is a probability sample in that every population member has a nonzero probability of selection. In a simple random sample, this probability is the same for all population members.

Random Selection and Random Assignment

Random selection and random assignment are not quite the same, but they are both used to obtain representativeness and eliminate bias. In *random selection,* the individuals are selected randomly as representing a population; in *random assignment,* commonly used in experiments, the individuals are randomly assigned to different groups or treatments. They may or may not have been initially selected from a larger population to participate in the experiment. Some examples follow.

An institutional researcher at a university selects a random sample of 250 from the freshman class of 6821 students, who are then surveyed about their attitudes toward certain factors of college life. This example involves random selection. The 250 students of the sample are representative of the 6821 in the freshman class.

A psychologist has 90 students in a sophomore-level psychology course. The psychologist is conducting a learning experiment using three different types of materials. All 90 students will participate, and 30 will be randomly assigned to each of the types of materials. In this way, the three groups of students assigned to the different materials vary only on a random basis. As the students are assigned, any student has the same probability of being assigned to any one of the three materials—namely, one in three or one-third.

In the latter example, what population do these 90 students represent? They were not randomly selected from a larger population. Their reason for participating in the experiment is that they enrolled in the psychology course. In a sense, they have self-selected themselves. In this situation, the psychologist would likely argue that the 90 students are representative of young adults attending college. If sophomore students at this university are much like those at other universities, the results may generalize to other populations of university students. It is not likely that the results would generalize to all young adults everywhere. Often, in studies of this type, representativeness is argued on a logical basis, depending on the individuals and variables involved.

The contrast between random selection and random assignment is diagrammed in Figure 11.1. When a defined group (such as the psychology class) is used, and the members are randomly assigned to treatments, there is no question about the assignment being unbiased or the results generalizing to the group involved. But the generalizability of the results to larger populations is done on a logical basis, in which questions of

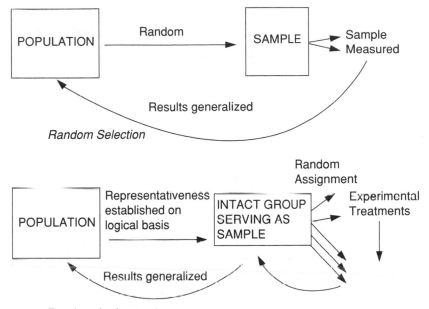

FIGURE 11.1   Contrast Between Random Selection and Random Assignment

unrepresentativeness may be raised. Of course, this is a matter of external validity, and the extent of representativeness and, correspondingly, the generalizability are always a matter of degree. Yet random assignment is commonly used in this way in educational research. Knowledge about the variables and individuals of the study is then used to make valid generalizations.

It might be mentioned that in a situation in which the number of individuals in the intact group does not equal the number required, the excess individuals are eliminated at random. (This is conceptually the same as selecting those for inclusion at random.) In the learning experiment example, if there were 94 students in the class and only 90 were required, 4 would be randomly selected not to participate. To avoid causing any apprehension, the psychologist could use all 94 in the experiment and then randomly eliminate the data of 4 individuals with the condition that each type of material would still have the data of 30 individuals.

Use of a Random Number Table

A simple random sample can be obtained by using a table of random numbers. (Table 11.1 is a sample page from a random number table.) Each member of the finite population is

TABLE 11.1 Sample Page from a Table of Random Numbers

	50–54	55–59	60–64	65–69	70–74	75–79	80–84	85–89	90–94	95–99
00	59391	58030	52098	82718	87024	82848	04190	96574	90464	29065
01	99567	76364	77204	04615	27062	96621	43918	01896	83991	51141
02	10363	97518	51400	25670	98342	61891	27101	37855	06235	33316
03	86859	19558	64432	16706	99612	59798	32803	67708	15297	28612
04	11258	24591	36863	55368	31721	94335	34936	02566	80972	08188
05	95068	88628	35911	14530	33020	80428	39936	31855	34334	64865
06	54463	47237	73800	91017	36239	71824	83671	39892	60518	37092
07	16874	62677	57412	13215	31389	62233	80827	73917	82802	84420
08	92494	63157	76593	91316	03505	72389	96363	52887	01087	66091
09	15669	56689	35682	40844	53256	81872	35213	09840	34471	74441
10	96116	75486	84989	23476	52967	67104	39495	39100	17217	74073
11	15696	10703	65178	90637	63110	17622	53988	71087	84148	11670
12	97720	15369	51269	69620	03388	13699	33423	67453	43269	56720
13	11666	13841	71681	98000	35979	39719	81899	07449	47985	46967
14	71628	73130	78783	75691	41632	09487	61547	18707	85489	69944
15	40501	51089	99943	91843	41995	88931	73631	69361	05375	15417
16	22518	55576	98215	82068	10798	86211	36584	67466	69373	40054
17	75112	30485	62173	02132	14878	92879	22281	16783	86352	00077
18	80327	02671	98191	84342	90813	49268	95441	15496	20168	09271
19	60251	45548	02146	05597	48228	81366	34598	72856	66762	17002
20	57430	82270	10421	05540	43648	75888	66049	21511	47676	33444
21	73528	39599	34434	88596	54086	71693	43132	14414	79949	85193
22	25991	65959	70769	64721	86413	33475	42740	06175	82758	66248
23	78388	16638	09134	59880	63806	48472	39318	35434	24057	74739
24	12477	09965	96657	57994	59439	76330	24596	77515	09577	91871
25	83266	32883	42451	15579	38155	29793	40914	65990	16255	17777
26	76970	80876	10237	39515	79152	74798	39357	09054	73579	92359
27	37074	65198	44785	68624	98336	84481	97610	78735	46703	98265
28	83712	06514	30101	78295	54656	85417	43189	60048	72781	72606
29	20287	56862	69727	94443	64936	08366	27227	05158	50326	59566
30	74261	32592	86538	27041	65172	85532	07571	80609	39285	65340
31	64081	49863	08478	96001	18888	14810	70545	89755	59064	07210
32	05617	75818	47750	67814	29575	10526	66192	44464	27058	40467
33	26793	74951	95466	74307	13330	42664	85515	20632	05497	33625
34	65988	72850	48737	54719	52056	01596	03845	35067	03134	70322
35	27366	42271	44300	73399	21105	03280	73457	43093	05192	48657
36	56760	10909	98147	34736	33863	95256	12731	66598	50771	83665
37	72880	43338	93643	58904	59543	23943	11231	83268	65938	81581
38	77888	38100	03062	58103	47961	83841	25878	23746	55903	44115
39	28440	07819	21580	51459	47971	29882	13990	29226	23608	15873
40	63525	94441	77033	12147	51054	49955	58312	76923	96071	05813
41	47606	93410	16359	89033	89696	47231	64498	31776	05383	39902
42	52669	45030	96279	14709	52372	87832	02735	50803	72744	88208
43	16738	60159	07425	62369	07515	82721	37875	71153	21315	00132
44	59348	11695	45751	15865	74739	05572	32688	20271	65128	14551
46	12900	71775	29845	60774	94924	21810	38636	33717	67598	82521
47	75086	23537	49939	33595	13484	97588	28617	17979	70749	35234
48	99495	51434	29181	09993	38190	42553	68922	52125	91077	40197
48	26075	31671	45386	36583	93548	48599	52022	41330	60651	91321
49	13636	93596	23377	51133	95126	61496	42474	45141	46660	42338

Source: Reprinted by permission from *Statistical Methods* (6th ed.), by G. W. Snedecor and W. G. Cochran, © 1967 by the State University Press, Ames, Iowa.

assigned a number, and then as many numbers as comprise the sample size are selected from the table. If there is a population of 70 members and 10 are to be selected at random, each of the 70 members is assigned a number from 1 to 70. The first 10 numbers that appear, wherever one begins in the random number table, determine the 10 sample members. Since there are only 70 members in the population, two-digit random numbers are used. Beginning with the first row in Table 11.1 and going across, taking two-digit numbers in sequence gives the following 10 numbers.

59, 39, 15, 80 (which is ignored, since our highest number is 70), 30, 52, 09, 88 (also ignored), 27, 18, 87 (also ignored), 02, and 48.

If a number exceeding 70 appears, it is ignored. If a number appears that has already been selected, it too, is ignored, because a single member of the population is not included twice in the sample. Any kind of sequencing in the table is random, and it is not necessary to go across the rows. The numbers could be selected in columns or by blocks. In Table 11.1, the numbers are grouped by fives to make it easier to locate them.

The random number table can also be used for random assignment. If 10 individuals are to be assigned at random, 5 to each of two treatments, single-digit numbers can be used, since (instead of 10) zero can be assigned to one individual. Using the random numbers of Table 11.1, if one begins with the first row of the second major block of five rows, the individuals with the first five numbers would be assigned to Treatment 1: 9, 5, 0, 6, and 8. This leaves the individuals with the following numbers for Treatment 2: 1, 2, 3, 4, and 7. If an individual's number repeats, it is passed over, because an individual can be assigned only once to a treatment.

Random number tables can be used for random selection and random assignment.

Sampling Error and Sampling Bias

Sampling error and sampling bias, two terms associated with sampling, at times are confused, although they have very different meanings. Sampling error is associated with random sampling and the term "error" does not mean making a mistake. Suppose we have a population of 1675 fifth graders and we select a random sample of 150 from this population. The sample is administered a science achievement test and the mean score on the test is 86.3. Would we argue that the mean of the population is *exactly* 86.3? No, but we are confident that the mean is a value around 86.3. The difference between the sample mean of 86.3 and the population mean, whatever it is, is an example of sampling error. Sampling error is related to variation, a concept introduced in Chapter 4 and discussed more fully in the chapters on statistical analysis. Sampling error is variation due to random fluctuation. In specific situations in which statistical analyses are used, we can obtain an estimate of sampling error. Generally, as sample size increases, the variation due to random fluctuation, and hence sampling error, decreases.

Sampling error is variation due to random fluctuation when random samples are used to represent populations.

Sampling bias is a different matter. Bias enters in when a sample fails to represent the population it was intended to represent. Bias can be due to any number of sources, and it is a threat whenever nonrandom (or nonprobability) sampling is used, or when random sampling is used with a biased source.

Consider again the previous example of the fifth-grade population. Suppose, instead of selecting a random sample, we selected five classes of fifth-graders, each class from a different school. The classes average 30 students per class so we again have 150 students in the sample. But the classes selected are the high-ability classes within the schools. For this sample the mean on the science achievement test is 103.8. Does this mean represent the science achievement of the population. Absolutely not. Sampling bias has occurred and this is a biased sample because of the way in which the sample was selected, in this case in a nonrandom manner.

Even though random sampling is used, sampling bias can occur if we have a biased source. The commonly cited survey in which a biased source was used was the 1936 survey by the Literary Digest which predicted that Alf Landon would win the presidential election over Franklin Roosevelt. Random sampling was used but the sample was selected primarily from telephone directories and automobile registration lists. In 1936 these lists were not representative of the voting population.

Consider another example. Suppose someone wanted to select a sample of the general population of U.S. adults. Country club membership lists are used for the source, and a random sample selected from such lists. This sample is not representative of the general, adult population. It was selected from a biased source.

Sampling bias is a distortion caused by the way the sample was selected or formed, so that the sample is no longer representative of the population.

As was discussed in Chapter 7, questionnaire surveys cause concern about possible bias due to nonresponse. Even though the original sample was selected randomly, the respondents, in essence, self-select themselves into the sample, possibly becoming a biased source. This may bias the sample causing those who respond to be no longer representative of the population. This, too, is an example of sampling bias.

Criteria for a Sampling Design

There may be any number of reasons why a researcher would depart from simple random sampling to use a more complex sampling design. Probably the most common reason is that the population from which the sample is to be selected is so large that simple random sampling cannot be conducted. The population may also be quite diverse and may consist of several subpopulations. Populations whose members are grouped or clustered are more readily sampled than individual members. If the population is very heterogeneous, an alternative to simple random sampling will tend to control some of the sampling variation.

Whatever the reason for using a more complex sampling design, a good sampling design should meet certain requirements. Kish (1965) identified four broad criteria for a good sampling design: (1) goal orientation, (2) measurability, (3) practicality, and (4) economy.

The first criterion, goal orientation, means that the sampling design should be tailored to the research design and should be based on the study's goals or objectives. The measurement necessary to obtain the data and the anticipated analyses, based on the research problem, also have important implications for sampling. These factors are considered in deciding what sampling design will best meet the goals and objectives of the study.

The criterion of measurability means that the sampling design provides the data for the necessary analyses. If a design has measurability, valid estimates of sampling variability, which are essential for the use of inferential statistics, can be made. (Inferential statistics are discussed in Chapter 14.) Measurability enables valid inferences to be made from the sample data to the population from which the sample was selected.

It is one thing to sketch a sampling design on paper theoretically and another to apply the design in a real situation. The criterion of practicality means that the actual activities of applying the sampling design have been identified and are feasible in the real situation. Practicality also means attempting to anticipate problems and devising methods for avoiding or circumventing them, and it involves making the conceptual design conform with the actual situation.

The criterion of economy is largely self-explanatory. Expenditures for educational research projects are usually limited, and economy requires that the research objectives be met with available resources: time, financial, personnel, and any other necessary resources. Since obtaining data for a research project can be time-consuming and expensive, a good sampling design is not wasteful of data-collection efforts.

Because it is not likely that all four criteria can be met maximally, attempting to meet these four criteria when developing a sampling design often becomes a matter of balance. For example, to enhance measurability, the researcher may increase the sample size to the extent that some economy is sacrificed. It may not be possible to anticipate all problems, but even with problems a design may be feasible and thus attain adequate practicality. The important overall criterion is that the design be feasible and adequately accommodate the research problem.

Stratified Random Sampling

Before discussing stratified random sampling, it is necessary to define the *sampling fraction*. This fraction is the ratio of sample size to population size, often designated n/N. Thus, if a sample of size 300 is selected from a population of size 2000, the sampling fraction would be 300/2000 or 3/20, which equals .15. For a simple random sample, the sampling fraction equals the probability of any member of the population being selected for the sample.

> The *sampling fraction* is the ratio of sample size to population size, expressed as n/N.

In some cases, the population to be sampled is not homogeneous but, in essence, consists of several subpopulations. Rather than selecting randomly from the entire population, the researcher might divide such a population into two or more subpopulations, called *strata*. This approach to sampling is called *stratified random sampling* because the population is stratified into its subpopulations. All strata are represented in the sample, and the sample members are selected from each stratum at random. Thus, the condition of random selection is included by the selection within the strata.

Allocation of Sample Size Among Strata

The decision must be made as to the number (that is, allocation) that will be selected from each stratum for the sample. One method of allocation, called *equal allocation,* is to select equal numbers from the strata. Thus, if there were five strata, one-fifth of the sample would be selected from each stratum. Unless the strata had equal population sizes, the sampling fraction would vary among strata.

A more commonly used method is *proportional allocation,* whereby each stratum contributes to the sample a number that is proportional to its size in the population. The allocation of strata members in the sample is proportional to the numbers of members in the strata of the population. Suppose that there are k strata to be sampled and that the respective population sizes of the strata are $N_1, N_2, \ldots, N_k$. Total population size can be indicated by N and total sample size by n. We can let $n_1, n_2, \ldots n_k$ be the sample sizes for the respective strata. Then:

$$\frac{n}{N} = \frac{n_1}{N_1} = \frac{n_2}{N_2} = \cdots = \frac{n_k}{N_k}$$

where $N_1 + N_2 + \cdots + N_k = N$ and $n_1 + n_2 + \cdots + n_k = n$. The sampling fraction is n/N, and this fraction (proportionality) is held constant for the allocation of the sample to the k strata.

Stratified sampling guards against wild samples, ensures that no subpopulation will be omitted from the sample, and avoids overloading in certain subpopulations. Stratified random samples are sometimes called *self-weighting samples.* Simple random samples have a tendency to distribute themselves according to the population proportions, and stratified random sampling with proportional allocation will build this proportionality into the sample.

Proportional allocation in stratified random sampling distributes the sample in such a way that the sampling fraction is the same for all strata.

Other allocations could be used if there is a compelling reason to do so. For example, if there is a large variable stratum a decision might be made to give it an allocation three times that of other strata. But from a practical standpoint equal allocation and proportional allocation are by far the most frequently used allocations, with proportional allocation often preferred because of its self-weighting characteristic.

EXAMPLE 11.1

We will present an example using proportional allocation. The director of institutional research at a university is conducting a survey of student opinion on the adequacy of facilities—the student union, the library, and so forth. The questionnaire is quite extensive, so rather than administer it to all students, a 5 percent stratified random sample will be selected. The university contains seven colleges, with a total enrollment of 15,823 students. The definition of an enrolled student is one who is presently registered to be taking at least one course for degree credit. College is the stratifying variable, and proportional allocation will be used. Because a 5 percent sample is selected, the sampling fraction is $\frac{1}{20}$, or .05. The information for this sampling example is presented in Figure 11.2.

Note that all strata (colleges) contribute to the sample. The sample members for each college are randomly selected within the college. Since colleges vary greatly in size, equal allocation would not be desirable if the opinions varied considerably among colleges.

The question might be raised, "What variables and how many can be effectively used for stratification?" More than one stratifying variable could be used, but this can substantially increase the number of strata because it involves combinations of the two variables. In the example, if the colleges of Arts and Sciences, Business Administration, Education, and Engineering have graduate as well as undergraduate programs, it might be desirable to stratify on the dichotomous variable undergraduate-graduate in these four colleges. Law would likely be considered a graduate program and thus would have no undergraduates. Community Services and Pharmacy have only undergraduates. If stratification were done in this manner, there would be 11 instead of 7 strata.

The number of strata that can be conveniently accommodated depends to some extent on the sample size. The larger the sample size, the more strata can be used. However, strata are not identified simply for the sake of having a large number of them. Unless a large survey is being conducted, stratification seldom involves more than two stratifying variables (usually only one), and the total number of strata would seldom exceed 20 and usually is considerably less.

Strata (college)	Strata sizes		Sample size by strata
Arts & Sciences	5,461		273
Business Administration	1,850		93
Community Services	2,092	A 1/20 random sample is selected from each stratum	105
Education	3,508		175
Engineering	2,112		106
Law	318		16
Pharmacy	482		24
	15,823 = N		792 = n

.05 of the total university population equals 15,823 x .05 = 791.15. The n of 792 includes any rounding off.

FIGURE 11.2   Sample Selection Using Proportional Allocation—University Example

Cluster Sampling

When the selection of individual members of the population is impractical or too expensive, it may be possible to select groups or clusters of members for the sample. *Cluster sampling* is a procedure of selection in which the unit of selection, called the cluster, contains two or more populations members. Each member of the population must be uniquely contained in one, and only one, cluster. Cluster sampling is useful in situations where the population members are naturally grouped in units that can be used conveniently as clusters. For example, pollsters doing surveys sometimes use city blocks as the cluster unit for selecting a sample. In educational research, a class can serve as a cluster. A school building, or possibly even a school system, might serve as a cluster in a large-scale study.

Cluster sampling differs from stratified random sampling in that the random selection occurs not with the individual members but with the clusters. The clusters from the sample are randomly selected from the larger population of clusters, and once a cluster is selected for the sample, all the population members in that cluster are included in the sample. This is in contrast to stratified random sampling, in which the individual members within strata are randomly selected. In cluster sampling, before selecting the sample, not only must all population members be identified in their clusters, but all the clusters must be identified. It is not necessary that all clusters have the same number of population members.

Cluster sampling involves the random selection of clusters from the larger population of clusters. All the population members of a selected cluster are included in the sample.

In cluster sampling, the exact sample size may not be known until after the sample is selected. This is because clusters usually are not the same size, and the final sample size depends on those clusters that are randomly selected. However, clusters are often somewhat similar in size, and if the researcher has a sample size in mind, the number of clusters required can be estimated.

EXAMPLE 11.2 _____

An example of a research situation for which cluster sampling would be appropriate is a survey of fourth-grade achievement in mathematics, using a standardized achievement test, conducted by the research director of a city system that contains 33 elementary schools. It is too expensive to administer the test to all fourth-graders in the system, and the logistics of selecting a simple random sample and administering the test would be quite extensive. Stratified random sampling might be feasible, but it has one disadvantage: the fourth-graders are in classes, and it is inconvenient to test some members of the class and not others. Since the fourth-graders are "naturally" assembled in classes, cluster sampling is to be used, using class as the sampling unit. Then all students in a selected class are to be tested.

There are 83 fourth-grade classes throughout the system, with an average enrollment of 27.3 students per class. A sample size of approximately 550 students is desired, so it is decided to select 20 classes or clusters. The sampling design is diagrammed in Figure 11.3.

All members of the 20 selected classes are tested on mathematics achievement. It so happens that 561 students are tested, which is a slightly larger than anticipated sample. (Some students may be absent on the testing day, but this is of no concern if the absence pattern is typical.)

The tendency is for cluster sampling to be used with large populations. Whatever the sampling unit, it is usually something that groups the population members naturally. As the size of the cluster increases, however, the sample size also becomes large, since all members of a selected cluster are in the sample. The sampling unit should be carefully selected and well defined so that there is no confusion as to what comprises a cluster. Cluster sampling has implications for the analysis of data in that the cluster may be used as the unit of analysis.

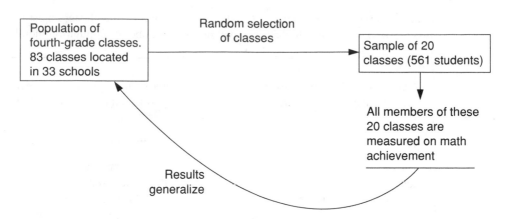

FIGURE 11.3   Sample Selection Using Cluster Sampling—Fourth-Grade Example

Systematic Sampling

The use of systematic sampling is quite common in educational research in which large populations are studied and alphabetical or possibly other lists of the population members are available. Directors of institutional research often use this technique in selecting a sample. The primary advantage of systematic sampling in educational research is convenience.

Systematic sampling is a procedure by which the selection of the first sample member determines the entire sample. The population members (that is, their names or type of identification) are in some type of order; for example, the names of the population members may be placed in alphabetical order on a list. The sample size is chosen and the sampling fraction determined. If the sampling fraction is 1/10, the first member of the sample is randomly selected from the first ten names on the list. Following this first selection, every tenth member of the population is selected for the sample. In the general case, if the sampling fraction n/N equals 1/k, the first member of the sample is randomly selected from the first k names on the list, and after that, every kth name on the list is selected. When the list is exhausted, the sample will have n members.

> *Systematic sampling* involves randomly selecting the first member of the sample from a list and from that point on taking every *k*th name on the list if 1/*k* equals the sampling fraction.

Possible Problem of Periodicity

Although the first member of a systematic sample is randomly selected, it is possible that this sampling design will yield a biased sample. The most serious and really the only threat of bias in systematic sampling is the existence of some type of periodicity in the ordering of the population members. *Periodicity* means that every kth member of the population has some unique characteristics that are related to, or have an effect on, the dependent variable. In that case, the sample becomes biased.

The likelihood of periodicity entering a list is generally quite small, though it could enter inadvertently. The following example illustrates how that might occur.

EXAMPLE 11.3 _____

A sample of fifth-graders is being selected from a large school system population. The sample is to be measured on an ability test to estimate the ability level of the fifth-grade population of the school system. The researcher in charge of the study decides to take a 1-in-30 sample and notes that class lists can be used conveniently, since the fifth-grade classes all contain about thirty students. The researcher calls for class lists, but instead of sending alphabetical lists, the fifth-grade teachers send lists on which the student names in each class are arranged from high to low according to performance on a recent achievement test. The researcher puts the lists together, one class following another, and selects the systematic sample. Since achievement and performance on an ability test are quite conclusively related, periodicity has entered into the sampling list. If the first random selection gives the third name on the list, it would mean that the third, thirty-third, sixty-third, and so forth students on the list would comprise the sample. This sample would differ from other samples, especially, for example, one beginning with the twenty-sixth name on the list. Whatever sample is selected would have the effect of periodicity in it.

_____

The foregoing example of periodicity, though possible, is quite unlikely, because for that type of research situation, another sampling design, possibly cluster sampling, would likely be used. Systematic sampling is convenient, for example, for an institutional researcher in a university who is to survey the student body (or some part of it) with a brief questionnaire to be returned by mail. Alphabetical lists of students for whatever population is being surveyed could be used.

Systematic sampling provides the condition of sampling throughout the population due to its spacing of selections over the entire list. A definite advantage of systematic sampling over, say, simple random sampling is that it requires less work. However, the researcher should be aware of how the list is ordered and check for the possibility of periodicity.

Considerations in Determining Sample Size—Random Sampling

Several factors can influence the size of the sample used in a research study, but with the exception of cost, information about such factors is often incomplete and it becomes difficult to set an exact size. Cost refers not only to the expenditure of money but also to the time and effort required to obtain the sample data. In any survey, the actual cost of obtaining the data per unit in the sample should be estimated as accurately as possible. If standardized tests are used, what is the cost per test? How much does it cost to score the tests and summarize the data? What, if any, costs will be encountered in locating the sample for testing? What is the cost of test administration? These are all examples of questions that can be raised. A researcher who is securing funds for a project from a funding agency usually is required to produce quite accurate cost estimates. Researchers who are university professors (and possibly graduate students) often receive funds from a funding agency or from a source within the university; thus, cost estimates are required. Even in the rare instances when facilities and resources are available through a university at no hard-dollar costs, costs of proposed projects should be estimated; at least time and effort estimates should be made.

Sample size also relates to what might be called the precision of statistical analyses. This deals with the concept of the magnitude of the differences between statistics necessary to attain statistical significance (discussed in Chapter 14). If enough prior information is available about the characteristics of the dependent variable, it may be possible to estimate the sample size necessary for a desired level of precision. Multiple factors must be considered simultaneously. Hinkle and Oliver (1983) discuss the determination of sample size given certain conditions. Generally, increasing sample size enhances statistical precision.

Although the determination of sample size can be somewhat complex from a statistical standpoint, there are some general guidelines, more or less based on empirical studies that have been conducted over the years. If statistical analyses are to be computed from a survey, for example, and the population is large, say 2000 or greater, the minimum sample size could be set around 200. Sometimes a certain percentage is suggested, but this may be misleading because for large populations, percentages may be quite small. For example, if a population of 25,000 teachers is surveyed, even with stratification, a sample of 500 or 600 should be adequate. Small populations tend to have higher sampling fractions. A sampling fraction of 10 percent would not be adequate for a population of size 50, but it likely would be for a population of 3500.

There may be several groups in a research study, such as an experiment for which the experimental variable has several levels forming several experimental groups. Generally, the more variable the dependent variable the greater the number required in each group. If a field experiment had several groups, say 8 or 10, 15 to 30 individuals per group should be adequate for sample size. However, if there were only two groups, we usually would not consider 15 or so per group an adequate sample. It would be desirable to get the total sample size across the groups to at least around 100. On the other hand, for a tightly controlled experiment, in a learning lab for example, 15 or so subjects per group, and a total of 60 or so subjects, might be adequate.

If a complex design is used, such as a factorial with two or more independent variables, and the number of cells or groups is large, a dozen or more, 10 or so subjects per cell may be an adequate minimum sample size. However, increasing the sample size does enhance the statistical analysis, and a total sample size of 240 would usually be preferred to one of size 120. But, the resources and the costs of doing the research must be considered, and of course, there is little point in having a large sample size if it is not feasible.

It should not be inferred that it is always desirable to increase the sample size to its maximum, since this may be unduly costly and wasteful of effort and information. For some surveys, the time required for the data collection of large samples may be so long that the timeliness of the results is ruined. Increasing sample size is not necessary to attain adequate representation. The method of selection and selecting from unbiased sources are the important determiners of attaining adequate representation. Probability sampling must include some aspect of random selection. The *Literary Digest* survey predicting the outcome of the 1936 presidential election mentioned earlier was based on a sample size of 2.4 million, which did nothing to counter the biased source. The annual Gallup/Phi Delta Kappa polls of the public's attitudes toward the public schools are national surveys, yet the twenty-fourth annual poll, for example, was based on a sample size of 1306 adults (Elam, Rose, and Gallup, 1992, p. 52).

With some types of research studies, there is the possibility that data will not be obtained from all sample members. Questionnaires mailed in survey research are susceptible to nonresponse, and studies conducted in a laboratory may lose subjects because of inability to perform. Replacement procedures may be implemented for individuals failing to participate in the study. However, if the likelihood of substantial nonresponse or nonparticipation by sample members is great, a certain percentage of oversampling may be included. This, of course, has direct implications for sample size. The percentage of oversampling to be used in a specific project will need to be estimated, possibly on the basis of previous experience or information from the research literature. It should be noted that oversampling does not solve the problem of possible sampling bias caused by nonresponse; it only tends to keep the amount of data at an originally desired level.

Purposeful Sampling

Probability sampling procedures that include some form of random selection are not always appropriate or desirable. We have seen that quasi-experimental designs are used when it is not possible to apply random selection or random assignment for an experiment. Ethnographic research and historical research, those toward the qualitative end of the research continuum, typically are not amenable to random sampling, at least not for the site selection.

There are a number of reasons why random sampling may not be appropriate or feasible. Sometimes a researcher simply does not have access to an entire group. It would be almost impossible logistically to select a random sample from all graduating high school seniors in the United States. Sampling or random assignment may not be appropriate for ethical reasons. In medical research, it is unethical to select randomly patients for treatment or nontreatment. Generalizability of the results may not be of great importance, at least it is not argued on a statistical basis. Most ethnographic research, for example, is more concerned with describing the specific situation than generalizing the results. External validity then is argued on a logical basis. Finally, there may be only one or a limited number of sites or groups relevant to the research problem, and sampling is not feasible.

> Random sampling is not appropriate or feasible in all educational research situations, for any of a number of reasons, both practical and conceptual.

When random sampling is not used, the researcher selects a sample to meet the purpose of the research, called a purposeful sample.[2] Purposeful samples are very different than random samples, not only in how they are selected but also in the logic of their use. The logic of random sampling is based on the sample being statistically representative of the population, thus allowing generalization to the population. The individuals of the population are assumed to be equivalent data sources. The logic of purposeful sampling is based on a sample of information-rich cases that are studied in depth. There is no assumption that all members of the population are equivalent data sources, but those selected are believed to be information-rich cases. Key informants in ethnographic research are examples of such selected individuals. Polkinghorne (1991) identifies two requirements of an adequate qualitative data base that are met by purposeful sampling:

> *intense descriptions of the phenomenon under investigation and enough variation in the data to develop a comprehensive structural description. (p. 11)*

Generalization is then based on assertoric argumentation as discussed in the ethnographic research chapter.

> Random sampling and purposeful sampling differ in their selection procedures and in the logic of their use.

It should not be inferred that purposeful sampling is haphazard. Selection of units is based on prior identified criteria for inclusion. Researchers must be knowledgeable about the characteristics of the units, such as variability and the existence of extreme cases. Units, whether sites or individuals, are selected because of the data they can provide relevant to the research problem. There are variations on purposeful sampling as discussed in the following sections.

Comprehensive Sampling

Comprehensive sampling is used when every unit is included in the sample. This type of sampling applies when the number of units is small. For example, six or so students might be in a special counseling program in a high school, and all would be included in the research. A study of one type of severely handicapped children in a school system likely would include all such children. When historians do biographies of individuals or do an analysis of a single event or issue, they essentially are using comprehensive sampling.

> Comprehensive sampling includes all units with specified characteristics in the sample.

Maximum Variation Sampling

Maximum variation sampling is a strategy by which units are selected for the sample because they provide the greatest differences in certain characteristics. An ethnographic researcher working in three high schools might select three that are quite different in terms of student characteristics, location, and other demographics. Maximum variation sampling is intended to generate two types of information: (1) the detailed descriptions of the cases that highlight their differences, and (2) the commonalities across the cases in spite of their variations.

Sometimes maximum variation sampling is associated with *quota sampling* because specified numbers of units are designated for the various categories of units. For example, in a study of social interaction among students in a racially mixed high school, an ethnographic researcher might designate certain numbers of black males, black females, white males, and white females to be interviewed as key informants.

> Maximum variation sampling is a selection process that includes units so that differences on specified characteristics are maximized.

Extreme Case Sampling

Extreme case sampling involves units that have a special or unusual characteristic. Studies of effective or exemplary schools typically involve extreme case sampling. The schools are included because they have been successful based on some specified criteria. The logic of using extreme case sampling is that what is learned from the extreme cases may be applied to typical cases.

Selecting extreme cases on both ends of a continuum may provide confirming and disconfirming units, so that comparisons may be made about the consistency or lack of consistency in characteristics and patterns. For example, a study of exemplary schools might involve one or more schools considered poor or unsuccessful based on the criteria used to define an exemplary school. Comparisons could be made to determine which practices, characteristics, etc., are relevant to an exemplary school. In essence, selecting on both ends for extreme case sampling becomes a special case of maximum variation sampling.

Extreme case sampling includes units with special or unusual characteristics.

Typical Case Sampling

In contrast to maximum variation and extreme case sampling, typical case sampling takes the "middle road," selecting units that are considered typical of the phenomenon under study. In a study of schools, in contrast to selecting very good or very poor schools, typical schools would be selected. Students interviewed in such a study would not be the extremely gifted or poorly performing students. Those interviewed would be typical on those characteristics under study.

Homogeneous Sampling

Homogeneous sampling is used when the purpose of the study is to focus on a particular subgroup, which in some sense is considered homogeneous. For example, in a study of teaching practices it may be decided to involve only a sample of beginning teachers. This is considered a homogeneous subgroup of the teacher population. From the sampling perspective, homogeneous sampling is considered the opposite of maximum variation sampling.

Other Variations of Purposeful Sampling

There are other variations of purposeful sampling, all of them involving a judgment as to who or what should be included in the sample. Network, chain, or "snowball" sampling is a process by which individuals initially selected suggest the names of others who might be appropriate for the sample. For example, in a survey of teachers who have strong pro-teacher union views, teachers initially selected suggest the names of others who have similar views on the issue.

Patton (1990) discusses critical case sampling and defines critical cases as:

> those that can make a point quite dramatically or are, for some reason, particularly important in the scheme of things. (p. 174)

Critical cases may not be easy to find, but when used they are identified on some logical basis. Critical cases may be viewed from two perspectives. For example, suppose a study is done on the implementation of a "new" instructional organization in an elementary school. One approach would be to select a school that has operational difficulties, poor student achievement, and low teacher morale. The idea is that if the instructional organization works in this school, it will work in any school. Another approach would be to do the implementation in a "highly" successful school; one with high teacher morale, good student achievement, and much resources. Selecting such a school would maximize the likelihood of the instructional organization's success.

Qualitative research often involves what Polkinghome (1991, p. 12) calls the "intermittent selection of subjects." That is, individuals may be selected for the sample as the research is in progress. Sometimes when getting into the research it becomes apparent that additional individuals or individuals initially not anticipated can provide useful data.

Although commonly used types of purposeful sampling have been described above, it should not be assumed that these types are always used in their "pure sense," so to speak. There may be variations and combinations. For example, typical case sampling or extreme case sampling may involve snowball sampling to extend the number of subjects with similar characteristics.

There may be random selection in connection with purposeful sampling. For example, in an ethnographic study, which had available fifty, equally qualified subjects for interviewing, five might be selected randomly. When random sampling is used in this manner, it is done to keep the data collection within feasible limits.

> Purposeful sampling has several variations and those used are done so in order to obtain information-rich units in the sample.

Sample Size of Purposeful Samples

Sample sizes in qualitative research are typically small. The numbers of sites at which the research is conducted is often one or a very limited number. But how many individuals or subjects are necessary? There is no general answer to this question. Very likely it is not possible at the beginning of the research to specify a number and intermittent sampling is common. Lincoln and Guba (1985) make the following comment about sample size:

> *In purposeful sampling the size of the sample is determined by informational considerations. If the purpose is to maximize information, the sampling is terminated when no new information is forthcoming from new sampled units; thus redundancy is the primary criterion. (p. 202)*

Although generally sample size cannot be specified as a number, it may be useful to consider sample selection in examples of qualitative research.

EXAMPLE 11.4 _____

In a study of the relationship between computer availability and classroom organization, Mehan (1989) observed four elementary school teachers as they introduced and used microcomputers in their classrooms. The selection of the sample for the study was described as follows:

> *Based on a demographic and ethnographic survey we conducted for the State of California Department of Education's Technology and Teacher Center, we iden-*

tified a small number of teachers to participate in the study. The teachers were selected because, at the time of the study, they all had teaching assignments at the same grade level, were teaching students from roughly the same socioeconomic background, and expressed willingness to participate in this study, investigating computer use for classroom instruction. (p.5)

This description indicates the criteria for selecting teachers. The report goes on to describe in greater detail the professional qualifications and activities of the teachers. The teachers varied in their knowledge about microcomputers and their experience in using microcomputers. So, in essence, this was a purposeful sample that deliberately introduced close to maximum variation relative to microcomputer knowledge and previous use, variables relevant to the problem under study.

EXAMPLE 11.5

Brady, Taylor, and Hamilton (1989) conducted a study of teachers' questioning behavior in mainstreamed classes. The description of selecting the sites and teachers for the study was as follows:

Middle school social studies teachers from two districts adjacent to the metropolitan Houston area served as subjects. Districts were matched for approximate equivalence in terms of (a) school population size, (b) SES of the community, (c) proximity, and (3) district policy toward mainstreaming in social studies classes. A total of 42 teachers was selected based on the following criteria: (a) currently teaching social studies in the sixth, seventh or eighth grade, (b) enrollment of at least one, but preferably two, student(s) certified as eligible for special education services mainstreamed into the social studies class, and (c) willingness to participate in the study. All teachers in the districts who met these criteria participated. Across the teacher sample, years of experience ranged from 1 to 20. (p. 12)

This example illustrates the use of criteria for site selection. The attempt at matching was done to increase the equivalence of the participating school districts. The selection of the teacher sample was essentially comprehensive sampling in that all teachers from the two districts meeting the teacher criteria participated in the study.

EXAMPLE 11.6

Hayes (1992) reports on attitudes toward education and an explanatory model as it pertains to Mexicans and Mexican-Americans. The research was conducted in a southern California suburban community at one site, the local high school which served approximately 2500 students, 16 percent of whom were Latinos. The methods of data collection consisted primarily of participant observation and ethnograph interviews, and some demograhpic data were collected about students and their families. Data collection was conducted over the period of one year.

Hayes describes the sample as:

> *The sample of this research consisted of 12 teenagers between the ages of 15 and 18. They all called themselves Mexican-Americans, and they all attended special education classes at Seaside High. There were five males and seven females . . . All of the sample members either were born in the United States or immigrated before the age of five. (p. 254)*

Hayes then goes on to describe the composition of the students' families and demographic characteristics of the families. The site for this study was selected because of its characteristics, especially the availability of Mexican-American students and their families. This may be considered an example of homogeneous sampling because the students all were enrolled in special education classes, in essence, being a specifically defined subgroup of the student population.

Summary

Sampling is an important consideration in any study in which there is concern about the sample providing adequate representation of a population. When probability sampling is used, some procedure of random selection must be applied in order to generalize from the sample to the population. When surveys are conducted, it is often necessary for logistical reasons to use some approach other than simple random sampling. This chapter described four approaches to sampling involving random selection. A summary of the general characteristics of those designs is provided in Table 11.2.

Purposeful sampling is associated with qualitative research and it is important to note that the logic of purposeful sampling differs from that of random sampling. Several variations on purposeful sampling were described in this chapter, variations designed to meet the needs of different research purposes.

Representativeness of the sample deals with the populations to which a researcher intends to generalize results. Random samples are representative, but what about nonrandom samples such as purposeful samples? When nonrandom samples are used, generalization cannot be argued on a probability basis. It must be argued on a logical basis. In some studies, generalizing to populations is not a big concern. In any event, when generalizing on a logical basis, how well the case can be made depends on the specifics of the study.

The discussion of this chapter essentially is an overview of some of the more common sampling designs used in educational research. Complex designs can be developed in which sampling procedures are used in combination and the sample is selected in multiple

TABLE 11.2   Summary of General Characteristics of Random Sampling Designs

Design	Random Selection	Other Characteristics
Simple random sampling	Sample members individually from the population.	The entire population serves as a single unit from which the sample is selected.
Stratified random sampling	Sample members individually within each of the subpopulations or strata.	All strata are represented in the sample; strata are allocated sample members, usually by one of two allocation systems: equal or proportional allocation. Proportional allocation is most frequently used.
Cluster sampling	Clusters of members selected from the larger population of clusters.	All members of a selected cluster are included in the sample. Not all clusters are included. Clusters need not be of equal size.
Systematic sampling	The initial sample member is individually selected.	The population is ordered in some manner and the designation of the initial sample member determines the entire sample.

stages. Entire books are written on sampling; if more detailed coverage is required, the reader is referred to texts such as that by Henry (1990). The discussion here was intended to provide the researcher with a basic knowledge of design characteristics, differences among designs, and the conditions under which they might be applied.

KEY CONCEPTS

Sample
Probability sampling
Random sample
Random assignment
Sampling error
Sampling bias
Stratified random sampling
Sampling fraction
Proportional allocation
Equal allocation
Self-weighting sample
Cluster sampling

Systematic sampling
Periodicity
Purposeful sampling
Information-rich cases
Comprehensive sampling
Maximum variation sampling
Extreme case sampling
Typical case sampling
Homogeneous sampling
Network or "snowball sampling"
Critical case sampling
Intermittent selection

EXERCISES

11.1 Suppose a researcher has a population of 839 members, and a simple random sample of size 50 is to be selected. Describe how a random number table would be used for selecting the sample. Use Table 11.1 to select the first ten members for the sample.

11.2 Describe the procedures involved in stratified random sampling using proportional allocation. Provide an example of a situation for which the sampling procedure might be used.

11.3 A study is proposed to determine the mathematics achievement of high school seniors in a statewide area. A sample of seniors is to be measured. Discuss some of the sampling difficulties that would be likely with such a large population. Discuss the possibilities of using stratified or cluster sampling. What would be possible stratifying variables if a stratified random sample were selected?

11.4 Discuss how the condition of random selection differs between stratified random sampling and cluster sampling in terms of including strata, clusters, and the members of the strata or clusters.

11.5 A population is divided into four strata. The population sizes of the four strata are 830, 660, 480, and 1030 for stratum 1 through stratum 4, respectively. A sample of size 450 is to be selected, using stratified random sampling with proportional allocation. What is the sampling fraction? Distribute the sample among the four strata using proportional allocation.

11.6 An educational psychologist has a population of 690 undergraduates available for participation in a concept-attainment experiment to be conducted in the learning lab. The experiment requires 120 individuals, including 60 men and 60 women. The population contains 381 women and 309 men. Describe how the individuals would be randomly selected for participation in the experiment. Suppose the experimental variable has four levels and equal numbers of men and women are to be assigned to each level. Describe how the individuals would be randomly assigned to levels.

11.7 The state department of a state containing approximately 500 school districts is planning a survey of the reading achievement of entering senior high school students (tenth grade). A sample of students is to be tested around mid-September. Develop a sampling plan using cluster sampling. What would be possible cluster sampling units and possible difficulties with this approach. Estimate the total sample size using your plan.

11.8 Describe the differences, both logistically and conceptually, between probability sampling, which involves some form of random selection, and purposeful sampling.

11.9 Describe the differences between comprehensive sampling and maximum variation sampling when using purposeful sampling. Provide an example for each type of sampling.

11.10 Describe the differences between typical case sampling and homogeneous sampling when using purposeful sampling. Provide an example for each type of sampling.

11.11 An educational research center of a state university has a contract to do a statewide ethnogaphic study of the nature of compensatory reading programs for first-graders deficient in reading performance. Basically, there are three different compensatory reading programs found throughout the 453 school districts of the state. The districts range in size from small rural districts to large city districts. The study has resources for including 50 sites for periodic observation, interviewing, etc., on a regular basis during one school year. Describe how a purposeful sample of sites would be selected for this study. After the study is under way, describe how intermittent sampling might be used.

11.12 Select an article from the research literature that reports on a study using purposeful sampling. Are there descriptions of the site selection (if applicable) and the unit selection? Are the descriptions for selection adequate? Is the sample size given? Does the author address generalizability or external validity and, if so, does the case seem adequate?

NOTES

1. If sampling is from a finite population without replacement, a slight adjustment in the definition is necessary. A sample is then considered to be a simple random sample if it is drawn in such a way that all possible samples of a given size have the same probability of being selected.

2. Such samples go by a variety of names such as judgmental or purposive samples.

REFERENCES

Brady, M. P., Taylor, R. D., and Hamilton, R. (1989). Differential measures of teachers' questioning in mainstreamed classes: Individual and classwide patterns. *Journal of Research and Development in Education,* 23(1), 10–17.

Elam, S. M., Rose L. C., and Gallup, A. M. (1992). The 24th annual Gallup/Phi Delta Kappa poll of the public's attitudes toward the public schools. *Phi Delta Kappan,* 74(1), 41–53.

Hayes, K. G. (1992). Attitudes toward education: Voluntary and involuntary immigrants from the same families. *Anthropology and Education Quarterly,* 23(2), 250–267.

Henry, G. T. (1990). *Practical sampling.* Newbury Park, CA: Sage.

Hinkle, D. E., and Oliver, J. D. (1983). How large should the sample be? A question with no simple answer? Or . . . *Educational and Psychological Measurement,* 43, 1051–1060.

Kish, L. (1965). *Survey sampling.* New York: Wiley.

Lincoln, Y. S. and Guba, E. G. (1985). *Naturalistic inquiry.* Beverly Hills, CA: Sage.

Mehan, H. (1989). Microcomputers in classrooms: Educational technology or social practice? *Anthropology and Education Quarterly,* 20(1), 4–22.

Patton, M. Q. (1990). *Qualitative evaluation and research methods,* (2nd ed.). Newbury Park, CA: Sage.

Polkinghorne, D. E. (1991). *Generalization and qualitative research: Issues of external validity.* Paper presented at the annual meeting of the American Education Research Association, Chicago.

C h a p t e r **12**

Measurement and Data Collection

When doing educational research, sooner or later something is measured, and this something includes the dependent variable. For example, if an experiment is conducted on different instructional approaches to teaching mathematics to sixth-graders, some measure of mathematics achievement or performance is necessary. The score on such a measure is the dependent variable of the study. The measure might be the mathematics subtest of a standardized achievement test or it might be a mathematics test constructed specifically for the experiment. Dependent variables may take on a variety of forms, so there are many different types of measurement used across the spectrum of educational research.

Because educational research encompasses a vast diversity of variables which are measured, a large variety of measurement devices is used in educational research—tests, inventories, observation schedules, and others. In some research projects, the measurement requirements can readily be met through the use of existing tests or instruments. For others, developing adequate measurement procedures may involve a substantial portion of the research effort. Whatever the case, the measurement instruments must adequately measure the variables, concepts, or phenomena under study, because a research study is only as well-done as the measurement that generates the required data.

The areas of educational measurement, indeed the measurement of educational variables such as achievement and attitude, are of themselves disciplines of study. It is the intent of this discussion to provide an overview of measurement as it is a part of conducting research, including basic measurement concepts. There are suggestions about sources of tests and other measurement instruments, sources that can be very helpful in locating examples of the more commonly used measurement instruments in educational research.

The questions of measurement in the context of educational research are basically twofold: What is to be measured and how is it to be measured?

Concepts of Measurement

A straightforward and widely accepted definition of measurement is given by Kerlinger (1986, p. 391):

> *The assignment of numerals to objects or events according to rules.*

A numeral is a symbol, such as 1, 2, or 3, that is devoid of either quantitative or qualitative meaning unless such meaning is assigned by a rule. The rules for a particular measurement are the guides by which the assignment of numerals proceeds. These may include, for example, the assignment of points for certain kinds of responses or the summing of numerals that have been assigned to the responses of two or more items.

> Measurement is a process of assigning numerals according to rules. The numerals are assigned to events or objects, such as responses to items or to certain observed behaviors.

Types of Measurement Scales

The four general levels of measurement scales—nominal, ordinal, interval, and ratio— were defined in Chapter 2 and are briefly reviewed here. The four scales comprise a hierarchy of measurement levels based on the amount of information contained in the score or the measure generated by the scales. The scales go from nominal to ratio in order from least to the most information contained. The four scales are defined as follows; in each case, an example of a variable that could be measured by the type of scale is given:

Nominal: This gives categorization without order; whatever is being measured is categorized into two or more classifications that indicate only differences with respect to one or more characteristics. Example: gender of the individual.

Ordinal: In addition to indicating difference, this scale also orders the scores on some basis, such as low to high or least to most. Although the scores are ordered, equal intervals between scores are not established. Example: attitude toward school.

Interval (also called equal unit): In addition to order, equal units or intervals are established in the scale such that a difference of a point in one part of the scale is equivalent to a difference of one point in any other part of the scale. Example: temperature.

Ratio: In addition to an equal unit, the scale contains a true zero point that indicates a total absence of whatever is being measured. Example: monetary expenditures for various school functions.

Although the descriptions of the scales seem straightforward enough, it is not always easy to categorize a variable into the hierarchy. The difficulty, when it appears, usually comes between the ordinal and interval scales. For example, Likert-scale items were introduced in Chapter 7. The scale of an individual item is ordinal; responses may be ordered but there is no equal unit. Later in this chapter a semantic differential is introduced. Like Likert-scale items, individual scales on a semantic differential are ordinal scale measurement. But suppose there is a substantial number of Likert-scale items, say 20 or so, that all measure a single concept such as a student's attitude toward school. Each item is scored 1 to 5 on a scale of "strongly dislike" to "strongly like," so that the higher the score the more positive the attitude. If the item scores (the numerals assigned to responses) are summed across the 20 items we have a total score which can range from 20 to 100. Does this total score attain interval scale measurement? It might be argued that the total score at least approaches having an equal unit in the scale, and thus could be considered interval scale measurement. Correspondingly, semantic differentials typically have several sets of bipolar adjectives (which correspond to items in Likert scales) applied to a single concept. The responses are then summed across the sets and the total score is treated as interval scale measurement.

Intervals in measurement scales such as those just described are established on the basis of convention and usefulness. The basic concern is whether the level of measurement is meaningful and that the implied information is contained in the numerals. The meaning depends on the conditions and variables of the specific study.

Many variables measured in educational research are human characteristics, attributes, or traits that are somewhat subtle. However, whatever is being measured must be defined operationally. This means that the variable will be represented or described by the score of the test or whatever measurement device is used. For example, mathematics achievement may be defined as the mathematics subtest score on the Iowa Test of Basic Skills. A student's perception of instruction may be the score on a ten-item rating scale developed specifically for the instruction under consideration. In doing research, such variables are defined in terms of what is used to measure them.

> The operational definition specifies the instrument or the operations to be used for measuring the variable.

Reliability of Measurement

Two essential characteristics of measurement that must be considered in establishing the appropriateness and usefulness of measurement instruments are reliability and validity. In a word, *reliability* means consistency—consistency of the instrument in measuring whatever it measures. It is the degree to which an instrument will give similar results for the same individuals at different times. In a conceptual sense, an observed score can be seen as consisting of two parts: one part the individual's "true" score and the other part an "error" score, which is due to the inaccuracy of measurement. Reliability is related to these parts. If scores have large error components, reliability is low; but if there is little error in the scores, reliability is high. Reliability is a statistical concept based on the association between two sets of scores representing the measurement obtained from the instrument when it is used with a group of individuals. *Reliability coefficients* can take on values from 0 to 1.0, inclusive. Conceptually, if a reliability coefficient were 0, there would be no "true" component in the observed score. The observed score would consist entirely of error. On the other hand, if the reliability coefficient were 1.0, the observed score would contain no error; it would consist entirely of the true score. Clearly, in educational measurement, it is desirable to obtain high reliability coefficients, although coefficients of 1.0 are very rare indeed.

> *Reliability* is the consistency of the instrument in measuring whatever it measures. Reliability coefficients can take on values of 0 to 1.0, inclusive.

Empirical Procedures for Estimating Reliability

Several procedures can be used to estimate reliability. All of them have computational formulas that produce reliability coefficients. The commonly used procedures are described as follows:

Parallel forms or alternate forms: This procedure involves the use of two or more equivalent forms of the test. The two forms are administered to a group of individuals with a short time interval between the administrations. If the test is reliable, the patterns of scores for individuals should be about the same for the two forms of the test. There would be a high positive association between the scores.

Test-retest: In this procedure, the same test is administered on two or more occasions to the same individuals. Again, if the test if reliable, there will be a high positive association between the scores.

Split-half: This procedure requires only one administration of the test. In computing split-half reliability, the test items are divided into two halves, with the items of the two halves matched on content and difficulty, and the halves are then scored independently. If the test is reliable, the scores on the two halves have a high positive association. An individual scoring high on one half would tend to score high on the other half, and vice versa.

Kuder-Richardson procedures: Two formulas for estimating reliability, developed by Kuder and Richardson (1937), require only one administration of a test. One formula, KR-20, provides the mean of all possible split-half coefficients. The second formula, KR-21, may be substituted for KR-20, if it can be assumed that item difficulty levels are similar.

Cronbach alpha: A formula developed by Cronbach (1951), based on two or more parts of the test, requires only one administration of the test.

Although all reliability coefficients are estimates of test consistency, there are different types of consistency. Procedures that involve only one test administration (split-half, KR-20, KR-21, Cronbach alpha) generate coefficients of internal consistency.

When two or more parallel forms of the test are used, the reliability coefficient is a coefficient of equivalence—the extent to which the forms are equivalent. Using the test-retest procedure gives a reliability coefficient that is a coefficient of stability—the extent to which the scores on the single test remain stable. Coefficients of equivalence and stability are based on more than one test administration.

> There are a number of procedures by which reliability can be empirically estimated. Those procedures that involve only one test administration give reliability coefficients of internal test consistency. If there is more than one test administration, the reliability coefficients are estimates of test equivalence or stability.

If published tests or inventories are used, the accompanying manuals should contain information about reliability, such as the type of reliability and the size of the reliability coefficients. When locally constructed instruments are used, reliability estimates should be computed. For example, suppose a group of teachers is conducting a study on students' attitudes toward school, measured by a locally constructed attitude inventory. The reliability of interest would most likely be internal consistency reliability. If the inventory contained 40 items, they could be divided into two halves of twenty items each, and the scores on the two halves could be correlated. (Correlation procedures are discussed in the next chapter.) The correlation coefficient between the scores on the two halves would then be used for estimating the reliability of the attitude inventory.

Expected Reliability Coefficients for Various Types of Tests

Although it is desirable to obtain reliability coefficients as close to 1.0 as possible, reliability is affected by a number of factors. One factor is the length of the test. Increased length tends to increase reliability, which is one reason total test reliability tends to be greater than the reliability of subtests that may be contained in the total test.

Size of the reliability coefficient also is affected by the variable being measured. Achievement tests in academic and skills areas, for example, tend to have higher reliability than interest and attitude inventories. Table 12.1 contains examples of typical reliability coefficients found with selected tests and inventories. When a range is given for the reliability coefficient (r), it indicates reliability estimates from multiple administrations of the test.

Validity of Measurement

Another essential characteristic of measurement is *validity*—the extent to which an instrument measures what it is supposed to measure. Simply stated, validity of measurement deals with the question, "Does the instrument measure the characteristic, trait, or whatever, for which it was intended?" Validity refers to the appropriateness of the

TABLE 12.1   Examples of Reliability Coefficients Reported for Selected Tests and Inventories

Test	r
Gray Oral Reading Tests—Diagnostic	.73–.99
Mathematics Anxiety Rating Scale	
Elementary Form	.88
Adolescent Form	.89–.96
Stanford Achievement Test, Eighth Ed., all subtests	.80 to over .90
California Diagnostic Reading Test	.73–.96
Wechsler Preschool and Primary Scale of Intelligence—Revised	
for Subtests	54.–.93
Consistency of IQs	.85–.97
Human Resource Development Report	
Short-Term Reliability	.81
Sutter-Eyburg Student Behavior Inventory	
Intensity Scores	.89–.92
Problem Scores	.86–.88
Test of Initial Literacy	
Orthographic Punctuation	.43
Letter Matching	.91
Survey of Functional Adaptive Behaviors	
Total Adaptive Behavior Score	.92
State-Trait Anger Expression Inventory—Research Ed.	.82
Reading Ability Series	
for Complete Subtests	.90 or greater
Individual Narrative	.83 or greater

Note: These coefficients were obtained from the *Eleventh Mental Measurement Yearbook,* Jack J. Kramer and Jane Close Conoley (Eds.). University of Nebraska at Lincoln (1992).

interpretation of the results of a test or inventory, and it is specific to the intended use. A test may be highly valid for some situations and not valid for others. For example, a science achievement test may be valid for measuring science knowledge but not valid for measuring logical reasoning skills.

There are basically two approaches to determining the validity of an instrument. One is through a logical analysis of content or a logical analysis of what would make up an educational trait, construct, or characteristic. This is essentially a judgmental analysis. The other approach, through an empirical analysis, uses criterion measurement, the criterion being some sort of standard or desired outcome. The criterion measure might be performance on a task or test, or it could be a measure such as job performance. Validity is then a measure of the association or correlation between the test validated and the criterion measure.

The traditional view of validity has been that there are basically three different types—content, criterion, and construct—with two variations of criterion validity, concurrent and predictive. A more current view is that validity is a unitary concept but that there are different types of evidence of validity. This is essentially a conceptual difference; the procedures for establishing validity are the same whether we consider different types of validity or different types of evidence for establishing validity. In the following discussion, the types-of-evidence view is used.

> *Validity* of measurement is the extent to which the instrument measures what it is designed to measure.

Content-Related Evidence.   Content validation is the process of establishing the representativeness of the items with respect to the domain of skills, tasks, knowledge, and so forth of whatever is being measured. Thus, content-related evidence deals with the adequacy of content sampling. Content validation is a logical analysis of the items, determining their representativeness. Validity of achievement tests is commonly based on content-related evidence.

Criterion-Related Evidence: Concurrent and Predictive.   Criterion validation establishes validity through a comparison with some criterion external to the test. The criterion is, in essence, the standard by which the validity of the test will be judged. If the scores of the measure being validated relate highly to the criterion, the measure is valid. If not, the measure is not valid for the purpose for which the criterion measure is used.

Concurrent and predictive validation are empirical approaches to establishing validity in which the relationship between the test scores and measures of performance on an external criterion are determined. Concurrent validation is used if the data on the two measures, test and criterion, are collected at or about the same time. Predictive validation involves the collection of the data on the criterion measure after an intervening period—say, six months—from the time of data collection for the test being validated. This is the basic operational distinction between the two. There also is a distinction in the objectives of validation. Concurrent validation is based on establishing an existing situation—in other words, what is—whereas predictive validation deals with what is likely to happen. Specifically, the question of concurrent validation is whether or not the test scores estimate a specified present performance; that of predictive validation is whether or not the test scores predict a specified future performance.

The criterion measure of concurrent validation is not necessarily the score on another test given at the same time as the test being validated. It may consist of concurrent measures, such as job success or grade-point average. The criterion measures used with predictive validation often are some types of job performance—certainly subsequent performance. Predictive validation is especially relevant when test results are used for the selection of personnel to fill positions. In school, predictive validation is associated with readiness and aptitude tests, such as reading readiness tests.

Construct-Related Evidence.   Construct validation can involve both logical and empirical analyses. The term *construct* refers to the theoretical construct or trait being measured, not to the technical construction of the test items. A construct is a postulated attribute or structure that explains some phenomenon, such as an individual's behavior. Because constructs are abstract and are not considered to be real objects or events, they sometimes are called hypothetical constructs. Theories of learning, for example, involve constructs such as motivation, intelligence, and anxiety.

Quite often, one or more constructs are related to behavior, in that individuals are expected to behave (or not behave) in a specified manner. A theory of frustration might include specific behavior patterns. For example, frustration increases as the individual unsuccessfully persists in a problem-solving task. The construct may be conceptualized informally with only a limited number of propositions, or it may be part or all of a fully developed theory. When using construct validation, the researcher initially suggests which constructs might account for test performance based on a logical analysis. Empirical procedures of construct validation involve relating scores on other tests that reflect the same general theory or constructs. Personality tests, for example, commonly are validated on the basis of construct-related evidence.

The different types of evidence all have their function, in educational measurement and, correspondingly, in educational research as measurement is involved. If published tests or inventories are used, validity information should be provided in the accompanying manual. However, published tests, especially those for school-age children, often are prepared for broad populations, and the validity (and reliability) information may not be generalizable to the subjects of the research study. Researchers should determine the validity and reliability of the test for the specific situation. The types of validity evidence and their characteristics are summarized in Table 12.2.

TABLE 12.2   Types of Evidence and Their Characteristics Used in Establishing Validity

Type	How Analyzed	Example of Use
Content	Logical analysis of item content	Achievement tests in academic and skills areas; a test of computational skills in fifth-grade mathematics
Criterion Concurrent	Empirical analysis—establishing the relationship between scores on the test and those on another measure obtained at the same time	Validations of a short history test against a long, standardized history exam that is known to be a valid measure of history achievement
Predictive	Empirical analysis—establishing the relationship between scores on the test and those on another measure obtained at a later time	A comparison of performance on a screening test for word processing specialists to a measure of job performance taken six months later
Construct	Logical and empirical analyses	Analysis of a personality test to determine whether it measures the major traits of a neurotic personality

Reliability is a necessary but not sufficient condition for validity. That is, a test or measuring instrument could be reliable but not valid. In that case, it would be consistently measuring something for which it was not intended. However, a test must he reliable to be valid. If it is not consistent in what it measures, it cannot be measuring that for which it was intended.

The discussion of reliability and validity in this chapter is only an overview and it is necessarily brief. Although procedures were named and described, no computational examples were given. Specific procedures can be quite extensive and can be found in several measurement and testing books.[1]

The Variables Measured in Educational Research

Since educational research covers a broad spectrum of phenomena, many different variables are measured. Research on student learning often focuses on student achievement in cognitive and skills areas, intelligence or some measures of inherent ability, and student attitudes. Sometimes, observations are made of student behavior in a classroom. The variables measured may include different behaviors that occur as well as the frequency of occurrence of certain behaviors. When field notes are taken in ethnographic research, they contain descriptions of numerous variables as found in the specific context. Educational research may involve the measurement of opinions or perceptions. Some examples are studies of teachers' perceptions of administrative practices and student opinions of teaching effectiveness.

Sometimes attempts are made to measure relatively abstract phenomena, such as how individuals learn to learn or how an individual's personality develops and changes. Many times, what is measured is very specific to the study. This is especially characteristic of surveys in which self-constructed questionnaires are used. Sometimes, physical skills or characteristics are measured. For example, a survey might be conducted on differences in personal habits related to health promotion. The list could go on. Individuals in practically any age range might be included in the measurement, although those measured are often of school age.

Tests and Inventories Used for Measurement

Tests, inventories, and scales commonly are used for obtaining the data in educational research studies, especially with research that is quantitative in nature. Often an available test or measuring instrument can be used; if this can be done, it greatly reduces the effort required to prepare for data collection. Many tests are available through commercial publishers of education tests, including achievement tests, intelligence tests, attitude inventories, self-concept inventories, and personality tests, among others. Sometimes, measuring instruments are available from other researchers who are working with similar variables.

In many situations, however, the researcher must construct an instrument because of the specific nature of the dependent variable. Sometimes, an existing instrument can be modified by changing the content of items, or a general format for the items can be used with only the content of the items being specific to the study. For example, a general form for an attitude scale may be used, but the items must be constructed for the study. In this section, some general forms are described and examples are included. Since construction of items for questionnaires was given considerable attention in Chapter 7, that discussion will not be repeated here. However, a questionnaire might include several items comprising an attitude scale, for example, and the comments on attitude scales would be relevant for a questionnaire as well as for an inventory administered in a classroom.

Achievement Tests in Academic and Skills Areas

Because achievement (or lack of it) is one of the principal outcomes of schooling, much research is done on this topic. Multitudes of *achievement tests,* commonly known as standardized achievement tests, are commercially available. These are generally norm-referenced tests; that is, performance on the tests is compared to the performance of some group, called the *normative group.* Information about the normative group is contained in the manual accompanying the test.

When a researcher uses a published test for a research study, the task is to select a test that measures what he or she wants to measure. This requires a careful review, preferably of the potential tests themselves, but at least of sources that describe the tests. The typical college library contains a number of sources that describe available tests.

One of the most extensive sources of information about tests are the publications of the Buros Institute of Mental Measurements at the University of Nebraska at Lincoln. *Tests in Print III,* edited by Mitchell (1983), catalogs 2672 tests, many of them achievement and scholastic tests. For example, the entries include 74 achievement batteries and 199 English tests (p. xxvi). *Tests in Print* provides descriptive listings and references of commercially published tests. However, it does not provide reviews of tests. *Tests in Print* has been published now for well over a decade so newly published tests and recent revisions of older tests are not covered.

The *Mental Measurements Yearbook* (*MMY*), also published by the Buros Institute, does contain reviews of tests. The *MMY*s are published more frequently than *Tests in Print*; in fact, there are only three years between the two most recent editions, and *Supplements to MMY* are published in intervening years. The *MMY*s contain descriptive listings, technical information, references, and reviews of commercially published tests. The *Eleventh Mental Measurements Yearbook* (Kramer and Conoley, 1992) contains reviews of tests that are new or significantly revised since the *Tenth MMY* was published in 1989. The *Eleventh MMY* covers 477 tests with 703 reviews because some are reviewed by more than one individual. There are eighteen major classifications of tests, such as Personality and Achievement, listed early in the volume. One classification, Behavior Assessment, has been added since the previous *MMY*. The amount of information varies across tests, but the *MMY* is an excellent test information source.

When using a standardized achievement test, the researcher should check carefully to determine the appropriateness of the test. If the researcher intends to use normative data, the manual should be carefully reviewed to make certain the norms are appropriate. Often it is not necessary to have norms, since comparisons are made between or among groups in the study, not with external groups.

> Published standardized tests often can be used effectively for research in achievement. The content of the test should be reviewed, as should any norms that may be used.

Published achievement tests are usually very well constructed—at least technically—and of course their use greatly reduces the effort needed to prepare for the measurement, compared to a study for which the test must be constructed. However, in some studies, the researcher may want to measure achievement in a very limited area for which a test is not readily available. Also, it may be that the standardized test is much longer than is actually needed and, therefore, would not be desirable. A self-constructed achievement test may then be used.

When a self-constructed achievement test is used, the items of the test should very closely reflect the objectives of the research. Usually, in achievement testing, finding an adequate fit between research objectives and test content is not very difficult because validity can be established through a logical analysis (content analysis). However, if at all possible, a pilot run of the test should be made, and reliability should be checked prior to the use of the test for the project. Then reliability can be checked using the research data. If reliability has not been previously checked and then turns out to be undesirably low, the entire project is in jeopardy.

Attitude Inventories

Achievement tests generally are designed to measure an individual's best or maximum performance, whereas an attitude inventory is intended to measure typical performance. Attitudes involve an individual's feelings toward such things as ideas, procedures, and social institutions. Note that the attitude is toward something. Most people think of attitudes in such terms as acceptance-rejection or favorable-unfavorable; however, the intensity of a person's feelings usually is not dichotomous but is on a continuum between the extremes. Measurement of the attitude is intended to place individuals on this continuum.

Attitude inventories are available from commercial publishers. The sources for information about tests discussed in the preceding section also contain information about available attitude inventories. However, it is usually more difficult to find an available attitude inventory than an achievement test for a research project. This is because attitude inventories used for research tend to be quite specific, and more general inventories may not be adequate. Often, it is necessary to construct an attitude scale. Several item formats may be used.

Likert Scale[2]   The *Likert scale* is a scale with a number of points or spaces, usually five, that represent a set of related responses, one for each point. The individual responds by checking a point or circling a letter (or number) representing a point on the scale. These points are assigned numerical values, 1 to 5 or 0 to 4, which are then totaled over the items to give the individuals an attitude score.

The Likert scale was introduced in Chapter 7 in connection with survey research and Table 7.4 contains several items from the Appalachia Educational Laboratory questionnaire. The responses in that table range from "Not at all" to "Much (very) (many)." There are any number of possible sets of Likert responses. The important characteristics of a set is that the responses be appropriate for the items. Following are some sample sets of Likert responses:

Very satisfactory	Very good
Satisfactory	Good
Undecided	No opinion
Unsatisfactory	Poor
Very unsatisfactory	Very poor
Highly appropriate	Highly favorable
Appropriate	Favorable
Neutral	No opinion
Inappropriate	Unfavorable
Highly inappropriate	Highly unfavorable
Very supportive	Definitely yes
Supportive	Probably yes
Neutral	Uncertain
Unsupportive	Probably no
Very unsupportive	Definitely no

Generally, Likert-scale items are written so that the positive end of the scale goes with points representing strongly agree or very satisfactory; for example, when this is the case, the higher scaled value (5) goes with the strongly agree and the lower value (1) is assigned to strongly disagree. However, in order to reduce response set, the directions of items may be reversed, and when this is done the scoring direction must be reversed also. For example, consider the following items from an attitude-toward-mathematics scale:

SA   A   U   D   SD   1. It is fun to work math puzzles.
SA   A   U   D   SD   2. I do not like to work fraction problems.

The first item would be scored with a 5 assigned to SA, and the second item would assign a 1 to SA. If the scale contained 20 items, the item scores could be summed with possible total scores ranging from 20 to 100; the greater the score the more positive the attitude.

In any event the scoring must be consistent, and usually Likert scales are scored so that the greater the score, the more positive the attitude.

A Likert scale contains a number of points on a scale, quite often five, but typically an odd number. The points have designations such as "strongly agree" to "strongly disagree."

Constructing an attitude inventory using Likert-scale items requires identifying the major topics or points to be addressed by the scale and then generating statements. These undoubtedly will need some revision to ensure clarity and relevance. Usually, items of both directions are used to provide more variety and breadth in the items. It also may make the items more interesting for the respondents. A pool of items is generated, and these items should be administered in a pilot run. On the basis of the pilot run, those items to be used in the inventory can be identified and put into final form.

Unlike achievement tests, it is possible for an individual to fake responses when taking an attitude inventory. The direction of the more positive attitude usually can be identified from the item, and the individual could deliberately respond in that direction regardless of true feelings. However, if the researcher is primarily interested in groups of scores, such as those for a class, and the respondent is aware of this, there is no reason to fake. Sometimes, very similar items are put in different parts of the inventory so that the consistency between responses can be checked.

Some individuals may develop a response set or tendency to respond in a certain manner as a reaction to the construction of the scale, independent of the item content. For example, the middle-of-the-roader will respond near the center of the scale regardless of true feelings. Sometimes, reversing the direction of items is used as a deterrent to response set.

It should be noted that Likert scales can be used for measurements other than attitude inventories. For example, a Likert scale could be used to measure teachers' perceptions of a program.

Semantic Differential. The *semantic differential* (Osgood, Suci, and Tannenbaum, 1957) is a measuring instrument that focuses on a single word or concept at a time to measure the connotative meaning of that concept. Then a series of bipolar adjective scales are given, and the respondents are asked to indicate their feelings (perceptions) on each scale with respect to the word or concept. Figure 12.1 contains an example of a semantic differential, taken from a study by Nussel, Wiersma, and Rusche (1988). This semantic differential was developed to measure professors' perceptions of college teaching as a profession. The pairs of bipolar adjectives were based on descriptors found in the job satisfaction literature. The semantic differential was tried out in a pilot run prior to its use in the research study.

SEMANTIC DIFFERENTIAL: COLLEGE TEACHING AS A PROFESSION

We are interested in how you feel about college teaching as a profession. Please respond to the items below, indicating your perception of your professional position. Mark *one X and one X only* for each pair of words. Place the *X* in the center of a space, not on the boundaries. For example:

If you feel your position is very stimulating , place the *X*

stimulating ⎯⎯⎯ X ⎯⎯⎯ : ⎯⎯⎯⎯ : ⎯⎯⎯⎯ : ⎯⎯⎯⎯ : ⎯⎯⎯⎯ : ⎯⎯⎯⎯ : ⎯⎯⎯⎯ dull

If you feel your position is very dull, place the *X*

stimulating ⎯⎯⎯ : ⎯⎯⎯⎯ : ⎯⎯⎯⎯ : ⎯⎯⎯⎯ : ⎯⎯⎯⎯ : ⎯⎯⎯⎯ : ⎯⎯ X ⎯⎯ dull

Or if you feel your position is neither very stimulating or very dull, place the *X* closer to the middle of the line, but on the side that you favor.

MY PROFESSIONAL POSITION

stimulating	____:____:____:____:____:____:____	dull
rewarding	____:____:____:____:____:____:____	unrewarding
exciting	____:____:____:____:____:____:____	monotonous
bad	____:____:____:____:____:____:____	good
secure	____:____:____:____:____:____:____	insecure
fair	____:____:____:____:____:____:____	biased
tiresome	____:____:____:____:____:____:____	interesting
menial	____:____:____:____:____:____:____	challeging
same	____:____:____:____:____:____:____	varied
stable	____:____:____:____:____:____:____	fluctuating
trivial	____:____:____:____:____:____:____	important
orderly	____:____:____:____:____:____:____	confused
active	____:____:____:____:____:____:____	passive
unpleasant	____:____:____:____:____:____:____	pleasant
simple	____:____:____:____:____:____:____	rigorous
valuable	____:____:____:____:____:____:____	worthless
nice	____:____:____:____:____:____:____	awful
tense	____:____:____:____:____:____:____	relaxed
flexible	____:____:____:____:____:____:____	rigid
routine	____:____:____:____:____:____:____	demanding
successful	____:____:____:____:____:____:____	unsuccessful
relevant	____:____:____:____:____:____:____	irrelevant
stereotyped	____:____:____:____:____:____:____	original
disorganized	____:____:____:____:____:____:____	systematic
vague	____:____:____:____:____:____:____	defined
autonomous	____:____:____:____:____:____:____	controlled
common	____:____:____:____:____:____:____	distinctive
boring	____:____:____:____:____:____:____	fun
satisfying	____:____:____:____:____:____:____	unsatisfying
isolation	____:____:____:____:____:____:____	interaction
noncompetitive	____:____:____:____:____:____:____	competitive
career	____:____:____:____:____:____:____	job

FIGURE 12.1   An Example of a Semantic Differential

Note: Reproduced with permission of the authors.

> The *semantic differential* provides a series of bipolar adjective scales relative to a word or concept; the respondents indicate their feelings on the continuum of each scale.

Scoring of the semantic differential can be done in different ways. The important thing about scoring is that it is consistent and meaningful. The usual scoring procedures are such that the greater the score, the more positive the attitude or perception.

One approach to scoring is to list all pairs of adjectives in a consistent direction, usually low to high or negative to positive. The position of the adjectives (whether the right or left side is negative) is an arbitrary choice, but if the negative adjectives are on the left, and the positive ones are on the right, then the values 0-1-2-3-4-5-6 (or any sequence of seven consecutive numbers) are assigned to the slots from left to right. Values of -3, -2, -1, 0, +1, +2, +3 could also be used, although this gives a possibility of a total score that is negative. Either way, the score is the sum of the values across the pairs of adjectives.

In the example of Figure 12.1, the adjective pairs are listed in both directions, and the order of direction was assigned randomly. For example, items 4 and 5 have reversed directions. Scoring was done by reversing the direction of assigning the numerical values, always keeping the 6 on the positive end and the 0 on the negative end. Since this semantic differential had 32 items, the maximum total score was 192; the greater the score the more positive the perception of college teaching as a profession.

Another scoring procedure can be used in which the values 6-5-4-3-2-1-0 are assigned left to right regardless of item direction. Then the score for the item is weighted either positive or negative, depending on its direction. A disadvantage of this procedure is the possibility of a negative total score. Sometimes semantic differentials are constructed to contain two or more subscales, called *dimensions* or *constructs*. For example, a semantic differential could be constructed to measure teachers' professional attitudes that might contain a subscale on feelings toward children and a subscale on feelings toward the school administration. A subset of the items in the semantic differential would make up the items for a subscale. Subscale scores would be generated in a manner similar to generating a total score. Of course, a subscale would involve fewer items than the total scale.

Aptitude Tests

Aptitude is considered to be the potential for achievement. Although actual achievement and the potential ability for achievement are not the same thing, operationally they may be difficult to separate. Intelligence tests are the most commonly known measures for aptitude in academic and skills areas, but other terms such as *general scholastic ability* and *general mental ability* are being used increasingly to replace the term *intelligence*. The difficulty with the term intelligence comes with the long-standing belief that intelligence tests somehow measure an inborn capacity, regardless of the individual's background, experience, and the like. Cronbach (1984, p. 198) comments on the problem with this perception of intelligence.

> *In British and American discourse, "intelligence" seemed usually to refer to potentiality as if the test score foretold what level the person would reach if given every educational advantage. The evidence is necessarily one-sided. Good ultimate performance proves capacity, but poor performance does not prove incapacity. The typical school-age test is best identified as a "test of general scholastic ability." It measures a set of abilities now developed and demonstrated (not a "potential"). It emphasizes abilities helpful in most schoolwork.*

The importance of Cronbach's remarks to the educator is that one must be cautious when using an aptitude test and not assume that the test is measuring inherent ability independent of other factors, such as existing achievement (or the lack thereof). When diverse groups, possibly those from subcultures within the larger culture, are being measured by aptitude tests, it should not be assumed that the tests are equally valid for all groups.

Aptitude tests come in a variety of forms, commonly designated as individual or group tests. Individual tests tend to be more elaborate and may involve manipulation of objects, whereas group tests are usually limited to items on paper. The Wechsler Adult Intelligence Scale (WAIS) is an example of an individual test, and the California Test of Mental Maturity is an example of a group test.

The tests mentioned here are largely designed to measure global intelligence or ability. There also are aptitude tests that focus more on specific abilities. For example, the Scholastic Aptitude Test (SAT) is highly oriented to the types of abilities learned in formal schooling, with an emphasis on verbal and mathematical abilities. Numerous batteries of aptitude tests measure multiple aptitudes through a series of subtests or subscores, an example being the Differential Aptitude Test. Such tests contain subtests of abilities, such as mechanical reasoning, numerical ability, and spatial relations, to mention just a few.

Scores on aptitude tests sometimes are used in educational research as control variables. For example, scores on an aptitude test may be used to classify individuals according to levels of ability if ability is used as an independent variable in the research design. Aptitude test scores also may be used as statistical controls.

The development of an aptitude test is a difficult task that requires a good deal of information, effort, and measurement expertise. For this reason, aptitude tests are seldom self-constructed for a research project. There are numerous aptitude tests available for both general and specific aptitudes. Information about specific aptitude tests can be found in sources such as the *Mental Measurements Yearbook* mentioned earlier in this chapter.

Aptitude is the potential for achievement. It may be difficult in the measurement to separate potential from actual achievement. In essence, an aptitude test gives indirect evidence of the existence of the potential.

Personality Measures

When characteristics such as motivation, attitudes, and emotional adjustment as a whole are considered, we are focusing on the individual's personality. Personality tests are generally designed to measure the affective or nonintellectual aspects of behavior.

The measurement of personality has certain inherent difficulties—for example, what to measure. Although there is some ambiguity associated with the term, the consensus is that personality measurement deals with the measurement of traits. In this sense, a trait is a tendency for the individual to respond to situations in a certain way. For example, a pessimistic individual will tend to respond by emphasizing the unfavorable aspects of almost any situation, and an honest person will tend to respond consistently in a certain manner in situations testing honesty. However, a trait is not usually so "pure" so that one response is consistent for all situations. Thus, a foremost problem of measuring personality is validity—the question of whether one is measuring what one intends to measure.

There are generally two kinds of personality tests: projective and nonprojective. *Projective tests* use a word, a picture, or some stimulus to elicit an unstructured response. A respondent might be asked to develop a story about a picture or to indicate what is seen in an ink blot. The response must then be interpreted by someone who scores the response. The Thematic Apperception Test (TAT) is an example of a projective test.

Nonprojective tests are paper-and-pencil tests that require the individual to respond to statements by selecting an option from a number of possible responses. The score is then generated from the options selected and certain patterns of options selected. Scores are indicative of identified personality characteristics. The Minnesota Multiphasic Personality Inventory (MMPI) is an example of a nonprojective test.

Personality tests are generally of two types: projective and nonprojective.

Constructing personality inventories is not a task for the novice. It requires extensive psychological knowledge and sophisticated psychometric methods. Satisfactory personality tests usually are commercially available. Personality tests often are listed and reviewed in psychological measurement publications. In educational research, which commonly includes "normal" individuals, traits are broadly defined—such as personal adjustment or social adjustment. Published inventories are available for measuring such broad traits.

Rating Scales

Rating scales are used frequently in educational research, and indeed they have already been introduced in connection with Likert scales. A rating scale presents a statement or item with a corresponding scale of categories, and respondents are asked to make judgments that most clearly approximate their perceptions. Rating scales may have three, four, five, or conceivably any finite number of points, and they may be presented in different formats. We have seen the Likert scale given with five points or options. Figure 12.2

PROFESSIONAL SATISFACTION SCALE
COLLEGE AND UNIVERSITY PROFESSORS

Below are listed numerous factors that may relate to the level of satisfaction or dissatisfaction that you find in your position as a professor in a college or department of education. Please reflect on your position over the past year or two and rate each factor as to the extent of satisfaction. If a factor had no influence on your extent of satisfaction please rate it NA (not applicable). DO NOT OMIT ANY FACTORS.

Please use the following numerical code for rating.

5 = Highly satisfied
4 = Satisfied
3 = Neither satisfied nor dissatisfied
2 = Dissatisfied
1 = Very dissatisfied

Rating

_____ 1. opportunities for promotion
_____ 2. process for promotion
_____ 3. opportunity for attaining tenure
_____ 4. opportunities for conducting research
_____ 5. opportunities for doing professional writing
_____ 6. opportunities for professional recognition
_____ 7. status of my work within the college or department
_____ 8. status of my work outside the college or department
_____ 9. recognition for a job well done
_____ 10. responsibility in my work
_____ 11. opportunities to use my best abilities
_____ 12. amount of effort required to do my work
_____ 13. type of work
_____ 14. challenging nature of my work
_____ 15. working with my immediate superior
_____ 16. working with other administrators
_____ 17. working with colleagues (nonadministrators)
_____ 18. working with students
_____ 19. working with professionals in the field
_____ 20. potential for growth either through training or experience
_____ 21. supervision of my work
_____ 22. management policies
_____ 23. working conditions
_____ 24. job security
_____ 25. available equipment
_____ 26. employee fringe benefits program
_____ 27. salary; base amount
_____ 28. merit increase in salary
_____ 29. privileges associated with being a professor
_____ 30. opportunities for additional income (e.g., consulting)

FIGURE 12.2   Sample Items from a Rating Scale

Note: Reproduced with permission of the authors.

contains another format for which the respondent places a number in a blank. These are sample items from a scale used by Nussel, Wiersma, and Rusche (1988).

Any number of variables can be measured using rating scales, including perceptions of instruction, adequacy of facilities, perceptions of program effects, and so forth. The descriptors used for the categories of the scale are selected to fit the particular variable being rated. Rating scales also can be used by observers who are observing an activity such as teaching.

Rating scales can vary in length, but usually they contain several statements, called *items,* that use the same descriptors and relate to a single concept, activity, phenomenon, experience, or physical object. If it is desirable to obtain a total score over all items or groups of items, this can be done in the usual manner by summing the item scores. The scoring usually is done so that the greater the score the higher the respondent's rating.

> *Rating scales* contain items related to a concept, phenomenon, activity, or physical object; the respondent is asked to select a descriptor on a scale that most closely approximates his or her assessment of whatever is described in the item.

Observation Systems

Tests and inventories used for measuring achievement, attitudes, scholastic ability, etc., are for the most part paper-and-pencil instruments, many of them administered simultaneously to an entire group. There also are educational research situations in which the data are collected through an *observation system*—a procedure by which an observer records what is occurring in some situation or setting, such as a classroom.

Observation systems take on a variety of forms; however, those for observing teacher and student behavior or classroom interaction roughly fall into two categories. One category consists essentially of a rating scale, for which observed behaviors are judged qualitatively. Then the ratings are combined in some manner in an attempt to quantify behavior. The Teaching Performance Profile developed by Rasmussen, Lindner, and Johnson (1986) is an example of this type of system.

The second category of observation systems consists of those made up of a matrix. The cells of the matrix represent behaviors or combinations of behaviors that may be exhibited in a classroom. The observer records the presence of behaviors and, in some systems, also the frequency of behaviors. The Classroom Observations Keyed for Effectiveness Research (COKER) system, as described by Medley, Coker, and Soar (1984, p. 72), is an example of a matrix-type observation system.

> An *observation system* is used for recording preselected behaviors in an attempt to quantify behavior in the situation being observed.

Collecting data using observation systems is a relatively demanding task. It requires considerable training of observers, who must be consistent in recording what they observe. Thus, agreement of observation is always a concern, not only between different observers, but also between the different observations of a single observer. For a detailed discussion of observation, both rationale and method, the reader is referred to Evertson and Green (1986).

Measures Involving Holistic Scoring

Dependent variables in educational research commonly are scored in an analytic manner. That is, some type of point system is used which generates a numerical score on the dependent variable. These scores are then analyzed as quantitative data.

There are educational research situations in which a dependent variable takes on a more qualitative characteristic, such as the overall quality of an essay written in response to a question or series of questions. Holistic scoring may then be used either singly or in combination with analytic scoring.

Holistic scoring, as the name implies, scores a response as a whole rather than by parts. It focuses on global quality and is based on a general impression of the overall adequacy of the response. Holistic scoring is more subjective than analytic scoring, and it may be difficult to justify the score. Holistic scores usually are ordinal in nature, placing responses into two or more categories, such as excellent, good, fair, or poor.

Analytic scoring is based on assigning points to individual parts or components of a response. In contrast, holistic scoring considers the response in its entirety, as a whole.

Holistic scoring, because of its subjectivity, has some inherent difficulties in generating consistent scores. But there are procedures that can and should be implemented to enhance consistency in scoring. These procedures are:

1. Summarize the qualitative aspects desired in the response; this may be done by developing a model response, or an outline of a model response.

2. All responses should be scored anonymously and in random order.

3. Have two (or more) equally competent (apparently) scorers score the responses independently.

4. If there are discrepancies in the scores of two scorers have them resolved by either a third independent scorer or through a discussion between the two scorers to resolve their differences.

5. If there are two or more items to be scored, have all responses to one item scored before moving on to another item. Also, reorder the responses before scoring the next item.

6. Make scorers cognizant of irrelevant factors that may affect the score. These include factors such as length and neatness of the response. They also may include factors such as a tendency to score responses higher if they are preceded in the scoring by poorer-quality responses.

7. Be aware of factors such as fatigue and boredom that may affect the scorer. Do not persist with the scoring over long periods without taking breaks for other activities.

Holistic scoring must be recognized for what it is; it is qualitative and by its very nature subjective. Analytic and holistic scoring can be used effectively in combination. When this is done, responses first are scored holistically to get a feel for their overall quality, and thus order or rate them into relatively broad categories. Then the responses are scored analytically, focusing more on specific characteristics or components.

Where to Find Test Information

There are a number of sources for information about tests and inventories in almost all areas of education. Two of these from the Buros Institute already have been mentioned: *Tests in Print III* and the *Mental Measurements Yearbooks* and their supplements. The Buros Institute also provides a computerized database service, Biographic Retrieval Service, Inc. (BRS), which is useful for obtaining information about new and revised tests. Libraries that offer the BRS service can conduct computer searches of the database.

Dissertation Abstracts International (DAI) can be searched online for test information, but the abstracts have been included online only since 1980. For tests used in dissertations prior to 1980, Fabiano (1989) has compiled a volume titled *Index to Tests Used in Educational Dissertations*. This volume lists over 40,000 tests used in dissertations from 1938 to 1980. The tests cover achievement, aptitude, personality, physical fitness, vocational ability, and almost any other area of educational testing.

The *Educational Testing Service (ETS) Test Collection Catalog* is a six-volume set published by Oryx Press. The names and publication dates of the six volumes are:

Volume 1: *Achievement Tests and Measurement Devices* (1986)

Volume 2: *Vocational Tests and Measurement Devices* (1989)

Volume 3: *Tests for Special Populations* (1989)

Volume 4: *Cognitive, Aptitude and Intelligence Tests* (1990)

Volume 5: *Attitude Tests* (1991)

Volume 6: *Affective Measures and Personality Tests* (1992)

These volumes as a group describe thousands of tests. Each volume contains an Introduction, a Main Subject Section, a Subject Index, an Author Index, and a Title Index. The test profiles are brief but they contain valuable information about subtests, descriptors, identifiers, availability, and target audiences. ETS itself maintains a collection of more than 10,000 tests and publishes a monthly newsletter, *News on Tests,* which describes revised tests or new tests added to the collection. The newsletter also includes references to reviews and general news about testing. ETS also publishes an annotated index of tests in microfiche.

A volume that has been around for some time but merits mentioning because it is one of the few sources for observation instruments is *Mirrors for Behavior III* (Simon and Boyer, 1974). This is an informative anthology of observation instruments focusing on teacher and student behavior. There are ninety-nine instruments listed and described, many highly specific, such as the Biology Teacher Behavior Inventory and the Medical Instruction Observation Record. The description of an instrument is complete, including information about the conditions of its use. One volume contains an extensive bibliography.

Many test publishers provide promotional brochures and catalogs about their tests. An example is the Publishers Test Service of CTB/McGraw-Hill. Virtually all published tests are accompanied by a manual, which is a valuable source of detailed information about the test under consideration. Many school systems and universities have counseling centers or testing centers in which such manuals are available and, sometimes, examples of tests.

Information about tests is contained throughout the periodical literature. Tests occasionally are reviewed in professional journals. Journals such as the *Journal of Educational Measurement* often contain reports about the use of exploratory approaches to measurement. Thus, there is a good deal of test information available, much of which can be located through the use of indices (see Chapter 3).

Quantitative Data Preparation

Scores on tests and attitude inventories usually are considered quantitative data and ultimately are analyzed by some statistical procedure. Before analysis can take place, tabulation is necessary and it may be desirable to make some type of data transformation. If answer sheets or tests are hand-scored, routine precautions include supervised practice for scorers and accuracy checks.

Research projects that require the collection of considerable data using standardized tests or inventories use machine-scored answer sheets. Test publishers typically provide a scoring service. Even locally constructed tests can be machine-scored because companies such as IBM and NCS sell standardized machine-scored answer sheets. It is possible to have special-purpose machine-scored answer sheets developed, but the process is quite expensive. Test-scoring machines not only provide the actual scores, they commonly provide tabulations, summaries, and conversions to various types of standard scores. In some cases, the machines are connected to a computer to provide certain kinds of analyses.

Machine scoring of tests is usually less expensive and more accurate than hand scoring and makes it easier to prepare the data for computer analysis. Not all educational research data are collected in a form that can be machine-scored, however, and the organization of data for analysis when transmitting data by hand from the answer sheet to the computer is an important part of the research procedure.

Coding Data

With the general availability of computers, any research project involving even a small amount of data or requiring anything but very simple statistical analysis should allow for the use of a computer. Data must be transmitted from answer sheets or data sheets to the computer through a computer terminal. A format for the data must be specified in order to complete this task.

A computer terminal screen contains rows, and the spaces in the rows correspond to columns. A typical row contains seventy-two spaces. The process of developing the format for identifying the information in each column is called *coding* the data. Information is commonly of two types: identification and scores or responses. The identification information consists of such things as the individual's classification on the independent variables and an identification number. Usually, the identification comes in the early columns, although this is not required. The scores, commonly the scores on the dependent variables, are entered using as many columns as necessary. A two-digit score, for example, requires two columns. If there are ten different tests, each giving a two-digit score, these data would require twenty columns. If tests with varying numbers of digits in the scores are used, the number of columns for each score is sometimes held constant—that is, the greatest number of digits for any score. This may facilitate setting up the analysis. If the data for an individual require more than the number of columns in the row, simply use additional rows for that individual. A row contains data from only one individual even if the row is not completely filled.

Coding data consists of developing a system by which the data and identification information are specified and organized in preparation for the analyses.

An example of coding information is presented in Figure 12.3. This is a sample data layout. The information is from a research study involving an experimental and a traditional reading program in 14 elementary schools. The first ten columns contain identification information. The first two columns identify the school, and the next two columns the class in the school. Since no school contains more than 1000 students, three columns are reserved for the student identification number. Columns 8, 9, and 10 contain classifying information. If the numbers in the first ten columns were

$$1 \quad 1 \quad 0 \quad 6 \quad 1 \quad 3 \quad 1 \quad 1 \quad 5 \quad 1$$

These mean: student 131 from school 11 in class 6, who is a fifth-grade girl in the experimental reading program. Columns 11 and 12 contain the number in the class,

Column Number	Column Information
1, 2	School code; 14 numbers possible
3, 4	Class number in the school
5, 6, 7	Student identification number
8	Sex 1 = female 2 = male
9	Grade level 3, 4, 5, or 6
10	Type of reading program 1 = experimental 2 = traditional
11, 12	Number in class
13, 14, 15	Score on recent IQ test
16, 17, 18	Score on attitude toward school inventory
19, 20	Total score on reading test
21, 22	Reading comprehension subscore
23, 24	Reading word attack subscore
25, 26	Score on comprehension math test involving written or "story" problems
27, 28	Score on science test
29, 30	Score on social studies test
31, 32	Score on English usage test
33, 34	Score on logical reasoning test
	Remaining columns blank

FIGURE 12.3   Sample Coding of Information

information that may be used in analyses. The remaining 22 columns contain the various test scores.

An Example of a Data File

The data should be organized so that minimum effort is required to transmit the data from their original form to the computer. Sometimes data can be transmitted directly from the measuring instrument to the computer. If this is not convenient, because reorganization of the data is necessary or the process is too complex, a computer recording form can be used, which is readily available at computer centers and stationery stores. These forms may contain eighty columns, a throwback to the days when eighty-column data cards were used. Either way, the data for each individual should be presented on a line or a row in the exact order they are to be transmitted. It is inefficient to be fishing around for information when transmitting data. When data have been transmitted, they should be checked for possible errors. When all the data have been transmitted into the computer, we have a data file.

Suppose a school system has fifty-four teachers in grades three through six and a study is being conducted on the extent to which these teachers demonstrate six selected teaching competencies. The six competencies are as follows:

C-1 Uses a variety of instructional strategies.
C-2 Uses convergent and divergent inquiry strategies.
C-3 Develops and demonstrates problem-solving skills.
C-4 Establishes transitions and sequences in instruction that are varied.
C-5 Modifies instructional activities to accommodate identified learner needs.
C-6 Demonstrates ability to work with individuals, small groups, and large groups.

The teachers are observed using a classroom observation inventory, and scores are obtained for each teacher on the six competencies.

The data are recorded on a computer recording form, as illustrated in Figure 12.4. Teachers are identified only by number; the information for six teachers is given in Figure 12.4. The coding is straightforward: The first two columns are for identification, and then the six competency scores are given in order. The scores are two-digit numbers, and one-columns spaces (which are not necessary) are inserted between scores for easier reading. Thus, the identification number, the scores, and the spaces use twenty columns. The data for each teacher are placed on a row.

When putting the data into the computer, we create a data file. The file needs a name. This file will be called **File: TCHRCOMP DATA.** Usually, the name is descriptive of the data and is used in locating the file for future analyses. Abbreviations are used because there usually is a limit on the number of characters that can be used in a file name. The data file is given in Figure 12.5. Note that there are fifty-four rows, one for the data on each teacher, and that the format for the rows is consistent. The file is now ready to be used in analyzing data; we will use it for a sample analysis in Chapter 13.

If the data are to be analyzed using a hand or desk calculator, it is important to classify and organize all scores so there is no confusion as to the identification of a score. The scores should be presented so errors are minimized in transmitting them from data sheets to the calculator. The computations on the calculator should be performed in such a manner that several internal checks can be made during the calculations.

Summary

This chapter provided an overview of some of the more common types of measurement used in educational research. For many research studies, adequate measurement devices—in the form of tests, inventories, scales, or observation schedules—are available, and suggestions were provided about information sources. Because the measurement instruments used provide the operational definition of the data, their selection merits attention.

Because some research projects have measurement needs that cannot be met readily by existing instruments, it is sometimes necessary to construct the instruments, and this increases the total research effort. Commonly constructed instruments such as rating

CODING FORM

ID	C-1	C-2	C-3	C-4	C-5	C-6
1 2 3	4 5	6 7 8	9 10 11 12	13 14 15	16 17	18 19 20 21
01	61	36	35	49	40	61
02	53	49	61	47	54	58
03	57	48	46	51	51	58
04	34	51	50	47	38	38
05	58	45	47	45	51	41
06	53	35	34	45	52	55

FIGURE 12.4 Sample Computer Recording Form Used for Coding Data

```
FILE:  TCHRCOMP  DATA
       A  UNIVERSITY  OF  TOLEDO  TIME-SHARING  SYSTEM
```

01	61	36	35	49	40	61		28	36	43	53	43	37	47
02	53	49	61	47	54	58		29	42	71	56	45	42	51
03	57	48	46	51	51	58		30	55	51	56	43	67	56
04	34	51	50	47	38	38		31	39	55	39	57	45	36
05	58	45	47	45	51	41		32	48	50	55	47	43	38
06	53	35	34	45	52	55		33	52	67	50	45	65	80
07	39	62	51	49	43	56		34	58	45	46	28	54	56
08	44	46	43	32	48	76		35	36	43	43	43	45	41
09	58	61	66	56	72	66		36	46	53	49	69	44	47
10	56	73	59	79	56	44		37	40	44	68	43	56	52
11	53	36	36	43	50	36		38	36	38	43	49	39	54
12	53	42	36	45	41	37		39	48	47	54	75	74	55
13	45	49	40	45	61	50		40	52	61	76	79	59	45
14	40	37	39	45	38	50		41	88	75	66	61	75	60
15	41	38	48	45	66	49		42	42	49	37	47	47	56
16	61	65	53	49	40	58		43	55	63	62	51	52	46
17	57	60	73	51	53	52		44	49	47	57	51	53	52
18	51	41	39	47	38	38		45	61	50	52	54	50	44
19	51	47	44	43	53	47		46	53	67	52	51	41	52
20	56	45	41	45	48	39		47	45	49	49	47	60	64
21	66	43	54	45	64	52		48	49	44	46	49	48	44
22	38	51	39	43	39	45		49	58	59	48	74	50	48
23	38	45	54	45	37	69		50	52	45	55	47	42	34
24	36	56	54	47	36	36		54	55	47	45	65	47	43
25	43	47	44	43	60	45		52	58	54	63	49	58	53
26	58	49	63	49	47	56		53	63	51	50	49	48	57
27	35	42	40	45	40	45		54	49	31	38	57	44	37

FIGURE 12.5   Sample Data File for the Six Competency Scores of 54 Teachers

Note: These are hypothetical data.

scales were discussed. Before embarking on the development of an instrument, however, the researcher should check for available instruments and estimate the magnitude of the development task. In some areas, such as the measurement of personality, instrument development requires sophisticated knowledge and skills.

The concepts of reliability and validity of measuring instruments were discussed. Whenever an instrument is used, its validity in the context of its use—the extent to which the instrument is measuring what it is intended to measure—must be considered. Reliability is consistency of measurement. There are a number of procedures for establishing reliability, as discussed in this chapter.

Since education includes so many variables, measurement is very broad and varied. Entire books are written on even limited areas within measurement, so this chapter did not go into detail about the theoretical concepts of measurement or some of the infrequently used procedures. The amount of effort that must be put into obtaining the measurement instrument and collecting the data depends on the conditions of the specific research study.

It is important to plan the data collection carefully and to identify the specific measurement requirements of the research study. Collecting a mass of data and then trying to fit a research problem to it is not acceptable practice. After data are collected, they must be assembled for analysis. Coding and construction of a data file were illustrated in this chapter; these procedures are done so that analysis can proceed in an appropriate and efficient manner. Although good measurement does not ensure good research, it is a necessary but not sufficient condition for good research.

KEY CONCEPTS

Measurement	Achievement tests
Scales of measurement	Aptitude tests
Reliability of measurement	Personality measures
Parallel forms procedures	Projective tests
Split-half procedure	Nonprojective tests
Kuder-Richardson procedures	Likert scale
Cronbach alpha procedure	Semantic differential
Reliability coefficient	Rating scales
Validity of measurement	Observation systems
Content-related evidence	Test information sources
Criterion-related evidence	Coding data
Construct-related evidence	Data file

EXERCISES

12.1 Discuss the distinction between the concepts of validity and reliability. Why do we say that measurement can be reliable without being valid, but that the reverse cannot be true?

12.2 A researcher plans to do a study about the extent of hostility in upper elementary classrooms taught by teachers classified as autocratic or democratic. Discuss the problem of establishing validity in measuring hostility. Assume that hostility can go both ways: from students to teachers and vice versa. What are possible approaches to measuring hostility? For example, would observation be used? If so, what would be included in the observation schedule? What is a possible operational definition of hostility? Is it possible to quantify hostility in any way?

12.3 Suppose a guidance counselor wants to do a study on the attitudes of junior high students toward a compulsory "orientation to the school" program. Students who have completed the program are to respond to an attitude inventory. Construct five items for such an inventory. Designate the scoring for your items.

12.4 A researcher is doing research on the science achievement of students in grades five through seven. Another researcher is doing research on personality characteristics of junior high students. Contrast the measurement of these two research studies with respect to the:

  a. availability of published measuring instruments.
  b. type of validity of major concern.
  c. data-collection procedures.

12.5 Suppose a researcher is doing research on the attitudes of junior high school students toward their teachers. Construct a semantic differential that might be used to measure such attitudes.

12.6 Construct five items for a rating scale that might be used with high school teachers to measure faculty perceptions of the central administration of the school system.

12.7 Contrast the use of a Likert scale and a semantic differential. In what ways are they operationally different in terms of the manner in which an individual responds? Describe any differences and similarities in the scoring procedures.

12.8 A research director for a large city school system conducts an extensive study of achievement in grades three through eight. Achievement in several areas is measured, with subscores in the areas, so that there are eighteen different achievement scores for each participating student. Ten of the scores require two digits each and the remainder, three digits each. The sample of students is drawn from seventy-four city schools. The total sample size is over one thousand, and each student in the sample is to be identified by a number. In addition to the specific school and grade level, the students are classified according to sex. The student's age is recorded to the nearest month. There are nine high schools in the city, and each of the seventy-four elementary schools is in only one high school district. This information also is recorded in terms of the high school district in which the student's school is located. Develop a possible coding scheme that includes all of the foregoing information. Consider the number of columns you would use for identification information and achievement scores. The order of providing information is somewhat arbitrary, but identify a specific order. Assume that the data will be put into the computer through a terminal and that seventy-two columns are available. Would it be necessary to use more than one row for the data of a single student?

12.9 Select an article from a professional journal that involves the measurement of attitudes or personality characteristics. Read the article carefully and check to see whether the author discusses such things as validity, reliability, and type of measuring device. Are the data quantified in some way? Were standardized tests used for the study? If so, were norms available?

12.10 In the research literature on teacher evaluation or teacher performance, locate two or more studies using classroom observation systems. If the observation systems are reproduced, inspect them for similarities and differences. If they are not reproduced, there should at least be descriptions of the systems. Identify the specific classroom interaction variables measured by the systems. Is any reliability information provided, and if so, is the specific type of coefficient indicated used to estimate reliability? How is the issue of validity addressed?

NOTES

1. See, for example, W. Wiersma and S. Jurs, *Educational Measurement and Testing*, 2nd ed. (Boston: Allyn and Bacon, 1990), or N.E. Gronlund and R.L. Linn, *Measurement and Evaluation in Teaching*, 6th ed. (New York: Macmillan, 1990). For a comprehensive reference on many concepts and issues of

measurement, *Educational Measurement,* 3rd ed. (Phoenix: Oryx, 1989) edited by R.L. Linn, is recommended.

2. The terms *index* and *scale* commonly are used interchangeably, although some authors make a technical distinction between them. Both scales and indices are composite measures of variables based on responses to more than one item, and both typically provide ordinal measurement for the individual items.

An index is obtained through the simple cumulation of scores to responses over the items. A scale is obtained through the assignment of scores to response patterns, thus taking into account any intensity structure that may exist in the items. By these technical definitions, most of the scales used in educational research are indices, but this discussion will continue with the more common term *scale.*

REFERENCES

Cronbach, L. J. (1951). Coefficient alpha and the internal structure of tests. *Psychometrika, 16,* 297–334.

Cronbach, L. J. (1984). *Essentials of psychological testing* (4th ed.). New York: Harper & Row.

Evertson, C. M., and Green, J. L. (1986). Observation as inquiry and method. In M. C. Wittrock (Ed.), *Handbook of research on teaching* (3rd ed.), (pp. 162–213). New York: Macmillan.

Fabiano, E. (1989). *Index to tests used in educational dissertations.* Phoenix, AZ: Oryx Press.

Kerlinger, F. N. (1986). *Foundations of behavioral research* (3rd ed.). New York: Holt, Rinehart and Winston.

Kramer, J. J., and Conoley, J. C. (Eds.) (1992). *The eleventh mental measurements yearbook.* Lincoln: University of Nebraska Press.

Kuder, G. F., and Richardson, M,W. (1937). The theory of the estimation of test reliability. *Psychometrika, 2,* 151–160.

Medley, D. M., Coker, H., and Soar, R. S. (1984). *Measurement-based evaluation of teacher performance: An empirical approach.* New York: Longman.

Mitchell, J. V. (Ed.). (1983). *Tests in Print III.* Lincoln: University of Nebraska Press.

Nussel, E. J., Wiersma, W., and Rusche, P. J. (1988). Work satisfaction of education professors. *Journal of Teacher Education, 39*(3), 45–50.

Osgood, C. E., Suci, G. J., and Tannenbaum, P. H. (1957). *The measurement of meaning.* Urbana: University of Illinois Press.

Rasmussen, R. E., Lindner, K. E., and Johnson, M. A. (1986). *The teaching performance profile.* Minneapolis: Digicator Systems, Inc.

Simon, A., and Boyer, E. G. (Eds.). (1974). *Mirrors for behavior III. An anthology of observation instruments.* Wyncote, PA: Communication Materials Center.

Chapter 13

Data Analysis: Descriptive Statistics

This chapter and the following chapter describe a variety of statistical procedures used for data analysis. Data can take many forms, and when they take numerical forms such as scores or frequencies, the usual course of action is to perform an appropriate type of statistical analysis.

When data take numerical forms, they usually are accorded some level of quantitative meaning. Thus, statistical analyses are commonly associated with research on the quantitative end of the research continuum: experimental, quasi-experimental, and survey research. In the chapters dealing with those types of research, specific analysis procedures were not emphasized because statistical procedures have broad application. With qualitative research, the analysis is more of an ongoing activity that is integrated with other steps in the research process, and this was reflected in the chapters on historical and ethnographic research. Analysis in qualitative research relies heavily on induction, and the product, rather than being a statistical result, is description. However, statistical procedures may be appropriate for some parts of data analysis in historical and ethnographic research, but they certainly are not the major thrust of analysis in qualitative research.

Statistical analysis has been greatly facilitated by the availability of both mainframe and personal computers. Software for analyses is widely available, and some comments about software will be made later. Thus, computational accuracy is pretty well assured, and the student can concentrate on the underlying reasoning of the procedures and the meaning of the results.

The Multiple Meanings of Statistics

The term *statistics* has multiple meanings in educational research, but probably its simplest meaning is "bits of information." If one says that 632 students are enrolled in a specific school, this can be considered a statistic. The salary schedule and the numbers of teachers at each salary level for a district are sometimes called salary statistics.

Statistics has a much broader meaning than simply bits of information, however. It also refers to the theory, procedures, and methodology by which data are summarized. It has been suggested that to some people, the terminology of statistics seems like a foreign language; although, this may be true, the understanding and use of statistics is not so much a matter of identifying new terminology and symbols for already known concepts as it is a way of reasoning and drawing conclusions. Although the lay person often views statistics as an accumulation of facts and figures, the researcher sees statistics as the methods used to describe data and make sense of them.

Many different specific statistical analyses are available to the educational researcher, but it is not the intent of this discussion to cover statistical analysis in detail. Rather, the following two purposes will be addressed by this chapter and Chapter 14: (1) to provide the reasoning underlying the use of statistical analysis and (2) to list the more commonly used statistical procedures and the conditions under which they apply. The discussion is intended to emphasize the logic of analysis, not computational procedures

Descriptive statistics, discussed in this chapter, are exactly what the name implies: procedures and measures by which we describe quantitative data. Suppose values or scores on some variable have been collected; one of the first tasks is to describe these scores. If fifty fourth-grade students have been tested on arithmetic achievement and their fifty scores comprise the data of the research study, how will these scores be described? Simply listing them on a sheet of paper is not adequate. They must be summarized somehow. Certain information is generated that describes these scores as a group. This information and the process by which it is obtained are called *descriptive statistics*.

Distributions

The group or set of all scores or observations on a variable is called a *distribution*. The fifty arithmetic achievement scores mentioned earlier would be a distribution. If measurement were on an interval scale, rather than listing all fifty scores individually, one would tabulate them according to frequency. That is, each possible score would be listed, and the frequency of its occurrence would be listed, as in Table 13.1. The *f* stands for frequency, and the content of Table 13.1 is called a *frequency distribution*.

Arranging the scores as in Table 13.1 does not provide much information. The largest and smallest scores, sixty and ninety-nine, can be determined, and they cover a total of forty points on the scale of measurement. Thus, the scores have a range of forty points. Instead of a tabular form, the scores could be put into graphic form by indicating frequency on the vertical axis and the values of the scores on the horizontal axis. Such a representation is called a *histogram*. The histogram for the arithmetic test scores is quite flat and spread out because of relatively small frequencies and a wide range of scores. The histogram brings out the general shape of the distribution, as illustrated in Figure 13.1.

TABLE 13.1   Frequency Distribution of Arithmetic Test Scores

Score	f	Score	f	Score	f	Score	f
60	1	70	0	80	2	90	1
61	1	71	0	31	2	91	1
62	0	72	4	82	3	92	1
63	0	73	0	83	2	93	2
64	0	74	2	84	2	94	1
65	0	75	3	85	1	95	2
66	3	76	1	36	2	96	0
67	1	77	1	87	1	97	1
68	0	78	2	88	0	98	2
69	1	79	1	89	2	99	1

Describing a Distribution of Scores

Although a frequency distribution and a histogram pull together the scores, they are hardly adequate for describing a distribution. All research results cannot be reported by merely producing frequency distributions and constructing related histograms. Measures that more efficiently and fully describe a distribution are needed.

Basically, there are three requirements for describing a distribution of scores or observations. One is that something must be known about where the distribution is located on the scale of measurement. Second, there must be information about how the distribution is spread out—how it is dispersed. The third requirement is the identification of its shape.

To describe a distribution is to provide information about its location, dispersion, and shape.

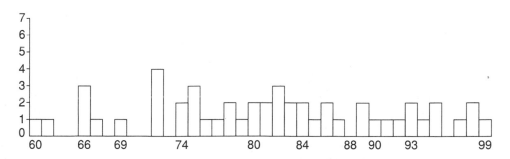

FIGURE 13.1   Histogram for the Frequency Distribution of the Raw Scores on an Arithmetic Test

Statistics called *measures of central tendency* indicate the location of a distribution. Correspondingly, statistics can be computed to indicate the dispersion of the distribution; these are called *measures of variability.* A histogram could be generated to determine the shape of a distribution, but it would be more common to infer a shape from knowing something about the variable under study. Many educational variables—for example, achievement scores in academic areas—tend to have symmetrical, bell-shaped distributions, which approximate what is known as a normal distribution.

Measures of Central Tendency.   Measures of central tendency are commonly referred to as *averages.* In this sense, they give an indication of what a typical observation in the distribution is like. Measures of central tendency are locators of the distribution; that is, they locate the distribution on the scale of measurement. They are points in the distribution that derive their name from a tendency to be centrally located in the distribution.

The mean, median, and mode are the most commonly used measures of central tendency. *Mean,* used in this context, refers to the arithmetic mean. The mean is determined by simply adding the scores in a distribution and dividing by the number of scores in the distribution. The *median* is the point on the scale of measurement below which one-half of the scores of the distribution lie. The *mode,* which is used infrequently, is simply the score with the greatest frequency.

The following illustrates the idea of a locator. There are two distributions of weights, one for adult men and one for adult women. The mean weight of the distribution is 170 pounds for the men and 132 pounds for the women. Both distributions have the same measurement scale—pounds—and both can be located on the measurement scale by their means. If the distributions are set on the measurement scale, the distribution for the men would be located to the right—that is, farther up the scale—than the distribution for the women.

Measures of *central tendency* are points in the distribution used to locate the distribution. The *mean* is the most commonly used measure of central tendency; it is the arithmetic average—the sum of all the scores divided by the number of scores. The *median* is the point below which one-half of the scores lie.

Measures of Variability.   In describing a distribution, it also is necessary to know something about its dispersion, or spread of the scores; dispersion is indicated by measures of *variability.* In contrast to measures of central tendency, which are points, measures of variability are intervals (or their squares); that is, they designate a number of units on the scale of measurement.

There are several measures of variability. The *range* is a crude measure, since it provides little information. It gives the number of units on the scale of measurement necessary to include the highest and lowest scores, but it provides no information about the pattern of variation between these scores.

The measures of variability most commonly used are the *variance* and the *standard deviation*. Before these measures can be defined, the meaning of a deviation must be considered. *Deviation* means the difference between an observed score and the mean of the distribution. To determine the variance, the squares of these deviations are summed and divided by the number of scores.[1] If *n* is the number of scores and $\overline{X}$ (read "*X*bar") the mean of the distribution, the variance is then given in symbol form by:

$$\text{Variance} = \frac{\Sigma(X_i - \overline{X})^2}{n}$$

That is, the deviation of each score from the mean is squared, the squares of these deviations are then summed, and this sum is divided by the number of observations in the distribution. Thus, the variance is the average of the squared deviations from the mean. The *standard deviation* is defined as the positive square root of the variance.

> The *variance* and the *standard deviation* are the most commonly used measures of variability. They are intervals (or their squares) on the scale of measurement, and they indicate the dispersion in the distribution.

This discussion of measures of central tendency and measures of variability has indicated the need for both types of measures, as well as knowing something about the shape, for describing distributions. When distributions are described as being alike, for example, it is important to specify in what way they are similar. Figures 13.2 and 13.3 illustrate distributions that are alike in one respect yet very different in the other.

Shapes of Distributions.   Distributions may take on a variety of shapes. The shape of the histogram in Figure 13.1 has no specific name, but there are distributions whose shapes have been named. A distribution that (at least theoretically) occurs frequently in educational research is the *normal distribution*. The normal distribution is not a single distribu-

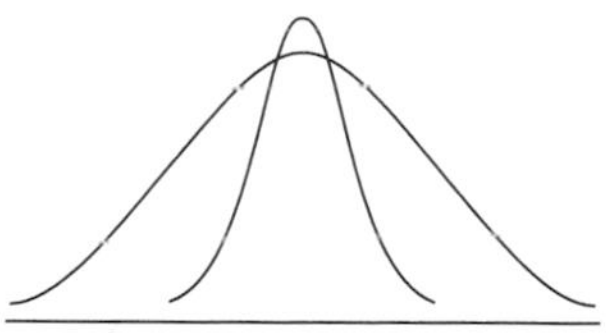

FIGURE 13.2
Distributions with Like
Central Tendency but
Different Variability

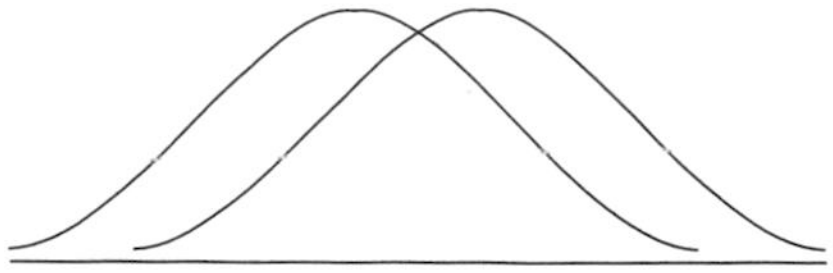

FIGURE 13.3
Distributions with Like Variability
but Different Central Tendency

tion with a specific mean and standard deviation. Rather, it is a smooth, symmetrical distribution that follows the general shape of the distributions in Figure 13.4 (sometimes called bell-shaped). The specific normal distribution depends on characteristics such as its variability.

When considering the shape of a distribution of scores comprising the data of some research study, the important consideration is not identifying the exact shape of the distribution. Histograms, for example, are seldom actually constructed. The important questions about the distribution's shape are: Theoretically, what shape should the data from this variable take? Can it be assumed that a variable will maintain a specified shape if all possible scores for the group under study are known? What kind of assumed distribution is required for the intended procedures to be applied to the data? These are the relevant questions to be raised about the shape of the distribution of observed scores. In contrast to working with measures of central tendency and variability, for which the specific values are computed, a researcher usually is less concerned with the actual shape of the distribution of observed scores and more concerned with its assumed or theoretical shape.

Standard Scores

Suppose an instructional experiment is being conducted, and there are two dependent variables, performance on a mathematics test and performance on a science test. If a subject in the experiment has a score of 78 on the mathematics test and a score of 92 on the science test, which is the better performance? There is no way to tell simply from the raw or observed scores, because the tests may be on different scales and have different numbers of items. What can be done is to transform the scores to a common equal-interval scale, and such scores are called standard scores. Standard scores are obtained by using the standard deviation as the unit of measure and then indicating the relative position of a single score in the entire distribution of scores in terms of the mean and standard deviation. Specifically, a standard score is the number of standard deviations that an observed score is located from the mean.

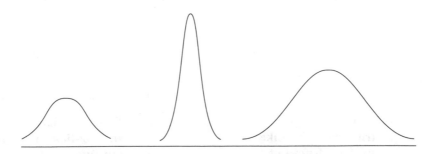

FIGURE 13.4   Examples of Normal Distributions

> Standard scores are obtained by a transformation so that the unit of measurement is the standard deviation and the score is expressed in standard deviation units from the mean.

Properties of Standard Scores.   The commonly used symbol for a standard score is a lower case *z* (*z*-score). When converting to standard scores, a z-score is calculated for each score in the original distribution. The distribution of z-scores has the following properties:

1. The shape of the distribution of z-scores is identical to that of the original distribution of scores.
2. The mean of the distribution of z-scores equals zero regardless of the value of the mean in the original distribution.
3. The variance of the distribution of z-scores is 1, and because the standard deviation is the positive square root of the variance, it too is 1. This is true regardless of the value of the variance of the original distribution.

> The distribution of standard scores has the same shape as the original distribution, a mean of zero, and a standard deviation of 1.

Determining Standard Scores. A z-score is computed by subtracting the mean from the observed score and dividing the result by the standard deviation. This process can be expressed by:

$$\text{Standard score} = \frac{\text{Observed score} - \text{mean}}{\text{Standard deviation}}$$

or in symbol form:

$$z = \frac{X - \overline{X}}{s}$$

where:

> *X is the observed score*
> $\overline{X}$ *is the mean of the observed distribution*
> *s is the standard deviation of the observed distribution.*

Going back to the two dependent variable scores mentioned earlier, the 78 on the mathematics test and the 92 on the science test, what would these scores be as standard scores? First we need to know the means and standard deviations of the original distributions of scores. Suppose the distribution of mathematics test scores has a mean ($\overline{X}_m$) of 76 and a standard deviation (s_m) of 4. The science test score distribution has a mean ($\overline{X}_{sc}$) of 94 and a standard deviation (s_{sc}) of 6. Converting the subject's scores of 78 and 92, respectively, to z-scores we have:

for the mathematics test score: $z_m = \dfrac{X_m - \bar{X}_m}{s_m}$

$$z_m = \frac{78 - 76}{4}$$

$$z_m = +.50$$

and for the science test score: $z_{sc} = \dfrac{X_{sc} - \bar{X}_{sc}}{s_{sc}}$

$$z_{sc} = \frac{92 - 94}{6}$$

$$z_{sc} = -.33$$

These are the two standard scores of one individual or subject. Note that the relative position of the mathematics test score with a z-score of +.50 is considerably better than that of the science test score with a z-score of −.33, even though the original scores were 78 and 92, respectively.

The above illustration shows that z-scores take on both positive and negative values. In fact, in a symmetrical distribution there will be as many negative as positive scores. A score at the mean of the original distribution will be a z-score of zero. So, attractive as z-scores are, they do have some undesirable features.

To avoid negative and zero scores we can transform a distribution of standard scores to a distribution with an arbitrarily selected mean and standard deviation. A transformation sometimes used is one to a distribution with a mean of 50 and a standard deviation of 10. This way negative scores are avoided and the scores tend to locate around 50. The transformation process is expressed by:

Transformed score = (10)(z) + 50

Transforming the previous science test score in this manner would give:

$$
\begin{aligned}
\text{Transformed science test score} &= 10(-.33) + 50 \\
&= -3.3 + 50 \\
&= 46.7
\end{aligned}
$$

So now, instead of a negative z-score, the original score of 92 is transformed into a score of 46.7.

Test publishers often use transformed standard scores to a distribution with a designated mean and standard deviation. A mean of 500 and a standard deviation of 100 are sometimes used. Distributions with a mean of 100 and a standard deviation of 15 have been used for intelligence test scores.

Standard scores are useful for showing the relative positioning of scores in a distribution. They also are used for finding values in statistical tables, as will be discussed later.

Correlation—A Measure of Relationship

Thus far, this discussion has been concerned mainly with describing the scores on a single variable, those of one distribution or set of data. However, in education, researchers are often interested in two variables simultaneously, to determine how they relate to one another. An example might be the relationship between student achievement in language arts and scores on a self-concept inventory.

This extent of relationship is approached through the distributions of scores that represent the two variables. The two distributions are commonly made up of paired scores from a single group of individuals. In any event, the distributions make up sets of ordered pairs of scores. The researcher is interested in how the scores in the distributions correlate or covary. To *covary* means to vary together—high scores with high, low with low, high with medium, whatever the case may be. The relationship between the two distributions (and, hence, the variables represented by the distributions) is based on how the pairs of scores vary together—that is, how changes in one variable compare with changes in the other variable. The degree of relationship or association between two variables is referred to as *correlation*. Thus, correlational studies are concerned not with a single distribution but with two distributions of scores.

The measure of correlation is called the *correlation coefficient* or the *coefficient of correlation*. The correlation coefficient is an index of the extent of relationship between two variables, which can take on values from –1.00 through 0 to +1.00, inclusive. The greater the absolute value of the coefficient, the stronger the relationship. The end points of the interval indicate a perfect correlation between the variables, whereas a correlation of 0 indicates no relationship between variables, in which case it is said that the variables are independent. The sign on the coefficient, plus or minus, indicates the direction of the relationship. If the sign is plus, high scores on one variable go with high scores on the other variable. The same is true for low scores on both variables going together. If the sign is minus, the relationship is reverse. That is, low scores on one variable go with high scores on the other variable, and vice versa.

The *correlation coefficient* is a measure of the relationship between two variables. It can take on values from –1.00 to +1.00, inclusive. Zero indicates no relationship.

A plot of the scores of the two variables in a two-dimensional space or plane illustrates the concept of correlation. Each individual has two scores, one for each variable. For the scores to be plotted, the scale of one variable is assigned to the horizontal axis and the scale of the other variable to the vertical axis. The variables may be called X and Y, and each individual's pair of scores may be plotted as a point in the plane. There will be as many points as there are individuals measured on both variables. Such a plot is called a *scattergram*.

Figure 13.5 illustrates a positive relationship between variables and, hence, a positive correlation coefficient. The high values of variable X are associated with high values of

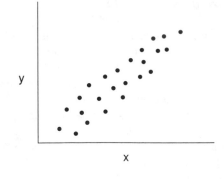
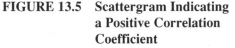

**FIGURE 13.5 Scattergram Indicating
a Positive Correlation
Coefficient**

variable Y. The opposite situation is true for a negative correlation; that is, high values of variable X go with low values of variable Y, and vice versa, as shown in Figure 13.6. To have a perfect correlation (+1.00 or –1.00), the points of the scattergram must fall on a straight line, although such a relationship is extremely rare in education.

For example, intelligence and achievement in science are two variables that seem to be positively correlated; that is, students who score high on IQ tests tend to be the highest scorers on science tests. An example of a negative correlation coefficient might be the relationship between intelligence scores and time to perform a learning task. That is, the more intelligent individuals should tend to perform the task in less time. Two variables that probably have zero correlation are foot size of fourteen-year-old girls and performance on a mathematics test.

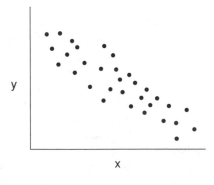
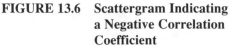

**FIGURE 13.6 Scattergram Indicating
a Negative Correlation
Coefficient**

The scatter or dispersion of the points in the scattergram gives an indication of the extent of relationship. As the positions of points tend to deviate from a straight line, the correlation tends to decrease. If a relationship exists but is not +1.00 or −1.00, the points generally fall in an elliptical ring. As the ring becomes narrower—that is, approaches a straight line—the relationship becomes stronger, and the absolute value of the correlation coefficient increases. The direction of the ring indicates whether the relationship is positive or negative, lower left to upper right being positive and upper left to lower right being negative. When the points of the scattergram fall within a circle, there is a correlation of zero. Figure 13.7 presents some examples of scattergrams, with the corresponding magnitude of the correlation coefficient given by *r*.

The correlation coefficient does not necessarily indicate a cause-and-effect relationship between the two variables. That is, it does not necessarily follow that one variable is causing the scores on the other variable. For example, there usually exists a positive correlation between the salaries paid to teachers and the percentage of graduating seniors going on to college in a particular school or system; that is, schools with higher teachers' salaries tend to have greater percentages of graduating seniors going on to college. However, it would be difficult to argue that paying higher teachers' salaries is causing

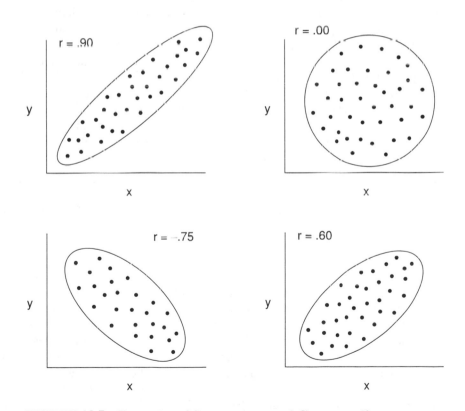

FIGURE 13.7 **Examples of Scattergrams and Corresponding Correlation Coefficients**

greater percentages of seniors to go on to college or, conversely, that sending seniors to college increases teachers' salaries. A third factor or a combination of external but common factors may be influencing the scores on both variables. Multiple causation is not uncommon when dealing with educational variables.

Uses of Correlation

The correlation coefficient is used extensively as a descriptive statistic to describe the relationship between two variables. It is also used for *prediction*—the estimation of one variable from a knowledge of another variable. The variable from which one predicts is called the *predictor variable,* and the variable being predicted is called the *criterion variable*.

For a prediction study, an equation of the form $Y = bX + a$ can be developed, in which Y is the criterion variable and X is the predictor variable. This is the equation of a straight line that is fit to the scattergram of points representing the scores of the two variables. (It is also called the equation of the regression line of Y on X.) The values of b and a are constants for a given set of data.

The correlation between X and Y has a definite effect on the prediction— specifically, the errors of prediction. The greater the absolute value of the correlation coefficient, the more accurate the prediction. What is meant by accuracy of prediction? Consider the criterion variable, Y. For each Y score, there is a paired X score that can be used in the prediction equation to generate a predicted score, say $\hat{Y}$. Then the difference would be symbolized by $(Y - \hat{Y})$, and this difference is an error in prediction. If all the errors of prediction are computed, these would comprise a distribution of error scores. This distribution has a standard deviation, called the *standard error of estimate*. The smaller this standard deviation, the more accurate the prediction. Correspondingly, the greater the correlation between the criterion and predictor variables, the smaller the standard deviation of the distribution of error scores.

Prediction is the estimation of one variable from a knowledge of another. Accuracy of prediction is increased as the correlation between the predictor and criterion variables increases.

Prediction in education is used in a multitude of ways—for example, predicting achievement (criterion) from scores on an intelligence test (predictor). Guidance counselors often use prediction equations composed of more than one predictor variable in attempting to predict success in college or success on a job. Scores on tests such as the Scholastic Aptitude Test (SAT) and the American College Testing (ACT) program are considered predictors of success in college. Often, predictor variables are used in combination rather than singly; for example, SAT score and high school grade-point average are used to predict success in college. The correlation coefficient also can be used in inferential statistics, which are discussed in the next chapter.

Different Correlation Coefficients

Although the concept of correlation is consistent, different correlation coefficients are used under varying conditions. The most commonly used correlation coefficient is the *Pearson product-moment,* which requires at least interval scale measurement, because the means of the distributions must be computed. The most important consideration affecting the choice of a coefficient is the level of measurement of the variables. Table 13.2 lists five of the more commonly used correlation coefficients and the minimum measurement scales required of the variables being correlated.

EXAMPLE 13.1 USE OF DESCRIPTIVE STATISTICS—
MEANS AND STANDARD DEVIATIONS

Three sixth-grade teachers in a school are conducting a study involving two types of instruction: individualized and traditional. Both boys and girls are involved in the study; thus, type of instruction and sex of the student are independent variables. The dependent variable is score on a reading achievement test.

The purpose of the study is to describe the distributions of reading achievement scores. It would be important to know the means of those distributions to determine the relative positions. However, knowledge about the variability or dispersion of the distributions is also important. It may be that individualized instruction spreads out the students more than traditional instruction. This would be evidenced by a greater standard deviation for the distribution of reading test scores of those taught by individualized instruction. The research questions can be stated as follows:

1. *What are the means and standard deviations of the distributions of reading test scores for type of instruction: individualized and traditional?*
2. *What are the means and standard deviations of the distributions of reading test scores for sex: boys and girls?*
3. *What are the means and standard deviations of the distributions of reading test scores for the four types of instruction and sex combinations?*

Table 13.2   Correlation Coefficients and Minimum Required Measurement of the Variables

Correlation Coefficient	Measurement of Variables (minimum required)
1. Pearson product-moment	1. Both variables on interval scales.
2. Spearman rank order	2. Both variables on ordinal scales.
3. Point biserial	3. One variable on interval scale; the other a genuine dichotomy on a nominal or ordinal scale.
4. Biserial	4. One variable on interval scale; the other an artificial dichotomy on an ordinal scale. The dichotomy is artificial because there is an underlying continuous distribution.
5. Coefficient of contingency	5. Both variables on nominal scales.

There is a total of 86 sixth-grade students enrolled in the school, 47 girls and 39 boys. The teachers can accommodate 40 students in the individualized instruction, so 20 boys and 20 girls are randomly assigned to this type of instruction. (This means that the remaining 46 students are also randomly assigned to traditional instruction.) The instruction proceeds and after one semester all students are measured on reading achievement. Since type of instruction is an experimental variable, the research design can be described as a posttest-only control group design.

Using the notation developed in the chapter on experimental designs, the experiment can be diagrammed as follows:

$$R\ G_1\ (boys)\ldots\ldots X \ldots\ldots O_1$$
$$R\ G_2\ (girls)\ldots\ldots X \ldots\ldots O_2$$
$$R\ G_3\ (boys)\ldots\ldots\ldots\ldots O_3$$
$$R\ G_4\ (girls)\ldots\ldots\ldots\ldots O_4$$

In this design, X represents individualized instruction. Although boys and girls within the type of instruction were not separated, they are in the design to show that sex of the student is an independent variable. The Os represent the measurement on the reading achievement test.

The following results appeared.

Distribution	Mean	Std. Dev.
Individualized inst.—both boys and girls	82.1	12.6
Traditional inst.—both boys and girls	76.0	17.2
Individualized inst.—boys	80.6	14.1
Individualized inst.—girls	83.6	11.3
Traditional inst.—boys	71.8	8.0
Traditional inst.—girls	80.2	6.8
All boys	76.2	16.3
All girls	81.9	12.7

Various combinations generated eight distributions that contained varying numbers of scores. For example, the first distribution, individualized instruction for both boys and girls, contained 40 scores, but the second distribution, for traditional instruction, contained 46 scores.

Although distributions with 40 scores and 46 scores would not be distributed as exact normal distributions, the teachers probably would not be much concerned about the distribution shapes, because there would be adequate evidence from previous use of the reading test that sixth-grade scores tend to be normally distributed. Thus, attention would focus on the location and variability of the distributions of scores.

The scores of those students receiving individualized instruction had a higher mean than the scores of those receiving traditional instruction. Overall, girls had a mean score higher than boys, and this pattern was consistent for both individualized and traditional instruction. However, the gap between boys and girls was much greater for traditional instruction than for individualized instruction, the difference between the means being 8.4 and 3.0 points, respectively.

The scores of the boys were more variable than those of the girls overall, and again this pattern was consistent for the two types of instruction. Considering the distributions of boys and girls singly within the types of instruction, the scores for individualized instruction were more variable. However, when the scores of boys and girls were combined, traditional instruction had the greater standard deviation. This was most likely caused by the fact that within traditional instruction, the girls' performance was considerably higher than that of the boys.

EXAMPLE 13.2 USE OF DESCRIPTIVE STATISTICS— MEANS AND STANDARD DEVIATIONS

The research office of a school system conducts a survey of the 366 teachers in the system, comprised of: 172 elementary school teachers, 102 junior high school teachers, and 92 senior high teachers. All teachers respond to an "attitude toward the central administration" scale. This scale contains 18 items, each scored from 1 to 5, so total scores on the scale can take on possible values from 18 to 90 inclusive. The greater the score, the more positive the attitude toward the central administration.

Total scores are computed for all teachers and then separated by level taught, elementary, junior high, and senior high school, giving three distributions of scores. The three distributions are plotted and they all are approximately normally distributed; the means ($\overline{X}$), variances (s^2), and standard deviations (s) for the three distributions are as follows:

Elementary	*Junior High*	*Senior High*
$\overline{X}_E = 73.2$	$\overline{X}_{JH} = 71.6$	$\overline{X}_{SH} = 50.3$
$s^2_E = 44.9$	$s^2_{JH} = 151.3$	$s^2_{SH} = 240.3$
$s_E = 6.7$	$s_{JH} = 12.3$	$s_{SH} = 15.5$

Considering the means of the total scores, it is apparent that the elementary and junior high school teachers have substantially more positive attitudes toward the central administration than the senior high school teachers. The means of 73.2 and 71.6 average out to be about 4 on the 5-point scales of the individual items. (An average of 4 on individual items would give a total score of 18 times 4 or 72.) So, in absolute terms, the elementary and junior high school teachers have quite positive attitudes.

However, the junior high school teachers' scores are more variable than those of the elementary school teachers. The standard deviation of 12.3 is almost twice that of 6.7. This result indicates that there are some junior high school teachers with quite low scores on the attitude scale, and some with quite positive scores. But as a group, the junior high teachers are not as uniformly positive as the elementary school teachers. The small standard deviation of the elementary school teachers' scores indicates that their scores are bunched around the mean.

The senior high school teachers not only have the lowest mean scores, but their scores also are the most variable. The scores are spread, indicating that the senior high school teachers within their group differ substantially on their attitude toward the central administration. Apparently, some think highly of the central administration, others have a very low opinion. If the central administration is interested in improving the attitude, the information above should be useful. Clearly, it is the high school teachers, especially those in senior high, that require efforts to improve attitudes. But the variability within these groups implies the less positive attitudes are not uniform throughout the groups of high school teachers and attention must be given to possible factors causing the variability. (Note: the variances were given above only for illustration.) Because the standard deviation was used as the measure of dispersion, it was not necessary to discuss the variances in this example.

Using the Computer for Data Analysis

Before continuing with additional examples, a discussion of computer use is presented, so that examples can be presented using computer solutions. Most researchers have access to a computer for data analysis, and although limited analyses can be done on a hand calculator, computers greatly facilitate data analysis. For some sophisticated analyses, such as factor analysis and multivariate analysis of variance (not discussed in this chapter), a computer is a practical necessity because the complex operations cannot be done by hand calculator, simply because it is too time-consuming.

Computers are extremely useful for data analysis because of their functionality, speed, accuracy, and accessibility. Functionality deals with the variety and sophistication of what the computer can do through its hardware (that is, the actual machines) and the software (the programs that give the computer instructions). Speed concerns the time, often in seconds, it takes the computer to perform the analysis. If the data are prepared without error and the appropriate analyses are used, the solution will be errorless. So, we have complete accuracy. Finally, computers generally are accessible; a researcher can use a mainframe computer at an institution such as a university or use a microcomputer, also called a personal computer (PC).

> Computers are extremely useful for data analysis because they are functional, fast, accurate, and accessible.

Fortunately, for behavioral sciences research, computer programs are available for commonly used analyses, and even for some used less frequently. Undoubtedly, the three most commonly used statistical packages for behavioral sciences research are:

Statistical Package for the Social Sciences (SPSS-X), distributed by SPSS, Inc., 444 North Michigan Avenue, Chicago, IL 60611

Statistical Analysis System (SAS), distributed by SAS Institute Inc., Box 8000, Cary, NC 27512-8000

BMDP Statistical Software, 1440 Sepulveda Boulevard, Suite 316, Los Angeles, CA 90025

There are manuals and users' guides available for these packages. Because of the changes and advancements made in computers and software, the publications with the packages are being updated almost continuously. Users such as university computer centers usually have the latest versions; at least, they have the versions that fit the programs used by their computer systems.

Several mainframe software packages have been prepared for microcomputers. Examples of microcomputers are the IBM PC and the Apple Macintosh. The corresponding microcomputer software packages of the three statistical programs listed previously are: SPSS/PC +, PC SAS, and BMDPC. They are distributed by the organizations listed for the packages. These statistical programs run on IBM and IBM-compatible microcomputers.

However, statistical programs are available for microcomputers. One of the more popular packages is SYSTAT (available from Systat, Inc., 2909 Central Street, Evanston, IL 60201). SYSTAT can perform almost every statistical procedure needed by educational researchers. For equipment, the program requires 256K of random access memory (RAM) and two floppy disk drives. A program such as SPSS/PC + has an option that includes an advanced statistics package. However, the program is more costly than SYSTAT and it requires 384K of RAM.

Another PC statistical package is StatView 512+, designed specifically for the Macintosh microcomputer. The program includes all the usual descriptive and inferential statistical analyses. It is available from Brain Power, Inc., 24009 Ventura Boulevard, Calabassas, CA 91302.

If a researcher uses the mainframe computer at a university or institution, the program used can be selected from those available and such selection is straightforward. However, with all the PC programs available, how is one to make a selection? First of all, the program must be capable of doing the necessary analyses and, of course, it must be compatible with the hardware, the specific PC being used. It is an asset if the microcomputer has a mathematics co-processor; otherwise the statistics package may require a relatively long time to process the analysis. These are technical matters. There are vendor services to be considered, such as the availability of training or consultation and maintenance assistance. Considering all of these factors, a researcher can decide which program(s) meets the needs of the situation.

Various publications contain information about PCs and their software. Some journals review statistics packages either on a regular or ad hoc basis. *Evaluation Practice,* a journal published by Sage Publications and sponsored by the American Evaluation Association, contains articles about the use of microcomputers in evaluation. The monthly journal, *Personal Computing,* is a large publication with a variety of information. It also contains advertising, so features and prices of PCs and software packages are available. *InfoWorld* is a weekly publication for personal computing professionals. Much information is available and it is being updated continually.

General Procedure for Computer Use

Whether a mainframe computer or a microcomputer is used, it must be told what to do. This is done through a computer program (software) which is a series of explicit instructions for the various operations required by an analysis. Computer communication is done through a terminal, which consists of a screen and keyboard similar to that of a typewriter. (The terminal screen was described in Chapter 12.) Commands are typed onto the screen in rows. When using a microcomputer, the statistical program is usually on a floppy disk or diskette which can be copied from the disk to the microcomputer disk drive. When this transformation takes place, the program appears on the screen and additional information may be typed in directly.

The tasks in using a computer for data analysis are illustrated in Figure 13.8. To the right are indicated the individuals who do the tasks, with possible sources for assistance. For the most part, the tasks are sequential from the top to the bottom of the figure. Since so many statistical programs are available, it would be very rare not to have one available; however, if special programming is required, assistance usually can be obtained at a computer center. The remaining tasks in completing an analysis are straightforward. Once the appropriate program is selected, the instructions to use the program, along with the data file, are put into the computer. The analysis is then run and the output produced. The

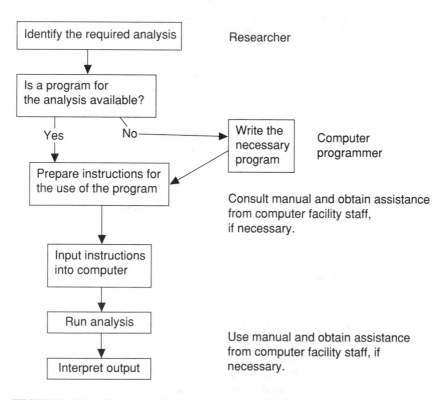

FIGURE 13.8   Tasks in Using a Computer for Data Analysis

output is the product of the analysis and contains the results. Output will be displayed on the screen, and if a printer is available, output can be obtained on large sheets of paper (printouts). The latter also is called hard copy and is nearly always available when mainframe computers are used.

> Data analysis by computer involves a series of sequential steps, using a program available in a statistical package.

EXAMPLE 13.3 USE OF DESCRIPTIVE STATISTICS— ANALYSIS OF TEACHER COMPETENCY DATA

Consider again the data file introduced in Chapter 12—the file consisting of scores on six competency measures for 54 teachers. This is the data file named **FILE: TCHRCOMP DATA.** The research question is:

> *What are the correlation coefficients among the six competency scores of these teachers?*

This question implies descriptive statistics; there is no indication that these teachers were a random sample of some larger population and that inferences are to be made to a population. We will compute the correlation coefficients and also obtain the means and standard deviations of the six scores.

The computer program used for the analysis is for the Pearson product-moment correlation coefficient and is from the SPSS-X package. It is described in the *SPSS-X User's Guide,* (3rd ed., 1988, pages 418–428). To communicate with the computer—that is, inform it of what to do—it is necessary to write a program. For this example, the task consists of typing onto the computer terminal screen the instructions that specify the program from the statistical package the computer is to use and the data file. These instructions are given in Figure 13.9. The information contained on each line is also given in the figure.

The analysis is now ready to run. If it were being done through a computer terminal, the command **SPSSX TCHRCOMP** would be typed onto the screen, the ENTER key would be hit, and the analysis would be completed.[2]

When the analysis is completed, the computer will create a file of the results. That file would have the name **TCHRCOMP LISTING.** It would be called up onto the screen and reviewed. Most likely, a printout of it on paper (hard copy) would be desired; it can be obtained by giving the computer the following commands:

ROUTE PRINTER XPRT7
PRINT TCHRCOMP LISTING

The **XPRT7** designates the specific printer to be used—usually the one closest to the computer terminal. Thus, the **XPRT7** here is an example, not a general command.

```
FILE: TCHRCOMP SPSSX   A UNIVERSITY OF TOLEDO TIME-SHARING SYSTEM

TITLE   TCHRCOMP ANALYSIS
FILE HANDLE TCHRCOMP NAME='TCHRCOMP DATA A'
DATA LIST   FILE=TCHRCOMP RECORDS=1
            /1 ID 1-2 C1 4-5 C2 7-8 C3 10-11 C4 13-14 C5 16-17 C6 19-20
PEARSON CORR C1 TO C6
STATISTICS 1
FINISH
```

Information:

Line 1: File name: programs are also files and since this is an analysis, it must contain SPSSX in the name, which indicates an analysis type file. TCHRCOMP is the descriptive term used earlier.

Line 2: Name given to the analysis.

Line 3: File handle identifies the data file; that name must be the data file name exactly, with DATA as indicating the type of file; A is a necessary notation for the computer.

Lines 4 and 5: Data list indicates how the data are listed: Line 4 shows the file name RECORDS = 1; indicates that the data for any individual are contained on one line. Line 5 indicates how the data are coded; the ID number is in columns 1 and 2, score for C1 in columns 4 and 5, etc.

Line 6: Tells the computer to use the program for the Pearson product-moment correlation coefficient, and to correlate the scores for the variables C1 to C6.

Line 7: Statistics 1 tells the computer also to compute the means and standard deviations for the variables.

Line 8: Indicates the program is finished.

FIGURE 13.9   The Analysis Program File for the Teacher Competency Example (SPSS-X)

The computer output containing the results for this analysis is given in Figure 13.10. Actually, the computer output consists of several large sheets. The earlier part of the output contains routine information, including the program file. After the results, there is a page with such information as the date and time of the analysis and the amount of computer time required for the analysis.

To consider the results more conveniently, recall the six competencies:

C-1 Uses a variety of instructional strategies.

C-2 Uses convergent and divergent inquiry strategies.

C-3 Develops and demonstrates problem-solving skills.

C-4 Establishes transitions and sequences in instruction that are varied.

```
            TCHRCOMP ANALYSIS
            THE UNIVERSITY OF TOLEDO          NAS 6650      VM/SP2



VARIABLE     CASES        MEAN         STD DEV

C1            54        50.0000         9.9868
C2            54        49.9630         9.9829
C3            54        49.9444         9.9516
C4            54        49.8704        10.0227
C5            54        50.0185        10.0179
C6            54        50.0926        10.0269
```

--- P E A R S O N   C O R R E L A T I O N   C O E F F I C I E N T S - -

	C1	C2	C3	C4	C5	C6
C1	1.000	.3058	.2954	.2422	.4720	.1877
	(54)	(54)	(54)	(54)	(54)	(54)
	P= .	P= .012	P= .015	P= .039	P= .000	P= .087
C2	.3058	1.0000	.5865	.3961	.2466	.2326
	(54)	(54)	(54)	(54)	(54)	(54)
	P= .012	P= .	P= .000	P= .002	P= .036	P= .045
C3	.2954	.5865	1.0000	.3340	.4003	.2033
	(54)	(54)	(54)	(54)	(54)	(54)
	P= .015	P= .000	P= .	P= .007	P= .001	P= .070
C4	.2422	.3961	.3340	1.0000	.2336	-.1499
	(54)	(54)	(54)	(54)	(54)	(54)
	P= .039	P= .002	P= .007	P= .	P= .045	P= .140
C5	.4720	.2466	.4003	.2336	1.0000	.3687
	(54)	(54)	(54)	(54)	(54)	(54)
	P= .000	P= .036	P= .001	P= .045	P= .	P= .003
C6	.000	.3058	.2954	.2422	.4720	.1877
	(54)	(54)	(54)	(54)	(54)	(54)
	P= .087	P= .045	P= .070	P= .140	P= .003	P= .

```
(COEFFICIENT / (CASES) / SIGNIFICANCE)     " . " IS PRINTED IF A
COEFFICIENT CANNOT BE COMPUTED
```

FIGURE 13.10   Computer Output of Results for the Teacher Competency Example (SPSS-X)

C-5 Modifies instructional activities to accommodate identified learner needs.

C-6 Demonstrates ability to work with individuals, small groups, and large groups.

The results in Figure 13.10 are quite straightforward. For this particular scoring procedure of the competency data, the scores of a normative group of teachers have been transformed to a distribution with a mean of 50.0 and a standard deviation of 10.0. The means and standard deviations of the six competency scores for this group of 54 teachers are close to these transformed values.

The primary focus of interest is on the results of the correlation analysis. The correlation matrix contains three bits of information:

1. The correlation coefficient,
2. The number of scores correlated, and
3. The P-value, which is a level of significance, testing the null hypothesis, that in the population the correlation coefficient is zero.

The final information is of no concern to us in this analysis, since we are interested only in descriptive statistics and not in inferring to a population. The number of scores (cases) correlated here is 54 for all coefficients, since there were no missing data. However, this information can be useful in analyses for which data are missing.

The correlation matrix is a 6×6 square, showing all correlation coefficients between variables in combinations of two. The matrix is symmetrical about the diagonal, and diagonal entries are all 1.00 (the correlation of a variable with itself), so basically there are 15 coefficients of interest, those located above (or below) the diagonal.

The competencies reflect instructional strategies and techniques actually demonstrated in the classroom; they do not deal with activities such as lesson planning or writing test items. Results can be summarized as follows:

1. All coefficients except one are positive, and the negative coefficient is modest (−.15) and the smallest in absolute value of all coefficients.
2. Overall, the coefficients are not large; the largest .586, between C-2 and C-3, is the only coefficient above .500. The next largest coefficient, .472, is between C-1 and C-5.
3. Overall, C-6 tends to have the lowest coefficients with the other competencies, and it is included in the only negative coefficient (with C-4).

The conclusions that can be drawn from these results are as follows:

1. The performance of these 54 teachers is very close to that of the normative group, both in mean scores and in variability of scores.
2. Scores on C-6 had the lowest overall coefficients with other scores, except for C-5. Ability to work with groups of differing sizes has little to do with the skills in the other competencies, except for modifying instructional activities to accommodate learner needs.
3. When different sized groups are used, there is a tendency to have fewer transitions and sequences in instruction (indicated by the −.15 coefficient).

4. Using convergent and divergent inquiry strategies goes with problem-solving skills.

5. Using a variety of instructional strategies goes with modifying instructional activities.

6. Working with different sized groups is close to being independent of using a variety of instructional strategies (evidenced by the .188 coefficient).

7. Generally, teachers performing well on one competency have a tendency to do so on others; at least, there is little evidence of inverse relationships.

These conclusions apply to the performance of these 54 teachers; no use is made of inferential statistics. Any generalizability of these conclusions would have to be argued on a logical basis.

Summary

This chapter has provided an overview of descriptive statistics, one of the broad categories of statistics used in analyzing quantitative data. Descriptive statistics are used to describe distributions and relationships between variables. Characteristics of one or more distributions of scores are computed.

In general, descriptive statistics are measures of central tendency, measures of dispersion, and measures of relationship. To describe adequately a distribution we need to know its shape, its location on the scale of measurement, and its variability. We can plot the scores and develop a histogram to determine shape, but more commonly we know from the research literature or other sources, the shape of distributions. For example, many educational variables are either known or assumed to have normal distributions. Measures of location are points on the scale of measurement, and the most commonly used are the mean and median, measures of central tendency. Finally, the most commonly used measures of variability, also called measures of dispersion, are the variance and the standard deviation. Measures of variability are intervals (or their squares) on the scale of measurement.

The relationship between two variables is described by the correlation coefficient. Correlation coefficients can take on values from −1.00 to +1.00 inclusive; the greater the absolute value of the coefficient, the stronger the relationship. A correlation coefficient of zero indicates no relationship or independence of the variables.

If descriptive statistics are being computed, "What is being described?" Central tendency, dispersion, relationship—any or all three of these descriptors. The specific descriptive statistics that can be computed depend on the level of measurement of the variables. Table 13.3 contains a summary of descriptive statistics for levels of measurement. Essentially, the same statistics can be computed for interval scale and ratio scale measurement. As we go up in the hierarchy of measurement scales, the statistics become more sophisticated; that is, they contain more information. For example, with nominal scale measurement, the lowest level, we can determine the category of greatest frequency, but because nominal scales only categorize without order, the concept of dispersion does not apply.

Descriptive statistics are useful in analyzing data, but they are only part of the statistics story. Inferential statistics comprise another broad category of statistics and these

TABLE 13.3   Descriptive Statistics by Level of Measurement

Level of Measurement	Central Tendency	What Is Being Described? Dispersion/ Variability	Relationship
Nominal	Mode	(—)	Contingency coefficient
Ordinal	Median Mode	Range	Rank order correlation coefficient
Interval/Ratio	Mean Median Mode	Standard Deviation Variance Range	Pearson product-moment correlation coefficient

are discussed in the next chapter. Often descriptive and inferential statistics are used in combination when analyzing research data. It is not the intent of this text to provide computational procedures or have the reader perform statistical analysis. Rather the intent is to provide a rationale for statistical analysis of data, and to describe the reasoning of some of the more commonly used statistical procedures. Numerous applied statistics texts are available that describe computational procedures for both descriptive and inferential statistics commonly used in educational research. A sampling of such texts is provided at the close of Chapter 14.

KEY CONCEPTS

Statistics	Variability
Descriptive statistics	Standard deviation
Distribution	Variance
Frequency distribution	Shape of a distribution
Histogram	Correlation
Central tendency	Prediction
Mean	Criterion variable
Median	Standard error of estimate

EXERCISES

13.1 Discuss the difference between measures of central tendency and measures of variability. Why are both types of measures necessary in describing a distribution? Present some examples of educational variables that are alike in measures of central tendency but different in variability, and some that are alike in dispersion but different in location.

13.2 Suppose a small company has around fifty employees working in the plant and office that earn around $30,000 per year. However, there are five executives, the president and four vice presidents, that earn over

$175,000 each per year. Why would the median be a more informative measure of central tendency than the mean, for this salary distribution?

13.3 Identify the three types of information necessary to describe a distribution.

13.4 The fourth-grade teachers in an elementary school want to compare the relative performances of individual students on tests of reading, mathematics, and science. Why is it necessary for them to use some type of standard score? Would the z-score be a desirable score? Why or why not? If the z-score is not used, what would be a desirable and useful transformed score?

13.5 The correlation coefficient is an index of the relationship between two variables. A positive correlation coefficient indicates a direct relationship, a negative correlation coefficient, an inverse relationship, and a correlation coefficient of zero, no relationship. For the following pairs of variables, indicate whether the correlation between the two variables would be expected to be positive, negative, or zero.

    a. Performance on an intelligence test and time required to solve concept attainment problems.
    b. Scores on an anxiety measure and those on a statistics test.
    c. Scores on the reading and mathematics subtests of a standardized test battery.
    d. Scores on an intelligence test and distance a baseball can be thrown.
    e. Shoe size and performance on a high school geometry test.

13.6 In a small high school, an attitude toward mathematics and mathematics-related professions scale is administered to the students. The mean score on the scale is 52.6 for boys and 50.9 for girls. The standard deviation of the distribution of scores for boys is 5.7, and that for girls 14.6. The maximum possible score on the scale is 130. The scores in each distribution are normally distributed. Interpret these descriptive statistics.

13.7 Locate an article in the research literature that involves descriptive statistics in the analysis of data. Are the statistics described clearly? Are the interpretations of the statistics reasonable, and are the interpretations complete? Are the statistics used when making recommendations?

NOTES

1. The symbol Σ is the summation operator and indicates to sum what follows, in this case the deviations. The i on the X_i indicates the individual scores used, in this case the first through the nth. When no numbers are indicated over the Σ, it indicates that i takes on values 1 through n.

2. If there were an error in the program instructions, the analysis would not run, but an error message would appear on the terminal screen, indicating that there was an error and where it was located in the instructions (program file).

REFERENCE

SPSS, Inc. (1988). *SPSS-X users' guide* (3rd ed.). (pp. 418–428). Chicago: SPSS, Inc.

$$C\ h\ a\ p\ t\ e\ r\quad 14$$

Data Analysis: Inferential Statistics

In many research situations, a specific group is studied with the intention of generalizing to some larger group. For example, surveys are conducted of large populations, not by surveying everyone in the population, but by surveying a subgroup of that population, called a sample, and then using the sample data to generalize to the population. As another example, a research director for a large city school system might set up five third grades and expose them to some experimental treatment with the purpose of generalizing to all third-grade students in the system. In a more ambitious vein, the goal might be to generalize to third-grade students in all school systems. In any event, an attempt is made to infer something about a relatively large group by using a subset of that group.

Different types of samples were discussed in Chapter 11, including random samples. Inferential statistics are based on random sampling; essentially the concept being that the data of the sample, which are the only data available, reflect the population data within random sampling fluctuation. Sample data are collected, and from these, generalizations are made to the population.

Thus, the researcher has a distribution consisting of sample scores. The descriptive measures, such as the mean and standard deviation computed from the sample data, are called statistics. Correspondingly, there are descriptive measures of the population (these measures are called *parameters*). Of course, parameters are not computed, because data are not collected from the entire population. Rather, inferences are made and conclusions are drawn about parameters from the statistics of the sample—hence, the name inferential statistics.

In *inferential statistics,* statistics are measures of the sample and parameters are measures of the population. Inferences are made about the parameters from the statistics.

The basic idea in making inferences from statistics to parameters is to obtain the sample distribution and then to use accepted statistical techniques to make the inferences to the the population. Statistics are computed from the sample data; on the basis of these statistics, generalizations to the parameters (population measures) are made. The theory and methodology underlying this procedure are known as inferential statistics. To construct the reasoning for inferential statistics, some basic concepts of probability and distributions (for the most part theoretical) related to probability must be employed. In this way, the researcher arrives at an established and conceptually sound procedure for making inferences from research data now summarized by statistics—inferences made from the sample to some larger population.

Testing Hypotheses and Estimating Parameters

In analyzing data by means of inferential statistics, we can use one or both of two general procedures: *testing hypotheses* or *estimating parameters*. Hypothesis testing is the more common procedure reported in the research literature. A hypothesis in the context of inferential statistics is a statement (conjecture) about one or more parameters. The researcher goes through a procedure of testing the hypothesis to determine whether or not it is consistent with the sample data. If it is not consistent, the hypothesis is rejected (note that the sample data are not discarded). If the hypothesis is consistent with the sample data, the hypothesis is retained as a tenable value for the parameter.

> In inferential statistics, a hypothesis is a statement about one or more parameters.

A second general procedure of inferential statistics is estimating a parameter. Given a set of sample data, the question can be asked, "What are tenable estimates of the parameter?" There are actually two types of estimates, a *point estimate* and an *interval estimate,* also called a *confidence interval.* A point estimate is simply a single-value estimate of the parameter. It is the value of the corresponding statistic from the sample. An interval estimate is an interval on the scale of measurement that contains tenable estimates of the parameter. Interval estimation is used much more than point estimation.

> Estimating a parameter in inferential statistics can be done by point estimation or interval estimation. Point estimation consists of estimating the parameter by a single value. Interval estimation consists of defining an interval (confidence interval) on the scale of measurement that contains tenable values of the parameter. Either way, the estimate is made from sample data.

The procedures of hypothesis testing and related concepts are discussed in the following section and illustrated with examples.

Concept of Sampling Distribution

Developing the chain of reasoning in inferential statistics requires some concepts of random sampling fluctuation and probability. For example, a researcher might be asked to determine the mean reading achievement score of a large population of eighth-graders. Rather than measuring the entire population, a random sample of 225 students is selected and administered an appropriate reading achievement test. The mean score for the sample is 55.3, and the sample distribution has a standard deviation of 21. This sample mean is a statistic computed from the distribution of 225 reading test scores.

If the curriculum director in charge of reading for this population of eighth-graders hypothesizes, "The population mean is 90," would the researcher go along with this hypothesis? Most likely not. If the curriculum director hypothesizes that the population mean is 56, would the researcher be supportive of this hypothesis? Very likely so.

Why would the researcher go along with the second hypothesis but not the hypothesis that the population mean is 90? The sample mean of 55.3 reflects the population mean, whatever it is. However, the researcher would not expect it to equal the population mean exactly, because the sample mean also reflects random sampling fluctuation. If a population mean of 56 is hypothesized, getting a sample mean of 55.3 is well within the bounds of sampling fluctuation. However, getting a sample mean of 55.3 if the population mean is 90 is very unlikely, because sampling fluctuation is not likely to account for such a difference. The sample mean of 55.3 is a fact that cannot be thrown away, so the researcher rejects the hypothesis that the population mean is 90. Another way of considering this is, "The probability that a sample mean of 55.3 would appear due to random sampling fluctuation, if the population mean is 90, is too small."

However, more than intuition is needed for deciding whether or not probability is too small. The researcher must connect probability with the statistic, using the concept of the sampling distribution of the statistic.

What is the *sampling distribution?* The sample mean of 55.3 will again be considered. If the means of all possible samples of size 225 of the eighth-grade population are computed, they would make a distribution of means. Conceptually, one mean from this distribution was selected when the sample mean of 55.3 was determined. This distribution of means is the sampling distribution of the sample mean. *Sampling distributions* are distributions of statistics, and for the most part they are theoretical—defined for the researcher by mathematical statisticians. Note that the sampling distribution of the mean is *not* the sample distribution.

Conceptually, a *sampling distribution* consists of the values of a statistic computed from all possible samples of a given size.

Continuing the example, the researcher needs to know about the sampling distribution of the mean, which is to know its shape, location (central tendency), and variability (dispersion). The *central limit theorem* describes the sampling distribution of the mean as follows:

Given any population with mean μ *and finite variance* σ^2, *as the sample size increases without limit, the distribution of the sample mean approaches a normal distribution with mean* μ *and variance* σ^2/n *where n is sample size.*

This theorem specifies that the sampling distribution of the mean has a mean equal to the population mean, a variance equal to the population variance divided by the sample size (thus, its standard deviation is $\sigma/\sqrt{n}$), and is normally distributed. Since σ is a parameter, it is usually not known, but it can be estimated by the sample standard deviation.

Probability traditionally has been expressed as a proportion between 0 and + 1.00; if something has no chance of happening, the probability is 0. In the flip of an unbiased coin, the probability of obtaining a head is .50, which is also the probability of obtaining a tail. The probability of obtaining either a head or a tail is .50 + .50 = 1.00, since one or the other will happen in a flip.

Knowing the sampling distribution, the researcher can bring in the concept of probability. If the area of the sampling distribution is set equal to 1.00, then any area in the distribution between two points on the scale of measurement would correspond to the probability of selecting a value from the distribution between those two points. For the purpose of testing hypotheses about the mean, the researcher is concerned about area as it is located away from the mean of the sampling distribution, where probability will be small.

A new term associated with testing hypotheses, *significance level* or *level of significance,* is now required. Significance level (also designated alpha level or α-level) is a probability such that if the probability that the statistic would appear by chance (due to random sampling fluctuation) if the hypothesis is true, is less than this probability, the hypothesis will be rejected. Thus, a significance level is a criterion used in making a decision about the hypothesis. Commonly used significance levels in educational research are .05 and .01. (Occasionally, .10 will be used as a significance level, and the smaller levels of .001 and .0001 may also appear, but they are rarely used.) The significance level is established by the researcher prior to testing the hypothesis, although some researchers report the smallest level attained after testing one or more hypotheses.

The *significance level* (α-level) is a probability used in testing hypotheses. Commonly used α-levels are .05 and .01.

The sampling distribution can now be connected with the level of significance. In the example, the researcher hypothesized about a population mean. The corresponding statistic is the sample mean, and the central limit theorem describes its sampling distribution (normally distributed, located at μ, with standard deviation $\sigma/\sqrt{n}$). If the α-level is set at .05, 5 percent of the area in the sampling distribution will be designated as the rejection region for the hypothesis. Since the researcher will reject the hypothesis if the sample mean is much larger or much smaller than the hypothesized value, the rejection region must be placed in both tails of the distribution, 2.5 percent in each tail. Figure 14.1

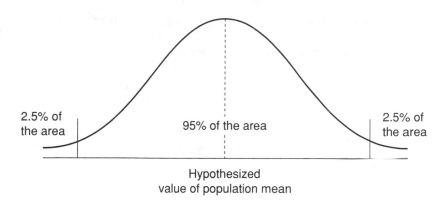

2.5% of
the area

95% of the area

2.5% of
the area

Hypothesized
value of population mean

**FIGURE 14.1   Area of the Sampling Distribution of the Mean with a
Significance Level of .05**

illustrates the sampling distribution of the mean, with 2.5 percent of the area in each tail as a rejection region. Sample means that occur within the central 95 percent of the area would not result in rejecting the hypothesis.

A question arises: How far from the mean in the sampling distribution must one go to reach the cutoff points or critical values that determine the rejection region? From the central limit theorem, it is known that the distribution is a normal distribution, but there are an infinite number of specific normal distributions, depending on the means and standard deviations. Thus, a conversion procedure is needed by which we can go to a *common* or *standard normal distribution*. The procedure consists of using standard scores as was discussed in Chapter 13. The values in a normal distribution are converted to a distribution with a mean of 0 and a standard deviation of 1.0. Such a converted distribution is called the standard normal distribution and this distribution is given in Table A of Appendix 3. (It is called the *normal curve* in the table title.) The values or scores in this distribution are given in standard deviation units from the mean, designated by x/σ in the table. The x is a score in deviation form; $x = (X - \overline{X})$, where X is the mean of the distribution. Corresponding to the x/σ value is given the area in the distribution between the mean and the score or value. Thus, if there is a x/σ value (also called a standard score or z-score as it was in Chapter 13) of .25, .0987 or 9.87 percent of the area in the distribution is contained between the mean and a score of .25. With a mean of 0, one-half of the scores in the standard normal distribution will be negative. However, because the normal distribution is symmetrical, the areas for the negative scores will be exactly the same as those for corresponding positive scores, so the table contains only the positive half of the distribution.

> The *standard normal distribution* has a mean of 0 and a standard deviation of 1.0.
> Scores in the standard normal distribution are given in standard deviation units from
> the mean.

Why would the researcher reject the hypothesis of the population mean being 90 when the sample mean was 55.3? Recall that the sample distribution had a standard deviation of 21; therefore, the standard deviation of the sampling distribution of the mean[1] is estimated as:

$$s_{\bar{x}} = \frac{s}{\sqrt{n}} = \frac{21}{\sqrt{225}} = 1.40$$

If the hypothesis of the population mean being 90 is true, the sample mean, 55.3, has a standard score of

$$\frac{55.3 - 90.0}{1.4} = -24.8$$

This means that it lies almost 25 standard deviations below the mean. A check of the area in the standard normal distribution shows that it requires 1.96 standard deviation units to leave 2.5 percent of the area in each tail. Thus, the value of –24.8 is far beyond this criterion or critical value. Therefore, the researcher rejects the hypothesis of the population mean being 90. The probability is less than .05 that a sample mean of 55.3 would appear due to random sampling fluctuation if the population mean is 90. It should be noted that the probability is on the statistic and that the conclusion rests on the hypothesis. In this case, the researcher would say that the statistical test is significant, since the statistic fell in the rejection region as determined by the significance level.

The other hypothesis—of the population mean being 56—also can be considered. If this hypothesis is true, the standard score for the sample mean of 55.3 is:

$$\frac{55.3 - 56.0}{1.4} = \frac{-.7}{1.4} = -.5$$

A check of the normal distribution table shows that a standard score of –.5 is well within the standard scores of ±1.96, which contain the central 95 percent of the area. Thus, the hypothesis of the population mean being 56 is not rejected; it is tenable. The probability that a sample mean of 55.3 would appear due to random sampling fluctuation if the population mean is 56 is greater than .05. Figure 14.2 indicates the location of the sample mean in the sampling distribution if the population mean is 56.

Building a Confidence Interval— The Example Continued

Developing the concept of sampling distribution was done in the context of a hypothesis testing example. Another procedure in inferential statistics is building a confidence interval, which is an interval estimation of a parameter.

Consider again the example of the 55.3 sample mean on the reading achievement test. Instead of testing hypotheses about the population mean, we want to obtain an interval

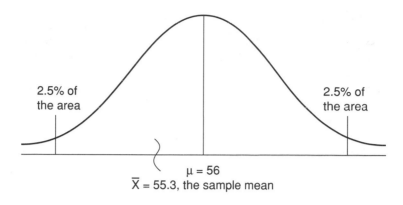

FIGURE 14.2   **Location of the Observed Sample Mean in the Sampling Distribution for the Example**

estimate of it. This requires a confidence level or a confidence coefficient, which is a defined probability that the interval will span the population mean.[2] Commonly used confidence levels in educational research are .95 and .99.

When a confidence interval for the mean is constructed, the interval is constructed symmetrically around the sample mean. If a 95 percent confidence interval (confidence level .95) for the example is constructed, the researcher wants an interval on the scale of measurement such that it includes 95 percent of the area of the sampling distribution. Because the sampling distribution is the normal (known from the discussion of hypothesis testing), it is necessary to go 1.96 standard deviation units on either side of the mean. The standard deviation of the sampling distribution of the mean was 1.4. Therefore, to construct the interval, the two points are determined by:

$$55.3 \pm 1.96\,(1.4)$$

This gives the interval 52.56 to 58.04, and we are 95 percent confident that this interval spans the population mean.

In general, when constructing confidence intervals, the researcher constructs the interval around the statistic by using the following formula:

$$\text{Statistic} \pm (\text{C.V.})\,(\text{standard deviation of the statistic})$$

The C.V. is the critical value from the sampling distribution in standard score form, which is required to include the proportion of area equal to the confidence level. Then this critical value is multiplied by the standard deviation of the sampling distribution of the statistic to convert from the standard distribution to the scale of measurement for the particular variable. This product is one-half the span of the confidence interval, since its length is contained on either side of the statistic.

Possible Errors in Hypothesis Testing

As mentioned earlier, in inferential statistics a hypothesis is a statement about one or more parameters. The term *null hypothesis* is often used in statistical analysis to describe the hypothesis of no relationship. (The hypothesis of no relationship is the hypothesis of independence of the variables.) In testing a hypothesis about a population mean, mu (μ), a researcher might have the null hypothesis, H_0: $\mu = 56$, which can be rewritten H_0: $\mu - 56 = 0$, which technically is a hypothesis of no difference. If a researcher is testing a hypothesis about two population means being equal, the hypothesis can be written in the null form as H_0: $\mu_1 = \mu_2$ or H_0: $\mu_1 - \mu_2 = 0$. The null hypothesis is used to locate the sampling distribution for the statistical test.

> The *null hypothesis,* often called a *statistical hypothesis,* is the hypothesis of no difference or no relationship.

Whenever a statistical test is used to test a hypothesis, a decision is made either to reject or not to reject the hypothesis. In either case, there is the possibility that an error has been made because the true value of the parameter(s) will not be known, since the entire population is not measured. If a researcher rejects the hypothesis, it is possible that a true hypothesis is being rejected. If a hypothesis is not rejected, it is possible that a false hypothesis is not being rejected.

The test of a specific hypothesis will yield one of four possible results, based on the actual situation in the population and the decision of the researcher. This may be diagrammed in a 2×2 table, as in Figure 14.3. The columns in this figure represent the situation in the population, which will never be known for certain. The rows indicate the researcher's decision relative to the hypothesis, and the statements in the box indicate whether the researcher's decision is correct or in error.

If a true hypothesis is not rejected or a false hypothesis is rejected, there is no error. The other two alternatives result in errors—namely, a true hypothesis is rejected or a false hypothesis is not rejected. The error of rejecting a true hypothesis is referred to as a *Type I* or alpha (α) error. This is because if a null hypothesis is rejected, the probability of

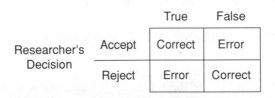

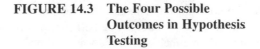

**FIGURE 14.3   The Four Possible
Outcomes in Hypothesis
Testing**

having made an error equals the significance (α) level. The error of failing to reject a false hypothesis is called a *Type II* or beta (β) error. Its probability is somewhat complicated to calculate and depends on a combination of factors. In any one statistical test, there is the possibility of making only one type of error, since the researcher either rejects or fails to reject the hypothesis. Generally, when a statistical test is computed, reducing the risk of one type of error increases the risk of the other type of error.

> In hypothesis testing there are two possible errors, rejecting a true hypothesis or failing to reject a false one. Once the decision is made on the hypothesis, there is the possibility of having made only one type of error.

Inferences from Statistics to Parameters: A Review

Considerable space has been devoted to the discussion of the basic ideas of inferential statistics and relatively elementary examples. The reason for this is that these concepts provide the foundation for testing hypotheses using statistical analyses, which are used so extensively in educational research. There are many specific inferential statistical procedures, and there are numerous statistics texts that describe these very well. Some statistical procedures are quite complex, at least computationally, but whenever inferential statistics are used, the basic reasoning is the same. It is a chain of reasoning used to make decisions when testing hypotheses and estimating parameters. Any reader who masters this reasoning is well on the way to understanding statistical analysis.

When a random sample is used to represent a population, the inference is from the statistics of the sample to the parameters of the population. The chain of reasoning, illustrated in Figure 14.4 is linked as follows: The researcher has a population and wants to know something about the descriptive measures of this population—the parameters. It is not feasible to measure the entire population, so a random sample is drawn. The descriptive measures of the sample are statistics, which are calculated. Since the sample is a random sample, the statistics reflect the parameters within the limits of random sampling fluctuation. It is at this point that the sampling distributions of statistics come in. If the sampling distribution of a statistic is known, it is also known how the statistic behaves—that is, how it fluctuates due to random sampling. The appropriate sampling distribution for a specific statistic has been determined by mathematical theory, and commonly used sampling distributions have been tabled in standard form.

From the information of the statistic and its sampling distribution, we reason back to the parameter. The parameters are never known for certain (unless the entire population is measured, in which case there is no inference or need for inferential statistics). Decisions about parameters are made through testing hypotheses and estimating parameters, the latter with a confidence interval.

As mentioned earlier, there are many specific statistical tests used in analyzing data. There are also numerous sampling distributions that are used, depending, of course, on

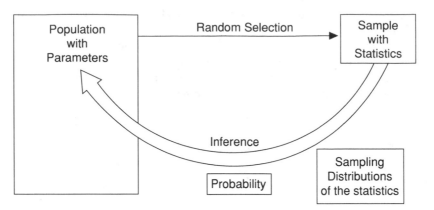

(a)   We have a population and we want to make decisions about measures of the population, namely, parameters.

(b)   We select a random sample and compute measures of the sample, which are statistics.

(c)   The statistics reflect the corresponding parameters and sampling fluctuation.

(d)   We observe the statistics, which are the facts that we have, and infer back to the parameters in the light of the sampling distributions and probability.

FIGURE 14.4   Chain of Reasoning for Inferential Statistics

the specific statistic. This is not a statistics text, so there is no intent to develop statistical mastery. However, in the remaining part of the chapter, a compendium of some of the more commonly used statistical procedures is provided. The different statistical tests that apply under different conditions are discussed. Sampling distributions other than the normal distribution are also mentioned as they apply for specific tests. In each case, the hypothesis will be indicated. Most data analyses for research projects are done on a computer, so the important point for any researcher is to understand the analysis.

Parametric Analyses

Undoubtedly the most frequently used analyses in educational research are *parametric analyses,* so called because a set of assumptions, called the parametric assumptions, are required for their application. The example of testing the hypothesis about the reading achievement mean, discussed earlier, involved a parametric analysis.

The parametric assumptions can be summarized as follows:

1. Measurement of the dependent variable, the variable whose data are being analyzed, is on at least an interval scale.

2. The observations or scores are independent, which means that the score of one individual is not influenced by the score of any other.[3]

3. The scores (dependent variable) are selected from a population distribution that is normally distributed. Actually, this assumption is required only if sample size is small—less than thirty.

4. When two or more populations are being studied, they have homogeneous variance. This means that the populations being studied have about the same dispersion in their distributions.

With more complex parametric procedures, additional assumptions may be required, but those listed here are the basic assumptions. (Any assumptions involving distributions refer to the population distributions.)

The t-Distribution—Another Sampling Distribution

In the discussion about a hypothesized population mean, the normal distribution was used as the sampling distribution of the sample mean—the statistic. Actually, if the sample standard deviation is used to estimate the population standard deviation, the appropriate sampling distribution is not the normal distribution. Rather, it is a family of distributions called the Student *t*-distributions or, simply, *t*-distributions.

The *t*-distributions are identified by *degrees of freedom (df)* values. In an analysis, the degrees of freedom are the number of ways the data are free to vary. Operationally, degrees of freedom are determined by subtracting the number of restrictions placed on the data from the number of scores. When testing a hypothesis about a population mean, the sample mean is computed, which requires the summing of the sample scores. Once $n - 1$ of the scores are determined, the *n*th score, too, is uniquely determined, because it must provide the remainder for the sum. Thus, the degrees of freedom are $n - 1$.

Like the normal distribution, the *t*-distributions are symmetrical and bell-shaped. As degrees of freedom increase, the *t*-distributions become more and more like the normal. Usually, if the degrees of freedom exceed 120, the normal distribution is used as an adequate approximation for the *t*-distribution. Therefore, in the reading achievement example, where sample size was 225, the normal distribution was used as the sampling distribution of the sample mean. The t-distributions are given in standard form in Table B of Appendix 3. Degrees of freedom must be considered in their use; this will be illustrated in the following example.

> The *t*-distributions comprise a family of distributions that are the sampling distributions for many statistics. Each *t*-distribution is determined by a degrees-of-freedom value.

EXAMPLE 14.1 A SCIENCE ACHIEVEMENT
EXAMPLE INVOLVING THE *t*-DISTRIBUTION _____

Suppose that it is known that over the years the science achievement of seventh-graders in a school has stabilized, and this is evidenced by a mean performance of 82.5 on a standardized end-of-the-year, science test. The teachers are interested in whether or not individualized science instruction will affect this measure of achievement. A random sample of 31 seventh-graders is selected for a class taught by individualized instruction. At the close of the school year, these students are tested using the standardized test.

The null hypothesis being tested is "The population science test mean of seventh-graders taught by individualized instruction equals that of seventh-graders taught by the usual instruction in this school." The mean of students taught by usual instruction is known to be 82.5, so the null hypothesis can be written:

$$H_0: \mu_I = 82.5 \text{ or } H_0: \mu_I - 82.5 = 0$$

It should be noted that the population of seventh-graders taught by individualized instruction is a hypothetical population, but the 31 students in the class so taught do comprise a sample of that population. Also, at the beginning of the study, it was not hypothesized that individualized instruction would be less or more effective than the usual instruction. So, when testing the null hypothesis, the rejection region will be located in both tails of the sampling distribution. The .05 level of significance is used.

The sample data are as follows: the mean, $\overline{X} = 87.0$, and the standard deviation of the 31 science test scores is 9.5. The statistic to be tested is the sample mean, and the standard error of this statistic (the standard deviation of its sampling distribution) is found by:

$$s_{\overline{X}} = \frac{s}{\sqrt{n}} = \frac{9.5}{\sqrt{31}} = \frac{9.5}{5.56} = 1.71$$

The appropriate sampling distribution is the *t*-distribution with *n*–1 or 30 degrees of freedom.

The computation for the statistical test is:

$$t = \frac{\overline{X} - \mu_I}{s_{\overline{x}}} = \frac{8.70 - 82.5}{1.71} = \frac{4.5}{1.71} = 2.63$$

The μ_I is the hypothesized value of the population mean if H_0 is true. The computation provides a value (sometimes called the *t*-value) in standard score form. It is the standard score of the statistic, in this case the sample mean, in its sampling distribution.

To check the value of 2.63 in the *t*-distribution table we use the *t*-distribution with 30 degrees of freedom. Going to Table B and to the row for 30 *df*, we find the critical value for level of significance .05, two-tailed test (the rejection region for H_0 is in both tails as noted above), to be 2.042. The computed test statistic (the *t*-value above) of 2.63 exceeds this critical value, hence, the statistical test is statistically significant and we reject the null hypothesis.

The probability statement is, "The probability that the sample mean of 87.0 would have appeared due to random sampling fluctuation, if the population mean of seventh-graders taught by individualized instruction is 82.5, is less than .05. Hence, we reject the null hypothesis and conclude that the population mean on the science test is not 82.5. The difference of 4.5 points between the sample mean and the hypothesized value of the mean is too great to attribute to chance (random sampling fluctuation). Because the sample mean is greater than the mean for the usual instruction, and the statistical test was significant, we can conclude that individualized science instruction is more effective than the usual instruction for seventh-graders in this school.

Analysis of Variance (ANOVA)

Analysis of variance (ANOVA) is an inferential statistics procedure by which a researcher can test the null hypothesis that two or more population means are equal ($H_0: \mu_1 = \mu_2 = \cdots = \mu_k$). Usually, it is not used for only two means, because a t-test for the difference between two means can be used. The sample means, one corresponding to each population mean, are computed and tested simultaneously for any statistically significant differences between them.

The null hypothesis in ANOVA is tested by comparing two estimates of variance.[4] These are put into a ratio form, called the F-ratio or F-value. The sampling distribution for the ratio of two variances is the F-distribution (named after R.A. Fisher). The F-distribution is a family of distributions that are generally not symmetrical. They are located between zero and plus infinity, so the numerical values of the distribution are all positive. It requires two degrees-of-freedom values, one for each of the variance estimates in the ratio, to determine the correct distribution. The F-distributions are given in Table D of Appendix 3; their use is illustrated with a subsequent example.

ANOVA tests the null hypothesis that two or more population means are equal. A ratio of two variance estimates is computed, and this ratio has as its sampling distribution the F-distribution, determined by two degrees-of-freedom values.

ANOVAs can include one or more independent variables. If one independent variable is included, the ANOVA is a *one-way* ANOVA. If an experiment were conducted in which there were four experimental treatments, there would be the four levels of the independent variable, experimental treatment. The null hypothesis would be $H_0: \mu_1 = \mu_2 = \mu_3 = \mu_4$; a sample mean for each of the four treatments would be computed and these means would be tested. This would be a one-way ANOVA because only one independent variable is included.

If two independent variables are included simultaneously in an ANOVA, the analysis is called a *two-way* ANOVA. In this case, there is a null hypothesis for each of the independent variables, and an F-ratio is computed for each of the groups of sample means from the two independent variables. It may also be possible to compute a statistical test for the interaction between the two independent variables. (Interaction is a combined effect of the independent variables on the dependent variable.) If this is done, the null hypothesis of no interaction is tested. As many *F*-ratios are computed as there are null hypotheses tested. In a two-way ANOVA, there are at most three null hypothesis, one for each independent variable and one for the interaction.

There are also three-way and more complex ANOVAs, which means that more independent variables are included in a single analysis. When more complex ANOVAs are used, increasing numbers of independent variables are included, although in educational research it would be rare to include more than four or five independent variables in a single analysis. The numbers of possible interactions and their complexities (including more than two independent variables in a single interaction) also increase. Data from the factorial designs discussed in the chapter on experimental designs are usually analyzed by what are called *factorial ANOVAs*. This simply means including the two or more independent variables simultaneously in the same analysis.

EXAMPLE 14.2 ONE-WAY ANOVA— A TEACHING HISTORY EXAMPLE

Consider an experiment in which three types of instruction are used for teaching American history—T_1, T_2, and T_3. Random samples of history students are assigned to the three types and, after a period of instruction, are tested on a common history exam. The independent variable is type of instruction. The dependent variable is performance or score on the history exam. The three random samples contain 25, 30, and 33 students, respectively, for T_1, T_2, and T_3.

The null hypothesis is H_0: $\mu_1 = \mu_2 = \mu_3$; that is, the population means of students taught by the three types of instruction are equal. The level of significance is set at .05. The sample means are found to be $\overline{X}_1 = 83$, $\overline{X}_2 = 72$, and $\overline{X}_3 = 80$, and the *F*-ratio from the ANOVA is $F = 4.93$.

To determine whether or not this *F*-ratio is statistically significant, we first need to identify the appropriate degrees of freedom associated with it. In this case, the *df* for the numerator of the *F*-ratio is 2, one less than the number of sample means. In determining the variance among sample means, the mean of all scores (called the *grand mean*) is computed, so one restriction is introduced. In general, for a one-way ANOVA, there are $k - 1$ *df* for the numerator if k is the number of sample means.

The *df* associated with the denominator of the *F*-ratio is 85. There is a total of 88 scores in the entire ANOVA. When computing the variance estimate for the denominator of the *F*-ratio, all 88 scores are used, but the mean for each sample is also used in the computation, so three restrictions are introduced. For a one-way ANOVA, there are $N - k$ *df* for the denominator of the *F*-ratio if N is the total number of scores in the analysis and k is the number of sample means.

Now we have a computed *F*-ratio of 4.93, with 2 and 85 degrees of freedom. Turning to Table D in Appendix 3, we go down the column for 2 *df* (the *df* for the numerator) to the row for 85 *df* (the *df* for the denominator). There is no row for 85 *df*, but there are rows for 60 *df* and 120 *df*. For each of these *df* values, there are actually four rows of critical values given, one for each of four significance levels. We select α-level .05 and find that the critical value for 60 *df* is 3.15 and that for 120 *df* is 3.07. Since we have 85 *df*, the critical value is about 3.12, based on a straight-line interpolation between the two table values. Our computed *F*-ratio exceeds 3.12; therefore, it is statistically significant and the null hypothesis is rejected. The probability statement and the conclusion are as follows:

> Probability statement: *The probability that the sample means would have occurred due to random sampling fluctuation, if the null hypothesis is true, is less than .05.*

> Conclusion: *The null hypothesis is rejected, and it is concluded that the population means are not all equal. This is the inference to the parameters. The types of instruction are not all equally effective, and we can conclude, at least, that T_1 is more effective than T_2.*

If more than two sample means are tested and if the *F*-ratio is statistically significant, the ANOVA does not indicate where the significance lies; that is, only one pair of means may be significantly different, all pairs may be significantly different, or some pairs may be different. We know that at least the two extreme sample means are significantly different (hence, the foregoing conclusion). However, subsequent tests, *post hoc tests,* can be computed to determine specifically which means are significantly different from others. Statistics texts such as those listed near the end of the chapter contain descriptions of such post hoc tests.

A summary ANOVA table commonly is used for presenting results of an analysis of variance in a research report. A summary ANOVA table for the example above is found in Table 14.1. The content is described below the table. The "total" line may or may not be included. It shows that the *SS* and *df* of "between" and "within" add to those of "total." We do not compute a mean square for "total" because it is not used.

TABLE 14.1   Example Summary ANOVA Table

Source	SS	*df*	MS	*F*-value
Between	36.48	2	18.24	4.93*
Within	314.50	85	3.70	
Total	350.98	87		

*p < .05

In a one-way ANOVA the total variation is partitioned into two sources; (1) Between the levels (groups) of the independent variable, in the example T_1, T_2, and T_3, and (2) Within the groups of the independent variable.

SS stands for sum of squares, the numerator of a variance estimate.

Dividing SS by df gives a mean square, MS, which is a variance estimate.

The F-value is obtained by dividing the MS Between by the MS Within. The p < .05 (probability less than .05) indicates the F-value, 4.93, is statistically significant at the .05 level of significance.

Nonparametric Analyses

As indicated earlier, the use of parametric analyses requires certain assumptions about the populations under study. Interval scale measurement is also required so that means can be computed. If these assumptions are not met, it is more appropriate to use nonparametric analyses. These analyses do not require interval scale measurement; ordinal and nominal scale data can be analyzed. Also, for most nonparametric analyses, assumptions about the shape of the population distribution are not required. For that reason, they are often used when small sample sizes are involved.

Nonparametric analyses are part of inferential statistics, so the chain of reasoning for inferential statistics applies. Hypotheses are tested and can be stated in null form. The statistics involved are not means but statistics, such as frequencies. Whatever the case, the statistics are still measures of the one or more samples.

> *Nonparametric analyses* require few if any assumptions about the population under study. They can be used with ordinal and nominal scale data.

The Chi-Square (χ^2) Test and Distribution

The most commonly used sampling distribution for statistics generated by non-parametric analysis is the chi-square (χ^2) distribution. Like the *t*-distribution, the χ^2 distribution comprises a family of distributions, each specific distribution identified by one degrees-of-freedom value. Unlike the *t*-distribution, the χ^2 distribution is not symmetrical. Theoretically, it extends from zero to plus infinity. The basic reasoning for using the sampling distribution is the same for the χ^2 distribution as for other distributions, such as the normal and *t*-distributions. However, because of the nonsymmetrical nature of the χ^2 distribution, the rejection region when testing hypotheses is usually contained entirely in the right-hand tail of the distribution.

Numerous hypothesis can be tested by computing a statistic called the χ^2 value. This statistic involves the comparison of observed and expected frequencies— the latter being anticipated on the basis of a null hypothesis—within categories. The χ^2 value is then distributed as the χ^2 distribution with the appropriate degrees of freedom. If a computed χ^2 value exceeds the tabled value (critical value) for a designated significance level, the statistical test is significant and the null hypothesis being tested is rejected. A statistical test involving the χ^2 distribution is commonly called a χ^2 test.

A χ^2 test can be used to test hypotheses about how well a sample distribution fits some theoretical or hypothesized distribution. Such a test is also called a *goodness-of-fit test;* that is, it tests how well the sampling distribution fits the hypothesized distribution. For example, we could test a hypothesis that a population distribution from which a sample was selected is normally distributed. The null hypothesis is that the population distribution is normally distributed or stated as a hypothesis of no difference: "There is no difference between the population distribution and the normal distribution." The statistical test tests whether the sample observations are within random sampling fluctuation of coming from a normal distribution. If the χ^2 value is statistically significant, we would reject the null hypothesis.

One common use of the χ^2 test is with *contingency tables,* which are two-dimensional tables with one variable on each dimension. Each of the variables has two or more categories, and the data are the sample frequencies in the categories. The null hypothesis of independence—that is, no relationship—between the variables is tested. The following example involves a contingency table.

EXAMPLE 14.3 CONTINGENCY TABLE
USING THE c² TEST _____

At a liberal arts college, a researcher is interested in student attitude toward compulsory attendance at college convocations. A random sample of students is drawn from each of the four undergraduate classes at the college. Equal numbers need not be selected from the classes. The students in the sample then respond to "agree," "undecided," or "disagree" to compulsory attendance.

The null hypothesis is that the four class populations do not differ in their attitude toward compulsory attendance. Another way of stating the null hypothesis is that class and attitude toward compulsory attendance are independent. This hypothesis does not imply what the extent of agreement or disagreement is; it only implies that the class populations do not differ. Table 14.2 represents sample data in a 3×4 contingency table.

Table 14.2 contains observed frequencies or sample data. To compute a χ^2 test, expected or theoretical frequencies are required. These expected frequencies are calculated from the sample data by using the marginal totals. The calculations will not be presented here, but Table 14.3 contains these expected frequencies, based on what would be expected if the null hypothesis is true.

In general, contingency tables have $(r - 1)$ times $(c - 1)$ degrees of freedom, where r and c are the number of rows and the number of columns, respectively, in the contingency

TABLE 14.2 Observed Sample Frequencies of Response to Compulsory Attendance at College Convocations

Class	Category			
	Agree	Undecided	Disagree	Total
Freshman	12	48	20	80
Sophomore	7	20	33	60
Junior	6	19	35	60
Senior	5	3	32	40
Total	30	90	120	240

TABLE 14.3   Expected Frequencies of Response to Compulsory Attendance at College Convocations

	Category			
Class	Agree	Undecided	Disagree	Total
Freshman	(12) 10	(48) 30	(20) 40	80
Sophomore	(7) 7.5	(20) 22.5	(33) 30	60
Junior	(6) 7.5	(19) 22.5	(35) 30	60
Senior	(5) 5	(3) 15.5	(32) 20	40
Total	30	90	120	240

Note: Observed frequencies from Table 14.2 are in parentheses.

table. For the example, the χ^2 test has 6 degrees of freedom. Suppose that we set the significance level at .05. The formula for computing the χ^2 value is given by:

$$\chi^2 = \sum_{i=1}^{k} \frac{(O_i - E_i)^2}{E_i}$$

where O = observed frequency
E = expected frequency
k = number of categories, groupings, or cells.

When a contingency table is used, $k = r \times c$, the number of cells in the table, which for the example is 12.

The computed χ^2 value for testing the null hypothesis is 33.59, based on the data in Table 14.3. We turn to Table C of Appendix 3, which contains the χ^2 distributions. This table contains critical values. The columns represent area to the right of the critical value point. The rows vary by degrees of freedom. The drawing of the distribution shows how the area is divided.

We set the level of significance at .05, so we go down the column headed .05 to the row corresponding with 6 *df* and find a critical value of 12.59. Thus, the statistical test is significant and the probability statement and conclusion are as follows:

Probability statement: *The probability that the sample responses would have occurred by chance if class and attitude toward compulsory attendance at college convocations are independent in the population is less than .05.*

Conclusion: *Class and attitude toward compulsory attendance at college convocations are related (not independent) in the college student population. The null hypothesis is rejected.*

An inspection of the frequencies shows that upper-class students tend to have higher frequencies of "disagree" than expected, and lower-class students have higher frequencies of "undecided" than expected.

The foregoing example illustrates the use of a nonparametric analysis involving the χ^2 test. There are numerous nonparametric analyses, some of which are listed in a table later in this chapter. Specific formulas for computation can be obtained from any applied statistics text. However, the underlying reasoning of inferential statistics still applies.

Correlational Analyses

Correlation was discussed previously as a descriptive statistic that is a measure of the relationship between two variables. Correlational analyses can also be conducted in the context of inferential statistics; that is, hypothesis can be tested about the relationship of the variables in the population based on the correlation coefficient(s) of the sample.

One null hypothesis involving correlation is that the correlation in the population is zero. This is the null hypothesis of independence of the variables in the population, essentially the same as the hypothesis for the contingency table discussed earlier. However, the contingency table itself does not give a measure of the extent of relationship. Also, contingency tables usually deal with ordinal or nominal scale measures, and often the correlation coefficient is a Pearson product-moment coefficient, which has the variables measured on at least an interval scale (see Table 13.2).

The null hypothesis of no relationship between the variables in the population can be tested directly, since the sampling distribution of the sample correlation coefficient is known if this hypothesis is true. The required size of the sample coefficient for a specified significance level depends on the sample size. The larger the sample, the smaller the absolute value of the sample coefficient required to reach statistical significance.

The minimum or critical values of the correlation coefficient required for statistical significance are given in Table E of Appendix 3. Various levels of significance are given in the columns, and degrees of freedom are given on the rows. The degrees-of-freedom value associated with a particular statistical test is $n - 2$. Two degrees of freedom are lost because a mean is computed for each variable when calculating the correlation coefficient. If the absolute value of the coefficient equals or exceeds the tabled value for the α-level, the null hypothesis is rejected. If not, the null hypothesis is not rejected.

> The hypothesis of independence or no correlation in the population can be tested directly using the sample correlation coefficient.

EXAMPLE 14.4 TESTING THE HYPOTHESIS OF NO CORRELATION IN THE POPULATION

The band director of a large high school is interested in whether or not there is a relationship between scores on a divergent thinking test, purported to be a measure of creativity, and scores on a musical aptitude test. The null hypothesis is $H_0: \rho = 0$. (This null hypothesis is read "rho equals zero, where rho is the parameter that corresponds with r, the sample correlation coefficient.") That is, the correlation in the population is zero. A random sample of 37 freshmen is selected, and these students are measured using both tests. The level of significance is set at .05.

The sample correlation coefficient, *r,* equals .21. To test the null hypothesis, we turn to Table E. We use the column headed .05 for level of significance for a two-tailed test, since no direction was hypothesized for the correlation. (It could have been positive or negative.) Since $n = 37$, $df = 35$, we go to the row for 35, and the critical value for the correlation coefficient is .325. The sample *r* of .21 is less than the critical value; therefore, the null hypothesis cannot be rejected. The probability statement and conclusion are as follows:

Probability statement: *The probability that a sample correlation coefficient of .21 would appear by chance if the correlation in the population is zero is greater than .05.*

Conclusion: *Scores on the divergent thinking test and scores on the musical aptitude test are uncorrelated in the population.*

EXAMPLE 14.5 CORRELATIONAL ANALYSIS— COMPUTER SOLUTION

An educational psychologist is interested in the relationship between scores on a verbal performance test and reading comprehension in a population of students in the middle school grades. A random sample of 150 students is selected from the population and administered the verbal performance test and the reading comprehension subtest of a standardized achievement test battery. The researcher is interested in both the descriptive statistics of the sample relative to the tests and in testing the null hypothesis, $H_0:\rho = 0$, that the correlation between scores on the two tests in the population is zero. The .05 level of significance is used for testing the null hypothesis.

The computer solution using a SPSSX program is found in Figure 14.5. The score on the verbal performance test is designated variable X, and that on the reading comprehension subtest, variable Y. The upper part of the computer solution or printout contains the raw or observed score, sample statistics. There are 150 scores (cases) for each variable, and the means and standard deviations are given. Although the means are quite different, the standard deviations of the two variables are quite close, less than one point apart.

The "correlation coefficients" part of the output actually contains only one correlation coefficient of interest, because in a correlation matrix the part above the diagonal contains the same information as the part below the diagonal. The diagonal contains 1.0000 because the correlation of a variable with itself is 1.0.

The sample correlation coefficient between scores on the verbal performance test and scores on the reading comprehension subtest is .6384, which rounded to two places is .64. The asterisks on the coefficient indicate the statistical test of the null hypothesis, and this correlation coefficient is statistically significant at both the .05 and .01 levels (LE stands for level). If a statistical test is significant at the .01 level it also is significant at the .05 level.

VARIABLE	CASES	MEAN	STD DEV
X	150	85,8000	12,2323
Y	150	62,0600	11,6777

- - CORRELATION COEFFICIENTS - -

	X	Y
X	1.0000	.6384**
Y	.6384**	1.0000

* - SIGNIF. LE. .05   **SIGNIF. LE .01   (2-TAILED)

FIGURE 14.5   Computer Output for Correlational Analysis—Example 14.5

Thus the educational psychologist can make the following observations and conclusion:

1. The means on the two variables, the scores on the verbal performance test and the reading comprehension subtest, are quite different—almost 23 points apart. This may be due to substantial differences in the scales for the two variables and an inspection of the test and subtest should be informative.

2. The distribution of the scores on the test and subtest have similar dispersions as evidenced by the similar standard deviations.

3. The null hypothesis, H_0: $\rho = 0$, is rejected, and it can be concluded that in the population of middle school students from which the sample was selected, performance on the verbal test and reading comprehension are related.

The probability statement with testing the null hypothesis is, "The probability that a sample correlation coefficient of .64 would appear by chance, if the correlation in the population is zero, is less than .05." Actually, the probability is less than .01, as indicated on the computer output. Some researchers report the most conservative level at which a statistical test is significant, and this is acceptable. Others report whatever level was initially established, even if there is significance at a more conservative level.

There are other hypotheses that can be tested about correlation coefficients. One such hypothesis is that the correlation coefficient in the population is a specified value other than zero, which can be written, H_0: $\rho = a$, $a \neq 0$. Another hypothesis is that two population correlation coefficients are equal, which can be written, H_0: $\rho_1 = \rho_2$ or H_0: $\rho_1 - \rho_2 = 0$. However, testing these hypotheses requires a transformation of the statistics, called the Fisher z-transformation, whose sampling distribution is normally distributed. The procedure for testing hypotheses using the Fisher z-transformation is not discussed here but can be found in most applied statistics texts.

Analysis of Covariance

A parametric statistical analysis that involves correlation is the *analysis covariance*. In Chapter 4, the matter of using a statistical adjustment to enhance control when conducting research was discussed. Analysis of covariance is a procedure for statistical adjustment or statistical control over variation.

Analysis of covariance is closely related to analysis of variance. Essentially, it is analysis of variance with the dependent variable scores adjusted on the basis of the dependent variable's relationship to some other relevant variable. This relationship, of course, involves the correlation between the dependent variable and the other variable. The adjusted dependent variable scores are adjusted so they are independent of the influence of this other relevant variable, called the *covariate*.

Analysis of covariance is a procedure by which statistical adjustments are made to a dependent variable. These adjustments are based on the correlation between the dependent variable and another variable, called the covariate.

The null hypothesis in the analysis of covariance is that the *adjusted* population means are equal. It can be written as the null hypothesis in analysis of variance, H_0: $\mu_1 = \mu_2 = \cdots = \mu_k$ except that now the μ's represent adjusted population means. As in the analysis of variance, the statistic generated is the ratio of two variances, and the appropriate sampling distribution is the F-distribution. The statistical reasoning is the same, except that conclusions and inferences are now made to adjusted population dependent variable means.

Analysis of covariance is especially useful for situations in which experimental or design control over an extraneous or mediating variable is impossible or undesirable. A researcher, especially one who works in a school setting, often must take intact groups such as classes for research studies. Analysis of covariance may be used to make adjustments, although it should be noted that analysis of covariance does not make the groups equivalent.

EXAMPLE 14.6 ANALYSIS OF COVARIANCE _____

A researcher is conducting an experiment involving four different types of materials for teaching sixth-grade mathematics. Several sixth-grade classes participate in the experiment, but it is not possible to have random assignment of students to classes or to type of material. Instruction using the materials takes place over one semester, and at the close of this period all participating students are tested by means of a common mathematics test. The intent of the research is to determine whether the different materials have differing effects on mathematics achievement. The null hypothesis is that the means of the populations of sixth-graders taught using the four different materials are equal.

Since there was no random assignment, it is possible that the four groups (samples) taught with the different materials are not equal in academic ability. Thus, if a difference appeared between the group means, it might be due to different abilities rather than different materials, which would be an example of confounding of ability and type of material.

It would be well if the mathematics test scores could be adjusted to remove the effect of different abilities. This could be done through analysis of covariance if a measure of academic ability were available to serve as a covariate. Such a measure would be an IQ test score, preferably one obtained prior to the experiment. (This way the IQ test score could not be affected by the experimental procedure.) The analysis of covariance would adjust the mathematics test score on the basis of the correlation between the IQ test score and the mathematics test score. The null hypothesis tested would be that the adjusted population means are equal. Adjusted means would be those with the effect of academic ability removed. The dependent variable now becomes the math test scores, adjusted for differing IQ test scores.

Using the notation described earlier, this experiment (or quasi-experiment) is diagrammed in Figure 14.6. Note that X_1, X_2, X_3, and X_4 represent the four different types of materials (the levels of the independent variable). There is no random assignment to groups. The Os with odd-number subscripts are measures on the covariate, and the Os with even number subscripts are adjusted scores on the mathematics test. Actually, the analysis of covariance does the adjusting. The IQ test scores and the mathematics test scores would be entered into the analysis simultaneously.

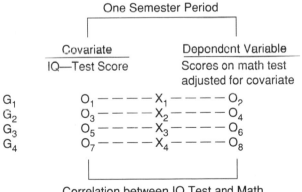

FIGURE 14.6   **Design of Research Example**
               Involving Analysis of Covariance as
               a Means for Adjusting for Possible
               Initial Differences in the Group

The study is conducted with 28, 32, 24, and 29 students in groups G_1 through G_4, respectively. Thus, a total of 113 dependent variable scores are analyzed. The level of significance is set at .05 for testing the null hypothesis. Suppose the following results appear: The adjusted, sample means are $\overline{X}_1 = 78.6$, $\overline{X}_2 = 75.3$, $\overline{X}_3 = 80.4$ and $\overline{X}_4 = 77.1$, and the F-ratio from the analysis of covariance is 1.93. This F-ratio has 3 and 108 degrees of freedom. An additional degree of freedom is lost due to the covariate for the variance estimate of the denominator of the F-ratio, relative to the degrees of freedom had no covariate been used. Referring to Table D of Appendix 3, a critical value of about 2.70 is required for statistical significance. Because the computed F-ratio is less than this critical value, it is not statistically significant and the null hypothesis cannot be rejected. The probability statement and the conclusion are as follows:

Probability statement: *The probability that the adjusted sample means would appear by chance if the adjusted population means are equal is greater than .05.*

Conclusion: *The adjusted population means are equal. More generally, the different types of materials have the same effect in the population.*

The Role of Statistical Analyses

Statistical analyses should be selected to meet the requirements of the research study: describing distributions and relationships, testing hypotheses, estimating parameters, and whatever is required. In essence, analyses assume a service function in the research process. Of course, it is well to plan research so that acceptable analyses can be applied. But a research study should not be done solely because some analysis procedure is available.

> Statistical analyses should not be an end in themselves, but a means to an end. They assume a service function in the research process.

With many research studies, statistical analyses can be applied in a straightforward manner. For example, when a factorial design is used for an experiment, an analysis of variance usually can be applied to the data of the dependent variable. Some studies may require multiple analyses; for example, several parameters may be estimated in a single survey. Different analyses may be used in the same study. For example, in a survey, if data from two groups are compared, a t-test might be used; if classification on another variable produces more groups for the data, a one-way analysis of variance might be applied.

Sometimes the research study yields data that are not amenable to a straightforward statistical analysis, and it is necessary to explore possible analyses that will reveal the information contained in the data. An example of this is data from the time-series designs, described in the chapters on experimental and quasi-experimental research. There may be more than one analysis done, and the specific analyses may depend on the pattern of results and prior knowledge of possible effects or relationships of variables.

EXAMPLE 14.7 ANALYSIS OF TIME SERIES DESIGN DATA _____

A junior high school science teacher has a ninth-grade science class of thirty-two students. The class is of heterogenous ability and includes both boys and girls. The teacher is conducting a study on health practices beliefs, or attitudes toward health practices. A thirty-item health practices inventory is used, and there are two parallel forms available, so the same form does not have to be used for every measurement. The scoring of responses is such that the greater the score, the more positive the attitude. The items of the inventory focus on beliefs and attitudes, not actual behaviors. (An individual might believe that certain practices are beneficial yet not engage in them.)

The teacher includes a three-week instructional unit on health and science during the course. The research question can be stated as:

Does the instruction of the health and science unit have an effect on the health practices attitudes of the students?

The design for the study is a single-group time series design. The health practices attitude inventory is administered seven times during the academic year: shortly after the beginning of school, close to the end of school, and five times in between. The measurement occasions are about equally spaced at approximately six-week intervals. Between the third and fourth measurements, the health and science unit is taught. This is the experimental treatment. Students respond anonymously to the inventory, since the interest is in the pattern of group scores, not individual scores.

The mean scores for each of the seven measurement occasions are computed and the pattern is given in Figure 14.7. The means for the seven Os are:

$$\overline{X}_1 = 45.3, \overline{X}_2 = 46.2, \overline{X}_3 = 46.4, \overline{X}_4 = 57.1, \overline{X}_5 = 61.2,$$
$$\overline{X}_6 = 58.5, \overline{X}_7 = 56.8$$

An inspection of the pattern indicates an increase from O_3 to O_4, a continuing increase but at a slower rate to O_5, and then a tapering off of the mean scores. A one-way analysis of variance[5] is computed using the seven measurement occasions as the levels of the independent variable for the ANOVA. The F-ratio from the ANOVA was statistically significant ($\alpha = .05$), and a subsequent post hoc test showed the following:

$\overline{X}_1, \overline{X}_2, \overline{X}_3$ are not significantly different.
$\overline{X}_4, \overline{X}_5, \overline{X}_6, \overline{X}_7$ are not significantly different.
$\overline{X}_1, \overline{X}_2,$ and $\overline{X}_3$ are significantly different from $\overline{X}_4, \overline{X}_5, \overline{X}_6,$ and $\overline{X}_7$.

Thus, the conclusion is that there is an effect of the instructional unit on the health practices attitudes of the students. An inspection of the pattern of means indicates that the

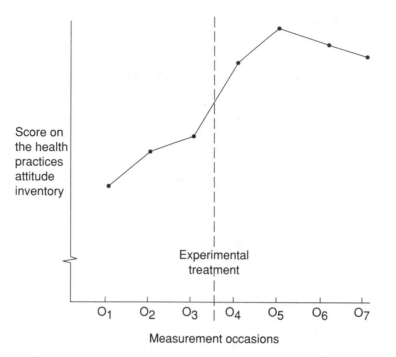

FIGURE 14.7   Pattern of Results for the Time Series Design Example

greatest effect is immediate, but there is a continuing effect to the next measurement. Then, for the final two measurements, there is a decline in the means, although not to the preexperimental treatment level.

This result would undoubtedly be of major concern, but other points also can be made about this analysis. The teacher may be interested in other information contained in the data. Consider the following question:

Is there a difference in the mean attitude scores of boys and girls?

Some kind of composite score could be computed for each of the students across the seven measurements. Then the mean for girls and the mean for boys could be determined. Suppose that the results were $\overline{X}_G = 54.8$, $\overline{X}_B = 51.2$. A t-test is computed, and the t-value is statistically significant. Therefore, we could conclude that girls have the higher attitude scores.

When analyzing time series design data, if at all possible, use all of the data in some manner. A t-test for the difference between the mean for O_3 and the mean for O_4 would not be adequate. Such an analysis would omit a good bit of the data and the pattern. If two composite scores were obtained for each student, one preexperimental treatment and the other postexperimental treatment, the overall pattern would be lost. Also, if such a comparison were made, a short-term effect might be lost, since the subsequent decline of the scores might wash it out in the analysis.

Finally, although the analysis procedures suggested here are inferential statistics, there was no random sampling of students for the class. Analyses could have been limited to descriptive statistics—computing means and standard deviations, for example. However, it likely could be argued on a logical basis that the students of the class are representative of some larger populations. If there is no special grouping for the students of this class, they may well be representative of ninth-grade students in the school and possibly of ninth-grade students enrolled in the school over a period of years. Therefore, inferential statistics often are used for such analyses even though a random sample is not used.

The analysis of data from time series designs can be quite complex and is beyond the scope of this book. More extensive analyses are discussed in such sources as McCain and McCleary (1979) and Gottman and Glass (1978).

Selecting an Appropriate Statistical Analysis

Selecting an appropriate statistical analysis depends on a number of factors, which can be summarized by the answers to three questions:

1. What information do we want?
2. What are the levels of measurement of the variables, especially the dependent variable?
3. What assumptions are met?

The answer to the first question determines whether descriptive statistics or inferential statistics will be used, or possibly both. The statement of the research problem usually gives adequate direction to answer this question. The answers to questions 2 and 3 determine the kinds of analyses (the statistics and statistical tests that can be computed) appropriate given the data.

When inferential statistics are to be used, the specific statistical analysis or statistical test depends on the hypotheses to be tested, the levels of measurement of the variables, and the assumptions that can be met. If the dependent variable is measured on an interval scale and the independent variable is categorical, either ordinal or nominal measurement, parametric analyses would be used. Testing hypotheses about means would be examples of using a parametric analysis. When less than interval scale measurement is attained or the parametric assumptions cannot be met, nonparametric analyses are used. If we are testing hypotheses about the relationship of two variables, we would use a correlation test, the specific test depending on the measurement of the variables. Table 14.4 contains a summary of statistical tests and hypotheses that can be tested by the tests. When a *t*-test is indicated, a statistical test involving the *t*-distribution as the sampling distribution is being used. If sample size is large (around 120), the normal distribution is used as an adequate approximation for the *t*-distribution. The table also contains two nonparametric tests not discussed earlier.

TABLE 14.4   Some Common Statistical Tests Used in Inferential Statistics

Statistical Test	Hypothesis Tested
Parametric Tests	
t-test (or use of normal distribution)	About a single mean H: $\mu = \alpha$
	Difference between two means H: $\mu = \mu_2$ or H: $\mu - \mu_2 = 0$, used for both independent and dependent samples but formulas differ
Analysis of variance (one-way)	Two or more population means are equal. H: $\mu_1 = \mu_2 \ldots = \mu_k$, from the levels of a single independent variable
Analysis of variance (two-way)	Two or more population means are equal; two independent variables included, and there is a hypothesis for each and their interaction.
Analysis of covariance	Two or more population means are equal after being adjusted for the effect of the covariate.
Nonparametric Tests	
x^2 test, goodness of fit	A population distribution has a hypothesized shape.
x^2 test, independence (contingency table)	Two variables are independent in the population.
x^2 test, median test	The medians of two or more populations are equal.
Mann-Whitney U-test	There is no difference in the scores from two populations.
Correlational Tests	
t-test (or use of normal distribution)	The population correlation coefficient is zero. H: $\rho = 0$
Fisher's z-transformation test, which uses the normal distribution	The population correlation coefficient is a specified value. H: $\rho = \alpha$
	Two population correlation coefficients are equal. H: $\rho_1 = \rho_2$ or H: $\rho_1 - \rho_2 = 0$.

Figure 14.8 contains a decision tree for selecting an appropriate statistical test. There are many statistical tests in inferential statistics, and this figure presents a limited number of those most commonly used. The top row of boxes indicates what the hypotheses are about. For example, if we are testing a hypothesis about four means, the parametric assumptions are met, and we are not adjusting the means, we would use ANOVA. Whatever the statistical test used, the underlying reasoning of inferential statistics remains the same, that of making inferences from the sample statistics to the population parameters. It is important to keep this reasoning in mind and not lose it in the technicalities of doing the statistical test.

Comments About Statistical Analysis

The foregoing discussion of statistical analysis was brief and considered only more commonly used and relatively elementary procedures. In fact, the analyses discussed in

What is the hypothesis and/or the conditions?

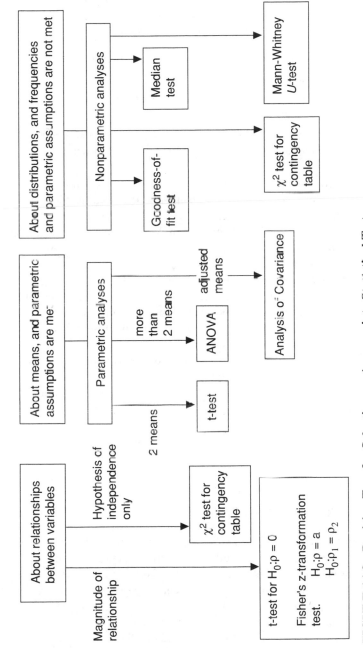

FIGURE 14.8 Decision Tree for Selecting an Appropriate Statistical Test

this chapter are limited to univariate analyses, which means that only one dependent variable is included in an analysis. There are analyses, called multivariate analysis, that include two or more dependent variables simultaneously. Multivariate analyses require quite complex statistical calculations, and the interpretations of results also are complicated because often the analyses create artificial variables from combinations of the dependent variables. Advanced statistics texts and entire books deal with the topic of multivariate analysis. Examples of the latter are:

> Everitt, B. (1992). *Applied multivariate data analysis.* New York: Oxford University Press.

> Johnson, R.A. (1992). *Applied multivariate statistical analysis* (3rd ed.). Englewood Cliffs, NJ: Prentice-Hall.

> Tatsuoka, M.M. (1988). *Multivariate analysis: Techniques for educational and psychological research* (2nd ed.). New York: Macmillan.

Additional sources are available in any university library.

Multivariate analyses are mentioned because they are appearing with increasing frequency in the research literature. The use of computers with speed and capability has greatly enhanced their application. Without computers, and even with relatively primitive computers, the computation was, for all practical purposes, prohibitive. But presently, all of the major statistical packages contain multivariate procedures, especially for mainframe computers. Multivariate analysis of variance and factor analysis are examples of multivariate analyses. Factor analysis especially is used quite extensively in the behavioral sciences, with considerable application in psychological research.

The original analysis of the data from a research study is called a *primary analysis,* and often this is the only analysis ever done. *Secondary analysis* may be useful, and these are basically of two forms. One is to reanalyze the data for the purpose of addressing the original research question with better statistical procedures. The other form is to answer new research questions by additional analysis of the original data—in essence, extracting more information from the data. Doctoral dissertation research often produces large quantities of data, and all of the information is not used for the dissertation. Secondary analyses can be useful for extended analyses of such data.

Meta-Analysis

Chapter 3 discusses the review of literature. Such a review requires a synthesis of the results of related studies, often done through a narrative approach that Mason and Bramble (1989, p. 249) called a "boxscore" format. This format is a descriptive procedure of classifying research studies as to the direction of results. Meta-analysis is a statistical procedure for synthesizing research results across studies. Over the past two decades or so, this procedure has been advocated by several writers, particularly Glass, McGraw, and Smith (1981). As Glass (1976, p. 3) pointed out in some of his early writing on the subject, meta-analysis is the analysis of analyses and requires a statistical analysis of a large collection of results from individual studies in order to synthesize the findings and draw general conclusions. More recently, Cook et al (1992), have emphasized the trend toward utilizing meta-analysis for explanatory purposes. The *Journal of Educational Statistics* recently devoted a special issue to meta-analysis (Winter 1992, 17 [4], B.J. Becker and L.V. Hedges, guest editors). This issue explores some of the latest thoughts on applications of meta-analysis and extensions of methodology.

Meta-analysis requires a common measure for expressing the results across studies, and the measure typically used is effect size (*ES*) as suggested by Glass (1977). Essentially, an effect size is a standard score (*z*-score) of the mean of one group referenced in the distribution of another group, often a control group. Thus, an effect size is a score expressed in standard deviation units. When results are being summarized across studies involving experimental and control groups, the effect size may be defined as:

$$ES = \frac{\overline{X}_E - \overline{X}_c}{S_c}$$

where $\overline{X}_E$ = mean of the experimental group
$\overline{X}_c$ = mean of the control group
S_c = standard deviation of the control group.

However, not all meta-analyses use the standard deviation of one group in computing effect size. In a meta-analysis of studies of gender differences in self-confidence when involved in physical activity, Lirgg (1991) computed effect size by subtracting the mean for females from the mean for males, and dividing by a "pooled" standard deviation, which was an "averaged" standard deviation across the sexes. In that meta-analysis there was no reason to use either the standard deviation of the females or that of the males, singly as the basis for the effect size.

One possible difficulty with meta-analysis is that results may be combined from studies so different that they should not be combined. In an attempt to avoid this difficulty, it is necessary to establish criteria for the inclusion of studies in a meta-analysis. Criteria are necessary in order to ensure some level of similarity across studies, and also to avoid including poorly done studies that may bias the results of the meta-analysis. The Lirgg meta-analysis mentioned above required that four criteria be met in order for a study to be included. These were, studies must have:

1. Been published after 1977.
2. Employed males and females as subjects.
3. Measured confidence before any manipulation.
4. Included proper statistics so that effect sizes could be calculated. (p. 296)

The author then goes on to discuss the reasons for these criteria. For example, the publication after 1977 criterion was included because 1978 was the year that Title IX was mandated to be in full effect, and prior to that time female participation in physical activity was limited due to inequalities in opportunities and budgets for males and females. The Lirgg meta-analysis yielded forty-six separate effect sizes from thirty-five studies.

Meta-analysis requires a quantitative measure of effect size and criteria should be established for including studies in the meta-analysis.

Bourhis and Allen (1992) report on a meta-analysis of the relationship between communication apprehension and cognitive performance. They reviewed twenty-three research studies yielding thirty effect sizes. Their criteria for including a study were:

1. The study had to contain quantitative information measuring the association between some measure of cognitive performance (eg., test scores) and communication apprehension.

2. The report of the study had to be accessible to the authors.

3. The study had to contain information permitting the estimation of an effect size. (pp. 69–70)

The metric used for the meta-analysis was the correlation coefficient. In the analysis, an average correlation was estimated, weighted for sample size.

Meta-analysis provides a quantitative synthesis procedure that can be used to supplement the descriptive summary of research results. It is an attractive procedure because of its "pulling together of results" characteristic. However, meta-analysis is not without potential pitfalls. Research results in education are sometimes inconsistent, at times even contradictory, and studies must be reviewed carefully for possible explanations of inconsistent results. There may be a tendency to exclude studies that do not support the conclusions of interest to the person doing the meta-analysis. Statistically nonsignificant results may be overlooked, or indeed not reported in the literature.

Conducting a meta-analysis requires a substantial effort. Meta-analysis is not done by including five or so studies; some include upwards of sixty to seventy studies. Yet meta-analysis has proven useful and there is continued interest in conducting meta-analysis and extending its methodology. Detailed discussions of meta-analysis and arguments for its use can be found in the references cited.

Meta analysis is a statistical procedure used to synthesize the results across numerous independently conducted research studies.

Summary

This chapter provided an overview of inferential statistics, undoubtedly the most widely used collection of procedures for analyzing quantitative data in educational research. In inferential statistics, we attempt to infer from statistics, computed from sample data, to parameters, the measures of the population from which the sample was selected. In general hypotheses about parameters are tested or parameters are estimated. The chain of reasoning in inferential statistics was identified and discussed in the chapter.

Descriptive statistics (discussed in Chapter 13) and inferential statistics provide for the researcher effective means for analyzing quantitative data. Statistics are a means to an end, they are not ends in themselves. In this sense they have a service function in educational research. Data analysis is greatly facilitated by the use of computers, and within recent years computers have become widely accessible, especially with the availability of microcomputers and computer terminals conveniently located for the user. Numerous programs, both for mainframes and for microcomputers, are available for statistical analysis.

As with Chapter 13, the intent of this chapter was to provide a rationale for the analyses of data and to review some of the more common analyses. There was no intention to elaborate on computational procedures or to have the reader perform statistical analyses. Numerous applied statistics texts are available that include detailed discussions of statistical procedures including computational formulas. The following is a sampling of such texts:

1. Glass, G.V., and Hopkins, K.D. (1984) *Statistical methods in education and psychology* (2nd ed.). Englewood Cliffs, NJ: Prentice-Hall.

2. Hays, W.L. (1994). *Statistics* (5th ed.). New York: Holt, Rinehart and Winston.

3. Heiman, G.W. (1992). *Basic statistics for the behavioral sciences*. Boston: Houghton Mifflin.

4. Hinkle, D., Wiersma, W., and Jurs, S. (1994). *Applied statistics for the behavioral sciences* (3rd ed.). Boston: Houghton Mifflin.

5. Keppel, G., and Zedeck, S. (1989). *Data analysis for research designs*. New York: W. H. Freeman.

6. Kuzma, J.W. (1992). *Basic statistics for the health sciences* (2nd ed.). Mountain View, CA.: Mayfield.

7. Popham, W.J., and Sirotnik, K.A. (1992). *Understanding statistics in education.* Itasca, IL: F.E. Peacock Publishers.

8. Shavelson, R.J. (1988). *Statistical reasoning for the behavioral sciences* (2nd ed.). Boston: Allyn and Bacon.

KEY CONCEPTS

Central limit theorem	Sampling distribution
Standard normal distribution	Level of significance
t-distribution	Confidence level
Analysis of variance (ANOVA)	Statistical significance
F-distribution	Type I error
Nonparametric analysis	Type II error
Null hypothesis	Parametric analyses
Testing hypothesis	Parametric assumptions
Estimating parameters	Chi-square (χ^2) distribution
Interval estimate	Contingency table

Correlation analyses
Analysis of covariance
Computer output
Univariate analysis

Primary analysis
Secondary analysis
Meta-analysis
Effect size

EXERCISES

14.1   The end-of-year reading level of approximately 1000 first-grade students of a city school system is to be estimated. The entire population cannot be tested. Discuss how sampling and inferring from statistics to parameters would be used. Identify the statistic and parameter involved in this situation. Reconstruct the chain of reasoning used to arrive at some conclusion about the the level of the entire first-grade population.

14.2   Distinguish between a statistic and a parameter in the context of inferential statistics. Discuss the role of the sampling distribution. Describe what is meant by a sampling distribution, and give an example of a sampling distribution.

14.3   Suppose a group of 150 teacher education students has been measured on three measures of scholastic achievement and a measure of performance on a professional knowledge exam. Thus, there are four dependent variables. In connection with what research questions would we do the following:

   a.   Compute only descriptive statistics for the four dependent variables?
   b.   Use inferential statistics?
   c.   Compute correlation coefficients between pairs of the dependent variables?

14.4   The mean science achievement on an objective test of a ninth-grade student population is hypothesized to be 85. A sample of twenty students is randomly selected from the population and given the science test. A *t*-test is then computed using the sample data, and the *t*-value is found to be 3.12. Using the .05 level of significance, find the appropriate *t*-distribution and decide whether or not you would reject the hypothesis. What value of *t* is necessary to reject the hypothesis at the .05 level?

14.5   A researcher is estimating the mean performance score of a large fifth-grade population on a science achievement test. A large sample size of 400 is selected and tested, and the sample mean is found to be 88. A 95 percent of confidence interval is constructed to be 86.5 to 89.5. Suppose the standard deviation of the population was estimated by the sample standard deviation. What is the appropriate sampling distribution for constructing the interval? Would this sampling distribution change if the sample size had been 25? If so, how? Suppose, with the given mean, the researcher had constructed a confidence interval of 85.5 to 89.5. Do you think there might have been an error, and if so, why? If a 90 percent confidence interval had been constructed, would this interval be shorter or longer than three units?

14.6   A study is being done in which the professional attitudes of four different populations of teachers are being surveyed. Random samples are selected from the populations and measured on an attitude inventory that has interval scale measurement. Thus, means are computed for all samples. An analysis of variance is used to analyze the data. What is the null hypothesis being tested? Suppose we are interested not only in differences in attitudes among the four populations, but also in differences between male and female teachers. Could the possibility of such a difference be determined in the same analysis? If so, explain how the ANOVA would be extended.

14.7   Suppose we have a variable measured on an ordinal scale with five categories. Four independent samples are measured on this variable. The hypothesis is that these four samples were drawn from a common population. A chi-square test is computed and found to be statistically significant at α = .05. What is the conclusion about the populations from which the samples were selected? Give the associated probability statement.

14.8   Suppose in Exercise 14.7 the variable is attitude toward school and that the four samples were students selected from grades four through seven. (The data are in a 5×4 contingency table.) State the hypothesis of independence. If the χ^2 test is significant at $\alpha = .05$, what is the conclusions? What if the χ^2 test is not statistically significant?

14.9   For the following situations, identify the descriptive statistics or the statistical test that would be computed. If a statistical test is used, identify the hypothesis being tested.

   a. All fifth-grade students in a school are measured with an achievement test, and the teachers want to know where the scores are located on the scale of measurement and the spread of the scores. The test scores have interval scale measurement.

   b. Math test scores are available for all students in a junior high school, and an attitude-toward school inventory is administered to the entire student body. The teachers want to know if there is a relationship between math test performance and attitude.

   c. A random sample of fifty students enrolled in a high school is administered a math test and an attitude-toward-school inventory. The teachers want to know if there is a relationship between math test performance and attitude.

   d. An experimenter selects a random sample of one hundred individuals and randomly assigns twenty-five to each of four experimental treatments. After participating in the treatments, the individuals perform a cognitive task that is measured on an interval scale. The parametric assumptions are met. The experimenter wants to know if the treatments have differing effects on ability to perform the task.

   e. Researchers measure a random sample of 200 students, aged 8 to 17 years, on a physical performance test. They want to know if the population distribution of test scores is uniformly distributed, that is, follows a flat, box like distribution.

14.10 Define the two possible types of errors in hypothesis testing. Why is there always a possibility of making an error when a decision is made about a hypothesis in inferential statistics?

14.11 Briefly review the meaning of a correlation coefficient and describe how the correlation coefficient can be used as a descriptive statistic and how it can be used in inferential statistics.

14.12 A researcher tests the performance of two random samples of individuals on a task. The performance of each is scored as poor, fair, good, or excellent. A t-test for the difference between means is then computed on the sample data. This result is interpreted as being significant at the .01 level but not at the .05 level. However, it is decided to reject the null hypothesis and conclude that the sample measures are in fact different. The researcher is then concerned about the probability of having made a Type II error. There are several errors in reasoning and procedures in this example. Identify these errors.

14.13 A researcher conducts an experiment in which there are five experimental treatments. The dependent variable is a performance score measured on an interval scale. Twenty individuals are assigned at random to each of the experimental treatments. The data are analyzed by an ANOVA and the summary ANOVA table is as follows:

Source	SS	*df*	MS	*F*-value
Between Exp. Treatments	122.76	4	30.69	3.11
Within Exp. Treatments	937.65	95	9.87	
Total	1060.41	99		

a. What is the null hypothesis tested by this ANOVA?

b. Using the .05 level of significance, complete the statistical test of the ANOVA. Give the conclusion about the null hypothesis.

c. Give the probability statement after the completion of the ANOVA.

14.14 In the research literature, review a report that includes inferential statistics for the analysis of the data. Identify the hypotheses tested and the statistical procedures for testing the hypotheses. Were those procedures appropriate? Were the conclusions from the statistical analyses appropriate? Is the author's chain of reasoning in using inferential statistics apparent and correct?

14.15 Briefly review the chain of reasoning in hypothesis testing. Consider such points as the meanings of statistic and parameter, the probability, and the inference to the population.

14.16 In the research literature, identify a report of a meta-analysis. (Journals, such as the *Review of Educational Research,* are good sources.) Review the meta-analysis. Does it seem to be well done? How many studies were included? Is effect size discussed? Do the summary conclusions follow from the results of the individual studies reviewed?

NOTES

1. The standard deviation of the sampling distribution of the mean also is called the *standard error of the mean.* In general, the term *standard error* is used in inferential statistics to indicate the standard deviation of the sampling distribution of a statistic.

2. This probability statement is not quite technically correct. If there is a 95 percent confidence level, for example, and if all possible intervals for a given sample size are constructed, 95 percent of those intervals would span the population mean. In practice, for a specific problem, only one interval is constructed, and that interval either does or does not span the population mean. However, there is 95 percent confidence that it does span the population mean.

3. Scores from the same individual in a repeated measures analysis violate this assumption, but there are ways to deal with the lack of independence in the analysis.

4. Estimates of variance in ANOVA are called *mean squares,* commonly symbolized by MS.

5. In this situation, the parametric assumption of independence of the observations is violated, since the students are measured seven times. The ANOVA would have to be computed as a repeated measures analysis. It is not necessary to provide the computational details of such an analysis here, since we are focusing on the interpretation of results.

REFERENCES

Bourhis, J., and Allen, M. (1992). Meta-analysis of the relationship between communication apprehension and cognitive performance. *Communication Education,* 41, 68–76.

Cook, T.D., Cooper, H.M., Cordray, D.S., Hartman, H., Hedges, L.V., Light, R.J., Louis, T.A., and Mosteller, F. (1992). *Meta-analysis for explanation: A casebook.* Newbury Park, CA: Sage.

Glass, G.V. (1976). Primary, secondary, and meta-analysis of research. *Educational Researcher,* 5(10), 3–8.

Glass, G.V. (1977). Integrating findings: The meta-analysis of research. In L. Shulman (Ed.), *Review of research in education,* Itasca, IL: Peacock Publishers.

Glass, G.V., McGraw, F., and Smith, M.L. (1981). *Meta-analysis in social research.* Beverly Hills, CA: Sage.

Gottman, J.M., and Glass, G.V. (1978). Analysis of interrupted time-series experiments. In T.R. Kratochwill (Ed.), *Single subject research: Strategies for evaluating change.* New York: Academic Press.

Lirgg, C.D. (1991). Gender differences in self-confidence in physical activity: A meta-analysis of recent studies. *Journal of Sport and Exercise Psychology, 8,* 294–310.

Mason, E.J., and Bramble, W.J. (1989). *Understanding and conducting research: Applications in educa-tion and the behavioral sciences* (2nd ed.). New York: McGraw-Hill.

McCain, L.J., and McCleary, R. (1979). The statistical analysis of the simple interrupted time-series quasi-experiment. In T.D. Cook and D.T. Campbell (Eds.), *Quasi-experimentation: Design and analysis issues for field settings* (pp. 233–294). Chicago: Rand McNally.

Chapter *15*

Communicating About Research

This text emphasizes how to do educational research; it describes the methods and procedures that apply to the various types of research. A part of doing research is communicating about research. Much of the communication takes place through the written word, such as research proposals and reports, although there also is some verbal communication, for example, through presentations at conferences. Formal communication is focused at two points: at the beginning of the research endeavor with a research proposal and at the close with a research report.

Sooner or later, graduate students prepare theses or dissertations, which have been preceded by proposals for the research reported in them. Funding agencies require proposals and reports, and publishing in professional journals is certainly widespread. Thus, the use of the written word in communicating about educational research is extensive.

This chapter discusses two types of written documents: the research proposal, which involves writing about intended research, and the research report, which describes completed research. Although there is a difference of intent, research proposals and reports do have many common characteristics. Within each there also is variation, especially in length, depending on such factors as the extent of the research, the audience for whom it is being prepared, and, if funded, the requirements of the specific funding agency. Although the general format may be similar, there are some differences between proposals and reports prepared for qualitative research and those for quantitative research. It is not feasible to include an entire proposal, journal article, or dissertation in this chapter, but the focus will be on those characteristics that constitute good proposals and reports.

Graduate students, especially those in doctoral programs, are required to defend their research proposals and completed dissertations, usually before faculty committees. Such defense involves verbal exchange. Presenting papers or giving other presentations at professional conferences and meetings is another form of verbal communication, although it involves more telling and not so much discussion as a dissertation defense. Some suggestions and guidelines are given for these types of communication.

Major Sections of the Research Proposal

Preparing a research proposal involves writing about a proposed rather than a completed research project. In proposal writing, we discuss what research is contemplated, why it is being contemplated, and how we intend to do it. The sections of the research proposal reflect answers to these assertions. The headings and subheadings within the research proposal may differ somewhat for different institutions or agencies. For example, some may require a section entitled "Procedures," others "Description of Activities," and still others "Methodology." Sometimes, a "Narrative" section is suggested for which the writer can supply subheadings. However, there is a general format for the content of a research proposal that develops a logical sequence from the statement of the problem in an adequate context and continues through concluding sections, which often provide a justification for the research. (Concluding sections for proposals submitted to funding agencies usually consist of budgets and resumes of the researchers.)

Research proposals discuss what research is intended, how it is intended to be done, and why the research is intended; the sections of the proposal are then directed to these issues.

Research proposals vary in length depending on a variety of factors, including the magnitude of the proposed research and the complexity of the intended procedures. However, the general format and sectioning or proposals are consistent and an outline for the sections of a research proposal is provided in Figure 15.1. Proposals generally follow this format in order, although in some cases topics may be interchanged. For example, sometimes a major section called "Introduction" is used with such subheadings as "Identification of the Problem" and "Definition of Terms." The significance of the proposed research may be discussed earlier in the proposal. In some instances, a discussion of need for the research is included early in the proposal.

The topics for the major body of the research proposal are contained between the dashed lines in Figure 15.1. Usually, preliminary information is required in the form of a cover page that consists of the title of the proposed research, the names of the investigators, and the institution or agency where it will be conducted. An abstract also may be required.

The same general criteria apply for all sections of a research proposal. Writing should be concise, with continuity between and within the sections. The description of what is to be done should be comprehensive but not wordy. The sections should be arranged so that the reader can follow the train of thought. At this point, comments will be made about the various sections.

Cover Page ⎤
Abstract ⎦   Preliminary information as required

– – – – – – – – – – – – – – – – – –

Identification of the Research Problem ⎫
    Introduction   ⎬ What research is
    Definition of Terms   intended
Review of the Literature ⎭

Methodology or Procedures ⎫
    Design   ⎬ How the research will
    Data Collection Procedures   be done
    Data Analysis ⎭

Significance of the Proposed Research ⎫
             ⎬ Why tho roooaroh io
    Anticipated Outcomes   intended
    Relevance to Education ⎭

– – – – – – – – – – – – – – – – – –

(Other items as required)
    Budget
    Staff Resumes
    Appendices

FIGURE 15.1   **General Outline for the Sections of a Research Proposal**

Identification of the Problem

Considerable discussion about stating research problems and hypotheses was presented in an earlier chapter, and those comments are not repeated here. It is important in a proposal that the problem stand out—that the reader can easily recognize it. Sometimes, obscure and poorly formulated problems are masked in an extended discussion, and a reviewer has difficulty recognizing the problem. If that happens, the remainder of the proposal suffers severely in the review.

The extent of the elaboration of the problem varies with the magnitude of the intended study. Research studies on the qualitative end of the research continuum tend to have somewhat more general problem statements than those for quantitative research.

Experiments and surveys typically have explicit, stated hypotheses, whereas ethnographic research, for example, may have foreshadowed problems.

The statement of the problem typically comes very early in the research proposal. There are usually some introductory comments, possibly including a few references to the related literature, to provide a context for stating the research problem. Then the problem is explicitly identified. The introductory phrase may be one of the following:

The problem of this proposed research is . . .
The research question to be addressed is . . .
The purpose of the research is . . .
Specifically, the research problem is . . .

The related hypotheses and/or research questions and operational definitions then follow in the proposal, usually quite closely. Occasionally, the hypotheses statements may appear later in the proposal if the measurement and data description might enhance the understanding of the hypotheses. However, unless somewhat unusual data are to be generated and uncommon analysis procedures are to be used, there is no point in separating the statement of the problem and the hypotheses.

Because both research reports and proposals require identification of the problems, examples can be selected from the research literature. Kuh (1993) identified the problem and three research questions as:

> *The purpose of this study was to discover, by asking undergraduates to reflect on their college years, the impact of out-of-class experiences on their learning and personal development. Three research questions guided the study: (a) What did students learn from their experiences outside the classroom? (b) In what ways have they changed since starting college? and (c) Do the outcomes considered by students to be important differ by type of institution attended and student background characteristics? (p. 279)*

Like any problem statement, this must be presented within a context and such a context is provided, including a discussion of the conceptual framework about what happens to students during college.

This example of an ethnographic research problem statement is taken from Dillon (1989, p. 227):

> *The purpose of this ethnographic study was to construct a description and interpretation of the social organization of one rural secondary, low-track English-reading classroom using an inducive analysis of the actions of, and interactions between, the low socioeconomic predominantly black students and their white male teacher.*

This problem statement describes the context for the study and it also identifies the general analysis approach. Although the author does not identify foreshadowed problems specifically, some are implied in the introduction. The social organization of the classroom and effective teaching and meaningful learning were mentioned, along with the theoretical underpinnings of symbolic interactionism (p. 228).

As necessary, terms used in describing the research problem should be defined, especially any terms that otherwise may be ambiguous. However, the identification of the problem should not become too cluttered with operational definitions. Such definitions of variables to be measured can be provided in the methodology section, where the measurement is described, rather than in the statement of the problem, especially if operational definitions are somewhat complex.

Review of the Literature

The review of the literature provides the background and context for the research problem. Proposals may vary considerably in the length of the review. Dissertation proposals often contain fifteen or more double-spaced pages in the review. In any event, it is seldom, if ever, possible to include every potentially relevant study in the review. Thus, the proposal writer must be selective. The following points are important to remember in preparing the review:

1. Select studies that relate most directly to the problem at hand.

2. Tie together the results of the studies so that their relevance is clear. Do not simply provide a compendium of references, devoting a paragraph or two to each without connecting the ideas and results.

3. When conflicting findings are reported across studies—and this is quite common in educational research—carefully examine the variations in the findings and possible explanations for them. Ignoring variation and simply averaging effects loses information and fails to recognize the complexity of the problem.

4. Make the case that the research area reviewed is incomplete or requires extension. This establishes the need for research in this area. (*Note:* This does not make the case that the proposed research is going to meet the need or is of significance.)

5. Although information from the literature must be properly referenced, do not make the review a series of quotations.

6. The review should be organized according to the major points relevant to the problem. Do not force the review into a chronological organization, for example, which may confuse the relevance and continuity among the studies reviewed.

7. Give the reader some indication of the relative importance of results from studies reviewed. Some results have more bearing on the problem than others, and this should be indicated.

8. Provide closure for this section. Do not terminate with comments from the final study reviewed. Provide a summary and pull together the most important points.

With survey and experimental research, those on the quantitative end of the research continuum, results from studies reviewed and specific results can be incorporated into the review. For qualitative research, such as ethnographic research, the review will tend to focus on more general or broad concepts. For example, the researcher might identify possible theoretical concepts that may become useful during data collection and analysis. As McMillan and Schumacher (1989, p. 520) point out, this is a preliminary review that explicitly describes the conceptual framework with which the researcher enters the field. The review should justify the need for an in-depth descriptive study. Possibly the phenomena have not been studied using a qualitative approach, and the case can be made that such an approach is appropriate and useful. If the approach has been used, it is necessary to identify gaps and deficiencies in other studies.

Some authors (McMillan & Schumacher, 1989, for example) recommend addressing the significance of the study in the review of literature section. This is appropriate in that the need for the study should be discussed here, and need is related to significance. When the case for significance is particularly crucial, such as in a dissertation proposal, it is a good idea to have a special section in addition to any comments about significance in the review. If that section is placed near the end of the proposal, the proposal reader is better informed about the research, and the case for significance may be stronger.

One of the marks of a knowledgeable reviewer is the ability to select pertinent information, tie it together to provide an understandable and accurate background for the problem, and demonstrate the continuity between the ideas in the literature and the research problem. The proposal writer should avoid statements implying that information on the problem is very limited or that the review has revealed no information about the problem. The proposal reader will be very suspicious of such statements (and rightly so) and will likely interpret them as a lack of knowledge on the part of the writer rather than as a gap in the literature. The review of literature should reveal that the writer has a good grasp of the area in which research is intended.

> The review of the literature provides the background and context for the research problem. It should establish the need for the research and indicate that the writer is knowledgeable about the area.

Methods or Procedures

This section of the research proposal will vary considerably depending on the type of proposed research. It will vary not only in content but in length. To the extent that subheadings are appropriate, it is well to use them. Subheadings such as "Design," "Site Selection," "Sample," and "Data Analysis" will not only aid the writer in identifying and describing the various activities, but should also help the proposal reader understand the continuity of the various activities.

In an ethnographic research proposal this section should address the following issues:

1. Site selection and any sampling, purposeful or random, that will be done at the site.
2. The role of the researcher.

3. Data-collection procedures: observation, interviewing, use of questionnaires, and the application of triangulation.

4. Presentation of data and inductive data analysis.

5. Limitations of the design.

When describing the site selection, the case must be made that the site will provide an appropriate setting for the research. To do this, it is helpful to show the correspondence between the foreshadowed problems and the characteristics of the site. For example, if a foreshadowed problem deals with social interaction, then the site must provide an opportunity to observe social interaction. If key informants are to be used, then make the case why certain types of individuals can assume this role.

The role of the researcher, for example, privileged observer, should be described along with possible data-collection procedures. It should be clear that multiple methods will be used, and that results will be validated through triangulation, but the specific methods (items, etc.,) will be identified in the field. The anticipated length of the data collection should be stated, along with its intensity. For example, will the researcher be on site every day, three days per week? On a given day will data collection take place for one hour, several hours?

Ethnographic research involves field notes along with other data, so there should be a description of how this information will be analyzed, even if only a general, inductive analysis is described. What are possible category systems or ways of ordering the data? The reader should be given some indication of the extent of the anticipated descriptive analysis: the ethnography that will be the product of this research.

Regardless of the type of research, the limitations of the design should be described. If limitations are not addressed specifically, the proposal reader may well infer that the researcher is expecting results from the study that are not possible. Restricting the statement of the research problem will aid in defining the limits of the design. The extent of generalizability should be addressed in this section. Extensive generalizability typically is more important for quantitative research than for qualitative research.

Ethnographic and historical research are, to a large extent, case studies: not necessarily of individuals, but of a site, an issue, a phenomenon, or an event. As such, it is well to identify the research as a case study which cues the reader to expect certain design characteristics. For more quantitative research, the design can be described by a specific name. For example:

> *A pretest-posttest control group design will be used involving four groups, three experimental and one control, with sex and grade level included as independent variables giving a 4 × 2 × 4 factorial design.*

Many designs have relatively common usage in the research literature, and their descriptive titles can be used. A title can be coined for a design so long as it is descriptive and appropriate.

For experiments and surveys, as applicable, the following project activities, materials, and so forth should be described in this section in addition to the general research design:

1. Measurement instruments to be used or developed.
2. Individuals participating in the research (subjects).
3. Sample (design and numbers).
4. Experimental procedure if the intended project is an experiment.
5. Data-collection procedures.
6. Data analysis (specific analyses to be used).

If there are potential weaknesses in the design or potential difficulties in doing the research, the writer should describe what will be done to compensate for or eliminate them. For example, there might be the possibility of extraneous variables being confounded with independent variables. Their possible effects should be discussed, and the discussion should indicate how they will be controlled or eliminated. Occasionally, writers are under the misconception that it is sufficient to identify a difficulty without providing a solution. Identifying a potential problem is not the same as solving it and, certainly, indicating that nothing can be done about the problem is no solution.

The matter of sampling is an example of the need for specific detail. The sampling plan must be viewed in terms of the external and internal validity of the research project. When sampling is used, the researcher invariably is attempting to make inferences to a larger population, so care must be taken in selecting the sample so that it represents the population.

In a study involving a sample of high school seniors from a single state, for example, it is not adequate to say that a random sample of seniors will be selected from the high schools of the state; the sampling plan should be described in detail. Assuming an adequate operational definition of a high school senior, the writer should indicate how all members of the population will be identified. What types of information will be available that will include all seniors who fit the definitions? Are stratifying variables to be used? If so, what are they and why are they important? Will it be necessary to sample through an intermediate unit? What will the replacement procedure be if selected units decline to participate?

These types of questions should be carefully answered. For example, if stratified random sampling with proportional allocation is the sampling design, the stratifying variables should be operationally defined, and it should be clear to the reader that students can be identified in terms of stratifying variables from the population information. It would not be adequate to indicate simply that size of district will be a stratifying variable. The definition of the categories for the stratifying variable would have to be given—for example, less than 2000 students, 2000–5000 students, and so on. Information should be provided about the source, probably a state document, on which the size of the district will be based, and it would be well to provide a rationale for the specific categories of the stratifying variable. A complete description of this type will provide the reader with evidence regarding how and why the sample will be selected.

The discussion of the procedures usually follows a somewhat chronological order of how they will be done. This makes it easier for the reader to recognize the continuity of the various procedures. If the intended research is adequately conceptualized by the proposal writers, they should be able to explain what they intend to do. The important thing is to have an appropriate and complete description.

> The methods or procedures section is really the heart of the research proposal. The activities should be described with as much detail as possible, and the continuity between them should be apparent.

Significance of the Proposed Research

Although empirical results certainly may be important, research is seldom conducted solely for the purpose of generating data. Regardless of the type of research, the study should contribute to the extension of knowledge in the area. Gaps in the existing knowledge may be filled, and the present study may answer questions raised by preceding research studies. Correspondingly, one contribution of a study is the suggestion or identification of questions for future research.

Other anticipated outcomes relate to the practical significance of the research. What will the research results mean to the practicing educator? Will the results, regardless of outcome, influence programs or methods? If the research will set the stage for deciding on alternative courses of action for improving education, this can be a significant contribution. What will be improved or changed as the result of the proposed research? How will the results of the study be implemented, and what innovations will come about?

Answers to these questions suggest outcomes that may take different forms. One outcome, in ethnographic research, for example, is a detailed description, an ethnography, of a naturalistic, educational phenomenon. Possibly the description will generate a theoretical explanation of the phenomenon. If such an outcome is anticipated, it should be mentioned in this section.

A revised curriculum or a description of how a segment of a curriculum in a specific area might be changed are examples of outcomes. Another product might be a process for the improvement of learning. A program is a possible product, such as one for dealing with disruptive behavior or reducing the number of dropouts. The research in and of itself may not generate a curriculum or program—these would likely have to be developed after the research is completed—but the research provides the basis for such development. It is important to indicate the potential relevance of the research to such outcomes.

Results of research may be useful for policy formation. For example, a school board may use survey results for determining board policy. When research is conducted on the roles of educational specialists, especially relatively new ones such as computer education specialists, the results can aid in the identification of necessary skills and in the definition of the role.

The case for the relevance to education is made, to some extent, when the need for the research is established through the review of the literature. When discussing the significance of the research, it is important to indicate how the anticipated results of this research will tie in to the research results already reported in the literature. The proposal writer should not hesitate to use previously cited or additional references at this point.

The relevance of the research problem to education is pretty well established through the review of the literature and the background for the problem. The case for the results being relevant to education rests on the effects of the anticipated outcomes. If these outcomes have potential benefit or impact, either practically or theoretically, the case can be made. Since this connection exists, the potential relevance to education depends on the likelihood that the anticipated outcomes will be attained.

The significance of the proposed research will be established on the basis of the anticipated outcomes, which may be in the form of products or processes.

Other Sections of the Research Proposal

The sections of a research proposal described thus far comprise the major parts or body of the proposal, but other sections may be appropriate for specific proposals. Indeed, funding agencies often require certain routine informational sections and, certainly, a budget. Brief comments on these sections are provided here.

Cover Page.   The cover page contains introductory information for the proposal: the names of the proposed project, the author of the proposal or principal investigator, and the institution. Some funding agencies have standardized cover pages that may contain additional information, such as a budget total.

Abstract.   An abstract is a brief summary statement of the proposal content. At the very least, it contains a statement of the research problem. Abstracts usually are limited to a maximum number of words; seldom do they exceed one page.

Budget.   When a proposal is submitted to a funding agency, a budget is required; it is usually placed near the end of the proposal. When a budget is prepared, the proposal writer should use the guidelines of the funding agency to which the proposal will be submitted and those of the institution through which it is being submitted. This should take care of such matters as overhead and benefit rates. Failure to follow guidelines usually results in considerable budget recalculation later and, possibly, unanticipated negotiations. An inappropriate or poorly constructed budget may result in rejection of the proposal.

Research conducted for theses and dissertations, usually is not externally funded, so budget preparation is not a concern. A graduate student may be doing research for a dissertation through some larger, externally funded project. However, in such situations a separate budget is seldom developed for the dissertation research.

Staff Resumes.   Staff resumes or vitae consist of summaries of the experience, education, publications, and research activities of individuals who will work on the proposed project. Again, resumes are commonly required for externally funded research.

Appendices.   If there is considerable supplementary information that may be relevant to the proposal content, it can be placed in an appendix. Appendices contain information that would distract from the continuity of the proposal if it were contained in the main body of the proposal. In a proposal submitted for external funding, an appendix might contain a description of the resources of the researcher's institution, such as the library and computer facilities.

The Evaluation of Proposals

When a graduate student submits a proposal for research (dissertation or other) typically it is reviewed by a professor or a committee of professors. The usual criteria of a relevant problem, evidence of knowledge in the area, appropriate methodology, and good continuity in the proposal apply when a proposal is reviewed. Funding agencies also develop criteria for the evaluation of proposals, and these often appear in guidelines for proposal preparation.

Evaluation criteria of funding agencies are quite general and quite similar across agencies. Except for special criteria, such as the reasonableness of the budget, the evaluation criteria of funding agencies are similar to those for any proposal, including a dissertation proposal. The evaluation focuses primarily on two characteristics: (1) the significance of the proposed research and (2) the quality of the proposed research. The following kinds of issues are considered in evaluating proposals relative to those two characteristics:

Significance of the Proposed Research

1. Contribution to basic knowledge relevant to the solution of educational problems.
2. Contribution to educational theory.
3. Contribution to the development of methodological tools, either for educational practice or research.
4. Contribution to the solution of educational problems, either long range or short range.
5. The potential generalizability of anticipated results.
6. The potential of anticipated results to influence the improvement of educational practice.

Quality of the Proposed Research

1. The extent to which the writer shows a thorough knowledge of relevant prior research.
2. The extent to which prior research is related to the proposed research.
3. The comprehensiveness and appropriateness of the research design.

4. The appropriateness of the instrumentation and the methodology.

5. The appropriateness of the anticipated analyses.

6. The likelihood that the proposed research can be completed successfully as described.

Funding agencies usually consider the qualifications of the principal investigator and other research project staff, and they may require a statement about facilities and resources available to the researcher. The reasonableness of the budget has already been mentioned. However, this characteristic usually receives few points, because budgets can be negotiated if they do not seem appropriate to fiscal officers of the funding agency.

Implicit criteria also are applied in evaluating any proposal. The writing should be technically correct and neat. The content of the proposal should be well organized, and there should be good continuity from section to section and within sections. Generally accepted formats, including sizes of margins and spacing, should be followed.

The preparation of a good research proposal is no small task. When submitting a proposal to a funding agency, it is important to follow the proposal preparation guidelines of that agency. Some agencies do not have guidelines; they will accept any standard format. Private foundations and funding programs within large agencies often fund projects for specific purposes or only in certain areas. It is important to be aware of these limitations; there is little point in submitting proposals that do not correspond to agency interest.

When submitting a proposal for dissertation research, it is important to describe as much of the procedural detail as possible. The proposed research should be within the capabilities, resources, and time of the researcher. Thinking things through carefully will avoid difficulties and delays later.

Major Sections of the Research Report

One distinguishing characteristic of the different types of research reports is length. The professional journal article may vary from five to twenty pages, occasionally longer, especially for reports of qualitative research. Restrictions of space for individual publications limit the length of journal articles. Dissertations and technical reports submitted to funding agencies usually are longer, commonly around one hundred pages and, in some cases, considerably longer. (Sometimes appendices contain substantial amounts of supplementary information that increase the length.) The length of a paper prepared for a professional meeting depends on the time allocated for presentation. However, such papers tend to be similar in length to journal articles, and many papers later appear as journal articles.

Even with the different types of research reports, there are some common characteristics in the way they are organized and presented. The sections follow, to some extent, the same sequence as those in a research proposal. However, a research report contains sections dealing with results and conclusions, which are not found in a proposal. In a proposal, there is a great deal of emphasis on how the research will be done. The emphasis for a report shifts to the results and the implications of those results.

In a *research report*, the writer describes completed research. There are discussions of what research was done, how it was done, and the results and conclusions of the research. The significance of the research also is addressed.

The sections of the research report begin with the identification of the problem and continue through the conclusions and implications. The sections have different formats for different types of reports. For dissertations or long reports, they usually take the form of chapters, whereas journal articles and papers commonly contain headings. Typically, dissertations contain five or so chapters, beginning with an introduction that contains the statement of the research problem, the review of literature, a methods chapter, a results chapter, and a final chapter of conclusions and recommendations. A dissertation about a qualitative research study may be organized differently with more integration of method, results, and conclusions. A journal article runs together the introduction and review and emphasizes the results and conclusions.

The general criteria for preparing a good proposal also apply to writing a good research report. Additional comments on the major sections of a research report are provided here.

Introduction, Including the Statement of the Problem

A dissertation usually has a several-page buildup to the problem statement, providing quite a complete introduction to the research. If hypotheses are appropriate, they too are introduced at this point. Articles in professional journals do not have space for a long buildup to the problem, so the context for the research must be established concisely. This introduction may include a brief review of the literature as well, unless the article deals with historical research or, for some reason, the results of numerous other studies must be brought in.

Problem statements were given in the section on writing proposals, and two more examples will be given here. In a study concerning teachers' grading practices, and the meanings and values associated with such practices, Brookhart (1993) identifies the research problem in terms of three questions:

The research questions for this study were designed to address both the meaning (Question 1) and values (Question 2) issues as well as the degree to which these questions are related to instruction in measurement (Question 3).

1. *What meaning do teachers wish to convey when they assign grades to their students? That is, for teachers, what is the nature of the construct* grade?
2. *To what degree are value judgments part of the grading process? What kinds of value judgments do teachers make when assigning their grades?*
3. *Do the construct meaning and value judgments underlying grades vary with whether or not the teacher has had instruction in educational measurement? (p. 124)*

Before describing the methods used in conducting the research, Brookhart discusses Messick's theory of validity applied to grading. This discussion provides an extended context for the research, in addition to the context provided prior to listing the research questions.

Stanovich and Cunningham (1993) conducted a study on associations between print exposure and information acquisition. The subjects for the study were 268 college students. The research problem was identified as:

> *In this study we examined whether individual differences in print exposure—and differences in exposure to other media—can account for individual differences in acquired declarative knowledge. Our test of the cognitive efficiency hypothesis occurs in the context of a research program in individual differences in quantity of reading. (p. 212)*

Earlier in the report, the authors provide a well-documented background of cognitive efficiency explanations for knowledge acquisition.

Review of the Literature

In professional journal articles, the literature review often does not have a separate heading; it is incorporated with the introduction and background. Because of space limitations, the writer must make decisions about which references to include and cite. The pertinent information must then be provided succinctly and tied together to provide a context for the problem.

As indicated earlier, dissertations typically have an entire chapter reserved for the review of the literature, which may cover thirty-five or more double-spaced pages. The headings in the chapter are specific to the study. Of course, the number of headings will vary. Qualitative studies that rely heavily on description tend to have fewer headings than quantitative studies, the latter having as many as ten or twelve headings. The important characteristic is not the number of headings, but the way the headings are placed to partition the review into appropriate segments.

The ideas from the various studies referred to in the review should relate to each other, as should the parts designated by the headings. This is called transition, and transition is facilitated by keeping the writing focused on the research problem. A common error is to present ideas from individual studies as little packages within themselves, which makes for a disjointed presentation. A related error is to treat each study in a mechanical way, regardless of relative importance.

The writer should avoid excessive use of quotations. In the context of the research problem, the ideas from several sources usually can be tied together better by the writer's own words than by a series of quotations. The ideas from the review of the literature should be integrated into a logical discussion focusing on the research problem.

The writer is not obligated to discuss information from every source listed in the bibliography. Often, in an article, three or four main points are brought in from an equal number of sources. Additional references may be listed in the bibliography to complement the information from the sources discussed. In the discussion of the review of the literature, the writer should demonstrate an adequate knowledge of the problem and the research related to it. An extensive bibliography with almost no discussion is not evidence of an adequate review of literature.

Methods or Procedures

The parts of this section describe how the research was done. How much description is necessary? A good rule to follow is that the description should be detailed enough so that a reader could replicate the study. Descriptions in dissertations tend to be very detailed, because the writer is demonstrating mastery of the methodology as well as the appropriateness of the methods used.

Consider the introductory paragraph of the methods section from the ethnographic study of Dillon (1989) referenced earlier:

> *The school site, as well as the teacher and students in the observed classroom, were chosen in a purposive manner (Miles and Hubermann, 1984; Patton, 1980) during an exploratory research phase prior to the study proper (Alvermann and Hayes, 1989). This exploratory phase served several functions: (a) I gained access to the school site and identified the teacher and class of students I wanted to study, (b) I collected initial data, and (c) I started to build the trusting, teacher–researcher and student–researcher collaborative relationship needed for ethnographic research. The classroom was located in a consolidated high school set in a rural area in the southeastern part of the United States (p. 231).*

Note the narrative description, and the author also documents her procedures, reinforcing the case for their appropriateness. The entire methods section is about six pages long, with three major headings: "Selection of Site and Participants," "A Description of the Site and Participants" and "Researcher Role, Data Collection and Analysis." All of this was in descriptive narrative form, with the exception of a figure giving the time line for data collection.

In contrast, the methods section in a report of quantitative research by Chalifour and Powers (1989) was slightly longer than one page. The early part of the section describes how a list of content characteristics was developed. Then the analysis was identified as follows:

> *The primary method of analysis was multiple regression analysis using each of two dependent variables. The dependent variables were:*
>
> 1. *item difficulty, as reflected by the delta index, a normalized transformation of the percentage answering each item correctly, and*
> 2. *item discrimination, as reflected by biserial correlations of each item with a total analytical score (transformed to Fisher's z). (p. 124)*

The statistical procedure was then described more fully as to how the variables were placed into the analysis.

Although they are quite different, each of these methods sections is well done and appropriate for the study. The point being made is that methods sections may vary considerably, not only in length and content, but also in the writing approach. Methods sections in qualitative research reports tend to be more descriptive than those in quantitative reports. For quantitative research, statistical procedures are discussed at some point.

Methods sections show a lot of variability across research reports in length, content, and the writing approach. The important criterion is that enough information is given so the reader can understand what was done.

The methods section describes instrumentation, data collection, sampling, experimental procedure, materials, and statistical analysis as these topics apply. The order of presenting the various topics in a methods section is somewhat arbitrary. One logical order is the sequence in which the activities of the topics occurred in conducting the research. It is possible that two or more of the activities were worked on simultaneously. However, the research project usually progresses from the development of the design and selection of the participants through data analysis.

Results

Results are the products of data analysis and they come in various forms. They may consist of summary statements synthesized from other documents, as in a historical study, or from field notes, as in ethnographic research. When statistical analysis is used, descriptive statistics and those generated by statistical tests are results.

Consider again the ethnographic study reported by Dillon (1989). The results and discussion section covers some seventeen pages, all of it in descriptive form. The opening paragraph sets the tone for how results are reported:

> *The major assertion generated from the data analyses was that the social organization in the observed classroom was constructed jointly by Appleby and his students; Appleby assumed the role of translator and intercultural broker (Erickson, 1986a) during teacher and student interactions. In this role, Appleby worked to bridge students' home culture with school culture. He also interacted with students in ways that met their cognitive and affective needs. Thus, Appleby established an environment in the classroom that resulted in reduced resistance to learning and increased active participation during lessons. (pp. 236–237)*

Dillon continues describing her perceptions based on field notes and interviews. The results section contains direct quotes from interviews with the teacher and selected students. Verbal and nonverbal actions in the classroom are described.

Reporting quantitative results is quite straightforward. An example excerpt from the Chalifour and Powers (1989) report is as follows:

*Generally, the correlations among the variables were relatively low (less than
.20 in absolute value). Only 20 of the total of 741 intercorrelations were greater
than .30 in absolute value. An inspection of the intercorrelation matrix revealed
several clusters of variables that seemed to relate both logically and empirically.
(p. 126)*

The writers then go on discussing various patterns of correlation coefficients. They also
present two tables: one with correlation coefficients representing reliabilities of expert
judgments, and the other containing regression weights for prediction.

Use of Tables

Tables can be used effectively for summarizing results, especially if a report involves a
large amount of statistical material. The content of a table should be clear to the reader.
This may seem to be an obvious statement, but tables are sometimes confusing and puzzle
the reader.

There are some relatively straightforward rules to follow when constructing tables:

1. The title should state specifically what the table contains, including the referent or
source of the content.

2. Appropriate subheadings should be included for rows and columns.

3. The number of different types of information a table contains should be limited. For
example, means and standard deviations may go together, but correlation coefficients
probably would not be included in the same table.

4. Spacing in the table should be such that numbers are clearly separated. Do not crowd.

5. If possible, tables should be limited to a single page. A table that will fit on one page
should not be split over two pages.

6. The table should follow the first reference to it as closely as possible.

7. Table formats should be consistent within a report.

8. An excessive number of lines should not be included. Horizontal lines may be used
to set off headings, but vertical lines are seldom necessary. The information should not
appear as if it is being "caged."

Figure 15.2 contains a sample results table, showing the title and headings. Note that
the title does not simply state that the table includes means and standard deviations; it
indicates the source of the means and standard deviations.

> Tables can be used effectively for summarizing results, but their content must be
> adequately labeled and logically organized.

The important concern in writing a results section is to present the results in a clear,
well-organized manner. Results can be organized in a number of ways. For example, when

Table 0.0
Means and Standard Deviations of Fifth-Grade Students
on Academic Measures

Measure	Experimental Group 1		Experimental Group 2		Control Group	
	Mean	Standard Deviation	Mean	Standard Deviation	Mean	Standard Deviation
Reading						
Arithmetic						
Spelling						
Science						
Social Studies						

FIGURE 15.2   Example of Title and Headings for a Table Containing Results

reporting on an ethnographic study, one possible organization is around foreshadowed problems. Or the results may be presented in a sequential narrative describing what happened. If several dependent variables are included in the study, the results may be grouped according to dependent variables—for example, grouping achievement measures separate from attitude measures. Sometimes, results are reported in the order of the hypotheses, if there are specific hypotheses. If several experiments were included in a study, the results could be organized in the order in which the experiments occurred. This is often done in dissertations based on a series of experiments. Whatever organization makes the most sense and facilitates the reader's understanding should be used.

Conclusions, Recommendations, and Implications

The final section of the research report consists of conclusions, recommendations, and implications. Commonly called the "Conclusions" section, it may also go by such names as "Conclusions and Discussion" or "Conclusions and Recommendations." In any event, the term *conclusions* almost invariably appears in the title of the section.

This section usually begins with a brief restatement of the research problem and, possibly, the main points of how the study was done. The conclusions must follow logically from the results and should avoid undesirable repetition of the results section. One common error in dissertations is that the writer is reluctant to draw conclusions and, instead, repeats results and passes them off as conclusions.

> The results of a research study are the products of the data analysis. Conclusions are the inferences and the like that the researcher draws from the results.

The number of conclusions drawn depends in part on the complexity of the results. Supposedly, at least one substantial conclusion can be drawn; otherwise, it hardly would be worth conducting, much less reporting, the research.

The following should be done in preparing the conclusions part of a research report:

1. Identify all noteworthy results in order of importance.

2. Interpret these results relative to the research problem and in the context of related research and/or theory; that is, draw conclusions.

3. Discuss other plausible interpretations of the results and explain why these are less likely than the interpretation of item 2.

4. Tie your results in with results from related research studies.

5. Explain any inconsistencies between your results and results from related research studies.

6. Discuss any limitations of your study, such as design limitations or problems in the procedures of conducting the research.

7. Identify directions for future research questions raised by the study.

8. Address the external validity of the conclusions, being specific about the generalizability of the conclusions and how generalizability may be limited.

9. Provide a summary of the research study.

The extent to which each of these items will be addressed depends on the magnitude of the study. Research conducted for a dissertation typically results in several conclusions, and in the final chapter of the dissertation, there may be an extensive discussion of questions for future research and recommendations for such research. Journal articles, because of space limitations for one reason, usually do not have extensive discussions of questions for future research.

This final section of a research report likely will require more rewriting than earlier sections. Transition and continuity between ideas are especially important in this section. A good procedure is to let the report sit for a few days, then go through it again completely and see if the conclusions still seem reasonable. There also should be a check for possible omissions. Rewriting should take off any "rough edges" and generally improve the quality of writing.

Other Sections of the Research Report

Preliminary sections, such as a title page, a table of contents, and an abstract, often are found in a research report. A bibliography and possibly an appendix often follow the conclusions section. These latter sections are called "backmatter." (A journal article would not contain a table of contents or an appendix and, when published, would not have a separate title page.) The title page usually follows a prescribed format similar to that of the title page of a proposal. Acknowledgments, a table of contents, and any necessary lists are self-explanatory. This leaves the abstract for the preliminary information.

Abstract

The abstract of a research report is similar to that of a research proposal, except that it describes what was done instead of what is contemplated. It contains a brief summary of the results. Again, abstracts can vary in length, depending on the report, but they usually do not exceed one double-spaced typed page.

Many professional journals require abstracts for published reports. These abstracts tend to be quite brief. An example of such an abstract, from Monk and Haller (1993), is as follows:

> *Relationships between high school structural characteristics and curricular of-ferings are examined in this study using survey data from* High School and Beyond. *Emphasis is placed on the role played by high school size. The study's central thesis is that the effects of school size on the curriculum will vary depending on subject area, the character of the course being offered (e.g., advanced versus remedial), and the setting in which the school is located. The influence of other structural features most notably socioeconomic status (ES), unionization, urban location, and grade configuration, are also examined. Find-ings are consistent with the basic proposition that the effects of size are differen-tiated within high schools. The findings have implications for assessments of equality of educational opportunity as well as for the renewed debate over optimal high school size. (p. 3)*

The abstract identifies the sources of the data, which were survey data from a large study. Variables are identified and results are summarized without going into detail.

Biography and Reference List

Toward the end of a research report, following the conclusions section, appears the list of references and, possibly, a bibliography. The American Psychological Association (1983) distinguishes between a reference list and bibliography as follows:

> *Note that a reference list cites works that specifically support a particular article. In contrast, a bibliography cites works for background or for further reading. (p. 111)*

Professional journals commonly require reference lists, not bibliographies. An extensive report such as a dissertation would require a bibliography.

A bibliographic entry contains a full description of the work, the name of the first author, inverted with last name first, followed by the names of co-authors. Titles of books, monographs, and journals are underlined. There are slight variations in format, as suggested in different editorial style sources. One format given in the *Publication Manual of the American Psychological Association* (1983) has all authors' names inverted with last name first, the year of publication following the author(s) names, and article titles with only the first words of the title, subtitles, if any, and proper names capitalized. No quotation marks are placed around articles titles. Sample entries for an article and a book are as follows:

Bell, T. H. (1993). Reflections one decade after *A Nation at Risk*. *Phi Delta Kappa*, 74(8), 592–597.

Sizer, T. R. (1984). *Horace's compromise: The dilemma of the American high school.* Boston: Houghton Mifflin.

The format used by the American Psychological Association is widely accepted, especially among professional journals in the behavioral sciences.

Entries are placed in the bibliography in alphabetical order, using the last name of the first author. If two or more works by the same author are included, the last name is not repeated in subsequent entries but is substituted for by a long dash, followed by a period. The two or more listings for an author are alphabetized by initial letter of the title, excluding "A," "An," or "The." If entries include publications of which the author is sole author and others co-author, those of sole authorship appear first.

Appendix

An appendix is included only if it is necessary—for example, when there are materials that do not fit well in the main body of the report. Several types of materials can be placed in an appendix: self constructed measuring instruments, such as tests or questionnaires; tables of raw scores; or related data. A large volume of related results tends to make the main report cumbersome and difficult reading, and such results can be placed in the appendix. Separate appendices should be used for different types of materials. The appendices appear at the end of the report, following the references or bibliography.

Putting a Report Together

A research report, especially a long one, is seldom conceptualized and written in one sitting. It usually is helpful to work from an outline. Sections often need reworking and rewriting. Generally, revision is a normal part of the task, and the report usually is improved by subsequent revisions, additions, and deletions. Critical reviews (conducted in a positive sense) of initial drafts by knowledgeable colleagues are helpful. Self-criticism or review is also valuable, but it is usually most valuable after the writer has let the report sit for a short time, perhaps a week to ten days. Explanations may not be so obvious and logical as they seemed to be during the initial writing, and omissions and confusing statements may become more apparent.

There are always several technical considerations when preparing a research report. Correct grammar and spelling and accepted uses of tenses are required. The past tense is used to report research findings, both one's own and those reported by others. For example:

> *Students in grades five and seven obtained mean scores of 25.3 and 31.6, respectively.*

The present tense is used to refer to the presentation of data and well-accepted generalizations, for example, "Table 1 contains the mean of all grades, separated by geographic region."

There are acceptable formats for presenting content in a report. Some institutions and associations have their own requirements about such things as margin size, table format, and presentation of graphs and figures. These are technical concerns, and it is simply a matter of knowing the rules and following them. Most institutions will accept any recognized standard format.

There are a number of publications dealing with format and style for preparing reports. The reference desks of most college and university libraries have copies of several such publications. The content of these manuals, guides, or handbooks includes explicit detail about format and style, including how to handle variations of the usual references, and sections. The following are examples of such publications:

American Psychological Association. (1983). *Publication manual of the American Psychological Association* (3rd ed.). Washington, DC: Author.

Campbell, W. G., Ballou, S. V., and Slade, C. (1990). *Form and style: Theses, reports, term papers* (8th ed.). Boston: Houghton Mifflin.

Giltrow, J. L. (1990). *Academic writing: How to read and write scholarly prose.* Lewiston, NY: Broadview Press.

Van Wagenen, R. K. (1991). *Writing a thesis: Substance and style.* Englewood Cliffs, NJ: Prentice-Hall.

Walker, M. (1993). *Writing research papers: A Norton guide* (3rd ed.). New York: W.W. Norton.

Williams, J. M. (1990). *Style: Toward clarity and grace.* Chicago: University of Chicago Press.

This chapter provides an overview on communicating about research, but there are entire books written about the preparation of proposals and research reports including dissertations and theses. For those readers who desire additional resources on this topic, the following books are recommended.

Dees, R. (1993). *Writing the modern research paper.* Boston: Allyn and Bacon.

Furst, E. J. (1990). *The writing requirement for the doctorate in education.* Lanham, MD: University Press of America.

Hubbuch, S. M. (1992). *Writing research papers across the curriculum* (3rd ed). Fort Worth: Harcourt Brace Jovanovich.

Locke, L. F., Spirduso, W. W., and Silverman, S. J. (1993). *Proposals that work: A guide for planning dissertations and grants proposals* (3rd ed). Newbury Park, CA: Sage.

Madsen, D. M. (1992). *Successful dissertations and theses: A guide to graduate student research from proposal to completion* (2nd ed). San Francisco: Jossey-Bass.

Mauch, J. E. (1989). *Guide to the successful thesis and dissertation: Conception to publication: A handbook for students and faculty* (2nd ed). New York: M. Dekker.

Rudestam, K. E., and Newton, R. R. (1992). *Surviving your dissertation: A comprehensive guide to content and process.* Newbury Park, CA: Sage.

Tallent, N. (1993). *Psychological report writing* (4th ed). Englewood Cliffs, NJ: Prentice-Hall.

Software for Word Processing

With the use of personal computers has come the capability of word processing and text editing, which greatly facilitates the mechanics of putting together a report. Like software for statistical analyses, numerous excellent programs for word processing are available. Word processing programs with editing capabilities have become a real boon to researchers when writing about research. They provide the researcher with the capability to automate what is often a difficult part of any project—actual presentation of a coherent and formally professional study. Following is a listing of the functions that are automated by word processors:

1. Online checks of spelling.
2. Providing online thesaurus.
3. Printing/nonprinting comment boxes for reviewing work.
4. Red-lining of text changes.
5. Automatic generation of footnotes.
6. Automatic generation of endnotes.
7. Automatic recalculation of numbering of footnotes and endnotes.
8. Automatic generation of indexes.
9. Automatic generation of table of contents.
10. Boilerplating paragraphs.
11. Cutting and pasting for easy shifting of paragraphs or whole pages.
12. Cutting and pasting between at least two documents.
13. Pagination.

14. Column control.
15. Database functions for ease of inserting data.
16. Database functions for ease of tracking journals for possible publication and submission records.
17. Mail merge functions for the creation of form letters.
18. Sorting, alphabetizing, and electing (this includes simple list management).
19. Automatic calculation of headings and subheadings.
20. Formatting controls from italicizing to centering, and margin and line space changes.

Most of the major commercial software packages provide these functions. The MicroSoft Corporation[1] has developed the "Windows" package. This is a graphical interface which provides a WYSIWYG environment, which simply means, "what you see is what you get." WYSIWYG allows for accurate editing and previewing, thereby cutting down on the number of preview points required to edit a report.

The graphics capability provided by Windows is considered multitask, which means that several documents or parts of documents can be opened simultaneously in the word processing, allowing for cutting and pasting between the documents. Spreadsheets, databases, charts, graphs, and calculations also can be accommodated, so that these can be cut and pasted directly from the original software into the document being processed. Immediate updates can be accommodated through Object-linking and Embedding (OLE) and Dynamic Data Links (DDL), so as charts, graphs, etc., are updated in the original software the updates will appear automatically in the word-processing document.

Most major, IBM compatible software for word processing has been ported to the Windows environment. These include MicroSoft Word, Word Perfect, and Lotus Ami-Pro. These bring with them extensive dictionaries, thesaurus capabilities, and grammar checkers. Most Windows-based, word processing packages also include desktop publishing capability. With this capability comes functions such as graphics management and color management. The desktop publishing capability allows for the preparation of essentially typeset-quality documents.

For the most part, word processing packages operate on IBM or IBM compatible hardware. The requirements may vary somewhat, and anyone thinking about using a specific package should make sure hardware requirements are met. Word processing packages are compatible with most printers, and laser printers are preferred because of the high-quality hardcopy (the written copy that comes from the printer).

Guidelines for Presenting Papers at Meetings

As professionals, educators participate in professional meetings or conferences, examples being the annual meetings of organizations such as the American Educational Research Association (AERA) and the National Council for Measurement in Education (NCME). At these meetings, participants present papers about research or other professional activities, and take part in symposia. Associations typically have a "call for papers," which goes out in a professional journal several months before the meeting. The call for papers will include forms to be completed. An abstract about the research to be reported on may be required, along with other information about the topic and the presenter. There will be a deadline for responding to the call, and it is important to follow the directions to the letter, so the proposed paper is not rejected on some technicality.

The first step in getting a presentation accepted for a professional meeting is to respond to the "call for papers" of the association sponsoring the meeting.

Assuming the association's proposal review committee accepts the paper proposal, following are the guidelines for preparing and presenting the paper.

1. Prepare a draft of the paper so that the research described in the paper has closure. Sometimes this research is part of a larger study, but it must not be "left hanging," so to speak.

2. Accurately estimate the time required to read the paper. The association will have time limits and these must be honored. It may be possible to have a more extended paper for distribution than what is actually read, but what is read must have continuity and closure.

3. Have one or more colleagues critique the draft of the paper.

4. Prepare a final draft of the paper. (It may be necessary to repeat step 3, depending on the status of the original draft.)

5. Anticipate the size of the audience and prepare enough copies for distribution at the meeting.

6. Familiarize yourself with the content of the paper, so presenting it can be done with audience eye contact.

7. At the meeting, check the room in which the presentation will be given to make sure that any necessary equipment, etc., is available. If any AV equipment is necessary, this would have been requested in the response to the call for papers.

8. Arrive at the presentation room several minutes before the session is to begin, so that you can meet the chairperson and other presenters.

9. If tables or charts are to be distributed with the presentation, arrange to have them distributed efficiently and without wasting time.

10. When it is your turn, give your presentation in a straightforward manner, speaking at a normal rate. You should be familiar enough with the paper so that you can talk to the audience, not read the paper verbatim. *Do not* attempt to give the presentation from memory or extemporaneously give a condensed version.

11. If for some unforeseen reason time does not allow reading the entire paper, make a decision about what part will be omitted, inform the audience, and mention that the omitted part is covered in the available copies.

12. Let the audience know that copies of the paper are available if they have not been distributed earlier. After the session, remain a few minutes to be sure there are adequate copies of the paper. If you run out of copies, have a signup sheet for the names and addresses of those desiring copies. (Be sure to follow up immediately in mailing these copies when you return to your home institution.)

Often presentations will have discussants or reactors to the papers. If this is the case, be sure to send that individual a copy of the paper several weeks in advance. It is very embarrassing to have a discussant fail to react to a paper because it was not sent in time. To the extent possible, it is well to anticipate a discussant's reaction or questions, as well as possible questions from the audience. If the research discussed in the paper was well done, and the paper is written without loose ends, questions should cause no difficulty.

Presentations to Dissertation and Theses Committees

There are two points in a graduate program when presentations are given to committees of graduate faculty members: the defense of a dissertation (thesis) proposal and the defense of the dissertation (thesis). Although these are oral presentations, they are very different than presenting papers at professional meetings. For one thing, committee presentations are much longer; those for dissertation defense typically require about two hours. The audience is usually small, three or four committee members for a dissertation and as few as two for a thesis. The committee members usually have considerable interaction with the graduate student (candidate).

Whether the defense is of a proposal or a dissertation, there are numerous similarities in giving the presentation. For the proposal defense, the candidate makes a case that the intended research is well designed and worthwhile, and that the candidate is knowledgeable about research in the area. For the dissertation defense, the candidate makes a case for the adequacy and importance of the completed research. Either way, the secret to a successful presentation lies in the preparation that takes place before the committee meeting.

The candidate should be very knowledgeable about the research area and research methodology that applies to the research problem. Before the meeting, prepare an organized and efficient presentation that provides the committee members with an overview of the research, highlighting important points. Overhead projectors can be helpful in presenting tables, diagrams, and lists. This introductory presentation should be twenty to thirty minutes in length and should be brought to closure after such time. Do not go on about trivial information or tangential issues in order to use up time.

Knowing the research in the area includes being able to anticipate the relevant questions. The questioning by the committee members usually will proceed in a somewhat predictable sequence. Certain questions will lead to other questions, and although the exact questions may not be anticipated beforehand, the candidate should have a good idea about the content of the questions. With regard to questions, the following are suggested:

1. Listen to the question carefully and answer the question asked. Too often candidates will give prepared responses regardless of whether or not they fit the questions.
2. Respond to a question succinctly but completely. In a dissertation defense, refer to research results if they are appropriate.

3. If you do not understand the question, ask for a repeat or an elaboration of the question.

4. If you do not know the answer to a question, say so. Do not try to bluff through a response.

5. Formulate a response in your mind and select your words carefully. Do not hurry your response. Use precise and appropriate terminology.

With regard to the latter point, precision in the use of terminology is often lacking, especially in terminology about the research methodology. For example, candidates often interchange the use of "sample" and "population" or make statements such as "testing hypotheses at the .05 level of confidence." Lack of precision in using terminology shows incomplete knowledge about the issue.

In the defense of a dissertation proposal, suggestions for improving the research may come from the committee members. Indeed, giving suggestions is one of the functions of committee members. But these suggestions should be viewed as "fine-tuning" rather than major revisions. The candidate should be aware of any research design limitations and must be able to make the case that these limitations will not jeopardize the validity of the research or the successful completion of the research.

In the defense of a dissertation, the candidate should distinguish explicitly between results and conclusions. One of the greatest weaknesses of first drafts of dissertations is the lack of conclusions. Candidates should address the external validity of the research and work from that to conclusions. Drawing conclusions requires effort; it takes a thorough knowledge of the research in an area and a projection of the research results into the appropriate context, usually an educational context.

Recognize the limitations of completed research in the dissertation defense. However, there should not be serious limitations in the research methods. It is not adequate to explain poorly done research by, "I did the best I could." Limitations most likely will apply to the external validity of the research. Any study should have some external validity, or a strong case must be made for why external validity is not of importance.

Overall, the defense of a research proposal or dissertation should be a learning experience for the candidate. It provides the opportunity for a relatively high level, professional discussion. Most candidates are unduly anxious about this experience, although understandably so. The advisor or major professor is unlikely to go ahead with the meeting if the candidate is not prepared for it. Remember that, very likely, the candidate is the most knowledgeable about the research of all the people participating in the defense.

Summary

Communicating about research is generally the concluding activity of a research project. Certainly, much is written about research, either in the form of a proposal for contemplated research or as a research report of completed research. This chapter provided suggestions for writing about research. Also, comments were made which hopefully will be helpful to anyone making an oral presentation about research.

Research is a never-ending activity, and the results of one study often lead to new research problems and projects. Conducting research is a valuable learning experience regardless of the level of sophistication of the research procedures. The field of educational research is expanding; for example, there is increasing use of qualitative methods. There are opportunities for all education professionals to participate in research activities. Often there is a tendency to associate educational research only with universities or special agencies designed for conducting research. But, increasingly, teachers and other professionals in the schools can participate in research of their own or as members of a research team. There is a trend toward university and school partnerships in conducting educational research. An example is the activity of the Institute for Research on Teaching at Michigan State University. Research conducted at this institute often involves the teacher as an equal participant in the research, providing the teacher with adequate time and resources for participation. Readers interested in knowing more about the studies conducted at the institute should subscribe to the *Communication Quarterly,* an institute publication. Information can be obtained by contacting:

> The Institute for Research on Teaching
> College of Education
> Michigan State University
> East Lansing, MI 48824–1034

In conclusion, it is important to recognize that one book is not going to cover all educational research methods. This text provides discussions of various types of research, with specific procedures, as well as a general introduction to educational research.

Educational evaluation, like any evaluation, involves making value judgments about the worth of something—something educational such as a curriculum or program. Educational research and educational evaluation have a lot of overlap in methodology. Evaluators use many of the same designs, measurement tools, and analyses, both qualitative and quantitative, as researchers. When the term *evaluation research* is used, it means using research procedures for the process of evaluation, that is, collecting data and making decisions (value judgments) about some educational program, policy, phenomenon, or the like. The research methods discussed in this text also have application in educational evaluation, depending on the specific situation. For whatever purposes it is conducted, educational research should be viewed as a continuing activity in which each specific project adds to the store of knowledge or provides solutions to educational problems.

KEY CONCEPTS

Research proposal	Abstract
Research report	Budget
Identification of the problem	Staff resumes
Review of the literature	Appendix
Methods section	Conclusions and recommendations
Significance of the research	Bibliography
Cover page	Reference list

Transition
Presenting research papers
Call for papers
Word processing

Text editing
Defense of a dissertation
Evaluation research

EXERCISES

15.1 Select a research problem of limited magnitude and write a proposal about doing a research project on the problem. Include in your proposal a statement of the problem, a context for the problem, and a brief (about two double-spaced pages) review of the literature. Comment on the anticipated procedures, the analysis that would be used, and the potential significance of the project. Be brief and concise, and pay special attention to the continuity of ideas. Use your mastery of the content of previous chapters to present an adequate and correct methodology for doing the research study. Include a bibliography. This is a writing task of the magnitude of a short-term paper.

15.2 Select a research report, probably an article, that deals with an educational topic in your area or one about which you have some knowledge. Read the report through the results (or data analysis) section, but do not read the conclusions. Write a conclusions section of your own. After you have completed your conclusions, compare them to the conclusions of the report.

15.3 Obtain a copy of a research paper presented at a professional meeting. The meeting program of a recently held annual meeting of a professional organization such as AERA is a good source. Review the paper for its format, completeness, and closure. Compare the sections of the paper with those of a research article on somewhat the same topic. How are they similar and how do they differ?

15.4 Suppose you were conducting a research study in which the scores of school-age children, grades three through six inclusive, on a battery of ten academic and skills areas tests (dependent variables) were analyzed. Within each grade, there was an experimental and a control group, with one-half of the students in each group. Means and standard deviations for each grade, separated by experimental and control groups, were calculated. The analysis also included a series of t-tests on the differences between the means of the experimental and control groups within each grade. After this was completed, all scores on the ten tests were correlated in combinations of two. Develop an organization for presenting these results in tables. Provide names and headings for your tables. Number the tests 1 through 10 for convenience.

15.5 Consult a form and style manual such as the *Publication Manual of the American Psychological Association* (3rd ed.) and indicate the editorial style for entries in a reference list for the following:

    a. A book that has a corporate author (rather than one or more persons).
    b. An English translation of a book.
    c. An edited book.
    d. An article or chapter in an edited book.
    e. An article in a professional journal that has five authors.
    f. A revised edition of a book.

NOTE

    1. MicroSoft Corporation, 16011 N.E. 36th Way, Box 97017, Redmond, VA 98073–9717.

REFERENCES

American Psychological Association. (1983). *Publication Manual of the American Psychological Association* (3rd ed.). Washington, DC: Author.

Brookhart, S. M. (1993). Teacher's grading practices: Meaning and values. *Journal of Educational Measurement.* 30(2). 123–142.

Chalifour, C. L., and Powers, D. E. (1989). The relationship of content characteristics of GRE analytical reasoning items to their difficulties and discriminations. *Journal of Educational Measurement,* 26(2), 120–132.

Dillon, D. R. (1989). Showing them that I want them to learn and that I care about who they are: A microethnography of the social organization of a secondary low-track English-reading classroom. *American Educational Research Journal,* 26(2), 227–259.

Kuh, G. D. (1993). In their own words: What students learn outside the classroom. *American Educational Research Journal* 30(2), 277–304.

McMillan, J. H., and Schumacher, S. (1989). *Research in education: A conceptual introduction* (2nd ed.). Glenview, IL: Scott, Foresman.

Monk, D. H., and Haller, E. J. (1993). Predictors of high school academic course offerings: The role of school size. *American Educational Research Journal* 30(1), 3–21.

Stanovich, K. E., and Cunningham, A. E. (1993). Where does knowledge come from? Specific association between print exposure and information acquisition. *Journal of Educational Psychology,* 85(2), 211–229.

Appendix 1

Ethical and Legal Considerations in Conducting Research

Much educational research involves the use of human participants who may be involved in a variety of ways. Those participating in experiments usually have some type of treatment administered to them. With survey and ethnographic research, it is the human participant from whom or about whom the data are collected. Sometimes, school or other records are used as sources of data that, of course, contain information about people. Since human participants are involved, ethical and legal considerations are of concern.

Not only are there ethical considerations that apply to conducting educational research, but in 1974, legislation was passed that applies to educational research. The Family Education Rights and Privacy Act of 1974, also known as the Buckley Amendment, protects the privacy of students' educational records. The impact for research is that when school records are used, the researcher must guard against unauthorized identification of students. If it is necessary to have personal identification, written consent must be obtained, and the identification information must be destroyed following its use for research.

The National Research Act of 1974 addressees legal considerations for conducting research. One stipulation of the act is that universities and agencies engaging in research with human participants have an institutional review board (IRB) for proposals. The IRB must approve the proposal and certify that the project will be conducted in accordance with the law. IRBs are committees through which proposals are channeled and they go by names such as the Human Subjects Research Committee (HSRC). These committees have guidelines and statements about the policies and requirements for protecting human subjects involved in research. Such statements usually are several pages in length and they conform to the legislation and the policies of the agencies. IRB statements tend to contain similar content and they are too long for inclusion here. However, some key requirements from a typical IRB statement, that of the University of Toledo, are:

- Projects should be carefully designed to minimize risk to the subjects and to anticipate risk.
- Participation of human beings as subjects in research must be voluntary.
- Consent processes and documentation must conform to the HSRC requirements and comply with applicable law and sponsor guidelines.
- Confidentiality of identifiable information is presumed and must be maintained unless the investigator obtains express permission of the subject to do otherwise.
- All research projects involving human subjects must be submitted for prior review unless certain specified instructional exemption criteria are fully met. The attached checklist may be used to assist in determining whether a project must be reviewed by the HSRC. (p. 1)

For each proposed project, a five-page form must be completed that provides a summary of the project and explicit information about possible risks to subjects. Any researcher working with human subjects at a university or agency or in a school system must follow the institution's rules and procedures. It is a serious breach of professional etiquette to avoid going through the established channels when proposing research in a school system. Not only is this unethical, but failure to follow established approval procedures practically ensures that the research will not be approved.

Another stipulation of the National Research Act is that of "informed consent" of research participants. Essentially, this means that participants be informed about their role in the research and that they give their written consent for participation. Again, from the University of Toledo policy statement, there are five requirements to be met by all consent documents:

1. The consent may not include any exculpatory language through which the subject is made to waive, or appear to waive, any of his or her legal rights, including any release of the institution or its agents from liability or negligence.

2. The consent must comply with applicable federal, state, and local laws or regulations requiring additional information to be disclosed.

3. The consent cannot place limits on the authority of a physician to provide emergency medical care, to the extent the physician is permitted to do so under applicable federal, state, and local laws.

4. When children, incompetent adults, prisoners, or wards of the state are to be subjects, the consent requirements of federal regulations 45 CFR 46 must be met. In addition, any subjects capable of assent (agreeing to participate) must be given the option to assent, despite permission of the parent or guardian. (A person may not be forced to participate.)

5. Where participation as human subjects of students enrolled in a course of instruction at the University of Toledo forms an integral part of the conduct of the course, the official University bulletins and timetables, as well as the course syllabus, shall state that fact in the description of the course. If the student's grade will be directly affected by participation in the projects, that must be explained as well, with a description of how the grade is

affected, and whether alternative means are available to obtain the same grade effect. (pp. 10–11)

The requirement of informed consent may be waived under certain conditions. Surveys involving questionnaires, for which data are recorded anonymously and reported in composite, usually have what is called implied consent. That is respondents have the option of refusing participation (failure to return the questionnaire), and if they return a completed questionnaire they have, in essence, given consent to participation. In the final analysis, the IRB has the responsibility for decisions about waiving the requirement.

The researcher is obligated to protect the participants from risk. Risk has a broad definition as exposure to the possibility of physical, social, or psychological harm. With most educational research there is little if any possibility of harm. However, in some areas, such as studies of the effects of drugs, there may be considerable potential for harm, especially psychological and social, even if no experiment with drugs is conducted. Foster (1988) comments on the issue of protecting children in the schools. In a survey of school boards, private schools, and other educational institutions, it was found that many institutional guidelines were general, and it could not be concluded that the personal autonomy of children in the schools is well protected by practices and policies of educational authorities. The survey was conducted in Canada, but the implication is clear wherever educational research is conducted; it is the responsibility of the researchers to protect the subjects in the specific research project.

There are any number of publications in the educational and psychological literature that comment on the ethics of research and the relevant legal interpretations. The American Psychological Association has a comprehensive statement, "Ethical Principles of Psychologists and Code of Conduct," which appeared in the December 1992 issue of the *American Psychologist* (pp. 1597–1611). Essentially, this statement addresses all aspects of the practice of psychology and several standards deal with conducting research. Those which apply most to educational research are listed below. (Of course, the term psychologist is used, but educational researcher may be substituted in an educational context.)

Planning Research

  a. *Psychologists design, conduct, and report research in accordance with recognized standards of scientific competence and ethical research.*
  b. *Psychologists plan their research so as to minimize the possibility that results will be misleading.*
  c. *In planning research, psychologists consider its ethical acceptability under the Ethics Code. If an ethical issue is unclear, psychologists seek to resolve the issue through consultation with institutional review boards, animal care and use committees, peer consultations, or other proper mechanisms.*
  d. *Psychologists take reasonable steps to implement appropriate protections for the rights and welfare of human participants, other persons affected by the research, and the welfare of animal subjects.*

Responsibility

> **a.** *Psychologists conduct research competently and with due concern for the dignity and welfare of the participants.*
>
> **b.** *Psychologists are responsible for the ethical conduct of research conducted by them or by others under their supervision or control.*
>
> **c.** *Researchers and assistants are permitted to perform only those tasks for which they are appropriately trained and prepared.*
>
> **d.** *As part of the process of development and implementation of research projects, psychologists consult those with expertise concerning any special population under investigation or most likely to be affected.*

Research Responsibilities

> *Prior to conducting research (except research involving only anonymous surveys, naturalistic observations, or similar research), psychologists enter into an agreement with participants that clarifies the nature of the research and the responsibilities of each party.*[1]

The American Educational Research Association (1991), in proposing its ethical standards, has a section on conducting research with research populations. In the preamble appears the following statement:

> *It is of paramount importance that educational researchers respect the rights, privacy, dignity, and sensitivities of their research populations and also the integrity of the institutions within which the research occurs. (p. 32)*

Ten "standards" are then given which summarize conditions and criteria for involving human subjects in research.

Any number of articles, monographs, and books comment on the ethics and procedures for conducting research with human subjects. Fowler (1984) identifies eight procedures for protecting respondents when conducting survey research. Tobin (1992) discusses conducting research in science classrooms, and an important point made in this article is that ethical questions ought to be considered within a cultural context, and a classroom is considered a culture. Tobin also comments on collaborative research with teachers. A guideline on this matter is:

> *To the extent possible, involve teachers in discussions of the data as they are collected, as research questions are formulated and pursued, and as interpretations are made. (p. 115)*

Protecting the rights of research participants and conducting research in an ethical manner are, to a large extent, matters of common sense. The researcher must protect the dignity and welfare of the participants. The individual's freedom to decline participation

---

[1]*The American Psychologist*, 47(2), 1608. Copyright (1992) by the American Psychological Association. Reprinted by permission.

must be respected, and the confidentiality of research data must be maintained. The researcher must guard against violation or invasion of privacy. The responsibility for maintaining ethical standards remains with the individual researcher, and the principal investigator also is responsible for actions of coworkers or assistants.

The researcher should inform participants about the purpose of the research and indicate the extent of commitment required of participants. Precautions should be taken against misuse and misinterpretation of the research results. The researcher should communicate the results of the study to participants, or at least offer to do so in a timely manner.

Most educational research studies focus on group data rather than individual data. For example, an experiment may emphasize how the groups receiving different treatments differ in performance, not the performance of a particular individual. In ethnographic research the emphasis is on describing the context, organization, cultures, and perspectives. Even if individual performance were described, it would not be necessary to identify anyone by name. Yet to collect group information, data must be collected from individuals, and the individuals' rights must be respected. Almost all educational research is conducted under the auspices of some institution, such as a university, school system, or related agency. When human participants are involved, the rules and procedures of that institution must be reviewed and followed. Generally, these will be in keeping with the intent of federal legislation.

REFERENCES

Ad Hoc Committee, American Educational Research Association. (1991). Proposed ethical standards for AERA. *Educational Researcher,* 20(9), 31–35.

Foster, W. F (1988). The protection of subjects of educational research . . . Is it adequate? *Education Canada,* 28, 10–13.

Fowler, F. J., Jr. (1984). *Survey research methods.* Beverly Hills, CA: Sage.

Human Subjects Research Committee, University of Toledo. *Protection of human subjects in research and investigational activities.* (undated and no copyright).

Tobin, K. (1992). Ethical concerns and research in science classrooms: Resolved and unresolved dilemmas. *Science Education,* 76(I), 105–117.

$Solutions$ to $Exercises$

Note: Solutions are not provided here for exercises (1) that have flexible answers; (2) that direct the reader to some type of extended activity, such as reading a journal article; or (3) that indicate considerable discussion. The purpose of this appendix is to help the reader make the solution of exercises a more profitable learning experience. Answers are brief; not all possible discussion is presented for some exercises.

Chapter 1

1.1 The essential difference between basic and applied research is in the orientation of the research. Applied research is oriented to the solution of a specific, often immediate, problem. Basic research is oriented to the extension of knowledge in the discipline.

1.2 Internal validity involves the extent to which we can interpret the results of a research study. It considers the conditions of the study that make the results interpretable (or uninterpretable). External validity involves the extent of generalizability of the results—the populations, conditions, and so forth to which the results can be generalized.

1.3 If the results cannot be interpreted, they cannot be validly generalized.

1.4 **a.** Internal
    b. Internal
    c. External
    d. Internal

1.5 Reliability means consistency; when applied to research, it is the extent to which research (the methods, conditions, results) are replicable. For (a) there may be inconsistency in the way the four experimenters administer the treatment; for (b) observers may not be consistent when interpreting the teacher behaviors.

1.6 In an experiment, at least one variable is deliberately varied or manipulated by the researcher.

1.7 Inductive inquiry involves reasoning from the specific (situation, etc.) to the general situation, etc. When conducting qualitative research something specific such as an educational phenomenon, issue, etc., is studied in detail and holistically, and to the extent possible, generalizations are made to similar phenomena, issues, etc.

1.8 Grounded theory is theory generated from data. To develop a grounded theory of principal evaluation, descriptions of evaluation systems used for evaluating principals would be obtained, along with data that might have been collected when the systems were used. The descriptions and the data would be analyzed for similarities and differences in methods, kinds of data, purposes, outcomes, etc. Possible components might be: (1) the extent of interaction with students, (2) methods and skills in conducting faculty meetings, and (3) public relations efforts with parents of students, and the community in general.

1.9 Historical research focuses on a description and interpretation of past events or facts; ethnographic research focuses on a holistic description of some present phenomenon.

Chapter 2

2.1 The constants are grade level, gender, and school. The independent variable is instructional materials. The teacher is an intervening variable, and the effect of the teacher variable cannot be separated from the effect of instructional materials, since each teacher uses only one type of instructional material with only one group. The dependent variable is reading achievement.

2.2 Gender of the student is an organismic variable that may also serve as a control variable if the reading scores for boys and girls are separated. School and grade level are likely to be included as control variables. (In essence, they become additional independent variables.) Class and method cannot be separated within schools, so within the schools, class (and also teacher, assuming that each teacher uses only one method) is an intervening variable.

2.3 Hypotheses would be directed to the variables under study. An example is, "The reading achievement of fourth-grade girls is equal to that of fourth-grade boys." This is a nondirectional hypothesis. A directional hypothesis might be, "The reading achievement of fifth-graders is higher than that of fourth-graders." There are other possible hypotheses.

2.4 Examples of foreshadowed problems might be:

a. Extent of play among children of different races.
b. Social interaction among children and teachers.

2.5 A nondirectional hypothesis does *not* specify a direction for the results; for example, it does not specify that one mean score will be greater than or less than another. A directional hypothesis specifies the direction (or order) of the results, for example, that one mean score will be greater than another.

2.6 It would be more appropriate to use directional hypotheses because the science educator is interested in whether or not the constructivist approach improves science achievement, not whether its effect simply is different than that of other approaches. The dependent variables are achievement scores (possibly final exam scores) in biology, chemistry, and physics. Certainly the approach to science instruction (constructivist versus other approaches) is the independent variable of primary interest. The gender of the student might be another independent variable, included as a control variable. The school is a constant. Student learning style and student study habits are intervening variables.

2.7 Open classroom is a rather general term that may have varied meanings, so it would need to be defined specifically for this study. Scholastic performance is the dependent variable, but most likely there would be several dependent variables such as the scores on specific tests of scholastic subjects, for example reading. The grade levels of elementary school students included in the study would need to be specified.

2.9 a. Ordinal
   b. Ordinal
   c. Ratio
   d. Interval
   e. Nominal
   f. Socioeconomic level usually is considered to be ordinal.

Chapter 3

3.2 The major descriptors to use are Instruction, Curriculum, and Education. More specifically, use Mathematics Curriculum (subheadings Arithmetic Curriculum and Elementary School Math.), Curriculum (Mathematics Curriculum and Elementary School Curriculum), Education Programs (International Programs), and Comparative Education (International Education). The foregoing descriptors would be used in combination when referencing in the following ERIC publications: *Educational Documents Index, Resources in Education* (Subject Index), and *Current Index to Journals in Education* (Subject Index).

3.3 Descriptors to use are Teacher Behavior, Teacher Performance, Teacher Competency, Science, and Science Achievement. To broaden the search, suppose that the results of searching on Teacher Behavior and Science Achievement produced few references. Then Teacher Behavior or Teacher Performance or Teacher Competency and Science Achievement could be used. An example of narrowing the search would be to use High School and Science Achievement. Note the connectors—"and" generally narrows the search; "or" broadens it.

Chapter 4

4.1 Possible variables that may contribute to the variance in performance test scores are: age, general physical health, differences in physical "shape," strength, weight, height.

4.2 a. Built into the design as an independent variable
   b. Constant
   c. Built into the design as an independent variable
   d. Randomization
   e. Randomization
   f. Constant

4.3 To some extent, level of school is confounded with school as is age of the students. The "geographic region," which includes socioeconomic factors, etc., may have some impact upon attitude, and region is confounded with school. Any effects that individual teachers, administrators, counselors, etc., have on attitude would be confounded with school.

4.4 No independent variables are manipulated by the researcher; attitude is measured as it occurs in the natural setting.

4.5 The following points should be noted in developing the research design: (a) Since each teacher teaches two classes, each teacher should use both packets, one for each class; in this way, teacher and instructional materials are not confounded. (b) Unless some measure of learning style is available, learning style would likely be controlled by randomization. (c) Gender of the student and teacher could be included as independent variables, although gender of the student could also be controlled through randomization. (d) The available GPA could serve as a measure of ability and could be used as a statistical control.

4.6 The ability level of the participants is a likely variable that may have an effect on the dependent variable. An ability level measure could be administered to the participants and then a statistical adjustment made on the basis of ability level score. There may be some difference in the performances of boys and girls or in the manner in which they respond to the motivational techniques. Therefore, the gender of the participant could be included as an independent (control) variable. Assuming that conditions for conducting the experiment are consistent across participants, any variables controlled would be organismic variables.

4.7 When two or more variables are confounded in a research study, their effects cannot be separated.

Chapter 5

5.1 (This exercise is similar to Exercise 1.2.) Internal validity concerns the basic minimum control, and so forth, that is necessary for the results of the experiment to be interpretable. External validity is the extent to which the results of the experiment are generalizable to existing conditions, populations, and the like. Internal validity is often enhanced by increasing control, which may include reducing the number of factors operating in the situation. This tends to jeopardize external validity. The reverse may also occur when the experiment is essentially a replication of the real situation (has high external validity), but so many factors are operating that it is impossible to interpret the cause and effect.

5.2 The fact that the teachers can assign students at random within the school gives a measure of control that would be missing if existing classes had to be taken. Existing classes may differ on ability and on other factors related to achievement. Control can be enhanced by building school into the design as an independent variable. Since each teacher teaches four classes, one of each size can be assigned per teacher. However, the teacher variable would be confounded with the independent variable school, since any one teacher would teach in only one school. The school variable might have several uncontrolled but relevant variables associated with it, such as extent of lab facilities. These variables are essentially confounded with the school variable.

5.4 The primary gain in internal validity is being able to check on an effect of pretesting. A possible interaction between pretesting and experimental treatment can also be checked.

5.5 The pretest-posttest control group design applies. Because the teacher is interested in the amount of algebra learned during the semester, pretesting is necessary. The pretest score may also be used as a statistical control. This experiment would most likely be quite high in external validity, since testing could occur at natural times and the experiment would be carried on in a natural educational setting. The population to which the results are generalized would have to be carefully defined in terms of the students enrolled in advanced algebra classes in this specific type of high school.

5.6 a. No, because the groups have been formed by random assignment.
  b. No, because there is no pretesting of any groups.
  c. (1) There are experimental treatment effects: the four experimental treatments all have differing effects. (2) There are experimental treatment effects: X_1 and X_3 have equal effects: X_2 and X_4 have equal effects (or the same effect), but their effects differ from those of X_1 and X_3. (3) X_1 and X_2 have effects and they are the same. (4) X_4 is the only treatment that has an experimental effect.

5.7 a. The researcher can determine the possible effect of X extended in time, along with a comparison group extended in time. Also, a possible diminishing effect of pretesting could be checked.

   b. Compare O_2 and O_9; compare O_4 and O_{10}.

   c. (1) If an experimental effect exists, it is a function of time. There is no long-term experimental effect. No pretesting effect appears in the short-run posttest results of experimental groups. (2) There is an experimental effect that is not affected by the different posttest times of the design; the experimental effect is the same in the short and long run. (3) In the short run, there is no change due to experimental treatment for pretested groups. (4) In the short run, there is no experimental effect, nor is there an effect of pretesting; there is an experimental effect in the long run with the pretested groups.

5.8 a. Gain scores can be analyzed; if necessary, we could also check on subject mortality.

   b. No; an effect of pretesting cannot be checked because there are no nonpretested groups with which to make a comparison.

   c. O_3 and O_6 compared with O_9; O_1 with O_3, and O_4 with O_6; O_2 with O_3, and O_3 with O_6.

   d. No, because random assignment was used.

   e. We would conclude that some external factor is causing the control group to change between measurement occasions.

   f. (1) There are experimental effects in the short run, and they are the same for X_1 and X_2. The effects do not persist for the long run. (2) There are experimental effects in the short run that are not the same for X_1 and X_2. (3) There are no experimental effects in the short run. There are experimental effects in the long run, but we cannot tell whether or not X_1 and X_2 effects are the same. We know that $O_2 \neq O_5$ and $O_5 \neq O_6$, but it is possible that $O_3 = O_6$. (4) There are experimental effects in the short run, and the effects are different for X_1 and X_2. There are also effects in the long term, but they do not remain constant between the short and long terms. The long-run effects of X_1 and X_2 are not the same.

Chapter 6

6.1 The primary difficulties that may be introduced when using intact groups are associated with possible lack of equivalence of the groups on factors related to the dependent variable. Such factors may be confounded with experimental treatments, threatening the internal validity of the research.

6.2 There are three sets of laboratory materials, and one set could be designated the traditional or control set, since it is unlikely that a class would do the lab work with no materials. The design can be diagrammed as follows:

$$G_1 \text{------} X_1 \text{------} O_1$$
$$G_2 \text{------} X_2 \text{-----} O_2$$
$$G_3 \qquad\qquad\qquad O_3$$

The pretest-posttest, nonequivalent control group design would be applied by administering a pretest at the beginning of the semester. The pretest might cover biology content, but if this study were conducted during the first semester of the school year, it might be a Scholastic Aptitude Test or a science achievement test. The advantages of pretesting are (1) that the preexperiment equivalence of the classes on the pretest can be checked and (2) that pretest scores may be used as a statistical control in the analysis. Internal validity is threatened if the classes are not equivalent, and other variables affecting the dependent variable are confounded with the materials. There is also the possibility that contamination across the classes may occur if students from different classes discuss or share materials. Assuming that the results can be interpreted, they generalize to the biology students in this school taught by this teacher, probably over a period of years if the characteristics of the student body do not change. Generalization to other schools, students, and teachers would have to be argued on a logical basis.

6.3   There is no random assignment of students to the practice treatments. The teacher variable is very apparent and essentially uncontrolled. The assumption is that teachers are most effective with the techniques they prefer. Even if this is true, there is no evidence that different teachers, independent of practice method, are equally effective. With only three schools, it would be difficult to make a case for the assumption that the teachers of each method are a representative sample of fifth-grade teachers, either in general or as a more specific group. There may be other relevant uncontrolled factors within the schools, and since the method is optional to the teacher, there is no reason to assume a balance between schools on such factors. Thus, internal validity is low because of lack of control. External validity is also low because of poor internal validity and questions that might be raised about the representativeness of the teachers. It would be important to have information about the characteristics of the teachers and their similarities across the two practice methods.

6.4   This is an example of a time series design. A design such as this is susceptible to multiple-treatment interference. In this case, detailed effects may begin appearing on subsequent observations. The pattern of results may be difficult to interpret. The advantage of using such a design is that it can be applied in a natural setting and can provide information on the reading achievement profile of a specific class. A special measurement problem would be attaining equivalent difficulty levels for the various tests given at four-week intervals. Suppose that there was a marked drop in performance after one period. This would be interpreted as an effect of the method of instruction, when in fact the drop might be due to a more difficult test.

6.5   **a.**   There are short-term effects of the training programs but no long-term effects. In the short term, the effects of the programs are not the same, with X_1 being most effective and X_3 least effective.
   b.   There are short-term effects that persist for the long term, and the effects are the same for the three training programs.
   c.   The groups were not equivalent initially, and they retain their relative positions in the short term. We cannot tell if there is a short-term effect. Apparently, there is no long-term effect, and the long term has also eliminated initial differences among the groups.
   d. O_3 with O_1 and O_2, O_6 with O_4 and O_5, and O_9 with O_7 and O_8.
   e.   No, because all groups are pretested. There is no comparison group that was not pretested.

6.6   **a.**   The experimental treatment has a positive effect, at least an immediate effect, but the effect diminishes over time.
   b.   There is a short-term effect of the experimental treatment, which continues for an additional three weeks but then disappears.
   c.   Check G_2 across O_8 to O_{14}. If there are changes in the attitude scores, normal class instruction is having an effect.

6.7   The study would be conducted over an eight-week period, with four observations (O_1 through O_4) taken when no logs were being kept and four observations (O_5 through O_8) taken when logs were kept. If O_5 through O_8 showed improvement in the student's subjects over performance from O_1 through O_4 the treatment is having an effect. If it were a one-time effect, O_5 would be greater than O_1 through O_4, but consistent with O_6, O_7 and O_8. If there were an accumulative effect, O_5 would be greater than O_1 through O_4 and O_6 would be greater than O_5, O_7 greater than O_6, and O_8 greater than O_7.

6.9   The essential differences are that for (a) we have two or more behaviors, for (b) two or more subjects, and for (c) two or more situations.

Chapter 7

7.1 There may be any number of independent variables of interest (some would serve as control variables). Examples are: grade level, sex of the student, at the high school level, subject taught, location of the school in terms of socioeconomic level of the community, size of the school, region of the state. Scholastic achievement in numerous subjects and areas would serve as dependent variables, at least some dependent variables measured by standardized achievement tests. Scores on attitude inventories could serve as dependent variables. One value of a longitudinal study is that there may be a check on long-range effects.

7.2 One advantage of the longitudinal study is the option of studying change occurring in the class as it goes through college. The longitudinal study would take four years or so to complete; the cross-sectional could be done in a much shorter time period, requiring data collection at only one point in time.

7.3 As a cohort study, the present freshman class would be the cohort and a random sample of this class would be selected each year as it goes through its four-year college experience. As a panel study, a random sample (the panel) of the present freshman class would be selected, and this same sample or what remains of it would be surveyed each of the four years. A disadvantage of the panel study is possible attrition in the panel, especially if the college has a high dropout rate. An advantage of the cohort study is avoiding the attrition problem. An advantage of the panel study is that individual change could be checked, whereas a cohort study would measure only group change.

7.4 The panel study allows for the opportunity of collecting data from the same group of teachers at different times. In this way, changes over time within specific teachers could be detected. A panel study is always susceptible to the difficulty of keeping the panel intact, and five years is a long period for maintaining a panel. It is also possible that over time the remaining members of the panel are no longer representative of the teacher population. The stability of the teacher population in this school system would impact upon the effectiveness of the panel.

7.5 To the extent possible, it would be well to use selected-response items because students who have dropped out would have little motivation for devoting much thought to responding to the questionnaire. For this reason, nonresponse very likely would be a problem. Some procedure for personal contact with nonrespondents, such as a telephone call, may be necessary.

7.6 The cover letter should be signed by the director of, or assistant superintendent in charge of, the Department of Guidance and Counseling.

7.7 Since all schools or guidance offices have telephones, all guidance counselors selected could be contacted by telephone. The advantage of using the telephone over a mailed questionnaire is the direct contact, which might increase response rate and would allow for more flexibility in the questioning, if this is desirable. Using the telephone would essentially shift the study from a questionnaire to an interview. A disadvantage of the telephone survey is that it may interrupt the work of the guidance counselors and responding by telephone may not allow adequate time for thinking about responses. It would be desirable—almost necessary—to provide prior information and to schedule the telephone call in advance. The additional effort of the telephone survey may not be merited, since the response rate with a mailed questionnaire would probably be quite good for this professional sample.

7.8 Very likely an independent variable would be position of the educator, teacher, principal, superintendent, etc. Their opinions would have policy implications and the implications would be different if such groups had similar opinions versus diverse opinions.

7.9   Possible sources of nonresponse that should be identifiable: position of the educator, region of the state, location of the school—rural, city, suburban, size of the school system.

7.10   In order to provide more focus for the items (on the curriculum, student issues) and to make response easier, use selected-response items to the extent possible. The president of the board of education likely would sign the cover letter.

7.11   A longitudinal design would be used if there is an interest in opinion change over time. In the interest of positive, school-community relations, it would be well to survey the entire parent population.

7.12   There would be little likelihood of success with mailed questionnaires (or distributed for students to take) because many would not be returned and those that are returned most likely would be completed as a group activity, or at least in consultation with others. It might be possible to administer the questionnaire to a "captive audience" such as a class, but the members of the class would not be a random sample of the student population. Careless or dishonest response might be a problem; for one reason, students might report more variable or positive eating habits than are being followed. Checking for possible careless or dishonest response could be done by checking for impossible or implausible responses or unlikely response combinations. The respondents could be asked how honest (or accurate) they were when responding.

7.13   The interview has the advantages of (1) allowing for deeper probing of the respondent and possibly pursuing a response, (2) clearing ambiguities, and (3) securing information that would not be forthcoming with a written questionnaire. Also, the problem of nonresponse is reduced and is usually not as great as with a questionnaire. The primary disadvantage of the interview is that it requires considerable resources in terms of time, effort, and personnel. Questionnaires can all be sent at the same time, so that there is no large lapse of time such as may occur between interviews. This could be a disadvantage of the interview if external factors or events associated with time affect responses. A problem with the questionnaire may be securing an adequate response rate. If a great deal of written material is necessary to communicate to the respondent and elicit response, the length of the questionnaire may be a disadvantage. Also, if communication breaks down, there is no opportunity to eliminate ambiguities at the time.

Chapter 8

8.1   Among the decisions that would be made at this initial step of the research design are: (a) the site selection, that is, the specific school(s) whose principal(s) will be observed; (b) who in addition to the principal will be observed or interviewed, that is, school staff and students; and (c) duration of the study (at least a tentative decision) and the schedule for data collection in the school(s). One of the initial decisions would be whether data collection will be done in one or more schools.

8.2   A working hypothesis might be, "The principal's role is more that of policy implementor than instructional leader." A foreshadowed problem might be, "The professional interaction between the principal and teachers."

8.3   Examples of documents that might be collected are (a) minutes of faculty meetings and (b) copies of reports prepared by the principal for the central administration of the school system. The principal would be observed conducting routine activities, and certainly a faculty meeting would be observed when the opportunity arises.

8.4 a.   A general question might be, "What are teacher perceptions of the efficiency effectiveness and feasibility of site-based management?"

    b. Schools—elementary, secondary, or whatever—where site-based management has been implemented would be candidates for sites. Because a limited number of schools could be included, criteria for inclusion would need to be considered. Possible subjects include teachers, principals, students, etc. Interview data, observation, and school records are examples of potential sources of data.

    c. The funnel approach would begin with general questions and, as data collection proceeds, it would become increasingly focused on specific phenomena.

    d. An example of a specific phenomenon is the principal's role (tasks) in site-based management.

8.6 The modified analytic approach works from a specific research problem, in this case a study of teacher's perceptions about a model for teacher evaluation, to a comprehensive description of the "phenomenon." As the study is conducted in this school system, a grounded theory of teacher evaluation as applied or practiced may emerge from the data. This theory, undoubtedly, would have several components, thus providing a comprehensive description.

Chapter 9

9.2 a. Survey

    b. Experiment

    c. Historical

    d. Survey (ex post facto in nature)

    e. Historical

    f. Survey (ex post facto in nature)

    g. Survey

9.4 An educational term that may have a problem of definition over the years is progressive education.

Chapter 10

10.1 Experimental research involves the direct manipulation of at least one independent variable; ethnographic research focuses on variables as they occur in the natural setting without any intervention by the researcher.

10.2 Perspectives form the cultures and the cultures collectively make up the organization.

10.3 Triangulation is qualitative cross-validation; it involves comparisons (among sources or data-collection procedures, for example) to determine the extent of consistency.

10.5 Relative to external validity, it probably would not be of much direct concern, and any external validity would need to be argued on a logical basis.

10.7 As a participant-observer, the researcher assumes the role of an active participant in the situation. A privileged observer does not assume the role of participant but has access to the activities of the situation. Limited observers are not participants, and they can observe only some of the activities. A young adult, actually enrolled in law school, doing research on what it is like to be a law school student is an example of a participant-observer. A researcher in a school observing all aspects of school operation—instruction, faculty meetings, lunch-room activity, and so on—but not actually being a teacher or student would be a privileged observer. A researcher in a school who observes only junior high science instruction two days per week would be considered a limited observer.

10.9   The concepts of reliability and validity are consistent with their meaning for types of research other than ethnographic research. Reliability is concerned with replicability of research procedures and results. Validity concerns the interpretation of results (internal) and their subsequent generalizability (external).

10.10   Assertoric argumentation is general-type generalization, applying to every member of a group or population rather than to the entire population as a whole. Such argumentation is based on reasonableness and rationality given acceptable assumptions and evidence. Aggregate-type generalizations are made about the entire population, not individuals, and they are often based on random sampling probability models.

10.11   Because ethnographic research is so situation- or context-specific, generalizability and, hence, external validity may be limited. Broadening the scope of an ethnographic research study to multiple sites tends to enhance external validity. Generalizability usually is not as big a concern as with quantitative research studies, and in ethnographic research the case for generalizability typically is made on a logical basis.

Chapter 11

11.1   Since there are 839 population members, three-digit random numbers are necessary. Any numbers selected between 840 and 999 inclusive can be disregarded.

11.2   For stratified sampling, we divide the population into nonoverlapping subpopulations called strata. When proportional allocation is used, the sample sizes selected from the strata are proportional to the sizes of the corresponding strata populations.

11.4   In stratified sampling, all strata are represented in the sample, and the random sampling is done within strata according to some allocation. Thus, individuals, not strata, are randomly sampled. In cluster sampling, the clusters are randomly selected from the population of clusters, but if a cluster is selected, all its members are included in the sample.

11.5   The sampling fraction is $\frac{450}{3000}$, which equals $\frac{3}{20}$ or .15. Sample sizes for strata 1 through 4, respectively, are 124.5, 99, 72, and 154.5. Since partial units probably cannot be included, the researcher must arbitrarily decide whether to select 125 from stratum 1 or 155 from stratum 4.

11.6   Sixty men and sixty women would be randomly selected from their respective populations. There would be fifteen men and fifteen women assigned to each of the four levels of the experimental variable. Since selection is random from each population, the first fifteen of each sex selected could be assigned to level 1, the second fifteen to level 2, and so on.

11.9   Comprehensive sampling is such that all units with specified characteristics are included in the sample. Maximum variation sampling includes units in the sample so that they provide the greatest differences in specified characteristics.

11.10   Typical case sampling involves selecting units judged to be the "average or middle road" units relative to the phenomenon under study. Homogeneous sampling involves selecting units that are similar; they may not be typical units, but are units belonging to some defined subgroup.

Chapter 12

12.1   Validity has to do with whether or not a test measures what it is supposed to measure; reliability concerns whether or not it is consistent in measuring whatever it does measure. A test can be reliable but not valid by consistently measuring something it was not designed to measure or by failing to measure what it was designed to measure. An unreliable test cannot be valid, because lack of consistency eliminates the possibility of measuring what it is supposed to measure.

12.4 a. Published measuring instruments are available to both researchers, but the one working on achievement would have greater choice. It would likely be easier to find an instrument specifically suited to the needs of the science achievement study.

   b. Content-related evidence would be of concern in establishing validity for the measurement of achievement; construct-related evidence would be of most interest for the validity of personality measurement. Evidence for the former would come from a logical analysis; evidence for the latter would most likely be based on information from the test manual, especially if the researcher is attempting to establish the constructs that underlie the junior high personality.

   c. Achievement could be measured by a paper-and-pencil test; personality data might be obtained by some type of written group test or might require individual testing.

12.7 A Likert scale is a scale used with individual items; it contains a number of points, usually four or more, with intervals between the points assumed to be equal. The respondents respond to individual items. The semantic differential, on the other hand, contains a series of pairs of bipolar terms (usually adjectives); each pair is located on the end points of the scale (continuum), usually with seven or nine intervals. The respondent is asked to judge the word or phrase (which represents a concept) at the top of the page by checking the scale for each of the bipolar pairs.

12.8 Consider the following coding scheme, listing the identification information first:

   a. Student identification number: four columns, since there are more than 1000 students and we can assume that there are fewer than 10,000 in the sample, provide numbers from 0001 to however many students are in the sample.

   b. City school number: two columns; there are 74 schools, and each would be assigned a two-digit number.

   c. Grade level: one column; assign numbers 3 through 8.

   d. Sex: one column; boys assigned 0, girls 1.

   e. High school district: one column; assign numbers 1 through 9.

   f. Age: three columns; age is to be given in months, and eighth-graders, the oldest students in the study, are typically around 13 or 14 years old, or around 156 to 168 months.

   Thus, identification would require twelve columns. The achievement variables would require a minimum of 44 columns, since the 10 two-digit variables would require 20 columns and the remaining eight variables would require 24 columns. The actual achievement scores would be recorded. This scheme requires a total of 56 columns for all information, so the information for a single student would fit on a row.

   Variations of this coding scheme could be used. For example, if no school has more than 100 students in the sample, the school code could be incorporated into the student number such that the first 2 columns of the student number indicate the school and the final 2 columns indicate the student in the school. For example, 1205 would indicate the fifth student in school number 12. This coding would reduce the number of columns required. Since the row is not filled, there is no great concern about reducing the number of columns. If it is desirable to allow three columns for each achievement score, this could be done, and the achievement data would then require 54 columns. In that case, the two-digit scores would have their scores preceded by a zero (or blank); for example, a score of 86 would be recorded as 086.

Chapter 13

13.1 Measures of central tendency are points that locate the distribution on the scale of measurement. Measures of variability are intervals that indicate the dispersion or spread in the distribution. In describing a distribution, measures of central tendency indicate where the distribution is located on the scale of measurement; measures of variability are indicators of the spread of scores in the distribution.

13.2 The mean is sensitive to extreme scores and the median is not. The salaries of the president and vice presidents are bunched at the extreme end of the distribution and would put the mean salary around $45,000. The median salary would be around $30,000 or so, which is more indicative of what most employees earn in this company.

13.3 To describe a distribution, it is necessary to know: (1) its shape, (2) its location on the scale of measurement, and (3) its dispersion or variability.

13.4 Some type of standard score is necessary in order to put the scores from the school subjects on a common measurement scale so that the scores of an individual student can be compared. The z-score would not be desirable because its distribution has a mean of zero and many scores (about one-half) would be negative. Any number of transformed scores could be used; for example, one with a mean of 100 and a standard deviation of 20.

13.5 a. Negative, those scoring higher on the intelligence test would likely require less time.
   b. Possibly a low, negative correlation.
   c. Positive
   d. Zero
   e. Zero

13.6 The mean scores show little difference, that for the boys being less than 2 points greater than the mean for girls. However, the distribution for girls is more variable (spread out more) than that for boys. This indicates that, relatively speaking, some girls have very positive attitudes and others quite negative attitudes. The boys are more homogenous in attitude. However, with a total possible score of 130, both means are more than 10 points below the midpoint of the scale, indicating in absolute terms quite low or negative attitudes.

Chapter 14

14.1 A random sample would be selected and statistics computed from this sample. The sample measures would reflect the population measures within the limits of sampling fluctuation. Hence, the statistics are used to infer to the parameters, again within the bounds of sampling fluctuation. The statistic involved would be the mean reading level of the sample of first-graders measured; the corresponding parameter is the mean reading level of the entire first-grade population. The chain of reasoning follows the implied inference. The population has certain measures, called parameters. The statistics are determined, and from them we reason back to the corresponding parameters and draw conclusions about the parameters. In this situation, conclusions are drawn about the population mean from the observed sample mean.

14.2 A statistic is a measure of a sample, and a parameter is a measure of a population. The sampling distribution is the distribution of the statistic, usually a theoretical distribution. (It is the distribution of all possible values of the statistic for the given sample size.) The sampling distribution provides the theoretical base for how the statistic under study behaves; that is, it identifies the shape, location, and dispersion of the distribution of the statistic of which the researcher has one observation.

14.3 a. If we were interested only in describing the distribution of scores for these 150 students.
   b. If inferences were being made to a larger population of teacher education students and the 150 students consisted of a random sample of this population.
   c. If the relationships between the variables were of interest.

14.4 We would reject the hypothesis because with 19 degrees of freedom and a two-tailed test (no direction is hypothesized) a t-value of 2.09 is required for significance at the .05 level.

14.5 The sampling distribution of the mean is used; this would be the t-distribution with 399 degrees of freedom (df), but since the df are so large, the normal distribution would be used. If sample size were 25, the t-distribution with 24 df would be used. There would be an error, because the confidence interval is constructed symmetrically about the sample mean; therefore, it must be the midpoint of the interval. The interval would be shorter if it were a 90 percent confidence interval.

14.6 In this case, the difference between the four sample means could be analyzed simultaneously, rather than analyzing only the difference between two means at a time with a t-test. The null hypothesis is that the four population means are equal—H_0: $\mu_1 = \mu_2 = \mu_3 = \mu_4$. Differences between male and female teachers also could be analyzed by extending the ANOVA to a two-way ANOVA.

14.7 Since the χ^2-value was significant, the conclusion is that the four samples were not drawn from a common population, or that the population distributions differ with respect to this variable. The probability that the sample distributions would have appeared due to random sampling fluctuation if the population distributions were the same is less than .05.

14.8 Grade level and attitude toward school are independent. If the χ^2 test is significant, we conclude that grade level and attitude toward school are related (not independent) in the student population sampled. If the χ^2 test is not significant, we cannot reject the hypothesis of independence and conclude that grade level and attitude toward school are not related to the population.

14.9　**a.** The mean would be computed as a measure of central tendency and the standard deviation as a measure of dispersion. The teachers also might compute the median and mode as additional information about central tendency, and the range as a second measure of dispersion.
　　b. The correlation coefficient between math test performance and attitude inventory score.
　　c. In contrast to the situation in (b) above, a random sample was selected so this situation involved inferential statistics. The correlation coefficient between math test scores and attitude inventory scores would be computed. This coefficient is a statistic and it would be used to test the null hypothesis that in the high school population the correlation is zero.
　　d. The cognitive task means of the four groups would be computed and used to test the null hypothesis; H_0: $\mu_1 = \mu_2 = \mu_3 = \mu_4$ by computing an ANOVA.
　　e. A goodness-of-fit test is called for; use a chi-square test, testing the sample distribution against the uniform distribution.

14.10 The two types of possible errors are rejecting a true hypothesis and failing to reject a false hypothesis. In inferential statistics, we do not know the values of the parameters about which we are hypothesizing; therefore, there is always the possibility of making an error. Inferences are made to the parameters from the statistics on the basis of probability. Although the probability of making an error may be very small, it is never zero.

14.12 Errors of reasoning or procedure:
　　a. A t-test does not apply to data measured on an ordinal scale, and means should not have been computed with ordinal data.
　　b. There is confusion on significance; a test that is significant at the .01 level is also significant at the .05 level.
　　c. Rejecting the null hypothesis would result in concluding that the population measures, not the sample measures, are different.
　　d. Since the null hypothesis is rejected, there is no probability of having made a Type II or beta error. The possibility does exist of having made a Type I or alpha error—that is, rejecting a true hypothesis.

14.13 **a.** H_0: $\mu_1 = \mu_2 = \mu_3 = \mu_4 = \mu_5$. The population means of the five experimental treatments are equal. The null hypotheses also could be stated as: The five experimental treatments are equally effective in the population.

  b. The computed F-value of 3.11 exceeds the critical value of F from Table D in Appendix 3, for 4 and 95 df and a significance level of .05. The critical value is about 2.49. Therefore, we reject the null hypothesis and conclude that the population means are not all equal.

  c. The probability that the five sample means would appear by chance, if the population means are all equal, is less than .05.

14.15 We want to make some decisions about the population characteristics, which are parameters. We draw a sample and compute characteristics of the sample, which are statistics. The statistics reflect the corresponding parameters within the bounds of random sampling fluctuations. We hypothesize about parameters, and the statistics have a certain probability of appearing by chance if the hypotheses are true. It is not necessary to determine the exact probability, only whether it is less than or greater than the significance level. We infer from the statistics and the results of hypothesis testing to the parameters and thus make decisions about the population.

Chapter 15

15.4 This situation suggests a considerable quantity of results. Since there are ten test scores, four grades, and two groups within each grade, there are eighty means and eighty standard deviations ($10 \times 4 \times 2$). Forty t-tests are computed, so there are forty t-values. There are forty-five correlation coefficients to report. Thus, to avoid excessively large or complicated tables, the minimum number of tables necessary is four. One way to organize the results would be a table for means, with eight columns for the four grades (experimental and control columns for each grade). The means for a specific test would then be in a row. We would have a similar table for standard deviations; a table of t-values containing four columns, one for each grade (it would be well to have this table near the table of means, since the difference between means is being tested); and a table (sometimes called a matrix) of correlation coefficients. The following is an example of a title and headings for the table of means:

TABLE A.1 Means for Experimental and Control Groups by Grade and Test

				Grade				
	4		5		6		7	
Test	E	C	E	C	E	C	E	C

Appendix *3*

Tables

TABLE A   Ordinates and Areas of the Normal Curve (in terms of s units)

$\frac{x}{\sigma}$	Area	Ordi-nate	$\frac{x}{\sigma}$	Area	Ordi-nate	$\frac{x}{\sigma}$	Area	Ordi-nate	$\frac{x}{\sigma}$	Area	Ordi-nate
.00	.0000	.3989	.35	.1368	.3752	.70	.2580	.3123	1.05	.3531	.2299
.01	.0040	.3989	.36	.1406	.3739	.71	.2611	.3101	1.06	.3554	.2275
.02	.0080	.3989	.37	.1443	.3725	.72	.2642	.3079	1.07	.3577	.2251
.03	.0120	.3988	.38	.1480	.3712	.73	.2673	.3056	1.08	.3599	.2227
.04	.0160	.3986	.39	.1517	.3697	.74	.2703	.3034	1.09	.3621	.2203
.05	.0199	.3984	.40	.1554	.3683	.75	.2734	.3011	1.10	.3643	.2179
.06	.0239	.3992	.41	.1591	.3668	.76	.2764	.2989	1.11	.3665	.2155
.07	.0279	.3980	.42	.1628	.3653	.77	.2794	.2966	1.12	.3686	.2131
.08	.0319	.3977	.43	.1664	.3637	.78	.2823	.2943	1.13	.3708	.2107
.09	.0359	.3973	.44	.1700	.3621	.79	.2852	.2920	1.14	.3729	.2083
.10	.0398	.3970	.45	.1736	.3605	.80	.2881	.2897	1.15	.3749	.2059
.11	.0438	.3965	.46	.1772	.3589	.81	.2910	.2874	1.16	.3770	.2036
.12	.0478	.3961	.47	.1808	.3572	.82	.2939	.2850	1.17	.3790	.2012
.13	.0517	.3956	.48	.1844	.3555	.83	.2967	.2827	1.18	.3810	.1989
.14	.0557	.3951	.49	.1879	.3538	.84	.2995	.2803	1.19	.3830	.1965
.15	.0596	.3945	.50	.1915	.3521	.85	.3023	.2780	1.20	.3849	.1942
.16	.0636	.3939	.51	.1950	.3503	.86	.3051	.2756	1.21	.3869	.1919
.17	.0675	.3932	.52	.1985	.3485	.87	.3078	.2732	1.22	.3888	.1895
.18	.0714	.3925	.53	.2019	.3467	.88	.3106	.2709	1.23	.3907	.1872
.19	.0753	.3918	.54	.2054	.3448	.89	.3133	.2685	1.24	.3925	.1849
.20	.0793	.3910	.55	.2088	.3429	.90	.3159	.2661	1.25	.3944	.1826
.21	.0832	.3902	.56	.2123	.3410	.91	.3186	.2637	1.26	.3962	.1804
.22	.0871	.3894	.57	.2157	.3391	.92	.3212	.2613	1.27	.3980	.1781
.23	.0910	.3885	.58	.2190	.3372	.93	.3238	.2589	1.28	.3997	.1758
.24	.0948	.3876	.59	.2224	.3352	.94	.3264	.2565	1.29	.4015	.1736
.25	.0987	.3867	.60	.2257	.3332	.95	.3289	.2541	1.30	.4032	.1714
.26	.1026	.3857	.61	.2291	.3312	.96	.3315	.2516	1.31	.4049	.1691
.27	.1064	.3847	.62	.2324	.3292	.97	.3340	.2492	1.32	.4066	.1669
.28	.1103	.3836	.63	.2357	.3271	.98	.3365	.2468	1.33	.4082	.1647
.29	.1141	.3825	.64	.2389	.3251	.99	.3389	.2444	1.34	.4099	.1626
.30	.1179	.3814	.65	.2422	.3230	1.00	.3413	.2420	1.35	.4115	.1604
.31	.1217	.3802	.66	.2454	.3209	1.01	.3438	.2396	1.36	.4131	.1582
.32	.1255	.3790	.67	.2486	.3187	1.02	.3461	.2371	1.37	.4147	.1561
.33	.1293	.3778	.68	.2517	.3166	1.03	.3485	.2347	1.38	.4162	.1539
.34	.1331	.3765	.69	.2549	.3144	1.04	.3508	.2323	1.39	.4177	.1518

Source: Educational Statistics, by J. E. Wert. Copyright 1938 by McGraw-Hill Book Company. Used by permission of McGraw-Hill Book Company.

TABLE A *Continued*

$\frac{x}{\sigma}$	Area	Ordinate	$\frac{x}{\sigma}$	Area	Ordinate	$\frac{x}{\sigma}$	Area	Ordinate	$\frac{x}{\sigma}$	Area	Ordinate
1.40	.4192	.1497	1.80	.4641	.0790	2.20	.4861	.0355	2.60	.4953	.0136
1.41	.4207	.1476	1.81	.4649	.0775	2.21	.4864	.0347	2.61	.4955	.0132
1.42	.4222	.1456	1.82	.4656	.0761	2.22	.4868	.0339	2.62	.4956	.0129
1.43	.4236	.1435	1.83	.4664	.0748	2.23	.4871	.0332	2.63	.4957	.0126
1.44	.4251	.1415	1.84	.4671	.0734	2.24	.4875	.0325	2.64	.4959	.0122
1.45	.4265	.1394	1.85	.4678	.0721	2.25	.4878	.0317	2.65	.4960	.0119
1.46	.4279	.1374	1.86	.4686	.0707	2.26	.4881	.0310	2.66	.4961	.0116
1.47	.4292	.1354	1.87	.4693	.0694	2.27	.4884	.0303	2.67	.4962	.0113
1.48	.4306	.1334	1.88	.4699	.0681	2.28	.4887	.0297	2.68	.4963	.0110
1.49	.4319	.1315	1.89	.4706	.0669	2.29	.4890	.0290	2.69	.4964	.0107
1.50	.4332	.1295	1.90	.4713	.0656	2.30	.4893	.0283	2.70	.4965	.0104
1.51	.4345	.1276	1.91	.4719	.0644	2.31	.4896	.0277	2.71	.4966	.0101
1.52	.4357	.1257	1.92	.4726	.0632	2.32	.4898	.0270	2.72	.4967	.0099
1.53	.4370	.1238	1.93	.4732	.0620	2.33	.4901	.0264	2.73	.4968	.0096
1.54	.4382	.1219	1.94	.4738	.0608	2.34	.4904	.0258	2.74	.4969	.0093
1.55	.4394	.1200	1.95	.4744	.0596	2.35	.4906	.0252	2.75	.4970	.0091
1.56	.4406	.1182	1.96	.4750	.0584	2.36	.4909	.0246	2.76	.4971	.0088
1.57	.4418	.1163	1.97	.4756	.0573	2.37	.4911	.0241	2.77	.4972	.0086
1.58	.4429	.1145	1.98	.4761	.0562	2.38	.4913	.0235	2.78	.4973	.0084
1.59	.4441	.1127	1.99	.4767	.0551	2.39	.4916	.0229	2.79	.4974	.0081
1.60	.4452	.1109	2.00	.4772	.0540	2.40	.4918	.0224	2.80	.4974	.0079
1.61	.4463	.1092	2.01	.4778	.0529	2.41	.4920	.0219	2.81	.4975	.0077
1.62	.4474	.1074	2.02	.4783	.0519	2.42	.4922	.0213	2.82	.4976	.0075
1.63	.4484	.1057	2.03	.4788	.0508	2.43	.4925	.0208	2.83	.4977	.0073
1.64	.4495	.1040	2.04	.4793	.0498	2.44	.4927	.0203	2.84	.4977	.0071
1.65	.4505	.1023	2.05	.4798	.0488	2.45	.4929	.0198	2.85	.4978	.0069
1.66	.4515	.1006	2.06	.4803	.0478	2.46	.4931	.0194	2.86	.4979	.0067
1.67	.4525	.0989	2.07	.4808	.0468	2.47	.4932	.0189	2.87	.4979	.0065
1.68	.4535	.0973	2.08	.4812	.0459	2.48	.4934	.0184	2.88	.4980	.0063
1.69	.4545	.0957	2.09	.4817	.0449	2.49	.4936	.0180	2.89	.4981	.0061
1.70	.4554	.0940	2.10	.4821	.0440	2.50	.4938	.0175	2.90	.4981	.0060
1.71	.4564	.0925	2.11	.4826	.0431	2.51	.4940	.0171	2.91	.4982	.0058
1.72	.4573	.0909	2.12	.4830	.0422	2.52	.4941	.0167	2.92	.4982	.0056
1.73	.4582	.0893	2.13	.4834	.0413	2.53	.4943	.0163	2.93	.4993	.0055
1.74	.4591	.0878	2.14	.4838	.0404	2.54	.4945	.0158	2.94	.4984	.0053
1.75	.4599	.0863	2.15	.4842	.0395	2.55	.4946	.0154	2.95	.4984	.0051
1.76	.4608	.0848	2.16	.4846	.0387	2.56	.4948	.0151	2.96	.4985	.0050
1.77	.4616	.0833	2.17	.4850	.0379	2.57	.4949	.0147	2.97	.4985	.0048
1.78	.4625	.0818	2.18	.4854	.0371	2.58	.4951	.0143	2.98	.4986	.0047
1.79	.4633	.0804	2.19	.4857	.0363	2.59	.4952	.0139	2.99	.4986	.0046
									3.00	.4987	.0044

TABLE B Critical Values of *t*

	Level of significance for one-tailed test					
	.10	.05	.025	.01	.005	.0005
	Level of significance for two-tailed test					
df	.20	.10	.05	.02	.01	.001
1	3.078	6.314	12.706	31.821	63.657	636.619
2	1.886	2.920	4.303	6.965	9.925	31.598
3	1.638	2.353	3.182	4.541	5.841	12.941
4	1.533	2.132	2.776	3.747	4.604	8.610
5	1.476	2.015	2.571	3.365	4.032	6.859
6	1.440	1.943	2.447	3.143	3.707	5.959
7	1.415	1.895	2.365	2.998	3.499	5.405
8	1.397	1.860	2.306	2.896	3.355	5.041
9	1.383	1.833	2.262	2.821	3.250	4.781
10	1.372	1.812	2.228	2.764	3.169	4.587
11	1.363	1.796	2.201	2.718	3.106	4.437
12	1.356	1.782	2.179	2.681	3.055	4.318
13	1.350	1.771	2.160	2.650	3.012	4.221
14	1.345	1.761	2.145	2.624	2.977	4.140
15	1.341	1.753	2.131	2.602	2.947	4.073
16	1.337	1.746	2.120	2.583	2.921	4.015
17	1.333	1.740	2.110	2.567	2.898	3.965
18	1.330	1.734	2.101	2.552	2.878	3.922
19	1.328	1.729	2.093	2.539	2.861	3.883
20	1.325	1.725	2.086	2.528	2.845	3.850
21	1.323	1.721	2.080	2.518	2.831	3.819
22	1.321	1.717	2.074	2.508	2.819	3.792
23	1.319	1.714	2.069	2.500	2.807	3.767
24	1.318	1.711	2.064	2.492	2.797	3.745
25	1.316	1.708	2.060	2.485	2.787	3.725
26	1.315	1.706	2.056	2.479	2.779	3.707
27	1.314	1.703	2.052	2.473	2.771	3.690
28	1.313	1.701	2.048	2.467	2.763	3.674
29	1.311	1.699	2.045	2.462	2.756	3.659
30	1.310	1.697	2.042	2.457	2.750	3.646
40	1.303	1.684	2.021	2.423	2.704	3.551
60	1.296	1.671	2.000	2.390	2.660	3.460
120	1.289	1.658	1.980	2.358	2.617	3.373
χ	1.282	1.645	1.960	2.326	2.576	3.291

Source: Abridged from Table III, p. 46 of R. A. Fisher and F. Yates, *Statistical Tables for Biological, Agricultural and Medical Research,* 6th edition, published by Longman Group, Ltd., London, 1974 (previously published by Oliver & Boyd, Ltd., Edinburgh), and reprinted by permission of the authors and publishers.

TABLE C   Upper Percentage Points of the χ^2 Distribution

df	.99	.98	.95	.90	.80	.70	.50	.30	.20	.10	.05	.02	.01	.001
1	$.0^3157$	$.0^3628$	.00393	.0158	.0642	.148	.455	1.074	1.642	2.706	3.841	5.412	6.635	10.827
2	.0201	.0404	.103	.211	.446	.713	1.386	2.408	3.219	4.605	5.991	7.824	9.210	13.815
3	.115	.185	.352	.584	1.005	1.424	2.366	3.665	4.642	6.251	7.815	9.837	11.345	16.266
4	.297	.429	.711	1.064	1.649	2.195	3.357	4.878	5.989	7.779	9.488	11.668	13.277	18.467
5	.554	.752	1.145	1.610	2.343	3.000	4.351	6.064	7.289	9.236	11.070	13.388	15.086	20.515
6	.872	1.134	1.635	2.204	3.070	3.828	5.348	7.231	8.558	10.645	12.592	15.033	16.812	22.457
7	1.239	1.564	2.167	2.833	3.822	4.671	6.346	8.383	9.803	12.017	14.067	16.622	18.475	24.322
8	1.646	2.032	2.733	3.490	4.594	5.527	7.344	9.524	11.030	13.362	15.507	18.168	20.090	26.125
9	2.088	2.532	3.325	4.168	5.380	6.393	8.343	10.656	12.242	14.684	16.919	19.679	21.666	27.877
10	2.558	3.059	3.940	4.865	6.179	7.267	9.342	11.781	13.442	15.987	18.307	21.161	23.209	29.588
11	3.053	3.609	4.575	5.578	6.989	8.148	10.341	12.899	14.631	17.275	19.675	22.618	24.725	31.264
12	3.571	4.178	5.226	6.304	7.807	9.034	11.340	14.011	15.812	18.549	21.026	24.054	26.217	32.909
13	4.107	4.765	5.892	7.042	8.634	9.926	12.340	15.119	16.985	19.812	22.362	25.472	27.688	34.528
14	4.660	5.368	6.571	7.790	9.467	10.821	13.339	16.222	18.151	21.064	23.685	26.873	29.141	36.123
15	5.229	5.985	7.261	8.547	10.307	11.721	14.339	17.322	19.311	22.307	24.996	28.259	30.578	37.697
16	5.812	6.614	7.962	9.312	11.152	12.624	15.338	18.418	20.465	23.542	26.296	29.633	32.000	39.252
17	6.408	7.255	8.672	10.085	12.002	13.531	16.338	19.511	21.615	24.769	27.587	30.995	33.409	40.790
18	7.015	7.906	9.390	10.865	12.857	14.440	17.338	20.601	22.760	25.989	28.869	32.346	34.805	42.312
19	7.633	8.567	10.117	11.651	13.716	15.352	18.338	21.689	23.900	27.204	30.144	33.687	36.191	43.820
20	8.260	9.237	10.851	12.443	14.578	16.266	19.337	22.775	25.038	28.412	31.410	35.020	37.566	45.315
21	8.897	9.915	11.591	13.240	15.445	17.182	20.337	23.858	26.171	29.615	32.671	36.343	38.932	46.797
22	9.542	10.600	12.338	14.041	16.314	18.101	21.337	24.939	27.301	30.813	33.924	37.659	40.289	48.268
23	10.196	11.293	13.091	14.848	17.187	19.021	22.337	26.018	28.429	32.007	35.172	38.968	41.638	49.728
24	10.856	11.992	13.848	15.659	18.062	19.943	23.337	27.096	29.553	33.196	36.415	40.270	42.980	51.179
25	11.524	12.697	14.611	16.473	18.940	20.867	24.337	28.172	30.675	34.382	37.652	41.566	44.314	52.620
26	12.198	13.409	15.379	17.292	19.820	21.792	25.336	29.246	31.795	35.563	38.885	42.856	45.642	54.052
27	12.879	14.125	16.151	18.114	20.703	22.719	26.336	30.319	32.912	36.741	40.113	44.140	46.963	55.476
28	13.565	14.847	16.928	18.939	21.588	23.647	27.336	31.391	34.027	37.916	41.337	45.419	48.278	56.893
29	14.256	15.574	17.708	19.768	22.475	24.577	28.336	32.461	35.139	39.087	42.557	46.693	49.588	58.302
30	14.953	16.306	18.493	20.599	23.364	25.508	29.336	33.530	36.250	40.256	43.773	47.962	50.892	59.703

Source: Taken from Table IV, p. 47 of Fisher and Yates: *Statistical Tables for Biological, Agricultural and Medical Research,* published by Longman Group, Ltd., London (previously published by Oliver and Boyd, Ltd., Edinburgh), and reprinted by permission of the authors and publishers.

For df > 30, the expression $\sqrt{2\chi^2} - \sqrt{2df - 1}$ may be used as a normal deviate with unit variance.

TABLE D Upper Percentage Points of the *F*-distribution

df for de-nomi-nator	α	df for numerator											
		1	2	3	4	5	6	7	8	9	10	11	12
1	.25	5.83	7.50	8.20	8.58	8.82	8.98	9.10	9.19	9.26	9.32	9.36	9.41
	.10	39.9	49.5	53.6	55.8	57.2	58.2	58.9	59.4	59.9	60.2	60.5	60.7
	.05	161	200	216	225	230	234	237	239	241	242	243	244
2	.25	2.57	3.00	3.15	3.23	3.28	3.31	3.34	3.35	3.37	3.38	3.39	3.39
	.10	8.53	9.00	9.16	9.24	9.29	9.33	9.35	9.37	9.38	9.39	9.40	9.41
	.05	18.5	19.0	19.2	19.2	19.3	19.3	19.4	19.4	19.4	19.4	19.4	19.4
	.01	98.5	99.0	99.2	99.2	99.3	99.3	99.4	99.4	99.4	99.4	99.4	99.4
3	.25	2.02	2.28	2.36	2.39	2.41	2.42	2.43	2.44	2.44	2.44	2.45	2.45
	.10	5.54	5.46	5.39	5.34	5.31	5.28	5.27	5.25	5.24	5.23	5.22	5.22
	.05	10.1	9.55	9.28	9.12	9.01	8.94	8.89	8.85	8.81	8.79	8.76	8.74
	.01	34.1	30.8	29.5	28.7	28.2	27.9	27.7	27.5	27.3	27.2	27.1	27.1
4	.25	1.81	2.00	2.05	2.06	2.07	2.08	2.08	2.08	2.08	2.08	2.08	2.08
	.10	4.54	4.32	4.19	4.11	4.05	4.01	3.98	3.95	3.94	3.92	3.91	3.90
	.05	7.71	6.94	6.59	6.39	6.26	6.16	6.09	6.04	6.00	5.96	5.94	5.91
	.01	21.2	18.0	16.7	16.0	15.5	15.2	15.0	14.8	14.7	14.5	14.4	14.4
5	.25	1.69	1.85	1.88	1.89	1.89	1.89	1.89	1.89	1.89	1.89	1.89	1.89
	.10	4.06	3.78	3.62	3.52	3.45	3.40	3.37	3.34	3.32	3.30	3.28	3.27
	.05	6.61	5.79	5.41	5.19	5.05	4.95	4.88	4.82	4.77	4.74	4.71	4.68
	.01	16.3	13.3	12.1	11.4	11.0	10.7	10.5	10.3	10.2	10.1	9.96	9.89
6	.25	1.62	1.76	1.78	1.79	1.79	1.78	1.78	1.78	1.77	1.77	1.77	1.77
	.10	3.78	3.46	3.29	3.18	3.11	3.05	3.01	2.98	2.96	2.94	2.92	2.90
	.05	5.99	5.14	4.76	4.53	4.39	4.28	4.21	4.15	4.10	4.06	4.03	4.00
	.01	13.7	10.9	9.78	9.15	8.75	8.47	8.26	8.10	7.98	7.87	7.79	7.72
7	.25	1.57	1.70	1.72	1.72	1.71	1.71	1.70	1.70	1.69	1.69	1.69	1.68
	.10	3.59	3.26	3.07	2.96	2.88	2.83	2.78	2.75	2.72	2.70	2.68	2.67
	.05	5.59	4.74	4.35	4.12	3.97	3.87	3.79	3.73	3.68	3.64	3.60	3.57
	.01	12.2	9.55	8.45	7.85	7.46	7.19	6.99	6.84	6.72	6.62	6.54	6.47
8	.25	1.54	1.66	1.67	1.66	1.66	1.65	1.64	1.64	1.63	1.63	1.63	1.62
	.10	3.46	3.11	2.92	2.81	2.73	2.67	2.62	2.59	2.56	2.54	2.52	2.50
	.05	5.32	4.46	4.07	3.84	3.69	3.58	3.50	3.44	3.39	3.35	3.31	3.28
	.01	11.3	8.65	7.59	7.01	6.63	6.37	6.18	6.03	5.91	5.81	5.73	5.67
9	.25	1.51	1.62	1.63	1.63	1.62	1.61	1.60	1.60	1.59	1.59	1.58	1.58
	.10	3.36	3.01	2.81	2.69	2.61	2.55	2.51	2.47	2.44	2.42	2.40	2.38
	.05	5.12	4.26	3.86	3.63	3.48	3.37	3.29	3.23	3.18	3.14	3.10	3.07
	.01	10.6	8.02	6.99	6.42	6.06	5.80	5.61	5.47	5.35	5.26	5.18	5.11

TABLE D *Continued*

				df *for numerator*									df *for de-nomi-nator*
15	20	24	30	40	50	60	100	120	200	500	χ	α	
9.49	9.58	9.63	9.67	9.71	9.74	9.76	9.78	9.80	9.82	9.84	9.85	.25	
61.2	61.7	62.0	62.3	62.5	62.7	62.8	63.0	63.1	63.2	63.3	63.3	.10	1
246	248	249	250	251	252	252	253	253	254	254	254	.05	
3.41	3.43	3.43	3.44	3.45	3.45	3.46	3.47	3.47	3.48	3.48	3.48	.25	
9.42	9.44	9.45	9.46	9.47	9.47	9.47	9.48	9.48	9.49	9.49	9.49	.10	2
19.4	19.4	19.5	19.5	19.5	19.5	19.5	19.5	19.5	19.5	19.5	19.5	.05	
99.4	99.4	99.5	99.5	99.5	99.5	99.5	99.5	99.5	99.5	99.5	99.5	.01	
2.46	2.46	2.46	2.47	2.47	2.47	2.47	2.47	2.47	2.47	2.47	2.47	.25	
5.20	5.18	5.18	5.17	5.16	5.15	5.15	5.14	5.14	5.14	5.14	5.13	.10	3
8.70	8.66	8.64	8.62	8.59	8.58	8.57	8.55	8.55	8.54	8.53	8.53	.05	
26.9	26.7	26.6	26.5	26.4	26.4	26.3	26.2	26.2	26.2	26.1	26.1	.01	
2.08	2.08	2.08	2.08	2.08	2.08	2.08	2.08	2.08	2.08	2.08	2.08	.25	
3.87	3.84	3.83	3.82	3.80	3.80	3.79	3.78	3.78	3.77	3.76	3.76	.10	4
5.86	5.80	5.77	5.75	5.72	5.70	5.69	5.66	5.66	5.65	5.64	5.63	.05	
14.2	14.0	13.9	13.8	13.7	13.7	13.7	13.6	13.6	13.5	13.5	13.5	.01	
1.89	1.88	1.88	1.88	1.88	1.88	1.87	1.87	1.87	1.87	1.87	1.87	.25	
3.24	3.21	3.19	3.17	3.16	3.15	3.14	3.13	3.12	3.12	3.11	3.10	.10	5
4.62	4.56	4.53	4.50	4.46	4.44	4.43	4.41	4.40	4.39	4.37	4.36	.05	
9.72	9.55	9.47	9.38	9.29	9.24	9.20	9.13	9.11	9.08	9.04	9.02	.01	
1.76	1.76	1.75	1.75	1.75	1.75	1.74	1.74	1.74	1.74	1.74	1.74	.25	
2.87	2.84	2.82	2.80	2.78	2.77	2.76	2.75	2.74	2.73	2.73	2.72	.10	6
3.94	3.87	3.84	3.81	3.77	3.75	3.74	3.71	3.70	3.69	3.68	3.67	.05	
7.56	7.40	7.31	7.23	7.14	7.09	7.06	6.99	6.97	6.93	6.90	6.88	.01	
1.68	1.67	1.67	1.66	1.66	1.66	1.65	1.65	1.65	1.65	1.65	1.65	.25	
2.63	2.59	2.58	2.56	2.54	2.52	2.51	2.50	2.49	2.48	2.48	2.47	.10	7
3.51	3.44	3.41	3.38	3.34	3.32	3.30	3.27	3.27	3.25	3.24	3.23	.05	
6.31	6.16	6.07	5.99	5.91	5.86	5.82	5.75	5.74	5.70	5.67	5.65	.01	
1.62	1.61	1.60	1.60	1.59	1.59	1.59	1.58	1.58	1.58	1.58	1.58	.25	
2.46	2.42	2.40	2.38	2.36	2.35	2.34	2.32	2.32	2.31	2.30	2.29	.10	8
3.22	3.15	3.12	3.08	3.04	3.02	3.01	2.97	2.97	2.95	2.94	2.93	.05	
5.52	5.36	5.28	5.20	5.12	5.07	5.03	4.96	4.95	4.91	4.88	4.86	.01	
1.57	1.56	1.56	1.55	1.55	1.54	1.54	1.53	1.53	1.53	1.53	1.53	.25	
2.34	2.30	2.28	2.25	2.23	2.22	2.21	2.19	2.18	2.17	2.17	2.16	.10	9
3.01	2.94	2.90	2.86	2.83	2.80	2.79	2.76	2.75	2.73	2.72	2.71	.05	
4.96	4.81	4.73	4.65	4.57	4.52	4.48	4.42	4.40	4.36	4.33	4.31	.01	

Continued

TABLE D *Continued*

df *for denominator*	α	1	2	3	4	5	6	7	8	9	10	11	12
						df for numerator							
10	.25	1.49	1.60	1.60	1.59	1.59	1.58	1.57	1.56	1.56	1.55	1.55	1.54
	.10	3.29	2.92	2.73	2.61	2.52	2.46	2.41	2.38	2.35	2.32	2.30	2.28
	.05	4.96	4.10	3.71	3.48	3.33	3.22	3.14	3.07	3.02	2.98	2.94	2.91
	.01	10.0	7.56	6.55	5.99	5.64	5.39	5.20	5.06	4.94	4.85	4.77	4.71
11	.25	1.47	1.58	1.58	1.57	1.56	1.55	1.54	1.53	1.53	1.52	1.52	1.51
	.10	3.23	2.86	2.66	2.54	2.45	2.39	2.34	2.30	2.27	2.25	2.23	2.21
	.05	4.84	3.98	3.59	3.36	3.20	3.09	3.01	2.95	2.90	2.85	2.82	2.79
	.01	9.65	7.21	6.22	5.67	5.32	5.07	4.89	4.74	4.63	4.54	4.46	4.40
12	.25	1.46	1.56	1.56	1.55	1.54	1.53	1.52	1.51	1.51	1.50	1.50	1.49
	.10	3.18	2.81	2.61	2.48	2.39	2.33	2.28	2.24	2.21	2.19	2.17	2.15
	.05	4.75	3.89	3.49	3.26	3.11	3.00	2.91	2.85	2.80	2.75	2.72	2.69
	.01	9.33	6.93	5.95	5.41	5.06	4.82	4.64	4.50	4.39	4.30	4.22	4.16
13	.25	1.45	1.55	1.55	1.53	1.52	1.51	1.50	1.49	1.49	1.48	1.47	1.47
	.10	3.14	2.76	2.56	2.43	2.35	2.28	2.23	2.20	2.16	2.14	2.12	2.10
	.05	4.67	3.81	3.41	3.18	3.03	2.92	2.83	2.77	2.71	2.67	2.63	2.60
	.01	9.07	6.70	5.74	5.21	4.86	4.62	4.44	4.30	4.19	4.10	4.02	3.96
14	.25	1.44	1.53	1.53	1.52	1.51	1.50	1.49	1.48	1.47	1.46	1.46	1.45
	.10	3.10	2.73	2.52	2.39	2.31	2.24	2.19	2.15	2.12	2.10	2.08	2.05
	.05	4.60	3.74	3.34	3.11	2.96	2.85	2.76	2.70	2.65	2.60	2.57	2.53
	.01	8.86	6.51	5.56	5.04	4.69	4.46	4.28	4.14	4.03	3.94	3.86	3.80
15	.25	1.43	1.52	1.52	1.51	1.49	1.48	1.47	1.46	1.46	1.45	1.44	1.44
	.10	3.07	2.70	2.49	2.36	2.27	2.21	2.16	2.12	2.09	2.06	2.04	2.02
	.05	4.54	3.68	3.29	3.06	2.90	2.79	2.71	2.64	2.59	2.54	2.51	2.48
	.01	8.68	6.36	5.42	4.89	4.56	4.32	4.14	4.00	3.89	3.80	3.73	3.67
16	.25	1.42	1.51	1.51	1.50	1.48	1.47	1.46	1.45	1.44	1.44	1.44	1.43
	.10	3.05	2.67	2.46	2.33	2.24	2.18	2.13	2.09	2.06	2.03	2.01	1.99
	.05	4.49	3.63	3.24	3.01	2.85	2.74	2.66	2.59	2.54	2.49	2.46	2.42
	.01	8.53	6.23	5.29	4.77	4.44	4.20	4.03	3.89	3.78	3.69	3.62	3.55
17	.25	1.42	1.51	1.50	1.49	1.47	1.46	1.45	1.44	1.43	1.43	1.42	1.41
	.10	3.03	2.64	2.44	2.31	2.22	2.15	2.10	2.06	2.03	2.00	1.98	1.96
	.05	4.45	3.59	3.20	2.96	2.81	2.70	2.61	2.55	2.49	2.45	2.41	2.38
	.01	8.40	6.11	5.18	4.67	4.34	4.10	3.93	3.79	3.68	3.59	3.52	3.46
18	.25	1.41	1.50	1.49	1.48	1.46	1.45	1.44	1.43	1.42	1.42	1.41	1.40
	.10	3.01	2.62	2.42	2.29	2.20	2.13	2.08	2.04	2.00	1.98	1.96	1.93
	.05	4.41	3.55	3.16	2.93	2.77	2.66	2.58	2.51	2.46	2.41	2.37	2.34
	.01	8.29	6.01	5.09	4.58	4.25	4.01	3.84	3.71	3.60	3.51	3.43	3.37
19	.25	1.41	1.49	1.49	1.47	1.46	1.44	1.43	1.42	1.41	1.41	1.40	1.40
	.10	2.99	2.61	2.40	2.27	2.18	2.11	2.06	2.02	1.98	1.96	1.94	1.91
	.05	4.38	3.52	3.13	2.90	2.74	2.63	2.54	2.48	2.42	2.38	2.34	2.31
	.01	8.18	5.93	5.01	4.50	4.17	3.94	3.77	3.63	3.52	3.43	3.36	3.30
20	.25	1.40	1.49	1.48	1.46	1.45	1.44	1.43	1.42	1.41	1.40	1.39	1.39
	.10	2.97	2.59	2.38	2.25	2.16	2.09	2.04	2.00	1.96	1.94	1.92	1.89
	.05	4.35	3.49	3.10	2.87	2.71	2.60	2.51	2.45	2.39	2.35	2.31	2.28
	.01	8.10	5.85	4.94	4.43	4.10	3.87	3.70	3.56	3.46	3.37	3.29	3.23

TABLE D *Continued*

15	20	24	30	40	50	60	100	120	200	500	χ	α	df for denominator
					df *for numerator*								
1.53	1.52	1.52	1.51	1.51	1.50	1.50	1.49	1.49	1.49	1.48	1.48	.25	
2.24	2.20	2.18	2.16	2.13	2.12	2.11	2.09	2.08	2.07	2.06	2.06	.10	10
2.85	2.77	2.74	2.70	2.66	2.64	2.62	2.59	2.58	2.56	2.55	2.54	.05	
4.56	4.41	4.33	4.25	4.17	4.12	4.08	4.01	4.00	3.96	3.93	3.91	.01	
1.50	1.49	1.49	1.48	1.47	1.47	1.47	1.46	1.46	1.46	1.45	1.45	.25	
2.17	2.12	2.10	2.08	2.05	2.04	2.03	2.00	2.00	1.99	1.98	1.97	.10	11
2.72	2.65	2.61	2.57	2.53	2.51	2.49	2.46	2.45	2.43	2.42	2.40	.05	
4.25	4.10	4.02	3.94	3.86	3.81	3.78	3.71	3.69	3.66	3.62	3.60	.01	
1.48	1.47	1.46	1.45	1.45	1.44	1.44	1.43	1.43	1.43	1.42	1.42	.25	
2.10	2.06	2.04	2.01	1.99	1.97	1.96	1.94	1.93	1.92	1.91	1.90	.10	12
2.62	2.54	2.51	2.47	2.43	2.40	2.38	2.35	2.34	2.32	2.31	2.30	.05	
4.01	3.86	3.78	3.70	3.62	3.57	3.54	3.47	3.45	3.41	3.38	3.36	.01	
1.46	1.45	1.44	1.43	1.42	1.42	1.42	1.41	1.41	1.40	1.40	1.40	.25	
2.05	2.01	1.98	1.96	1.93	1.92	1.90	1.88	1.88	1.86	1.85	1.85	.10	13
2.53	2.46	2.42	2.38	2.34	2.31	2.30	2.26	2.25	2.23	2.22	2.21	.05	
3.82	3.66	3.59	3.51	3.43	3.38	3.34	3.27	3.25	3.22	3.19	3.17	.01	
1.44	1.43	14.2	1.41	1.41	1.40	1.40	1.39	1.39	1.39	1.38	1.38	.25	
2.01	1.96	1.94	1.91	1.89	1.87	1.86	1.83	1.83	1.82	1.80	1.80	.10	14
2.46	2.39	2.35	2.31	2.27	2.24	2.22	2.19	2.18	2.16	2.14	2.13	.05	
3.66	3.51	3.43	3.35	3.27	3.22	3.18	3.11	3.09	3.06	3.03	3.00	.01	
1.43	1.41	1.41	1.40	1.39	1.39	1.38	1.38	1.37	1.37	1.36	1.36	.25	
1.97	1.92	1.90	1.87	1.85	1.83	1.82	1.79	1.79	1.77	1.76	1.76	.10	15
2.40	2.33	2.29	2.25	2.20	2.18	2.16	2.12	2.11	2.10	2.08	2.07	.05	
3.52	3.37	3.29	3.21	3.13	3.08	3.05	2.98	2.96	2.92	2.89	2.87	.01	
1.41	1.40	1.39	1.38	1.37	1.37	1.36	1.36	1.35	1.35	1.34	1.34	.25	
1.94	1.89	1.87	1.84	1.81	1.79	1.78	1.76	1.75	1.74	1.73	1.72	.10	16
2.35	2.28	2.24	2.19	2.15	2.12	2.11	2.07	2.06	2.04	2.02	2.01	.05	
3.41	3.26	3.18	3.10	3.02	2.97	2.93	2.86	2.84	2.81	2.78	2.75	.01	
1.40	1.39	1.38	1.37	1.36	1.35	1.35	1.34	1.34	1.34	1.33	1.33	.25	
1.91	1.86	1.84	1.81	1.78	1.76	1.75	1.73	1.72	1.71	1.69	1.69	.10	17
2.31	2.23	2.19	2.15	2.10	2.08	2.06	2.02	2.01	1.99	1.97	1.96	.05	
3.31	3.16	3.08	3.00	2.92	2.87	2.83	2.76	2.75	2.71	2.68	2.65	.01	
1.39	1.38	1.37	1.36	1.35	1.34	1.34	1.33	1.33	1.32	1.32	1.32	.25	
1.89	1.84	1.81	1.78	1.75	1.74	1.72	1.70	1.69	1.68	1.67	1.66	.10	18
2.27	2.19	2.15	2.11	2.06	2.04	2.02	1.98	1.97	1.95	1.93	1.92	.05	
3.23	3.08	3.00	2.92	2.84	2.78	2.75	2.68	2.66	2.62	2.59	2.57	.01	
1.38	1.37	1.36	1.35	1.34	1.33	1.33	1.32	1.32	1.31	1.31	1.30	.25	
1.86	1.81	1.79	1.76	1.73	1.71	1.70	1.67	1.67	1.65	1.64	1.63	.10	19
2.23	2.16	2.11	2.07	2.03	2.00	1.98	1.94	1.93	1.91	1.89	1.88	.05	
3.15	3.00	2.92	2.84	2.76	2.71	2.67	2.60	2.58	2.55	2.51	2.49	.01	
1.37	1.36	1.35	1.34	1.33	1.33	1.32	1.31	1.31	1.30	1.30	1.29	.25	
1.84	1.79	1.77	1.74	1.71	1.69	1.68	1.65	1.64	1.63	1.62	1.61	.10	20
2.20	2.12	2.08	2.04	1.99	1.97	1.95	1.91	1.90	1.88	1.86	1.84	.05	
3.09	2.94	2.86	2.78	2.69	2.64	2.61	2.54	2.52	2.48	2.44	2.42	.01	

Continued

TABLE D *Continued*

df for de-nomi-nator	α	\multicolumn{12}{c}{df for numerator}											
		1	2	3	4	5	6	7	8	9	10	11	12
22	.25	1.40	1.48	1.47	1.45	1.44	1.42	1.41	1.40	1.39	1.39	1.38	1.37
	.10	2.95	2.56	2.35	2.22	2.13	2.06	2.01	1.97	1.93	1.90	1.88	1.86
	.05	4.30	3.44	3.05	2.82	2.66	2.55	2.46	2.40	2.34	2.30	2.26	2.23
	.01	7.95	5.72	4.82	4.31	3.99	3.76	3.59	3.45	3.35	3.26	3.18	3.12
24	.25	1.39	1.47	1.46	1.44	1.43	1.41	1.40	1.39	1.38	1.38	1.37	1.36
	.10	2.93	2.54	2.33	2.19	2.10	2.04	1.98	1.94	1.91	1.88	1.85	1.83
	.05	4.26	3.40	3.01	2.78	2.62	2.51	2.42	2.36	2.30	2.25	2.21	2.18
	.01	7.82	5.61	4.72	4.22	3.90	3.67	3.50	3.36	3.26	3.17	3.09	3.03
26	.25	1.38	1.46	1.45	1.44	1.42	1.41	1.39	1.38	1.37	1.37	1.36	1.35
	.10	2.91	2.52	2.31	2.17	2.08	2.01	1.96	1.92	1.88	1.86	1.84	1.81
	.05	4.23	3.37	2.98	2.74	2.59	2.47	2.39	2.32	2.27	2.22	2.18	2.15
	.01	7.72	5.53	4.64	4.14	3.82	3.59	3.42	3.29	3.18	3.09	3.02	2.96
28	.25	1.38	1.46	1.45	1.43	1.41	1.40	1.39	1.38	1.37	1.36	1.35	1.34
	.10	2.89	2.50	2.29	2.16	2.06	2.00	1.94	1.90	1.87	1.84	1.81	1.79
	.05	4.20	3.34	2.95	2.71	2.56	2.45	2.36	2.29	2.24	2.19	2.15	2.12
	.01	7.64	5.45	4.57	4.07	3.75	3.53	3.36	3.23	3.12	3.03	2.96	2.90
30	.25	1.38	1.45	1.44	1.42	1.41	1.39	1.38	1.37	1.36	1.35	1.35	1.34
	.10	2.88	2.49	2.28	2.14	2.05	1.98	1.93	1.88	1.85	1.82	1.79	1.77
	.05	4.17	3.32	2.92	2.69	2.53	2.42	2.33	2.27	2.21	2.16	2.13	2.09
	.01	7.56	5.39	4.51	4.02	3.70	3.47	3.30	3.17	3.07	2.98	2.91	2.84
40	.25	1.36	1.44	1.42	1.40	1.39	1.37	1.36	1.35	1.34	1.33	1.32	1.31
	.10	2.84	2.44	2.23	2.09	2.00	1.93	1.87	1.83	1.79	1.76	1.73	1.71
	.05	4.08	3.23	2.84	2.61	2.45	2.34	2.25	2.18	2.12	2.08	2.04	2.00
	.01	7.31	5.18	4.31	3.83	3.51	3.29	3.12	2.99	2.89	2.80	2.73	2.66
60	.25	1.35	1.42	1.41	1.38	1.37	1.35	1.33	1.32	1.31	1.30	1.29	1.29
	.10	2.79	2.39	2.18	2.04	1.95	1.87	1.82	1.77	1.74	1.71	1.68	1.66
	.05	4.00	3.15	2.76	2.53	2.37	2.25	2.17	2.10	2.04	1.99	1.95	1.92
	.01	7.08	4.98	4.13	3.65	3.34	3.12	2.95	2.82	2.72	2.63	2.56	2.50
120	.25	1.34	1.40	1.39	1.37	1.35	1.33	1.31	1.30	1.29	1.28	1.27	1.26
	.10	2.75	2.35	2.13	1.99	1.90	1.82	1.77	1.72	1.68	1.65	1.62	1.60
	.05	3.92	3.07	2.68	2.45	2.29	2.17	2.09	2.02	1.96	1.91	1.87	1.83
	.01	6.85	4.79	3.95	3.48	3.17	2.96	2.79	2.66	2.56	2.47	2.40	2.34
200	.25	1.33	1.39	1.38	1.36	1.34	1.32	1.31	1.29	1.28	1.27	1.26	1.25
	.10	2.73	2.33	2.11	1.97	1.88	1.80	1.75	1.70	1.66	1.63	1.60	1.57
	.05	3.89	3.04	2.65	2.42	2.26	2.14	2.06	1.98	1.93	1.88	1.84	1.80
	.01	6.76	4.71	3.88	3.41	3.11	2.89	2.73	2.60	2.50	2.41	2.34	2.27
χ	.25	1.32	1.39	1.37	1.35	1.33	1.31	1.29	1.28	1.27	1.25	1.24	1.24
	.10	2.71	2.30	2.08	1.94	1.85	1.77	1.72	1.67	1.63	1.60	1.57	1.55
	.05	3.84	3.00	2.60	2.37	2.21	2.10	2.01	1.94	1.88	1.83	1.79	1.75
	.01	6.63	4.61	3.78	3.32	3.02	2.80	2.64	2.51	2.41	2.32	2.25	2.18

TABLE D   *Continued*

15	20	24	30	40	50	60	100	120	200	500	∞	α	df *for denominator*
				df *for numerator*									
1.36	1.34	1.33	1.32	1.31	1.31	1.30	1.30	1.30	1.29	1.29	1.28	.25	
1.81	1.76	1.73	1.70	1.67	1.65	1.64	1.61	1.60	1.59	1.58	1.57	.10	22
2.15	2.07	2.03	1.98	1.94	1.91	1.89	1.85	1.84	1.82	1.80	1.78	.05	
2.98	2.83	2.75	2.67	2.58	2.53	2.50	2.42	2.40	2.36	2.33	2.31	.01	
1.35	1.33	1.32	1.31	1.30	1.29	1.29	1.28	1.28	1.27	1.27	1.26	.25	
1.78	1.73	1.70	1.67	1.64	1.62	1.61	1.58	1.57	1.56	1.54	1.53	.10	24
2.11	2.03	1.98	1.94	1.89	1.86	1.84	1.80	1.79	1.77	1.75	1.73	.05	
2.89	2.74	2.66	2.58	2.49	2.44	2.40	2.33	2.31	2.27	2.24	2.21	.01	
1.34	1.32	1.31	1.30	1.29	1.28	1.28	1.26	1.26	1.26	1.25	1.25	.25	
1.76	1.71	1.68	1.65	1.61	1.59	1.58	1.55	1.54	1.53	1.51	1.50	.10	26
2.07	1.99	1.95	1.90	1.85	1.82	1.80	1.76	1.75	1.73	1.71	1.69	.05	
2.81	2.66	2.58	2.50	2.42	2.36	2.33	2.25	2.23	2.19	2.16	2.13	.01	
1.33	1.31	1.30	1.29	1.28	1.27	1.27	1.26	1.25	1.25	1.24	1.24	.25	
1.74	1.69	1.66	1.63	1.59	1.57	1.56	1.53	1.52	1.50	1.49	1.48	.10	28
2.04	1.96	1.91	1.87	1.82	1.79	1.77	1.73	1.71	1.69	1.67	1.65	.05	
2.75	2.60	2.52	2.44	2.35	2.30	2.26	2.19	2.17	2.13	2.09	2.06	.01	
1.32	1.30	1.29	1.28	1.27	1.26	1.26	1.25	1.24	1.24	1.23	1.23	.25	
1.72	1.67	1.64	1.61	1.57	1.55	1.54	1.51	1.50	1.48	1.47	1.46	.10	30
2.01	1.93	1.89	1.84	1.79	1.76	1.74	1.70	1.68	1.66	1.64	1.62	.05	
2.70	2.55	2.47	2.39	2.30	2.25	2.21	2.13	2.11	2.07	2.03	2.01	.01	
1.30	1.28	1.26	1.25	1.24	1.23	1.22	1.21	1.21	1.20	1.19	1.19	.25	
1.66	1.61	1.57	1.54	1.51	1.48	1.47	1.43	1.42	1.41	1.39	1.38	.10	40
1.92	1.84	1.79	1.74	1.69	1.66	1.64	1.59	1.58	1.55	1.53	1.51	.05	
2.52	2.37	2.29	2.20	2.11	2.06	2.02	1.94	1.92	1.87	1.83	1.80	.01	
1.27	1.25	1.24	1.22	1.21	1.20	1.19	1.17	1.17	1.16	1.15	1.15	.25	
1.60	1.54	1.51	1.48	1.44	1.41	1.40	1.36	1.35	1.33	1.31	1.29	.10	60
1.84	1.75	1.70	1.65	1.59	1.56	1.53	1.48	1.47	1.44	1.41	1.39	.05	
2.35	2.20	2.12	2.03	1.94	1.88	1.84	1.75	1.73	1.68	1.63	1.60	.01	
1.24	1.22	1.21	1.19	1.18	1.17	1.16	1.14	1.13	1.12	1.11	1.10	.25	
1.55	1.48	1.45	1.41	1.37	1.34	1.32	1.27	1.26	1.24	1.21	1.19	.10	120
1.75	1.66	1.61	1.55	1.50	1.46	1.43	1.37	1.35	1.32	1.28	1.25	.05	
2.19	2.03	1.95	1.86	1.76	1.70	1.66	1.56	1.53	1.48	1.42	1.38	.01	
1.23	1.21	1.20	1.18	1.16	1.14	1.12	1.11	1.10	1.09	1.08	1.06	.25	
1.52	1.46	1.42	1.38	1.34	1.31	1.28	1.24	1.22	1.20	1.17	1.14	.10	200
1.72	1.62	1.57	1.52	1.46	1.41	1.39	1.32	1.29	1.26	1.22	1.19	.05	
2.13	1.97	1.89	1.79	1.69	1.63	1.58	1.48	1.44	1.39	1.33	1.28	.01	
1.22	1.19	1.18	1.16	1.14	1.13	1.12	1.09	1.08	1.07	1.04	1.00	.25	
1.49	1.42	1.38	1.34	1.30	1.26	1.24	1.18	1.17	1.13	1.08	1.00	.10	∞
1.67	1.57	1.52	1.46	1.39	1.35	1.32	1.24	1.22	1.17	1.11	1.00	.05	
2.04	1.88	1.79	1.70	1.59	1.52	1.47	1.36	1.32	1.25	1.15	1.00	.01	

TABLE E   Critical Values of the Correlation Coefficient

	Level of significance for one-tailed test			
	.05	.025	.01	.005
	Level of significance for two-tailed test			
df	.10	.05	.02	.01
1	.988	.997	.9995	.9999
2	.900	.950	.980	.990
3	.805	.878	.934	.959
4	.729	.811	.882	.917
5	.669	.754	.833	.874
6	.622	.707	.789	.834
7	.582	.666	.750	.798
8	.549	.632	.716	.765
9	.521	.602	.685	.735
10	.497	.576	.658	.708
11	.476	.553	.634	.684
12	.458	.532	.612	.661
13	.441	.514	.592	.641
14	.426	.497	.574	.623
15	.412	.482	.558	.606
16	.400	.468	.542	.590
17	.389	.456	.528	.575
18	.378	.444	.516	.561
19	.369	.433	.503	.549
20	.360	.423	.492	.537
21	.352	.413	.482	.526
22	.344	.404	.472	.515
23	.337	.396	.462	.505
24	.330	.388	.453	.496
25	.323	.381	.445	.487
26	.317	.374	.437	.479
27	.311	.367	.430	.471
28	.306	.361	.423	.463
29	.301	.355	.416	.456
30	.296	.349	.409	.449
35	.275	.325	.381	.418
40	.257	.304	.358	.393
45	.243	.288	.338	.372
50	.231	.273	.322	.354
60	.211	.250	.295	.325
70	.195	.232	.274	.303
80	.183	.217	.256	.283
90	.173	.205	.242	.267
100	.164	.195	.230	.254

Source: Abridged from Table VII, p. 63 of Fisher and Yates: *Statistical Tables for Biological, Agricultural and Medical Research,* published by Longman Group Ltd., London (previously published by Oliver and Boyd, Ltd., Edinburgh), and reprinted by permission of the authors and publishers.

Glossary of Research Methods Terms

Analysis of covariance   A method of statistical control through which scores on the dependent variable are adjusted according to scores on a related variable.

Analysis of variance   A statistical technique by which it is possible to partition the variance in a distribution of scores according to separate sources or factors; although variance is partitioned, the statistical test tests for differences between means.

A posteriori judgment   A judgment based upon actual observation (data), after the fact, so to speak.

Applied research   Research conducted for the primary purpose of solving an immediate, practical problem.

A priori decision   A decision made prior to collecting data; for example, deciding what comparisons will be made before collecting data.

Aptitude   The potential for achievement.

Assertoric argumentation   Making the case for generalization (external validity) using a general-type argument that something is true for each and every member of a population.

Attitude   A tendency to possess certain feelings toward a specified class of stimuli.

Basic research   Research conducted for the primary purpose of adding to the existing body of knowledge, for example, research for theory development.

Case study   A study characterized by an investigation of a single individual, group, event, institution, or culture.

Census (in survey research)   A study that includes all members of a population.

Central limit theorem   A theorem that states that given any population with a mean and finite variance, as sample size increases, the distribution of the sample means approaches a normal distribution, with mean equal to the population mean and variance equal to the population variance divided by sample size.

Cluster sampling   The selection of groups of elements, called clusters, rather than single elements; all elements of a cluster are included in the sample, and the clusters are selected randomly from the larger population of clusters.

Coding   Process of organizing data, specifying designations and symbols as appropriate. Usually, the process results in data reduction.

Cohort studies   Longitudinal designs (in survey research) in which a specific population is studied over time by taking different random samples at various points in time.

Concurrent-related validity of a test   The extent to which scores on a test match performance scores on one or more criterion measures obtained at about the same time the test is given.

Confidence interval   An interval estimate of a parameter constructed in such a way that the interval has a predetermined probability of spanning the parameter.

Confounded variables   Variables operating in a specific situation such that their effects cannot be separated.

Constant   A characteristic that has the same value for all individuals in a research study.

Construct-related validity of a test   The extent to which a test measures one or more dimensions of a theory or trait.

Content-related validity of a test   The extent to which the content of the test items reflects the academic discipline, behavior, or whatever is under study.

Contextualization (in ethnographic research)   The requirement that data be interpreted only in the context of the situation or environment in which they were collected.

Contingency table   The array into which a set of numeration data may be grouped according to two or more classification variables.

Continuous variable   A variable that can take on any value within an interval on the scale of measurement.

Control group (in an experiment)   A group of subjects who do not receive any experimental treatment; the group is included for comparison purposes.

Control variable   A variable, other than the independent variable(s) of primary interest, whose effects are determined by the researcher. Control variables are included in designs as independent variables for the purpose of explaining variation.

Correlation   The extent of relationship between two variables.

Correlation coefficient   The measure of the extent of relationship between two variables.

Covariate   The measure used in an analysis of covariance for adjusting the scores of the dependent variable.

Criterion-related validity of a test   The extent to which scores on a test correlate with scores on some external criterion measure.

Cronbach alpha   An internal consistency or reliability coefficient for a test, based on two or more parts of the test but requiring only one test administration.

Cross-sectional studies   Surveys in which the data are collected at one point in time from a random sample of a general population that contains two or more subpopulations, with the intention of comparing the data from the subsamples or noting trends across such subsamples.

Data file   The organized array of data and identification information commonly placed in a computer prior to analysis.

Degrees of freedom   The number of ways in which the data are free to vary; the number of observations minus the number of restrictions placed on the data.

Dependent variable   The variable being affected or assumed to be affected by the independent variable.

Descriptive statistics   That part of statistical procedures that deals with describing distributions of data and relationships between variables.

Directional hypothesis   A hypothesis stated in such a manner that a direction, usually indicated by "greater than" or "less than," is hypothesized for the results.

Distribution   The total observations or a set of data on a variable; when observations are tabulated according to frequency for each possible score, it is a frequency distribution.

Ecological psychology   Psychology focusing on naturally occurring human behavior and relationships between human behavior and the environment.

Error variance (in a statistical context)   Inherent or natural variance due to random assignment or random selection; also called random variance.

Ethnographic research   Research that is intended to provide scientific descriptions of (educational) systems, processes, and phenomena within their specific contexts.

Ethnography   A branch of anthropology that deals with the scientific description of individual cultures; also, the written account that is the product of an ethnographic study.

Evaluation research   Research procedures used for the process of evaluation, that is, collecting data and making decisions (value judgments) about an educational program, policy, etc.

Experiment (in educational research)   A research situation in which one or more independent variables are systematically varied according to a preconceived plan to determine the effects of this variation.

Experimental mortality   The dropping out of subjects participating in an experiment; the failure of certain subjects to continue in the experiment until its conclusion.

Ex post facto research   Research in which the independent variable or variables have already occurred and in which the researcher begins with the observations on a dependent variable, followed by a retrospective study of possible relationships and effects.

Foreshadowed problems (in ethnographic research)   Specific research problems, possibly stated in question form, that provide a focus for the research.

Grounded theory   Theory based on a study of the data rather than on some prior set of axioms and theorems.

Hardware   Computer equipment including related equipment such as printers.

Histogram   A graphical representation, consisting of rectangles, of the scores in a distribution; the areas of the rectangles are proportional to the frequencies of the scores.

Historical research   Research directed to the study of a problem, event, etc., of the past, using information from the past.

Historiography   The historical method of conducting research.

Holistic ethnography   The study of all or parts of a culture or community by describing beliefs and practices of the group and considering the various parts as they contribute to the culture as a unified, consistent whole.

Hypothesis A conjecture or proposition about the solution to a problem, the relationship of two or more variables, or the nature of some phenomenon.

Independent variable A variable that affects (or is assumed to affect) the dependent variable under study and is included in the research design so that its effect can be determined.

Inferential statistics That part of statistical procedures that deals with making inferences from samples to populations.

Interaction The effect of one independent variable on another; the lack of the effect of one independent variable remaining constant over the levels of another.

Interval scale A measurement scale that, in addition to ordering scores, also establishes an equal unit in the scale so that distances between any two scores are of a known magnitude; also called *equal-unit scale.*

Intervening variable A variable whose existence is inferred but that cannot be manipulated or measured.

Key-informant (in ethnographic research) An individual in whom one invests a disproportionate amount of time because that individual appears to be particularly well informed, articulate, approachable, or available.

Kuder-Richardson methods Procedures for determining the reliability of a test from a single form and single administration of the test without splitting the test.

Latin square An $n \times n$ square array that includes different letters or symbols so arranged that each symbol appears once and only once in each row and column.

Level of confidence The probability associated with a confidence interval; the probability that the interval will span the corresponding parameter. Commonly used confidence levels in educational research are .95 and .99.

Level of significance A probability associated with the test of a hypothesis using statistical techniques that determines whether or not the hypothesis is rejected. Commonly used significance levels in educational research are .05 and .01, also called *alpha level.*

Likert scale A scaling procedure, commonly associated with attitude measurement, that requires a graded response to each item or statement. In scoring, the alternative responses to items are assigned numerical values, and the individual's score is the sum of the numerical values.

Linear relationship A relationship between two variables such that a straight line can be fitted satisfactorily to the points of the scattergram; the scatter of points will cluster elliptically around a straight line rather than some type of curve.

Longitudinal studies Studies that involve measuring the same or different individuals two or more times during a period of time (usually of considerable length, such as several months or years)—for example, measuring the mathematics performance of the same students at yearly intervals as they progress from the fourth grade through senior high.

Maturation Psychological and biological processes operating and causing systematic variation within individuals with the passing of time.

Mean The sum of the scores in a distribution divided by the number of scores in the distribution.

Measurement   The assignment of numerals to objects or events according to specific rules.

Measures of central tendency   Points in a distribution that locate the distribution on the measurement scale; points within the distribution about which the scores tend to group themselves.

Measures of variability   Measures of a distribution that indicate the amount of dispersion or spread in the distribution.

Median   The point in a distribution below which 50 percent of the scores lie.

Meta-analysis   A statistical procedure used to summarize the results across numerous, independently conducted research studies.

Mode   The point or score of greatest frequency in a distribution.

Moderator variable   A variable that may or may not be controlled but has an effect in the research situation.

Multiple-treatment interference   Carry-over or delayed effects of prior experimental treatments when individuals receive two or more experimental treatments in succession.

Multivariate analyses   Statistical data analyses in which two or more dependent variables are analyzed simultaneously.

Nominal scale   A measurment scale that simply classifies elements into two or more categories, indicating that the elements are different, but not according to order or magnitude.

Normal distribution   A family of bell-shaped, symmetrical distributions whose curve is described mathematically by a general equation; sometimes called the *Laplace-Gaussian normal probability function.*

Norms   Descriptive statistics that summarize the test performance of a reference group of individuals.

Null hypothesis (in inferential statistics)   A hypothesis stated such that no difference or no relationship is hypothesized.

Operational definition   A definition expressed in terms of the processes or operations that are going to be used to measure the characteristic under study.

Optimum allocation (in stratified random sampling)   Selecting the sample in such a manner that the strata contributions to the sample are proportional to the sizes of strata populations and the strata variances.

Ordinal scale   A measurement scale that classifies and ranks elements or scores.

Organismic variable   A variable that is an existing or natural characteristic of the individuals under study—for example, the sex of the individual.

Panel studies   Longitudinal designs (in survey research) in which the same random sample is measured at different points in time.

Parallel forms of a test   Two (or more) forms of a test that are equivalent in terms of characteristics.

Parameter   A characteristic or measure of a population—for example, the population mean.

Participant-observer   The role assumed by the researcher in ethnographic research such that the researcher becomes a participant in the situation being observed.

Periodicity (in systematic sampling)   A periodic characteristic that follows the listing of the elements and the selection interval so that a bias is introduced into the sample.

Personality   In general, the sum total of an individual's mental and emotional characteristics; in the context of psychological testing, personality inventories usually are designed to measure characteristics such as emotional and social adjustment.

Phenomenology   The study of phenomena through observation and description.

Pilot study   A study conducted prior to the major research study that in some way is a small-scale model of the major study; conducted for the purpose of gaining additional information by which the major study can be improved—for example, an exploratory use of the measurement instrument with a small group for the purpose of refining the instrument.

Population   The totality of all elements, subjects, or members that possess a specified set of one or more common characteristics that define it; in inferential statistics, the group to which inferences are drawn.

Portraiture   An ethnography that is a descriptive account of a culture, in essence, providing a portrait of the culture through words.

Prediction   The estimation of scores on one variable from information about one or more other variables.

Predictive-related validity of a test   The extent to which predictions made from the test are confirmed by subsequent data.

Primary source   An original or first-hand account of an event or experience.

Probability sample   A sample selected in such a way that each member of the population has some nonzero probability of being included in the sample.

Proportional allocation (in stratified random sampling)   Selecting the sample in a manner such that the sample size is divided among the strata proportional to population sizes of the strata.

Purposeful sample   A sample selected in a nonrandom manner, based on member characterstics relevant to the research problem.

Quasi-experimental research   Research involving an experimental variable with intact groups, or at least with groups that have not been formed through random selection or random assignment; single subjects, not randomly selected, may also be involved.

Random sample   A sample selected in such a way that the selection of one member of the population in no way affects the probability of selection of any other member.

Random (error) variance   The inherent variance in a distribution of scores, which includes variance due to sources such as random sampling (or assignment) and intervening variables.

Range   One plus the difference between the two extreme scores of a distribution.

Ratio scale   A measurement scale that, besides containing an equal unit, also establishes an absolute zero in the scale.

Regression (as a threat to experimental validity)   A tendency for groups, especially those selected on the basis of extreme scores, to regress toward a more average score on subsequent measurements, regardless of the experimental treatment.

Regression line   The straight line of best fit (usually according to the least squares criterion) for a set of bivariate data.

Reliability coefficient   A measure of the consistency of a test. There are several methods of computing a reliability coefficient, depending on the test and the test situation.

Reliability of measurement   The consistency of the measurement.

Reliability of research—external   The extent to which research is replicable.

Reliability of research—internal   The extent of consistency in the methods, conditions, and results of research.

Response set   The tendency for an individual to respond to items or other stimuli in a consistent manner, regardless of the content or context of the stimuli.

Sample   A subset of the population under study.

Sampling bias   A distortion caused by the way the sample was selected or formed so that the sample is no longer representative of the population.

Sampling distribution of a statistic   The distribution (usually theoretical) of all possible values of the statistic from all possible samples of a given size selected from the population.

Sampling error   Variation due to random fluctuation when random samples are used to represent populations.

Sampling ratio   The ratio of sample size to population size; also called the *sampling fraction*.

Scattergram   The plot of points determined by the cross-tabulation of a set of bivariate data.

Secondary analysis   Reanalysis of the data for the purpose of (1) addressing the original research problem with better statistical procedures and/or (2) answering new research questions.

Secondary source   An account that is at least one step removed from an event or experience.

Semantic differential   An attitude measuring technique in which the respondent is asked to judge a word or concept using a set of bipolar adjective scales.

Significant statistic   A statistic whose appearance by chance in the light of the hypothesis is less than the probability designated by the significance level—for example, a significant difference; a difference too large to be attributed to chance (random sampling fluctuation) if the hypothesis is true.

Simple random sample   A sample selected in such a way that all members of the population have an equal probability of selection; in the case of sampling without replacement from a finite population, all possible samples of a given size have the same probability of being selected.

Software   Programs used to provide instructions to the computer concerning analyses, procedures, or operations.

Split-half method   A procedure for determining the reliability of a test by which a single form of the test is divided into comparable halves, the scores on the halves are correlated, and the reliability coefficient is computed by applying a special formula known as the Spearman-Brown step-up formula.

Standard deviation   A measure of variability that is the positive square root of the variance.

Standard error of a statistic   The standard deviation of the sampling distribution of the statistic.

Standard normal distribution   The normal distribution with a mean of zero and a standard deviation of 1.0.

Standard score   A score given in terms of standard deviation units from the mean of the distribution. A negative score indicates below the mean and a positive score indicates above the mean.

Statistics   In descriptive statistics, measures taken on a distribution; in inferential statistics, measures or characteristics of a sample; in a more general sense, the theory, procedures, and methods by which data are analyzed in a quantitative manner.

Stratified random sampling   A sampling procedure in which the population is divided into two or more subpopulations, called *strata,* and elements for the sample are then randomly selected from the strata.

Survey research   Research that deals with the incidence, distribution, and relationships of educational, psychological, and sociological variables in nonexperimental settings.

Systematic sampling   A selection procedure in which all sample elements are determined by the selection of the first element, since each element on a selection list is separated from the first element by a multiple of the selection interval.

Test-retest method   A procedure for determining test reliability by correlating the scores of two administrations of the same test to the same individuals.

Trait   A tendency to respond in a certain way to situations.

Trend studies   Longitudinal designs (in survey research) in which a general population is studied over time by taking different random samples at various points in time.

Triangulation (in ethnographic research)   Qualitative cross-validation of data using multiple data sources or multiple data-collection procedures.

Two-stage sampling   A general term referring to any sampling procedure that requires two steps in the sample selection.

Type I (or alpha error)   In inferential statistics, the error of rejecting a true hypothesis.

Type II (or beta error)   In inferential statistics, the error of failing to reject a false hypothesis.

Unbiased statistic   A statistic computed in such a manner that the mean of its sampling distribution is the parameter that the statistic estimates.

Validity of measurement   The extent to which a measurement instrument measures what it is supposed to measure.

Validity of research—external   The extent and appropriateness of the generalizability of results.

Validity of research—internal   The basic minimum control, measurement, analysis, and procedures necessary to make the results interpretable.

Variable   A characteristic that takes on different values for different individuals.

Variance   A measure of variability that is the average value of the squares of the deviations from the mean of the scores in a distribution.

Name Index

Subject Index